Industrial Relations in the New Europe

Industrial Relations in Context

General Editors: Paul Edwards, Richard Hyman and Keith Sisson

Titles previously published

Industrial Relations in Britain
Edited by George Sayers Bain

Labour Law in Britain
Edited by Roy Lewis

Employment in Britain
Edited by Duncan Gallie

Personnel Management in Britain
Edited by Keith Sisson

Industrial Relations in the New Europe

Edited by

Anthony Ferner and Richard Hyman

BLACKWELL
Business

First published 1992

Blackwell Publishers
108 Cowley Road
Oxford OX4 1JF
UK

238 Main Street
Suite 501
Cambridge, Massachusetts 02142
USA

British Library Cataloging in Publication Data

A CIP catalogue record for this book is available from the British Library.

Library of Congress Cataloging-in-Publication Data

A CIP catalogue record for this book is available from the library of Congress.

ISBN 0-631-185925
ISBN 0-631-185933 (pbk)

Prepared on PageMaker in 10 on 11.5 pt Palatino by Simone Dudley, Industrial Relations Research Unit, University of Warwick, CV4 7AL, Coventry.

Printed in Great Britain by T.J. Press Ltd, Padstow, Cornwall.

This book is printed on acid-free paper.

Contents

Note: A list of abbreviations is found at the end of each chapter

Contributors

José Barreto, Research Assistant, Instituto de Ciências Sociais, University of Lisbon

Jon Erik Dølvik, Norwegian Trade Union Centre for Social Science and Research (FAFO), Oslo

Paul Edwards, Deputy Director, Industrial Relations Research Unit, University of Warwick

Anthony Ferner, Principal Research Fellow, Industrial Relations Research Unit, University of Warwick

Janine Goetschy, Chargée de Recherche at CNRS (Centre National de la Recherche Scientifique), Université de Paris-Sud

Mark Hall, Research Fellow, Industrial Relations Research Unit, University of Warwick

Beat Hotz-Hart, Professor of Economics, University of Zürich; Head of Technology Policy, Federal Office for Economic Policy in the Federal Department of Economic Affairs, Berne

Richard Hyman, Professor of Industrial Relations, School of Industrial and Business Studies, University of Warwick

Otto Jacobi, formerly of the Institut für Sozialforschung, Frankfurt, now German correspondent for the European Commission's European Observatory of Industrial Relations

Berndt Keller, Professor of Labour and Social Policy, University of Konstanz

Anders Kjellberg, Associate Professor, Department of Sociology, University of Lund

Nicos D. Kritsantonis, Personnel Director of a Greek company

Kari Lilja, Professor of Business Economics, Helsinki School of Economics and Business Administration

Paul Marginson, Lecturer in Industrial Relations, School of Industrial and Business Studies, University of Warwick

Miguel Martínez Lucio, Lecturer in Industrial Relations, Cardiff Business School, University of Cardiff

Walther Müller-Jentsch, Professor of Social Sciences, University of Paderborn

Patrick Rozenblatt, Chargé de Recherche at CNRS (Centre National de la Recherche Scientifique), Travail et Mobilité, Université de Paris X – Nanterre

Steen Scheuer, Lecturer, Institute of Organization and Industrial Sociology, Copenhagen Business School

Keith Sisson, Professor of Industrial Relations and Director, Industrial Relations Research Unit, University of Warwick

Dag Stokland, Norwegian Trade Union Centre for Social Science and Research (FAFO), Oslo

Franz Traxler, Professor of Economic and Industrial Sociology and member of the Institute of Sociology of the Faculty of Economy and Social Sciences at the University of Vienna

Gary Tunsch, Inspector at the Ministry of Labour and Secretary of the National Conciliation Office, Luxembourg

Jim Van Leemput, Research and Training Assistant, Department of Sociology, and Researcher at the Study Group in Technological, Economic and Social Change and Labour Market Research (TESA), Vrije Universiteit Brussel

Jacques Vilrokx, Professor of Industrial Relations and Labour Economics, Director of the Centre for Sociology and Head of Study Group in Technological, Economic and Social Change and Labour Market Research (TESA), Vrije Universiteit Brussel

Jelle Visser, Sociology of Organisations Research Unit (SORU), Sociologisch Instituut, University of Amsterdam

Ferdinand von Prondzynski, Professor of Law, University of Hull

Jeremy Waddington, Research Fellow, Industrial Relations Research Unit, University of Warwick

David Winchester, Senior Lecturer in Industrial Relations, School of Industrial and Business Studies, University of Warwick

Foreword

The 'Industrial Relations in Context' series was launched in 1983 by George Bain. This is the first volume to appear since he ceased to be the general editor, and it is appropriate to record our debt to him for creating the series. Its aims remain unchanged. It complements the established series of research monographs, 'Warwick Studies in Industrial Relations', by providing a series of broadly-based textbooks on themes related to industrial relations.

'Industrial Relations in Context' is designed for teaching and wider dissemination. The volumes in the series analyse current problems and issues in industrial relations, informed by empirical research and scholarship, and by an awareness of recent trends and developments in industrial relations and their wider social, economic, political and international contexts.

The series aims to provide a clear, comprehensive, authoritative and up-to-date analysis of the entire field of employment relations. It is intended for students doing diploma, undergraduate, or postgraduate courses in personnel management and industrial relations at colleges, polytechnics or universities, as well as for those studying industrial sociology, labour economics and labour law. It is also addressed to those in adult education, to those seeking membership of professional bodies like the Institute of Personnel Management, to industrial relations practitioners in both unions and management, and to the general reader who wants to find out more about industrial relations today.

The hallmarks of the series are clarity, comprehensiveness, authoritativeness and topicality. Each chapter of each volume is an original essay that brings together theoretical and empirical knowledge and understanding. Each is stamped with the views of the authors who are experts in their field. Each emphasizes analysis and explanation as well as description. Each focuses on trends over the past two or three decades and says something about likely future developments. And in each case the complete text is welded into a coherent order by editors who combine a distinguished research record with a proven ability to communicate to a wider audience.

The series began with *Industrial Relations in Britain*, edited by George Bain. It continued with the publication of *Labour Law in Britain*, edited by Roy Lewis, *Employment in Britain*, edited by Duncan Gallie, and more recently with *Personnel Management in Britain*, edited by Keith Sisson.

On the eve of completion of the single European market, the publication of *Industrial Relations in the New Europe* is recognition of the growing importance of the European context for an understanding of British industrial relations. The volume contains chapters on all twelve European Community countries, and on the other five major west European countries. The rich detail and analysis from such a comprehensive group of countries gives an unrivalled appreciation both of cross-national developments and of the causes of continuing diversity in European industrial relations. Across Europe, one of the key trends since the early 1980s has been the shift in the focus of attention to decentralized, company-level industrial relations. *Industrial Relations in the New Europe* contains the fullest and most up-to-date empirically-based accounts available of the impact of this important phenomenon. A companion volume, due to appear in 1994, will examine some of the major themes of European industrial relations in a comparative cross-national way.

Paul Edwards
Richard Hyman
Keith Sisson

Preface

This book is the first of two volumes on industrial relations in Europe. It presents a range of national studies, while its companion, due to appear in early 1994, will provide comparative analysis of a variety of issues of practical and theoretical importance.

Our contributors cover a total of seventeen countries: all the member states of the European Community and the five other principal countries of western Europe: Austria, Finland, Norway, Sweden and Switzerland. It is by far the most comprehensive volume of its kind. When we first planned it, in the summer of 1989, the physical boundary between western and eastern Europe was brutally clear, and the institutional division was equally stark. The very concept of industrial relations was not translatable into Russian, Polish, Hungarian, Czech.... Collective bargaining, or even trade unionism independent of the state (despite the brief flowering of *Solidarnosc* a decade earlier), had no place in the eastern system. A focus on western Europe, covering all countries of any size (the largest exclusion, Iceland, has only a quarter of a million inhabitants), required little justification.

Even as we began to plan this book, Mazowiecki had been elected premier in Warsaw; by the end of the year, the Berlin Wall and the 'iron curtain' had fallen. New autonomous unions sprang up, and the old 'official' unions rapidly declared their independence from the collapsing regimes and communist parties; employers emerged from the tutelage of the state; the first hesitant steps were taken towards western-style collective bargaining. We had to consider whether to enlarge the volume to take account of these developments. On reflection, we decided to retain the original focus. It would have been impossible to have provided individual country studies without unduly increasing the size – and the price – of the volume. In any case, events were moving at such bewildering speed that there existed few social scientists with the necessary expertise; and even these could produce nothing but a preliminary account which would be rapidly overtaken by events. Our intention is therefore to use the second volume to provide a systematic overview of developments in east/central Europe; by the time this is written, there will, we hope, have been time for the dust to settle.

Why is it necessary to add to the stock of literature on European industrial relations? First, we were anxious to examine a far wider range of countries than is normal in such enterprises. We believed, and have been confirmed in our view by our authors' contributions, that the stereotypical models of industrial relations in Europe are distorted by being based on a limited and repetitive range of cases. The sheer variety and diversity of practice comes as a salutary antidote to simplistic generalization. On the other hand, it also provides the wealth of empirical material needed to sustain and deepen – or revise – existing models. Thus discussions of the 'Nordic model', for example, will be better informed for having side-by-side the four country studies, so that the paradigmatic Swedish case may be compared and contrasted with the rather different experiences of the other Nordic countries. Similarly, the impact of dictatorship and transition to democracy in southern Europe can be explored in terms of the specific evolution of Spanish, Portuguese and Greek industrial relations.

Second, we were sensitive to debates on the transformation of British industrial relations in the 1980s. How did the obvious changes – new legislation, declining union membership, high unemployment, the end of tripartism – actually impinge on the shop floor? How did the rhetoric of 'macho management' translate into the day-to-day search for employee compliance and commitment? Such questions have guided much of the recent research in the Industrial Relations Research Unit. Reading accounts of industrial relations elsewhere in Europe, we felt the lack of similar information. Hence while much recent writing places considerable emphasis on the themes of decentralization and flexibility, few studies give more than passing and impressionistic attention to the actual strategies and practices of the large companies that have moved to centre stage in a more decentralized environment. We have exhorted our contributors to redress this balance, and while in many cases the paucity of empirical data has hampered them, we feel that our volume gives a much more detailed, rounded view of developments in management strategy and in workplace industrial relations than has typically been the case in country studies.

This relates to a third consideration. Most multi-country volumes are out-of-date as soon as they are published, because of the extreme diplomatic and logistical problems inherent in coordinating international collaborative ventures of this kind. We have been determined at all costs to avoid this 'lag'. As a result, the accounts in the volume deal with events at least up to the end of 1991 and in some cases up to the spring of 1992; for example, the German chapter contains a sustained account of the impact of German (re)unification on industrial relations. This achievement has been made possible, not only by the impressive commitment of our contributors, but also by the capabilities of the Industrial Relations Research Unit's 'desk-top publishing' facilities which have enabled us to circumvent the entire stage of conventional type-setting and thus reduce production time.

Our rapport with our contributors has been an essential ingredient in the completion of the project on schedule. It has been made possible by the extensive contacts that IRRU maintains with European colleagues, and particularly by the 'Industrial Relations in the European Community' network set up at Richard Hyman's initiative following an inaugural conference hosted by IRRU in March 1989. With one exception, the chapters have been written by national experts, many of them already well-known internationally, others whose contribution will undoubtedly bring them to a wider audience. The exception is Italy. Unfortunately, this proved to be the single casualty of the relentless demands of the project. Our original Italian authors had to withdraw from the project at a late stage and, given the practical problems of finding a replacement, we saw no alternative to writing the chapter ourselves. We were greatly helped in this by the committed support and advice of our colleague Michael Terry. Mike has had a long acquaintance with Italian industrial relations, and has recently returned from a three-month study visit to Milan and Bari. He was able to send us up-to-date information and material and above all to offer his incisive commentary on our early drafts. We are extremely grateful for his invaluable help in 'keeping the show on the road'. We have also received very considerable and much appreciated advice from Italian colleagues, although their professional reticence prevents us from naming them here.

In one other case, that of Spain, our original team of authors felt obliged by the pressure of other commitments to withdraw at an early stage. We are most grateful to Miguel Martínez for taking over the burden of writing the Spanish chapter.

Despite maintaining firm overall editorial control, we tried to allow our authors relative discretion in the treatment of their subject. We decided early on not to impose a rigid structure on each chapter. In our view, attempts to do so invariably lead to a disjunction between content and organization, since what is appropriate for one country will not be so for another. Instead, we supplied contributors with guidance on the themes and issues to be covered. Some areas of guidance are worth mentioning specifically. First, as mentioned, we exhorted authors to offer a detailed consideration of corporate industrial relations strategy, and of change at the workplace. Second, we encouraged them to carry historical threads of explanation through their accounts, relating present-day developments to the critical phases and factors in the evolution of a country's industrial relations. Third, we asked authors to suggest likely future scenarios for the development of industrial relations in their country; in particular, on the eve of completion of the single European market, to consider the impact of European integration and the 'social dimension' on the strategies of employers, unions and government. Fourth, while a systematic comparative approach must await the second volume of the project, authors were encouraged occasionally to raise their sights from their own country, and to draw out the similarities and differences between it and its comparators in Europe. Finally, we requested extensive bibliographical references, both in English and in the original language – another point of distinction with many ventures of this kind. We did so not only on grounds of academic respectability, but also in the hope and expectation that this book will appeal (in English or in translation) to a wide market throughout Europe. Moreover, we would expect (perhaps naively!) increasing numbers of scholars and students to be acquiring a reading knowledge of the language of the countries they are studying in today's integrating Europe.

In addition to the guidance to authors, another factor of 'cohesion' has been the series of international meetings that we held to discuss issues and drafts. An inaugural meeting in Madrid in July 1990 was attended by most of the contributors, and we must express our gratitude to Víctor Pérez Díaz and his colleagues at the Instituto Juan March for the facilities they provided. Subsequent meetings with groups of authors were held in Lund, Brussels, Vienna and Bari, and again we thank those who assisted with arrangements.

As for the editorial process itself, we realized early on that it was better for us to adopt a 'stereoscopic' approach rather than a clear division of labour. Thus at each stage both of us read and commented on every chapter. Only in the final phase of major editorial revision did we divide up the chapters between us, each taking primary responsibility for a group of countries; even then, we subjected our efforts to each other's detailed scrutiny. In the Warwick tradition, we have been extremely interventionist editors where necessary in order to ensure that our guidelines were followed as far as possible, and to ensure a certain homogeneity of treatment – though not, we believe, to the exclusion of the individual concerns and eccentricities of authors. We would like to thank all our contributors for their considerable patience in the face of our tiresome demands for further revisions, and for our own sometimes significant amendments to their texts. But we would like to think that on the whole our interventions have been the outcome of negotiation rather than the unilateral exercise of editorial prerogative!

Guidance was also given to authors on chapter length. We applied a crude rule of thumb that might be seen as an analogue of 'qualified majority voting'. The four largest countries were given between 20,000 and 30,000 words each, the smallest around 10,000 or less. It did not work out quite so neatly in practice. Some countries produced fewer words than their allotted quota, and the resulting redistribution allowed some smaller countries more space where we felt that the intrinsic interest of the account merited it. A major exception to the 'QMV' rule was Sweden; partly because we regarded it as paradigmatic of a whole model in the throes of crisis, partly because we commissioned its author, Anders Kjellberg, to write an introductory overview to the four Nordic countries.

We have tried to order the chapters according to a logic other than that of the alphabet, grouping them together in blocs of countries that appear closely related. This was inevitably a somewhat arbitrary undertaking in some cases: clear for the Nordic group, less so for, say, France, which we have treated as a bridge to the southern European group of Italy, Portugal, Spain and Greece.

Finally, we must record our debts of gratitude to numerous people and institutions. The Industrial Relations Research Unit has, as usual, provided an indispensable intellectual and administrative infrastructure for our efforts. We are grateful for the financial support that has enabled us to hold meetings with contributors. We would also like to acknowledge the generous support of the British Council towards expenses for visits to Brussels and Lund in the spring of 1991. Many people within the IRRU have made our task much easier than it might have been. The Director, Keith Sisson, has offered continuous and firm support to the project, even when it threatened to absorb more resources than anticipated. Paul Edwards acceded graciously to our requests for him to coordinate the British team of authors, all of whom are members of the IRRU. Simone Dudley has, as IRRU Publications Assistant, put a prodigious amount of work into getting to grips with the intricacies and whims of the PageMaker desk-top-publishing system that we have used to set the book. Norma Griffiths has acted as an efficient secretary to the project, and Annemarie Flanders translated the Swiss chapter into English as well as performing much useful editorial work. Jo Smithies typed some chapters for us and Margaret Morgan prepared several of the tables. Beyond IRRU, we would like to thank Joyce Lewis for efficient proof-reading under considerable time pressure, and to Michael Heary for preparing the index.

Finally, we would end in customary fashion by accepting entire responsibility for the finished product; and by thanking our partners Diana Foster and Judy Hyman for their immense patience and support while we struggled to complete this mammoth enterprise.

Anthony Ferner
Richard Hyman

Introduction

Industrial Relations in the New Europe: Seventeen Types of Ambiguity

Anthony Ferner and Richard Hyman

We write this introduction in the spring of 1992 – a year which has come to serve as a symbol, for some a promise, for others a threat. A few months after the publication of this text, as 1992 becomes 1993, the free movement of goods and services, labour and capital within the territories of the European Community will be confirmed. The dynamic unleashed by the completion of the internal market obliges more and more governments outside the twelve current member states to seek admission to the club. As recent controversies in Britain have made painfully clear, 'Europeanization' challenges long traditions of national autarchy and institutional distinctiveness. What is also evident is that economic transnationalism is a potent force, shaping and constraining the options available in individual national contexts, whatever the political structures that evolve within the EC.

How will industrial relations be affected? Systems which in most countries have evolved incrementally over the course of many decades – even centuries – have each acquired a distinctive coloration, adapted to the idiosyncrasies of national socio-economic structure, national political regimes, and perhaps also national temperaments. How will these be affected by the spread of supranationalism – the intensification of global competitive pressures, and the transnational activities of major companies, quite apart from any regulatory initiatives of the EC institutions? We do not attempt here to survey the current controversies over the EC 'social dimension', elaborated in the 1989 'Social Charter' and accompanying Action Programme, and in the 'social chapter' of the treaty revisions agreed at Maastricht in December 1991: that is a subject for our next volume. Whether 'harmonization' of national industrial relations systems is a realistic possibility must therefore be left to subsequent analysis. However, such policy discussion certainly needs to be informed by an understanding of the similarities and differences between national systems, the evidence of convergence and divergence in recent years, and possible explanations for these trends and characteristics. This is a major objective of the seventeen national studies in this volume.

In this introductory chapter, we begin the task by examining three interrelated questions concerning European industrial relations. First, from the vantage point of the early 1990s, what are the main common trends that emerge from our country studies, and how far do they represent departures from earlier patterns? Our intention is not to provide a comprehensive overview of developments – such an enterprise would require a volume in itself – but rather to pick out some key themes that are manifest across most if not all European countries. Second, what sorts of explanations account for these tendencies? We attempt to disentangle short-term and transitory causes, whose effects may well be reversed, from more long-term factors whose current effects are likely to be indicators of future developments. Our judgements are cautious, and we try to guard against too deterministic an analysis by also pondering how far the actors are able to preserve 'strategic choice' even when structural conditions constrain their options. Third, the story that unfolds in our studies is one not only of common trends but of continuing and in some respects increasing variety and heterogeneity of national models. We ask, therefore, how we may account for persistent national diversity in the face of cross-national pressures towards convergence.

The Common Background: Structural Change and Conjunctural Crisis

From the 1970s European countries have faced a number of common economic developments of both a long-term and a more conjunctural nature. These have provided a context shaping – but not determining – the evolution of industrial relations.

First, the western European economies have been undergoing a continuing structural transformation. There has been a continued transition from manufacturing towards services: in every country in this study, both industry and agriculture accounted for a lower proportion of employment at the end of the 1980s than at the beginning. Services continued their relentless advance, and in several countries now account for nearly 70 per cent of employment; in only two do they still represent less than half (see tables A.4-A.6 in the statistical Appendix to this chapter). Generally, as our contributors recount, this has been accompanied by a move from manual to white-collar employment. Within manufacturing industry, traditional sectors such as textiles, steel and heavy engineering have lost ground, sometimes dramatically, while 'new' sectors such as microelectronics-based consumer and capital goods industries have expanded.

At the international level, the European economies are becoming increasingly integrated into a global economy dominated by large multinational companies which account for a growing share of output; within Europe, the completion of the single market is a major element in this process as

European business – outside the EC as well as in the twelve member states – seeks to assure its competitiveness in world markets (Ramsay 1990). In recent years there has been a significant increase in cross-border mergers and joint ventures in the EC (Hall 1992: 2). Competition is reflected not only in the continuing growth of global markets for products, but also in an accelerated rate of product innovation and technological change, leading to a move from what Sorge and Streeck (1988) call 'standardized price-competitive' production to 'customized quality-competitive production'.

Large companies are major employers of labour. In 1986, more than 13,000 EC enterprises employed at least 500 people each: this represented 0.1 per cent of total EC enterprises, but 28 per cent of employment. A recent study has identified over 8,000 enterprises employing at least 1,000 workers each in EC member states in 1991; and over 900 multinational corporate groups based in the EC having at least 1,000 employees in two or more EC countries. There are also at least 280 non-EC multinationals with 1,000 or more employees in the EC (Sisson et al. 1992). These and other large companies are changing their corporate structures to cope with the demands of international competitiveness: not only through mergers and joint ventures but through new organizational forms that devolve greater financial and operational responsibility to 'strategic business units' in specific product markets.

Second, superimposed on these long-term structural developments – and partly a manifestation of them – have been the major international recessions of the early 1980s and the early 1990s. Economic crisis has been reflected in periods of declining or stagnating GDP (table A.8), and of continuing high unemployment (table A.7). Unemployment is now rising even in countries with traditionally very low levels.

At a more fundamental level, it has been fashionable in recent years to analyse such trends in capitalist economies in terms of a transition from 'Fordism' to 'post-Fordism'. The argument derives from what is usually known as *régulation* theory, based on the thesis that there have historically existed distinctive 'regimes of accumulation', each complemented and supported by a specific 'mode of regulation'. Put simply, the proposition is that the middle decades of this century were dominated by a Fordist regime of accumulation, based on the mass production with largely semi-skilled labour of standardized products for price-competitive mass markets. The accompanying mode of regulation involved state macro-economic regulation, public welfare provision, and the standardization of employment relations. This encouraged on the one hand the rapid growth of employment in public services, on the other the legitimation of trade unionism and the spread of collective bargaining. More recently, however, it is argued that the regime of accumulation has changed to one based on quality-competitive production for shifting and differentiated markets, with a greater need for qualified labour. This has required a transformation in the mode of regulation, with less state intervention in the labour market, greater personal or corporate responsibility for welfare provision, and a more flexible and differentiated management of employment relations.

This analytical model was used by some writers in Britain, for example Jessop et al. (1988), to insist that the initiatives of the Thatcher government were not simply a reflection of political ideology but were 'required' by the trend to post-Fordism in the national economy. More generally, this type of analysis could be used to suggest that certain trends identifiable across western Europe – the weakening of statutory labour market regulation, declining union membership, the decentralization or even dismantling of collective bargaining – were not the reversible outcome of conjunctural trends but rather stemmed from fundamental changes in the regime of accumulation.

We are unimpressed by some of the accoutrements of regulation theory, and find the stark polarization between Fordism and post-Fordism far too simplistic (cf. Hyman 1991a). Nor do we accept the mechanistic linking of changes in the economic model to those in the polity and in other 'institutional' arrangements. Nevertheless, we see value in a more modest theoretical framework which identifies the functionality of a 'fit' between economic structure and regulatory institutions, and hence suggests that a change in the former will have an impact on the latter. Below, we examine the varying nature of that relationship in different national contexts.

At the political level, the balance of power has swung generally, although not universally, against labour over the past decade or so. The economic context has encouraged policies, from governments of left and right, of retrenchment, control of public expenditure, and restructuring of labour markets. Social-democratic approaches have been in general retreat. In Spain and France, nominally socialist governments have presided over conservative economic strategies, and in the former, the governing party's natural allies in the labour movement have been progressively alienated to the point of anti-government general strikes - one imminent as we write. In Scandinavia, the retreat of social democracy, signalled in the early 1980s by the accession in Denmark of a centre-right administration that remains in power, has been compounded by the precarious position of a minority social-democratic government in Norway and the election in 1991 of a right-wing conservative government in Sweden. The ideological challenge to social democracy was, of course, taken furthest by the Thatcherite programme of economic liberalism and deregulation in Britain; and while her successor has signalled a commitment to 'capitalism with a human face', the new government's options and horizons have been fundamentally constrained by the political assumptions established over the previous thirteen years. However, in other countries where the right has been in power, it has not necessarily mounted a fundamental challenge to consensual accommodations; this is most obvious in Germany, but in Holland, Denmark and elsewhere, centre-right administrations which have made significant inroads into welfare state assumptions have none the less pulled back from rampant liberalization and deregulation.

Employers: The Search for Flexibility and the Decentralization of Industrial Relations

Against this background of long-term structural transformation, conjunctural economic crisis, and an altered balance of political power, two of the major, interrelated, trends in industrial relations have been towards greater flexibility and the decentralization of decision-making.

First, there is a tendency, by no means universal, to a devolution of industrial relations issues to lower levels; in some cases through the exercise of managerial prerogative, but more generally through collective bargaining. The major structural impetus to this development has come from the growth of international competition, requiring companies to respond flexibly to rapidly evolving markets. Conditions of escalating uncertainty (cf. Streeck 1987) have encouraged employers to seek increased flexibility in the recruitment, deployment and reward of labour, through the now familiar panoply of measures: part-time, fixed-term and other non-standard forms of employment contract (EIRR 1990); new forms of work organization such as team-working and 'just-in-time' production; and individual and performance-related pay.

Decentralization today contrasts with earlier episodes in one major respect: it is driven by the requirements and strategies of employers, rather than being the expression of workplace union power. One need only compare, for example, current decentralized industrial relations in Britain or in Italy with the situation in the two countries in the late 1960s.

The tendency to decentralized industrial relations and the pursuit of flexibility has been compounded by companies' organizational changes, particularly the creation of 'strategic business units' with their own profit targets and considerable operational autonomy over many aspects of labour management. The growing dominance of large corporations means that employers are less dependent on the services of interest associations acting at industry (or higher) level (cf. Crouch 1991: 2). Furthermore, the nature of current product markets – fast-changing and often dependent on rapid technological innovation – highlights issues of work organization that are more naturally determined at company or workplace, rather than at industry or sector level. The recession has also encouraged more conjunctural moves towards decentralization, since it makes sense for employers to conduct relationships at a level where the unions cannot bring their national organizational and political strengths to bear; and recession has given added weight to the search for 'numerical' flexibility in particular as a means of containing labour costs. Finally, decentralization has often been encouraged by political choice, as in the case of the Thatcher government's exhortation to 'let the market decide'. Governments have also provided the framework for greater employer flexibility by labour market deregulation notably in Spain and Portugal – but also in Britain, Italy, and many other countries.

Second, however, there has been great variation between countries in the nature and extent of decentralization of industrial relations and of employers' flexibility initiatives. In Switzerland or Austria, for example, there has been a notable continuity in the structures and levels of collective bargaining; and a remarkable absence of new 'human resource management' initiatives for motivating and controlling the work force. In both countries, this reflects the traditional assumption that such matters are already the prerogative of management. Innovative personnel policies are rendered unnecessary by the 'functional equivalent' provided by strong employee identification with the company and its aims, as both Hotz-Hart and Traxler imply in this volume. In many countries – Italy is a prime example – higher-level bargaining structures have continued to provide a framework for extensive company-level bargaining. In Germany, too, devolved bargaining has been accommodated within existing procedures at enterprise level, and has been 'embedded' within a solid structure of national and industry-level arrangements; a format which appears to have transferred successfully to the former DDR. The search for flexibility has taken the form of what Windolf (1989) and others (see e.g. Brünnecke et al. 1991) have referred to as 'productivity coalitions' - collaborative joint approaches to change and flexibility in the interests of corporate competitiveness and hence of the permanent work force of the company; this phenomenon – within a far less institutionalized framework – has also been increasingly characteristic of large Italian firms since the 1980s. In Britain, in contrast to most European countries, decentralization has been paralleled by the 'collapse of associational control' (Crouch 1991) and hence of multi-employer bargaining, a process already well under way in the 1970s and virtually complete by the beginning of the 1990s.

One problem in assessing the impact of decentralization is that the connotations of the term vary markedly in different national contexts. Thus in Denmark the past decade has seen what Scheuer terms a 'return to decentralization' largely in the sense of a devolution of pay bargaining from the national multi-industry level to individual sectors. In Scandinavia as a whole, decentralization, even in the sense of a move to industry bargaining, has been problematic. In Sweden, the 1980s were marked by a continual see-sawing between centralized and industry bargaining, with the employers pressing for the further decentralization of relations to company level, where possible on management's own terms. The ambivalence of Nordic decentralization appears to reflect employer concerns over the dangers of wage drift resulting from an established union presence in the workplace and (in the context of still relatively low unemployment, especially in Sweden) local labour market pressures. On other issues, such as work organization, Scandinavian employers have been more wholehearted in their commitment to decentralization, successfully overcoming union efforts (as in Sweden) to retain a strong central framework of 'codetermination' at company level.

There has also been considerable variation in the 'style' in which management has implemented decentralization and flexibility strategies. While even in countries with 'successful' and flexible industrial relations models, employers' organizations may generally have pursued objectives designed to strengthen their position *vis-à-vis* organized labour and to 'individualize' employment relations, 'macho' management has been the exception at the level of the individual enterprise. Even in Britain, where Thatcherism produced such a marked shift in the balance of power in favour of employers, aggressive anti-union management strategies have been evident only in isolated pockets of the private sector – in the publishing industry, for example – and in a public enterprise sector driven by political pressures; although less radical exclusionary strategies, bypassing or ignoring weakened unions, have been more common. In other countries, notably France and Italy, where capital-labour relations in the enterprise have traditionally been determined by raw power relations, an increasing 'institutionalization' of relationships has taken place; in the former under the impulse of a new legislative framework, in the latter through a combination of national political exchange and the wide variety of more or less formal, pragmatic structures of collaboration within the firm that have sprung up since the early 1980s. Nor, in general, has the pursuit of flexibility led to thoroughgoing 'human resource management' strategies aimed at individualizing the relationships between management and employees. Unlike the United States, where HRM has often accompanied a marginalization of the unions, in the countries studied here it has operated in parallel, usually accepting the constraints imposed by a union presence, sometimes actively involving the unions in its operation. In many cases, the adoption of HRM seems confined to changing the name of the personnel departments whose essential functions remain unaltered. The one area which has seen an individualization of relationships in many countries is that of the management of managerial and professional staff.

Within a broad pattern of industrial relations changes, therefore, there has been considerable variation, despite the common background. Some developments may reflect the conjunctural shift in the balance of power towards the employer resulting from recession or from governments hostile in varying degrees to trade unionism, and are thus likely to be reversed in periods of sustained economic recovery or when more sympathetic governments are returned to power. Other aspects of decentralization and flexibility, however, appear to reflect long-term developments in the dynamic of international competition, and the pressures they exert are likely, if anything, to intensify towards and through the millennium. It is worth reiterating that the pressures are not all in the direction of decentralization: for example, the centralized control of labour costs may well be a major concern as the EC economies converge within a single economic and monetary system. Moreover, space is still left for strategic choice: for example, as Dølvik and Stokland insist, one viable strategic option for Norwegian employers is to pursue with the unions a coordinated collaborative approach to the strengthening of international competitiveness.

The Unions: Has the Union Movement a Future?

The trade unions have, in most if not all the countries analysed in this volume, emerged from the 1980s to all appearances weaker than at the beginning of the decade. One manifestation is the general, but again not universal, trend towards lower union density; and in nearly all cases, the unions face severe problems of 'representativeness', finances, organization and mission. Again, the combination of structural change and conjunctural economic crisis can be used to explain current developments. The relationship between the two is, however, unclear. It seems likely that the weakening of unions at the point of production in Britain and elsewhere is in large part a reflection of recession and may hence be reversed in the economic upturn, especially where the balance of power is relatively 'uninstitutionalized' (see below). However, longer-term changes have undoubtedly occurred, and these may tempt the observer to extrapolate current trends into the future: the composition of the labour force in all the European countries has moved away from the strongholds of traditional unionism towards new sectors and occupational categories which have less of a union heritage (if any) and which in some cases may appear to be inherently more difficult to organize. As in Sweden, structural changes have thrown up new union constituencies – white-collar, service-sector and public employees – whose interests can no longer be accommodated within previously dominant union structures; the result has been an increase in disruptive inter-union competition, and notably in the Scandinavian context, a decline in traditional 'solidaristic' strategies.

The country studies, however, demonstrate that simple deterministic analyses of union decline or disintegration are inadequate. Leaving aside the issue of whether the traditional union movement was ever as strong, solidaristic and purposeful as is sometimes implied, evidence of current union debility is very variable. In some cases – the four Nordic countries, for example – unionization has increased. Elsewhere it has declined far less sharply in some cases than others. Thus factors other than the underlying structural changes must be at work. Important elements in the explanation are the influence of specific institutional and ideological factors. Thus union-controlled unemployment insurance funds in Denmark, Sweden, Belgium and elsewhere are seen as contributing to high union density, as is the role of Danish unions in enforcing individual employment rights through the labour courts. Ideological divisions have seriously weakened the French unions, although similar divisions has been far less detrimental in the Italian case, and more ambiguously so in Spain. In countries such as Luxembourg, Belgium or Holland, divisions based on the split between socialist or communist and catholic unionism have been contained and institutionalized. Once more, it must be stressed that independent explanatory factors constrain but do not determine outcomes, still leaving space for strategic choice of the actors.

Indeed, institutional leverage may in some cases be seen as a functional substitute for the strength inherent in high union density. In many countries union influence is exerted through industrial relations institutions in a way that is little dependent on levels of membership. For example, the more or less conventional wisdom on Germany – shared by Jacobi et al. in this volume – is that the extension of the outcomes of collective agreements negotiated by industry unions to all affected workers obviates the need for high unionization, while unions are protected by a structure of powerful institutions that gives them *de facto* influence at both workplace and industry levels. In Spain, and to a lesser degree in France, the unions' influence is demonstrated by their high vote in elections to workplace representative bodies. The limitations of union density as a measure of 'strength' are further shown by the power of apparently weak unions with low membership – again the Spanish case is illustrative – to attract considerable work-force support at times of 'mobilization': as in the highly successful general strike of December 1988. Conversely, high density does not necessarily indicate union strength, especially in national contexts where membership is often semi-compulsory (through the closed shop or analogous arrangements). Numbers are important, but not all-important.

Inter-union relationships also influence trade union strength and effectiveness. Many of our authors emphasize how increasing divisions are emerging between economism and 'solidarity'. A variant of this is explored by the Danish and Swedish contributions to this volume: the pursuit of 'solidarity' *within* union blocs (white-collar, blue-collar) has led to a widening of the gulf *between* blocs. Thus further fuel is added to the question (Crouch 1990: 359; cf. Hyman 1991b: 630): do union *movements*, as opposed to unions, have a future? The question is given added point by the generally declining influence of unions at national political level with the dismantling of corporatist arrangements (see below).

Union structure is important in a different respect. As Kjellberg emphasizes in his chapter, and has stressed in his previous work, a major reason for the strength of Scandinavian unionism lies in the integration of powerful central organizations and effective workplace representative mechanisms. The active system of workplace 'clubs' and workshop delegates provides an organic link between workers and national unions, helping sustain density levels in a more adverse climate. In very different national contexts, the resilience of German and Austrian trade unionism in the 1980s owes much to the *de facto* integration of statutory workplace representatives within the national union structures; while the looser but still real connections between Italian factory councils and the national confederations have likewise proved a source of strength. Two counter-examples reinforce the point. In Britain, self-confident and relatively autonomous shop steward organization was a potent force in favourable economic circumstances, despite the structurally chaotic and under-resourced system of national trade unionism; in hard times, this distinctive decentralization has proved a source of weakness. In France, the reverse pattern of superficially influential national organizations without an effective workplace base has proved even less capable of weathering the storm.

The role of the law as a support for trade union organization – particularly within the workplace – has an obvious bearing in this respect. In very different ways, in three of the national contexts mentioned above, legislative innovations in the 1970s helped reinforce the position of shop floor unionism in the 1980s. In Italy, the 1970 Workers' Statute provided an extensive array of rights for unionized employees within the workplace, both in terms of positive supports for collective representation and negative prohibitions on employer anti-union action. This has made it very difficult for employers to implement desired changes in the organization of production except by agreement with union representatives. In Germany, legislation in 1972 and 1976 considerably reinforced the system of codetermination, and gave statutory backing to the links between unions and works councils which had already been cemented in practice in the previous two decades. Here too, employers can hardly escape the need to manage by agreement. In Sweden, various pieces of legislation – most notably the 1976 Codetermination Act, bitterly opposed by the employers – reinforced the already strong position of shop-floor unionism, again encouraging micro-corporatist processes in the 1980s. So long as such legislative supports remain – and the complexities of the political process mean that in none of these cases is a radical alteration probable – trade unions are cushioned against the impact of pressures which in other national contexts have proved far more debilitating and disruptive.

Hence structural factors may be of crucial importance in explaining the contrasting experience of unions in different countries. Nevertheless, more 'voluntaristic' themes are also relevant: how far have unions been able to 'break free' of underlying structural constraints through imaginative strategies capable of attracting new constituencies? One element of such an attempt has been the effort of unions in many countries to appeal to new work forces by offering new kinds of services geared to the specific needs, for example, of women, youth, casual or part-time workers and immigrants. A second has been the attempt to devise new organizational forms capable of encompassing a broad range of interests while managing the conflicts between them: the crucial objective here has been to contain the pressures of white-collar workers. The comparison of Austria (where white-collar employees are subsumed within the single union confederation) with the Scandinavian countries (where rival confederations organizing such employees have become increasingly powerful) and with Germany (where DGB unions have held off the challenge of separate white-collar organizations) suggests that structural problems can be accommodated if not eradicated by skilful manipulation of representational categories (and by relaxing other union goals such as the commitment to 'pure' industrial unionism). Finally, the mechanistic association of unionism and effective union action with traditional categories of workers may be challenged. Indeed, as the country studies reveal, groups of white-collar workers in public sector occupations – teaching, health, local government, posts and telecommunications, and so on – have often been in the forefront of worker and union militancy over the last decade or two (see below). At the same time, these groups have posed problems for existing unions by developing new organizations – notably *coordinations* and *cobas* – to push their sectional interests, adding to the fragmentation of worker representation. But this may be partly a conjunctural rather than a secular phenomenon, arising from the current process of redefinition of the role of the public sector in European countries, and the consequent painful readjustments of its organization and finances.

A further element of union strength and weakness is their ability to respond to the changing agenda of management, especially with regard to the organization of work at company and workplace level – and indeed, to the increasing demands of members for more flexible work arrangements. Streeck (1991) argues that unions will only be able to maintain their strength where they can make an active contribution to the restructuring of production and rein in companies' temptations to adopt low-wage options. Our country studies suggest that the 'productivistic' influence of unions has been apparent not only in the expected cases such as Germany, but has also emerged in more surprising ways, notably in large (and sometimes small) Italian enterprises where the unions have accepted managerial objectives in exchange for influence over their achievement.

One final major issue on which our contributors cast light is the impact on trade unionism and industrial relations of large-scale unemployment. As is obvious from table A.7, the degree to which countries have been affected has varied enormously, for reasons both of economic vulnerability and of political will (Therborn 1986). However, in most of Europe in the 1980s there has been sustained unemployment at a level unprecedented since the inter-war depression (or in some cases, immediate post-war dislocation). Even in those countries which maintained near-full employment throughout the 1980s, the current position is cause for concern, with recent sharp increases in Sweden, and (from an even lower initial rate) Luxembourg and Switzerland.

There has now been sufficient time to assess some of the effects of a deteriorating labour market. One clear conclusion is that there is no simple and direct relationship – as some economists might suppose – between unemployment and trade union strength. It is true that in many European countries there has been a traumatic loss of employment in traditional strongholds of 'proletarian' trade unionism – coalmining, docks, steelmaking, old staple manufacturing industries – bringing with it a corresponding decline of union membership and a weak bargaining position for the unions affected. Britain is, of course, an exemplary case. However, such 'de-industrialization' and the accompanying job losses represent only the acceleration of a much longer-term decline (previously cushioned, in most countries, by rapid employment growth elsewhere). Such traditional union strongholds have long lost their centrality – except perhaps in symbolic and emotive terms – to most national labour movements.

As a corollary, the fate of the victims of economic crisis and restructuring may have little practical bearing on trade unionists employed elsewhere. Miners laid off by pit closures in the Rhondda or the Ruhr do not affect the labour market position of engineers in Solihull or Stuttgart. The strength of labour market segmentation has been clearly demonstrated in the 1980s. In most countries, unemployment disproportionately affects the young, and in particular those who have never held regular employment and thus have never been part of the constituency of trade unionism. The increasing peripheral and irregular labour force – to a large extent composed of women and migrant workers – likewise falls outside the traditional framework of trade unionism in most countries. In many cases, indeed, it can be argued that the forms of job control pursued with some success by unions over the decades, through both collective bargaining and legal regulation, constraining the employer's freedom to hire and fire, have inhibited new recruitment in times of uncertain product markets and have encouraged the resort to alternatives in the secondary labour market. Meanwhile the unions in the primary labour market retain a relatively secure membership base, and may have lost little of their former bargaining power. Recession and instability have their effects, not through labour market competition but rather through the uncertainties which result from product market competition (Hyman 1989: 195–7). To the extent that the closure of all or part of the employing organization is a plausible risk, 'endangered primary' workers and their unions may feel obliged to acquiesce in management initiatives which might formerly have been resisted, and may indeed welcome attempts to restructure industrial relations within a framework of micro-corporatism.

The State and Industrial Relations

The common context of structural transformation and economic crisis has also had a cross-national impact on the role of the state as regulator, as employer, and as participant in political exchange. First, in many countries, even those whose industrial relations systems have shown great solidity and continuity, the state has played a role in deregulating labour markets. This has responded both to employer pressure for increased flexibility in forms of labour contract, hours of work, and so on; and to the desire to tackle massive unemployment by providing additional (if precarious) points of entry into the labour market for groups such as young workers or the long-term unemployed. In Britain, where these two ambitions of deregulation were mutually reinforcing in the grand Thatcherite project of 'setting the market free', a further aim of government intervention, particularly in the 1980s, was to remove 'imperfections' impeding the operation of markets, notably in the form of trade union power. Yet elsewhere, deregulation may be far more modest (as in Germany) or combined with new forms of re-regulation (as in Italy).

Second, there has been a general dynamic across Europe to control public expenditure and to make the operation of the state more effective. This has been reinforced in the EC countries by agreed targets for reducing public sector deficits as part of the process of economic 'convergence'. One effect has been to put general pressure on the state's own employees. In most of the countries in this study, the average wages of public sector employees fell relative to those in the private sector in the second part of the 1970s and throughout the 1980s (cf. Oxley and Martin 1991: 166–7). While employment in the public service has been relatively stable, the public enterprise sector throughout Europe has borne the brunt of cuts in jobs: a reflection not only of the restructuring of state-owned traditional heavy industries such as steel, coalmining and shipbuilding, but of pressures for greater efficiency and more 'commercial', market-oriented approaches. Increasingly, the same pressures are also leading to the reorganization of central and local government, health and education, often according to techniques such as devolved management and 'internal markets' imported from the private sector (cf. Ferner 1991).

The third major tendency has been the weakening of corporatist or tripartite arrangements, and the withdrawal of the state from political exchange. This again reflects a confluence of conjunctural and more long-term factors. In recession, the state has been less able and willing to offer concessions to organized labour, especially when the concessions it has demanded of the unions in political exchange have encompassed painful economic restructuring and labour market liberalization as much as pay moderation. While few countries pursued market policies with the vigour of the British Conservatives, the renewed emphasis on market solutions was also a deterrent to state participation in political exchange: the frac-tured history of tripartism in Spain in the 1980s provides an example. More permanent underlying changes also contributed to the decline of tripartism. Streeck (1991) emphasizes the growing assertiveness of new interest groups within an increasingly fragmented labour movement, undermining one of the conditions of corporatist solutions, the effective centralized mediation of interests. Tripartism, by imposing moderation and compromise at cen-tral level, itself further encourages dissenting challenges from below. In addition, the interests of employers lie far more in issues of rationalization and competitiveness at decentralized, company level – affecting such ques-tions as the organization of production, flexibility of labour, and the motivation and involvement of staff – and rather less in the central control of labour costs at national level; though as suggested above, this interest may be renewed with the economic upturn and the resurgence of wage pressures, or – as recent Italian developments suggest – in the context of the exigencies of European monetary union.

Yet, again, despite these broad tendencies and their common origins in the changing economic and political context of the 1980s, it is the variability of our country studies that attracts attention. Tripartite institutional ar-rangements have unravelled in The Netherlands and are collapsing in Sweden, but in Austria they appear, despite considerable external strains, to be as strong as ever. Once more, the independent influence of strong and flexible institutions, able to withstand or adapt to change, appears to be confirmed. In Belgium, tripartism is severely stressed, but as a result of the centrifugal forces of the Belgian state rather than of factors common to other European countries. The radical exclusion of organized labour from political exchange in Britain during the 1980s contrasts with the unsettled oscillations in Spain or Italy; while in Portugal, 'social concertation' is seen by some (though not by our own more sceptical contributor) as the emerging new paradigm of Portuguese industrial relations. Corporatist bargaining is also robust in Ireland, where national concertation is seen as a major contributory factor in recent economic renewal.

Neither is liberalization and 'deregulation' of industrial relations a uniform trend. At one end of the spectrum, the radical British initiatives have hobbled union power through legal controls on industrial action and internal union organization. In the middle, the much more restrained measures of the Christian Democrats in Germany have imposed only limited constraints on the ability of unions to conduct industrial disputes. Both these cases contrast with situations where the state has intervened rather to establish or complete the institutional framework of industrial relations: in France with the Auroux laws, in Spain and Portugal after the fall of their dictatorships, in the Italian public sector. All these initiatives may be seen as going against the grain of more flexible, less constraining (for employers) institutional arrangements. Finally, trends to deregulation and re-regulation coexist within the same country. In the Latin countries generally, labour market liberalization has run in parallel with the consolidation of the legal and formal framework of industrial relations.

Patterns of Conflict

A notable common feature of the past decade is the considerable decline in strike activity in almost the whole of western Europe, as table A.11 indicates. It would be as foolish now as it was when Ross and Hartman (1960) coined the term to speak of a 'withering away of the strike'. Nevertheless, on all the familiar dimensions – number of stoppages, workers involved, days lost – there has been a sharp reduction in most of the countries with a previous high strike record, such as Britain, France, Ireland and Italy. Finland, Greece and Spain stand out as the heavily strike-prone countries of western Europe today. In the first of these at least, the evidence is that disputes are very concentrated in a small number of traditional 'proletarian' workplaces; in the latter two cases, the heritage of authoritarian dictatorship remains relevant, with weakly institutionalized bargaining institutions and a continuing tradition of politicized mobilization and contestation.

These exceptions aside, how is the general decline in strike-proneness to be explained? Have the realities of a tougher competitive environment, and the policies of conservative governments, encouraged a 'culture shift' towards cooperation and productivism? Or have circumstances in the 1980s merely caused a pragmatic (and reversible) adaptation to a shift in the balance of power and in the calculus of the costs and benefits of militant action? Such a debate has been common in Britain in the past decade, and in other countries also. Other factors can be brought into the explanatory matrix. The creation of new institutions of dispute resolution, or the fine-tuning of old mechanisms, is emphasized by a number of our authors. Most crucially, the crystallization of new structures of workplace representation can serve the dual function of damping discontents arising from the intra-firm restructuring of production, and of encouraging tendencies to 'wildcat cooperation' (Streeck 1984).

The significance of 'new actors' in industrial relations is less easy to assess. There is a long sociological tradition of identifying strike-proneness with 'mass workers' – the manual labour force of large manufacturing and analogous establishments. Trends towards smaller work units, from manu-facturing to services, and from manual to white-collar employment (and the associated feminization of the workforce) are commonly linked to declining strike activity. The new actors, it is argued, bring new attitudes, new identities and new interests: if they identify with trade unionism at all it is with one which de-emphasizes the role of militancy and struggle in its agenda. Yet there is a converse argument, particularly familiar in Italy, which speaks of a 'tertiarization of conflict': the theme here is that the service sector, and in particular public services, have become the new cockpit of conflict. As we suggest in our account of Italian industrial relations, this position can be overstated; what appears to have occurred is a relative stabilization of service-sector strikes, at a time when those in manufacturing have subsided dramatically. Nevertheless, a growing pro-portionate role of public services in the strike pattern is evident in many countries, including some where disputes in general have formerly been at a low level. Even as we write, the first major public-service strike for eighteen years is taking place in Germany. It is not difficult, of course, to analyse such 'tertiarization' in terms of the constraints on public budgets, the application of management approaches previously confined to the private sector, and perhaps also the relative sense of security among public employees.

What emerges clearly from the broad scope of our studies, however, is the diversity of national experience, in the public services and more gener-ally. Nor is the lack of a uniform pattern surprising. Strikes are necessarily the outcome of a relationship, of the interaction of the strategies and tactics of two (or more) parties each attempting to interpret ambiguous signals from their counterparts. Institutions may contain, or at times amplify, the explosive consequences of incompatible objectives or simple miscalcula-tions; and institutions vary between and within countries. This is a theme to which we now turn.

Forms of Explanation

The discussion so far suggests that, despite common contexts and general trends, considerable variety persists. There has been convergence of sys-tems in some respects, but increased diversity in others (cf. Streeck 1991;

Crouch 1991). This applies equally within blocs or 'models' as between more disparate groups of countries. One of the virtues of setting the four 'Nordic' cases side-by-side, for example, is to emphasize considerable diversity within the overall features of the model, as can be seen from Kjellberg's introduction to the Nordic group of countries in this volume. Within individual countries, one observes patterns of change, but also of considerable continuity. Some cases – Austria, Switzerland, Luxembourg – have appeared as islands of relative stability, tranquillity even, in a turbulent sea of change. Radical transformations have been few: even in Britain, despite the attempt to uproot the traditional ethos of industrial relations, the system retains many of its former characteristics of 'muddling through', as Edwards et al. demonstrate.

How then, are we to explain these patterns of diversity and convergence between countries, of change and continuity within countries? What *kinds* of explanations can be put forward?

First, while the international economic background has been a common one, it has not been straightforwardly so. It has differential impact on countries that vary in their productive base, in their sectoral distribution of output and employment, in their orientation to the international economy, in the extent of foreign and state ownership of industry, and so on. In some respects, these differences reflect, or are bound up with, very long-term economic factors, such as the timing of industrialization, that continue to have pervasive consequences. Taking the Nordic countries, for example, the economies of Finland and Norway, dominated by scattered forest industries, contrast with the more highly industrialized Swedish economy, with its large, powerful and internationally oriented engineering industry. While all are highly dependent on the export sector, Finland has until recently been oriented more towards its giant eastern neighbour than to the west. Such variations have thrown up their own amalgam of class interests and alliances, leading to particular accommodations and conflicts: while in Denmark capital and labour were reaching a basic settlement at the end of the last century that was to lay the foundation of Danish industrial relations up to the present, in Finland, unresolved class antagonisms in the wake of independence from Russia were manifested in the civil war of 1918 and cast a shadow over subsequent decades.

Second, the political sphere has an independent impact on countries' responses to cross-national pressures for change. In many respects, of course, the 'political' cannot be separated from the 'economic'. Thus, as Fulcher (1988) argues, the nature and evolution of unionism and industrial relations are influenced by the *combination* of the timing of industrialization and the appearance of socialist political parties. The dispersed rural economic structure in some of the Nordic countries has given rise to some characteristic amalgams of class interests and accommodations. Similarly, the geo-politics of Italy are intimately bound up with the distribution of economic activity and resources between north and south. None the less, politics has its own (relatively) autonomous and irreducible influence. As with the economy, there are different 'layers of variation' in the political environment, each with specific effects on the response of industrial relations to external pressures (cf. Ferner 1988: 160–2). At the most general level, long-term historical features of the political system leave a persistent legacy – affecting such factors as the degree of centralization, the sorts of relationships between the state and civil society, and forms of political action. For example, the centralized, authoritative interventions of the French state may be compared with the weak Italian state, operating in symbiosis with political parties through clientelistic relationships. In all cases they continue to influence profoundly the possibilities of current industrial relations.

A second layer of explanation is provided by shorter- or medium-term phases, based on political alliances that have some degree of stability over time: the post-war 'Butskellite' consensus in Britain, the social-democratic hegemony in Sweden from the 1930s to the 1980s, the Francoist dictatorship in Spain, the Salazarist in Portugal, or the briefer regime of the colonels in Greece. In each case, the political context influenced the agenda of industrial relations, and in a sense continues to do so: not only are the institutions sometimes retained (albeit in modified form), but when a new phase commences, its agenda tends to be shaped by what has gone before – defined in terms either of its differentiation from or its continuity with the core features of the earlier period.

These phases may in turn be sub-divided into shorter, 'conjunctural' periods, caused by changes of government, transitions from one regime to another, and so on. While throughout the polities of Europe, governments may have been wrestling with the political requirements of economic restructuring, the precise form of the political project devised is contingent. Thus, while Thatcherism or the recently elected conservative administration in Sweden may be seen as logical outcomes whose advent was heralded by gradual changes in economic structure, class composition and the nature of the labour movement (for example, the decline of 'solidarity' in the Swedish model), and by political and economic crisis, they were not *necessary* outcomes; alternative scenarios were perfectly imaginable, and their specific effect would have been significantly different. Even political projects of market liberalization – such as the British and the Spanish – with marked similarities, are based on quite different political alliances and bases of support that constrain their action in different ways.

The effects of such political conjunctures may likewise be transient: in Spain, Portugal and Greece, for example, the politics of the transition from dictatorship, with the emphasis on the primacy of democratic consolidation, put off economic readjustment, but only temporarily. But the consequences of political (or for that matter economic) conjunctures may be longer-lasting. This is especially the case when the division between the short and the medium term is naturally blurred, and when conjunctural developments turn out to mark a 'watershed' or 'sea-change', defining a rupture with the previous phase of development: as indeed in the case of many aspects of the democratic transition in southern Europe, or Thatcherism in Britain. In other cases, the conjuncture may be so traumatic as to leave a durable if not permanent imprint on industrial relations. Examples include the impact of war, and particularly of civil war: as Traxler's contribution makes clear, Austro-corporatism reflects a deep desire to escape the fatal divisions that rent apart Austrian society in the 1930s and prepared the ground for Nazism.

As the last example suggests, one way in which political conjunctures or longer-term phases leave a concrete 'residue' is in the form of industrial relations institutions. 'Institution' is a term which we employ flexibly: it encompasses highly formalized structures backed by legislation, as in Germany; or as in The Netherlands, Belgium and Switzerland, where 'pillarized' arrangements are attempts to sublimate deep-seated religious or linguistic divisions; formal arrangements established in historic framework agreements, as in the 'basic agreements' that govern the industrial relations of Nordic countries; and more informal, albeit customary and established, structures typified by workplace representation in British industry in the 1960s and 1970s.

Institutions may be the crystallization of specific class forces and balances of power, but once established they have a life and reality of their own, independent of political (or economic) fluctuations or caprices; they are, in Streeck's term, 'sticky', especially when enshrined in law (1987: 287–8; 296). This institutional persistence appears to explain much of the variability in countries' responses to common influences in the 1980s.

As indicated above, while accepting the 'relative autonomy' of institutions, we take from the 'regulation' approach the notion that changes in economic structure since the 1970s will have had a substantial impact on 'regulatory institutions'. Yet, as the history of the last decade or so underlines, the institutions mediate intensifying external pressures with greater or lesser degrees of success. We suggest that three broad types of national context can be distinguished, in terms of the strength and rigidity of the social regulation of employment relations; and that the differences can help us understand different trajectories in the 1980s and anticipate different fates in the 1990s.

The first variant involves industrial relations institutions which in relative terms are both strong and inflexible. Here, the pressures of structural change in markets and employment cannot be accommodated by evolutionary adaptation: the consequence is crisis and breakdown or enforced transformation. The British and Dutch cases seem to meet this model; perhaps Sweden too should be interpreted in these terms. Indeed, the Thatcherite case suggests that part of the ideological battle has been to *depict* existing institutions as barriers to change that must be systematically destroyed; the same appears increasingly true of the new centre-right political project in Sweden. Institutional rigidity, in other words, may be a question of subjective perception and not merely objective reality.

It is worth noting, therefore, that despite the support of employers at national level for such radical projects, their practice at the workplace may be somewhat different. In Britain, for example, the evidence is that most employers have refrained from a frontal challenge to the institutions of collective bargaining; they have been willing to sustain unions' representative status so long as the latter do not seriously obstruct management initiatives. In practice, it seems clear, the former strength of workplace union institutions in Britain was crucially dependent on favourable economic circumstances. Deprived of their environmental support, they no longer function as barriers to management strategies. Thus previously strong institutions may become 'facades', whose structures and formal mechanisms remain in place, but whose vital processes no longer function.

It can be argued that the same disjunction between formal structure and effective functioning is true of newly institutionalized industrial relations systems such as Spain, Portugal or Greece (not to mention France) where the structures established in the initial democratic upsurge have not so far generated any great strength or depth of bargaining in practice; observers talk of the 'impoverishment' of bargaining, although future developments may perhaps breathe new life into existing institutions. Other countries have shown a more fluctuating pattern, with institutions being temporarily neutralized, only to reassert themselves subsequently. This was the case, as Vilrokx and Van Leemput show, in Belgium where for much of the 1980s the state intervened directly to regulate pay determination, only to withdraw again at the end of the decade (although leaving its interventionary mechanisms in place).

In the second variant, institutional regulation is relatively weak. Transformations in economic structure therefore create little pressure for institutional change in industrial relations, and to the extent that such changes do occur the explanation lies more in the 'relative autonomy' of the political process. In poorly institutionalized systems, changes are much less mediated by persistent structures. Traditionally, Italy and France have been depicted as examples (though in the former case, as we suggest, 'informal institutionalization' is actually strong). Several consequences have flowed from under-institutionalization. First, as mentioned, the interaction of capital and labour tends to be determined far more by 'raw' power relations than in more mediated, institutionalized systems, where fluctuations are dampened by institutional process. Another way of putting this is that the weaker or more brittle the institutions, the more scope there is for strategic choice by the actors, notably management. In the highly institutionalized German environment, the limitations on German employers' adopting the tenets of 'macho' management are strong. Conversely, French or British managers may be able to choose whether to exclude, ignore, confront or collaborate with the unions.

Second, as the Italian case illustrates, relatively under-institutionalized systems may undergo bewilderingly rapid transformations. The rampant workplace power of the years following the 'hot autumn' of 1969 proved to be transient, while an observer of the scene at the beginning of the 1980s would have been hard put to predict the mushrooming of collaborative relationships between managements, unions and work forces in many if not most large Italian companies in the course of the decade. Indeed, researchers have spoken of the recent institutionalization and 'proceduralization' of company industrial relations, through dense formal structures of joint committees and networks of collective agreements. However, one may see such developments as being made possible by the previous relative institutionalization of industrial relations in the area of workplace rights, through the Workers' Statute. This indicates the importance, when talking of institutionalization, of differentiating between levels and areas of the industrial relations system. In several countries since the 1980s, the deregulation or re-regulation of labour market institutions in the direction of greater flexibility has gone hand-in-hand with a greater procedural institutionalization in the sphere of industrial relations, particularly collective bargaining and participation.

The third variant of national responses to economic structural change involves regulatory institutions which are strong but flexible. Here, industrial relations can be adapted in a relatively gradual, consensual and painless manner. The classic case of flexible adaptation is that of the dual German system of sectoral bargaining and workplace representation. As Jacobi et al. explain in this volume, it has proved capable of handling not only the challenge of employer demands for flexibility, but that of German unification as well. In such systems, institutional arrangements have acted as a brake on employers, preventing them from fully exploiting the changing balance of power between capital and labour resulting from the recession and structural transformation. But in Scandinavia, The Netherlands, and in some ways Belgium, among others, there have been signs of analogous adaptability, even though the institutions have proved somewhat less resilient.

The actual process and character of change in this third type of context will be influenced both by the sources of the system's strength and the directions of its flexibility. Streeck (1991) has suggested that where existing institutional arrangements are based on welfare-state, redistributional, assumptions, they have been more open to challenge in the conditions of the 1980s and 1990s. Those that have survived have demonstrated a flexibility in responding to companies' needs in an era of intense international competition. Concomitantly, the ability of the unions to maintain their strength within the system is a function of their ability to make a contribution to the restructuring of production. Streeck points to the increasing 'productivistic' role of unions not only in Germany, but also in Sweden – a development described in detail in Kjellberg's chapter in this volume – and in Italy. This assessment may be questioned partly on the ground that an active productivistic orientation appears not to be a necessary condition for institutional flexibility. In Switzerland, and more particularly in Austria, the role of the unions in the organization of work has been limited and flexibility has been achieved through the undisputed exercise of managerial prerogative. Moreover, the long-term stability and effectiveness of the productivistic orientation is still in doubt. Even in the 'strong' case of Germany, tensions exist. In a context of rapid technological innovation and changes in work organization, relations at the point of production threaten to outstrip the capacity of company-level worker representation to monitor and control developments, while 'productivity coalitions' are achieved at the expense of non-core employees (cf. Hyman 1988). More generally, observers have raised doubts about the ability of the unions to respond effectively to the conflicting demands of consensus and flexibility: for example, the assumption that employer demands can be accommodated may be erroneous and unions may be unable to control their members' dissatisfaction with the new pressures – for example, for flexible but highly inconvenient new hours of work (cf. Saba 1992: 134–7).

Arguably, the differing recent experiences in those countries with strong but flexible institutions are partly attributable to the particular make-up of 'flexible rigidities' (Dore 1986) within the industrial relations system: in other words, which aspects are relatively open to change, which are far more resistant. In Germany, as Streeck has emphasized, it is extremely difficult for employers to follow policies of 'hire-and-fire'; but the corollary accepted by management and unions alike is a flexible approach to work organization, vocational training and task allocation. In Italy, substantial rigidities in legally permissible recruitment practices have been eroded by the growth of the 'underground economy'; as a reaction, a distinctive form of flexible adaptation has ensued in which the derogation from established statutory restrictions is conditional on collectively bargained alternative arrangements. Here is perhaps the clearest example of a process familiar in a number of national contexts: what may be termed 'regulated deregulation', whereby the procedural commitment to negotiated change is the fixed principle, while the specific content of regulation is treated flexibly. Often related is what may be termed 'centrally coordinated decentralization': the trend in much of northern Europe towards a controlled devolution of power from central confederations, on both the union and the employer sides, to lower levels. Here the principle of articulation between levels remains a firm point of reference; the actual distribution of functions between the levels has become flexible. In systems which have accommodated change rather than suffering disruptive transformation, adaptation has tended to follow the grain of systemic flexibility.

What of the 1990s? It is certainly possible that new changes in economic structure may generate forces for different types of institutional adaptation. In some cases, perhaps, the directions of flexibility which proved adequate in the 1980s may be inappropriate for the new decade – let alone the new century. Conversely, industrial relations systems which were transformed painfully in the 1980s may evolve more easily in the 1990s. Will European integration itself generate a Euro-level mode of regulation? We will not speculate here, but the authors in our subsequent volume will be encouraged to address such issues in ways which are firmly grounded yet imaginative.

References

Brünnecke, K. Faust, M., Jauch, P. and Deutschmann, C. 1991: Operative Decentralisation – The Influence of Different National Systems. Paper presented to Workshop on Centralisation and Decentralisation of Labour Management in The Euro-Company, University of Warwick, 13–15 December 1991.

Crouch, C. 1990: Afterword. In G. Baglioni and C. Crouch (eds), *European Industrial Relations. The Challenge of Flexibility*. London: Sage, 356–62.

Crouch, C. 1991: Ambiguities of Decentralisation. Paper presented to Third European Regional Congress of IIRA, Bari, September 1991.

Dore, R. 1986: *Flexible Rigidities: Industrial Policy and Structural Adjustment in the Japanese Economy 1970–1980*. London: Athlone.

European Industrial Relations Review (EIRR) 1990: *Non-Standard Forms of Employment in Europe*. London: Eclipse.

Ferner, A. 1988: *Governments, Managers and Industrial Relations*. Oxford: Blackwell.

Ferner, A. 1991: Changing Public Sector Industrial Relations in Europe. Warwick Papers in Industrial Relations, 37. Coventry: IRRU.

Fulcher, J. 1988: On the Explanation of Industrial Relations Diversity: Labour Movements, Employers and the State in Britain and Sweden. *British Journal of Industrial Relations*, 26, 2.

Hall, M. 1992: Legislating for Employee Participation: A Case Study of the European Works Councils Directive. Warwick Papers in Industrial Relations, 39. Coventry: IRRU.

Hyman, R. 1988: Flexible Specialization: Miracle or Myth? In R. Hyman and W. Streeck (eds), *New Technology and Industrial Relations*, Oxford: Blackwell, 48–60.

Hyman, R. 1989: Dualism and Division in Labour Strategies. In R. Hyman, *The Political Economy of Industrial Relations. Theory and Practice in a Cold Climate*, Oxford: Blackwell, 188–201.

Hyman, R. 1991a: *Plus ça change?* The Theory of Production and the Production of Theory. In A. Pollert (ed.), *Farewell to Flexibility?*, Oxford: Blackwell, 259–83.

Hyman, R. 1991b: European Unions: Towards 2000. *Work, Employment & Society*, 5, 4, 621–39.

Jessop, B., Bonnett, K., Bromley, S. and Ling, T. 1988: *Thatcherism: A Tale of Two Nations*. Cambridge: Polity.

OECD 1991: *OECD Economic Outlook. Historical statistics 1960–1969*. Paris: OECD.

Oxley, H. and Martin, J. 1991: Controlling Public Spending and Deficits: Trends in the 1980s and Prospects for the 1990s. *OECD Economic Studies*, 17, Autumn, 145–89.

Ramsay, H. 1990: 1992 – The Year of the Multinational? Corporate Behaviour, Industrial Restructuring and Labour in the Single Market. Warwick Papers in Industrial Relations, 35. Coventry: IRRU.

Ross, A. and Hartman, P. 1960: *Changing Patterns of Industrial Conflict*. New York: Wiley.

Saba, L. 1992: Il sindacato e la partecipazione: forme, istituti e organismi partecipativi nel rapporto con l'impresa. In M. Ambrosini, M. Colasanto and L. Saba (eds), *Partecipazione e Coinvolgimento nell'impresa degli anni '90*, Milan: FrancoAngeli, 51–115.

Sisson, K., Waddington, J. and Whitston, C. 1992: The Structure of Capital in the

European Community: The Size of Companies and the Implications for Industrial Relations. Warwick Papers in Industrial Relations, 38. Coventry: IRRU.

Sorge, A. and Streeck, W. 1988: Industrial Relations and Technical Change: The
Case for an Extended Perspective. In R. Hyman and W. Streeck (eds), *New
Technology and Industrial Relations*, Oxford: Blackwell, 19–47.

Streeck, W. 1984: Neo-Corporatist Industrial Relations and the Economic Crisis in
West Germany. In J. Goldthorpe (ed.), *Order and Conflict in Contemporary Capitalism*, Oxford: Clarendon, 291–314.

Streeck, W. 1987: The Uncertainties of Management in the Management of Uncertainty: Employers, Labor Relations and Industrial Adjustment in the 1980s. *Work,
Employment & Society*, 1,3, 281–308.

Streeck, W. 1991: Industrial Relations in a Changing Western Europe. Paper presented to Third European Regional Congress of the IIRA, Bari, September.

Therborn, G. 1986: *Why Some Peoples Are More Unemployed Than Others. The Strange
Paradox of Growth and Unemployment*. London: Verso.

Windolf, P. 1989: Productivity Coalitions and the Future of European Corporatism.
Industrial Relations, 28, 1, 1–20.

Table A.1 Total labour force as percentage of population aged 15–64 1960–89

Country	1960	1968	1974	1979	1980	1981	1982	1983	1984	1985	1986	1987	1988	1989
Austria	70.7	67.4	68.7	64.9	64.6	64.5	66.4	65.6	66.3	65.8	66.2	66.9	66.8	67.1
Belgium	60.7	61.7	62.8	62.8	63.0	63.0	63.0	62.8	62.3	62.0	61.8	61.8	62.0	62.1
Denmark	71.2	74.9	76.6	79.8	80.3	80.1	80.4	80.9	80.3	81.0	82.5	82.6	83.8	83.4
Finland	78.0	72.0	72.8	75.5	76.4	76.9	77.5	77.4	77.4	77.7	77.7	77.2	76.9	77.2
France	70.4	67.2	68.0	68.4	68.1	67.6	67.3	66.4	66.1	65.8	65.8	65.8	65.6	65.7
Germany	70.3	69.2	68.5	66.8	68.5	68.3	68.0	67.5	67.2	67.6	68.2	68.6	68.9	68.6
Greece	65.8	58.7	57.0	55.4	55.9	58.7	58.7	59.9	59.8	59.6	59.1	58.7	59.5	59.2
Ireland	67.3	66.9	63.0	62.4	62.3	62.6	63.0	62.7	62.0	61.3	61.4	61.6	61.0	60.3
Italy	66.6	60.4	58.8	60.2	60.8	60.8	60.2	60.1	59.8	59.8	60.5	61.0	60.9	61.2
Luxembourg	61.8	59.5	65.2	64.4	64.4	64.2	63.9	63.3	63.4	63.9	64.9	66.4	68.0	70.3
The Netherlands	61.7	59.7	57.2	56.5	57.7	59.7	60.2	59.0	58.8	58.6	58.5	64.1	65.2	65.5
Norway	64.3	63.7	68.6	75.6	75.3	76.1	76.3	76.5	76.7	77.5	79.3	80.3	80.1	78.7
Portugal	59.4	62.4	73.5	73.5	73.9	72.5	71.6	74.3	72.9	71.9	71.4	71.4	71.6	71.9
Spain	61.6	61.6	61.5	57.7	57.1	56.8	56.7	56.6	56.2	55.9	56.2	57.7	58.4	58.6
Sweden	74.3	73.5	76.9	80.5	81.0	81.0	81.2	81.3	81.4	82.0	81.3	81.7	82.3	82.8
Switzerland	75.5	77.2	77.4	73.8	74.4	75.1	74.7	74.5	74.7	75.5	75.8	76.1	76.2	76.4
United Kingdom	72.0	72.4	73.0	74.3	74.4	73.7	73.1	72.4	73.5	74.6	74.5	74.9	75.5	76.1

Source: OECD 1991.

Table A.2 Female labour force as percentage of female population aged 15–64, 1960–89

Country	1960	1968	1974	1979	1980	1981	1982	1983	1984	1985	1986	1987	1988	1989
Austria	52.1	49.8	52.8	49.1	48.7	49.0	50.2	49.7	51.5	51.0	51.7	53.0	53.7	54.3
Belgium	36.4	39.4	42.4	46.3	47.0	47.7	48.3	48.7	48.9	49.3	49.9	50.6	51.4	51.6
Denmark	43.5	56.4	63.2	69.9	71.4	71.8	72.6	74.2	73.8	74.5	76.5	76.8	77.6	77.3
Finland	65.6	60.1	65.5	68.9	70.1	71.1	72.4	72.7	72.9	73.7	73.4	72.9	73.0	73.3
France	46.6	47.1	50.6	54.2	54.4	54.4	54.7	54.4	54.8	54.9	55.3	55.7	55.8	56.2
Germany	49.2	47.7	49.8	49.6	51.4	51.7	51.8	51.6	51.7	52.3	53.4	54.4	54.8	54.7
Greece	41.6	33.4	32.6	32.8	33.0	36.9	36.4	40.4	40.9	41.8	41.6	41.7	43.5	43.4
Ireland	34.8	34.7	34.2	35.2	36.3	36.9	37.6	37.8	36.9	36.6	37.2	38.5	37.6	37.5
Italy	39.6	33.6	34.1	38.7	39.6	40.0	39.8	40.3	40.7	41.0	42.3	43.4	43.7	44.3
Luxembourg	32.6	30.7	37.3	39.8	39.9	41.9	41.2	41.7	42.5	43.2	44.3	45.7	47.6	49.8
The Netherlands	26.2	27.5	29.7	33.4	35.5	37.9	39.0	40.3	40.7	40.9	41.3	48.8	50.6	51.0
Norway	36.3	37.7	50.0	61.7	62.3	63.9	64.3	65.5	66.3	68.0	71.0	72.3	72.8	71.2
Portugal	19.9	25.7	52.4	57.3	57.0	57.3	56.6	59.1	58.1	58.0	57.1	58.1	59.1	59.6
Spain	26.0	27.7	33.0	32.6	32.2	31.8	32.5	33.2	33.1	33.3	34.2	37.4	39.3	39.9
Sweden	50.1	56.6	64.9	72.8	74.1	75.3	75.9	76.6	77.3	78.1	78.3	79.4	80.1	80.5
Switzerland	51.0	51.0	54.0	53.0	54.1	55.4	55.3	55.2	55.7	56.2	56.6	57.3	57.9	58.5
United Kingdom	46.1	49.8	54.3	58.0	58.3	57.2	57.1	57.2	59.1	60.5	61.3	62.4	63.7	65.4

Source: OECD 1991.

Table A.3 Female labour force as percentage of total labour force 1960–89

Country	1960	1968	1974	1979	1980	1981	1982	1983	1984	1985	1986	1987	1988	1989
Austria	39.4	38.9	39.8	38.9	38.7	38.9	38.7	38.8	39.7	39.5	39.7	40.1	40.5	40.7
Belgium	30.2	32.0	33.7	36.7	37.2	37.7	38.2	38.7	39.1	39.7	40.2	40.7	41.2	41.3
Denmark	30.9	37.7	40.9	43.5	44.1	44.5	44.9	45.4	45.6	45.6	45.8	46.0	45.7	45.7
Finland	43.7	42.9	45.7	46.0	46.1	46.4	46.9	47.0	47.1	47.3	47.1	47.1	47.2	47.2
France	33.3	35.1	37.0	39.4	39.8	40.1	40.5	40.9	41.4	41.7	42.0	42.4	42.6	42.8
Germany	37.3	36.1	37.2	37.6	37.8	38.0	38.2	38.4	38.6	38.7	39.0	39.4	39.4	39.4
Greece	32.6	29.3	29.3	30.1	30.0	31.9	31.5	34.1	34.6	35.4	35.6	35.9	36.9	36.9
Ireland	25.6	25.6	26.8	27.8	28.7	29.1	29.5	29.8	29.5	29.6	30.0	30.9	30.5	30.7
Italy	30.7	28.5	29.7	32.8	33.3	33.5	33.7	34.2	34.6	34.9	35.5	36.1	36.3	36.6
Luxembourg	26.5	26.0	28.1	30.8	30.9	32.7	32.3	33.1	33.6	33.9	34.1	34.3	34.7	35.0
The Netherlands	21.5	23.0	25.7	29.2	30.4	31.4	32.0	33.8	34.2	34.5	34.8	37.6	38.3	38.4
Norway	28.2	29.4	36.1	40.3	40.9	41.4	41.6	42.2	42.6	43.2	44.1	44.3	44.6	44.4
Portugal	17.8	21.8	37.8	40.2	39.7	40.7	40.7	40.9	41.0	41.4	41.0	41.7	42.3	42.4
Spain	21.8	23.0	27.3	28.6	28.4	28.3	28.9	29.5	29.6	29.9	30.5	32.5	33.8	34.1
Sweden	33.6	38.1	41.8	44.7	45.2	46.0	46.2	46.6	46.9	47.1	47.6	48.0	48.0	47.9
Switzerland	34.1	33.4	34.5	35.8	36.2	36.7	36.8	36.9	37.1	37.0	37.0	37.3	37.6	37.8
United Kingdom	32.7	34.7	37.4	39.1	39.2	38.9	39.1	39.5	40.2	40.5	41.0	41.6	42.1	42.8

Source: OECD 1991.

Table A.4 Employment in agriculture as a percentage of civilian employment 1960–89

Country	1960	1968	1974	1979	1980	1981	1982	1983	1984	1985	1986	1987	1988	1989
Austria	22.6	16.0	11.4	10.7	10.5	10.3	10.0	9.9	9.4	9.0	8.7	8.6	8.1	8.0
Belgium	8.7	5.5	3.8	3.3	3.2	3.2	3.1	3.2	3.1	3.1	3.0	3.0	2.8	2.8
Denmark	18.2	12.7	9.6	7.2	7.1	7.3	7.5	7.4	6.7	6.7	5.9	5.7	5.8	5.7
Finland	35.2	25.6	16.3	13.8	13.5	13.0	13.2	12.7	12.2	11.5	11.0	10.4	9.8	8.9
France	22.5	15.6	10.6	9.0	8.7	8.4	8.2	7.9	7.8	7.6	7.3	7.0	6.7	6.4
Germany	14.0	9.9	7.1	5.8	5.3	5.2	5.0	5.0	4.8	4.6	4.4	4.2	4.0	3.7
Greece	57.1	44.5	36.0	30.8	30.3	30.7	28.9	29.9	29.4	28.9	28.5	27.0	26.6	25.3
Ireland	37.3	29.4	22.8	19.6	18.3	17.3	17.0	17.0	16.7	15.9	15.7	15.3	15.4	15.1
Italy	32.6	22.9	17.5	14.9	14.3	13.4	12.4	12.4	11.9	11.2	10.9	10.5	9.9	9.3
Luxembourg	16.6	10.3	7.2	5.8	5.4	5.1	4.9	4.7	4.7	4.4	4.2	3.9	3.7	3.4
The Netherlands	9.8	6.8	5.7	5.3	4.9	4.9	5.0	5.0	5.0	4.9	4.8	4.9	4.8	4.7
Norway	21.6	15.4	10.6	8.6	8.5	8.4	8.1	7.7	7.4	7.4	7.4	6.7	6.4	6.6
Portugal	43.9	33.1	34.9	30.5	27.3	26.0	25.2	23.2	23.8	23.9	21.9	22.2	20.7	19.0
Spain	38.7	29.0	23.2	20.0	19.3	18.8	18.6	18.7	18.5	18.3	16.2	15.1	14.4	13.0
Sweden	15.7	9.1	6.7	5.8	5.6	5.6	5.6	5.4	5.1	4.8	4.2	3.9	3.8	3.6
Switzerland	14.5	9.4	7.5	7.2	6.9	6.6	6.4	6.4	6.2	6.1	5.9	5.9	5.7	5.6
United Kingdom	4.7	3.5	2.8	2.7	2.6	2.7	2.7	2.7	2.6	2.5	2.5	2.4	2.3	2.1

Source: OECD 1991.

Table A.5 Employment in industry as a percentage of civilian employment 1960–89

Country	1960	1968	1974	1979	1980	1981	1982	1983	1984	1985	1986	1987	1988	1989
Austria	40.3	40.9	42.3	40.5	40.3	40.0	39.9	38.8	38.1	38.1	37.8	37.7	37.4	37.0
Belgium	45.0	43.3	41.0	35.5	34.7	33.3	32.2	31.4	30.8	30.2	29.6	28.9	28.3	28.5
Denmark	36.9	37.4	32.3	32.5	30.4	29.3	28.3	28.4	26.8	28.1	28.2	28.2	27.2	27.4
Finland	32.6	33.3	36.0	34.7	34.6	35.0	33.8	33.2	32.6	31.9	32.0	31.2	30.6	30.9
France	37.6	38.6	39.4	36.3	35.9	35.2	34.6	33.8	32.9	32.0	31.4	30.8	30.3	30.1
Germany	47.0	47.1	46.7	44.2	43.7	43.0	42.1	41.5	41.2	40.9	40.7	40.3	39.9	39.8
Greece	17.4	22.9	27.8	30.0	30.2	29.0	29.2	28.6	27.8	27.4	28.1	28.0	27.2	27.5
Ireland	23.7	28.9	32.6	32.3	32.5	32.1	31.3	29.7	29.2	28.9	28.7	27.9	27.8	28.4
Italy	33.9	37.8	39.3	37.8	37.9	37.6	37.1	36.1	34.5	33.6	33.1	32.6	32.4	32.4
Luxembourg	44.9	46.6	44.9	38.5	38.1	37.2	36.4	35.4	34.7	33.8	33.5	32.9	31.9	31.2
The Netherlands	40.5	39.1	35.9	32.5	31.4	29.9	28.7	28.1	28.3	28.1	26.8	26.8	26.4	26.5
Norway	35.6	36.6	34.3	30.3	29.7	29.3	28.6	27.4	27.6	27.2	27.1	27.0	26.4	25.3
Portugal	31.3	32.9	33.8	35.0	36.6	37.0	37.5	35.3	34.1	33.9	34.1	34.9	35.1	35.3
Spain	30.3	34.4	37.2	36.6	36.1	35.3	34.1	33.5	32.7	31.7	32.0	32.3	32.5	32.9
Sweden	40.3	41.1	37.0	32.5	32.2	31.3	30.3	29.9	29.8	29.8	30.1	29.8	29.5	29.4
Switzerland	46.4	46.8	44.3	39.7	38.1	37.9	36.9	36.0	35.7	35.6	35.7	35.3	35.1	35.1
United Kingdom	47.7	45.2	42.0	38.7	37.7	35.8	34.6	33.4	32.3	31.6	30.8	30.2	29.7	29.4

Source: OECD 1991.

Table A.6 Employment in services as a percentage of civilian employment 1960–89

Country	1960	1968	1974	1979	1980	1981	1982	1983	1984	1985	1986	1987	1988	1989
Austria	37.1	43.1	46.3	48.8	49.3	49.8	50.0	51.3	52.4	52.9	53.6	53.7	54.6	55.1
Belgium	46.4	51.2	55.2	61.2	62.1	63.6	64.7	65.4	66.1	66.7	67.4	68.2	68.9	68.7
Denmark	44.8	49.9	58.0	60.3	62.4	63.3	64.2	64.2	66.5	65.2	65.9	66.1	67.1	66.9
Finland	32.2	41.1	47.6	51.6	51.8	51.9	53.0	54.2	55.2	56.5	57.0	58.4	59.6	60.2
France	39.9	45.8	49.9	54.8	55.4	56.4	57.3	58.3	59.3	60.4	61.3	62.2	63.0	63.5
Germany	39.1	43.0	43.2	50.0	51.0	51.8	52.8	53.6	54.1	54.5	54.9	55.5	56.1	56.5
Greece	25.5	32.6	36.2	39.2	39.5	40.4	42.0	41.5	42.8	43.7	43.4	45.0	46.2	47.1
Ireland	39.0	41.7	44.6	48.1	49.2	50.6	51.6	53.2	54.1	55.2	55.5	56.8	56.8	56.5
Italy	33.5	39.3	43.2	47.3	47.8	49.0	50.5	51.5	53.6	55.2	56.0	56.8	57.7	58.2
Luxembourg	38.4	43.1	47.9	55.7	56.5	57.7	58.7	59.9	60.6	61.9	62.3	63.2	64.4	65.4
The Netherlands	49.7	54.1	58.4	62.2	63.6	65.2	66.3	66.9	66.8	67.0	68.4	68.3	68.8	68.8
Norway	42.9	48.0	55.1	61.1	61.9	62.4	63.4	64.9	65.0	65.4	65.6	66.3	67.1	68.1
Portugal	24.8	34.0	31.3	34.4	36.1	37.0	37.3	41.5	42.2	42.2	43.9	42.9	44.2	45.7
Spain	31.0	36.5	39.6	43.4	44.6	45.9	47.3	47.8	48.8	49.9	51.9	52.5	53.1	54.0
Sweden	44.0	49.8	56.3	61.7	62.2	63.1	64.1	64.7	65.1	65.3	65.7	66.3	66.7	67.0
Switzerland	39.1	43.8	48.3	53.2	55.0	55.6	56.6	57.6	58.1	58.3	58.4	58.8	59.2	59.3
United Kingdom	47.6	51.3	55.1	58.6	59.7	61.5	62.7	63.9	65.1	65.8	66.7	67.4	68.0	68.4

Source: OECD 1991.

Table A.7 Standardized unemployment rates (percentage of total labour force) 1965–90

Country	1965	1970	1978	1979	1980	1981	1982	1983	1984	1985	1986	1987	1988	1989	1990	Average				
																1964–67	1968–73	1974–79	1980–89	1964–89
Austria*	1.9	1.4	1.8	1.8	1.6	2.2	3.1	3.7	3.8	3.6	3.1	3.8	3.6	3.1	3.3					
Belgium	1.8	2.1	7.9	8.2	8.8	10.8	12.6	12.1	12.1	11.3	11.2	11.0	9.6	8.1	7.3	2.0	2.5	6.3	10.8	6.5
Denmark*	–	–	7.3	6.2	7.0	9.2	9.8	10.4	10.1	9.0	7.8	7.8	8.5	9.2	9.5					
Finland	1.4	1.9	7.2	5.9	4.6	4.8	5.3	5.4	5.2	5.0	5.3	5.0	4.5	3.4	3.4	1.8	2.6	4.4	4.9	3.8
France	1.5	2.5	5.2	5.9	6.3	7.4	8.1	8.3	9.7	10.2	10.4	10.5	10.0	9.4	8.9	1.7	2.6	4.5	9.0	5.4
Germany	0.3	0.8	3.5	3.2	2.9	4.2	5.9	7.7	7.1	7.2	6.4	6.2	6.2	5.6	5.1	0.6	1.0	3.2	5.9	3.3
Greece*	–	–	–	–	–	–	–	7.8	8.1	7.8	7.4	7.4	7.7	7.5	7.2					
Ireland	–	–	–	–	–	–	–	13.7	15.4	16.8	17.1	16.9	16.3	15.0	13.7					
Italy	5.3	5.3	7.1	7.6	7.5	7.8	8.4	8.8	9.4	9.6	10.5	10.9	11.0	10.9	9.9	5.1	5.7	6.6	9.5	7.3
Luxembourg*	–	–	0.8	0.7	0.7	1.0	1.3	1.6	1.7	1.6	1.4	1.6	1.4	1.3	1.3					
The Netherlands	0.5	1.0	5.3	5.4	6.0	8.5	11.4	12.0	11.8	10.6	9.9	9.6	9.2	8.3	7.5	0.8	1.5	4.9	9.7	5.3
Norway	1.8	1.6	1.8	2.0	1.6	2.0	2.6	3.4	3.1	2.6	2.0	2.1	3.2	4.9	5.2	1.7	1.7	1.8	2.8	2.1
Portugal	–	–	–	–	–	–	–	7.9	8.4	8.5	8.5	7.0	5.7	5.0	4.6					
Spain	2.7	2.4	6.8	8.4	11.1	13.8	15.6	17.0	19.7	21.1	20.8	20.1	19.1	16.9	15.9	2.4	2.8	5.2	17.5	8.9
Sweden	1.2	1.5	2.2	2.1	2.0	2.5	3.1	3.5	3.1	2.8	2.7	1.9	1.6	1.3	1.5	1.6	2.2	1.9	2.4	2.1
Switzerland*	–	–	0.3	0.3	0.2	0.2	0.4	0.8	0.9	0.8	0.7	0.6	0.7	0.6	0.6					
United Kingdom	2.3	3.0	5.9	5.0	6.4	9.8	11.3	12.4	11.7	11.2	11.2	10.3	8.5	6.9	6.9	2.5	3.3	5.0	10.0	6.1

* Non-standardized definitions.
Source: OECD 1991, OECD *Economic Outlook*, various issues.

Table A.8 Real Gross Domestic Product/Gross National Product (% change) 1970–89

Country	1973–79	1979–89	1970	1975	1980	1981	1982	1983	1984	1985	1986	1987	1988	1989	1990
Austria	2.9	2.0	6.4	-0.4	2.9	-0.3	1.1	2.0	1.4	2.5	1.2	1.7	4.0	3.7	4.9
Belgium	2.2	2.0	5.5	-1.4	4.2	-0.9	1.5	0.4	2.0	0.8	1.6	2.3	4.9	3.8	3.7
Denmark	1.9	1.8	2.0	-0.7	-0.4	-0.9	3.0	2.5	4.4	4.3	3.6	0.3	0.5	1.2	2.1
Finland	2.3	3.7	7.5	1.1	5.3	1.6	3.6	3.0	3.1	3.3	2.8	3.3	5.4	5.4	0.4
France	2.8	2.1	5.7	-0.3	1.6	1.2	2.5	0.7	1.3	1.9	2.5	2.3	4.2	3.9	2.8
Germany*	2.3	1.8	5.1	-1.3	1.0	0.1	-1.1	1.9	3.1	1.8	2.2	1.5	3.7	3.8	4.5
Greece	3.7	1.6	8.0	6.1	1.8	0.1	0.4	0.4	2.8	3.1	1.6	-0.7	4.1	3.5	-0.1
Ireland*	4.9	2.9	3.2	2.1	2.7	2.6	-0.7	-1.6	2.3	1.0	-1.2	5.0	1.4	5.0	6.6
Italy	3.7	2.5	5.3	-2.7	4.2	1.0	0.3	1.1	3.0	2.6	2.5	3.0	4.2	3.0	2.0
Luxembourg	1.3	3.3	1.7	-6.6	0.8	-0.6	1.1	3.0	6.2	2.9	4.8	2.7	3.5	6.3	2.3
The Netherlands	2.7	1.5	2.5	-0.1	0.9	-0.7	-1.4	1.4	3.2	2.6	2.0	0.8	2.7	4.0	3.9
Norway	4.9	2.8	2.0	4.2	4.2	0.9	0.3	4.6	5.7	5.3	4.2	2.0	-0.5	0.4	1.8
Portugal	2.9	2.8	9.1	-4.3	4.6	1.6	2.1	-0.2	-1.9	2.8	4.1	5.3	3.9	5.4	4.2
Spain	2.2	2.7	4.1	0.6	1.3	-0.3	1.2	1.7	1.7	2.5	3.8	5.6	5.2	4.8	3.7
Sweden	1.8	2.0	6.7	2.7	1.4	0.0	1.1	1.8	4.0	2.2	2.2	2.8	2.3	2.1	0.3
Switzerland	-0.4	2.3	6.4	-6.7	4.4	1.4	-0.9	1.0	1.8	3.7	2.9	2.0	2.9	3.5	2.2
United Kingdom	1.5	2.3	2.2	-0.7	-1.7	-1.0	1.5	3.5	2.1	3.5	3.9	4.8	4.3	2.3	0.8

* GNP.
Source: OECD Economic Outlook, 50, December 1991.

Table A.9 Consumer price indices 1976–90

Country	1976	1977	1978	1979	1980	1981	1982	1983	1984	1985	1986	1987	1988	1989	1990	Average 1960–68	1968–73	1973–79	1979–89	1960–89
Austria	7.3	5.5	3.6	3.7	6.4	6.8	5.4	3.3	5.6	3.2	1.7	1.4	2.0	2.5	3.3	3.6	5.2	6.3	3.8	4.5
Belgium	9.2	7.1	4.5	4.5	6.6	7.6	8.2	7.7	6.3	4.9	1.3	1.6	1.2	3.1	3.4	2.8	4.9	8.4	4.8	5.0
Denmark	9.0	11.1	10.0	9.6	12.3	11.7	10.1	6.9	6.3	4.7	3.6	4.0	4.6	4.8	2.7	6.2	6.3	10.8	6.9	7.4
Finland	14.4	12.6	7.8	7.5	11.6	12.0	9.6	8.3	7.1	5.9	2.9	4.1	5.1	6.6	6.1	5.6	5.8	12.8	7.3	7.7
France	9.6	9.4	9.1	10.8	13.6	13.4	11.8	9.6	7.4	5.8	2.7	3.1	2.7	3.6	3.4	3.6	6.1	10.7	7.3	6.7
Germany	4.5	3.7	2.7	4.1	5.5	6.3	5.3	3.3	2.4	2.2	-0.1	0.2	1.3	2.8	2.7	2.7	4.6	4.7	2.9	3.5
Greece	13.3	12.1	12.6	19.0	24.9	24.5	21.0	20.2	18.4	19.3	23.0	16.4	13.5	13.7	20.4	1.9	5.6	16.1	19.4	11.3
Ireland	18.0	13.6	7.6	13.3	18.2	20.4	17.1	10.5	8.6	5.5	3.8	3.1	2.1	4.1	3.3	4.0	8.9	15.0	9.2	8.8
Italy	16.8	17.0	12.1	14.8	21.2	17.8	16.6	14.6	10.8	9.2	5.8	4.7	5.1	6.3	6.1	4.0	5.8	16.1	11.1	9.1
Luxembourg	9.8	6.7	3.1	4.5	6.3	8.1	9.4	8.7	5.6	4.1	0.3	-0.1	1.4	3.4	3.7	2.3	4.6	7.4	4.7	4.6
The Netherlands	8.8	6.4	4.1	4.2	6.5	6.7	5.9	2.7	3.3	2.3	0.1	-0.7	0.7	1.1	2.5	3.6	6.9	7.2	2.8	4.6
Norway	9.1	9.1	8.1	4.8	10.9	13.7	11.3	8.4	6.3	5.7	7.2	8.7	6.7	4.6	4.1	3.9	6.9	8.7	8.3	6.9
Portugal	19.3	27.2	22.5	23.9	16.6	20.0	22.4	25.5	28.8	19.6	11.8	9.4	9.7	12.6	13.4	3.2	8.4	23.7	17.5	13.0
Spain	17.6	24.5	19.8	15.6	15.6	14.5	14.4	12.2	11.3	8.8	8.8	5.2	4.8	6.8	6.7	6.6	7.1	18.3	10.2	10.3
Sweden	10.3	11.4	10.0	7.2	13.7	12.1	8.6	8.9	8.0	7.4	4.3	4.2	5.8	6.4	10.5	3.8	6.0	9.8	7.9	6.8
Switzerland	1.7	1.3	1.1	3.6	4.0	6.5	5.6	3.0	2.9	3.4	0.8	1.4	1.9	3.2	5.4	3.4	5.6	4.0	3.3	3.8
United Kingdom	16.5	15.8	8.3	13.4	18.0	11.9	8.6	4.6	5.0	6.1	3.4	4.1	4.9	7.8	9.5	3.6	7.5	15.6	7.4	8.0

Source: OECD 1991

Table A.10 Real hourly earnings in manufacturing 1976–89

Country	1976	1977	1978	1979	1980	1981	1982	1983	1984	1985	1986	1987	1988	1989	Average				
															1960–68	1968–73	1973–79	1979–89	1960–89
Austria	1.4	3.0	2.0	2.3	-0.1	0.4	0.7	1.5	-1.7	2.0	2.9	3.7	1.6	2.1		5.8	3.7	1.3	
Belgium	1.8	1.9	2.6	3.1	2.5	2.0	-1.5	-3.5	-0.9	-1.2	1.2	0.3	-0.3	2.4	4.7	7.2	3.8	0.1	3.3
Denmark	3.5	-0.8	0.4	1.5	-1.0	-2.0	-0.2	-0.3	-1.5	0.2	1.1	5.1	1.9	0.3			3.1	0.3	2.9
Finland	0.3	-3.2	-0.4	3.7	1.1	0.7	0.9	1.1	3.1	1.7	3.2	2.5	3.4	2.1	2.9	6.9	1.3	2.0	2.9
France	4.1	3.0	3.6	2.1	1.3	0.9	3.1	1.4	0.3	-0.1	1.2	–	0.4	0.2	4.0	5.3	3.7	0.9	3.1
Germany	1.9	3.7	2.3	1.3	0.7	-0.9	-0.3	–	-0.1	2.2	3.7	3.9	3.0	1.3	5.0	5.7	2.4	1.3	3.3
Greece	13.5	7.8	9.8	1.4	1.9	2.2	10.4	-0.7	6.6	0.4	-8.4	-5.8	-4.3	6.0		4.2	6.9	1.5	
Ireland	-0.8	4.3	6.4	1.9	2.5	-3.4	3.5	1.0	-0.3	2.7	2.8	2.6	2.4	1.0	3.7	6.3	3.5	1.5	3.3
Italy	3.5	9.3	3.6	3.7	-2.2	4.5	0.4	0.1	0.7	1.9	-0.9	1.6	1.0	-0.2	3.9	9.0	5.2	0.7	3.9
Luxembourg																			
The Netherlands	-0.2	0.9	1.5	0.1	-1.8	-3.2	0.8	-0.2	-2.1	2.6	1.5	2.1	0.5	0.3			2.1	–	
Norway	7.2	1.7	-0.1	-1.8	-1.0	-2.9	-0.1	-0.6	1.9	1.9	2.9	6.8	-0.9	0.8	3.5	3.6	3.6	0.9	2.6
Portugal																			
Spain	10.5	4.2	6.4	6.9	1.5	7.1	1.3	2.6	0.3	1.1	2.0	2.2	1.5	2.2		7.6	8.2	2.2	
Sweden	6.9	-4.3	-1.1	0.5	-4.3	-1.4	0.1	-1.7	1.4	0.2	3.0	2.2	2.0	3.3			1.2	0.5	
Switzerland	-0.1	0.4	2.3	-1.3	1.1	-1.4	0.6	3.7	-0.8	-0.1	2.7	0.9	1.1	0.5	1.8	1.9	0.9	0.8	1.3
United Kingdom	0.2	-4.8	5.7	1.9	-0.1	1.0	2.4	4.2	3.6	2.9	4.1	3.7	3.4	0.9		3.7	0.9	2.6	

Source: OECD 1991

Table A.11 Working days lost in industrial disputes per 1000 employees (annual averages)

Country[a]	1961–65	1966–70	1971–75	1976–80	1981–85	1986–90
Austria	85.4	11.9	14.7	2.1	1.8	1.2
Belgium	63.0	144.8	195.8	183.2	n/a	n/a
Denmark	107.6	42.7	354.5	75.9	262.3	79.6
Finland	143.7	104.8	595.5	520.7	271.2	343.2
France	146.3	134.0[b]	186.7	154.2	65.8	34.6
Germany	18.3	6.0	47.7	44.1	43.3	4.1
Greece	32.1	48.0[c]	n/a	n/a	36.0	126.4[d]
Ireland	337.5	625.6	292.7	716.1	360.6	183.7
Italy	648.4	933.6	1,063.9	940.0	536.8	218.2
The Netherlands	8.0	14.0	36.1	27.8	18.7	11.2
Norway	104.7	12.4	9.3	36.3	49.7	123.3
Spain	14.1[e]	37.1	95.6	1,089.8	400.9	433.6
Sweden	3.8	33.0	65.5	220.3	36.7	121.2
Switzerland	2.7	0.2	0.9	2.6	0.4	0.3
UK	127.0	222.6	538.6	521.7	387.4	117.5

[a]Luxembourg and Portugal omitted
[b]Excluding 1968
[c]1966–7 only
[d]1986–8 only
[e]1963–5 only

Source: ILO, *Yearbook of Labour Statistics*

1

Great Britain: Still Muddling Through

Paul Edwards, Mark Hall, Richard Hyman, Paul Marginson, Keith Sisson, Jeremy Waddington and David Winchester

Introduction

The election of the Conservative government under Mrs Thatcher in May 1979 is widely seen as marking a turning point in British industrial relations. A major challenge arose from the combined influences of mass unemployment, new managerial policies, and a government determined to run the economy on free market principles. Yet many features of industrial relations proved to be remarkably resilient. It was, for example, rare for employers to cease to bargain with trade unions (Millward and Stevens 1986; Claydon 1989). Deeper aspects of the British system, including a poor record on training (Keep 1989), low levels of productivity (Nolan 1989), and a lack of solidarity among employers (Sisson 1987), were still present. Wage increases continued to run at 7 or 8 per cent a year even in the depth of the recession. This contrasted sharply with the other major economy in which free market policies were most in evidence, the United States, where real wages fell steeply (Kassalow 1989).

This chapter is organized around the questions of what happened after 1979, how far these events represented a major change from the past, and how the complex balance of change and continuity can be understood. The focus is on Great Britain, with its work force of about 27.7 million, as distinct from the whole of the United Kingdom, which also includes Northern Ireland (with around 0.7 million workers). Northern Ireland is distinctive in some respects, notably labour law and the pattern of trade union organization, though it shares many of the broader features of the British situation.[1] Wherever possible, data are presented for Britain, though in a few cases they are available only for the UK as a whole.

A preliminary indication of the balance of continuity and change is provided by trends in the labour force. The 1980s were marked by a dramatic shift in the distribution of employment away from manufacturing. This was caused in particular by the deep recession of the early part

of the decade: between 1979 and 1981 manufacturing output and employment both dropped by 14 per cent, but a subsequent slow recovery of
output contrasted with a continued decline in employment. By 1990,
manufacturing accounted for only 23 per cent of all employment, compared with 30 per cent ten years earlier. Yet this decline was part of a
longer-term trend. From 1945 the service sector grew at the expense of all
other sectors. Manufacturing in the first industrial nation was never the
largest sector of employment: even in 1911 it accounted for only 35 per
cent of the work force (Routh 1980: 35, 42). None the less, the collapse in
the 1980s was widely experienced as marking a qualitative shift, as many
large industrial sites closed and as financial services grew in size and
significance. There was also a decline in the average size of manufacturing
plants which strengthened the tendency away from large concentrations
of workers. The extent of job loss in manufacturing was unusual among
advanced industrialized nations. Between 1973 and 1979, manufacturing
employment in Britain fell by 1.3 per cent a year, as against an OECD
average of 0.4 per cent. The accelerated decline in the early 1980s produced respective figures of 5.4 per cent and 1.3 per cent for 1979–84
(MacInnes 1987: 87).

There were associated developments in the composition of the work
force. As in other countries, the proportion of women in the work force
rose: from 33 per cent in 1951 to 48 per cent in 1990. The participation of
married women in the labour force increased particularly rapidly: from
26 per cent in 1951 to 57 per cent thirty years later (Walker 1988: 220).
What was particularly marked, however, was the growth in part-time
employment: female full-time employment remained relatively constant
from 1971 to 1986, while the number of part-timers increased by 45 per
cent (Rubery and Tarling 1988: 101). Virtually all part-timers were women.
Such trends led to concerns that part-time married women would be used
as a secondary labour force, being drawn in to employment during
prosperity and being expelled during recessions. In fact, it was male
unemployment which rose the more rapidly during the 1980s, reflecting
the decline in staple manufacturing industries and also rapid employment losses in other sectors, such as mining and railways, which had been
dominated by men. Women found jobs in services and the expanding
sections of manufacturing such as electronics.

As in other OECD countries, unemployment rose during the 1980s, but
the increase was more rapid, and the levels were higher, than elsewhere –
The Netherlands being the only significant exception (Tabatoni 1985: 7).
Rising unemployment was not, however, a new phenomenon, for a series
of crises during the 1970s pushed the total up to 1.5 million, and full
employment became a thing of the past. But the dramatic loss of jobs
during the early 1980s was unprecedented. Because of numerous changes
in definition consistent data are not available. But the peak of unemployment came in 1986, when 3.2 million people, representing 11.7 per cent of
the work force, were included in the figures. This national average concealed wide regional variations, with rates being much higher in Scotland,

Wales, and the north of England, and consistently the highest in Northern Ireland. Even previously prosperous areas such as the West Midlands experienced increases in unemployment to above the national average. After 1986 unemployment fell consistently, but it began to increase again in 1990 as the economy slowed and a new round of redundancies took place.

The recession had profound effects on many aspects of industrial relations. To analyse these effects, this chapter has seven sections. The longest are the third and fourth, which cover respectively employers and collective bargaining in the private sector of the economy, and trade unions. The public sector has differed significantly from the private and a fifth section therefore examines it in detail. The sixth section outlines the pattern of strikes. British industrial relations have, however, reflected, probably to a greater extent than those of any other country, a legacy of history. To understand current developments requires awareness of this legacy. A key feature was the abstention of the law from direct involvement in setting the rules of employment. The first two sections therefore review the historical background and assess how far legal developments in the 1980s marked a break from tradition. The concluding section draws together assessments of the balance of change and continuity and offers some pointers to the future.

Capital, Labour and the State

Origins of the System

It is often remarked that Britain, as the first industrial nation, has an industrial relations system of unique age. Yet age is not in itself distinctive: France, for example, had early industrial trades at least as developed as those in Britain. Three characteristics mark Britain out: the continuity of experience, the centrality of the workplace, and the role of the state. On the first, as Price (1982) has pointed out, problems that were 'discovered' during the 1960s, namely, unofficial strikes and 'restrictive practices on the shopfloor', had exact parallels in the 1890s. Indeed, the parallels can be traced even further back, for the early craft guilds also practised forms of restriction that would be recognizable to the modern shop steward (Rule 1981). In no other country has the legacy of history had such an important influence on contemporary developments.

Second, this legacy involved the handling of industrial relations at the level of the workplace. As described below, the alternative of legal regulation was never a serious possibility. The other alternative, of comprehensive industry-level agreements, existed in certain sectors such as clothing and building, but in the key industry of engineering there was no such system (Sisson 1987). There was no framework defining the rights and obligations of the parties. The rules of employment were settled on a day-to-day basis within the workplace. A major source of authority was 'custom and practice': the unwritten norms and understandings which established in a particular workplace the rules of work (Clegg 1972: 4–6). Workplaces developed their own sets of custom and practice rules, which naturally had some family resemblance with each other but which stemmed from negotiation at the point of production and not from any higher-level authority.

Considerable attention has been given to the role of the shop steward – a member of a work group elected to represent the group in dealings with management – in the conduct of workplace bargaining. By the 1960s stewards had come to prominence in large parts of engineering and, in large factories in particular, their organizations operated largely independently of official union hierarchies (Terry 1983). Yet, before then, large sectors of engineering had stewards only for limited numbers of craft workers, while, outside engineering, they were even less common. Workplace bargaining should not be equated with the specific presence of a shop steward. The general situation was one in which managers and workers reached an accommodation within the workplace without a framework of rules laid down either by the state or by industry-wide agreements. This is illustrated by a case study of one of the few industries in Britain where industry-wide bargaining has been important in the determination of terms and conditions of work, the footwear industry (Armstrong et al. 1981). Yet even here industry agreements were open to interpretation on the shopfloor: issues such as the length of the working week, holiday entitlements, and the setting of piecework rates depended as much on informal arrangements as on the formal agreement.

Shop stewards were certainly important. Their presence meant that informal understandings could be given some permanence. Stewards not only took up existing grievances with management but also acted to mobilize workers around certain issues and to maintain principles of trade union solidarity (Batstone et al. 1977). In industries with a strong steward system, managerial power was extensively challenged. But even elsewhere the shopfloor was the key level for the regulation of work.

The reasons for this state of affairs can be located in the structural conditions faced by employers and workers, and in the choices made at key junctures. The timing and pace of industrialization discouraged radical breaks with the past: the early start meant that factories grew up when craft skills were still crucial, whereas in Germany, for example, industrial growth occurred after these skills became less central; a slow pace of change permitted craft systems to remain. By the key period of the late nineteenth century, British firms were small and they produced for specialized markets, not for mass consumption. Compared with their American counterparts, their size made them less able to take on craft unions, while their market structure reduced the incentive to do so (Elbaum and Wilkinson 1979; Lazonick 1990). Moreover, the craft system brought considerable benefits, notably the use of skilled workers to supervise and discipline the less skilled (Littler 1982).

Choice was also important. A key juncture was the 1897–8 dispute in the engineering industry. The employers won the strike but failed to use their victory to root out craft practices from the shopfloor. They certainly did not welcome such practices, and they tried to tackle them aggressively when they had the chance; but this tactical toughness was not matched by any strategic vision, and the practices were able to re-emerge. The alternative, of a cooperative approach, was rejected because it was felt to undermine the cherished 'right to manage' (Zeitlin 1983, 1990). In contrast to their American counterparts, for whom the workplace was similarly important, employers relied more heavily on the stimulus of piecework and much less on the authority of management to induce workers to work hard (Lewchuk 1986). The result was two-fold: space was left to workers to develop their own shopfloor practices, and the oscillation between toughness and distancing from the shopfloor promoted distrust of management which allowed workers, when conditions permitted, to build on these practices an institutional challenge to managerial authority.

This explanation works well for industries where craft practices had existed. It is less applicable to those, such as chemicals or light engineering, where they had not been present (Coleman 1988). Less work has been done on these cases, but it is likely that they shared some features with the craft-dominated sectors. Protected markets and the limited use of mass production may have made employers less keen than those elsewhere to rationalize the shopfloor. The political environment was also the same: employers received no encouragement from the state to develop detailed, legally enforceable, collective agreements. This brings us to the third distinctive feature of Britain, the role of the state.

The State and the Tradition of Voluntarism

The approach adopted by organized labour – of a resistance to change and an adversarial posture in the workplace, combined with little wider political militancy – had parallels in the behaviour of the state. At various critical junctures from the late eighteenth century onwards the ruling classes could have chosen an authoritarian response to challenges from below. But at each point they rejected this route, fearing that it might so disrupt the political fabric that it would provoke even stronger challenges. Instead, they relied on a long tradition of the 'rule of law' (Fox 1985: 39–41). Their own political power had been forged in opposition to royal absolutism, and there was a strong commitment to due process and to the rights of 'freeborn Englishmen', a situation which they contrasted with Continental tyranny. Anti-union legislation was certainly passed, but it was not enforced with particular vigour. There was a strong distrust of statist solutions, and a preference for compromise and a search for social stability based on traditional methods. As Fox (1985: 168) argues, this grudging toleration of working class organization might have collapsed without the position of Britain in the world economy: foreign trade and imperialism provided the resources which allowed opposition at home to be accommodated. Early industrialization thus helped to reinforce the tradition of limited state intervention.

The result was the continued existence of the 'restrictionist' aspects of union activity outside any regulatory framework, together with a view of the state among workers as something that it was not necessary to attack directly. Because job regulation was practised within the workplace, all that was desired was that the state stand outside this process. Because, moreover, the state upheld the tradition of the rule of law, which meant above all that the law was not just an instrument of ruling class power but contained an element of justice, there was little sense of the need to mount a class project in the political arena.

This approach to the management of class conflict was reflected in labour law. The voluntary regulation of employment was more important than the law. This did not mean a complete absence of legislation, but its role was limited to protecting those outside the framework of collective bargaining, as in the regulation of the employment of women and children, and to supporting collective bargaining, for example the provision of conciliation and arbitration machinery. This tradition of voluntarism was supported by both sides of industry: unions wished to avoid what they saw as hostile intervention of the courts in industrial disputes, while employers were keen to avoid legislation which constrained their freedom to manage.

The era of voluntarism has its roots in the 1870s. Its fullest expression was the Trade Disputes Act of 1906. This Act removed the ability of employers to take legal action against trade unions and protected the organizers of industrial action from common law liabilities, notably for inducing a breach of employment contracts, provided they were acting 'in contemplation or furtherance of a trade dispute'. This was the famous 'golden formula': a negative immunity from common law liability, in contrast to other countries' positive right to strike (Wedderburn 1986). Other key aspects of the voluntary system were the absence of any obligation on employers to bargain with unions and the fact that collective agreements were not legally enforceable.

Employers and unions thus became locked into a relationship in which each could frustrate the other in the workplace but could not achieve a larger victory. As the role of the state became increasingly defined as that of maintaining the rule of law, the state was not available to employers to help them to resolve their problems. It would certainly act to try to contain union activity within legitimate bounds, but it could not be relied on to give any consistent support to a long-term policy of rationalizing control of the workplace. Employers, unions, and the state were all strong enough to maintain defensive positions while too weak to organize radical departures from the tradition of compromise and muddling through.

State and Economy in the Post-War Period

While Britain's economic position remained powerful, these problems did not matter very much. After 1945, however, competition from overseas grew dramatically. In 1953 the UK held 21 per cent of world exports of manufactures (the percentage for Germany was 13, for France 9, and for Japan 4). By 1980 the British share had halved to 10 per cent, while Germany's had gone up to 20 per cent, France's was steady at 10 per cent while Japan's had grown to 15 per cent (Williams et al. 1983: 116). During the 1980s, Britain's share stabilized, but imports grew much faster than exports: in 1988 imports were 65 per cent higher than they had been in 1980, compared with export growth of 32 per cent. A symbolic turning point came in 1983, when for the first time since the Industrial Revolution more manufactured goods were imported than were exported. A slow rate of economic growth was associated with unit labour costs that grew fast by international standards and continuing low levels of labour productivity. From the 1950s to the 1970s economic policy was characterized by a series of 'stop-go' cycles, that is economic expansion, producing inflation and a balance of payments crisis, which in turn led to a sharp recession. Some industries, notably the car industry, were used as macro-economic regulators, making long-term investment and production planning very difficult.

The consequences for industrial relations took time to sink in. In 1954 Kahn-Freund was able to celebrate the abstention of the law from the employment relationship. Twenty years later, Flanders (1974) was still speaking of voluntarism in positive terms: in particular, the massive mobilization of workers during the Second World War without much state compulsion was a major vindication of the approach. In fact, the war effort involved rather more conflict than Flanders implied. Some state regulations were overtly coercive, while on the shopfloor tensions mounted between managers who were unwilling to cede any real authority and an increasingly self-confident body of shop stewards (Croucher 1982).

These tensions continued into the period of post-war reconstruction. Employers maintained their wish to manage the shopfloor as they saw fit. Unlike their counterparts in Germany, who had suffered a major crisis of legitimacy and had to think carefully about their own authority, they could pursue a policy of business as usual, which meant that they neither rooted out the shopfloor challenge nor created a way of accommodating to it. The Labour government was more concerned with macro-economic policy than with detailed institutional reconstruction. It is true that there were worries about productivity, illustrated by a number of joint employer-union bodies which visited America to study production methods. But there were relatively few such bodies – France sent six times as many – and their findings were not implemented. The reasons were that employers were hostile to a joint approach, fearing that it would undermine their legitimacy and seeing little need to worry about productivity in a sellers' market, and that the Labour government lacked any understanding of the role of management and was unable to make itself an agency of modernization (Tomlinson 1989). This episode illustrates a key point: it was not a lack of information or will which constrained, and arguably continues to constrain, the actors in Britain but a set of structures and relationships in which no party could take a lead.

It was not only Labour administrations which used tripartite mechanisms to try to promote industrial regeneration. A Conservative government created, in 1962, one of the major institutions of British efforts at corporatist solutions, the National Economic Development Council. The Council, known as Neddy, brought together representatives of employers, unions, and the government to discuss economic policy; 'little Neddies' were also established for a range of industries. These industry-level bodies were quite widely supported by companies, and they were felt to produce useful recommendations. The problem was that there was no mechanism to turn these aims into action at the level of the firm. In the foundry industry, for example, the aim of rationalization and modernization was widely shared, but fragmentation on the employers' and the unions' sides prevented any serious progress; moreover, the government agencies involved were also too poorly staffed and organized to press through a modernization programme (Whitston 1989).

Difficulties of economic management were perhaps most apparent in attempts to establish incomes policies. The post-war Labour government made the first effort in 1948. The attempt set the pattern for the more ambitious efforts of the 1960s and 1970s (Panitch 1976; Crouch 1977). An economic crisis, in particular a severe balance of payments problem, led to demands for wage restraint. The government secured the compliance of union leaders for a time but it proved impossible to regulate the chaotic wage bargaining system, and the policy fell apart in acrimony.

In 1966 another Labour government instituted a more rigorous pay policy. It included statutory penalties for breaches of the policy and it established a new body, the National Board for Prices and Incomes, to review not just pay increases but also prices. The policy had some immediate success, but by 1969 it was beginning to decay (Clegg 1979: 345–77). In the private sector, it was possible to find ways round the policy, and powerful bargaining groups pursued their own sectional interests. In the public sector, pay restraint provoked discontent and hitherto quiescent groups began to use strikes, a development which accelerated during the 1970s.

The third major phase of incomes policy was the 'Social Contract' of 1975–9, so-called because it avoided the compulsion of the earlier policy, being based instead on the quasi-contractual exchange of wage moderation for tax concessions and other benefits in the field of labour legislation. It received strong support from the leaders of some unions, notably Jack Jones of the Transport and General Workers' Union. Yet it again proved impossible to regulate settlements in the private sector, and the collapse of the policy was symbolized by the defeat of Jones by his own union conference on the issue of whether to continue to co-operate with it. But particularly damaging was a series of highly visible disputes in the public sector which culminated in the 'winter of discontent' of 1978–9. The government appeared to have lost control of the economy, and the image of strikes in essential services seriously damaged its credibility.

Corporatism received considerable attention during the late 1970s, as union involvement in pay restraint seemed to be becoming more or less permanent. But the Thatcher government explicitly rejected such approaches by leaving wage regulation to 'market forces' and by refusing to become directly involved in industrial disputes. In retrospect, British corporatism can be seen to have been a very partial and ramshackle affair (Regini 1984; Cameron 1984). Its practices emerged out of attempts to manage economic crises, and not out of any deeper commitment to long-standing structural change. Not only were employer and union sides fragmented and divided, but the British state also lacked the structures to engage in long-term planning (Hall 1986). Its whole tradition of intervention had been to manage the economy rather than actively to regulate it. During the depression of the 1930s, for example, British state planners were far less willing to embrace Keynesian solutions than their counterparts in Sweden (Weir and Skocpol 1985).

Britain's fragmented bargaining structure exacerbated difficulties whose prime cause lay in the competitiveness of the economy. Debate has turned on how far institutional reform can resolve the weaknesses of the pay bargaining system. At the end of the 1960s, Fox and Flanders (1970) argued that the aspirations of workers had expanded and that institutions had failed to keep pace, the result being disorder or anomie, that is a lack of moral regulation over the wants and goals of individuals. New institutions could restore a balance. Goldthorpe (1974, 1978) by contrast argued that anomie went deeper: it could not be resolved by industrial relations reform because it was a fundamental characteristic of a society lacking any moral basis for wage restraint. Three features of Britain rendered it particularly vulnerable to inflationary pressure: the breakdown of normative order, a growth in citizenship rights, and the maturation of the working class (in the sense that the manual working class was recruited very heavily from the children of workers).

Sympathetic critics admit to difficulties with demonstrating a decline in normative consensus (Roche 1990), and institutionalists argue that inflation can be explained in institutional terms without having to invoke deeper aspects of the social structure (Brown 1990). Yet the essence of Goldthorpe's view, namely, that difficulties of industrial relations reform and economic management stemmed from a deeper fragmentation in the social fabric, remains suggestive: employers, unions and the state lacked the means to build a lasting system of political exchange, and this lack was exacerbated by institutional limitations. This issue is likely to be revived: in the early 1990s several commentators proposed a system of coordinated pay bargaining on the lines of the systems of Germany and Belgium. It is arguable that problems of anomie continue to run deep, and hence that such reforms might not have the results hoped for them because of the character of the industrial relations system.

Goldthorpe (1974: 233) was aware of the possibility of 'entirely authoritarian solutions' but felt that these would break down the traditional insulation of economic from political relations, which in turn carried 'the very real threat of extending economic into political instability'. Other commentators (e.g. Jessop 1980) were even clearer that an abandonment of corporatism and a return to free market principles was not feasible because of the political turmoil that mass unemployment would create. Such predictions look dated in the light of the experience of Thatcherism. There is debate as to how far Thatcherism was authoritarian, and authoritarianism was certainly no more than one element of a complex and not always coherent or planned approach. Yet the 1980s plainly showed that a non- and in fact avowedly anti-corporatist approach was politically feasible. The reason why it did not produce turmoil is two-fold. First, British workers have long had a limited view of politics and class action. Studies comparing Britain with Sweden (Scase 1974) and with France (Gallie 1978, 1983) have shown that British workers had a low level of resentment at economic inequality and saw the role of unions as restricted to the economic sphere. Second, there was a gap between beliefs about equality and the means available to pursue them. From their survey of social class in Britain, Marshall et al. (1988) conclude that Britons are characterized by an 'informed fatalism': fatalist because they tolerate what happens to them and informed because they are cynical about the ability of political parties to effect lasting change. The 1980s did not see any widespread move to accept individualism – ideas that Thatcherism had attained an ideological hegemony were seriously at odds with the evidence (Gamble 1988: 174–207) – and concern about class inequality remained largely as it had been. But people did not believe that there was any real means of dealing with this problem, and mass protest about unemployment seemed out of place (Westergaard et al. 1988).

Thatcherism was thus able to make significant changes in political rhetoric. It did not seem to change deeper views about the class structure. We may now consider its labour law project before assessing the impact on the conduct of industrial relations.

The Legal Framework

The law was a major instrument in the Conservative government's efforts to effect change during the 1980s. The objective was to limit the 'excessive' power of unions, in particular by curtailing the use of the strike, and to remove barriers to the free operation of labour markets. To place these efforts in context, the development of labour law up to 1979 needs to be understood. The origins of the Conservative government's project may then be considered before the details of the legislation are outlined; finally, the effects are assessed.

Regulation in the 1960s and 1970s

As noted above, the voluntary system came under increasing strain from the 1960s. The imposition of incomes policies was the most obvious break with the tradition. Intervention was also proposed in labour law. As early as the 1950s, some Conservative lawyers were proposing tighter control of unions and restrictions on the right to strike. In 1965 the Labour government appointed the Donovan Royal Commission to investigate industrial relations. When the Commission reported in 1968, it focused on the voluntary reform of collective bargaining, as discussed below; but it left open the possibility of more legalistic approaches. One such approach was attempted by the government when it proposed, towards the end of its period of office, laws to regulate unconstitutional strikes (that is, those in breach of procedure), but strong opposition from the unions forced the abandonment of the proposals. Some significant legislation was passed, notably the Redundancy Payments Act 1965, which for the first time required compensation to be paid to workers losing their jobs for economic reasons. But the voluntarist approach largely survived the challenges to it.

In 1971, however, the new Conservative government passed the Industrial Relations Act, which proposed a comprehensive legal framework. Closely modelled on American legislation, the Act replaced the unions' traditional legal immunities with restrictions on industrial action; tightly regulated arrangements for closed shops (that is, the practice that workers must belong to a union in order to keep their jobs); and endeavoured to make collective agreements legally enforceable. The Act was resisted by the unions, and it had only a very limited effect on day-to-day industrial relations, largely because employers did not put its provisions into practice (Weekes et al. 1975). Where it was invoked, it provoked some major clashes with the unions, in which its provisions seemed unworkable or counterproductive.

The Act lost its credibility, and the incoming Labour government returned the law on trade disputes and the status of unions broadly to what it had been before 1971. One significant feature was retained, namely, provisions against unfair dismissal. Important new individual rights, notably for women employees to return to their jobs after maternity leave, were included in the Employment Protection Act 1975; other legislation strengthened laws against sex and race discrimination. The most controversial aspects of the EPA, however, concerned collective matters. Hitherto, an employer could refuse to bargain with a union, but now a statutory procedure to aid unions seeking recognition was introduced. Section 11 of the Act also strengthened the rights of unions to use statutory mechanisms to require an employer to pay the recognized level of pay for a particular trade or industry (or, in the absence of such a rate, the 'general level' for comparable workers).

Though the recognition procedure lacked means of enforcement and was limited in its effects (Dickens and Bain 1986), it was interpreted by its opponents as a major concession to the unions. Together with other developments under the Social Contract, labour laws were seen as making unions into over-mighty subjects. The Conservative Party developed an alternative approach, which it began to put in place in 1979.

Origins of the 1980s Legislation

The 'Thatcher project' was neither a completely pre-planned strategy nor an opportunistic reaction to events. There were strong elements of opportunism: specific legal provisions were 'greatly influenced by the immediate experience of contemporary disputes' (Brown and Wadhwani 1990: 58). But there was a broad set of ideas guiding opportunistic action. The governments of the 1980s were 'the first . . . since the war to pursue a policy on industrial relations which [was] integrally geared into [their] overall economic policies' (Wedderburn 1985: 36). These policies had their intellectual origins in the New Right, with its emphasis on the free working of markets and the need to minimize state interference, as expressed in particular by Hayek (1982). During its period of opposition from 1974 to 1979 the Conservative Party reflected on the lessons of the 1971–74 Heath government, in two ways: strategically, it developed a more coherent statement of free market principles, and it thus criticized the interventions to rescue failing private sector firms which that government had made; and tactically, it was determined to be prepared for the battles which might be necessary to press through its approach. The Heath government had been defeated after the miners' strike of 1974. The spectre of industrial militancy haunted party thinkers, and they were determined to exorcize it. A senior figure, Nicholas Ridley, prepared a famous report, leaked to the press in 1978 (*The Economist*, 27 May 1978: 21–2). The report identified possible areas of conflict, with the mines as the most likely battleground, and sketched a policy to defeat strikes, including contingency plans to build up coal stocks, import coal and run power stations on alternative fuels (Gamble 1988: 93–4).

This renewal of ideology was able to build on the decay of corporatism and to present itself, not only as a break from Labour governments' concessions to the unions, but also as distinct from former Conservative approaches. The 'winter of discontent' provided the opportunity: corporatism had failed and the public popularity of unions reached unprecedented lows (Edwards and Bain 1988). There was no detailed blueprint for every piece of economic policy. Most notably, privatization emerged as a major strand only in the mid-1980s. But there was a theory guiding the overall direction. The government was assisted in effecting its programme by a widespread belief that its economic experiment could not survive the high unemployment of the early 1980s. Potential opposition was fragmented, and the government had the space in which to allow its policy to develop.

The Legislative Programme

As union bargaining strength was considered to stem from immunities in relation to industrial action and the 'coercive power' of the closed shop, these became central targets of the government's legislative programme. The government also saw union leaderships as being unrepresentative of the views of their (implicitly more 'moderate') members, and so legislated to prescribe the internal democratic procedures unions should adopt. A policy of 'enterprise confinement' (Wedderburn 1989: 27) was pursued not only in respect of the scope for industrial action, but also over procedures to extend collectively-bargained rates of pay to comparable groups of workers: measures such as Schedule 11 of the Employment Protection Act and the Fair Wages Resolution were seen as 'creating rigidities and inflexibility in pay' (DE 1988a: 26). The government also viewed employment protection provisions not as essential minimum standards but as 'burdens on business' (particularly in respect of small employers) which acted as a deterrent to the employment of more people. This led to a sustained government emphasis on the need to 'deregulate' the labour market.

Against this background, the Conservatives introduced a series of Acts of Parliament – most notably the Employment Acts of 1980, 1982, 1988, 1989 and 1990, the Trade Union Act 1984 and the Wages Act 1986 – and backed them with a number of statutory Codes of Practice. The key provisions of these complex and interlocking measures can be seen as having a number of distinct but complementary objectives: the legal regulation of industrial action; the eradication of the closed shop; the regulation of internal union government; the dismantling of statutory support for collective bargaining; and the curtailment of individual employment rights.

During the 1980s, legal restrictions were increasingly placed on industrial action. The statutory immunities from common law liabilities were seen as unique 'privileges' putting trade unions 'above the law', and were narrowed significantly by successive pieces of legislation. Picketing away from the pickets' own workplace, and 'secondary' industrial action (i.e. that by workers whose employer is not party to the dispute) other than in certain tightly defined circumstances, were made unlawful by the 1980 Act. More fundamentally, the 1982 Act introduced a narrower, enterprise-specific definition of what constituted a trade dispute and exposed unions as organizations to injunctions and damages in cases of unlawful industrial action, whereas previously only individuals organizing the action were so liable. The 1984 Act made it unlawful for unions to authorize or endorse industrial action called without a secret ballot. The 1990 Act made all secondary industrial action unlawful, extended the scope of union liability to include industrial action organized by shop stewards, and enabled employers to dismiss selectively any employee taking unofficial industrial action.

Repeated changes were made to the law concerning the operation of 'union membership agreements or arrangements'. The 1980 Act, for example, gave statutory exemption from a requirement to belong to a trade union to 'conscientious objectors' and to those who were non-members at the time such a requirement was introduced. The dismissal of such employees for non-membership thus became unfair. The 1988 Act made the dismissal of any employee on grounds of non-membership of a union automatically unfair. With the passage of the 1990 Act, all forms of the closed shop became unlawful. These successive steps were backed up by provisions outlawing commercial arrangements and industrial action to ensure that work would be done only by unionized labour (Lewis and Simpson 1986).

On union democracy, the government at first confined itself to providing public funds to encourage unions to use secret ballots. However, the measures introduced by the Trade Union Act 1984 and the Employment Act 1988 represented the most detailed statutory regulation of internal union affairs yet attempted in Britain, based on a highly individualist model of the rights and obligations associated with trade union membership (McKendrick 1988: 141). The 1984 Act required, among other things, five-yearly secret ballots of union members for the election of union executive committees and presidents and general secretaries with voting rights on such committees. The 1988 Act extended these requirements to all union presidents and general secretaries, and stipulated that election ballots should be fully postal and independently scrutinized. It also provided a range of statutory rights for individual union members enforceable against their union with the assistance of the new 'Commissioner for the Rights of Trade Union Members', including the right not to be 'unjustifiably disciplined' by a union for refusing to take part in industrial action. Much of the existing statutory support for collective bargaining was also dismantled during the 1980s. In 1980, the statutory recognition procedure was abolished, as was Schedule 11 of the Employment Protection Act.

In 1986 there was a significant illustration of how the government's free market philosophy did not always translate directly into practice. The case concerned the Wages Councils. The councils had been established in 1909 to provide statutory minimum wages and conditions for workers in certain industries where collective bargaining was weak; by 1986 they covered about 2.5 million workers (see Pond 1983). They were seen as an impediment to the free working of the labour market (DE 1988b); all protection for workers aged under 21 was removed, and other powers of the councils were reduced. Though the councils were apparently a prime target, complete abolition was eschewed. This reflected employer opposition (in turn stemming from a preference for some predictability in competitive markets), and possibly also a concern that an absence of any statutory system might fall foul of EC requirements on equitable pay (IPM 1991).

A number of steps were taken to curtail individual employment rights, notably the adjustment of the qualifying period of employment (from 6 months to 2 years) and of the procedural rules relating to unfair dismissal, and the erosion of working women's maternity rights. The 1989 Act continued the emphasis on 'deregulation' by repealing a range of laws which restricted the employment of women and regulated young people's hours of work (Deakin 1990).

Effects of the 1980s Legislation

Despite the extent of these statutory changes over the 1980s and the attendant political controversy, the available evidence concerning their practical impact on industrial relations has often been less than clear-cut. There has clearly been a substantial decline in the number of employees covered by closed shops, from a peak of 5.2 million in 1978 (Dunn and Gennard 1984) to around 2.6 million in early 1989 (DE 1989: 4). Much of this decline was due to changes in the structure of employment, as sectors where the closed shop had been prevalent experienced disproportionate employment losses. But the institution was less resistant to hostile legislation than might have been expected from its survival largely untouched under the Industrial Relations Act (Weekes et al. 1975). In the 1980s, the legislative attack was more determined, and, as shown below, employers were more willing to challenge the collectivism which the closed shop represented in extreme form. Unions also appear to have adapted to the constitutional and electoral requirements of the 1984 and 1988 Acts with little resistance; and the relative inactivity to date of the Commissioner for the Rights of Trade Union Members lends credence to union claims that the range of statutory rights for union members included in the 1988 Act was in practice unnecessary.

In the area of individual employment rights, research evidence has suggested that, despite government claims to the contrary, the unfair dismissal legislation has had only a marginal impact on employers' recruitment decisions (Daniel and Stilgoe 1978; Clifton and Tatton-Brown 1979). Legislative changes during the 1980s to lighten the perceived 'burden' have also had an insignificant employment impact (Evans et al. 1985). And the reform of the Wages Councils produced no clear moves to raise employment levels or lower the wages of those taken out of council protection (IPM 1991).

Although employees' rights were weakened in substantive terms, the basic *system* of individual employment rights was left largely intact. At the same time, the UK was forced by virtue of earlier European Community legislation and by rulings by the European Court of Justice to introduce important new regulatory measures in the employment sphere which were inconsistent with the government's deregulatory preferences, including the Transfer of Undertakings (Protection of Employment) Regulations 1981, the Equal Pay (Amendment) Regulations 1983, the Sex Discrimination Act 1986, and aspects of the Employment Act 1989, even though the UK systematically blocked the adoption of several new draft labour law directives during the 1980s. Moreover, draft directives proposed by the European Commission in 1990 and 1991 to implement aspects of the Community Charter of Fundamental Social Rights for Workers raised the prospect of a further extension of domestic labour law into new areas to reflect European norms.

Perhaps the major question, however, concerns the impact of the 1980s legislation on the conduct of industrial disputes. In several major industrial disputes during the 1980s, extensive use of the law had a major and possibly decisive impact. Examples included the 1983 dispute between Messenger Newspapers and the National Graphical Association, the 1986 dispute between News International and the print unions, and the 1988 dispute between P&O Ferries and the National Union of Seamen, all of which involved the sequestration of union assets as a result of union non-compliance with injunctions. More generally the law was used by employers during disputes with considerably higher frequency than during the 1970s (Evans 1985, 1987).

However, there is little doubt that recourse to the courts by employers occurs in only a small proportion of disputes in which the potential for legal action exists. For example, the 951 pre-strike ballots noted by ACAS during the three years 1987, 1988 and 1989 (Brown and Wadhwani 1990: 61) amounted to only a fraction of the overall number of industrial disputes. Employers appear willing to consider legal action – and certainly the threat of legal action – as a tactic in disputes, while legal constraints have affected union members' willingness to resort to industrial action and union officials' perception of their bargaining strength (Labour Research 1990). Yet employers have shown little interest in going beyond the injunction stage to pursue claims for damages against unions (Evans 1987), and very few have set out to use the law strategically to undermine effective industrial action during disputes.

As for the union response, there are indications that unions have become more cautious in the tactics that they adopt during disputes. Moreover, because of the greater risk of court action, union leaders have tended to strengthen central union control over how and when industrial action should be called and who should be empowered to authorize it (Evans 1987). Recent research (Martin et al. 1990) suggests that ballots can be valuable during negotiations, acting as a 'low cost' way of illustrating the strength of employee feeling to management. In 92 per cent of the strike ballots recorded by ACAS during 1987–9 the outcome was a vote in favour of industrial action; in the great majority of these cases the employer then settled without a strike (Brown and Wadhwani 1990: 61). Noting that 'where the rank-and-file decide a matter by direct vote, they will tend to respond more timidly in adversity and more aggressively in prosperity than their elected leaders', the same authors conclude that:

> In an economic upswing the greater use of strike ballots is thus likely to result in wage claims that are more extravagant, and in negotiators with less room for manoeuvre than would otherwise be the case. In times of rising expectations, governments may come to regret that the

1984 Trade Union Act was born of the politics of recession. (Brown and Wadhwani 1990: 63).

Some econometric studies have suggested that the number of strikes has been reduced by the legislation (Metcalf 1990), but the impact on the size and length of strikes has been less clear. There has also been debate as to how far the legislation as such had an effect: it may have been no more than a reflection of wider changes, and the connections between the statute book and shopfloor behaviour are indirect (McCarthy 1992). Unions have approached industrial action with greater caution but this is likely to have reflected many factors in addition to the law. It is impossible to separate out a 'pure' legal effect, but it does seem likely that the law played a significant part in redefining union approaches to industrial action.

Conclusions

After 1970, the law became deeply involved in industrial relations in ways which broke dramatically from the tradition of voluntarism. The newly re-elected Conservative government is likely to continue the incremental process of the 1980s. Even had Labour been successful in the 1992 election, there would have been no prospect of a return to voluntarism. Britain is among the countries in which observers detect a 'juridification' of industrial relations: though the political parties would use the law differently, the fact of legal involvement in processes formerly independent of the law is firmly established. The effects of the law are harder to judge: its specific impact is hard to disentangle from other political developments. But in certain well-publicized disputes it played a direct role, and it may have encouraged unions to be more circumspect in their behaviour, notably in the use of strikes, even though it did not fundamentally alter the conduct of industrial relations. One key limitation was that the law merely placed weapons in the hands of employers who had to choose whether to use them; as we now argue, many chose not to do so.

Employers and Collective Bargaining

Employers in Britain are unusual within Europe in having so fully turned their backs on multi-employer bargaining as the means of regulating basic terms and conditions. From the 1960s there was a trend in many industries for single-employer bargaining, at company or site level, to replace multi-bargaining at industry or district level. Industrial relations have become increasingly enterprise-specific. Jobs have come to be defined in terms of the internal requirements of companies rather than the occupational structure of the external labour market. Pay systems have been oriented towards rewarding individual and collective contribution to company performance. Both employer and trade union solidarity across companies have been weakened.

This section focuses on large companies, for several reasons. As shown below, these organizations accounted for a larger proportion of total employment than their counterparts elsewhere. More importantly, they have been the engine of most recent developments. They also dominate the main employers' body, the Confederation of British Industry. Small firms, by contrast, have lacked the organized voice of their counterparts in certain other countries.

There is a substantial amount of research on small firms, much of it producing findings that do not need further comment here. Such firms are, for example, less heavily unionized and strike-prone than large ones; they are also more likely to be involved in cases of unfair dismissal (Edwards 1983; Dickens et al. 1985). They came to prominence during the 1980s, however, with government claims that they could be a source of new jobs. These claims were sometimes associated with the view that small firms' industrial relations are particularly harmonious. There is little evidence that small firms did create significant numbers of new jobs (Johnson 1991). As for relations within them, it is certainly not the case that harmony prevails. Indeed, it has been claimed that they are particularly autocratic (Rainnie 1989). Neither view is correct. In many cases, managerial domination is qualified by a dependence on workers' skills and by paternalism (Ram 1991). There are distinctive dynamics in these firms, but these have not impinged significantly on the key developments in employer policy.

The section begins by outlining the key features of large firms. The next task is to put into context the key distinguishing features of the structure of collective bargaining and to account for their evolution. Finally, the largely management-inspired changes in the 1980s are considered, in particular the extent to which they represented a fundamental challenge to the 'traditional' practice of collective bargaining.

Who are the Employers?

Large companies in Britain account for a larger proportion of employment than is the case in most European countries. In 1987 more than half the manufacturing labour force worked in companies with more than 1,000 employees; one-quarter worked in the 48 companies with over 10,000 employees. The average number of establishments under the control of companies with over 1,000 employees was 12 in 1987, little changed from the 1979 figure of 13; in the case of companies with more than 10,000 employees it was 43 in 1987 and 40 in 1979 (Business Monitor 1982, table 13; 1989, table 12). No comparable figures are compiled for the service sector, but the available evidence suggests that the large company is dominant here too.

Diversification, Divisionalization and Decentralization

As well as dominating particular industries – electrical engineering, food and drink, and banking are good examples – many of these companies have also become increasingly diversified in their activities. Some, such as the four clearing banks, have moved into 'horizontally related' areas. Others, for example British Steel, have expanded into 'vertically related' areas. A third group has gone into 'unrelated' areas; it includes BAT from tobacco into insurance, and Unigate from dairy products into transport (see Channon 1973; Hill and Hoskisson 1987). There has also been considerable growth, largely through merger and takeover, in the number and size of 'conglomerate' companies such as BTR, Hanson and Lonrho.

Such diversification has not been restricted to the UK. During the 1980s many British-owned companies, for example, Lucas Industries, GKN and TI in engineering, and Cadbury Schweppes and United Biscuits in food and drink, rapidly expanded what were already significant overseas operations (United Nations 1988). Although a number of these recent acquisitions have been in Europe, critically important for attitudes to the Single European Market in general and its 'social dimension' in particular is the extent to which this expansion, including that of the above-mentioned companies, has been in North America.

The past thirty years have also seen major changes in the internal organization of these large and complex bodies. Many managements have introduced arrangements that disaggregate the enterprise into quasi-independent business units, emphasize the separation of strategic from operating management, and decentralize responsibility for day-to-day operations to the managers of the individual units (see Marginson et al. 1988). Survey evidence (Hill and Pickering 1986) suggests that over 80 per cent of the largest 200 companies in Britain have adopted such divisionalized arrangements.

The autonomy enjoyed by managers of individual units is not unqualified, however. Even in apparently highly decentralized organizations, a framework of planning and budgetary controls is laid down by company headquarters (Goold and Campbell 1987), and unit managers are held strictly to account for their financial performance. There is also evidence (Kinnie 1985a and b; Marginson et al. 1988) that many of the decisions that appear to be taken in the individual unit emanate from higher levels in the organization.

Ownership and Control

As well as being the 'home' of a large number of multi- or trans-national companies, Britain is 'host' to an equally large number of overseas-owned companies. North American-owned companies such as Alcan, Ford, IBM and Vauxhall (General Motors) have long had an established presence. Especially significant in recent years has been the growth of overseas investment in services and the coming of Japanese investment, notably in car manufacture (Nissan, Honda and Toyota), electrical components

(Toshiba) and banking and finance (Nomura). British capital, in short, has become truly internationalized.

Unlike other countries, the banks are not major shareholders in British industry. Fundamentally important are the investment trusts and the pension funds. Their holdings rarely amount to a controlling stake and yet it is widely argued that their influence on corporate policy has led to the elevation of short-term financial performance at the expense of longer-term business development (see, for example, Dore 1985; Cosh et al. 1990; Marsh 1991). 'Short-termism' has also been associated with a relatively 'open' market in the trading of shares, coupled with the threat of takeover by the conglomerate.

A further complication is the growing distinction between the firm as a legal entity and as a centre of economic decision-making (Cowling and Sugden 1987). An increasing volume of business activities has fallen under external control, as indirect forms of ownership such as licensing, franchising, subcontracting and joint ventures displace the direct form.

In terms of comparative experience, the processes of diversification, divisionalization and decentralization have gone much further in Britain than in other European countries (Chandler 1976; Chandler and Daems 1980). Indeed, the situation in Britain is much closer to that in the USA. The main difference from the US is that in many British companies, especially those organized on 'holding' company lines, there was no tradition of a strong corporate or divisional office (Payne 1967); the primary emphasis was on monitoring and control. The operation of divisionalization in Britain, coupled with pressure from institutional investors to deliver short-term financial results, is an important consideration in helping to explain the 'opportunism' and 'pragmatism' associated with British management's approach to industrial relations (Purcell and Sisson 1983; Thurley 1981).

A second feature of this context is important in understanding developments in the structure of collective bargaining. The decentralization of management accountability associated with changes in the internal structure of large companies has called into question the logic of negotiating collective agreements at levels higher than the accounting unit. If operating managers are to have 'bottom-line' responsibility for their costs and revenue, so the wisdom goes, they must be responsible for their own pay determination.

The Structure of Collective Bargaining

Like the other countries considered in this collection, Britain has a large number of employers' organizations to which individual companies belong. As well as the 'peak' organization or employers' confederation, the Confederation of British Industry, the Certification Officer for Trade Unions and Employers' Associations (1990) reports the existence of more than 250 such organizations. Their structure and government are also very similar to those of employers' organizations in other countries (Sisson 1987: 45–80).

The membership of these organizations is, however, very low compared with that in most of the other countries, and in many sectors it fails to reach 50 per cent of eligible companies. Significantly, many of the large multinational companies, which are members of employers' organizations in other countries, are not members in Britain. For example, none of the large car manufacturers – Ford, Peugeot-Talbot, and Vauxhall (General Motors) – are members of the Engineering Employers' Federation. GEC, which is the largest employer in the engineering industry, is no longer a member. Many of the large companies in the chemical industry, including ICI, are 'non-confirming' members of the Chemical Industries' Association: they belong to it but do not follow the terms of the multi-employer agreement that it negotiates. Paradoxically, it is the CBI which has the most representative membership, because it is essentially a pressure group and individual companies are eligible to join direct.

The explanation for the low membership of employers' organizations is inextricably bound up with the two key features of the structure of collective bargaining in Britain when compared with other countries in Western Europe. One is the form and status of collective bargaining. In Britain the relationship between employers and trade unions is built on procedural rules, whereas in most other countries it rests on a code of substantive rules which are intended to exhaust negotiations for a specified period. In Britain priority has been given to 'voluntary' rather than 'compulsory' rules in collective bargaining. The procedural rules, in other words, are made by the parties themselves rather than being imposed by government. These procedural rules, and the substantive rules to which they give rise in subsequent negotiation, are, moreover, 'gentlemen's agreements', binding in honour only, rather than legally enforceable contracts. Collective bargaining in Britain thus approximates to a 'common law' model, whereas in most other countries it is much more like 'statute law' (Clegg 1979: 116–9; Flanders 1970: 94–9; Sisson 1987: ch. 5).

As noted above, the explanation for these characteristics lies in past patterns of conflict, compromise and cooperation between management and labour. The resort to 'procedural' as opposed to 'substantive' rules in sectors such as engineering recognized that district and workplace negotiations had already given rise to a very considerable and complex body of practices and rules. Equally importantly, the relative 'success' of the compromise which was struck – for example, the 'Provisions for Avoiding Disputes' of 1898 in the engineering industry – reinforced those who favoured 'voluntarism' as opposed to 'compulsion' in collective bargaining matters. This was profoundly important in the period immediately following the First World War, when collective bargaining spread its net from the craft-based industries to manufacturing industries more generally (see Sisson 1987: 162–9; Zeitlin 1990).

A second distinguishing characteristic of the structure of collective bargaining in Britain is the level. In most other Western European countries, companies deal indirectly with trade unions through the intermediary of employers' organizations. The predominant pattern is multi-employer bargaining; company bargaining, if it occurs, is largely administrative or supplementary. In Britain, single-employer bargaining is increasingly the rule. Table 1.1 summarizes the situation in the mid-1980s. At first sight, the importance of single-employer agreements seems limited. Overall, pay was set by managerial decision rather than collective bargaining in the majority of establishments. In the case of manual workers in manufacturing, who have been the focus of most discussions of single-employer bargaining, such bargaining was 'most important' in only 32 per cent of establishments, compared with 22 per cent where national or regional levels were most important. These figures underline the fact that, particularly for non-manual workers, pay setting often depends on managerial decision with no underpinning of law or collective agreement. Where bargaining occurs, the table underestimates the significance of plant and company bargaining. First, this becomes more significant the larger the establishment: for manual workers in manufacturing, the plant level alone was 'most important' in 48 per cent of sites with 500 or more workers. Second, the trend has been for single-employer bargaining to grow. Multi-employer agreements increasingly set only minimum terms, and during the 1980s several were terminated altogether (IRRR 1989a and b; Brown and Walsh 1991). Third, the major company and plant agreements increasingly set the 'going rate' in annual pay rounds, with the Ford agreement being particularly prominent. These agreements directly cover a minority of employees but they provide a major engine in the pay-setting process.

Two main phases may be identified in this shift from multi-employer to single-employer bargaining. The first is what the Donovan Commission of 1968 referred to as the growth of the 'informal system' of workplace bargaining. A key figure in this 'informal system' was the shop steward. As described above, shop stewards came to play an increasingly important role after the Second World War. By 1961, there were estimated to be about 90,000 stewards; seven years later research for the Donovan Commission put the number at 175,000; and by the late 1970s the figure had reached between 250,000 and 300,000 (Terry 1983). Stewards came to outnumber full-time officials by about 100 to 1.

The growth in the number and the influence of shop stewards was largely spontaneous (see Terry and Edwards 1988). Shop stewards received no support from the legal framework; even collective agreements had little to say about their role and functions. Against a background of full employment and relatively 'soft' product markets, where demand exceeded supply, they were able to exploit the institutional framework of collective bargaining to draw managers into workplace negotiations. In some industries, such as clothing or printing, this workplace bargaining was largely administrative and supplementary and not dissimilar to the workplace bargaining in other countries. In industries such as engineering and chemicals, however, it went much further and, in effect, took over from the multi-employer bargaining or 'formal' system as the main source of joint regulation.

Table 1.1 Basis of most recent pay increase in 1984 – private sector

Percentage of establishments	Manufacturing		Services		All	
	manual	non-manual	manual	non-manual	manual	non-manual
Result of collective bargaining	55	26	38	30	44	29
Most important level:						
Plant/establishment	21	11	4	3	10	6
Company/division	11	9	12	15	12	13
National/regional	22	5	20	11	21	9
(Other)	1	1	2	(..)	2	(..)
Not result of collective bargaining	45	74	62	70	56	71
Decision about increase taken by:						
Management in establishment	33	53	30	45	31	48
Managment at higher level	10	21	21	24	17	23
National joint body	2	1	9	3	6	2
Wages Council	1	(..)	5	2	3	2
(Not stated)	(..)*	(..)*	1	1	(..)*	1

*(..) = less than 0.5 per cent but not zero. Under 'not result of collective bargaining' more than one reply was possible; hence sub-totals do not add to the overall total.
Source: Millward and Stevens (1986: Tables 9.2, 9.8; final 2 columns calculated from these 2 tables).

A second phase began in the late 1960s as public policy increasingly promoted the development of formal industrial relations arrangements at workplace level. With the encouragement of the government and other agencies, such as the National Board for Prices and Incomes (1965–70), the Commission on Industrial Relations (1968–74) and the Advisory, Conciliation and Arbitration Service (established in 1974), there were very considerable management-inspired reforms of workplace industrial relations in many British companies. There were three main aspects. First, firms introduced a wide range of workplace procedures dealing with such matters as negotiation, individual grievances and collective disputes, consultation, discipline and dismissal, and health and safety. Second, pay systems were reformed, with work-study-based group systems such as measured daywork or plant bonuses replacing the piecework systems which had been such a fertile breeding ground for workplace bargaining. Finally, job evaluation was widely adopted, with the aim of fixing pay differentials on 'rational' criteria intended to be immune to work-group pressure (see Purcell and Sisson 1983).

The impact of the reforms has been the subject of considerable discussion (Goldthorpe 1974; Batstone 1984). Three points are relevant here. First, the reconstruction of workplace industrial relations furthered the decline of multi-employer bargaining. Not only did a number of the large companies withdraw from employers' organizations to give themselves greater autonomy; the piecemeal way in which the reforms were introduced also made it difficult for companies to arrive at common positions. Second, little attempt was made to reconstruct multi-employer agreements in the light of changing circumstances; there were changes in the operation of multi-employer agreements in some industries – for example, basic rates of pay became a 'safety net' rather than a 'floor' – but they merely accelerated the decline of multi-employer agreements (see Sisson and Brown 1983). Third, with the exception of the shift from multi-employer to single-employer bargaining, reform did not lead to a radically different system. Much of it was directed at procedures and not at the substance of workplace trade union organization. The process of reform also promoted conflict, as workers challenged some of the changes, such as new payment systems; in many well-organized workplaces bargaining pressure switched from wages to effort. Studies in manufacturing (Batstone 1984) and coal (Edwards and Heery 1990) concluded that reform had brought few substantive benefits to management.

These characteristics are profoundly important. First, industrial relations in Britain is highly decentralized and is becoming ever more so for reasons which will be explored in more detail below. British employers may be in a strong position individually, but collectively they no longer possess the ability of their counterparts in many EC countries to influence the pattern of events in industrial relations. In particular, employers have no means of coordinating pay bargaining to avoid the leap-frogging which seems to be endemic in such a highly decentralized system (see IRRR 1991a).[2]

Second, Britain does not have a 'dual' system of industrial relations in the sense that many other EC countries have. There is no clear-cut distinction between, on the one hand, collective bargaining and the role which trade unions in other countries play outside the workplace and, on the other, the joint consultation and employee-based systems of representation which take place inside the workplace. In some sectors, notably the public services, the vestiges of such a 'dual' system remain; employee councils are also a feature of some of the Japanese-owned subsidiaries (see IDS 1988). In the great majority of cases where trade unions are recognized, however, managements deal direct with lay trade union representatives or shop stewards and there is little distinction between the processes of joint regulation, joint consultation and communications.

Third, there is enormous variety in the pattern of this workplace representation. In some cases, workplace bargaining is highly fragmented and management deals with a number of shop stewards each representing more or less independent groups of workers. In other cases, notably the larger workplaces, management deals with joint committees of shop stewards, some of whom will be engaged full-time in trade union activities, even though they are paid by the company. Typically, there will be one committee representing manual workers and one or more representing non-manual workers. Only in very rare cases will management deal with representatives of both manual and non-manual workers round a 'single bargaining table' (see Marginson and Sisson 1990).

The Challenge to Collective Bargaining in the 1980s

During the 1980s British management came under pressure to adapt industrial relations policies from three directions: economic, political and legislative. In the economic sphere, companies had to operate in product markets characterized by more intense international competition; they have had to become more responsive in terms of the price, quality and variety of the goods and services they produce, leading to the need to be more versatile in the organization of production and their use of labour (Rubery et al. 1987). In the political and legislative spheres, as discussed above, the government has pursued policies hostile to the collective organization of employment relations.

Companies' responses have been notable for their diversity. It is possible, however, to identify a number of common developments. These include not only changes in the conduct of collective bargaining itself but also policies designed to promote a more flexible labour force and adoption of human resource management practices. Each of these developments appears to challenge the traditional practice of collective bargaining.

A Flexible Work Force?

Managerial attempts to secure a more flexible work force have received widespread attention (Pollert 1988). Yet the extent of change over recent years appears to be relatively limited. 'Functional' flexibility involves broadening the range of tasks or skills undertaken in particular jobs. Here Cross (1988) finds that most management initiatives have been confined to increasing the range of tasks performed within existing occupational boundaries rather than moves to genuine multi-skilling. 'Numerical' flexibility increases the ability of companies to adapt the size of the effective labour force through use of temporary and fixed term contracts, and forms of outsourcing such as subcontracting and homeworking. Survey evidence suggests that, while there has been recent increase in the use of such practices, there are also important continuities over a longer time period (Marginson et al. 1988; Wood and Smith 1989). 'Time' flexibility involves moves to annualized hours arrangements, changes in full- and part-time shift patterns and increased use of part-time working. Again, the extent to which such changes are widespread is doubtful (IRRR 1991b).

How far these 'flexibilities' have been the subject of collective bargaining varies, however. In the case of 'functional' flexibility, Marsden and Thompson (1990) distinguish between changes in working methods, which are frequently management-inspired, and broader changes in working practices which increasingly have been the subject of collective bargaining. They note that, unlike the productivity agreements of earlier periods, recent 'flexibility' agreements promote a preparedness to undertake a broader range of tasks rather than a `buy out' of certain practices. The same rationale underlies agreements providing for more flexible working-time arrangements involving full-time work forces. Changes to working-time patterns of part-time workers and service workers more generally are rarely the subject of collective bargaining.

The impact of these changes on collective bargaining is likely to be profound. To begin with, it might be expected that they would reinforce the stress on organization-specific arrangements of decentralized negotiations discussed below. Perhaps even more importantly, however, traditionally widespread collective bargaining over 'managerial relations', that is, the deployment, organization and discipline of the labour force, has been undercut by new ways of organizing work. In short, the logic of flexibility is replacing the rules and procedures associated with 'custom and practice' which have hitherto held sway.

In Britain's highly decentralized arrangements, however, it is so-called 'numerical' flexibility which is posing the biggest challenge. This is rarely the subject of collective bargaining. Especially important has been the increase in the practice of putting out to tender such activities as cleaning, catering, maintenance and transport. Although considerable controversy surrounds the strategic significance of these developments (Atkinson 1984; Pollert 1988), the practical implications are clear enough. Where the activity is subcontracted, it very often means that the group falls out of the coverage of collective bargaining. Where the activity remains `in house', the tendering process may be used to drive down the pay or conditions of the groups involved (Bach 1989).

The Coming of Human Resource Management?

There has been considerable discussion about whether British managements have been inclining towards the 'human resource management'
approach, whether, in other words, they have been shifting the emphasis
from 'collectivism' (relations with trade unions) to 'individualism', that is
relations with individual employees (Guest 1987; Purcell 1987; Storey 1989).
Evidence points to an increased use of a range of practices which focus on
individual employees and their contribution to the enterprise. Thus, selection testing and appraisal are on the increase for manual as well as
non-manual workers (Long 1986). So is the use of pay systems related to
individual and organizational performance: merit pay, profit-sharing and
share-ownership show considerable growth. Greater efforts to involve
individual employees in the affairs of the business are also evident. Communications systems such as team briefing have been introduced into a
wide variety of organizations. So too have quality circles – the number of
organizations with them rose from a handful in the late 1970s to perhaps as
many as 700 to 800 by 1988 (Storey 1989; see also Sisson 1989).

Yet there is little evidence to suggest that these initiatives add up to a
widespread adoption of an integrated human resource management (HRM)
approach (see Guest 1987; Storey and Sisson 1989). Few companies seem
prepared to undergo the change in management approach and incur the
substantial expenditure involved. Examples of companies pursuing sophisticated 'union substitution strategies', although widely cited, are
rare. Nor have companies sought to articulate their initiatives towards
individual employees with their approach to trade unions in the way that
Kochan, Katz and McKersie (1986) report in the USA, where such companies as Ford, General Motors and some steel firms introduced trade union
joint consultation over a wide range of issues in an attempt to promote a
'new industrial relations' climate. A detailed study of 15 'mainstream'
firms found that, though new devices such as direct communication with
employees were widespread, there was little evidence that human resource policies were linked to traditional industrial relations concerns or
that the HRM policies themselves were deployed in a connected way
(Storey 1992). There was, moreover, little association between the number
of HRM initiatives and a company's economic performance.

As with attempts to increase flexibility, many of the initiatives are best
seen as essentially piecemeal reactions to the economic and political
context; British managements, faced with intensifying competition, are in
urgent need of the cooperation and commitment of individual workers
and they feel relatively confident of being able to introduce the measures
without strong opposition. The challenge to collective bargaining is implicitly rather than explicitly expressed.

The Conduct of Collective Bargaining

Contrary to what might have been expected in view of the economic and
political context, there has been no overt management 'offensive' against

trade unions in the 1980s. Thus there have only been a small number of cases of genuine derecognition (Claydon 1989). In manufacturing, there has been a decline in the numbers of workers covered by collective agreements, but the bulk of the trade union membership loss has come from redundancy rather than the withdrawal of recognition (Towers 1989). The report of the second Workplace Industrial Relations Survey (Millward and Stevens 1986) found little or no change between 1980 and 1984 in the proportion of workplaces recognizing trade unions; and few companies reported a change in policy towards trade unions over the previous five years. So-called 'new style' agreements involving some or all of single union recognition, flexibility of working, single status, an employee consultative council, 'no-strike' provisions which rule out industrial action even as a last resort, and 'pendulum' or 'straight-choice' arbitration affect a relatively small number of workers (see Bassett 1986; TUC 1988; IRRR 1989d.

The situation is not as straightforward as it seems, however. A number of groups of managers have been taken out of collective bargaining and put on individual contracts, which may have important implications for the future. Also few companies have been prepared to concede recognition on new sites, particularly in private services where employment growth has been strongest.

In workplaces where unions continue to be recognized, there is also evidence that managements have exploited the economic and political situation to limit their role. Scope for doing so exists because of the massive informality of collective bargaining in the UK. As noted above, the distinction between communications, joint consultation and joint regulation can easily become blurred depending on circumstances. In other words, it is not necessary to withdraw recognition to bring about significant changes in the relationship with trade unions.

Certainly there is case study evidence to suggest that attempts have been made to switch the emphasis from joint regulation to joint consultation and communications in a number of cases; meetings with shop stewards that in the 1970s involved the joint regulation of an issue have been turned into consultative or in some cases straightforward communication exercises (Terry 1989). In particular, unions which were well-organized to negotiate over wages and conditions in times of full or near-full capacity found themselves on weak ground as the agenda shifted to rationalization, job loss and organizational survival.

Similarly, although unions have been involved in negotiations over changes in working practices, their role in the introduction of new technologies which frequently pave the way for these changes has at best been consultative. Daniel (1987), for example, concluded that, as with much else, management's approach to the introduction of new technology was essentially opportunistic, consulting with unions where it felt constrained to do so, but not otherwise. Unions, for their part, appear to have been most concerned to negotiate over the employment and pecuniary implications of new technology.

Paralleling the long-running shift from multi-employer to single-employer bargaining mentioned earlier, there have also been significant changes in the level at which single-employer bargaining takes place in the large multi-establishment companies. In the relatively few companies with integrated production arrangements – for example the car manufacturers – there has been a shift from establishment to multi-establishment negotiations. The dominant trend, however, is towards the decentralization of collective bargaining. In some cases (for example, British Steel and Pilkington) it has meant the shift away from company negotiations to the individual business units; in others (for example, GEC) it has meant the break-up of site negotiations embracing a number of different businesses in favour of single unit negotiations (see IRRR 1989c and 1990).

The implications are far-reaching. For management, the coordination of apparently decentralized negotiations is relatively easy. For trade unions, such coordination is more difficult; they have yet to develop effective company-wide organization (Terry 1985). This helps to explain why the proposals in the EC's 'Social Charter' to grant information, consultation and negotiation rights at company level have generated so much opposition from British management. Moreover, decentralized negotiations increase the focus on workplace issues at the expense of occupational comparisons or notions of the 'going rate' (Gregory et al. 1985, 1986). The prospects of industry-wide campaigns are further diminished when the prohibition on secondary industrial action discussed above is taken into account; the engineering unions, for example, were obliged to wage their campaign for a reduction in the working week workplace by workplace rather than across the industry.

Conclusion

In the absence of a strong legally-supported framework of multi-employer bargaining, developments in collective bargaining in recent years have largely reflected changes in industrial and company structure. Especially important has been the growth in the large diversified company. In theory, the 'divisional' structures which have been adopted have given British managements a wide-ranging strategic capability to shape their industrial relations. For a variety of reasons – the historical legacy (both of corporate structure and industrial relations), the patterns of ownership, and the inability of trade unions to develop effective organization at company level – British management has undertaken little serious restructuring of industrial relations. The approach remains largely 'opportunistic' and 'pragmatic'.

There has been change in collective bargaining. The main imponderable is whether or not there have been fundamental changes in what might be termed bargaining 'awareness'. In the case of what was termed above managerial relations (the deployment, organization and discipline of the labour force), the indications are that the need to be flexible is becoming more accepted. In the case of 'market relations', that is, pay and hours of work, however, the extent of change is more questionable.

Above all, the persistent tendency for pay increases to outstrip increases in productivity – there was no year in the 1980s in which the growth in average earnings in manufacturing was less than 7 per cent – suggests there is considerable continuity. Moreover, as a later section will illustrate in more detail, the events of 1989 and 1990 call into question some of the more superficial judgements made about developments in the decade. A number of groups of workers, in the private as well as the public sector, resorted to industrial action in order to secure pay increases in line with rising inflation. The engineering unions did so to achieve a reduction in hours in many companies using a form of the 'rolling strike' which suggests they are beginning to adapt to the decentralization of collective bargaining. In short, the institutions and habits of British industrial relations die hard.

Trade Unions

British trade unions can trace their origins back two centuries; the predecessors of some modern unions were created at the time of the industrial revolution. In the intervening years, unions have often been restricted in their operations by the law, receiving damaging treatment by judges and the courts; but they have been free from systematic legal persecution, at least since the abolition of the Combination Acts in 1824. Similarly, while some employers have always been uncompromisingly hostile to trade unionism, others were prepared to recognize the independent collective representation of their employees at an early stage. By the 1880s, when Beatrice Webb coined the term 'collective bargaining', the practice that she identified was already well established in British industrial relations; and by the end of the nineteenth century, support for 'free collective bargaining' was an accepted element in British public policy.

Long historical continuity is thus a major consideration in the understanding of trade unionism in Britain. Particular organizations may over the years have fallen victim to recession, industrial restructuring, employer resistance, internal fragmentation or insolvency; but the movement as a whole, though experiencing periods of defeat and numerical decline, has never had to face a crisis so serious as to threaten its very existence. This long stability clearly differentiates Britain from most other European countries.

British trade unionism has none the less altered substantially during the past century in terms of numbers, structure and status. With only temporary setbacks, membership increased to roughly half the working population; the occupational and sectoral composition changed with the transformations in the economy; the movement became dominated by a dozen or so unions each with several hundred thousand members. The four decades from the outbreak of the Second World War saw a development of unions' place in industry: there was an unprecedented growth of membership; the scope of collective bargaining steadily expanded; and unions became increasingly involved in the formulation and implementation of government social and economic policy. But in the 1980s these advances were rapidly reversed: unions lost members, faced new challenges from employers, and were confronted by a passionately hostile government. As the social and political environment alters again in the 1990s, the future for British trade unionism is uncertain; but there can be no expectation that a simple return to the position of the 1970s is on the agenda.

This section examines the changing nature of trade unionism. First, it analyses patterns of union growth and decline; then it considers changes in structure; finally it looks at internal organization and responses to external challenge.

Membership

In contrast to most European countries, the right to belong to a trade union has only recently received (limited) legal support. Traditionally, the employer was free in law to obstruct a union's efforts to recruit. The Industrial Relations Act introduced the right to join a union, and this was re-enacted in the Social Contract legislation. But there was still only a series of individual rights, and no explicit guarantee of freedom of association (Lewis and Simpson 1986: 52). By the same token, there are few legal restrictions on membership. Unionism of military personnel is illegal, and there are major restrictions on collective organization and action in the police force; however the Police Federation, while debarred from affiliation to the TUC, is officially registered as a trade union and its membership is included in the aggregate statistics given below. In general civil servants (including civilian employees of the armed forces) are subject to no special restrictions.

For most purposes union *density* – the ratio of actual to potential membership – is the most useful measure of unionization. It can be calculated in a variety of ways (Kelly 1988). Most definitions of potential membership exclude the armed forces and the self-employed (who in Britain are unionized only in exceptional cases). Some measures only cover those in employment; others include the unemployed, who in Britain rarely join trade unions or retain membership which they may previously have held, even though some unions have recently made serious efforts to organize those out of work. In periods of high unemployment, such as the 1980s, different definitions of potential membership will entail very different density figures. We therefore present two sets of density statistics: the first basing potential membership on the labour force in employment or seeking employment (Labour Force Density); the second based only on those in employment (Employment Density).

As can be seen from table 1.2, in the post-war period there were three main phases of development. The years between 1949 and 1968 were a period of stagnation, when membership failed to keep pace with the expansion of employment. Then followed a decade of pronounced expansion: between 1969 and 1979 Labour Force Density grew from 43 to 53 per cent, and Employment Density from 44 to 57 per cent. During the 1980s both measures, in particular the former, show a sharp decline. In the latter part of the decade Employment Density declined faster than the labour force measure, an indication that unions were failing to make significant inroads in those areas of the economy where employment was expanding.

Disaggregated data (by sex and occupation) show the same trends, but also reveal how the composition of trade union membership has altered with the changing structure of employment. From table 1.3 it can be seen that the proportions of union members who are women (18 per cent in 1948, 35 per cent in 1987) and white-collar workers (23 per cent in 1951, 48 per cent in 1987) have both doubled.

Many explanations have been offered for trends in union density, involving some combination of such factors as shifts in the composition of employment, the business cycle, the changing environment of industrial relations, and institutional and strategic characteristics of unions themselves. The changing structure of employment, in particular a decline in traditional manufacturing industry, tends to weaken unions (Price and Bain 1983; Booth 1989; Waddington 1992b); but this alone does not explain the severity of the decline in the 1980s. Nor can it account for the rapid growth of the 1970s, achieved despite adverse shifts in employment composition (Price and Bain 1983; Kelly 1990). Business cycle indicators – movements in unemployment, retail prices and wages – explain much of the short-term fluctuation in union membership (Bain and Elsheikh 1976; Booth 1983; Carruth and Disney 1988; Disney 1990). Because some sectors and occupations are more vulnerable than others to unemployment, this explanation is linked to the compositional one.

The institutional framework of industrial relations is obviously important. In the 1970s, (modest) legal backing for union recognition, the lack of serious legal restrictions on the closed shop, and broad public-policy support for collective bargaining, all assisted union growth (Price and Bain 1983; Dunn and Gennard 1984). Conversely, Freeman and Pelletier (1990) claim that unfavourable legislation in the 1980s is the primary explanation of membership decline. This is an over-simplification. Though legal encouragement of 'de-collectivization' was a notable feature of the 1980s, the impact of the law has been far from uniform (Brown and Wadhwani 1990), and has occurred in combination with the effects of adverse economic conditions and new management policies. It may be noted that the most severe decline in membership took place in the early 1980s, before the most important elements of restrictive legislation took effect.

Trade Union Structure

The structure of contemporary British trade unions reflects their slow historical evolution and displays a complex pattern with no underlying organizational logic. As table 1.4 shows, in 1989 there were 313 trade unions in Britain with an aggregate membership of 10,158,000; the average size

Table 1.2   Aggregate union growth in Great Britain 1948–87

Period	Union Membership		Labour Force				Employment			
	Total change (000s)	Annual average change (000s)	Total change (000s)	Annual average change (000s)	Total change (% points)	Annual average change (% points)	Total change (000s)	Annual average change (000s)	Total change (% points)	Annual average change (% points)
1949–68	637	32	2,433	122	−2.1	−0.1	2,192	110	−1.7	−0.1
1969–79	2,900	264	984	89	10.5	1.0	125	11	12.8	1.2
1969–70	933	467	−163	−82	4.5	2.3	−193	−97	4.7	2.4
1971–73	281	94	194	65	0.8	0.3	189	63	0.8	0.3
1974–79	1,686	281	953	159	5.2	0.9	129	22	7.3	1.2
1980–87	−2,765	−346	418	52	−12.4	−1.6	−986	−123	−10.3	−1.3
1980–83	−1,873	−468	−72	−18	−7.8	−2.0	−1,567	−392	−4.8	−1.2
1984–87	−892	−223	490	123	−4.6	−1.2	581	145	−5.5	−1.4

Table 1.3   Unionization by sex and occupation 1948–87

	1948	1968	1979	1987
Male union membership (000s)	7,454	7,518	8,818	6,415
Male Labour Force (000s)	13,485	14,452	13,979	13,555
Male Employment (000s)	13,273	14,013	13,036	11,623
Male Labour Force Density (%)	55.3	52.0	63.1	47.3
Male Employment Density (%)	56.2	53.7	67.6	55.2
Female union membership (000s)	1,648	2,221	3,822	3,459
Female Labour Force (000s)	6,785	8,251	9,708	10,550
Female Employment (000s)	6,721	8,137	9,276	9,702
Female Labour Force Density (%)	24.3	26.9	39.4	32.8
Female Employment Density (%)	24.5	27.2	41.2	35.7
	1951*	1966	1979	1987
Manual union membership (000s)	7,097	6,842	7,517	5,120
Manual Labour Force (000s)	13,985	13,907	11,930	11,214
Manual Employment (000s)	13,818	13,682	10,772	9,495
Manual Labour Force Density (%)	50.7	49.2	63.0	45.7
Manual Employment Density (%)	51.4	50.0	69.8	53.9
White-collar union membership (000s)	2,149	2,811	5,122	4,754
White-collar Labour Force (000s)	6,725	9,141	11,559	12,891
White-collar Employment (000s)	6,708	9,105	11,539	11,830
White-collar Labour Force Density (%)	32.0	30.8	43.2	36.9
White-collar Employment Density (%)	32.0	30.9	44.4	40.2

* The Censuses of Population are the only source of manual and white-collar potential union membership data for Britain as a whole. The years 1951 and 1966 are used in this table for these categories of membership as in these years Censuses were conducted. The method of calculation of the data for 1979 and 1987 is provided in Waddington, forthcoming.
Sources: Waddington, forthcoming.

was thus 32,500. However, the distribution of membership was very uneven: at one extreme, 234 unions (76 per cent of the total) each had fewer than 10,000 members, and together included only 3 per cent of total membership. At the other extreme, the ten largest unions contained over 60 per cent of all trade unionists.

This uneven pattern has always been characteristic of British unions. In 1948 the proportion of members in the ten largest unions was over 53 per cent. However, the composition of the numerically dominant unions has changed as the sectoral and occupational composition of employment has altered. Formerly prominent unions like those of coalminers and railway workers have, like the textile unions in earlier times, declined rapidly in numbers. Those representing workers in education, the health services and other public services have replaced them in the 'league table'.

There have been other noteworthy changes. The number of very small unions, though still striking, has declined with a reduction in the total number of unions: by over 40 per cent between 1949 and 1979. At the same time, the number of unions with over 100,000 members increased from 17 to 27. In consequence, the average size of unions – only 13,000 in 1948 – more than doubled. Within the Trades Union Congress, the number of affiliated unions fell by 41 per cent over the same period, despite the affiliation of some major public-sector white-collar unions such as NALGO and NUT. By 1980, 90 per cent of all British trade unionists were members of a TUC-affiliated union. This increased concentration of membership reflected both more successful recruitment by larger unions, and a process of acquisition and amalgamation whereby the 'giants' absorbed numerous smaller organizations.

The number of unions continued to fall during the 1980s. However, the large TUC-affiliated unions are no longer the beneficiaries of change. The TGWU and AEU, the two largest unions in 1980, each lost some 40 per cent of their membership during the decade. While some large TUC affiliates have held steady or even expanded during the 1980s, they are a fairly small minority. The main success stories in a depressing decade for trade unions have been outside the TUC: among some large organizations such as the Royal College of Nursing and the Police Federation, and also among many smaller professional and staff associations. Hence the proportion of members included in TUC affiliates has fallen to 85 per cent: a decline only partially attributable to the expulsion of the Electricians.

The principal reason for the declining number of small unions is a 'merger wave' (Waddington 1992a) which has occurred since 1966. In this period a total of 347 unions have been absorbed by amalgamation; 84 per cent of these had less than 5,000 members. A facilitating factor was the Trade Union (Amalgamation) Act of 1964, which eased the previous legal requirements, in particular making it possible for smaller unions to 'transfer engagements' to a larger organization by a simple majority of those voting in a special ballot. In addition, several precipitating causes can be identified: company restructuring and tougher employer policies (Buchanan 1974); competition from non-TUC unions and staff associations after the repeal of the 1971 Industrial Relations Act, which had privileged such bodies (Dickens 1975; Morris 1986); a rise in the threshold of union solvency with the diversification of the range of services which unions sought to provide (Hyman 1983); and, in some cases, numerical decline resulting from the contraction of a union's recruitment base. Also important has been the active pursuit of smaller merger partners by some large unions. Under the 'Bridlington principles' adopted by the TUC in 1939, affiliates are precluded from commencing recruitment where another affiliate already has a presence; but merger with an established organization (whether or not TUC-affiliated) offers a route round this restriction. In the 1970s the TGWU and ASTMS were noted for extending their recruitment bases in this manner (Undy et al. 1981); other unions followed suit in the 1980s. In some cases, such mergers, which may allow

Table 1.4 The changing structural dimensions of British unionism 1948–89

	By size group of membership						Ten largest unions	TUC affiliated unions
	Below 500 members	500–9,999 members	10,000–24,999 members	25,000–99,999 members	100,000 and more members	Total		
1948								
Number of unions	335	281	39	34	17	706		187
Total membership (000s)	57	742	587	1,695	6,220	9,301	4,997	7,937
% of all unions	47.5	39.8	5.5	4.8	2.4			26.5
% of all members	0.6	8.0	6.3	18.2	66.9		53.7	85.3
1968								
Number of unions	235	235	37	35	19	561		155
Total membership (000s)	38	600	569	1,946	7,034	10,187	5,338	8,875
% of all unions	41.9	41.9	6.6	6.2	3.4			27.6
% of all members	0.4	5.9	5.6	19.1	69.0		52.4	87.1
1979								
Number of unions	197	172	26	34	27	456		109

Total membership (000s)	34	439	448	1,715	10,811	13,447	7,681	12,173
% of all unions	43.2	37.7	5.7	7.5	5.9			23.9
% of all members	0.3	3.3	3.3	12.8	80.4		57.1	90.5
1987								
Number of unions	138	116	17	31	24	330*		79
Total membership (000s)	23	287	294	1,429	8,441	10,474	5,745	8,797
% of all unions	41.8	35.2	5.2	9.4	73			23.9
% of all members	0.2	2.7	2.8	13.6	80.6		54.9	84.0
1989								
Number of unions	121	113	17	31	23	309*		78
Total membership (000s)	21	311	291	1,372	8,163	10,158	6,131	8,652
% of all unions	39.1	36.5	5.5	10.1	7.4			24.9
% of all members	0.2	3.0	2.9	13.5	80.4		60.4	85.2

*4 unions membership unknown, but assumed to be insignificant.
Source: Department of Employment Gazette, TUC Report, IRRU trade union membership record, Annual Reports of the Certification Officer.

the junior partner to function as a semi-autonomous section of the larger union, have reflected no obvious industrial relations logic, but rather have stemmed from the political allegiances of the leaderships involved or from a simple desire to extend recruitment bases. The merger of the AEU and EETPU in early 1992 united the principal right-wing-led unions. It remains to be seen whether the merged union will re-affiliate to the TUC following the EETPU's expulsion in 1988. Several major unions have already written to the TUC's general secretary pointing out areas of dispute with the EETPU and expressing concern regarding the union's re-affiliation, but it is in any case possible that the merged union may wish to operate outside the TUC.

Such processes have further complicated an already confusing structure of unionism. Traditionally, writers on British industrial relations classified trade unions into three broad categories: craft, industrial and general. Historically, societies of skilled artisans were the first to emerge; their membership was restricted to those qualified to exercise a specific craft, often across a range of industries. In the mid-nineteenth century there developed unions organizing all grades of worker within a single industry, notably in the rapidly expanding coal industry. Around the turn of the century, general unions were formed; they did not confine their recruitment to a single industry or by occupation. But the competition amongst these different types of unions, their responses to sectoral shifts in employment, and in the present century the creation of new unions catering specifically for public sector employees and for non-manual workers, have all increased diversity.

Today, most significant unions are to some extent general unions: multi-occupational and often multi-industrial. Former craft unions have opened their membership in one direction to lower-skilled workers, in another to white-collar staff. Most bodies with a single-industry base have, like employers, diversified. In face of the overall decline in membership in the 1980s, recruitment strategies have become increasingly opportunistic, and inter-union conflict has inevitably resulted.

In one respect, the pattern of British trade union organization is simpler than in many other European countries: there is only one central confederation in Britain, the TUC. This unitary characteristic reflects the facts that British unions have never been radically differentiated on ideological grounds and that the unionization of public employees and white-collar grades has largely evolved out of the traditional union structure. Some relatively large unions (notably NALGO, representing local government officers, and the largest teachers' union, the NUT) were originally outside the TUC, but joined during the 1960s in order to gain a voice in the developing machinery of tripartism. By the end of the 1970s, as has been seen, 90 per cent of all trade unionists were members of TUC affiliates. Though the proportion has now fallen to 80 per cent, there have been no serious attempts to create a rival federation to the TUC.

Internal Organization and Finance

The internal organization of unions in Britain is also distinctive. By comparison with most Northern European countries, they charge relatively low levels of membership contribution (on average, roughly 0.5 per cent of members' income), and possess a relatively undeveloped bureaucracy. The ratio of full-time officials to members is comparatively low (in general, ranging between 1:100 and 1:500); most unions depend heavily on 'lay' rank-and-file activists to recruit new members, undertake local administrative tasks, and perform workplace-level collective bargaining. Specialist functions at national level, such as research, education and communications, have traditionally been very poorly resourced. As shown below, however, since the 1960s some unions have significantly increased their staffing in these areas in an attempt to become more 'professional'.

Increased expenditure on staffing and administration has obvious implications for unions' financial stability, particularly in a context of membership decline. Some details are given in table 1.5. Union solvency – the ratio of income to expenditure – has fluctuated over the post-war years, and deteriorated over much of the 1970s and 1980s. Overall, British unions remain solvent, but within far narrower margins than in the early post-war years; and some individual unions are in serious financial straits.

The pattern of both income and expenditure has altered significantly over the years. Traditionally, many unions – particularly those with craft origins – paid extensive financial benefits to members (for disputes, sickness, retirement, accidents, and unemployment). Over the present century the relative importance of such benefits has declined, as state welfare benefits have been provided; this process has been accentuated in the last half-century, partly because of rapid price inflation which has devalued unions' 'friendly' benefits. Today, almost 90 per cent of expenditure goes on administration – in other words, such items as premises, staff salaries, correspondence and publications, and transport.

For most of the post-war period, the proportion of income received directly from members in subscriptions has declined. It is probable that competition from rival unions for members has encouraged the tendency to keep subscriptions low. In addition, in most unions an increase in subscriptions requires approval by a delegate conference, and raising fees in line with increased prices and incomes can provoke resistance (though some unions have now introduced automatic wage-indexation of members' contributions). Only in the 1980s were most unions forced to introduce substantial increases in real subscription levels in order to remain solvent in the face of declining membership.

With rising expenditure and static subscriptions during much of the past quarter-century, how have unions survived? To an important extent they have been sustained by income from property and other investments. This in turn has tended to erode the 'real net worth' (Willman 1990) of British unions, that is the real value of assets minus liabilities. The figure was stable in the 1950s, increased for much of the 1960s, but fell

Table 1.5 The changing composition of union finances

Year	Union solvency[a] from members (%)	Proportion of Income		Proportion of Expenditure Disposed		Real subscription level per member	Index of real 'net worth'[b]
		from members (%)	from other sources (%)	on benefits to members (%)	on administration and other outgoings (%)		
1948	132.8	89.8	10.2	33.5[c]	66.5[c]	2.7	100
1968	106.4	83.7	16.3	29.5[c]	70.5[c]	2.9	114
1979	110.4	84.4	15.6	16.0	84.0	2.9	75
1987	106.6	81.8	18.2	12.8	87.2	4.2	80

[a]Income/expenditure ratio
[b]Real value of assets minus liabilities (1948 = 100)
[c]excludes expenditure and political funds
Sources: Reports of the Chief Registrar of Friendly Societies and Certification Officer.

sharply in the 1970s. In the 1980s, despite falling membership there are signs of recovery; but net worth is still 14 per cent below the 1948 level.

As has been noted, British unions are distinctive for the degree of rank-and-file involvement in policy and organization. Most unions are governed by lay executive committees, to which the national leaders (normally general secretaries) are technically subordinate; the supreme policy-making body is normally a conference composed predominantly or exclusively of rank-and-file delegates. Many would argue that the relatively amateur basis of union organization in Britain both reflects and reinforces an approach to industrial relations which is pragmatic and opportunistic, uninformed by explicit strategy.

A more positive evaluation of this tradition would emphasize its democratic ethos. Activists and officials commonly stress the importance of membership participation in the formulation and implementation of policy, and are suspicious of too much dependence on a cadre of professional experts. Part of the logic of this philosophy of participatory democracy is a conviction – far older than the sociological presentation of the argument by Offe and Wiesenthal (1980) – that trade union strength depends crucially on the members' 'willingness to act'; and that this can best be nurtured by discussion and decision-making at the grass roots.

One aspect of the tradition of decentralized rank-and-file initiative is the role of the shop steward. From the nineteenth century, craft unions in several industries had workplace representatives responsible for monitoring the employer's observance of union working rules, for ensuring the recruitment and retention of members, and in some cases for collecting their weekly contributions. In the present century, such stewards became increasingly concerned with negotiations with the employer, particularly where systems of payment by results were introduced; and procedures of workshop representation spread from the craft organizations to many other unions. The fragmentation of bargaining was linked in turn to the characteristic British pattern of numerous small, short strikes, usually conducted without the sanction or often even the knowledge of full-time union officials. At the same time, the large body of workers representing their fellows as shop stewards played a vital part in the official decision-making structures of many trade unions.

The moves away from the pattern of fragmented decentralization described by Donovan had significant effects on unions in the workplace. The first phase was marked by a formalization of the machinery of plant-level representation, often involving management's explicit agreement that certain senior stewards could perform their union role full-time while remaining on the company payroll, and the provision of a range of facilities to assist them. In a number of industries without a previous tradition of workplace collective bargaining, similar procedures were introduced. At the same time, many unions drafted clearer rulebook definitions of the rights and responsibilities of shop stewards, and in some cases established new policy-making bodies at company and industry level, with the aim of increasing stewards' integration within their official structures. The past decade has seen a new climate of company-level industrial relations, and in some cases a management challenge to 'shop steward power'. As discussed above, the actual effects within the workplace have been mixed, but the self-confidence of the 'rank and file' does seem to have been eroded.

Developments in the 1980s: Union Democracy and the Role of the TUC

The internal politics of British unions, and the relationships with actual and potential members, have altered in a variety of ways during the past decade. The most obvious stimulus to change was the legislation of the 1980s, which reflected the government's conception of trade union democracy. Though in the past 'the internal affairs of trade unions were regulated more by the unions' own rule books than by external legal regulation' (Lewis 1986: 4), the legislative changes reviewed above make this no longer true. Underlying the 1984 Act, and argued explicitly in the 1983 Green Paper 'Democracy in Trade Unions', was the view that in many unions the traditional forms of collective and delegatory decision-making allowed policy to be dictated by 'militant' leaders or shop stewards. By requiring secret individual ballots as the central mechanism of union democracy, it was assumed that 'moderate' policies would prevail.

The 1980 Employment Act provided for public subsidies to unions which used secret postal ballots, in order to encourage the practice. However the TUC, as part of its initial policy of non-cooperation with the government's initiatives, instructed affiliates not to apply for these funds. In 1985 this provoked a crisis when the AEU and EETPU, unions which already made extensive use of postal ballots, declared that they would apply for government funds regardless; and the TUC modified its policy at a special conference in February 1986.

A major administrative burden has been placed on unions by the provisions of legislation requiring elections of officers by secret postal ballot. In some unions, membership records in the past were notoriously unreliable, and the spur to greater efficiency might perhaps be welcomed. But in view of problems of membership turnover, the absolute requirement to maintain up-to-date registers of members eligible to vote, together with current home addresses, is difficult for any union to satisfy.

More substantively, many unions have been forced to transform their electoral systems. In many unions, notably white-collar organizations in the public sector, general secretaries were not elected but appointed by the executive committee or the conference; executive committees themselves were sometimes elected by conference delegates rather than the membership as a whole. In other unions national officers were initially elected by a membership ballot, but were not subject to re-election; examples are the Railwaymen (now merged with the Seamen to form a new union) and the National Union of Mineworkers. Across the movement as a whole, despite increased use of postal ballots in the 1970s, branch or workplace voting remained the norm. It was also common for executive committee members representing specific occupational interests to be appointed by the relevant union committee rather than directly elected by the membership (for example, trade group representatives in the TGWU).

With varying degrees of reluctance, unions have been forced to comply with the new legal requirements. The consequences have probably been less marked than the government anticipated. In few unions have the new election methods brought radical changes in the political disposition of the executive. However, because postal balloting often seems to result in far lower voting figures than other methods, the outcome can be greater unpredictability and fluctuation. Two general secretaries have failed to pass the new electoral test; in NATFHE the victor was a leftist, in the NUJ an opponent of a proposed merger with other print unions.

The second area in which the 1984 Act introduced new balloting requirements, political funds, resulted in a clear defeat for the government. Under the 1913 Trade Union Act, unions undertaking political activities (including affiliation to the Labour Party) were required to ballot members to establish a separate fund. The 1984 Act required new ballots to confirm support for existing funds. Despite expectations that these would result in widespread rejection of political activities, gravely damaging the Labour Party, an effective campaign resulted in confirmation of all existing political funds, usually by very large majorities. Some unions which had not previously had political funds also held successful ballots to establish them – a reaction to the section of the Act which extended the range of campaigns and propaganda which might be construed as political activity.

Although the legislation may have failed to transform the political characteristics of British unionism, many would argue that it has helped encourage a more individualistic conception of trade union democracy. Paradoxically, opinion polls suggest that the principle of secret ballots is very popular among union members, who are receptive to the argument that leaders and activists are out of touch with the opinions of the majority, even though they have shown no marked disposition to vote these leaders out of office. For critics, the statutorily imposed procedures reflect an individualistic model of unionism and thus subvert the collective character of trade union organization and action. Such 'privatization' is also reflected in the growing tendency of most unions to develop an appeal to prospective members on the basis of individual services: advice and representation in the case of individual problems at work, but also discounts for banking, insurance, pensions and other personal expenditure. Some dismiss such initiatives as 'credit card unionism'; others see it as an inevitable reflection of reduced strength in collective bargaining, and the need to appeal to workers in the secondary labour market who have little basis for collective militancy.

In the face of this change in the character of unions' links with their members, the TUC has attempted to coordinate the responses of its affiliates. To the extent, however, that the internal authority of Congress depends on the status derived from dealing with the government (cf. Martin 1980), its ability to exert effective leadership in policy formulation has if anything diminished. In 1987, Congress established a Special Review Body (SRB) to consider future policy for the movement. Its deliberations have concentrated on two problems: recruitment and retention of members, and inter-union relations. Its reports have emphasized the need for more targeted recruitment methods, encouraging increased attention in membership campaigns and in bargaining priorities to vulnerable groups with distinctive needs, such as women, young workers, and ethnic minorities.

The TUC has also encouraged unions to offer a wider range of individual services, and has taken initiatives of its own in this respect. In conjunction with the Cooperative Bank it has established the Unity Trust Bank, which offers to trade unionists financial services such as pensions, insurance, credit cards and discount schemes; a trade union advice service on legal matters not connected with employment has also been launched.

Another notable TUC initiative was to commission six studies of union membership and non-membership in local labour markets where employment had recently expanded, often in small high-technology companies. On the basis of the findings, the SRB attempted to coordinate the recruitment efforts of its members in such areas, on the grounds that unrestricted competition among affiliates for new members would prove counterproductive. However, some of the larger TUC unions effectively vetoed such intervention, since they felt able to gain more from a recruitment 'free-for-all' than smaller and less well-resourced competitors. Highly publicized efforts were also made to recruit members in specific localities such as Trafford Park in Manchester; the results were very limited.

The TUC has also amended its 'Bridlington' rules on inter-union relations. In 1988 substantial modifications, together with a new Code of Practice, were approved by Congress. The new rules restrict the freedom of affiliates to seek recognition, in particular where this involves a single-union agreement, where this might infringe the bargaining rights of other member unions. It was because of breaches of these rules that the EETPU was expelled from the TUC in 1988 (Waddington 1988).

A further index of, and influence on, the political process within the TUC is the constitution of its executive committee, the General Council. Traditionally this was elected by a complicated procedure which, in effect, over-represented the older private-sector manual unions at the expense of newer white-collar and public-sector organizations; and it allowed the leaders of a handful of major unions considerable 'patronage' in elections to contested seats. Changes introduced in 1982 gave every union with over 100,000 members an automatic seat on the General Council (with extra seats for the largest unions), and allowed smaller unions the right to elect a limited number of their own representatives. In 1989 this was modified again: a new procedure substantially increased the number of seats reserved for women trade unionists, but the electoral procedure shifted the balance of influence once more towards the largest unions.

There has thus been a significant effort to come to terms with the changes of the 1980s. Yet many observers would conclude that unions, like managements, have found it difficult fundamentally to alter their structures and attitudes. This characteristic is also evident in unions' approaches to politics.

Trade Unions and Politics

Most of the larger unions affiliate to the Labour Party (though the TUC itself does not); party membership via national trade unions is one of the many unique features of the British system. However, the relationship between unions' 'political' and 'industrial relations' involvements is complex and often contradictory. Traditionally a tacit division of labour existed between party and unions. Although affiliated unions provided most of the party's funds, and had potentially the decisive vote at its conference, the parliamentary leadership was allowed a virtually free hand on policy issues except where these affected the conduct of collective bargaining. Conversely, the party did not seek to interfere in industrial relations; and unions often deployed the rhetoric of class to legitimate industrial militancy in defence of their members' particularistic employment interests.

This division of labour has been subject to many strains. In the 1940s and 1950s a group of major union leaders (the so-called 'praetorian guard') used their block votes to support the parliamentary leadership against left-wing challenges. The situation altered as a more left-oriented group of union leaders began to question the efforts of a new 'revisionist' party leadership to imitate continental social democracy and to abandon many of the traditional symbols of socialist class politics. Key issues on which union votes influenced party policy in the 1960s were unilateral nuclear disarmament and opposition to EC membership. On questions of more material importance union influence was far weaker: under Labour governments of the 1960s unions exerted some negative power, notably in vetoing proposals in 1969 to legislate to control unofficial strikes, but they had no influence over the general direction of economic policy. After the 1970 election defeat, a TUC-Party Liaison Committee was established to try to develop more constructive relationships; during the 1974–9 Labour government this was an important body in defining the 'Social Contract'.

After the election of the Conservative government in 1979, Labour Party and union leaderships considered that a looser relationship was desirable: the latter because many of their members, and particularly those groups that they wished to attract into membership, were hostile to the party; the former, because the charge that policy was dominated by the 'union bosses' was seen as an electoral liability. Thus in the 1980s the relationship became far more detached. Some union leaders have helped to initiate moves to reduce the weight of the union block vote at conference, and in the longer run to weaken the role of conference itself in policy determination. Perhaps most notably, the policy review launched after the 1987 election defeat has brought the abandonment of a range of traditional commitments with deep symbolic resonance – unilateralism, nationalization, Keynesian economic management – with minimal union criticism. On the specific issue of trade union legislation, moreover, the unions have accepted party aims which would retain many of the key changes of the 1980s – compulsory secret ballots for strikes and for union elections, prohibition of the closed shop – with only modest amendments to meet their wishes.

If most union leaders have accepted the party's move towards a dilute form of continental social democracy, this has not however been matched by any agreement on incomes policy. Except in periods of exceptional economic crisis (1948–50, 1975–6) British unions have always vigorously resisted any notion of wage restraint. The Wilson government incomes policy was supported as part of an optimistic expansionary programme (and was made acceptable under the label of 'planned growth of incomes'), and was further legitimated by the government's efforts to control prices as well as pay. Today the very term 'incomes policy' has become taboo; even the recent euphemism 'national economic assessment' has aroused suspicion in some influential unions. How unions might conduct their bargaining under any future Labour government has not therefore been deemed a proper matter for explicit discussion. Recently there have been a few signs of change – notably, proposals from some important union leaders for the synchronization of national pay bargaining – but the rhetoric of 'free collective bargaining' remains potent.

A marked development of the late 1980s was the transformation in union attitudes towards the European Community. Ever since the issue of UK membership of the Community was first debated, the great majority of unions were uncompromisingly hostile. During the referendum of 1975, the TUC called for British withdrawal, and this remained its formal policy. In the 1980s, however, with their strength in collective bargaining reduced, and with their aspirations to represent a new and more vulnerable constituency, British unions have come increasingly to see legislation as a necessary and desirable method of achieving employee rights. Given the hostility of the government towards such legislation, unions have looked to Brussels for what Westminster denies. The TUC became an enthusiastic supporter of European integration, in particular of a 'social dimension' to the single market.

As part of the growing influence of the EC, the issue of industrial democracy may be returning to the agenda. The traditional view of most British unions was that 'free collective bargaining' was incompatible with any statutory system of employee representation; and even 'voluntary' structures of worker participation were suspect, unless very firmly integrated into trade union machinery. In the early 1970s, EC proposals in the area, together with leftist notions of workers' control and managerialist interest in harnessing employee support for productivity initiatives helped stimulate increased attention to industrial democracy. The enthusiasm of

Jack Jones, general secretary of the TGWU, was an important stimulus to the creation of the Bullock Committee and its recommendations for a statutory procedure for board-level employee representation. At that time, however, trade unions were deeply divided on the issue, while employers were bitterly hostile, and more urgent priorities soon took over. But after a decade in which unions have lost some of their traditional confidence in their industrial muscle, while employers have increasingly taken the initiative and the centres of corporate decision-making appear increasingly transnational, EC debates over employee rights of representation, information and consultation have acquired new resonance.

Conclusion

During the 1980s unions made considerable efforts to re-orient their policies and methods in the light of the changing structure of the work force, employer attempts to redefine the employment relationship, and legal and political challenges. As yet there is little consensus on the responses to be adopted, and the effectiveness of new policy initiatives remains unclear. Unions have certainly survived, and there is no evidence that most workers have abandoned collectivism as a general principle (Gallie 1989). Yet the meanings and constituencies of collectivism may well have altered. Some recent policy initiatives may be seen as adaptations to increasing differentiation among trade unionists and within the labour force more generally. At one level, it can involve increased attention to the needs of those whose labour market position is weak. At the other extreme, though, a concern of many unions in the 1980s was how to appeal to relatively advantaged groups with scarce skills or secure careers. Allowing such groups scope for policy-making autonomy has become in particular an important feature of the trade union merger process. The implications of such sectionalization – particularly when allied to more bureaucratic modes of union organization and administration – are deeply ambiguous. Unions have survived, but they have not created a new identity, and the idea of a labour 'movement' is perhaps more distant than ever.

Public Sector Industrial Relations

Public sector employment, by definition, is more closely regulated by state policies than that in the private sector. While Britain is unusual in the very limited extent to which employment legislation differentiates between the two, the character of public sector industrial relations has been shaped by government policies (Fredman and Morris 1989). These include the strategic decisions that determine the scope of public ownership and the coverage of the 'welfare state'; the legal and administrative rules and informal political pressures that limit the discretion of local service managers; and government expenditure policies that exert a crucial influence on pay determination because salaries consume up to 70 per cent of current expenditure in labour intensive public services.

Six million employees, 22 per cent of the labour force in employment, worked in the British public sector in 1990. Local authorities employed just under 3 million staff, mainly in education, police, and social services, and there were 1.2 million staff in the National Health Service. Approximately 0.75 million civilian staff were employed by central government and the same number in public corporations, mainly nationalized industries. Public sector employment fell from a peak of nearly 30 per cent of the work force in 1977. This was caused by a gradual reduction in central government staff, and the rationalization and privatization policies that halved employment in nationalized industries in the 1980s (CSO 1990).

Much of the growth in women's employment in Britain has been located in the public sector, especially in education, health and social services where women outnumber men. In these services, a substantial number of women are employed in full-time, relatively well-paid jobs in the 'caring professions', while many others are employed part-time in less secure and low paid 'domestic' and 'ancillary' grades. Trade unions have been more successful in recruiting women employed both in professional and ancillary jobs than have unions operating in the private sector; they have achieved only partial success, however, in reducing gendered occupational segregation.

Patterns of industrial relations were plainly different in sectors as varied as health, education, public utilities and coal (Ferner 1989). One common theme, however, was the intractable problem of the control of public sector pay. This issue forms the focus of the following discussion since it most clearly illustrates the ways in which successive governments have tried to manage the sector.

The Traditional Pattern

Until the late 1960s, public sector industrial relations attracted very little academic and political interest. A broad consensus supported the continued public ownership of major power, transport and other industries, and the expansion of education, health, and social services within the welfare state. Steady economic growth and low levels of inflation facilitated the expansion of public expenditure and employment.

In this favourable environment, public sector industrial relations were fairly stable. Centralized collective bargaining, and a commitment to the principle of 'fair comparison', led to pay movements broadly in line with those of the private sector. When pay and conditions grievances arose, potential conflicts were settled mainly through arbitration procedures. Trade union membership density was high, union policy-making was centralized, and most of the unions representing non-manual employees had modest policy objectives which they pursued cautiously and outside the mainstream of the labour movement; that is, they were not affiliated to the TUC. There was little incentive to develop management expertise in industrial relations; various forms of 'consensus management' were based on formal consultation with staff representatives and a bureaucratic style of decision-making. The ideology and rhetoric of 'public service' values encouraged a tacit understanding that if government and public sector managers sustained a long-established obligation to be 'model employers', then staff and their unions would accept a reciprocal obligation to preserve industrial peace.

During the 1970s, far more conflictual patterns of industrial relations emerged. In most countries, high and fluctuating levels of inflation threatened existing methods of pay determination and expenditure planning and control in the public sector. In the British context of weak economic performance and volatile electoral politics, however, public sector disputes generated unpredictable and dramatic political consequences. The general elections of 1974 and 1979 were influenced decisively by industrial disputes in the public sector; indeed, the 'winter of discontent' legitimized a sharp and intensely ideological challenge to the remnants of the post-war consensus on the position of the public sector in the British economy (Winchester 1983).

Wage Militancy in the 1970s

From the mid-1960s, higher levels of inflation led to the introduction and collapse of a series of incomes policies. A cyclical pattern of public sector pay movements *vis-à-vis* the private sector emerged. In the first phase, governments were able to impose incomes policy norms more rigorously on the large, centralized, and politically sensitive bargaining units of the public sector. After several years of relative pay deterioration, trade unions developed national wage campaigns, culminating in disputes and the disruption of services. This militancy was rewarded by large pay awards, often legitimized by public inquiries, which enabled public sector workers to 'catch up' with pay movements elsewhere. These pay settlements often disturbed public sector pay relativities, added a new twist to the inflationary spiral, and contributed significantly to the problems of public expenditure control, thus encouraging a new phase of pay restraint.

It was not, of course, inevitable that this cyclical pattern of pay movements and conflict would develop. The grievances of workers had to be organized, and government ministers and public sector employers had some choice in the way in which they responded to the demands and disruption. The policies and tactics of the parties changed during the 1970s, and the consequences of the disputes varied significantly.

At the beginning of the 1970s, at a time of relatively low unemployment and weak public expenditure control, trade unions embarked on radically new strategies. The leadership of the National Union of Public Employees (NUPE), for example, organized pay campaigns that succeeded in mobilizing a previously quiescent membership of low-paid manual workers. The union was able to develop more effective workplace organization and bargaining, and to coordinate a series of selective strikes, protests, and publicity campaigns that succeeded in winning a remarkable degree of public support during the disputes in local authorities and the health service. Equally important but rather different changes took place in many non-manual public service unions. The national leadership of these traditionally hierarchic and moderate unions was challenged by a form of 'radical professionalism'; and schoolteachers, social workers, and civil servants engaged in selective strike action for the first time.

What stands out in retrospect was the extent of management and government uncertainty in responding to the conflict of the early 1970s. Trade unionists had demonstrated 'a willingness to act' in unprecedented ways, and the 'public service values' and limited management expertise of their employers left them quite unprepared for the conflict. The strategy of the 1970–4 Conservative government was also uncertain; it fluctuated between corporatist and coercive approaches to union leaders in implementing incomes policies and industrial relations legislation. On several occasions, ministers failed to anticipate the impact of disputes on public opinion, and the ultimate political miscalculation was made by the prime minister when he chose to call a general election in 1974 during the second miners' strike.

The form and consequences of public sector wage conflict in the late 1970s were quite different. There were few disputes during the early years of the Labour government because most public sector workers received large pay settlements – the classic 'catching-up' phase of the cycle, intensified by the demand for compensation for the rapid price inflation of the period. This contributed substantially to the crisis in public expenditure planning and control in 1975, and paved the way for the introduction of cuts and cash limits that would have profound consequences in later years. Active trade union support for the incomes policies of 1975–7 was undermined over the following year by declining real incomes and the deterioration in pay relativities with the private sector. Despite union opposition, the government tried to sustain a pay limit of 5 per cent in the autumn of 1978. Government ministers refused to sanction public service settlements above the pay norm, and widespread industrial disruption took place in the early months of 1979.

The 'winter of discontent' was not merely a repeat performance of the early 1970s disputes. First, the strikes exposed severe inter-union conflict, and tensions between the leadership, activists and members within some unions. Second, the unions were faced by a more confident group of public service managers following the major reorganizations of local government and the health service in the mid-1970s. Third, the public hostility to the simultaneous disruption of essential health, education, and community services was intensified by the press coverage of the unresolved disputes in the months before a general election.

The disputes transformed the political context of public sector industrial relations. The Labour government had miscalculated the ability of trade union leaders to 'deliver' another year of pay restraint; it thus lost its prime electoral asset – the ability to sustain an understanding with the trade union movement. The disruption of public services contributed significantly to the Conservative Party's election victory and legitimized the policies it had developed during five years of opposition. Its general commitment to confront trade union power included a specific hostility to public sector unions. Strict controls on public expenditure, leading to job losses and pay restraint, would be accompanied by a policy of privatization, involving the sale of public enterprises and the contracting out of public services. These developments cannot be reviewed in detail here. In brief, contracting out tended to reduce wage levels and worsen conditions of service, though productivity gains were also claimed (Bach 1989). Privatized firms faced many of the issues discussed above in relation to the private sector, including the abandonment of national pay bargaining (Colling 1991). The remaining public sector was also subjected to commercial principles, but the problem of pay setting was not resolved.

Conservative Government Policies in the 1980s

The determination of the new Conservative government to confront public sector unions was first delayed, and then intensified, by the experience of its first year in office. The reports of the Pay Comparability Commission, set up in the last months of the Labour government, recommended large pay increases for several million public service workers, partly to allow them to 'catch up' with pay movements in the private sector over the previous three to four years, and partly to keep pace with the high rate of inflation (17 per cent in 1980). As soon as it was politically feasible, the government abolished the Commission and systematically attacked the principle of comparability, by substituting the 'ability to pay' as the key criterion for public sector pay determination. Cash limits and other financial controls defined this 'ability to pay'. The macro-economic implications of cash limits were profound. The government virtually abandoned the previous system of volume planning of public services; from 1981, cash planning implied that the volume of public services emerged as a residual after taking account of pay increases, work force changes, and other costs. The collective bargaining implications of cash limits were equally significant; in comparison with the incomes policies of the 1970s, the new system offered a more flexible form of government intervention.

First, in contrast to the fixed pay norms of previous policies, where a single publicized breach often undermined the credibility of the whole policy, cash limits allowed unequal pay awards to reflect the potential industrial power or labour market position of different groups. Second, cash limits forced union and employer negotiators to confront income-employment trade-offs more explicitly; they could exceed the pay assumption of the cash limits, but only if the extra cost could be recovered by job losses, efficiency savings, or service reductions. Thirdly, cash limits encouraged public sector managers to seek a more direct influence on negotiations. At the very least, this required more effective feedback between employers' representatives involved in the national negotiations and local service managers who had to reconcile pay awards with tightly controlled budgets. Variations in local labour market conditions and housing costs, as well as in the financial circumstances of individual employers, also encouraged demands for greater flexibility in national agreements, or more decentralized collective bargaining structures.

The imposition of tight cash limits in the early 1980s led to a number of protracted disputes in the steel industry, civil service, health service, schools, and water supply industry. All of these disputes revealed that the Conservative government had recalculated the political costs of public sector conflict and had developed a more strategic approach to conflict management. First, government ministers rejected traditional methods of conciliation and mediation; opportunities for compromise were repeatedly scorned as a sign of weakness. Second, the government was willing to pay substantial financial costs to defeat public sector unions; the estimated £5 billion cost of defeating the 1984–5 coalminers' strike was merely the most dramatic example of the government's determination to win (Adeney and Lloyd 1986). Third, public sector employers were encouraged to adopt a more abrasive and confrontational style of management in negotiations and disputes.

For most of the 1980s, this strategy seemed to be successful. Few union leaders and activists had the inclination or organizational capacity to contemplate national strikes, and many public sector unions adopted a version of 'new realism' based on the recognition that militancy was unlikely to be rewarded. While the frequency of nationally coordinated strikes over pay declined, especially in the middle of the decade when most workers' real incomes rose, public sector conflict did not disappear altogether. For instance, ambulance staff sustained an effective programme of non-strike sanctions (various forms of 'working-to-rule') and a sensitive media campaign in their pay dispute of 1989–90. More generally, a number of disputes arose from defensive union action to preserve bargaining procedures or conditions of service. These have been threatened by more assertive management proposals designed to increase 'flexibility', cut labour costs, and remain within tight budgets (Ferner 1991).

Central government control of aggregate pay movements and a determined resistance to union pay demands have been accompanied by constant ministerial exhortation in favour of more decentralized methods of pay determination that would be more sensitive to local labour market conditions and individual employees' performance. The government can claim some success in undermining national bargaining structures. Throughout the public sector, senior managers have been removed from the coverage of collective bargaining; national agreements are now less prescriptive than in the past; some local authorities have withdrawn from the national machinery; and legal and administrative changes have been introduced to allow a devolution of pay and personnel policies to separate 'executive agencies' in central government, separate 'businesses' in nationalized industries, 'self-governing trusts' in the health service, and 'locally managed' schools and colleges in education. These changes reflect the substantial devolution of managerial authority in all parts of the public sector.

The future structure of public sector collective bargaining, however, remains a matter of dispute. Predictable trade union objections to the weakening of national agreements have been accompanied by management reservations. Most public sector managers have welcomed increased flexibility in the implementation of national agreements, but many fear that local bargaining could produce higher pay settlements, increased conflict, and additional costs in developing the necessary management expertise. It can be argued also that government policies have not always matched ministerial rhetoric on decentralization and flexibility.

More than 1.5 million employees, including nurses (since 1983) and schoolteachers (since 1991), are covered by Pay Review Bodies. While the pay review system formally ends 'free collective bargaining', permitting the government to accept, modify or reject the review bodies' recommendations, it sustains a 'quasi-bargaining' process in practice. Trade unions, employers, and government departments submit evidence and arguments covering the usual pay determination criteria, and the possibility that the government might reject the review bodies' recommendations is minimized by the potential political costs involved. Although the pay awards for nurses have been deferred or staged on several occasions, their relative pay has improved under the pay review procedure during the 1980s.

More generally, the overwhelming priority attached to centralized financial control has limited the scope and efficacy of flexibility initiatives. The 'flexible pay supplements', introduced to reduce recruitment and retention problems in tight labour markets, have often proved to be expensive, or trivial in relation to the overall supply-side problem, or regional imbalances, that they are trying to redress (Thornley and Winchester 1991). Similarly, government insistence that performance-related pay supplements should be added to national salary structures in many parts of the public sector have been restricted mainly to senior staff, and seem to have generated more grievances concerning the adequacy and equity of performance appraisal procedures than motivational and retention benefits (Bailey 1989).

The data on pay movements in the 1980s could, however, be cited in support of Conservative governments' public sector pay policies. Public service employees received increases in real income in the last decade, but their pay relative to that of private sector employees declined. This was accompanied by increasing variation in the treatment of different services and occupational groups. In general, pay differentials between staff with professional qualifications and their administrative, clerical, and ancillary support staff widened. Police prospered more than teachers, and teachers in schools were treated more favourably than their colleagues in further education or universities (Brown and Rowthorn 1990).

These data are broadly consistent with the stated aims of government policy, namely, control of public sector pay aggregates and the exposure of particular services and occupations to market forces. The relative decline in the pay of ancillary workers, many of whom work in services subject to compulsory competitive tendering, can be explained by a greater exposure to market forces. Given the very low levels of pay received by such groups, it is a matter of political judgement whether their further relative decline should be celebrated or regretted.

The notion of a local labour market for many public service occupations, however, is inherently problematical. As Brown and Walsh (1991: 56) have argued, the public authority is more or less the exclusive provider of the service, and the predominant employer of key occupational groups, such as teachers, nurses, and police officers. Moreover, the quality of the service may depend upon an occupational or professional integrity that is expressed most effectively in a national salary structure, and may be undermined by the decentralization of pay determination. This suggests that relative pay movements can be explained only by a combination of political, institutional, and short-term supply-side factors rather than by ambiguous references to market forces.

In conclusion, only the most sanguine of commentators can believe that Conservative governments have discovered a convincing and enduring solution to the problem of public sector pay determination in Britain. The evidence of the last twenty-five years suggests that governments have succeeded only rarely, and for brief periods, in their attempts to balance conflicting pay criteria. However, the never-ending flood of legislation and administrative intervention designed to restructure services, modify financial control systems, and reshape management values and practices, has transformed the organizational context in which public sector pay problems will be confronted in the future.

Strikes

A final curiosity of Britain is the attention that has been given to strikes, even though the country has never been at the top of the international league table of days lost through industrial action, and even though most British strikes have always been small and short. Strikes merit some attention, however, partly in their own right and partly as an index of how far the 1980s marked a break from the past.

Table 1.6 gives some indices of the strike pattern. Figures are given separately for coal mining and for other industries because of the domination of the overall figures by coal: in 1957, as many as three-quarters of all strikes occurred in this one industry. Because trends here often ran in a different direction from those in the rest of industry, the overall strike figures obscure what was happening outside coal.

The number of strikes outside coal was fairly constant during the 1940s and 1950s. During the 1960s, numbers increased, reaching a peak of 3746 in 1970. This increase reflected economic circumstances, with tight labour markets giving workers bargaining leverage. But underlying it was a

Table 1.6 Strikes in the United Kingdom, 1945–91

	All industries				Non-Coal		Coal Mining	
	Strikes	% Strikes lasting 3 days	Days lost (000s)	Days lost per 1000 employees	Strikes	Days lost (000s)	Strikes	Days lost (000s)
1945–9	1,881	77.3	2,235	110	745	1,597	1,136	639
1950–4	1,701	78.2	1,903	91	519	1,443	1,182	460
1955–9	2,530	81.2	4,602	211	659	4,013	1,871	588
1960–4	2,512	74.7	3,180	142	1,237	2,747	1,275	433
1965–9	2,380	65.1	3,929	172	1,961	3,584	419	346
1970–4	2,885	49.2	14,077	630	2,684	10,544	201	3,533
1975–9	2,310	42.6	11,663	510	2,033	11,560	277	104
1980	1,330	51.4	11,964	521	1,028	11,812	302	152
1981	1,338	55.5	4,266	195	1,036	4,031	302	235
1982	1,528	60.1	5,313	248	1,125	4,939	403	374
1983	1,352	55.6	3,754	178	997	3,270	355	484
1984	1,206	51.7	27,135	1,280	1,128	4,652	78	22,483
1985	903	56.9	6,402	298	743	2,260	160	4,142
1986	1,074	67.6	1,920	89	723	1,777	351	143
1987	1,016	66.7	3,546	164	720	3,329	296	217
1988	781	64.8	3,702	166	627	3,480	154	222
1989	701	69.8	4,128	181	555	4,078	146	50
1990	630	69.2	1,903	83	543	1,844	87	59
1991	354	–	759	–	–	–	–	–

Note: 1945–79 figures are annual averages. Official figures exclude strikes involving fewer than 10 workers or lasting less than one working day, unless a total of 100 days were 'lost'.
Source: Employment Gazette.

change in bargaining structure: the decentralization of collective bargaining and the growth in the number of shop stewards meant that there were many more separate bargains and that workers had the organization to sustain their demands (Edwards 1983). The Donovan Commission hoped that procedural reform would contain what was widely perceived to be a problem of small-scale unofficial action. Though strike numbers fell during the 1970s, they stabilized at a level substantially above that of the 1950s. Reform was often too limited to affect the use of strikes, and in other cases the process actually stimulated strikes as workers first resisted changes in bargaining arrangements and then used plant-wide organizations to press their demands. One indication of this was a decline in the proportion of strikes which were over within three days: from about 1970 onwards, strikes tended to become longer, indicating that they were over less immediate grievances.

With the onset of the recession in 1980, the number of strikes fell sharply. The number recorded in 1990 was the lowest since 1935. There was, moreover, an increase in the proportion of short strikes: not only were there fewer strikes, but those that took place were over sooner. The issues of strikes also changed, with a decline in the proportion over pay and a rise in the percentage over work allocation and other workplace matters. The absolute number of strikes over workplace issues fell only slightly. This suggests that the focus of industrial conflict shifted towards the organization and control of work. It does not, however, mean that conflict levels in the workplace were unchanged. As we have seen, widespread changes in working practices were introduced: the proportion of such cases involving industrial action is likely to have been lower than in the past.

A good deal of the decline in strikes reflected the effects of the recession. Declining employment in the strike-prone sectors, notably coal, the docks, and cars, was also a factor. And Britain was not alone in seeing a reduction in strike levels. As noted above, some studies suggest that legislation may also have had an effect. Legal immunities for industrial action were narrowed, and ballots were required before official action was legal. In one survey of union representatives, one-fifth reported calling off industrial action because of the law, and two-thirds believed that the law had had an effect in reducing workers' willingness and ability to strike (Labour Research 1990). As we have also seen, it is hard to point to specific legal provisions which have directly stopped strikes from occurring. Strike ballots, for example, have rarely led to industrial action. It seems likely that, as Brown and Wadhwani (1990) argue, the law was one factor making union leaders more cautious in disputes and in making any strike more disciplined. This might suggest that strikes would grow longer. The fact that they actually became shorter may be due to a willingness of employers to concede demands rapidly in the face of demonstrated support for industrial action.

The number of 'days lost' in strikes did not, however, show a parallel decline: there was a fall during the 1980s, but only to a level similar to that of the 1960s. The explanation turns on the role of the large official dispute. Between 1932 and 1954 there were no national stoppages. From the mid-1950s several such strikes took place, but they remained relatively rare until the 1970s. During that decade, they became more common. The most famous examples are the miners' strikes of 1972 and 1974 and the series of stoppages in the public services in the winter of discontent. Several other public sector disputes involved groups which had hitherto rarely struck, including teachers and nurses. Large strikes were certainly not limited to the public sector, but, as explained above, they had a particular salience there: incomes policies impacted most forcibly, and the growth of workplace union representation assisted in the mobilization of workers and in the organization of strike action.

In the 1980s, the public sector was the site of even more fundamental struggles. In some cases, managers were able to impose change without overt challenge, in others, notably some disputes in the railways, resistance collapsed. But in others there were full-scale confrontations, the most massive and significant being the miners' dispute of 1984–5 (Adeney and Lloyd 1986; Goodman 1985). This year-long dispute was over a programme of colliery closures. The union was defeated for a complex set of reasons including the careful preparations of the government, the fact that about one-third of coal capacity remained operational, and the lack of support from other unions (the last two factors being attributed by the miners' leaders to a lack of courage and solidarity, and by working miners and other unions to the vagueness of the strike's aims and the naive militancy of the miners' leadership). But underlying this strike, and many others in the public sector, was the willingness of the government to confront industrial action. In the past, governments had striven to avoid strikes in the public sector because of the political costs involved. But the Conservatives were able to attach the blame to the unions. Their approach had two effects: a direct one, as in the decision to fight the miners, and an indirect one, in that public sector managers knew that it was legitimate to 'take on' the unions, a series of strikes in British Rail over new working practices being a good example (Ferner 1985).

Yet not all strikes ended in government or employer victories. A strike of railway workers in 1989 was widely seen as a union victory, as wage concessions were made by management, and the ambulance workers' dispute in 1989–90 also produced significant gains for the unions; the latter strike also demonstrated that it was still possible for industrial action to be sustained for long periods. In the private sector, the most significant dispute involved demands for shorter working hours in the engineering industry. As mentioned above, the unions marked out certain key employers for industrial action, and claimed widespread success. They were able to exploit the lack of solidarity among British employers and, on this occasion at least, to turn the decentralization of bargaining to their own advantage.

Strikes are not the only form of collective pressure. Several studies (reviewed by Edwards 1992) showed that other forms of action, notably a ban on overtime working, were up to twice as common as strikes. There are, moreover, many small strikes which escape inclusion in the official statistics. One study of manufacturing indicated that, at the end of the 1970s, official figures included only a quarter of all strikes and one-ninth of all cases of industrial action (Brown 1981). There are some indications that during the 1980s the use of non-strike action fell more slowly than the number of strikes, suggesting that overt conflict remained more entrenched than might appear. There was, moreover, a tendency for new groups such as public service workers and white-collar employees to engage in strikes.

The decline in the formerly strike-prone sectors makes it very unlikely that strike rates will ever reach the level of the early 1970s. But there has been a fragmentation of the strike pattern, with the decline in traditional areas and some rise elsewhere, and not a fundamental elimination of strikes from the system. A study of a highly strike-prone plant in the 1970s concluded that 'the strike is simply a further tactical extension' of collective opposition to management (Batstone et al. 1978: 218). The British system, with its absence of legal enforceability of collective agreements and with employers who were often willing to cede responsibility to shop stewards, imposed few restraints on such a tactical extension. By the end of the 1980s, more limits were in place. Some were legislative: balloting requirements, and the new restrictions on unofficial action. Others stemmed from managers' desire to shape the workplace order, so that, instead of a vacuum filled by informal bargaining which could spill over into strikes, rules and expectations were clearly defined. This could range from a restructuring based on new payment systems and individualism to a simple reassertion of managerial prerogative. But in either case industrial action is likely to have become more divorced from the day-to-day conduct of industrial relations. This is one illustration of the wider ways in which industrial relations have been re-shaped while retaining some of their essential characteristics.

Conclusions

There is little doubt that the 1980s marked a significant change in the ways in which industrial relations were perceived: the government claimed to have curtailed the excessive power of the unions; managers were more self-confident, and were able to implement change in many areas; and unions had to respond to a loss of membership and their exclusion from political influence. There has been much debate about how far these developments constituted a sharp break from the past and about the characteristics of the emerging system.

There was a clear break between the 1970s and the 1980s in such areas as labour law. But, seen in longer perspective, many of the developments of the 1980s had historical parallels and did not disrupt some of the enduring features of the British system, notably the absence of detailed

legally enforceable collective agreements. Some developments, in particular the decline of national- and industry-level bargaining, continued
previous trends. Others, such as the widespread introduction of new
technology and new working practices, were less distinctive than might
appear. Surveys in the 1980s showed that these changes were introduced
with little trade union opposition (Daniel 1987). Yet out-and-out opposition to technical change has always been rare in British unions (Hilton et
al. 1935). It was not a matter of the sudden removal of restraints on
management during the 1980s, but of changes in economic conditions
(which increased the pressure to change or face collapse) and of a re-
discovered sense of will among managers themselves: in the 1970s union
or worker opposition, sometimes anticipated rather than actual, could
provide a convenient excuse for managerial inaction.

A focus on management leads to two further points. First, managers
were, either through commission or omission, active agents in the creation of the traditional pattern of industrial relations. Consider the most
extreme case of shopfloor bargaining and apparent restraints on management, the car and related industries. It has consistently been shown that
managers often willingly ceded control to shop stewards and gained
benefits from doing so, and that stewards did not resist all forms of
change (Hyman and Elger 1981; Terry and Edwards 1988). Management
made little clear-cut effort to establish any system to regulate the shopfloor
until existing habits had become entrenched. Second, efforts to make such
change often pre-dated Thatcherism. In the car industry, more autocratic
styles of management were introduced from the late 1970s, notably under
Michael Edwardes, who was appointed as Chairman of the then British
Leyland in 1977. Similar trends occurred in less celebrated cases. The
employees of the food manufacturer, Cadbury, for example, were not
noted for industrial militancy, yet managers increasingly perceived industrial relations as a problem, and they introduced an assertive approach
in 1977 (Smith et al. 1990).

Thatcherism reinforced certain trends that were already evident and
helped to generalize them, particularly in the public sector where there
was a consistent effort to remove existing bargaining arrangements and to
reassert managerial authority. As for the private sector, there was more
variety, but certain trends are discernible. There was much use of terms
such as 'involvement' and 'participation'. But this did not imply that
employers had embraced industrial democracy in the sense of the representation of workers on company boards. Involvement meant giving
workers a sense of the goals of the enterprise and expecting them to
recognize the extent to which their own objectives were dependent on
corporate success. Few firms made direct attacks on the position of trade
unions, but many hoped to introduce a new climate in which unions were
rendered irrelevant. The emerging system was not a leap forward to a
new age of flexibility or sophisticated human resource management:
firms adopting advanced styles of personnel management remained very
much in the minority, even in sectors such as electronics. Yet neither was

there a simple return to the past. The use of communications systems, merit pay, and performance appraisal has no close parallels in the past, and new forms of work organization reshaped jobs and the way workers were expected to perform them. Cadbury's is again a good example: under old technology, workers used a mix of craft skill and informal knowledge to operate machines, whereas the new computerized system not only eliminated jobs but also controlled and monitored the production process so that the worker was less of a machine operator and more of a general adjunct to a technically driven process.

The consequences for workers were often profound. In addition to job losses in many of the key sectors of the economy, systems for the utilization of labour were changed. New patterns of shift working were introduced, and surveys suggested that workers felt that they were working harder than before (Batstone and Gourlay 1986; Edwards and Whitston 1991). Workers did not necessarily resent these changes: though there was little evidence of a keen acceptance of an ideology of individualism, there was also little to suggest sustained, principled opposition, and workers seem to have acquiesced in changes with a mixture of resigned acceptance and recognition that they could not be prevented (Kelly 1990).

Perhaps the largest question about these developments concerns their long-term effects. Central here is the approach of management. There is little evidence that British firms have developed a strategic approach to industrial relations. This is exemplified, within the firm, in a poor record on training despite numerous exhortations to change, and in the tendency of firms to adopt new devices such as quality circles only for enthusiasm to wane rapidly. Outside the firm, employers showed little interest in coordinating pay bargaining, so that the system of wage determination remained anarchic. During the recession at the start of the 1980s survival was the prime impulse, and long-term thinking was eschewed. During the latter half of the decade those firms which had survived gave more attention to the longer term, but by the early 1990s there were concerns that a new recession was again inducing firms to neglect training. Two outstanding concomitants of employer behaviour were the often-remarked tendency for money wages to continue to grow and the less noticed fact that, talk of a core and periphery and of a management concern with engendering commitment notwithstanding, very few efforts were made to develop any form of job security for manual or routine clerical employees. Firms may have sought commitment but for workers there was little positive in return. The other part of the core-periphery model, namely the emergence of insecure jobs of a temporary, part-time or subcontract nature, had more applicability. In the public sector, competitive tendering tended to reduce wages and worsen conditions of service in the independent contractors and, as a result of competition from contractors, in public sector organizations themselves. The compatibility of short-term financial pressures with long-term service goals, and with employee commitment, became an issue in several organizations.

The impact of these developments on trade unions was profound. Particularly striking is the fact that employment growth has been concentrated in sectors with little union presence; to the extent that this trend continues, unions will face further membership losses. As noted above, such a trend is not inevitable: membership grew during the 1970s despite unfavourable shifts in employment composition. Trends during the 1980s were possibly more adverse, however, being reinforced by an unfavourable environment of law and employer policy. It is not surprising that unions came to pin their hopes on developments at the EC level as well as on the re-election of a Labour government. More surprising, in view of the long tradition of voluntarism, was their acceptance of legal regulation, even in areas (such as a statutory minimum wage) where unions had generally been hostile to such 'interference'. In one sense, unions had changed more than employers in that they now welcomed a legally-backed framework for industrial relations while employers remained as disunited as ever. Yet this contrast was at the level of policy, not practice. At the day-to-day level unions had to respond to membership losses, legal restraints, and employer challenges. These pressures had weakened unions, but perhaps to a smaller extent than might have been imagined in 1980; certainly, there was no parallel to the steep decline in unionization that occurred in the United States.

As in the past, the future of unions is likely to depend on the political climate and employer policy. The former is hard to predict, but on the latter it seems unlikely that many employers will be as welcoming to unions as they were during the post-Donovan period of industrial relations reform. This, together with shifts in the employment structure, suggests that, even with a favourable political situation, unions will find it hard to increase density levels. An additional imponderable is the impact of the single European market. To the extent that fears of job losses in the weaker economies are realized, British unions will face a further challenge.

British industrial relations are thus likely to continue to change in the face of new economic and political circumstances. During the 1980s they altered dramatically while retaining many features from the past. The fact that change has been complex and uneven reflects one key aspect of continuity, namely, that neither employers nor unions, nor for that matter the state, have been able to press through a coherent strategy of renewal and rationalization. All parties still labour under a legacy of the past.

Notes

[1]   The main differences from Great Britain in terms of the legal framework are that statutory procedures for union recognition remain in force and that a Fair Employment Agency operates to promote equal opportunities for members of the two religious communities. Beaumont (1987: 55–87) reviews the recognition procedures. Black (1984) offers an overall survey which argues that the day-to-day conduct of industrial relations is very similar to that in Great Britain.

[2]   It might be asked why these problems are not apparent in the even more decentralized system of the USA. One obvious difference is the level of union membership, with density in Britain being nearly three times that of the US. But more important is the link between national and local developments. In Britain, there is a clear annual wage round, and public sector employees in particular compare themselves with others in the public and private sectors. In the US, wage determination depends far more on local labour market conditions, and the 'going rate' is much less firmly established.

References

Adeney, M. and Lloyd, J. 1986: *The Miners' Strike, 1984–5: Loss without Limit*. London: Routledge.

Armstrong, P.J., Goodman, J.F.B., and Hyman, J. 1981: *Ideology and Shop-floor Industrial Relations*. London: Croom Helm.

Atkinson, J. 1984: Manpower Strategies for Flexible Organisations, *Personnel Management*, August, 28–31.

Bach, S. 1989: Too High a Price to Pay? *Warwick Papers in Industrial Relations*, 25. Coventry: Industrial Relations Research Unit.

Bailey, R. 1989: Pay and Industrial Relations in the UK Public Sector. *Labour*, 3, 2, 31–56.

Bain, G. and Elsheikh, F. 1976: *Union Growth and the Business Cycle*. Oxford: Blackwell.

Bassett, P. 1986: *Strike Free: New Industrial Relations in Britain*. London: Macmillan.

Batstone, E.V. 1984: *Working Order*. Oxford: Blackwell.

Batstone, E.V., Boraston, I. and Frenkel, S. 1977: *Shop Stewards in Action*. Oxford: Blackwell.

Batstone, E., Boraston, I. and Frenkel, S. 1978: *The Social Organization of Strikes*. Oxford: Blackwell.

Batstone, E.V. and Gourlay, S. 1986: *Unions, Unemployment and Innovation*. Oxford: Blackwell.

Beaumont, P.B. 1987: *The Decline of Trade Union Organisation*. London: Croom Helm.

Black, B. 1984: Industrial Relations in Northern Ireland: A Survey. *Industrial Relations Journal*, 15, 1, 29–36.

Booth, A. 1983: A Reconsideration of Trade Union Growth in the United Kingdom.*British Journal of Industrial Relations*, 21, 3, 379–91.

Booth, A. 1989: What Do Unions Do Now? *Discussion Papers in Economics*, 8903, Brunel University.

Brown, W. (ed.) 1981: *The Changing Contours of British Industrial Relations*. Oxford: Blackwell.

Brown, W. 1990: Class and Industrial Relations. In J. Clark et al. (eds), *John H. Goldthorpe*, London: Falmer, 213–22.

Brown, W. and Rowthorn, R. 1990: *A Public Services Pay Policy*. Tract No. 452. London: Fabian Society.

Brown, W. and Wadhwani, S. 1990: The Economic Effects of Industrial Relations Legislation since 1979. *National Institute Economic Review*, 131, 57–70.

Brown, W. and Walsh, J. 1991: Pay Determination in Britain in the 1980s: The Anatomy of Decentralization. *Oxford Review of Economic Policy*, 7, 1, 44–59.

Buchanan, R. 1974: Merger Waves in British Unionism. *British Journal of Industrial Relations*, 5, 1, 37–44.

Business Monitor. 1982: *Report on the Census of Production 1979*, Summary volume, PA1002. London: Business Statistics Office.

Business Monitor. 1989: *Report on the Census of Production 1987*, Summary volume, PA1002. London: Business Statistics Office.

Cameron, D. 1984: Social Democracy, Corporatism, Labour Quiescence and the Representation of Economic Interest in Advanced Capitalist Society. In J. H. Goldthorpe (ed.), *Order and Conflict in Contemporary Capitalism*, Oxford: Clarendon, 143–78.

Carruth, A. and Disney, R. 1988: Where Have Two Million Members Gone? *Economica*, 55, 1, 1–19.

CSO (Central Statistical Office). 1990: Employment in the Public and Private Sectors. *Economic Trends*, 446, 92–8.

Chandler, A.D. 1976: The Development of Modern Management Structure in the US and UK. In L. Hannah (ed.), *Management Strategy and Business Development*, London: Macmillan.

Chandler, A.D. and Daems, H. 1980: *Managerial Hierarchies*. Cambridge, Mass: Harvard University Press.

Channon, D.F. 1973: *The Strategy and Structure of British Enterprise*. Cambridge, Mass: Harvard University Press.

Claydon, T. 1989: Union Derecognition in Britain in the 1980s. *British Journal of Industrial Relations*, 28, 2, 214–24.

Clegg, H. A. 1972: *The System of Industrial Relations in Great Britain*. Oxford: Blackwell.

Clegg, H. A. 1979: *The Changing System of Industrial Relations in Great Britain*. Oxford: Blackwell.

Clifton, R. and Tatton-Brown, C. 1979: *Impact of Employment Legislation on Small Firms*. Department of Employment Research Paper 6. London: HMSO.

Coleman, D. C. 1988: [Review of Elbaum and Lazonick, 1986]. *Business History*, 30, 1, 130–1.

Colling, T. 1991: Privatisation and the Management of Industrial Relations in the Electricity Industry. *Industrial Relations Journal*, 22, 2, 117–29.

Cosh, A., Hughes, A., Singh, A., Carty, J. and Pender, J. 1990: *Takeovers and Short-termism in the UK*. London: Institute of Public Policy Research.

Cowling, K. and Sugden, R. 1987: *Transnational Monopoly Capitalism*. Brighton: Wheatsheaf.

Cross, M. 1988: Changes in Working Practices in UK Manufacturing, 1981–88. *Industrial Relations Review and Report*, 415, 2–10.

Crouch, C. 1977: *Class Conflict and the Industrial Relations Crisis*. London: Heinemann.

Croucher, R. 1982: *Engineers at War, 1939–1945*. London: Merlin.

Daniel, W.W. 1987: *Workplace Industrial Relations and Technical Change*. London: Pinter.

Daniel, W. W. and Stilgoe, E. 1978: *The Impact of Employment Protection Laws*. London: Policy Studies Institute.

Deakin, S. 1990: Equality under a Market Order: The Employment Act 1989. *Industrial Law Journal*, 19, 1, 1–19.

DE (Department of Employment). 1988a: *Employment for the 1990s*. Cm 540. London: HMSO.

DE. 1988b: *Wages Councils: Consultation Document*. London: DE.

DE. 1989. *Removing Barriers to Employment*. Cm 655. London: HMSO.

Dickens, L. 1975: Staff Associations and the Industrial Relations Act: The Effect on Union Growth. *Industrial Relations Journal*, 6, 3, 29–41.

Dickens, L. and Bain, G. S. 1986: A Duty to Bargain? In R. Lewis (ed.), *Labour Law in Britain*, Oxford: Blackwell, 80–108.

Dickens, L., Hart, M., Jones, M. and Weekes, B. 1985: *Dismissed: A Study of Unfair Dismissal and the Industrial Tribunal System*. Oxford: Blackwell.

Disney, R. 1990: Explanations of the Decline in Trade Union Density in Britain: An Appraisal. *British Journal of Industrial Relations*, 28, 2, 165–78.

Dore, R.P. 1985: Financial Structures and the Long-Term View. *Policy Studies*, 6, 1, 10–29.

Dunn, S. and Gennard, J. 1984: *The Closed Shop in British Industry*. London: Macmillan.

Edwards, C. and Heery, E. 1990: *Management Control and Union Power*. Oxford: Clarendon.

Edwards, P. K. 1983: The Pattern of Collective Industrial Action. In G. S. Bain (ed.), *Industrial Relations in Britain*, Oxford: Blackwell, 209–34.

Edwards, P. K. 1992: Industrial Conflict: Themes and Issues in Recent Research. *British Journal of Industrial Relations*, 30, 3, forthcoming.

Edwards, P. K. and Bain, G. S. 1988: Why Are Trade Unions Becoming More Popular? Unions and Public Opinion in Britain. *British Journal of Industrial Relations*, 26, 3, 311–26.

Edwards, P. K. and Whitston, C. 1991: Workers Are Working Harder: Effort and Shopfloor Relations in the 1980s. *British Journal of Industrial Relations*, 29, 4, 593–602.

Elbaum, B. and Wilkinson, F. 1979: Industrial Relations and Uneven Development. *Cambridge Journal of Economics*, 3, 3, 275–303.

Elbaum, B. and Lazonick, W. (eds) 1986: *The Decline of the British Economy*. Oxford: Clarendon.

Evans, S. 1985: The Use of Injunctions in Industrial Disputes. *British Journal of Industrial Relations*, 23, 1, 133–7.

Evans, S. 1987: The Use of Injunctions in Industrial Disputes, May 1984–April 1987.*British Journal of Industrial Relations*, 25, 3, 419–35.

Evans, S., Goodman, J.F.B. and Hargreaves, L. 1985: *Unfair Dismissal Law and Employment Practice in the 1980s*. Department of Employment Research Paper 53. London: HMSO.

Ferner, A. 1985: Political Constraints and Managerial Strategies. *British Journal of Industrial Relations*, 23, 1, 47–70.

Ferner, A. 1989: Ten Years of Thatcherism: Changing Industrial Relations in British Public Enterprises. *Warwick Papers in Industrial Relations*, 27. Coventry: IRRU.

Ferner, A. 1991: Changing Public Sector Industrial Relations in Europe.*Warwick Papers in Industrial Relations*, 37. Coventry: IRRU.

Flanders, A.D. 1970: Industrial Relations: What is Wrong with the System? *Management and Unions: The Theory and Reform of Industrial Relations*. London: Faber.

Flanders, A. 1974: The Tradition of Voluntarism. *British Journal of Industrial Relations*, 12, 3, 352–70.

Fox, A. 1985: *History and Heritage*. London: Allen and Unwin.

Fox, A. and Flanders, A. 1970: Collective Bargaining: From Donovan to Durkheim. In Flanders, *Management and Unions*. London: Faber.

Fredman, S. and Morris, G. 1989: *The State as Employer: Labour Law in the Public Services*. London: Mansell.

Freeman, R. and Pelletier, J. 1990: The Impact of Industrial Relations Legislation on British Union Density. *British Journal of Industrial Relations*, 28, 2, 141–64.

Gallie, D. 1978: *In Search of the New Working Class*. Cambridge: Cambridge University Press.

Gallie, D. 1983: *Social Inequality and Class Radicalism in France and Britain*. Cambridge: Cambridge University Press.

Gallie, D. 1989: *Trade Union Allegiance and Decline in British Urban Labour Markets*. Working Paper 9, Oxford: ESRC Social Change and Economic Life Initiative.

Gamble, A. 1988: *The Free Economy and the Strong State*. London: Macmillan.

Goldthorpe, J.H. 1974: Industrial Relations in Great Britain: A Critique of Reformism. *Politics and Society*, 4, 4, 419–52.

Goldthorpe, J. H. 1978: The Current Inflation. In F. Hirsch and J. H. Goldthorpe (eds), *The Political Economy of Inflation*, London: Martin Robertson, 144–78.

Goodman, G. 1985: *The Miners' Strike*. London: Pluto.

Goold, M. and Campbell, A. 1987: *Strategies and Styles: The Role of the Centre in Managing Diversified Corporations*. Oxford: Blackwell.

Gregory, M., Lobban, P. and Thomson, A. 1985: Wage Settlements in Manufacturing 1979–84. *British Journal of Industrial Relations*, 23, 3, 339–57.

Gregory, M., Lobban, P. and Thomson, A. 1986: Bargaining Structure, Pay Settlements and Perceived Pressures in Manufacturing, 1979–84. *British Journal of Industrial Relations*, 24, 2, 215–32.

Guest, D. 1987: Human Resource Management and Industrial Relations. *Journal of Management Studies*, 24, 5, 503–21.

Hall, P.A. 1986: The State and Economic Decline. In Elbaum and Lazonick, 1986, 266–302.

Hayek, F.A. von 1982: *Law, Legislation and Liberty*. 3 vols. London: Routledge.

Hill, C.W.L. and Hoskisson, R.E. 1987: Strategy and Structure in the Multi-product Firm. *Academy of Management Review*, 12, 2, 331–41.

Hill, C.W.L. and Pickering, J.F. 1986: Divisionalization, Decentralization and Performance of Large UK Companies. *Journal of Management Studies*, 23, 1, 26–50.

Hilton, J. et al. 1935: *Are Trade Unions Obstructive?* London: Gollancz.

Hyman, R. 1983: Trade Unions: Structure, Policies and Politics. In G. Bain. (ed.), *Industrial Relations in Britain*, Oxford: Blackwell, 35–66.

Hyman, R. and Elger, T. 1981: Job Controls, the Employers' Offensive and Alternative Strategies. *Capital and Class*, 15, 115–49.

Incomes Data Services (IDS). 1988: *Company Councils*. Study No. 437. July.

Industrial Relations Review and Report (IRRR). 1989a,b: Developments in Multi-Employment Bargaining: 1, *Report 440*, May, 6–11; Developments in Multi-Employment Bargaining: 2, *Report 443*, July, 6–12.

Industrial Relations Review and Report. 1989c: Decentralised Bargaining in Practice: 1, *Report 454*, December, 570.

Industrial Relations Review and Report. 1989d: Single Union Deals. *Report 442*, June, 5–11.

Industrial Relations Review and Report. 1990: Decentralised Bargaining in Practice: 2, *Report 457*, February, 13–14.

Industrial Relations Review and Report. 1991a: Co-ordinating Bargaining: The Debate. *Report 485*, April, 4–7.

Industrial Relations Review and Report. 1991b: Annualised Hours: The Concept of the Flexible Year. *Report 488*, May, 4–8.

IPM (Institute of Personnel Management). 1991: *Minimum Wage: An Analysis of the Issues*. London: IPM.

Jessop, B. 1980: The Transformation of the State in Post-war Britain. In R. Scase (ed.), *The State in Western Europe*, London: Croom Helm, 23–93.

Johnson, S. 1991: The Small Firm and the UK Labour Market in the 1980s. In A. Pollert (ed.), *Farewell to Flexibility?*, Oxford: Blackwell, 239–58.

Kassalow, E.M. 1989: Labour Market Flexibility and New Employment Patterns. Proceedings of the Eighth World Congress of the International Industrial Relations Association, Brussels, Vol. 1, 75–98.

Keep, E. 1989: A Training Scandal? In K. Sisson (ed.), *Personnel Management in Britain*, Oxford: Blackwell, 177–202.

Kelly, J. 1988: The Decline of Trade Unionism? *The Industrial Tutor*, 4, 7, 5–17.

Kelly, J. 1990: British Trade Unionism, 1979–89: Change, Continuity and Contradictions. *Work, Employment and Society*, Additional Special Issue, May, 29–66.

Kinnie, N. 1985a: Local Managers' Control Over Industrial Relations: Myth and Reality. *Personnel Review*, 14, 2, 2–10.

Kinnie, N. 1985b: Changing Management Strategies in Industrial Relations. *Industrial Relations Journal*, 16, 4, 17–24.

Kochan, T.A., Katz, H. and McKersie, R.B. 1986: *The Transformation of American Industrial Relations*. New York: Basic.

Labour Research. 1990: Are the Anti-strike Laws Working? *Labour Research*, 79, 9, 26–9.

Lazonick, W. 1990: *Competitive Advantage on the Shop Floor*. Cambridge, Mass.: Harvard University Press.

Lewchuk, W. 1986: The Motor Vehicle Industry. In Elbaum and Lazonick, 1986, 135–61.

Lewis, R. 1986: The Role of the Law in Employment Relations. In R. Lewis. (ed.), *Labour Law in Britain*, Oxford: Blackwell, 3–46.

Lewis, R. and Simpson, B. 1986: The Right to Associate. In R. Lewis (ed.), *Labour Law in Britain*, Oxford: Blackwell, 47–79.

Littler, C.R. 1982: *The Development of the Labour Process in Capitalist Societies*. London: Heinemann.

Long, P. 1986: *Performance Appraisal Revisited*. London: Institute of Personnel Management.

McCarthy, W.E.J. 1992: The Rise and Fall of Collective Laissez Faire. In W.E.J. McCarthy (ed.), *Legal Intervention in Industrial Relations*, Oxford: Blackwell.

MacInnes, J. 1987: *Thatcherism at Work*. Milton Keynes: Open University Press.

McKendrick, E. 1988: The Rights of Trade Union Members. *Industrial Law Journal*, 17, 3, 141–61.

Marginson, P., Edwards, P.K., Martin, R., Sisson, K. and Purcell, J. 1988: *Beyond the Workplace: Managing Industrial Relations in Multi-Establishment Enterprises*. Blackwell: Oxford.

Marginson, P. and Sisson, K. 1990: Single-Table Talk. *Personnel Management*, May, 46–9.

Marsden, D. and Thompson, M. 1990: Flexibility Agreements and their Significance in the Increase in Productivity in British Manufacturing Since 1980. *Work, Employment and Society,* 4, 1, 83–104.

Marsh, P. 1991: *Short-termism on Trial.* London: Institutional Fund Managers' Association.

Marshall, G., Newby, H., Rose, D. and Vogler, C. 1988: *Social Class in Modern Britain.* London: Hutchinson.

Martin, R. 1980: *TUC: The Growth of a Pressure Group, 1868–1976.* Oxford: Oxford University Press.

Martin, R., Morris, H., Fosh, P., Smith, P. and Undy, R. 1990: The Decollectivization of Trade Unionism? Kingston: Kingston Polytechnic, mimeo.

Metcalf, D. 1990: Industrial Dispute Incidence, Laws, Resolution and Consequence. Working Paper 65, Centre for Economic Performance, London School of Economics.

Millward, N. and Stevens, M. 1986: *British Workplace Industrial Relations 1980–1984.* Aldershot: Gower.

Morris, T. 1986: Trade Union Mergers and Competition in British Banking. *Industrial Relations Journal,* 17, 2, 129–40.

Nolan, P. 1989: Walking on Water? Industrial Performance and Industrial Relations under Thatcher. *Industrial Relations Journal,* 20, 2, 81–92.

Offe, C. and Wiesenthal, H. 1980: Two Logics of Collective Action: Theoretical Notes on Social Class and Organisational Form. *Political Power and Social Theory,* 1, 1, 67–115.

Panitch, L. 1976: *Social Democracy and Industrial Militancy.* Cambridge: Cambridge University Press.

Payne, P.L. 1967: The Emergence of the Large-Scale Company in Britain, 1870–1914. *Economic History Review,* 20, 4, 519–42.

Pollert, A. 1988: The Flexible Firm: Fixation or Fact? *Work, Employment and Society,* 2, 3, 281–316.

Pond, C. 1983: Wages Councils, the Unorganised, and the Low Paid. In G.S. Bain (ed.), *Industrial Relations in Britain,* Oxford: Blackwell, 179–208.

Price, R. 1982: Rethinking Labour History. In J. Cronin and J. Schneer (eds), *Social Conflict and the Political Order in Modern Britain,* London: Croom Helm, 179–214.

Price, R. and Bain, G. 1983: Union Growth in Britain: Retrospect and Prospect. *British Journal of Industrial Relations,* 21, 1, 46–68.

Purcell, J. 1987: Mapping Management Styles in Industrial Relations. *Journal of Management Studies,* 24, 5, 533–48.

Purcell, J. and Sisson, K. 1983: Strategies and Practice in the Management of Industrial Relations. In G.S. Bain (ed.), *Industrial Relations in Britain,* Oxford: Blackwell, 95–120.

Rainnie, A. 1989: *Industrial Relations in Small Firms.* London: Routledge.

Ram, M. 1991: Control and Autonomy in Small Firms: The Case of the West Midlands Clothing Industry. *Work, Employment and Society,* 5, 4, 601–19.

Regini, M. 1984: The Conditions for Political Exchange. In J. H. Goldthorpe (ed.), *Order and Conflict in Contemporary Capitalism,* Oxford: Clarendon, 124–42.

Roche, W. 1990: Social Class, Social Integration and Industrial Relations. In J. Clark et al. (eds), *John H. Goldthorpe,* London: Falmer, 191–212.

Routh, G. 1980: *Occupation and Pay in Great Britain, 1906–79.* London: Macmillan.

Rubery, J., Tarling, R. and Wilkinson, F. 1987: Flexibility, Marketing and the Organisation of Production. *Labour and Society,* 12, 1, 131–51.

Rubery, J. and Tarling, R. 1988: Women's Employment in Declining Britain. In J. Rubery (ed.), *Women and Recession,* London: Routledge, 100–34.

Rule, J. 1981. *The Experience of Labour in Eighteenth Century England.* London: Croom Helm.

Scase, R. 1974: Relative Deprivation: A Comparison of English and Swedish Manual Workers. In D. Wedderburn (ed.), *Poverty, Inequality and Class Structure,* Cambridge: Cambridge University Press, 197–216.

Sisson, K. 1987: *The Management of Collective Bargaining: An International Comparison.* Oxford: Blackwell.

Sisson, K. 1989: Personnel Management in Transition? In K. Sisson (ed.), *Personnel Management in Britain*, Oxford: Blackwell, 22–52.

Sisson, K. and Brown, W. 1983: Industrial Relations in the Private Sector: Donovan Revisited. In G.S. Bain (ed.), *Industrial Relations in Britain*, Oxford: Blackwell, 137–54.

Smith, C., Child, J. and Rowlinson, M. 1990: *Reshaping Work: The Cadbury Experience*. Cambridge: Cambridge University Press.

Storey, J. (ed.). 1989: *New Perspectives on Human Resource Management*. London: Routledge.

Storey, J. 1992: *Developments in the Management of Human Resources*. Oxford: Blackwell.

Storey, J. and Sisson, K. 1989: Limits to Transformation: Human Resource Management in the British Context. *Industrial Relations Journal*, 20, 1, 60–5.

Tabatoni, P. 1985: The Market Economies Tack Against the Wind. In H. Juris et al. (eds), *Industrial Relations in a Decade of Economic Change*, Madison: Industrial Relations Research Association, 1–40.

Terry, M. 1983: Shop Steward Development and Managerial Strategies. In G.S. Bain (ed.), *Industrial Relations in Britain*, Oxford: Blackwell, 67–94.

Terry, M. 1985: Combine Committees: Developments of the 1970s. *British Journal of Industrial Relations*, 23, 3, 359–78.

Terry, M. 1989: Recontextualising Shopfloor Industrial Relations. In S. Tailby and C. Whitston (eds), *Manufacturing Change*, Oxford: Blackwell, 192–216.

Terry, M. and Edwards, P.K. (eds) 1988: *Shopfloor Politics and Job Controls*. Oxford: Blackwell.

Thornley, C. and Winchester, D. 1991: The Remuneration of Nursing Personnel in the United Kingdom. A research report commissioned by the International Labour Office, Geneva.

Thurley, K. 1981: Personnel Management in the UK – A Case for Urgent Treatment? *Personnel Management*, August, 24–8.

Tomlinson, J. 1989: A Missed Opportunity? Labour and the Productivity Problem, 1945–51. *Discussion Papers in Economics 8904*, Brunel University.

Towers, B. 1989: Running the Gauntlet. *Industrial and Labor Relations Review*, 42, 2, 178–87.

Trades Union Congress (TUC). 1988: *Meeting the Challenge: First Report of the Special Review Body*. London: Trades Union Congress.

Undy, R., Ellis, V., McCarthy, W.E.J. and Halmos, A. 1981: *Change in Trade Unions: The Development of U.K. Unions Since the 1960s*. London: Hutchinson.

United Nations 1988: *Transnational Corporations in World Development*. New York: UN Centre for Transnational Companies.

Waddington, J. 1988: Business Unionism and Fragmentation within the TUC. *Capital and Class*, 36, 7–15.

Waddington, J. 1992a: Restructuring Representation: Trade Union Mergers, 1980–1988. In D. Cox and J. Morgan (eds), *Facing the Future*, Nottingham: University of Nottingham Press.

Waddington, J. 1992b: Trade Union Membership in Britain, 1980–1987: Unemployment and Restructuring. *British Journal of Industrial Relations*, 30, 2.

Walker, J. 1988: Women, the State and the Family in Britain. In J. Rubery (ed.), *Women and Recession*, London: Routledge, 218–52.

Wedderburn, K.W. (Lord). 1985: The New Policies in Industrial Relations. In P. Fosh and C. Littler (eds), *Industrial Relations and the Law in the 1980s*, Gower: Aldershot, 22–65.

Wedderburn, K.W. (Lord). 1986: *The Worker and the Law*. 3rd edn. Harmondsworth: Penguin.

Wedderburn, K.W. (Lord). 1989: Freedom of Association and Philosophies of Labour Law. *Industrial Law Journal*, 18, 1, 1–38.

Weekes, B., Mellish, M., Dickens, L. and Lloyd, J. 1975: *Industrial Relations and the Limits of Law*. Oxford: Blackwell.

Weir, M. and Skocpol, T. 1985: State Structure and the Possibilities for 'Keynesian' Response to the Great Depression in Sweden, Britain and the US. In P.B. Evans et al. (eds), *Bringing the State Back In*, Cambridge: Cambridge University Press, 107–68.

Westergaard, J., Noble, I. and Walker, A. 1988: After Redundancy. In D. Rose (ed.), *Social Stratification and Economic Change*, London: Hutchinson, 153–73.

Whitston, C. 1989: Rationalizing Foundries. In S. Tailby and C. Whitston (eds), *Manufacturing Change*, Oxford: Blackwell, 23–59.

Williams, K., Williams, J. and Thomas, D. 1983: *Why Are the British Bad at Manufacturing?* London: Routledge.

Willman, P. 1990: The Financial Status and Performance of British Trade Unions, 1950–1988. *British Journal of Industrial Relations*, 28, 3, 313–28.

Winchester, D. 1983: Industrial Relations in the Public Sector. In G. Bain (ed.), *Industrial Relations in Britain*, Oxford: Blackwell, 155–78.

Wood, D. and Smith, P. 1989: *Employers' Labour Use Strategies: First Report on the 1987 Survey*. DE Research Paper No.63. London: Department of Employment.

Zeitlin, J. 1983: The Labour Strategies of British Engineering Employers, 1890–1922. In H.F. Gospel and C.R. Littler (eds), *Managerial Strategies and Industrial Relations*, London: Heinemann, 25–54.

Zeitlin, J. 1990: The Triumph of Adversarial Bargaining. *Politics and Society*, 18, 3, 405–26.

2

Ireland: Between Centralism and the Market

Ferdinand von Prondzynski

Introduction

In January 1991, the Irish government, the trade unions, and the main employers' associations concluded an agreement to be called the Programme for Economic and Social Progress (PESP). This agreement has two parts, the first dealing with a range of issues of social and economic policy, and the second – entitled Agreement on Pay and Conditions Between the Irish Congress of Trade Unions and Employer Organisations – with the more traditional subjects of collective bargaining. The PESP is the successor agreement to the Programme for National Recovery (PNR) negotiated by employers and unions in 1987, and both of these are at least to some extent modelled on the National Wages Agreements and National Understandings of the 1970s.

The PESP confirms Ireland as a country in which industrial relations are still influenced by corporatist tendencies; however, as we shall see, these tendencies have been qualified to a large extent by other trends, and the PESP is very different from the national agreements negotiated in the early 1970s in particular. During the 1980s the various actors on the industrial relations stage were searching for an opportunity to return to centralized, national bargaining, but at the same time Ireland was affected by the trends of recession and free-market politics which were in evidence in other countries as well. The result has been a new system of centralization which is, nevertheless, much more local in many of its aspects, and much more market-driven in many of its rules.

Irish industrial relations are therefore interesting in that they exhibit characteristics associated with a variety of quite different systems in other countries. These characteristics betray the diverse strands of Irish political and social history, as well as the growing importance of new political structures. However, the Irish system is still primarily derived from the

British model of industrial relations, even if current trends are moving it away from this source. The traditional features of the Irish system owe much to its origins in the United Kingdom before Ireland[1] achieved independence in 1922; the British characteristics were kept alive after independence by the fact of geographical proximity, the close cultural relations between Ireland and Britain, and by the fact that British trade unions continued to organize a substantial minority of workers in Ireland (McCarthy 1977).

Before we go on therefore to consider the current trends of Irish industrial relations, it may be useful to list the main characteristics of what we may call the 'traditional' model, and to indicate the effects they have had on industrial relations practice over the years. The main features of the Irish industrial relations framework could be described as follows:

Voluntaristic. The Irish system of industrial relations is built on the premise that it will for the most part be regulated by the voluntary collective bargaining of the social partners. To put this another way, there is, as the Commission of Inquiry on Industrial Relations remarked in its 1981 Report, an assumption by all parties that legal regulation should be avoided (Commission of Inquiry 1981: 114; von Prondzynski 1985). This tradition, usually described as voluntarism (Flanders 1974), grew out of the evident hostility towards organized labour which lawyers and judges exhibited in the nineteenth century; it still tends to influence trade union thinking (Kerr 1989). The idea of voluntarism however not only led trade unions to avoid the law, it also persuaded successive governments to avoid legal intervention where possible, and most employers were also willing to accept an alternative regulatory framework based on collective bargaining.[2]

Antagonistic. The Irish system of industrial relations is based strongly on the pluralist assumption that the interests of employers and organized labour are in constant conflict. This conflict can be temporarily resolved by means of collective bargaining, and such bargaining may indeed make possible stable and extensive cooperation between the social partners, but the basic relationship between the two sides of industry is an antagonistic one. This is further made possible by, and in turn encourages, high trade union density compared with many other countries. According to the most recent information available, 57 per cent of employees at work in Ireland are trade union members.

Non-participative. In Ireland the post-war movements towards various experiments with industrial democracy were not followed, and both employers and trade unions tended to be suspicious of any formalized worker participation schemes. There is still no general legal provision for participative or consultative machinery which gives employees a formal say in the organizational decision-making processes of the bodies which employ them. The sole exception relates to certain public sector organizations under the Worker Participation (State Enterprises) Acts of 1977 and 1988. Under these Acts one-third of the directors of the organizations concerned are elected for a fixed period by the employees from candidates nominated by trade unions or other representative bodies. The experience of some of the elected worker directors has demonstrated the limited extent to which the idea of participation has taken root in Ireland – they were in some organizations largely excluded from the real decisions, and in return they felt more motivated by solidarity with fellow workers than management concerns (Kelly 1989). Although it remains government policy to stimulate worker participation (Department of Labour 1980), it has to be said the climate is not favourable to its success.

Centralized. A very strong feature of Irish industrial relations is the tendency to deal with issues in a centralized way. For example, since the early 1970s almost all pay agreements for the entire national work force have either been centrally negotiated, under the aegis of a body known as the Employer–Labour Conference, or have followed a general norm, often established as a result of agreements between the government and public service employees. Local pay bargaining either has not taken place at all, or if it has, it has almost universally followed the general trend set elsewhere. This tendency to centralize comes naturally in a country like Ireland where there are almost no devolved political or economic powers. It shares this characteristic with countries such as Austria, and this is one important context in which the British tradition is of no importance.

Non-flexible. Irish employment has, in the past at any rate, tended to be centred around a number of restrictive practices. Jobs were constructed on the basis of rigid demarcation lines, with job descriptions which excluded the possibility of flexible work practices (von Prondzynski 1989). It could of course be said that this only mirrored the wider social traditions of what one might call a demarcation society, with restrictive practices carried on by the various professional bodies in areas such as legal practice, medicine, accountancy, and so forth.

Institutionalized. All the parties to the industrial relations process rely to a large extent on the ability of various institutions to solve their problems, not only trade unions and employers' associations, but also state-sponsored dispute resolution agencies, government departments, and so forth. This, as has been noted by some writers, is a typical feature of a pluralistic industrial relations system (Crouch 1982).

The picture of the traditional industrial relations model is one of a conservative, rigid, pluralistic and antagonistic system, characterized by powerful institutions and widespread restrictive practices. Perhaps its most significant feature, particularly from the perspective of some outside observers, is the degree of centralism. This partly reflects the small size of the country. It also owes something to the fact that, when the institutional framework matured to something like its present status in the late 1940s, Ireland was still in the grip of a particular form of corporatism which was derived in part from Roman Catholic social teaching and in part from some continental European models, including Salazar's Portugal and Franco's Spain. The first chairman of the Labour Court (see below), R.J.P. Mortished, also attempted to use the Court to install a centralized form of pay bargaining in the national economy. This historical legacy has been much modified in practice, but continues to have an influence on general structures and expectations.

Although there are today severe pressures on the traditional industrial relations model in practice, and changes are currently taking place, nevertheless it suited the generally conservative social partners in Ireland for many decades. However, the effect of a severe economic recession during the 1980s, a more hostile attitude by governments towards the traditional industrial relations pattern of conduct, and the arrival of often anti-union multinational companies in greater numbers, have called this traditional model into question (von Prondzynski 1987). We shall see below to what extent it still provides an accurate picture of industrial relations in Ireland.

The Economic Context and the Labour Market

The total labour force in Ireland, according to an estimate based on the Labour Force Survey of 1991, is 1,390,200, out of a population of 3.5 million. Ireland still has one of the largest agricultural sectors in Europe, employing 15.1 per cent of the labour force, compared with 28.4 per cent in industry and 56.5 per cent in services in 1991; even as recently as the late 1960s, nearly 30 per cent of the labour force were engaged in agriculture, twice the OECD average at the time (see table 2.1). The public sector is important, not only in general government, but in energy, steel, transport and communications and the financial sector, accounting for about one-third of non-agricultural employment in 1987.

Table 2.1 Employment in Ireland 1970–87

Year	Working population 000s	as % total population	% females in working population	agriculture	industry	services
				Sectoral distribution of working population		
1970	1,053	37.9	26.7	26.9	29.6	43.5
1975	1,073	36.4	28.1	22.2	31.4	46.4
1980	1,156	36.7	28.7	18.1	32.1	49.8
1985	1,103	36.9	31.3	15.8	28.4	55.8
1987	1,081	37.0	32.4	15.2	27.8	56.1

Source: Eurostat *Employment and Unemployment 1989*.

Foreign capital, especially from North America, has been playing an increasingly important role in the Irish economy. Attracted by favourable tax incentives and substantial capital grants, many multinational companies have established subsidiaries in pharmaceuticals, electrical engineering and the food industry, and most notably in advanced sectors such as consumer electronics, often on 'greenfield' sites in non-traditional industrial areas. In 1987, multinationals accounted for 43 per cent of employment and 65 per cent of net output of the Irish manufacturing sector (OECD 1991: 108).

Employment and unemployment have had a major and persistent influence on industrial relations developments in Ireland. In the period 1988–91, unemployment increased by nearly 30,000 despite an increase in the number of persons in work by a similar amount; at the same time, an increasing proportion of those affected were out of work for long periods (over a third had been unemployed for three years or more in 1985, although the burden has fallen heavily on older workers, rather than on the young as in other European countries). The number of unemployed reached 269,200 in 1991: the highest figure in the history of the Irish State and the second highest rate in the OECD area. The deterioration in the employment situation in the 1980s has been attributed to causes such as the weakening of international competitiveness following entry into the European Monetary System, and distorted relative factor prices as a result of tax incentives that have made it unattractive for foreign companies to increase employment in Ireland (OECD 1988: 46).

Unemployment levels have tended to be high compared with other European countries, but potentially higher rates have usually been avoided by the existence of the outlet of emigration, usually to the United Kingdom. In periods when Britain was itself in recession the emigration option was not so readily available: with renewed economic difficulties in Britain and the US at the beginning of the 1990s, net emigration for the twelve months to April 1991 fell to just 1,000, compared to 31,000 in the previous twelve-month period (EIRR 212, September 1991: 6). Periods of high unemployment have often been accompanied by greater management insistence on new work practices (von Prondzynski 1989).

Irish Trade Unions and Employers' Associations

Ireland is by international standards fairly highly unionized. In 1981 it was estimated that 85 trade unions organized a total membership of 498,900, a figure which represented almost exactly half of the national work force. Of these trade unions, 72 were affiliated to the Irish Congress of Trade Unions (the central umbrella body for the trade union movement), representing a total of 463,900 members. By 1989 the number of trade unions had shrunk to 60 (mainly as a result of mergers), with a total membership of 471,700; of these 54 were ICTU-affiliated, with a total membership of 441,300. This represents a drop in trade union membership, but one which is not as marked as might have been expected at the end of a decade of recession, growing employer militancy, and political ambivalence towards trade unions. This is evident also in the fact that, by 1990, ICTU-affiliated membership had risen again to 459,300. It may be that the status of the trade union movement, and of the Irish Congress of Trade Unions in particular, in a centralized, corporatist state has cushioned them from the trends visible elsewhere in recent times. This may also account for the greater willingness of some multinational employers investing in Ireland to recognize trade unions when, in other countries, they have a record of refusing to do so.

However, as economic conditions worsened in the early 1980s, successive governments were less willing than before to support trade unionism, thus leading to the political ambivalence referred to above. This was apparent in events such as the Fianna Fail government's violation of the agreement reached with public service trade unions in 1982, and the FitzGerald coalition government's dispute with the trade unions in 1985, leading to the unions' 'day of action' in October of that year.

Trade unionism in Ireland, since almost the beginning of the century, has been marked by the dominant position of large general unions. As in Britain, this reflects in part the strongly entrenched position of craft unionism in the formative stages of modern Irish trade unionism – effectively precluding continental patterns of industrial unionism. But it may also be attributed to the powerful impact, in the early decades of this century, of ideas of the 'one big union' as a vehicle for working-class interests.

From the foundation of an independent Irish state, trade unionism was dominated by the Irish Transport and General Workers' Union (ITGWU) – not to be confused with its British namesake (which organizes in Ireland under the name Amalgamated TGWU). In 1924 a split occurred, and the Workers' Union of Ireland (WUI – later Federated WUI) was for much of the subsequent period the country's second largest union. Since 1990, the two organizations have come together in the Services, Industrial, Professional and Technical Union (SIPTU). Amalgamations in the 1980s have reinforced the traditional skewed distribution of Irish union membership. Both the former general unions had merged with a number of smaller organizations, and the new SIPTU now claims 197,000 members – almost half the total membership of unions affiliated to the ICTU. The second largest union – the Irish Municipal, Public and Civil Trade Union (IMPACT) formed by amalgamation in 1991 – has some 25,000 members. Next largest, with just over 20,000 members in each case, are the Irish Distributive and Administrative Trade Union (IDATU), Manufacturing Science and Finance (MSF) and the Communication Workers' Union (CWU), with the Amalgamated Transport and General Workers' Union claiming exactly 20,000. At the other extreme are numerous small organizations: until recently, three-quarters of Irish unions had fewer than 3000 members, though many of these have been absorbed in the amalgamation movement of the 1980s.

It has already been noted that there are in Ireland a number of trade unions which have their headquarters in Great Britain. There are currently twelve unions with members in Ireland which have their head office outside the jurisdiction, with a total membership of 63,700, including the fourth and sixth largest unions in Ireland (MSF and ATGWU). The proportion of Irish trade union members represented by British-based unions is in fact growing slightly. All of the British-based trade unions are affiliated to the Irish Congress of Trade Unions. British-based trade unions now have a secure place in Irish industrial relations, but historically their role has been controversial, and their presence contributed to a split in the Irish trade union movement (McCarthy 1977). During the 1940s special legislative provisions were introduced (Part III of the Trade Union Act 1941) to make it difficult for British-based unions to represent Irish workers; however, the provisions were eventually declared to be unconstitutional by the Supreme Court in 1947. The hostility on the part of some Irish unions to the British presence has now largely evaporated.

As in Britain, the basic administrative unit of trade union organization is the local branch, while shop stewards act as union representatives within the workplace. However, stewards in Ireland have traditionally been more integrated into the official union structure, and hence enjoyed less autonomy, than has often been the case in Britain.

The central umbrella body for Irish trade unions is the Irish Congress of Trade Unions (ICTU) (Cassells 1989). The ICTU is the product of the merger between the Irish Trades Union Congress (ITUC) and the Congress of Irish Unions (CIU) in 1959, as a result of which the ICTU is the central trade union body for both the Republic of Ireland and Northern Ireland; in Northern Ireland a separate committee provides a forum for local discussions and negotiations. Most of the affiliated unions in Northern Ireland are British-based. The ICTU regulates various aspects of inter-union relations, including transfer of membership (von Prondzynski 1987), and nominates trade union members on various official bodies and agencies.

Irish employers are also well organized (O'Brien 1989). When legislation was passed in 1941 requiring all bodies engaged in collective bargaining to have trade union status with so-called 'negotiation licences' (an aspect of the move to corporatist structures at the time), a large number of employers set up the Federated Union of Employers. Conceived initially as a private-sector association, the FUE eventually also admitted into membership various state bodies and public sector employers. In 1989 it changed its name to Federation of Irish Employers, largely in response to the changing patterns of industrial relations, and the growth of multinational enterprises for whom the designation 'union' was suspect. The FIE organizes employers with a total work force of approximately 250,000.

The FIE must be distinguished from the Confederation of Irish Industry (CII), which is a pressure group lobbying for member companies in all matters other than industrial relations; this demarcation between the FIE and the CII is a matter of occasional debate, but both bodies are anxious to retain their independence. Other employers' associations organize companies in specific sectors of the economy; the most influential of these is the Construction Industry Federation.

Institutions of the 'Middle Ground'

The Irish system of industrial relations is, as already noted, a highly institutionalized one. Most public interest is focused on the activities of the main organizations and institutions. Amongst these institutions are what the noted Irish academic and trade union leader, Charles McCarthy, described as the 'institutions...which take up the middle ground and which the public authority may have an interest in providing', particularly 'in the case of intractability' (von Prondzynski and McCarthy 1984). The 'institutions of the middle ground' are those bodies, usually (but not always) set up by the state, which provide dispute resolution facilities and which can offer advice to the social partners. Such institutions have always been heavily relied upon in Ireland to calm the waters in cases of industrial conflict, and their successes and failures have tended to contribute to or reflect the ups anddowns of national industrial relations performance.

Broadly speaking, one may classify these institutions as, first, those which have adjudicatory functions, particularly where they declare the legal rights and obligations of the parties; secondly, those whose task it is to provide dispute resolution facilities or give advice on good industrial relations; and thirdly those who provide a forum for general discussion or negotiation. In Ireland the first type can be seen in the form of the Employment Appeals Tribunal, which interprets and applies a number of employment protection statutes, and the Labour Court in its role as the tribunal to which sex discrimination cases are taken under the Anti-Discrimination (Pay) Act 1974 and the Employment Equality Act 1977; the second type is represented by the Labour Relations Commission and the Labour Court (in its other role); and the third by the Employer–Labour Conference. Of these bodies, the Labour Court, the Labour Relations Commission and the Employer–Labour Conference need to be explained a little further.

The Labour Court is a tripartite body originally created under the Industrial Relations Act 1946 to provide some direction for wage bargaining after the lifting of the pay freeze imposed during the Second World War. Its main function was to support the system of collective bargaining through conciliation and mediation, offered on a voluntary basis. Since 1990 some of these functions have been removed from the Court and transferred to the new Labour Relations Commission, to which we return. Before that, in 1974 and again in 1977, the Labour Court had also been given juridical functions under the sex discrimination legislation; these functions remain. But otherwise the Labour Court is not a 'court' at all, but rather a body which uses its good offices to persuade and cajole parties in dispute in order to achieve a peaceful settlement. In this function it has been largely successful, in that a large proportion of disputes taken to the Court in any year are resolved either at the conciliation stage or through mediation (called 'investigation' in the Court's terminology). However, the Court's task is not always easy, and in particular at times when the government has attempted to influence pay bargaining the Court has been subjected to apparent government pressure, often prejudicing its standing in the eyes of unions and employers. Experience indicates that the Court works well in what one might call 'average' disputes, but less effectively when the system comes under major pressure, as in the case of, say, disputes in public utilities such as energy and transport.

The Labour Relations Commission was set up under Part III of the Industrial Relations Act 1990 (EIRR 193, February 1990: 13–15). The Act gave the Commission the functions *inter alia* of providing a conciliation service and an industrial relations advisory service, preparing codes of practice, and conducting or commissioning research. The Commission is broadly modelled on the Northern Ireland Labour Relations Agency, or the British Advisory, Conciliation and Arbitration Service; however, given the tendency to centralize industrial relations issues in Ireland, it is likely that the Commission will have a greater role in setting norms than these two bodies. At the time of writing it is still too early to tell what its impact in practice will be. The Commission had been heralded in a number of discussion documents in the late 1980s. The institutional reform initially provoked a hostile response from the Labour Court, which saw the new Commission as diminishing the Court's effectiveness by divorcing it from the conciliation service that had always been a central part of its activity; the creation of yet another institution was widely regarded as reflecting a political aim of changing the balance of power between the Labour Court and the Department of Labour (EIRR 193, February 1990: 15). Eventually, however, the reform was largely accepted by all industrial relations practitioners.

The Employer–Labour Conference was set up in its present form in 1970. It is an *ad hoc* body, with no statutory foundation. Its original purpose was to rationalize pay bargaining after a period of great industrial relations turbulence in the late 1960s, and to remove the then government's threat to introduce a statutory incomes policy (McCarthy 1973). The Conference is bipartite or tripartite in nature: members are nominated in equal numbers by the ICTU and various employer bodies, but the employer nominees include government representatives; in any case, its conduct since the mid-1970s has been clearly tripartite, with the government taking a distinct line in its deliberations. During the 1970s the Conference was responsible for negotiating the succession of 'National Wages Agreements' (to which we return below), but since around 1980 it has merely been a forum for union–employer discussions: recent national bargaining has taken place elsewhere.

Collective Bargaining

As already noted, the voluntaristic nature of the Irish system of industrial relations has put collective bargaining at the centre of all activity. Most workers have their terms and conditions of employment settled by collective agreements, and it has been long-term public policy to support this process. However, support for collective bargaining, particularly on the part of the government, is not unqualified. Governments tend still to approve of voluntary bargaining and industrial relations self-regulation, but not in every context and at any price; in particular, recent years have seen the growth of a widespread belief that the inflationary effects of collective bargaining must be reined in, and that this is easier in the context of centrally determined pay norms. How to set these pay norms is however another matter. The FitzGerald government of the mid-1980s appeared to prefer a norm set by the government and backed up, if necessary, by the threat of retribution against employers minded to exceed the figure; the Haughey administrations from 1987 appeared to prefer the notion of a centralized, national agreement between the government and the social partners.

Historically collective bargaining in Ireland has proceeded on several levels. General pay increases have tended to be determined at the most centralized level available; so-called 'special' increases – i.e. all those pay increases justified by something other than inflation, such as productivity, changes in working practices, relativities, and so forth – have tended to be settled at the level of the firm or, sometimes, the plant; other terms and conditions of employment, and matters of local procedure, have been the subject of lower-level bargaining. Industry-wide bargaining, common in other countries, is rare in Ireland, although in evidence in certain sectors such as printing. Overall, there is no doubt that the main emphasis has always been on the centre.

Before 1970 there had been a number of attempts to reach national collective agreements covering the entire work force, but in each case the arrangement was beset by problems, and the outcome was invariably that a central, national agreement was not replaced by a similar arrangement on its expiry. The first centralized agreement was the 'National Wages Policy' of 1948; later attempts were made in 1952, 1957 and 1964. The last of these led directly to the major round of strikes of the late 1960s (McCarthy 1973). In this setting, when the government published a Prices and Incomes Bill in 1970, in which it threatened to exercise statutory control over wage and price increases, the employers and unions were sufficiently jolted to set up the Employer–Labour Conference, where they then negotiated a 'national wages agreement' to run from January 1971. This time the exercise worked, and the first national wages agreement (NWA) was followed by others in 1972, 1974, 1975, 1976 and 1978 (O'Brien 1981).

These agreements, which set the agreed rate of pay increase for the entire national work force in all industries and sectors, were initially deemed a success: they contributed to industrial peace, adopted recognizable principles of equity (including special provisions for the lower paid and for women), were generally non-inflationary, and stabilized what had previously been a chaotic picture. However, they coincided with the economic problems associated with the first oil crisis in the aftermath of the 1973 Yom Kippur war, and by 1975 the government was no longer prepared to let employers and unions fix pay increases which were unrelated to the needs of macro-economic policy. This led to a tripartite negotiation: following the conclusion of the 1975 NWA, the government offered the employers and unions budgetary concessions if they agreed the specified pay increases. The significance of this development was that a precedent had been set for a bargaining round between the government and interest groups, in which the subject-matter for negotiation included aspects of government policy and parliamentary initiative. Economic recession had pushed Ireland further down the road to corporatism, and established a tendency which has persisted since.

The NWAs continued for the next few pay rounds, but were beginning to run into problems. The trade unions found it increasingly difficult to persuade local officials and activists of the merits of a system where decisions were taken centrally, without much local input; furthermore, some unions had always taken the view that national agreements robbed them of the opportunity to realize their full bargaining potential, particularly in the case of craft workers and employees of the financial institutions. Many employers felt that centrally fixed pay norms were not appropriate, particularly for those with trading difficulties, and that too many trade unions or their officials breached the terms of the agreements. When the 1978 agreement was due to expire, a Special Delegate Conference of the ICTU voted not to negotiate a replacement agreement, and the NWAs thus came to an end.

Once again, the emergence of a problem tended to reinforce the corporatist trend. In 1979 the government was determined to secure industrial growth through centralized collective bargaining, and when the proposal for an NWA was rejected, it offered the social partners a new concept, described as a 'National Understanding'. This was to involve a moderate pay agreement, combined with a social-contract-style agreement on economic and social policy. For the first time, the government became directly involved in national negotiations with the social partners in its own right, rather than simply in its capacity as an employer represented on the Employer–Labour Conference. The arrangement was, after some difficulties, duly initiated: the 'National Understanding for Economic and Social Development' involved an NWA-type pay agreement, but with an added section covering such issues as employment, taxation, pay, industrial relations, social welfare and health. A second National Understanding was agreed in 1980 (O'Brien 1981). However, the concept did not survive beyond that, partly because the employers in particular were now determined to have local pay bargaining, and partly because the government had been almost completely unable – or in some cases unwilling – to deliver almost any of the commitments entered into in the areas of economic and social policy; job-creation targets in particular were not met.

Following the second National Understanding, from 1981 until 1987, there was no centralized or national agreement. That does not mean however that collective bargaining was conducted on a local, 'free-for-all' basis; rather, during each pay round a 'trend' or 'norm' emerged which set the standard for local negotiators. During the first two years or so of this period the norm was set by agreements between the government and the Public Services Committee of the Irish Congress of Trade Unions (of which the present author was at the time a member) for the public service; the pay increase reached there was almost invariably adopted in other negotiations. During later pay rounds the trend was set in the private sector, usually by those companies or sectors which were the first to conclude agreements. The government attempted at times to impose a norm through pay guidelines, but these guidelines were largely ignored in the private sector, and should more realistically have been seen as opening shots in the public service pay negotiations (von Prondzynski 1985).

It is clear that the FitzGerald coalition government of 1982–7 failed to establish the level of pay increase that was economically appropriate. When the government was urging employers to concede either no pay increases at all, or only very low ones, the actual statistics for the '26th Pay Round' in 1986–7 showed average increases of around 6 per cent. However, the government's attempt to re-model industrial relations practice in other respects bore more fruit, and the complicated framework of special pay awards based on productivity (often bogus) or relativity was largely dismantled during this period, with pay awards being related to what the employer could afford, rather than the market rate. This important structural change has been reinforced further in the subsequent period.

It has been stated by one writer that 'market control' in industrial relations has never been a strategic objective of the Irish state (Roche 1989). Nevertheless, market control came to dominate government thinking by 1982 at the latest, when the then Haughey administration unilaterally announced that it was proposing not to honour its commitments under a public service pay agreement because of macro-economic considerations; and has been the primary objective of public policy towards collective bargaining ever since. The policy was manifestly unsuccessful until 1987, but none the less real. In 1987, however, the new Fianna Fail minority administration embarked on a new attempt to enter into a national agreement, at the prompting of the ICTU, and in October of that year the government, unions, employers, and a small number of other interest groups (including a farmers' organization) entered into an agreement entitled the 'Programme for National Recovery' (PNR). This agreement might have indicated that monetarist economics were once again giving way to corporatist tendencies, but in reality the PNR was merely a different vehicle for achieving market control. Covering the period to the end of 1990, the Programme expressed the parties' commitment to providing an economic climate conducive to growth, constructing a more equitable tax system, reducing social inequalities, and creating employment. Pay rises were not to exceed 2.5 per cent in each of the three years 1988–90, and special provision was made for the low paid: there was a higher percentage increase for the first £120 of weekly pay, and a flat-rate minimum increase.

The basic similarity between the PNR and the National Understandings of the late 1970s lay in the fact that both dealt with pay and terms of employment on the one hand, and issues of social and economic policy on the other. There, however, the similarity largely ends. The PNR was an agreement covering three years; the pay terms of the PNR were not fixed norms, but guidelines which had, in the private sector at least, to be converted into agreed rates through local bargaining (thus meeting a major employer demand); and the terms on economic and social policy were to a much lesser extent government commitments, but rather targets for all relevant parties to the continuing corporatist process – for example, the job creation targets were largely for the private sector, particularly manufacturing. In summary, the PNR was an agreed framework of general guidelines, rather than a document of binding commitments. Furthermore, as it turned out, the PNR was to run side by side with a government programme of massive cost-cutting in the public sector, as well as a number of other measures to depress inflation and cut the budget deficit, which might, in earlier times, have met stiff trade union resistance. While a delegate to the 1988 Annual Conference of the ICTU might complain that 'we do not believe that the way the economy has been managed is in accordance with the letter or the spirit of the agreement', in practice the PNR locked the trade union movement into an alliance with the government which made difficult any serious opposition to other aspects of government policy.

The PNR was remarkably successful in that its terms were largely satisfied. Pay bargaining at a local level, which was to continue under the Programme, produced results which were almost invariably those suggested by the PNR; over the three-year period, these rates in turn were more or less in line with inflation, which fell steadily to under 3 per cent in early 1991. With strong manufacturing and export performance, job-creation targets were also generally met in the private sector, although the jobs gained were partly lost again in redundancies elsewhere. Economic growth of more than 4 per cent a year on average between 1987 and 1990 helped reduce the gap between Ireland and the stronger EC economies: GDP per head rose from 64 per cent of the EC average in 1987 to 68 per cent in 1990 (EIRR 207, April 1991: 17). One other aspect of the PNR, the general agreement that negotiations should take place on reductions in working hours, led to a framework agreement and local negotiations which resulted in the shortening of the working week for most workers by one hour to 39 hours.

However, while the FIE described the PNR as an 'unprecedented success', the agreement did not meet with much enthusiasm on the union side. At the 1988 Annual Conference of the ICTU three motions were submitted on the PNR, all largely critical; two were carried, and one was remitted. Furthermore, for the duration of the PNR's terms Congress in particular was constantly engaged in soul-searching over its role in the agreement, and over whether it should continue to operate it. In the end the PNR held together, and what is more, it has now been succeeded by a similar arrangement, the 'Programme for Economic and Social Progress' (PESP).

In 1990, against a background of Ireland's increasing integration into the international economy, in particular through the creation of the single European market and European Monetary Union, the ICTU again took the initiative in calling for tripartite national negotiations based around the notion of a ten-year development strategy. This strategy eventually formed the core long-term objective of the PESP, which refers to the development of 'a modern, efficient market economy with innate capacity for satisfactory and sustainable growth and discharge of the obligations of a developed social conscience'. Key objectives of the long-term strategy are increased competitiveness and a further reduction in the gap in living standards between Ireland and the rest of the Community (for details, see EIRR 207, April 1991: 17–19). PESP seeks to underpin the broad strategic goal with specific macro-economic and industrial policies, and reform of tax and social welfare systems: in the words of a senior figure in Ireland's largest union, SITPU, the agreement demonstrates that 'issues like taxation, inflation and economic growth are a legitimate and necessary part of the trade union agenda, since they all have bearings on the standard of living'.

As with the PNR, the PESP sets targets for job creation – 20,000 new jobs each year in manufacturing and a similar number in the international services sector. It also acknowledges the need for special measures to help the long-term unemployed. While many of the measures of the Programme are left to the social partners to implement, its tripartite nature is underscored by the government's commitment to implementing specific measures – for example, enacting as soon as possible legislation to protect part-time workers, amending equal opportunities and unfair dismissals law – and to reviewing other aspects such as conditions of employment, holidays and the control of employment agencies.

On the question of pay, the Programme recognizes the need for the long-term development strategy to be bolstered by 'consensus on responsible incomes developments at national level'. Moderate targets for pay increases, determined in a separate agreement between the ICTU and employers' organizations, are set for the three years to 1993; the increases are in line with those forecast for Ireland's European partners, again showing the underlying concern of the parties with the country's international competitiveness. Special provision is made under the agreement for helping the low paid, and the precise determination of pay increases within the agreed guidelines is left to local negotiations. Once again, the evidence is that the pay terms of this agreement are being adhered to in local bargaining, with 90–95 per cent of some 550 private sector companies in one survey complying with the PESP increases (*IDS European Report* 360, December 1991: 6). However, in the face of lower than expected growth, the government was hinting that it might be necessary for the partners to go 'back to the drawing board' to renegotiate the pay aspects of the Programme, and there have also been strains in public sector pay negotiations as a result of lower than expected growth. These differences provoked a dramatic confrontation at the beginning of 1992, when the government's decision to impose a flat-rate £5 pay increase in place of the 3 per cent rise due under the PESP led to a concerted protest strike throughout the public sector.

A final aspect of industrial relations covered by the PESP is employee participation. A joint declaration of the FIE and the ICTU encourages increased 'employee involvement' in firms, in the form of communication and consultation arrangements, financial participation schemes, quality of working-life programmes and quality circles. Such schemes are seen as a way of encouraging employees to identify with the objectives of the enterprise and of promoting competitiveness. Though the social partners look to government for financial incentives for profit-sharing schemes, the stress is on the voluntary nature of involvement 'in keeping with the (voluntary) industrial relations and collective bargaining systems in operation in Ireland' (cited in EIRR 210, July 1991: 6). The optimism of the signatories does not seem as yet borne out by the available evidence. Such schemes in Ireland have tended to be implemented as part of human resource management policies of foreign multinationals; case-study research in the electronics industry (Geary 1992a and 1992b) suggests that they have sat uneasily with 'harder' components of management strategy, such as the extensive use of part-time labour (which in the economy as a whole is well below European levels, at under 5 per cent in 1984), and continuing tight supervision and control of the work force. One of the most publicized experiments in participation was the profit-sharing scheme agreed in 1989 at one of Ireland's major companies, Waterford Crystal (EIRR 187, August 1989: 14–15). The scheme, introduced in the context of corporate financial difficulties, provided for profit-related pay and share ownership for the company's 2000 employees once it was back in profit; in return, the work force voted to accept cuts in pay and other benefits. However, in 1990 the company suffered a fourteen-week strike over the withdrawal of special payments – highlighting the difficult prospects for employee 'involvement' at times of economic stringency.

Industrial conflict

Until quite recently it was common for Ireland to be thought of – and to consider itself – as a strike-prone country. Whether this view of Irish industrial relations was ever entirely accurate could be a matter of some debate, but in any case there is no reason to suppose that it is accurate now. For much of the post-war era, Ireland has been regarded – by both foreign and domestic observers – as a strike-prone country. High strike levels in the late 1940s were followed by relative peace in the 1950s, but the 1960s were a 'decade of upheaval' (McCarthy 1973), and this turbulence was to continue through the 1970s. Conflict was reflected in large numbers of strikes – with a peak of 219 recorded stoppages in 1974 – and high figures of days lost – over 1.4 million in 1979. For much of the period, some two-thirds of strikes were unofficial; but there were also many protracted disputes – for example, the national stoppage which closed down the Irish banking system for six months in 1970.

In the 1970s, Ireland ranked consistently near the top of the European strike league table (as measured by the ratio of days lost to employment). But Irish strike-proneness declined consistently during the 1980s, and particularly rapidly from the latter part of the decade: an indication of the growing impact of centralized concertation. In 1980 a total of 404,000 working days were lost in 132 strikes; by 1988 days lost were down to 130,000, and in 1989, the number of recorded strikes fell to 38, and days lost to 50,000 – placing Ireland near the bottom of the European league table. Subsequently, however, there has been an increase in strike activity; most recently, a major public sector stoppage at the beginning of 1992.

It could be argued that the incidence of industrial conflict in recent years has been so low that it is not a serious feature of Irish industrial relations. Unofficial industrial action, which was once considered to be a major industrial relations problem (von Prondzynski 1982), is no longer seen as significant. As yet, however, it is unclear whether the low strike figures of the late 1980s were a temporary lull or the beginning of a new era of stability.

Nevertheless, there have been some serious disputes in Ireland in recent years, often in the public sector, but also in the private sector as with the Waterford Crystal strike mentioned above. Disputes are usually centred on pay and conditions, and the tendency visible up to the 1970s of challenging management's disciplinary and dismissal decisions in industrial action seems largely to have been dissipated by the provision of alternative statutory avenues.

Irish industrial relations, when put under stress in industrial conflict, rely heavily on state-run mechanisms to provide resolution facilities. The natural tendency of employers or trade unions is to turn to the Labour Court – or, now, the Labour Relations Commission – to offer a way out. A very large proportion of disputes are taken to these institutions, and many are settled there. Equally, however, when for some reason or other the institutions temporarily lose the confidence of the parties – as happened in the mid-1980s when the trade unions felt that the Labour Court was being put under pressure by the government to apply its pay guidelines – the ability of the system to relieve the stress is seriously compromised. In a recent major dispute in 1991 in the electricity service, the institutions failed to deliver a quick resolution, and the parties seemed at a loss to find one elsewhere.

Irish industrial relations law is still built on the basic notion of immunities first introduced under the (British) Trade Disputes Act 1906. That Act has now been replaced by the Industrial Relations Act 1990, which retains the principle of immunities available to trade union officials and members who are acting 'in contemplation or furtherance of a trade dispute'; the idea which had been floated by the government in 1986 of creating a system based on the 'right to strike' (Department of Labour 1986) was subsequently abandoned. However, some of these immunities are now more tightly drawn than under the 1906 Act (EIRR 193, February 1990: 13–15): for example, under the 1990 Act, unions failing to hold secret pre-strike ballots risk losing their negotiation licence, and restrictions are also placed on picketing. Another development encouraged by the Act is the widespread use of strike codes of practice. The Labour Relations Commission was granted powers to prepare industrial relations codes of practice. In 1991 it published a discussion paper on disputes procedures which stressed the function of the code as the means by which 'the community's interest in a dispute situation can be taken into account', especially in essential services or particular manufacturing operations; this implied a move towards the setting of agreed minimum levels of service or production in the event of a dispute.

Conclusion

From the perspective of the early 1990s, there are a number of influences at work in Irish industrial relations. First, there are the British origins of the system, visible in the trade union structures and traditions, employer preferences, bargaining tactics, industrial relations terminology, and so forth; these origins continue to have an impact, reinforced by such matters as the presence of British-based trade unions, and the strong cultural ties between these islands. Second, there is the now well established Irish trend to seek corporatist solutions to problems of an economic and social nature. Third, there is the influence of the (often American) multinational enterprises, with their sophisticated personnel management tactics and, frequently, their preference for a non-union environment. Fourth, there are the effects of recession, with a weakened trade union presence and a more confident management. And finally, there is the influence of the European Community, and its moves not only towards economic integration but also towards a stronger social policy in the context of what one might describe as a more 'Germanic' system of industrial relations (von Prondzynski 1990).

The above influences are largely at odds with each other. So for example, the British industrial relations tradition is not comfortable with either a move towards formal worker participation, or tripartite arrangements coming from the centre, or non-union personnel management, or minimum wage legislation; the Irish corporatist tendency does not sit easily with a tradition of grassroots trade union activism, or the recession-inspired management preference for local solutions and negotiations. And yet, the Irish genius for 'muddling through' has kept an industrial relations framework on the road which has apparently been able to absorb these contradictions and retain much greater levels of stability than those enjoyed by more homogeneous systems elsewhere.

The 1980s undoubtedly added new dimensions to the Irish model of industrial relations, partly through recessionary conditions and partly due to changes in government policy. The 1990s appear set to add a more dynamic European dimension. However, these developments seem certain merely to add new layers, rather than to create an entirely different system. If one looks at the characteristics of the traditional model of industrial relations listed earlier, then one can be confident in predicting that some of these will change: more flexibility and more participation, for example, seem likely. But the essence of the Irish system overall, rooted in a small society increasingly confident of its status internationally, is secure.

Notes

[1]   When the term 'Ireland' is used in this chapter it must be taken to be a reference to the state of that name established by the 1937 Constitution (*Bunreacht na hEireann*), or where appropriate, the Irish Free State of the period 1922–37. In other words, this chapter concerns itself solely with the 26 counties of the Republic of Ireland, and it does not deal with Northern Ireland.

[2]   References in this chapter are to the Irish Pound (or Punt), the value of which is slightly less than its UK namesake.

Abbreviations

CII	Confederation of Irish Industries
CIU	Congress of Irish Unions
EAT	Employment Appeals Tribunal
ELC	Employer–Labour Conference
FIE	Federation of Irish Employers
FUE	Federated Union of Employers (see FIE)
ICTU	Irish Congress of Trade Unions
ITGWU	Irish Transport and General Workers' Union
ITUC	Irish Trades Union Congress
LRC	Labour Relations Commission
NU	National Understanding
NWA	National Wages Agreement
PESP	Programme for Economic and Social Progress
PNR	Programme for National Recovery
PSPA	Public Sector Pay Agreement

References

Cassells, P. 1989: The Organisation of Trade Unions. In Murphy, T. et al. (eds), 13–20.
Commission of Inquiry on Industrial Relations 1981: *Report*. Dublin: Stationery Office.
Crouch, C. 1982: *Trade Unions: The Logic of Collective Action*. London: Fontana.
Department of Labour 1986: *Outline of Principal Provisions of Proposed New Trade Disputes and Industrial Relations Legislation*. Dublin.
Department of Labour 1980: *Discussion Paper on Worker Participation*. Dublin.
Flanders, A. 1974: The Tradition of Voluntarism. *British Journal of Industrial Relations*, 12, 3, 352–70.
Geary, J. 1992a: Employment Flexibility and Human Resource Management: The Case of Three American Electronics Plants. *Work, Employment & Society*, 6, 2.
Geary, J. 1992b: Pay, Control and Commitment: A Case Study Analysis of HRM Policies of Employee Appraisal and Reward. *Human Resource Management Journal*, 2, 4, Summer, forthcoming.
Kelly, A. 1989: The Worker Director in Irish Industrial Relations. In *Industrial Relations in Ireland: Contemporary Issues and Developments*, Dublin: University College Dublin, 305–10.
Kerr, T. 1989: Trade Unions and the Law. In Murphy, T. et al. (eds), 217–34.
McCarthy, C. 1973: *The Decade of Upheaval: Irish Trade Unions in the Nineteen Sixties*. Dublin: Institute of Public Administration.
McCarthy, C. 1977: *Trade Unions in Ireland: 1894–1960*. Dublin: Institute of Public Administration.
Murphy, T., Hillery, B. and Kelly, A. (eds) 1989: *Industrial Relations in Ireland: Contemporary Issues and Developments*. Dublin: University College Dublin.
O'Brien, J.F. 1981: *A Study of National Wage Agreements in Ireland*. Dublin: Economic and Social Research Institute.
O'Brien, J.F. 1989: The Role of Employer Organisations in Ireland. In Murphy, T. et al. (eds), 73–82.
OECD (Organisation for Economic Cooperation and Development) 1988: *Economic Surveys. Ireland 1987/1988*. Paris: OECD.
OECD 1991: *Economic Surveys. Ireland 1990/1991*. Paris: OECD.
Roche, W.K. 1989: In Murphy, T. et al. (eds), 115–31.
Von Prondzynski, F. 1982: Unofficial Strikes: Myth and Reality. *Administration*, 29, 400.
Von Prondzynski, F. 1985: The Changing Functions of Labour Law. In P. Fosh and C.R. Littler, *Industrial Relations and the Law in the 1980s*, Aldershot: Gower, 176–93.
Von Prondzynski, F. 1985: The Death of the Pay Round. *IRN Report*, 7, 11, 16.
Von Prondzynski, F. 1987: The Changing Face of Irish Industrial Relations. *IRN Report*, 9, 24, 16–20.
Von Prondzynski, F. 1989: Flexibility and New Work Practices. *IPM News*, 4, 2.
Von Prondzynski, F. 1990: Irish Labour Law and the European Community. *Comparative Labor Law Journal*, 11, 4, 498–510.
Von Prondzynski, F. and McCarthy, C. 1984: *Employment Law (Irish Law Texts)*. London: Sweet & Maxwell.

3

Sweden: Can the Model Survive?

Anders Kjellberg

Introduction: The 'Nordic Model' of Industrial Relations

Since the mid-1960s Swedish industrial relations have undergone such fundamental changes that the very existence of a 'Swedish model' is now questioned. Nevertheless, given the continuing similarities between Nordic countries, and the differences between them as a group and other European countries, the notion of a 'Nordic model'[1] of industrial relations still has descriptive and analytic value. First, therefore, the broad outlines of the 'Nordic model' will be presented. The main focus of the chapter, however, is on Swedish industrial relations: the roots of the 'historic compromise' between capital and labour in the 1930s, and the erosion of the Swedish model of 'self-regulation' and centralized bargaining by increased state intervention and pressures to decentralization.

Nordic industrial relations characteristically reflect a relative balance of power between capital and labour: compromises between employers' associations and unions were concluded at an early stage in the three Scandinavian countries, although Finland lagged behind. Political deals with other class forces – notably farmers' parties – allowed Scandinavian labour movements represented by strong social-democratic parties to extend their already considerable industrial and political strength to the governmental sphere (Therborn 1984; Katzenstein 1985). This occurred in the 1930s in Norway and Sweden, and considerably earlier in Denmark where the party of small farmers headed governments based on an alliance with the social democrats in 1909–10 and 1913–20. The political compromises bringing social democracy to power meant that the favourite weapon of Scandinavian employers – the large-scale lockout – could no longer be used as freely as in the past. This encouraged Swedish and Norwegian employers to conclude basic agreements.

The Danish government commission on labour law appointed in 1908 might be described as a compromise across the political and industrial arenas. The commission, made up of equal numbers of union and employer representatives, presented a proposal on compulsory arbitration, mediation and conflict procedures which was adopted in 1910. The real origin of the compromise was the so-called September Compromise of 1899 between the confederations of unions and employers (see below). Danish industrial relations were thus already institutionalized around the turn of the century. While the political developments of the 1930s did not therefore have the same significance as in Norway or Sweden, important legislation on union balloting rules, with centralizing effects on industrial relations, was passed in Denmark as well as Norway in this decade.

In the long run, however, the coalitions of the 1930s were of lesser significance. They were succeeded by a long era of 'bloc policy' with social-democratic parties as leaders of a 'socialist bloc' competing with a 'bourgeois bloc' (the phrases used in Sweden). Since the 1930s, governments led by social democrats have been in power in the following periods: 1932–76 and 1982–91 in Sweden; 1935–65, 1971–2, 1973–81, 1987–9 and since 1990 in Norway; 1929–43, 1947–50, 1953–68, 1971–3 and 1975–82 in Denmark. In Finland there were governments with social-democratic prime ministers in 1948–50, 1956–7, 1958–9, 1966–70, 1972–5 and 1977–87, but that did not always mean social-democratic dominance. In contrast to other Nordic countries, Finnish governments have generally consisted of coalitions bridging socialist and non-socialist blocs. Thus the agrarian/centre party has been a major component of governments for more than fifty years, and social democrats have been almost as often represented. Another distinct feature of Finnish governments is the participation of communists during the 'popular front' governments of 1945–8, in 1966–70, and in a 'third wave' in 1975–9.

The crucial element in Scandinavian compromises between capital and labour was the extension of cooperation into the industrial arena. The Danish September Compromise of 1899 was the first basic agreement in the world. Equivalent agreements were reached in Norway in 1936 and in Sweden in 1938, although there were important precursors: the 1907 Metal Agreement in Norway, the 1905 Engineering Agreement and the 1906 'December Compromise' in Sweden. Employer prerogative was accepted by the unions in exchange for recognition of basic trade union rights. Under Sweden's 'historic compromise' of the 1930s, it was agreed that the efforts of social- democratic governments to bring about economic growth should not challenge the capitalist nature of production (Korpi 1978; 1983). Class compromise in Finland was delayed by the civil war from which the bourgeois forces emerged victorious, and by the absence of a unified reformist labour movement.

In the Scandinavian countries, social-democratic hegemony within the labour movements was an essential precondition for the compromises of the 1930s and earlier. Their subsequent reformist strategy has been based on strengthening the position of workers and unions through economic growth, permitting 'full employment' and social reforms. The close links between manual workers' unions and social-democratic parties – in Norway and Sweden (until 1991) local branches of LO unions may 'collectively affiliate' their members to the party – have facilitated the acceptance of the measures necessary to implement this strategy.

The various basic agreements were reached in a climate of often intense industrial conflict. For example, the Danish basic agreement of 1899 and the Swedish compromises of 1905–6 followed major lockouts or threats of lockouts – and one of their most important aims was to regulate conflict between the 'labour market parties'.

The agreements promoted another distinctive feature of Nordic union movements and industrial relations: the combination of centralization and decentralization (Kjellberg 1983). The decentralized element already existed from an early stage in the form of union workplace organizations, which still represent the national unions at workplace level and have important functions including recruitment and bargaining. The centralized compromises in the industrial arena facilitated the unions' presence at the workplace by granting basic union rights. This has favoured high union density: mutual recognition at central level has curbed the fragmentation of trade unionism, while decentralization has brought workers into direct contact with the union at the workplace.

The basic agreements paved the way for the introduction of a three-tier system of collective bargaining. The traditional system of collective contracts concluded by national unions and their workplace organizations was supplemented by a third level of centralized agreements on wages and related issues (in Denmark from the 1930s, Norway from the 1940s and Sweden from the 1950s).

The introduction of centralized bargaining presupposed a certain centralization of the parties themselves. Almost from the start, the threat from powerful unions drove Scandinavian employers towards centralized organization and their confederations were given extensive powers over affiliated bodies. Large dispute funds were built up and had to be coordinated centrally, especially as extensive lockouts came to be the favourite weapon of Scandinavian employers. (In Finland a similar centralization of employers did not occur until the 1950s.) The centralization of Scandinavian union confederations took place later. In the 1940s, the Swedish LO was given considerably increased powers over affiliated unions, within which the authority of the leadership was strengthened at the expense of the members. Balloting on collective bargaining outcomes was abolished (although advisory balloting was retained for a period). Most Swedish unions still have more centralized decision-making today than their Norwegian and Danish counterparts.

The regular use of membership ballots on draft agreements in Denmark and Norway puts intense pressure on union negotiators to win concessions. This makes centralized bargaining a much more complicated affair than in Sweden and is probably the main cause of the considerably higher degree of state intervention in collective bargaining in Denmark and Norway. Danish and Norwegian state mediators are given the right to aggregate ballot results from different unions and sectors, and mediation proposals have often been transformed into law. The extensive use of compulsory arbitration in Norway should also be mentioned.

The more fragmented union structure in Denmark and Norway is also conducive to state intervention. Early industrialization in Denmark has left a legacy of craft unionism, while in Norway white-collar union organization is fragmented and union density for white-collar workers is much lower than in Sweden or Denmark.

The three-tier system of collective bargaining corresponds to a four-level system of union organization: the workplace; local union branches; national unions; and union confederations and bargaining cartels. Where workplace organizations are absent – particularly in small enterprises – local union branches take care of bargaining at this level. In other cases they assist workplace organizations if required.

From an international perspective the Nordic union systems are both comparatively centralized and decentralized. Nordic union confederations have an important role in centralized bargaining for manual workers in the private sector; however, this role has been undermined by the expansion of public sector and white-collar employment which has strengthened the role of bargaining cartels. At the same time, union workplace organizations have important decentralized bargaining funtions – in contrast to many European countries where bodies other than unions, such as works councils, are assigned these tasks. (Works councils in Nordic countries are exclusively union mechanisms.)

The absence of political and religious divisions in the union movement (with the exception of Finland in the late 1950s and 1960s) and the success of Nordic unions in avoiding dual systems of representation have facilitated the recruitment of members. Labour legislation in the 1970s further extended the role of union workplace organization. Furthermore, the collective character of Nordic labour law implies that unions and their workplace organizations – not individual workers – are legal entities (Bruun et al. 1990).

The characterization of Nordic unions as both centralized and decentralized does not imply that intermediate levels – the national unions and their local branches – are less important than elsewhere. Bargaining by national unions at industry level has increasingly replaced centralized agreements, and even where central agreements exist, sectoral bargaining is important in adapting their provisions to specific conditions within each industry. Without the consent of major national unions, no centralized negotiations will take place. The prominence of Nordic national unions is emphasized by the fact that union workplace representatives – in contrast to British shop stewards – are wholly integrated into the national unions and their branches.

Since the 1980s a clear tendency to the decentralization of collective bargaining can be seen in all Nordic countries, although there are differences. Swedish employers are aiming gradually to decentralize bargaining down to workplace level, contrary to the policy of the social-democratic government (1982–91) to preserve and even strengthen the role of centralized agreements; in principle no wage increases were allowed at workplace level in 1991–2. In Denmark (and to a lesser extent in Norway), where the state has intervened much more actively in collective bargaining, the unions have been successful in eroding government influence by decentralizing bargaining to industry level.

The Background to the Swedish Model: The Economy and Labour Market

Few if any economies are so concentrated and internationalized as the Swedish. Despite its small population – 8.6 million – a surprisingly large proportion of big companies are based in Sweden. Out of the top 500 European firms by capitalization, 29 were Swedish in 1991 (*Financial Times* 1992). Among the Nordic countries Sweden accounts for 15 out of the 20 largest enterprises, or 29 out of the top 50 (*Affärsvärlden*, 35, 1991). Swedish engineering firms occupy an especially prominent position. There is obviously a close correlation between size of firms and the degree of internationalization in a small country like Sweden: only by selling the greater part of production in foreign markets (through exports and production abroad) has the impressive expansion of the largest Swedish firms been possible. The share of production sold by Swedish transnationals in the domestic market was halved between 1965 and 1986 (*Produktivitetsdelegationen* 1991b). In addition, production abroad by Swedish enterprises increased faster than exports; by the mid-1980s almost as much was being produced abroad as exported by these companies. Long before that, the largest of them often employed far more workers abroad than in Sweden: 85 per cent of the workers of the Swiss-Swedish ABB are employed abroad, while Electrolux and SKF have more than 80 per cent of employment located outside Sweden. In 1985, the workers employed by Swedish subsidiaries abroad amounted to 43 per cent of those employed by Swedish manufacturing industry at home; compared with only 18 per cent in 1965 (Forsgren 1989: 12).

The size and internationalization of leading Swedish firms, combined with the smallness of the country, have given them a strategic position among the country's social forces. There is an increasing discrepancy between the increasing economic significance of the 'C-sector' (the sector competing on international markets) and the changing composition of the labour force. In 1963 the sector accounted for 30 per cent of the total number of working hours; by 1985 the figure had fallen to 20 per cent. In the same period, the public sector (excluding communications) grew from 14 to 30 per cent. The protected private sector (including public communications) declined slightly from 56 per cent in 1963 to 50 per cent in 1985.

Throughout the 1980s the public sector (excluding government-owned companies) accounted for about 40 per cent of employed workers (41 per cent in 1990). The overwhelming majority (71 per cent) are women. As many as 57 per cent of all female workers were employed in the public sector in 1990, but only one in four male workers. By international standards the activity rate of women in the Swedish labour force is very high: 83 per cent of the female population (16–64 years) in 1990, compared with 87 per cent of men. Female workers were divided equally between manual and white-collar employment (compared with 56 and 44 per cent respectively for men). More than 80 per cent of women manual workers were in the service sector, while 71 per cent of male manual workers were employed in manufacturing and construction. In 1985, 47 per cent of all wage and salary earners were white-collar workers (despite the fact that most shop workers and auxiliary nurses are classified as manual). The expansion of white-collar employment within the SAF area is shown by the fact that in the mid-1980s this category absorbed half the total wage costs of SAF firms, compared with 40 per cent in the early 1970s.

Swedish union structure reflects to an exceptional degree the division between manual and white-collar workers. Almost all national unions affiliated to LO (the Swedish Trade Union Confederation) are manual workers' unions. TCO (the Central Organization of Salaried Employees, founded in 1944) and SACO (the Swedish Confederation of Professional Associations, established in 1947) are composed exclusively of white-collar unions. In 1990 LO had 1,980,000 'active' members (i.e. excluding pensioners, students, etc.), TCO had 1,144,000 and SACO 260,000.

Extremely low unemployment – far below the OECD average – is another distinctive feature of the Swedish labour market. At the end of the 1980s unemployment was less than 2 per cent of the labour force: having peaked at 3.5 per cent in 1983, it reached a low point of 1.4 per cent in 1989, when the OECD-Europe average was 8.6 per cent. Since 1991, however, a profound change has occurred. Unemployment rose sharply, reaching 2.7 per cent in 1991 and 4.1 per cent in January 1992 (with 6 per cent forecast for autumn 1992), although it is still low in international terms. In contrast to earlier slumps in which the expansion of public services offset falling employment elsewhere, the public sector has itself been hit by redundancies.

Since 1974 Sweden's record on productivity has been below the OECD average. Productivity growth in Swedish manufacturing industry lagged behind that of a group of eleven important competitors in the periods 1974–7 and 1985–90. While Sweden was in third place in this group in the 1960s, it dropped to eighth in the 1970s and 1980s.

The Swedish Model of Industrial Relations: Centralized 'Self-Regulation'

The Swedish variant of the 'Nordic Model' of industrial relations was long distinguished by remarkably limited state regulation. This changed in the 1970s with an expansion of labour legislation, while in the 1980s the frequency of government intervention in collective bargaining accelerated. As a result, Swedish industrial relations have become more similar to those of other Nordic countries.

The relatively passive stance of the Swedish state reflects historical factors such as the relatively non-repressive character of the state in the early years of the union movement; the deep disunity of the bourgeois parties, vitiating several attempts at legislation; and the prominent role of employer and union confederations, paving the way for self-regulation as an alternative to state regulation (for different views with regard to the first point, see Fulcher 1988: 254; Sisson 1987: 157).

The fundamental compromises of 1905–6 represent an early institutionalization or self regulation of industrial relations, more than three decades before the 1938 Saltsjöbaden Agreement between LO and SAF (the Swedish Employers' Confederation). The 1905 engineering agreement and the 1906 LO–SAF December Compromise came about after massive trials of strength in which the employers failed to defeat the unions. SAF, and particularly VF (the Engineering Employers' Association), were already centralized. From the beginning, SAF alone rather than individual employers or affiliated associations had the power to decide on lockouts and the use of lockout funds. From 1905 collective contracts had to be approved by SAF's executive committee.

Centralization of Swedish employers was not so much a reflection (as Ingham 1974 suggests) of Sweden's highly concentrated and export-oriented industrial structure, as a response to the threat from a unified, socialist labour movement organizing unskilled as well as skilled workers (Fulcher 1988; Jackson and Sisson 1976; Kjellberg 1983). The character and strength of the Swedish labour movement are best understood as stemming from the timing of industrialization (late and rapid) relative to the rise of socialism (the SAP was founded in 1889) and universal suffrage (which was not conceded until after the First World War) (Kjellberg 1983: 167–9, 211–17; Fulcher 1988: 263–71; Therborn 1983). Until the establishment of LO in 1898, the social-democratic party fulfilled the double role of union confederation and party.

The formation of VF and SAF was triggered by the 1902 general strike as part of the campaign for universal suffrage. In addition to the unified character of the Swedish labour movement, manifested in the close cooperation between LO and SAP, the employers faced the strong workplace presence of such powerful national unions as the Metalworkers (Metall). The employers thus had to deal with a union movement active in both the industrial and political arenas, and at both national and workplace levels.

The emergence of centralized employer organizations and the SAF/ VF strategy in the period 1902–9 of escalating conflicts into large lock-outs reversed the advantage of the unions at workplace level, forcing the union movement to centralize in turn and to grant increased powers to LO. This process was interrupted by the defeat of the unions in the great strike and lockout of 1909, but eventually led to the conclusion of the basic agreement of 1938 (the 'Saltsjöbaden Agreement'), and to the introduction of centralized bargaining in the 1950s (cf. Fulcher 1988: 249–51).

Labour law did not play a significant role until the end of the 1920s. In 1928, legislation on labour courts and collective contracts imposed a peace obligation during the currency of collective agreements. However, subsequent developments discouraged the further extension of labour law: LO and SAF preferred self-regulation through the basic agreement to the state regulation of industrial relations threatened by the social-democratic government if employers and unions failed to reach agreement. An obvious advantage of self-regulation was that it gave employers and unions some freedom of manoeuvre. The unions could retain a function in the eyes of their members, while employers avoided regulation of industrial relations by a social-democratic government; and the government believed that union members were more likely to accept labour peace and pay restraint if the unions preserved a degree of autonomy.

Cooperation was facilitated by another common goal, economic recovery and expansion. One aspect of this was the perceived need for the 'labour market parties' to foster 'labour peace': Sweden had experienced very high, albeit declining, levels of industrial conflict by international standards (cf. Shorter and Tilly 1974: ch. 12). This made centralized and disciplined peak organizations necessary and, in particular, the powers of LO over affiliated national unions had to be strengthened. An important step was taken in the new LO constitution of 1941, which can be regarded as a logical organizational complement to the 1938 Saltsjöbaden agreement.

Peaceful industrial relations were promoted by a relative balance of power between employers and unions during a decade of social-democratic governments and rapid union growth (Fulcher 1987; Korpi 1978: ch. 4; Therborn 1984: 589; Åmark 1986). With the prospect of protracted social-democratic rule the employers were less confident about their principal weapon, the massive lockout. The rise of social democracy to political power and the close link between the political and union wings of the labour movement also encouraged a cooperative strategy by the unions. In exchange for social reforms and improved material conditions, the unions declared themselves prepared to show 'social responsibility'.

Despite self-regulation, the state intervened informally in several aspects of Swedish industrial relations. As mentioned, negotiations on a basic agreement took place under government pressure. In 1933–4 the government acted resolutely to bring to an end a dispute in the building industry which threatened the recovery programme. The intimate links between the social-democratic party and the union movement provided a two-way channel of discussion and influence between government and LO. As a consequence of the 'historic compromise' the employers also came to use informal channels, influencing government policy by means of 'non-political' experts and through representation on government agencies and commissions, rather than attempting to support the bourgeois parties in parliament and mounting a political challenge to social democracy (Söderpalm 1980). During the Second World War (when Sweden was neutral) the professional know-how of business representatives allowed them to dominate the important economic commission. Confrontation in the industrial and state arenas thus gave way to cooperation and corporatism. The 'spirit of Saltsjöbaden' paved the way for a series of 'cooperation agreements' (on safety representatives, time-and-motion studies, works councils, etc.).

The Establishment of Centralized Bargaining between LO and SAF

Centralized bargaining was not established until the 1950s, but then functioned for almost three decades as a successful alternative to open government intervention. LO had an interest in centralization as a means of implementing a 'solidaristic wage policy', combining membership demands with 'social responsibility' and economic stability (Meidner 1974): according to the Rehn-Meidner model, elaborated by LO economists Gösta Rehn and Rudolf Meidner, the union movement would contribute to economic policy by promoting a 'rational' (solidaristic) wage structure that would avoid inflationary wage competition between different groups. However, despite LO's increased central powers, centrifugal forces within the union movement were too strong to permit LO to take the initiative on centralized bargaining.

Paradoxically it was the employers' own lack of internal cohesion that led them to play this role: centralization was aimed at overcoming the lack of discipline and coordination between the individual SAF associations, as well as between individual employers. Especially in years of expansion SAF had an interest in avoiding wage explosions as a result of 'scissoring', in which indulgent employers' associations concluded collective agreements at different points of time (de Geer 1986: 325, 327).

As a consequence of centralized bargaining, government regulation of wages was never on the agenda in the following decades; the solidaristic wage policy functioned as an extra-governmental form of incomes policy. However, the 'active labour market policy' managed by the Labour Market Board (AMS, created in 1948) played an important supplementary role. The encouragement of geographical and occupational mobility allowed expanding industries to take on workers from declining regions and industries. The solidaristic wage policy accelerated the structural transformation by forcing up wages in low-paid industries like textiles, while the automobile industry and other export industries benefited from relatively low wage increases. The combination of active labour market policy and economic expansion made possible 'full employment', another prominent goal of the Swedish labour movement.

Full employment and solidaristic collective bargaining legitimized LO policy in the eyes of union members. At the end of the 1960s, however, dissatisfaction was mounting among workers hit by the rapid structural transformation of industry. Employers often failed to inform, let alone consult, union representatives before taking decisions on dismissals and plant closures. The basic agreement had confirmed employer prerogative, already conceded in the 1905–6 compromises, on matters concerning production; this state of affairs was now called in question.

Historic Compromise or Corporatist Integration?

Among sociologists and political scientists there have been two main theoretical approaches to the development of Swedish industrial relations since the 1930s (cf. Fulcher 1987). One, labelled 'labour movement theory' (e.g. Korpi 1978, 1983; Himmelstrand et al. 1981; Esping-Andersen 1985; and Stephens 1979) stresses the gains made by the labour movement, including improvements in social welfare; while the other – the 'corporatist' interpretation – emphasizes the integrative effects of corporatist deals and arrangements (e.g. Przeworski 1985 and Panitch 1981). Walter Korpi, a prominent advocate of the former view, considers the history of the Swedish labour movement as a successful example of the so-called three-stage road to reformist socialism, an idea common among Swedish social democrats in the interwar period (Korpi 1983: ch. 8). The first stage, *political* democracy, was achieved with the introduction of universal suffrage in the elections of 1921. The rise of social democracy to political power in the 1930s is a precondition of the second stage, a socially equitable distribution of welfare (*social* democracy). Following a long period of consolidation, indicated by the impressive growth of union density, *economic* democracy was put on the agenda; however, a more radical stance was required before this third 'step' on the road to socialism could be achieved.

In practice, the growing internal contradictions of the Swedish model in the 1960s appear to be the real cause of change, rather than the conscious implementation of a socialist strategy. The policy of economic growth and geographical mobility combined with managerial prerogative had a negative impact on employment security, and the working environment. Workers' discontent, manifested in wildcat strikes, stimulated a pronounced radicalization of the union movement; thus demands for economic democracy originated largely from the unions rather than from the social-democratic party. Indeed, the party was taken by surprise by the most radical demand, LO's 1975 proposal for wage-earner funds – that is union-administered investment funds made up of a proportion of corporate profits (Åsard 1978); these funds were seen as a way of protecting solidaristic wage policy by avoiding high wage claims in efficient, profitable industries (Martin 1985).

'Labour movement' theorists, who tend to consider the history of Swedish labour as a continuous progress towards socialist society, have problems in explaining discontinuities and contradictory elements in the 'model' and cannot account for the current political conjuncture in which the Swedish version of socialism has been almost completely removed from the agenda of the 1990s.

Some observers have seen corporatist arrangements as a mechanism for integrating the labour movement within capitalism. However, this interpretation seems misplaced. Corporatist representation is better understood as a mediating variable rather than the ultimate cause of capitalist integration. More significant influences are the development of power relations within the industrial and state arenas, the character of the labour movement and the strategy of employers. For example, the 1905 Metall-VF and 1906 LO-SAF compromises can hardly be explained by the corporatist integration of union leaders (although prominent union and employer representatives later became members of the National Welfare Board founded in 1912) (Rothstein 1988a).

The primary motive of the organizations concerned in corporatist arrangements was to increase their influence on government bodies, especially when the political climate was unfavourable – as in the case of SAF's adoption of a corporatist strategy in the 1930s, prompted by employers oriented to the domestic market against the opposition of exporters. Conversely, the employers might withdraw from such arrangements when power relations shifted in their favour: as in the early 1990s, when SAF saw the dismantling of the corporatist system of representation (see below) as a way of reducing union influence. Corporatist theories usually underestimate corporatism as a means of influence on the state, and neglect the significance of corporatist systems for employers (cf. Panitch 1981).

Both these aspects of corporatism are also relevant to unions. The Labour Market Board (AMS) is the first – and most notable – example of how the Swedish labour movement aspired to transform traditional state bureaucracies into vehicles for social reform (Rothstein 1986). The AMS is, however, exceptional in its composition (union representatives are in a majority), in its employment of many union activists, and in its ideological rather than bureaucratic methods of implementing decisions. The AMS was given an important and 'active' role in implementing the policy of 'full employment' and the 'solidaristic wage policy'. The Rehn-Meidner model saw the active labour market policy not only as a means of reducing unemployment but also of avoiding open state intervention in collective bargaining.

Despite extensive corporatist representation in Swedish government bodies – involving thousands of LO, TCO and (until their withdrawal in 1992) SAF representatives – the integrative effects upon unions should not be overestimated. Considerably greater importance has to be attached to the fact that for 44 years (1932–76), Sweden was ruled by social-democratic governments. It was government pressure (reinforced by the close relationship between LO and the social democrats), rather than corporatist arrangements, that promoted the policy of cooperation between LO and SAF manifested in the 1938 agreement. Furthermore, with the major exceptions of the AMS and the Board for Occupational Health and Safety, the Swedish model of industrial relations has been characterized by self-regulation, rather than by tripartite corporatist arrangements. State regulation did not make its entry on a massive scale until the 1970s, and then as a consequence of the radicalization of industrial relations.

From Self-Regulation to State Intervention

By the end of the 1960s, dissatisfaction among rank-and-file workers and employer resistance demonstrated the inadequacy of traditional means of solving problems through collective agreements (Kjellberg 1981). At the behest of the unions, and in the face of employer refusal to make concessions, the government implemented an extensive programme of labour legislation in the 1970s, including laws on job security (1974), union workplace representatives (1974) and co-determination (1976). The powers of safety representatives were strengthened in 1974, and the Work Environment Act 1978 updated the law on health and safety.

This development was a substantial departure from the Swedish model of cooperation, of 'agreement in preference to legislation'. Yet even the Co-determination Act in some ways respected historical continuity. As a framework law laying down procedures, it was to be put into effect through subsequent collective agreements. It reinforced negotiating rights in the event of major changes within enterprises, but beyond that it contained no substantive rules of co-determination. Hence the law was completely compatible with union desires to protect the traditional Swedish principle of autonomous industrial relations.

Another limitation of the new labour legislation was that it left the system of wage negotiations untouched. But by calling into question important parts of the 'historic compromise', it influenced the employers' bargaining strategy. The political cease-fire between LO and SAF, dating back to the Saltsjöbaden agreement, was at least temporarily broken, a development encouraged by the social democrats' loss of office after 44 years. SAF refused to conclude an agreement on co-determination until 1982 – five years after the law came into force. In addition SAF became deeply involved in political campaigns aimed at forestalling further union initiatives on labour legislation. As a result of the affiliation in the 1960s of employers' associations dominated by small firms, SAF's capacity for political and ideological mobilization increased considerably. Although the new militant leadership of SAF from 1976 was dominated by big firms, an important aspect of employer strategy was to prevent a revolt by small employers (Ehrenkrona 1991; cf. also Jerneck 1986: 166, 169). During the bourgeois governments of 1976–82 the labour movement was forced to retreat on wage-earner funds, not least as a result of the employers' successful campaign on the issue.

The labour legislation of the 1970s – and the plans to extend it further – thus transcended the boundaries of the basic compromise; in a more radicalized context, the policy of cooperation and the avoidance of state regulation simply did not work.

The Withdrawal of SAF from Corporatist Representation

From the mid-1980s, as the fissures in the Swedish model became more apparent, SAF increasingly called into question the corporatist system, although there was considerable hesitation especially by small employers and regional representatives who feared that the influence of employers would diminish. SAF failed, however, to convince LO and TCO (the white-collar union confederation) to dismantle corporatist arrangements, and at the beginning of 1992 it withdrew from almost all government bodies, at central as well as regional level. A notable exception was the Labour Court, on the grounds that it was a 'court' rather than a state agency. Subsequently, the bourgeois government announced plans to abolish corporatist representation.

The shift of the political climate to one more friendly to the employers has encouraged SAF to work for a profound 'change of system' by ideological and political means. Intense public campaigns have been used to spread the market ideology and to improve the electoral prospects of liberal and conservative parties. Withdrawal from government bodies has given SAF more freedom to pursue its aims, particularly since one of its targets is the state apparatus itself. SAF regards representation on government bodies as contributing to the legitimation of public sector expansion: while the confederation was attacking high taxes and advocating cuts in public expenditure, its representatives in the large welfare bureaucracies were consenting to levels of expenditure exceeding even those recommended by social-democratic governments! (Rothstein 1988b).

SAF's ideas on privatization and deregulation – which it sees as making representation on government bodies less important – have influenced not only the new bourgeois government but the former social-democratic administration as well: an indication of the effectiveness of SAF's strategy of influencing the ideological climate. This is manifested in the increasing pressures on the Post Office and other state-run organizations to 'professionalize' their boards by appointing people with business competence. Another example is the new 'Privatization Commission', made up exclusively of business representatives.

Another motive for ending corporatist arrangements has been to reduce the power of unions. In the discussion preceding SAF's final decision to withdraw from corporatist bodies, the Working Life Fund (financed by payroll taxes to support improvements in the working environment) was cited as an example of 'socialist economic planning under the guise of corporatism' (*SAF-tidningen* 26 and 38, 1990; 1, 1991); SAF argued that decisions over the allocation of such resources should be left to individual employers. The dismantling of the corporatist system is aimed at breaking economic and other bonds between unions and the state – as with the abolition of subsidies to unions (see below). The apparent success of the policy is shown in LO's decision to withdraw from most government bodies in 1992.

At the same time, growing internationalization and the increasing importance of the European Community make corporatist representation less urgent from the employers' point of view, by diminishing the significance of nation states especially in small countries dominated by large firms, like Sweden. Future Swedish membership of the EC will increase the importance of European bodies for Swedish employers, while that of Swedish government agencies is likely to diminish.

The decline of corporatism has meant that other means of influence, such as political campaigns, lobbying, and participation in informal advisory groups and expert commissions (by business representatives rather than SAF officials), have achieved greater prominence. The increased emphasis on influencing governments directly, rather than operating through state agencies, is closely related to SAF's new 'political' strategy. Its central principle is to intervene at a relatively early stage of the decision-making process in order to influence the policy agenda and avoid becoming a 'hostage' to policies devised elsewhere; in short, to move from a defensive to an offensive posture.

The Transformation of Swedish Industrial Relations

The erosion of the principle of self-regulation through the growth of legislation in the 1970s was followed in the 1980s by the undermining of another traditional pillar of the 'historic compromise': the value placed on industrial peace. The 'great conflict' of 1980 shocked those who believed that massive strikes and lockouts were a thing of the past. The 1980 dispute can be seen as a logical consequence of long-term processes, above all the rapid growth of public sector and white-collar employment, leading to growing heterogeneity and a change in power relations in bargaining (see below). The conflict also expressed a change of approach by employers, with the adoption of the more militant line of action advocated by big transnational firms. A few years later the same group of industrialists led the way in decentralizing collective bargaining with the aim of abolishing centralized wage negotiations.

From the LO-SAF Axis to a Multitude of Bargainers

The 1970s were a decade of fundamental change for the bargaining parties. Already in the 1960s, the expansion of white-collar and public sector employment had generated powerful new union blocs threatening LO's monopoly. A number of bargaining 'cartels' of white-collar unions were founded whose strength was based on high white-collar union density and the extensive rights to strike granted to public sector workers in 1966. Bargaining cartels are federations of national unions performing common negotiating tasks. Their bargaining functions are thus similar to those of LO. They have their own governing bodies, congresses, officials, strike funds, etc.

By the mid-1960s the government and SAF were no longer able to deal with white-collar and public sector unions on a different basis from LO unions. Employers encouraged centralized bargaining analogous to that between LO and SAF. In the public sector, only bargaining cartels and union confederations were allowed to negotiate under the 1966 reforms that granted full bargaining rights to state and municipal workers. In the private sector, the efforts of SAF to coordinate the negotiations of LO and TCO unions were less successful. With the growing capacity of white-collar workers to take strike action (Faxén et al. 1988: 404), SAF's constitution was amended in 1963 to permit lockouts of white-collar workers.

Coordinated private sector bargaining was not achieved until 1977, although gradual centralization within the ranks of white-collar workers had started well before then. From 1957, SIF (the Swedish Union of Clerical and Technical Workers in Industry, representing most technicians and other white-collar workers in manufacturing and construction) negotiated directly with SAF about general wage increases. In 1973, SIF and a number of other white-collar unions (including SALF, the TCO supervisors' union, and HTF, representing employees in commerce) founded the cartel PTK to bargain with SAF. The next step in the centralization process was the establishment of coordinated bargaining between LO, PTK and SAF in 1977, with SAF the driving force (Elvander 1988a: 49; Martin 1985).

In the public sector a considerably more complex pattern emerged despite the strong centralizing ambitions of the government. The main union cartel in the state sector, TCO-S, was founded in 1967, almost immediately after the concession of full bargaining and strike rights to government workers. The LO state employees' cartel was transformed into a new union, SF (Swedish State Employees' Union), in 1970. In 1977 the rapidly growing Municipal Workers' Union (Kommunal) replaced Metall as the largest LO union (excluding pensioners) (see table 3.1). The bargaining cartels KTK and SACO-K were founded in 1976, covering municipal white-collar unions affiliated to TCO and SACO respectively.

Coordination between the many public sector bargaining cartels left a great deal to be desired. In contrast to the private sector, no organized

Table 3.1 Membership of important union blocs and bargaining cartels in Sweden

Year	Private sector LO[a]	PTK	State sector SF	TCO-S[b]	Municipal sector Kommunal	KTK[b]
1970	1,149,308	-	145,305	175,926	231,247	-
1975	1,232,681	422,796	149,049	236,975	339,947	183,000[c]
1980	1,153,947	495,107	157,068	265,360	514,515	237,306
1985	1,184,967	516,432	160,341	266,414	632,941	297,719
1990	1,155,795	555,020	149,698	250,536	636,671	325,059

[a] Only private sector unions affiliated to LO, i.e. total membership except for Swedish Social Insurance Employees' and Insurance Agents' Union, SF, and Kommunal.
[b] 1 January 1991 reorganized and amalgamated into TCO-OF.
[c] 1976.
Source: A. Kjellberg (DUES project, Lund).

cooperation was established between TCO and SACO unions. The newly attained right to strike was used considerably more frequently, especially by white-collar workers, than the government had intended or anticipated: the majority of legal conflicts since 1966 have occurred in the public sector (Elvander 1988a: 39). A contributory factor is that white-collar unions within this sector do not embrace the ideology of cooperation with employers and the state. Within LO the balance of power has shifted in favour of public sector unions (Kommunal and SF).

Public sector unions and bargaining cartels gradually coordinated their actions (Martin 1985; Elvander 1988a). From 1970 to the early 1980s TCO-S and its LO counterpart, SF, jointly pursued a wage policy favouring low-paid workers. The high-water mark of union cooperation was reached in 1980 when for the first time LO and TCO public sector organizations (SF, Kommunal, TCO-S and KTK) coordinated wage negotiations. Together they comprised a substantial proportion of Swedish union members. Common action enabled them to seize the initiative and play a prominent role in the bargaining round, and they became known as the 'Gang of Four'. Their high wage demands led to the collapse of PTK's proposal for a 'social contract' combining low wage increases with reduced marginal taxes. LO, which had at first been prepared to accept low pay increases, was forced to adopt the high wage demands of the Gang of Four, provoking the 'great conflict' of 1980.

The Great Conflict of 1980 – At the Confluence of Centralizing and Decentralizing Forces

The great conflict of 1980 may be seen as the outcome of two contrary but parallel processes: centralization within the group of white-collar and public sector unions, and fragmentation of the union system into a few blocs relatively equal in strength: LO (manual workers, private sector), PTK (white-collar workers, private sector) and the 'Gang of Four' (LO and TCO public sector unions). Thus LO no longer occupied a dominant position. Instead a complicated pattern of alliances and conflicts between union blocs emerged. Likewise, in the employers' camp, while SAF continued to dominate the private sector, a number of parallel, and often badly coordinated, actors emerged. The growth of public employment increased the significance of SAV (the National Collective Bargaining Office), which represents the government as employer, and of the municipal employer organizations. In short, centralized bargaining between LO and SAF no longer occupied such a privileged position as in the 1950s and 1960s when the export sector was unchallenged as a wage leader. The large number of top actors resulted in considerably more complex negotiations.

In addition, the economic situation in 1980 was quite different from the earlier period of LO-SAF dominance. From 1976, real wages were falling. With inflation rising following the second oil price shock, political confrontation over wage-earners' funds, and a bourgeois government in power, SAF called for a pay freeze, and called a lockout of 750,000 LO members. The conflict accelerated the transition to decentralized industrial relations; indeed, it has been argued that SAF's lockout was intended to achieve such an outcome by provoking government intervention that would undermine the system of centralized negotiations (Martin 1985: 320–2).

The 1980 conflict also led to intensified tensions between union blocs, especially between public and private sector unions. It is remarkable that the bourgeois government did not assist the moderate bargaining approach of private sector unions (cf. Martin 1985: 318); by rejecting LO's calls for reduced taxation of low incomes it removed the incomes policy solution from the agenda. Disunity between LO (with its low-paid members) and PTK (with more highly paid members) on the question of income differentials prevented the two organizations from reaching a common negotiating position. Consequently, the LO-PTK cooperation established in the 1970s collapsed.

Disputes over Union Wage Policy – An Obstacle to Common Action

The 1970s and 1980s were decades of growing disunity between unions. LO's concept of solidaristic wage policy had already been modified in the 1960s to denote a general levelling of wages, rather than 'equal pay for the same job', and the new policy was successfully pursued from the mid-1960s through large increases in minimum wages (Jonsson and Siven 1986: 12). 'Compensation clauses' were introduced for LO groups less favoured by wage drift; subsequently, special low-wage elements began to be distributed among low-paid workers. As a result, wage dispersion with respect to industries, workplaces and individuals within workplaces declined. Equalization between industries ceased about 1980, but total wage dispersion continued to decrease for some years.

Table 3.2 Bargaining cartels and union blocs by sector and category

Category/sector	private sector	public sector
manual	LO (private sector unions)	SF (LO), Kommunal (LO)
white-collar	PTK (TCO/SACO)	TCO-S, KTK (TCO) SACO-S, SACO-K

LO's 1971 congress proclaimed that equalization of wages should be extended to the whole labour market (Elvander 1988a: 35–6). This presupposed that the white-collar unions would adopt a version of solidaristic wage policy. While these unions were, with the exception of SACO unions, influenced by solidaristic norms, they applied them only *within* their ranks and firmly opposed diminished wage differentials between white-collar and manual workers. The issue generated considerable tensions between LO and TCO/SACO unions. Upon this conflict was superimposed a further division between public and private sector unions and bargaining cartels.

One division over wage strategy concerned the treatment of wage drift, that is increases in earnings beyond those negotiated in collective agreements. In the mid-1970s, a number of technical devices were introduced to compensate white-collar and public sector workers for the fact that manual workers in manufacturing had greater opportunities to benefit from wage drift. The introduction of such clauses worked against LO's aspirations to decrease pay differentials between manual and white-collar workers. Since 1970 pay relationships between the main blocs – LO, PTK and the public sector – have been characterized by periodic swings of about 5 percentage points. On the whole, however, pay increases tended to develop in parallel (see table 3.3).

Intensifying Wage Competition and the Strengthening of Centrifugal Forces

The limited success in equalizing wages across union blocs caused increasing problems for LO in urging members to practise wage restraint and 'social responsibility'. With more militant groups demanding substantial wage increases, LO was forced in turn to revise its claims upwards. Thus solidaristic wage policy, based upon the privileged position of the LO-SAF axis, lost its role as an alternative to incomes policy. Accelerating pay competition between competing union blocs, combined with declining economic growth, resulted in a divergence between real and money wages, further sharpening conflicts between the blocs. After the wage explosion of the mid-1970s, real wages fell until the mid-1980s.[2] Increasing real wages since 1985 have meant that average hourly real wages after tax were about the same in 1990 as in

1980; however, real wages of households climbed 13 per cent in the 1980s owing to increased employment.

Another consequence of high nominal wage increases and inflation was to transfer the issue of income differentials from the industrial to the state arena. Conflicting interests of manual and white-collar unions were expressed in arguments about the reduction of marginal taxes (exceptionally high in Sweden). While the political parties, including the social democrats, were keen to attract the expanding number of white-collar voters through proposals for tax cuts, LO maintained its opposition to them.

The increasing proportion of workers in 'protected' industries – public and private – enabled them to challenge the traditional wage leadership of the competitive 'C-sector' under LO and SAF: as mentioned, the public sector took over the position of wage leader in the 1980 bargaining round. An explosive tension thus developed between the expanding weight of the protected sectors and the increasingly strategic role of the C-sector in the Swedish economy, manifested in conflict over the issue of wage leadership. The changed locus of union power, and the dimin-

Table 3.3 Contractual wage increases and wage drift in manufacturing industry, 1975–91

Year	Manual workers			White-collar workers		
	(A)	(B)	(C)	(A)	(B)	(C)
1975	10.5	7.5	18.0	14.3	2.2	16.5
1976	7.9	5.4	13.3	11.2	2.5	13.7
1977	3.7	3.5	7.2	7.1	1.8	8.9
1978	4.8	3.2	8.0	5.6	2.2	7.8
1979	4.4	3.8	8.2	5.9	1.9	7.8
1980	6.1	3.2	9.3	6.3	2.4	8.7
1981	5.9	4.2	10.1	4.5	2.9	7.4
1982	4.1	3.5	7.6	3.5	2.9	6.4
1983	3.8	2.9	6.7	3.3	3.5	6.8
1984	6.2	4.1	10.3	3.7	5.8	9.5
1985	3.8	3.7	7.5	2.6	3.9	6.5
1986	3.9	3.5	7.4	4.3	3.3	7.6
1987	-	-	6.4	2.0	4.1	6.1
1988	3.4	5.0	8.4	2.3	4.8	7.1
1989	4.5	5.6	10.1	4.1	6.3	10.4
1990	2.8	6.7	9.5	3.0	6.4	9.4
1991	2.3	3.1	5.4	-	-	-

(A) = contractual wage increase
(B) = wage drift
(C) = (A) + (B) = total wage increase
Source: *December Report, Konjunkturinstitutet* 1991: 66; and *Preliminär nationalbudget* 1992: 47.

ishing ability of LO to implement a policy of wage restraint, also reduced the value of 'centralized' bargaining for the employers.

Paradoxically, the partial success of solidaristic wage policy contained the seeds of decentralization. Decreasing wage differentials within each of the main blocs of workers but unchanged relations between them caused a widening gap between skilled workers and lower-level white-collar workers (Jonsson and Siven 1986: 14). The largest private sector LO union, Metall, feared losing members to SIF as a result of the growing wage gap; a concern aggravated by new labour processes blurring the boundaries between manual and white-collar work in several workplaces. Indeed, since terms of employment are determined by union membership in Sweden, many skilled workers left Metall to join SIF to benefit from more favourable contracts. This was one reason for Metall to accept the engineering employers' (VF) initiative for decentralization.

Employers experienced the 'distortion' of wage relations as problems in recruiting skilled workers, leading VF, the dominant body within SAF, to break away from economy-wide negotiations in 1983. Centrifugal forces also took hold within the 'LO family', although LO itself continued resolutely to defend centralized bargaining and solidaristic wage policy.

Decentralization as an Employer Strategy in the 1980s and 1990s

Since the beginning of the 1980s, Swedish employers have increasingly challenged centralized bargaining. One motive has been concern over general labour costs. In the 1950s, macro-economic considerations had led the employers to force the unions to accept centralized bargaining. Three decades later, it was argued that central agreement functioned as a 'floor' for wage increases, rather than as a 'ceiling' (even though in practice wage drift had been a phenomenon of earlier years as well), and total wage costs were seen as a serious problem for Swedish industry in its attempts to remain competitive. Moreover, the triumph of 'solidaristic' norms at local level meant that measures intended to reward skilled workers and other special groups have often been applied across the board (Faxén et al. 1988: 221, 236), leading to additional wage drift and aggravating the problem of total labour costs.

A second motive has been the desire for greater flexibility at local level. Workplace negotiation in Sweden, as in other Scandinavian countries, has played a prominent role, but it has taken place within a framework established by centralized bargaining, allowing central principles and norms to be transmitted to local level, and imposing uniform and inflexible provisions across a wide variety of different local conditions (Albåge 1987). As noted above, the erosion of differentials made it difficult for companies to recruit and retain skilled labour, and diminished employers' ability to use pay as a management tool for promoting economic performance and productivity within the enterprise (Östman

1987). In 1984, the difference between the wages of the highest and lowest decile of manual workers in manufacturing was 34 per cent (though it had risen to 45 per cent by 1990), compared with as much as 210 per cent in Britain and 490 per cent in the USA (*Produktivitets-delegationen* 1991a: 197). This compression has taken place, according to SAF, at a time of divergence in skill and knowledge requirements of different kinds of work. Increasingly, therefore, employers have argued that pay systems should be adapted to the specific conditions of the workplace through decentralized wage determination, free from the constraints imposed by higher levels.

While pure piecework systems have continued their long decline, result-based pay systems – both collective and individual – have become increasingly popular since 1980. There has also been a change in the nature of 'fixed' payment systems. New schemes reflect the blurring of the distinction between white- and blue-collar work. Manual workers increasingly receive the same type of fixed pay as white-collar employees, that is differentiated with respect to tasks and individual performance.[3] This has paved the way for the introduction of so-called employee agreements at local level (see below).

The growth of new pay systems for manual workers is illustrated by a recent survey by Metall (1992). In 1991, 55 per cent of employees received some form of payment by results, usually comprising a basic fixed component, with a personal supplement and a bonus. Twenty-seven per cent received fixed pay, while only 17 per cent were on piecework (of which under a third were on 'pure' piecework schemes). In some sectors, unions have successfully resisted new pay systems: in construction, for example, half of union members were on traditional piecework, the others received fixed wages. There has also been an expansion of performance-related systems among white-collar workers. Rare before the 1980s, 'bonus systems' affected one in four SIF members in 1989 (Nilsson 1990: 17–23).

Companies have introduced profit-sharing and convertible debenture schemes as devices for increasing employee commitment, and for retaining staff in tight labour markets. At the end of the 1980s, about one in eight manual workers and one in five white-collar workers in the private sector were covered by profit-sharing; the figure was as high as 22 per cent for Metall members but only 15 per cent for SIF members (LO 1989a: 43–5, 77–80; Elvander 1991b). Convertible debenture schemes, first introduced in 1983, spread very rapidly in 1987–8. In the enterprises where such schemes exist, 40 per cent of manual workers and 70 per cent of white-collar workers hold shares. The unions are divided in their attitudes to these developments. LO and TCO are critical, arguing that the schemes undermine solidaristic wage principles and risk increasing the power of employers, while workplace unions – reflecting the attitudes of employees – are often more positive. However, individual pay components cause serious difficulties for workplace unions (Metall 1992: 47–8): there is much discussion of the fairness of such elements and of whether they are consistent with solidaristic pay policy. As a result, some workplace clubs (local union organizations – see below) do not participate in the implementation of personal pay supplements, and control over this important element of local pay determination rests completely with supervisors.

However, the path to the ultimate goal of completely decentralized pay determination has been far from smooth. Externally, employers have faced resistance from union confederations, and the policy of social-democratic governments of 1982–91 aimed at preserving or even strengthening centralization. Internally, they have been undecided over objectives. The collective employer interest in wage restraint, implying a degree of central coordination of pay determination, appears to be incompatible with a full-blooded decentralization strategy, at least in countries like Sweden with high union density and low unemployment (Elvander 1988a; 1988b: 5). As a result, they have followed a 'zigzag' path towards decentralization, tacking between different priorities. Uncertainties and divisions over strategy also reflect the different interests among employers: notably, those competing in international markets, led by VF, and those in sectors oriented to the domestic market, for example distribution, hotels and restaurants. VF's insistence on the right to conduct pay bargaining autonomously – and to establish its own strike and lockout fund – reflected the dominance of large, export-oriented transnationals led by Volvo. These were particularly anxious to break with standardized pay determination in order to introduce wider skill differentials and local productivity-based increases. Some associations in SAF were more inclined to retain coordinated bargaining, at least in the form of central pay frameworks.

Despite the Metall-VF breakaway in 1983, the remainder of the private sector was still covered by centralized bargaining, and, at the insistence of LO, the compensation clause was retained. None the less, the 1983 agreement between LO and SAF, in contrast to its predecessors, did not contain detailed provisions circumscribing the scope of industry-level agreements (Elvander 1988a: 94). Another sign of the fragmentation of the centralized system was that SAF signed agreements of different duration with LO and with PTK, as a way of obstructing LO's proposal for coordinated bargaining between the three bodies (Elvander 1988a: 103–4; Faxén et al. 1988: 319). Finally, industry negotiations no longer took place under a peace obligation as in the 'era of centralization' from 1956 to 1982.

From 1984 onwards, Swedish bargaining rounds oscillated between centralization and decentralization (see table 3.4). Employer attitudes remained ambivalent. Apart from VF, most associations favoured some coordination of bargaining as a means of controlling total wage costs, especially when decentralized negotiation failed to deliver moderate pay settlements, as in 1984. Thus they adopted a positive stance on central agreements in the 1986–7 pay round. The Volvo president Pehr Gyllenhammar – despite having previously been the principal advocate of decentralized bargaining – played a leading role, holding an informal meeting with the LO president and the finance minister that resulted in a top secret agreement and paved the way for two-year central framework agreements (Borgström and Haag 1988: 240–1). Centralization was partly seen as a way of incorporating white-collar wage drift within the centrally determined pay norm. Since wage drift above a specified level would be deducted from the following year's contractual increases, this was a way of damping total wage costs. (PTK's willingness to regulate wage drift centrally was motivated by the weakness of white-collar

Table 3.4   Collective Agreements, 1980–93

| | | | Sector | |
| | | | National | Local |
Duration	LO-SAF	PTK-SAF	Government	Government
One year 1980	x	x	x	x
Two years 1981/1982	x	x	x	x
One year 1983	xᵃ		x	x
Two and a half years 1983/1985		x		
Two years 1984/1985			x	x
Varying lengths 1984-10–27 months)ᵇ	(x)			
One year suppl. contract 1984/85		x		
Recommendation one year 1985ᶜ	(x)			
Half a year 1985		x		
Two years 1986/1987		x		
Recommendation two years 1986/87ᶜ	(x)			
Two years 1986/1987			x	x
One year 1988ᵇ	(x)	(x)		
One year 1988			x	
Two years 1988/1989				x
Two years 1989/1990	x	x	x	
One year 1990				x
Renegotiationsᵈ		x	x	x
One and three-quarters of a year 1991/93ᵉ	(x)	(x)	x	x

ᵃ Excl. Metall-VF.
ᵇ No central agreements, decentralized negotiations between industry-level unions and employers' associations.
ᶜ LO-SAF recommendations to industry-level unions/employers' associations.
ᵈ PUG (*prisutvecklingsgaranti*) price indexation clause 1990.
ᵉ 1 July 1991 – 31 March 1993 with variations between national unions within LO-SAF and PTK-SAF areas.
Source: *Konjunkturläget hösten 1991* (*Konjunkturinstitutet* 1991): table 17.

workplace organizations.) While central agreements circumscribed the use of pay as a tool of management – as for example with the favourable treatment of low-paid workers in the 1986–7 round – reduced local pay supplements could also be used to encourage local unions to accept profit-sharing, bonuses, and other alternative pay systems, despite the continuing hostility of the national unions; and indeed, the rapid introduction of new wage systems at the workplace represented a breakthrough in the employers' strategy of decentralization.

On the other hand, employers experienced central pay norms – as in 1985 or 1986–7 – as a constraint on their freedom of manoeuvre at local level, particularly in a period of tight labour markets. When central bargaining in its turn failed to contain wage costs – as in 1986–7 when wage drift in the LO-SAF bargaining area exceeded the pay norm by several percentage points – pressure would once more be exerted for a return to decentralization, particularly by the export-oriented employers. Thus in 1988, negotiations were completely decentralized as they had been in 1984. In 1989, the tensions within the employers were manifested in a split between VF, which wanted to continue to bargain alone, and the other associations, which preferred central negotiations as a way of containing accelerating wage costs. In practice, VF's two-year agreement for 1989–90 was very similar to those negotiated centrally by SAF on behalf of other employers' associations.

Thus the transition to a decentralized system of pay determination in the private sector is uneven and incomplete. Moreover, enterprise-based pay systems are likely to generate new tensions. Pay differentials between firms may be eroded by the strong tendency to follow wage leaders – employer imitation has been a major factor in wage drift (Faxén et al. 1988: 110–11, 199–202), facilitated by the high concentration of Swedish industry and the coordination of pay between companies and plants within conglomerates (Olsson 1991: 103). Thus considerations related to the profitability or productivity of an individual unit may yield to external factors. According to econometric analyses of wage drift, three-quarters of the yearly variation is attributable to macro-economic variables (number of vacancies and unemployment, prices, etc.) and is unconnected to industry- or enterprise-specific factors (Faxén et al. 1988: 234–7).

Developments were less ambiguous in the public sector, where employers responded to expenditure constraints with management reforms aimed at promoting efficiency and lowering costs, often by the adoption of techniques borrowed from the private sector. These pressures led employers to adjust pay more closely to labour market conditions (especially to facilitate the recruitment of senior officials and technical experts), and to take the initiative in individualizing pay determination (Elvander 1988a: 230–2; 312–16). In 1986, compensation clauses, which had been contained in almost all public sector agreements since 1975, were abolished. Moreover, structural reforms led to the break-up of the state sector into a number of sub-sectors with separate bargaining systems, weakening the cartels organizing public employees.

From Self-Regulation to State Regulation

Paradoxically, while the government as employer had taken significant steps towards decentralized bargaining in the 1980s, government political intervention became a further recentralizing force. Intervention was motivated, as in the formative period of the 'Swedish model', by a concern for economic stabilization.

The escalation of direct government intervention in collective bargaining in the 1980s has to be seen in the light of a broad set of developments undermining the foundations of the classical Swedish model. First, as has been seen, the appearance of powerful organizations of white-collar and public sector workers weakened the basis of LO-SAF cooperation and of the solidaristic wage policy which had functioned as an alternative to a government incomes policy. Wage competition between the blocs accelerated, and Swedish wages began rising faster than in other European countries in the early 1980s. The increasingly transnational character of large Swedish enterprises magnified the significance of even moderate wage increases and accordingly the pressure on the government to intervene. Another consequence of the end of LO-SAF domination was that the potential for multiple conflicts increased; another facet of the Swedish model, industrial peace, was therefore undermined, giving the government another motive for intervention in pay determination.

In the 1970s, the threat of a wage-price spiral in the wake of the first oil shock had prompted the government to call the 1974–5 'Haga talks' at which the unions were asked to accept pay restraint in exchange for reduced marginal tax rates (Martin 1985: 285, 290–3). When the social democrats returned to power following the bourgeois interregnum of 1976–82, they were determined to pursue the economic policy of the 'third way' and to reject the austerity policies that were causing very high unemployment in several countries. They also rejected traditional Keynesian demand management as increasingly inappropriate for an internationalized economy. The essence of the 'third way' was to promote investments by high profits and low nominal wage increases. The principle means of transferring resources from wages to profits was a 16 per cent devaluation in 1982. In this respect social-democratic policy followed that of the preceding bourgeois governments which had devalued the krona in 1977 and 1981. Supported by LO and subsequently also by TCO, this devaluation proved to be the only substantial success of social-democratic 'incomes policy' in the 1980s (Elvander 1990: 16). Private sector employers were prepared to concede large rises to highly paid white-collar workers, despite reduced marginal tax rates: this was the case in 1983, when the government had to introduce additional tax changes benefiting LO groups – the so-called 'LO rebate'; in addition, since 1983, union subscriptions have been tax-deductible. More generally, decentralization in any case muted the impact of pay norms. Further problems were caused by the government's lack of success in restraining the pay of its own employees: in 1984, public employers broke the proposed 6 per cent pay norm which public sector unions took as a floor rather than ceiling, an event that prompted the reorganization of the body responsible for representing the state in pay negotiations.

These difficulties led the government to promote the return of centralized bargaining through the 'Rosenbad talks' before the 1985 bargaining round. The aim of the talks was to get unions and employers to agree a 5 per cent pay norm for 1985; and although no formal accord was reached, none of the parties opposed the norm. In return, the government offered tax concessions favouring low-paid workers: the 'purest instance of a fiscal policy trade-off during the 1980s', according to Elvander (1990: 14). It also legislated on 'renewal funds' which were to be used for training and research. They were intended to encourage pay restraint in sectors or firms with high profits (Rehn and Viklund 1990: 309–10); similar techniques had been adopted in earlier years to prevent high profits from influencing wage drift (Martin 1987: 113–14). The introduction of a much diluted version of wage-earner funds at the end of 1983 and of special investment reserve funds in 1983 and 1984 also forced firms to reduce disposable profits. Subsequently LO-SAF and PTK-SAF negotiations led to agreements within the norm, although they were considerably less detailed and restrictive than earlier central contracts.

Government intervention in the 1985 pay negotiations marked the high point of 'negotiated incomes policy'. The integration of wage negotiations and political decision-making challenged the principle of self-regulation. LO feared that union authority in the eyes of members might be undermined if state intervention were required to ensure coordination of bargaining. In addition, there was a danger that national unions would appear superfluous in a situation where low nominal wage increases were combined with relatively high wage drift (Elvander 1988a: 181). In 1986–7, therefore, although centralized bargaining was restored, the parties agreed to return to the Swedish model of 'free collective bargaining', and government action was less pronounced.

Despite the failure of both decentralization (as in 1988) and centralization (as in 1989–90) to slow wage drift in these years of economic expansion, the government's role was relatively passive towards the end of the 1980s. At the beginning of the 1990s, however, the picture changed completely. Early in 1990 it became clear that price rises would exceed the rate of 4 per cent at which the unions' right to renegotiate the 1989–90 contracts was triggered. The government convened a meeting (the Haga talks) at which it called for a return to centralized bargaining and a restrictive two-year agreement. But VF, and SAF, refused. Instead, the SAF president proposed a two-year pay freeze, in return for employer acceptance of a price freeze and dividend ceiling (Feldt 1991: 456). The social democrats then prepared the most far-reaching intervention in the history of Swedish industrial relations. In concert with top leaders of LO and affiliated unions (except Kommunal), in February 1990 the government announced a two-year general pay freeze and strike ban, with increased fines for wildcat strikes, and ceilings on prices and dividends. The proposal, widely regarded as a violation of basic trade union rights, aroused a wave of protests from rank-and-file members and from many local union branches and workplace organizations. This forced union leaders to dissociate themselves from the initiative, leading the government to resign (though a new social-democratic government was formed).

The collapse of its proposal forced the government to look for more consensual methods to contain the wage-price spiral. A 'national mediation commission', the Rehnberg Commission, composed of a national mediator and one representative each from SAF, LO, TCO and SACO, was appointed in March 1990. Having failed to get the parties to agree to low pay increases for re-negotiations in 1990 and for the new 1991 agreements, the commission was given a new mandate in September 1990: to persuade parties to accept a two-year 'stabilization agreement' (1991–2) intended to cover the whole labour market. Most organizations approved the 'Rehnberg agreement' setting out the framework of industry bargaining. The provisions prohibiting local negotiations in 1991 and stipulating that any wage drift would be subtracted from 1992 increases were initially resisted by PTK unions SIF and HTF; the 1988 SIF strike had been over the question of union influence on local wage-setting. The unions were forced back to the negotiating table by SAF. The efforts of the PTK unions to encourage their workplace clubs to conclude local deals exceeding the Rehnberg terms were thwarted by strong employer discipline and the downward turn in the economy. In engineering, the Metall-VF agreement was delayed by the union's argument that local wage increases related to changes in work organization and improved productivity should not be considered as wage drift.

At first sight, SAF's role in encouraging the Rehnberg agreement was ironic in view of its fervent adherence to decentralized bargaining. In practice, the Rehnberg agreement could be seen as encouraging a form of 'super-decentralization' since by avoiding local negotiations, local pay determination would be a matter for individual employer prerogative, and hence become a more effective tool of human resource strategy. In the breadth of its coverage, however, the Rehnberg agreement represented a 'super-centralization' of bargaining: all unions except CF and the Transport Workers' Union (a rebellious LO union) concluded agreements within its terms. But this too was in SAF's favour, since pay competition was reduced and a non-fragmented bargaining model temporarily restored, removing a major SAF objection to central negotiations. Private and public employers formed a close alliance to support the agreement which they saw as a way of holding back the high nominal wage rises of the previous years' tight labour markets. The abrupt move from economic boom into recession means that the aims of the agreement are likely to be achieved.

The Rehnberg agreement represents a new type of centralized industrial relations in Sweden. First, centralization was restored under the auspices of the state. Second, the absence both of central negotiations between employer and union confederations and of workplace bargaining meant a departure from the combination of centralized and decentralized elements characteristic of the Swedish model. The unions' room for manoeuvre was reduced in two ways: their normal role at the peak level was exclusively assumed by the commission itself; and at workplace level employers were assigned a monopoly role in wage-setting. The three-tier system of bargaining was thus replaced by negotiations at a single level – between national unions and employer associations – circumscribed by the central framework stipulated by the Rehnberg Commission.

The initiatives of the Rehnberg Commission might be described as a mixture of the 'negotiated income policy' of the mid-1980s and the proposed coercive measures of 1990. Before the commission – itself tripartite – presented its final proposal, it sounded out the views of the unions and employers. But 'tripartite' interaction was backed up by threats of more far-reaching state intervention should the parties fail to comply with the commission's demands. Thus collective bargaining in the early 1990s assumed a more 'corporatist' form than ever before in Sweden. Corporatist concertation on the Rehnberg model could be regarded as an attempt to counter the tendencies to a more and more 'disorganized' or fragmented system of collective bargaining (cf. Lash 1985; Lash and Urry 1987). More properly, however, the commission represented an expansion of state regulation of collective bargaining, in response to the increasing breakdown of the old system of centralized self-regulation. But elements of self-regulation were retained: the implementation of the Rehnberg agreement was left to the parties themselves. In the background, LO and SAF played an important supporting role; the SAF by putting pressure on affiliated associations not to permit local agreements, in close cooperation with public employers and the government. As a result, the alternative – of compulsory legislation – was avoided.

Everything seems to indicate that the Rehnberg agreement will be a parenthesis in Swedish industrial relations. Bourgeois governments have traditionally failed to win the trust of the LO unions – the last bourgeois government was unable, for example, to forestall the 'great conflict' of 1980. The current government, headed by a conservative prime minister, is committed to liberating market forces. However, despite rapidly rising unemployment which has in some cases depressed wages even during existing contracts, the deep-rooted 'full employment' ideal in Sweden is likely to prevent the government from using unemployment as a major tool of pay stabilization; thus state financial support for the Labour Market Board has continued to increase.

It is uncertain whether the Rehnberg approach will be followed by some new form of coordinated negotiations or by decentralized bargaining. In marked contrast to the 1970s, the employers have seized the initiative for change in the 1990s. They have launched an offensive aimed at reducing the power of the unions. One telling manifestation is that SAF is reducing the amount of data that it compiles on wages, which will make wage comparisons more difficult. The employers also want to weaken the unions' capacity to strike and sap their economic resources. The employers' objectives have influenced the policy agenda of the bourgeois government. A series of measures have been taken or are planned: union dues will no longer be tax-deductible; subsidies to unemployment funds have been reduced; and union education has been hard-hit by the suspension of 'co-determination money', the huge subsidies provided to unions for education related to the Co-determination Act. Planned changes in labour law, many of them drawn from an SAF list of desiderata, will make the law more oriented towards the individual worker and will further reduce union influence, particularly in the area of industrial conflict. Proposed changes include the strengthening of provisions for compulsory mediation through the mediation institute and greatly increased fines for wildcat strikes; these demands are almost identical to proposals put forward by a commission appointed by the social-democratic government, but withdrawn after union protests on that occasion, on condition that the unions accept the Rehnberg agreement! A third SAF proposal is for pre-strike ballots of union members. Furthermore, the right to strike of public sector workers is increasingly being questioned (SOU 1991: 109). One possible government measure, the introduction of compulsory unemployment insurance, would break the traditional link between the unions and unemployment funds, thus removing one of the strongest incentives for union membership.

Increased state regulation of union affairs, together with decreased state subsidies, is likely to facilitate the success of the employers' decentralization strategy. The significance of workplace industrial relations will increase, and it is clear that union priorities will have to change and organization will have to be decentralized. In contrast to the 1930s, when the parties agreed to the Saltsjöbaden agreement in order to forestall state intervention, in the 1990s SAF appears to prefer state regulation to a new basic agreement. An indication of this is the employers' cancellation in 1991 of the central LO-SAF-PTK agreement on the working environment. At the same time, SAF is planning an organizational concentration at the level closest to the individual enterprises, the industry associations. By mergers the number of affiliated associations will be reduced from 35 to 9 to form a 'massive front' for supporting firms under the decentralized pay determination anticipated after the

Rehnberg interlude. Thus a new combination of centralization and decentralization seems likely, posing a serious challenge to the unions.

Swedish Unions Between Cooperation and Disunity

Inter-union Tensions in the 1980s and 1990s

The union movement has experienced serious tensions since the early 1980s. The rise of the public sector 'Gang of Four' symbolized the end of private sector hegemony, while the divisions among private sector unions were demonstrated by the collapse of the LO-PTK alliance after only three years. This reflected strains between manual and white-collar unions over 'compensation clauses': should white-collar workers be fully compensated for the wage drift of manual workers in manufacturing? SAF was able to play off LO and PTK against each other (Elvander 1988a). In 1981, following a strike and lockout of 250,000 PTK members, SAF achieved its objective – supported by LO – to cut compensation to 80 per cent. Two years later, however, SAF allied with PTK against LO on the issue of pay differentials.

A rapprochement between LO and PTK took place following the Rosenbad talks, and in 1986 there was coordinated bargaining between LO, PTK and SAF for the first time since 1978. Closer relations reflected PTK's attempts to strengthen its own internal cohesion by giving priority to low-paid members. But this did not suppress the conflict of interests between the PTK unions. Given the weakness of workplace union organization, it was market forces and employer preferences, rather than union pay equalization policies, that determined local pay increases of white-collar workers. This led SIF to demand greater union influence on pay determination at local level. But despite a three-week strike in 1988, followed by a lockout, SIF failed to achieve its demands. VF stood firm, and the other PTK unions supported VF's views on pay differentiation. For the first time since 1973, each PTK union (SALF, CF, HTF and SIF) negotiated separately with SAF (although there was a degree of coordination between SIF and Metall in negotiations with VF). With all the PTK unions advocating, from their different perspectives, extended negotiating rights at local level (including in the case of the service sector union, HTF, the local right to strike), PTK was facing dissolution as a bargaining organization.

Cleavages also began to appear within the public sector 'Gang of Four', particularly between the more militant TCO cartels TCO-S and KTK, and the LO unions SF and Kommunal. In 1983 the issue of compensation clauses split the Gang of Four – the LO unions choosing loyalty to their confederation and to the newly-returned social-democratic government, rather than their public sector allies. Isolated, TCO-S failed to sustain the existing compensation ratio.

Tensions recurred during the 1980s, interspersed with phases of enhanced public sector collaboration. At the time of the Rosenbad talks, for example, the loyalty of SF and Kommunal to LO and the government again proved stronger than their public sector identity, leaving TCO-S to fight a lone strike and lockout. However, the strains within LO between public and private were merely postponed. Conflict broke out in 1986, yet again over compensation clauses. The two public sector LO unions in vain demanded clauses guaranteeing that their members' pay would not lag behind the private sector, and Kommunal, with its many low-paid members, also resisted increased decentralization of public sector bargaining which favoured the two SACO cartels.

Decentralization, and the transfer of teachers from the state sector to local government, led TCO-S and KTK to merge at the beginning of 1991 into a coordinating body, TCO-OF, comprising six 'mini-cartels', each with bargaining and strike rights. Similar decentralization has occurred in SACO: the cartels SACO-S and SACO-K have been replaced by smaller cartels or 'sectors'. Many of TCO-OF's mini-cartels are dominated by a single national union. Moreover, dissatisfied unions have the right to negotiate on their own (both the police and the nurses' unions had threatened to leave their respective cartels in the mid-1980s). These changes aroused fears of public sector dominance among TCO's private sector unions, and conflicts have been further complicated by the blurring of borders between the public and private sectors as a result of the conversion of state trading authorities to corporate status. However, efforts are being made to overcome such problems; for example, a merger of SIF and the Civil Servants' Federation (ST) is in preparation.

Thus the 1980s may be characterized as a period of growing inter-union tension,both between public and private and between manual and white-collar unions. The high union density of the expanding occupational groups of white-collar and public sector workers means that a substantial shift in the balance of power has been occurring within the union movement. This shift has been all the more visible for the fact that manual and white-collar workers are organized in separate unions, cartels and confederations in Sweden. The conflicts between unions have been played out, as was seen above, through increasingly intense scrutiny of each other's pay movements and bargaining outcomes.

The Rise and Decline of Union Density

Swedish union density is among the highest in the world, having grown almost continuously since the mid-1920s (Kjellberg 1983; 1990). While white-collar density at first lagged behind manual, by the 1970s the gap had been eliminated. Also notable is the fact that the female unionization rate, until the 1980s significantly below the male rate, has now overtaken it. This is associated with the fact that most women are employed in the public sector, where density in the 1980s outstripped that in the private sector (see table 3.5).

In 1986, density reached a peak of some 86 per cent. Since then, however, the figure has fallen, to about 82 per cent in 1990. The decline affected both manual and white-collar workers, especially in the private sector. How may one explain this new phenomenon? One argument commonly used to explain cross-national trends in union membership is the structural transformation of the labour force, with the contraction of traditional union strongholds and the expansion of occupations, industries and regions with low union densities. The high overall union density in Sweden reduces the explanatory power of this argument. Union decline in Greater Stockholm, the region where this tendency is most pronounced, might partly be attributed to the rapid expansion of high-tech industries and private services. This, however, is to obscure the role played by other, more basic processes, for example the introduction of new management techniques.

It is more plausible to see falling union density as the result of a combination of economic, political and ideological circumstances. The extremely tight labour market, especially in Greater Stockholm, has considerably improved the position of workers as individuals *vis-à-vis* employers, who tended to outbid each other to offer favourable terms of employment. The tight labour market, the decentralization of wage determination and the expansion of individualized wages for manual workers meant that an increasing proportion of wage drift escaped union control. Furthermore, absolute as well as relative wage drift (the ratio of wage drift to contractual wage increases) reached very high levels at the end of the 1980s (see table 3.2). With exceptionally low unemployment – less than 2 per cent in 1987–9, only about 1 per cent in Greater Stockholm – few people feared losing their jobs. Under these circumstances unemployment benefit funds lost some of their value as an incentive for union membership. In contrast to Denmark, where unemployment benefits are also administered by the unions, there has been a rise in the number of workers who are members of a fund without

Table 3.5 Union density (% membership/employed workers) in Sweden, 1975–91

	1975	1980/81	1986/87	1990	1991
Manual workers					
Men	84	86	87	82	80
Women	67	80	87	81	81
Both sexes	77	83	87	82	81
Private sector	78	82	84	78	77
Public sector	76	86	92	87	87
White-collar workers					
Men	80	84	83	78	78
Women	78	84	85	83	83
Both sexes	79	84	84	80	80

Sources: LO 1989: part 5 (refers to ULF, i.e. surveys on living conditions, SCB; annual averages); AKU (Labour Force Surveys, SCB; first quarter of the year).

being members of the associated union, indicating a weakening of collective norms. However, the overwhelming majority of members of unemployment funds remain union members as well.

The decline in union density has occurred in an ideological and political climate increasingly unfavourable to the unions, notwithstanding the presence of a social-democratic government until 1991. The ideology of equality and solidarity has entered a state of crisis, called into question in practice even by its traditional supporters: the unions by their acceptance of increased wage dispersion, and the social-democratic party by tax reforms particularly favouring those with high incomes. The dramatic widening of divisions between rich and poor during the 1980s was accentuated by the social-democratic policy of the 'third way' which stressed the importance of high profits. Wage competition and inter-union conflict have promoted 'group egoism' at the expense of common action and solidaristic norms, and have weakened the unions' public standing. The increase in demarcation disputes between unions, encouraged by new labour processes and the increasing 'corporatization' of public agencies, has also undermined their public image (Nilsson and Sandberg 1988).

The dissolution of established norms has also been hastened by conflict between the two wings of the labour movement. At times the relationship between LO and the social-democratic government has been so strained that it has been referred to as the 'Wars of the Roses'. Both have lost ground among their potential supporters. In the September 1991 elections, the social democrats suffered their most severe defeat since 1928; the share of votes for the 'socialist bloc' was the lowest since the introduction of universal suffrage. Part of the explanation is the reduced space for a traditional social-democratic reform policy since the 1980s, as a result of lower economic growth and accelerated internationalization: in 1989, the social-democratic government abolished exchange controls, and in 1991 it linked the Swedish krona to the ecu and applied to join the European Community. Changes in the social structure (expansion of white-collar workers, increased social heterogeneity) have led to a reappraisal of the traditional principle of equality in social policy and the taxation system. Thus the long social-democratic hegemony in Sweden has broken down, hastened by the successful ideological offensives of SAF and the bourgeois parties.

In parallel, solidaristic wage policy has gradually lost ground to market forces and new management strategies, a development facilitated by the decentralization of bargaining from 1983. By 1989–90 wage dispersion was back to the levels of the mid-1970s, reversing the substantial wage compression up to 1982–3 (Hibbs 1991). Greater inequality of incomes after 1983 may be one cause of the fall in union density four years later: the weakening of the cement of solidaristic norms is likely to have enlarged the space for individualistic behaviour.

A third trend break – from declining to increasing real wages – took place in the mid-1980s. It might appear paradoxical that union density turned downwards as real wages began to rise. However, as mentioned above, the average hourly real wage (after tax) was about the same in 1990 as in 1980, implying a stagnation of real wages during the decade as a whole. Moreover, the unions' role in wage increases was constrained by repeated government interventions resulting in fixed limits on contractual wage increases, and by the rising proportion of wage drift, promoted by the same factors which explain the increased wage dispersion: market forces, decentralization of collective bargaining and new management strategies.

Workplace Organization

Tasks of Union Workplace Organizations

In Sweden, as in other Nordic countries but in contrast to Germany, the Netherlands and other continental countries, union workplace organizations rather than works councils are the dominant form of worker representation at workplace level. Works councils existed in Sweden from 1946 to 1977 (and in one or two places thereafter), but employee representatives were elected by the unions, and their tasks were limited to exchanging information and advice. They were products not of legislation but of an agreement between LO and SAF, reflecting the spirit of cooperation following the Saltsjöbaden agreement. In the radicalized climate of the 1960s and 1970s, they proved completely inadequate to channel workers' increasing demands. Following the MBL (Law of Co-determination, which was passed in 1976 and came into effect the following year), LO and TCO withdrew from agreements on works councils as a way of putting pressure on the employers to conclude co-determination agreements (which were finally achieved in 1982). The unions shocked the employers by also withdrawing from the Saltsjöbaden agreement, although the sections on bargaining procedure and third-party intervention were retained.

Since the end of the nineteenth century, union workplace organizations have played a significant role in Sweden, especially among manufacturing workers. Almost from the beginning, workplace 'clubs' were completely integrated into the national unions and their local branches. In the phase preceding national collective agreements, the strategy of national unions was to play off individual employers against one another. This necessitated close cooperation between different levels of the union under the firm leadership of national headquarters.

Following the establishment of industry-wide bargaining at the beginning of the twentieth century, union workplace organizations retained important negotiating tasks. National contracts had to be adjusted to local conditions. In addition, the widespread use of piecework required more or less continuous activity on the part of workplace organizations. Another prominent function was membership recruitment, although it was weakened by the replacement of dues collectors with check-off arrangements. In recent decades 'production' issues have been given higher priority, but 'distribution' issues still are of outstanding importance; both these areas are to an extent regulated by law.

The *distribution* functions of union workplace organizations include the negotiation of workplace contracts (on pay, working hours, etc.) within central and/or industry agreements. These negotiations take place under a peace obligation, but they are sometimes backed up by spontaneous wildcat strikes. Union representatives are prohibited by law from encouraging or participating in such action. In those, mainly small, workplaces without union clubs, negotiations are carried out by officials from the local union branch, which also assists union clubs where necessary. In addition, workplace organizations have the task of protecting members' interests in the operation of piecework systems, the introduction of new pay systems, profit-sharing arrangements, and so on. Finally, under the 1974 Law on Employment Security, they negotiate about redundancies. The *production* role (cf. Sandberg 1989) of union clubs covers the election of health and safety representatives and committees; dealing with issues affecting the working environment; influencing the design of work organization and new technology and participating in project groups, joint committees and company boards.

Workplace organizations also have competence in the settlement of conflicts over the interpretation and application of laws and agreements (so-called 'legal disputes' or disputes of right, in contrast to 'conflicts of interest'). According to the MBL law, the union interpretation of the provisions of agreements on co-determination, and on those concerning the individual's obligation to work, takes preference over that of the employer in the event of disagreement (Edlund et al. 1989). This right also applies in some other areas, although not in pay issues. 'Central negotiations' conducted by national unions and employer associations are sometimes required to solve legal disputes. Ultimately they are settled by the labour court.

A final set of functions concerns the representation of members in the workplace, handling individual grievances and problems. In large workplace clubs, 'representative assemblies' are organized for elected representatives, with smaller clubs, and sub-units of large clubs ('group organizations'), arranging their own meetings of union members. Clubs organize workplace study circles and courses on union matters, labour law, and such other topics as languages. Workplace union organizations are responsible for coordination and information exchange with local union branches, and for cooperation with other workplace unions; in large enterprises, cooperation may take place across plants.

Since the 1970s the tasks of union workplace organizations have grown in scope and complexity. This reflects the decentralization of collective bargaining from the 1980s and the expansion of labour legislation in the 1970s. The latter has meant that negotiations often take place within a more legally defined context set by 'framework' laws, as on co-determination. A third factor is the growth in union aspirations to influence production issues. A recent survey of committee members of LO clubs indicates that 75 per cent are willing to spend more time on production issues, such as working environment, work content and job satisfaction, as well as on training (LO 1989b: 52–3). According to a general survey of LO members, the average member still considers that the most important tasks are the traditional ones of pay, job security, and protection against loss of income in case of sickness and unemployment (LO 1989a: part 1, 47–50, 61–2, 78). There is one exception – working environment – which is given almost the same priority, but when it is defined more narrowly in terms of issues relating to the labour process, such as 'influence over one's own work' and 'development of job content', its importance drops sharply. Thus there is a certain divergence of view between members and activists on the weight to be given to production issues.

Union workplace organization is widespread (Molin 1991), and deals with an expanding number of issues of increasing complexity. This activity requires a large number of union representatives. In 1988 nearly one in eight LO members performed some task for their union, about the same proportion as ten years earlier. For the white-collar members of TCO and SACO unions, usually employed in smaller workplaces than manual workers, the proportion of union representatives was even higher, about 20 and 22 per cent respectively (LO 1989a: part 4, 17, 30, 92). About 85 per cent of all LO clubs either failed to elect a complete club committee, or had difficulty in doing so, possibly a reflection of the onerous and complex nature of such work which requires considerable knowledge of labour legislation (LO 1989b: 116–17). However, as many as one in five LO members (excluding those already elected) are prepared to be union representatives if asked (LO 1989a: part 4, 29). Thus there is a substantial, if poorly exploited, reservoir of potential union activists.

The facilities of union clubs tended to improve in the 1980s. Employer resistance to union activities during working time was at least partly overcome, as a result of the new labour legislation of the 1970s (especially the 1974 Law on Shop Stewards) as well as subsequent agreements. A quarter of LO clubs hold all membership meetings during working time; in manufacturing industry the figure is as high as 40 per cent.

The availability of paid time off may contribute to the relatively high level of attendance at meetings, but may also conceal a lack of membership interest in union matters. An indication of increasing passivity is the declining participation in study circles arranged by unions. Calculations for LO show that one in seven LO members attended such circles in 1980–1, fewer than one in ten in 1988–9. Survey findings also reveal declining membership confidence in unions among manual as well as white-collar workers. Between 1980 and 1990 the proportion of members who were 'fairly' or 'very confident' in trade unions in general fell by about 10 percentage points (LO 1991b: 279). Despite the extensive network of union workplace organization, most Swedish workers see little scope for influencing the actions of the local union, a further expression of the cleavage between members and unions. A smaller but still significant proportion doubt the union's ability to influence workplace conditions (Petersson et al. 1989: 124–5): a reflection, no doubt, of the continued supremacy of employers only partially reduced by the legislation on co-determination.

Unions in the Workplace: Stagnating Influence or the Extension of Co-determination?

The first half of the 1970s, when the unions were on the offensive, saw the introduction of a body of labour legislation aimed at improving the position of labour at the expense of capital. Great hopes were invested in the 1976 MBL as a means of increasing the influence of union workplace organizations. The law recommended that employers and unions conclude agreements on 'co-determination' – on terms of employment, organizational and technical change, and so on; and it required employers to negotiate (a requirement enforceable through the labour court by largely symbolic fines) before coming to final decisions on major changes in operations, working conditions or terms of employment affecting union members. Unions were also entitled to negotiate on other issues of relevance to their members, and their right to information was reinforced.

The law contains a built-in contradiction between the legal *requirements* on employers to negotiate – reflecting the employers' resistance to negotiations on co-determination, and the *recommendation* to regulate co-determination by agreements. Although unions have a right to participate in the decision-making process, the employers are free to act as they think best provided that they have first informed the unions and given them an opportunity to present their views. Thus the unions faced the obvious risk that employers would refuse to negotiate seriously, creating the impression of powerless unions. Critics have called the MBL law a 'hooter': once the employers have hooted they have fulfilled their obligations.

Thus the impact of the law depended on the attitudes of the employers, and ultimately on power relations in society. While central co-determination agreements were concluded fairly quickly in the public sector (MBA-S 1978, for government workers; MBA-KL 1980, for municipal workers), the negative stance of private sector employers delayed agreement until 1982. The private employers were encouraged in their resistance by the presence of a bourgeois government for the first time in 44 years. The social democrats' removal from office meant that government intervention could not be used to put pressure on the employers (Simonson 1989: 136–7), and the new political and ideological climate allowed the militant new leadership of SAF to influence public opinion. The struggle against wage-earner funds played a significant role in this, knitting together the bourgeois camp around an issue of high symbolic value. The labour movement was forced on the defensive, partly because TCO divisions on wage-earner funds prevented a common front with LO.

The profound shift in the political and ideological climate was clearly reflected in the 1982 'Development Agreement' on co-determination (UVA), concluded between SAF and LO/PTK after six years of negotiations (Schiller 1988a: 101–25). The UVA represented a victory for the employers and the maintenance of the status quo (Schiller 1988b; 1988a: 118). The agreement stressed the common endeavour to improve the efficiency, profitability and competitiveness of enterprises, rather than specific rights of co-determination. Thus the unions were obliged to abandon their radical positions of the 1970s and return to the earlier policy of cooperation.

The UVA nevertheless implied some change of approach on the part of employers. At the political level, employers faced the prospect of a new social-democratic government; they also perceived a need to involve union workplace organizations in efforts to raise productivity and win back market shares lost by Swedish export industry. Another motive was to avoid the bureaucratization of decision-making caused by the MBL; an agreement was expected to facilitate smoother and more flexible arrangements. Finally, a number of labour court judgments on the implementation of the MBL had gone in the unions' favour.

The UVA emphasizes the common interest of employers and unions in realizing the potential of the individual worker and in changing work organization in order to increase productivity and pave the way for more stimulating jobs. As in the 1946 agreement on works councils and other earlier cooperation agreements, the economic performance of enterprises is given top priority; co-determination is seen as a means of attaining this goal, rather than a value in itself (Simonson 1989: 181). A section on the 'Development of the Enterprise' lays down information and co-determination procedures in the areas of work organization, technical development and the economic situation of enterprises. The area originally given highest priority by the LO and the PTK, personnel administration (that is issues of manpower planning, recruitment, employment, induction and training), is excluded (Simonson 1989: 152, 179–80, 185; Schiller 1988: 117–18). A wide array of forms of co-determination, through negotiations at different levels and through participation in joint bodies and projects, allows considerably more flexibility and adjustment to local conditions than the procedures established by the MBL law. Employer objectives of decentralized decision-making – and co-determination – are given due weight in the UVA. One example is the introduction of 'workplace representatives' within small enterprises (appointed by unions at workplaces without union organizations), reducing the need for MBL negotiations with local union branches.

The approach of the UVA was largely based on ideas on flexibility and decentralization originally drawn up by SAF's technical department in the mid-1970s. SAF had discussed devolution of decision-making to first-line supervisors and lower management as a way of forcing unions to decentralize their own activity within companies (Schiller 1988b). Improved contacts between workers and supervisors would reinforce the development of cooperative relationships within sub-units of plants. These ideas were followed up by experiments aimed at increasing the job satisfaction of the individual worker, and by the spread of systems of devolved management with relatively independent operating units coordinated by sophisticated central financial control systems.

For the unions, decentralization of decision-making and co-determination under the UVA brought the risk of fragmentation, and even the appearance of alternative forms of organization. From the unions' perspective, the UVA could be seen as an instrument for adapting the co-determination system to the employers' strategies of decentralization, while maximizing union influence on the process. The agreement acknowledges the right of unions to participate in the planning of work organization, with the aim of enriching and enlarging the jobs of individual workers, and in improving the work environment; in addition, workers 'should be given opportunities to participate in planning their own work'. According to Schiller (1988b) the unions were successful in maintaining their traditional position as representatives of the work force and the agents of co-determination.

None the less, the UVA appears potentially to open the way to a degree of dualism between unions and individual workers or groups of workers (cf. Hart and Hörte 1989: 66). Such dualism may also be the consequence of the new employer strategies of decentralization. Brulin (1989) argues that one management aim is to establish direct relationships with employees as a way of winning their loyalty and weakening the position of unions within the enterprise. Companies have used ideological as well as organizational means: for example, the creation of a corporate culture to increase workers' commitment to local managements, and the restructuring of organizational hierarchies into relatively autonomous units and work groups. Such developments might challenge the position of unions built on solidarity between workers across plant and enterprise borders, and the enterprise would then become a 'political arena' of struggle over the loyalties of workers. However, only one of Brulin's three case studies appears fully to support his thesis.

The concept of political arena is also suggestive of the potential conflict between the direct influence of workers on management, and their indirect influence, through the union. However, these two forms of influence do not necessarily conflict. Svensson (1984), in a case study of the single-establishment engineering company Almex, demonstrates a close interaction between influence through the representative union workplace organization, autonomous work groups and individual self-determination. The Almex case is special in that the initiative for democratization came from 'within' and 'below', from the workers themselves. Once the union workplace organization had been democratized, there was an upsurge in membership activity and the development of a multi-level union strategy to increase worker influence in the plant through high-level union co-determination, 'direct' influence via production groups, and the freedom of individual workers to plan their own work.

The Almex case illustrates how direct and indirect forms of influence may reinforce each other in the presence of an active union workplace organization; with a less active union, a dual structure may arise, undermining workers' support for the union. However, apart from some high-technology and service companies, the aim of new management strategies in Sweden – in contrast to the USA – has not been to create union-free enterprises but rather to encourage the union's loyalty to the individual enterprise: a local form of corporatism (Brulin 1989: 63). To the extent that these efforts are successful, they will erode the strong solidaristic element in Swedish unionism. The combined centralization and decentralization of the union system would be replaced by a far-reaching fragmentation, especially if wage negotiations are concentrated at enterprise and workplace level. Fears about the emergence of a multitude of disparate models at local level led the unions to postpone negotiation on local co-determination agreements until a central settlement had been reached. At the beginning of the 1980s, however, local developments were slipping away from LO control (Simonson 1989: 179). The UVA may thus be seen as a reflection of union efforts to secure as much uniformity of rules as possible in the circumstances.

None the less, central uniformity did not prevent a considerable diversity of arrangements at enterprise and workplace level. While the employers' aspirations for decentralized industrial relations have been one driving force of change, workplace unions have also at times been the promoters of new forms of work organization, improvements in the working environment, and other changes. There are, however, considerable differences between workplaces in the extent of union activity, particularly with respect to co-determination issues. The cases studies reported by Brulin (1989) suggest that in some case unions have acted to contain the erosion of worker solidarity as a result of the organizational initiatives of employers; in others, their aim has been to modernize workplaces (in order, for example, to secure jobs, improve the working environment); in still others, they have remained passive in the face of changes initiated by employers (probably these are not experienced as a threat to solidarity).

The heterogeneous pattern of co-determination may also reflect the slow growth of local agreements. In state and municipal sectors detailed central agreements on co-determination have restrained activities at local level, but even in manufacturing relatively few local agreements have been signed despite the flexible character of the central UVA; most have been in large workplaces with strong unions (Edlund et al. 1989). Instead informal arrangements are widespread, in accordance with the preferences of many employers. In many cases, both parties prefer informal solutions, as these may go beyond the scope of the UVA.

Edlund et al. (1989) argue that all bipartite arrangements, rather than just formal agreements, should be included in assessments of co-determination. On this basis they conclude that 'there has been a genuine shift in favour of more bipartite decision-making' at workplace level (p. 30).

However, these conclusions are based on only two case studies – the Swedish Post Office Administration and the Volvo plant in Olofström. In the former, co-determination is extensively formalized, with a concentration on form rather than content. In the second half of the 1980s decentralization took place within the Post Office. A large number of joint committees and expert groups on issues such as work organization resulted in the involvement of workers at an earlier stage in the decision-making process; however, regular negotiations continue to dominate employer-worker relations. On the negative side, the employer's 'de facto dominance is retained or accentuated' (Edlund et al. 1989: 48) by reorganization, as modern information technology increased the centre's control over financial and personnel management. At the same time, the transfer of co-determination activities from the centre to the periphery of the Post Office has fragmented the union perspective on change.

In contrast, co-determination at Volvo Olofström takes place largely through joint bodies rather than through traditional negotiations. This reflects the decentralized and flexible character of the UVA, compared with the state sector agreement, the MBA-S, which emphasizes the role of negotiations between local union and management. At Volvo there are a number of 'partnership and co-determination groups' parallel to the lower levels of line management, but management considers them too slow for communicating important information to subordinates. Information is therefore increasingly given directly to the workers. Thus line management is taking over the functions of co-determination groups, and direct participation of workers tends to replace union participation at this level. As a result, the decisive contact between management and unions has shifted to the top co-determination body in the plant. Another source of discrepancy between enterprise and unions concerns the existence of a multitude of unions at the plant: while Metall alone organizes manual workers, there are three white-collar unions (SIF, SALF and CF). Management would prefer a single union, particularly since inter-union boundaries are increasingly out of alignment with work organization.

The partial transition to the 'direct democracy' model at Volvo Olofström seems to contradict – or at least reduce the significance of – the conclusion of Edlund et al. that the long-term effect of the legislative reforms of the 1970s has been to expand bipartite decision-making at workplace level. They admit (1989: 67) that the initiative 'has for the time being passed to the employers, as regards both the transformation of production and work organisation and the machinery of co-determination'. The UVA may be seen as marking this shift away from the unions who were the driving force behind the introduction of the MBL law.

Surveys of the development of co-determination fill in the picture. The study by Hart and Hörte (1989) deals with 'the stagnation of co-determination' in 1978–85, while the empirical data used by Levinson (1991) stems from 1982–3. The first, based on surveys in 1978, 1980 and 1985, indicates a trend break about 1982, the year the UVA was concluded. A period in which co-determination became 'established' (1977–82) was followed by a 'phase of stagnation' from about 1982 through to the end of the period of study. Co-determination in the form of negotiation expanded rapidly in the early years of the MBL law (1978–80), but subsequently diminished somewhat in scope. The average number of co-determination negotiations per workplace union was 11 in 1978, 22 in 1980 and 19 in 1985. In contrast, the average number of negotiation *issues* declined over the period, partly as a result of the improved labour market situation. The scope of information given to the unions by employers decreased between 1978 and 1980; in the public ïctor this development continued after 1980.

In the 'phase of stagnation', the employers changed their strategy towards co-determination: the duties of negotiation and information were increasingly performed through 'integrated' arrangements, that is by joint negotiating committees established by management in coopera-tion with unions – for budgets and finance, personnel administration, rehabilitation of employees injured at the workplace, etc.; and by union representation on company boards and other management bodies. Un-ions also participated increasingly in project groups, possibly a manifestation of the employers' aspirations to increased flexibility ex-pressed in the 1982 UVA agreement.

The early years of the MBL law, indeed of the 1970s as a whole, meant a departure from the strong Swedish tradition of cooperation between unions and management at central level. The surveys demonstrate, however, a remarkable continuity of cooperative relations at the workplace. Despite the intention of the unions nationally to abolish the system of joint committees, which were seen as an outgrowth of works councils, committees in private-sector firms largely survived the intro-duction of the MBL; some works councils also continued to hold meetings. However, there was a fall in the proportion of joint bodies with deci-sion-making powers, particularly health and safety and personnel administration committees. These results suggest that the MBL reform did not fundamentally change the established system of co-determina-tion. Neither did the UVA agreement introduce a completely new model. More or less formal agreements on co-determination existed before the UVA and even before the 1976 MBL in many workplaces, although a sharp increase occurred 1980–5, especially in the public sector.

The system of co-determination has become more complex as a result of the growing number of decision-making organs. This has widened the scope for local union participation and influence, but at the same time has made additional demands on union resources, by requiring more union representatives and increased union coordination and monitoring. The growth of 'integrated' and decentralized forms of co-determination from the 'phase of stagnation' may have strengthened union workplace activities, but may also have led to increasingly heterogeneous union policies across workplaces. There is a risk that the growing involvement of unions in company decision-making processes will weaken their effectiveness as interest organizations in the eyes of their members.

The complexity of co-determination is emphasized by Levinson (1991). Management and unions in a large number of parent companies and their subsidiaries were asked about the role of unions in 'strategic changes' at company and local level. Somewhat surprisingly, there was fairly frequent cooperation between unions representing different subsidiaries or plants within big companies (38 per cent of both manual and white-collar unions); the proportion was much higher in companies with at least 500 employees. This indicates the creation of a new form of union structure based upon union workplace organizations. Unions appear to be more active in strategic decisions at central (corporate group) level than at local level. Union influence at central level is exercised predominantly through board representation, followed by informal contacts for LO unions and joint bodies for TCO unions. At local level negotiations are considered most important, followed by board representation. Finally, union influence is larger in big companies than in small ones. Taken together these results demonstrate a complex pattern of co-determination, most actively exerted at the central level of big companies (at least with respect to 'strategic changes'). The 1976 law giving rights of board representation to union representatives appears to play a significant role in this context.

Levinson's study confirms the findings of Hart and Hörte on the variety of co-determination methods, according to the level of decision. The survey by Levinson also demonstrates considerable variation in union activity and methods according to the different phases of the decision-making process: initiation, preparation or development, decision-taking, and implementation. Unions are not very active in the first two phases, although they often participate. At none of the parent companies or their subsidiaries investigated did unions initiate the change. Nor did they often take the initiative in preparing decisions: only in one in ten cases did unions prepare decisions or present alternative courses of action. Union participation and influence were at their peak in the phase of formal decision-taking, but by then management was often already committed. In this phase negotiation was the most common method used. LO and TCO unions tended to agree that their limited influence was at its greatest in stages three and – to a slightly lesser extent – four of the process, and their perceptions were roughly shared by management. There was also a consensus that the degree of union influence was modest: at its peak on decisions to do with the working environment (at both parent-company and local level), followed in descending order of importance by the introduction of new technology, major investments and the appointment of managers.

About 90 per cent of managers believed that union influence – exerted principally through their advisory functions – was neither too large nor too small. Seven out of ten managers saw union participation as facilitating work-force reductions. By contrast, about half LO union representatives, and 40 per cent of TCO activists, wished to increase union influence, especially on the relocation of business.

Levinson's conclusion is that 'co-determination has not led to any dramatic changes of power relations' (1991: 149). The unions' weak point appears to be their passivity in the early phases of decision-making. If they are to increase their influence, unions will have to be better prepared and able to put forward alternatives; this presupposes a deeper knowledge of the company and of the economic conditions under which it operates than is generally the case, although other studies have shown that unions are sometimes able to develop such knowledge (cf. Sandberg 1984).

The Transformation of Work Organization

Swedish employers have had several motives to change work organization. First, in a small export-oriented economy highly exposed to international competition, employers are under increased pressure to achieve flexibility and reduce costs. Second, extremely low unemployment – the principal objective of social welfare policy since the 1930s – has meant recruitment and retention difficulties and added to pressures on labour costs. Third, the highly developed welfare system has led to serious problems of sickness absence.

Berggren (1990: chs. 18–19) emphasizes such social and labour market factors as important agents of change in his study of the Swedish car industry (Volvo and Saab/Scania) between 1970 and 1990. Volvo's efforts to apply 'small-scale manual technologies', with long cycle times, autonomous work groups and no traditional first-line supervisors, most notably at the new Uddevalla plant, have been confined to its plants in Sweden. The new 'Swedish concept' of work organization and technology has not spread to the expanding Volvo plant in Ghent, Belgium, which operates in completely different social and labour market conditions of high unemployment, less generous unemployment benefits and lower job security.

Like Berggren, Auer and Riegler (1990) conclude that accelerated change in production concepts in the Swedish car industry in the 1980s was caused by an interplay of factors: social and labour market conditions favourable to workers and unions, high union density, the prevalence of union workplace organization, changing product demand, and the adoption of decentralization strategies by employers. In the course of the 1980s, employers increasingly considered Fordist and

Taylorist concepts ineffective. Growing dependence on workers' motivation, stability and competence, and the strength of Swedish unions, especially in tight labour markets, combined to promote change in the Swedish car industry.

In the 1970s the unions feared that the experiments initiated by employers could fragment and individualize co-determination at plant level (Auer and Riegler 1990: 20). The views of the employers gradually prevailed, even if union demands for participation at all levels of co-determination were met by the 1982 UVA. With little alternative but to accept employer-initiated change, the unions directed their energies towards exercising as much control as possible over the process of change. The strategy proved successful, particularly where unions were strong and had cooperative relations with management. At Volvo – in contrast to Saab – management gave very high priority to close, long-term cooperation with the unions: it was no accident that the first UVA at enterprise level was concluded at Volvo. According to Berggren (1990: 422), it was the specific combination of top management 'philosophy', cooperative labour-management relations, and the 'open' technological culture of the enterprise, as well as the social and labour market conditions in Sweden, that made the Uddevalla concept possible.

However, this complexity of causal factors means that Uddevalla may well prove an isolated experiment (Berggren 1990: ch. 19). Indeed, while important changes of work organization have been made in Volvo plants such as Olofström, Borås (buses) and Tuve/Gothenburg (lorries), as well as at the Saab-Scania plant in Katrineholm (buses), the highly traditional Volvo factory in Gothenburg still dominates Swedish car production. The recent impact of the recession on the General Motors-dominated Saab Automobile, as in the closure of the new Saab car plant in Malmö and the return to traditional production methods in Saab Trollhättan, indicates the vulnerability of the experiments in the Swedish motor industry (Svensson and Svensson 1991: 141–59). Changing economic and political circumstances may therefore bring further setbacks in the future.

Efforts of Employers and Unions to Integrate Work Organization and Pay Determination

Despite recent setbacks, leading employers seem prepared to continue and even intensify their efforts to transform work organization and not least to decentralize and individualize pay determination. So-called employee agreements (*medarbetaravtal*) with harmonized conditions for manual and white-collar employees were recently introduced at ABB Service and ABB Atom (the latter only for manual workers but with conditions similar to white-collar workers). These are subsidiaries of the largest 'Swedish' enterprise, the product of the merger between the Swedish transnational ASEA and the Swiss company Brown Boveri. One indication of ABB's prominent position in Swedish industrial relations is that the managing director of its Swedish operations is president of VF, while company representatives have headed SAF in the past. The conclusion of employee agreements at ABB complements another company-initiated project which introduced 'self-governing groups' as a way of drastically reducing delivery times (*SAF-tidningen*, 34 1991; Steen 1991: 45–61). At ABB Distribution the groups are responsible for the whole cycle of operations, from orders to delivery. The new system currently in operation in about half of ABB's 130 Swedish subsidiaries means more varied jobs, increased responsibility, fewer supervisors, and greater cooperation between manual and white-collar workers. A second objective is to develop a model of 'employee agreements' (starting with the agreement at ABB Service) and to expand their coverage, probably also to other enterprises in the engineering industry.

LO has accepted in principle the introduction of flexible, individualized wage systems among manual workers as a means of encouraging workers to enlarge their skills and open the way for more integrated and varied jobs (LO 1991). But the unions wish to relate wages exclusively to systematic job evaluation, and reject the 'subjective' appraisal of individual qualities which would turn pay into an instrument of managerial control. 'Individualized wage development' to promote the development of jobs is preferred to 'individualized wage setting' that creates or maintains job hierarchies (see below). Thus rival principles of pay determination are a potential source of conflict between unions and employers. However, the practical distinction between the concepts appears ambiguous. Unions are also worried that the introduction of employee agreements at enterprise and workplace levels on relatively easy terms may be part of VF (and SAF) strategy to decentralize collective bargaining completely: if agreements at higher levels appear unnecessary to local unions, the position of union confederations and national unions would be seriously weakened. In the current, introductory, phase of employee agreements, tensions have already arisen between Metall and its workplace club at ABB Atom, with the national union complaining that the local agreement incorporates elements of the white-collar workers' contract that are inferior to those of the national metalworkers' contract (*LO-tidningen*, 43–4, 45–6, 1991). The solution to this dilemma proposed by the president of Metall is the conclusion of common national manual and white-collar agreements, to be followed up by local agreements (*Metallarbetaren*, 44–5, 1991).

The accelerated integration of pay determination and work organization over the last few years is likely to lead to a shift in power within unions from national wage negotiators to workplace organizations. The latter will acquire more multi-dimensional or integrated tasks, at both company and workplace levels (cf. Torsten Björkman in *SAF-tidningen*, 36, 1991). Whether or not this process will create fragmented 'company unions' will depend on how successful the national unions are in coordinating and supporting the development of local union expertise to meet the new demands. On 'production issues' the task will be facilitated by the experience and knowledge gained as a result of the legislation on co-determination, and from local projects on improving work organization and the working environment (Sandberg 1984; Levie and Sandberg 1991; Sandberg et al. 1992). Furthermore, the national unions, especially Metall, have given these issues a considerably higher priority than before. In contrast to the 1970s, the main emphasis is on the content of working life, not on procedures of co-determination (cf. Sandberg et al. 1992): significantly, the first major report of Metall on reforming work organization was called 'Good Work' (*Det goda arbetet*, 1985, partly translated into English as *Rewarding Work*), and it outlined a strategy for the 'Development of Work' on the basis of group-based work organization, integral job training, and the encouragement of job enlargement through payment systems.

The 1989 Metall report 'Solidaristic Work Policy for Good Jobs' (*Solidarisk arbetspolitik för det goda arbetet*) further elaborates the connection between work organization and wage issues. Squeezed between the dismantling of centralized bargaining and employers' efforts to transform pay into an instrument of management, LO unions have to find a new formula of (solidaristic) wage policy; a new union strategy is necessary not only because of the growing problems of traditional solidaristic wage policy but also because of the efforts of employers to individualize wages. At a time of increasing wage differentiation, the union concept of solidarity is reformulated to cover 'production' as well as 'distribution' issues. The new formula is a combined policy on pay and work organization aimed at creating 'Good Jobs'. Through continuous training and a gradual expansion of tasks, the individual worker will benefit from enlarged job content as well as economic rewards. Thus pay differentials are to be used as incentives to encourage workers to climb a skills 'ladder', developing their competence in the performance of an increasing number of tasks within a more flexible and democratic work organization. Work groups in which tasks are horizontally and vertically integrated are recommended as a way of achieving 'rewarding jobs' (cf. Mahon 1991: 306–11).

LO strategy is to move away from the current polarization between a relatively small proportion of stimulating jobs and a growing number of monotonous and physically stressful jobs, often occupied by women, which are associated with high labour turnover and other employment problems. This polarization partly reflected the social-democratic policy of the 'third way' which, in particular through the large devaluations at the beginning of the decade, tended to decrease the pressures for transforming the structure of Swedish industry; but it was also a consequence of the decline of 'basic industries' (pulp and paper, mining) and the expansion of the 'industries of the future' (electronics, transport equipment, pharmaceuticals) with a low proportion of skilled manual jobs and a high proportion of less-skilled manual jobs and of qualified white-collar employment.

There are obvious difficulties in applying the union concept of good jobs. Even at the Volvo Tuve/Gothenburg plant, used as an illustration by the LO inquiry on 'Democracy and Influence', most workers never have the chance to develop their skills. They remain at the bottom of the skills ladder, whose rungs tend to operate as static units rather than offering a gradual enrichment of jobs (LO 1990a). Another problem, emerging at Alfa Laval in Lund, where job enrichment has been widely achieved, is that local pay determination tends to be monopolized by management. Pay rises that result from individual task enlargement are regarded by management as part of wage drift, removing the scope for wage negotiations at workplace level. A third problem, also evident at Alfa Laval, reflects the almost complete separation in Sweden of manual and white-collar workers into different national unions and union confederations. At the Alfa Laval plants in Lund, the dominant white-collar union, SIF, has resisted further development of work groups through fear of losing additional jobs to the manual metalworkers; but the interests of skilled manual workers might also be threatened by the introduction of democratic work organization. Finally, job enlargement is often limited to the use of 'multi-skilled' workers to attain greater flexibility within the framework of a work organization that is otherwise little changed (Mahon 1991: 305).

Powerful white-collar unions assist white-collar workers to resist the equalization of their conditions with manual workers. Elvander (1991b: 235–6, 239) argues that single-status agreements are less common in Sweden than in Britain because white-collar unions are stronger in Sweden.

The 1991 LO congress signalled a major reorientation in its priorities by adopting the 'Good Jobs' notion with the approval of the report 'Developing Work' (*Det utvecklande arbetet*), prepared under the guidance of the president of Metall. LO's attention now turned to pay determination and production issues at the workplace. Its objective was to integrate the two sets of issues, negotiating at the workplace on the quality and content of jobs, as a way of overcoming the quantitative bias of local pay determination (Metall 1992: 5). Both LO and TCO unions are today energetically attempting to develop appropriate forms of workplace union activities going beyond traditional negotiations on wages (cf. Utbult 1991). The employers' decentralization strategy and declining union density have led unions to stress workplace issues 'close to everyday life' and to the expressed wishes of the members. The pressure for change is reinforced by the changing attitudes of young workers and by a higher level of education. Only a minority of manual workers today rate 'economic equality' higher than 'personal liberty', considerably fewer than a decade ago (LO 1991b); while a growing proportion of both manual and white-collar workers emphasize the importance of jobs that promote personal development.

To some extent, workers, unions and employers have a common interest in creating 'good jobs'. On this basis, Brulin and Nilsson (1991a;

1991b) have proposed a new 'Swedish model' and 'historic compromise', based on decentralized industrial relations (a concession to employers) and guaranteeing union influence on work organization and local pay determination. They argue that such a model would promote economic growth (a common interest of the parties). To prevent increasing wage differentials and fragmented wage systems, Brulin and Nilsson recommend that the unions 'develop job classification systems, job evaluation systems and overall wage statistics' (1991b: 344). The proposal is very close to the policy adopted by LO on workplace industrial relations. However, LO still hopes to retain the centralized aspect of collective bargaining. Given employers' resistance, their efforts are likely to be unsuccessful, at least in preserving the old combination of centralization and decentralization.

Apart from the conflicting policies of LO and SAF on the issue of central negotiations, current Swedish industrial relations display co-operation rather than confrontation although with indications of a hardening of the climate (see Conclusions below). The 1982 UVA marked a new era of cooperation but with the employers holding the strategic initiative. The concept of solidaristic work, extending the notion of solidarity from pay to work organization, may be seen as the unions' strategic response. As argued above, however, the implementation of this policy would have potentially explosive consequences for issues of local pay determination and trade union structure, both as regards the distinction between manual and white-collar unions and between local and central levels. Above all, there are obstacles to making 'good jobs' accessible to all workers. If the polarization of jobs between and within workplaces continues, and the differentiation of wages increases, then the reformulated concept of solidarity will lose its substance.

Conclusions

In recent decades, the Swedish model of industrial relations has undergone profound change. First, private sector employers, headed by the big transnational engineering firms that dominate the Swedish economy, lost confidence in the centralized bargaining system following the abortive 1980 lockout, and have pursued a strategy of decentralization. They have succeeded in seizing the industrial relations initiative in the 1980s and 1990s. On co-determination, a compromise was reached, largely on the employers' terms, in the Development Agreement of 1982, acknowledging demands for flexibility and decentralization. At the workplace, management took the lead in integrating production and wage issues. This process has been facilitated by a general consensus on the need to increase productivity and change work organization. At national level, despite inevitable differences of perspective, the unions have accepted a greater spread of wages provided that individual workers are given the chance to develop their jobs and perform increasingly complex tasks.

'Solidaristic work policy' is replacing 'solidaristic wage policy' as the unions' slogan. At local level, changes in work organization, including such post-Fordist experiments as that at the Volvo Uddevalla plant, have been made possible by the survival, and in some cases the strengthening, of cooperative relations between unions and management at the workplace.

Employers' decentralization strategy proved problematic, however, exacerbating competitive pay bargaining in a system already complicated by conflicting interests among different groups of workers. As a result, employers have tended to oscillate between decentralized and centralized negotiating strategies; while at a decentralized level they have been concerned to increase the scope for management action.

Second, in the face of the disintegration of the established model of industrial relations since the 1980s, the state has increasingly intervened, pursuing two contrasting avenues. One approach, exemplified by the Rehnberg Commission in the last years of the social-democratic government, was to intervene directly in the increasingly fragmented and complex collective bargaining arena in an attempt to restore coordinated bargaining under state auspices, using more or less coercive measures to moderate pay increases in line with the strategy of the 'third way'. While state involvement in the 1980s represented a centralizing counterweight to the pressures of decentralization, more recently state intervention has followed a second avenue, abetting the decentralizing tendencies. Encouraged by SAF, the current bourgeois government has taken up earlier social-democratic proposals and extended them into what might be characterized as a general labour law offensive aimed at circumscribing union power, particularly through the regulation of industrial conflict at the workplace. Although the frequency of illegal strikes since the 1980s has been somewhat lower than in the 1970s, it is considerably higher than before 1970, and the mere prospect of such action may be a powerful incentive for employers to offer concessions to workplace unions. The old formula of centralized self-regulation no longer appears applicable, and the bourgeois government is to introduce massive increases in fines for illegal strikes. It is also planning such measures as compulsory industry-level mediation and pre-strike ballots to control legal conflicts. Legislative intervention is therefore directed at regulating the decentralized relationships that employer strategies have encouraged to develop.

Compared with the 1970s, therefore, the object of state regulation has shifted. Legislation introduced in that decade, in such areas as co-determination and job security, responded to union demands for restrictions on the power of employers with respect to production issues. This agenda has been replaced by employer demands for the weakening of the role of unions: at the political level, at the workplace, and in pay determination in general. In both phases, the traditional emphasis on cooperation and agreement through centralized self-regulation has been abandoned in favour of legislation.

These changes have intensified the challenges facing the unions. Their strength traditionally derived from the combination of high density, very low unemployment, and the absence of rival channels of workplace representation. In recent decades, the cohesion of the labour movement has been weakened and the union system increasingly fragmented by the emergence of new conflicts between different groups of workers – manual and white-collar, public and private. More recently, unemployment has risen sharply to nearer the average of other European OECD countries. Moreover, decentralization has upset the traditional balance of power between different union levels. The 1980 conflict marked the end of the centralized LO-SAF axis, and power has subsequently shifted from the confederations (and bargaining cartels) – additionally weakened by the dilution of corporatist arrangements – to the national unions and their workplace organizations. Other recent developments, such as the efforts of employers to harmonize conditions of white-collar and manual staff through 'employee agreements', are likely to accelerate the shift in union power to the workplace and to exacerbate tensions between different levels of the union hierarchy. Strains between manual and white-collar workers are also felt at this level: for example, the existence of separate manual and white-collar unions – each organizing an overwhelming majority of its respective groups of workers – is likely to inhibit the harmonization of working conditions in companies. The expansion of employee agreements will make more urgent the issue of mergers between manual and white-collar unions.

Increasingly, therefore, there is strong evidence that the model will not be able to survive, and indeed one may question whether it any longer exists even today. The expansion of legislative regulation looks like consigning centralized self-regulation – along with other salient features of the classic 'Swedish model' – to the past. Even were the current political conjuncture to give way to one more favourable to the social democrats, it seems unlikely that the political agenda would be radically revised since it is a manifestation of more profound, longer-term processes of structural change and decentralization that are not going to be reversed.

Notes

[1]   I would like to thank the authors of the other 'Nordic' chapters, Steen Scheuer, Kari Lilja, Jon Erik Dølvik and Dag Stokland, for their valuable comments on a draft of the section on 'The "Nordic Model" of Industrial Relations'. The chapter was written in the course of a research project on 'Trade unions and members in the 1990s', financed by the Swedish Work Environment Fund.

[2]   Calculations from SCB wage statistics, obtained from Lena Johansson, SCB Stockholm 1991, and *Preliminär nationalbudget 1991*.

[3]   Information from Lena Östman, VF, 1991.

Abbreviations

AMS	*Arbetsmarknadstyrelsen* – Labour Market Board
CF	*Civilingerjörsförbundet* - Swedish Association of Graduate Engineers
DOI	*Demokrati-och inflytandeutredningen* – Commission of Democracy and Influence LO
HTF	*Handelsjänstemannaförbundet* - Union of Commercial Salaried Employees
Kommunal	*Svenska Kommunalarbetareförbundet* (SKAF) – Swedish Municipal Workers' Union
KTK	*Kommunaltjänstemannakartellen* – Federation of Salaried Local Government Employees (bargaining cartel of TCO municipal unions)
LO	*Landsorganisationen* – Swedish Federation of Trade Unions
MBA-KL	*Medbestämmandeavtalet för kommuner och landsting* – Co-determination Agreement for Municipalities and County Councils
MBA-S	*Medbestämmandeavtalet för statliga sektorn* – Co-determination Agreement for State sector
MBL	*Medbestämmandelagen* – Act on Co-determination at Work
Metall	*Svenska Metallindustriarbetareförbundet* – Swedish Metalworkers' Union
PTK	*Privattjänstemannakartellen* – Federation of Salaried Employees in Industry & Services
SACO	*Centralorganisationen SACO (Sveriges Akademikers Centralorganisation)* – Swedish Confederation of Professional Associations
SACO-K	*SACOs kommunala förhandlingskartell* – SACO Section for Salaried Local Government Employees
SACO-S	*SACOs statliga förhandlingskartell* – SACO Section for State Employees
SAF	*Svenska Arbetsgivareföreningen* – Swedish Employers' Confederation
SALF	*Sveriges Arbetsledareförbundet* – Swedish Union of Clerical and Technical Employees
SAP	*Sveriges Socialdemokratiska Arbetareparti* – Swedish Social-Democratic Party
SAV	*Statens Avtalsverk* – National Collective Bargaining Office
SF	*Statsanställdas förbund* – Swedish State Employees' Union (founded in 1970 by amalgamations of LO state sector unions)
SIF	*Svenska Industrijänstemannaförbundet* – Swedish Union of Clerical and Technical Employees
ST	*Statstjänstemannaförbundet* – Federation of Civil Servants
TCO	*Tjänstemännens Centralorganisation* – Central Organization of Salaried Employees
TCO-OF	*TCOs förhandlingsråd för offentliganställda* – Negotiating Council of TCO for Public Employees
TCO-S	TCO Section for State Employees
UVA	*Utvecklingsavtalet* – Development Agreement
VF	*Verkstadsföreningen* – Swedish Engineering Employers' Association; from 1992: *Sveriges Verkstadsindustrier* – Association of Swedish Engineering Industries

References

Ahlén, K. 1989: Swedish Collective Bargaining Under Pressure. *British Journal of Industrial Relations*, 27, 3, 330–46.

Albåge, L.-G. 1987: Recent Trends in Collective Bargaining in Sweden. An Employer's View. In J.-P. Windmuller (ed.), *Collective Bargaining in Industrialised Market Economies: A Reappraisal*,

Geneva: ILO.

Auer, P. and Riegler, C. 1990: *Post-Taylorism: The Enterprise as a Place of Learning Organizational Change. A Comprehensive Study on Work Organization Change and its Context at VOLVO.* Berlin/Stockholm: Wissenschaftszentrum Berlin, Arbetsmiljöfonden.

Berggren, C. 1990: *Det nya bilarbetet. Konkurrensen mellan olika produktionskoncept i svensk bilindustri.* Lund: Arkiv förlag.

Borgström, H. and Haag, M. 1988: *Gyllenhammar.* Stockholm: Bonniers.

Brulin, G. 1989: *Från den svenska modellen till företagskorporatism?* Lund: Arkiv förlag.

Brulin, G. and Nilsson, T. 1991a: *Mot en ny svensk modell.* Stockholm: Rabén & Sjögren.

Brulin, G. and Nilsson, T. 1991b: From Societal to Managerial Corporatism: New Forms of Work Organization as a Transformation Vehicle. *Economic and Industrial Democracy,* 12, 3, 327–46.

Bruun, N. et al. 1990: *Den nordiska modellen. Fackföreningarna och arbetsrätten i Norden - nu och i framtiden.* Malmö: Liber.

Calmfors, L. and Forslund, A. 1990: Wage Formation in Sweden. In L. Calmfors (ed.) *Wage Formation and Macroeconomic Policy in the Nordic Countries,* Stockholm/Oxford: SNS/Oxford University Press.

Edlund, S. et al. 1989: *Views on Co-determination in Swedish Working Life.* Lund: Juristförlaget.

Ehrenkrona, O. 1991: *Nicolin. En svensk historia.* Stockholm: Timbro.

Elvander, N. 1988a: *Den svenska modellen. Löneförhandlingar och inkomstpolitik 1982–86.* Stockholm: Almänna förlaget.

Elvander, N. 1988b: Central och lokal lönebildning under 80-talet. In L. Holmstrand (ed.) *Den lokala lönebildningens roll och betydelse i den svenska lönebildningsmodellen,* Uppsala: A-Forum rapport no 3.

Elvander, N. 1989: Bargaining Systems, Income Policies and Conflict in the Nordic Countries. In *Current Approaches to Collective Bargaining.* Labour-Management Relations Series No. 71, Geneva: ILO.

Elvander, N. 1990: Income Policies in the Nordic Countries. *International Labour Review,* 129, 1, 1–21.

Elvander, N. 1991a: Den dubbla utmaningen mot fackföreningarna. In R. Andersson et al. (eds), *Internationalisering, företagen och det lokala samhället,* Stockholm: SNS.

Elvander, N. 1991b: *Lokal lönemarknad. Lönebildning i Sverige och Storbritannien.* Stockholm: SNS.

Esping-Andersen, G. 1985: *Politics Against Markets.* Princeton: Princeton University Press.

Faxén, K.-O., Odhner, C.-E. and Spånt, R. 1988: *Lönebildningen i 90-talets samhällsekonomi.* Stockholm: Rabén & Sjögren.

Feldt, K.-O. 1991: *Alla dessa dagar... I regeringen 1982–90.* Stockholm: Norstedts.

Financial Times 1992: *European Top 500. Financial Times* Supplement, 13 January 1992.

Forsgren, M. 1989: *Managing the Internationalization Process. The Swedish Case.* London: Routledge & Kegan Paul.

Fulcher, J. 1987: Labour Movement Theory Versus Corporatism: Social Democracy in Sweden. *Sociology,* 21, 2, 231–52.

Fulcher, J. 1988: On the Explanation of Industrial Relations Diversity: Labour Movements, Employers and the State in Britain and Sweden. *British Journal of Industrial Relations,* 26, 2, 246–74.

de Geer, H. 1986: *SAF i förhandlingar.* Stockholm: SAF.

Hart, H. and Hörte, S.-Å. 1989: *Medbestämmandets stagnation. Medbestämmandets utveckling 1978–1985.* Arbetsvetenskapliga Kollegiet i Göteborg.

Hibbs, D.-A. 1991: Market Forces, Trade Union Ideology and Trends in Swedish Wage Dispersion. *Acta Sociologica,* 34, 2, 89–102.

Himmelstrand, U. et al. 1981: *Beyond Welfare Capitalism.* London: Heinemann.

Ingham, G. 1974: *Strikes and Industrial Conflict. Britain and Scandinavia.* London: Macmillan.

Jackson, P. and Sisson, K. 1976: Employers' Confederations in Sweden and the U.K. and the Significance of Industrial Infrastructure. *British Journal of Industrial Relations,* 14, 3, 306–23.

Jerneck, M. 1986: *SAFs framtidssyn: förutsägelser, målsättningar och dilemman.* Stockholm: SAF.

Jonsson, L. and Siven, C.-H. 1986: *Why Wage Differentials?* Stockholm: SAF.

Katzenstein, P.-J. 1985: *Small States in World Markets*. Ithaca and London: Cornell University Press.

Kjellberg, A. 1981: Från industriell demokrati till medbestämmande - fackliga utvecklingslinjer 1917–80. *Arkiv*, 21–2, 53–82.

Kjellberg, A. 1983: *Facklig organisering i tolv länder*. Lund: Arkiv.

Kjellberg, A. 1990: The Swedish Trade Union System: Centralization and Decentralization. Paper presented at XIIth World Congress of Sociology, 9–13 July 1990 Madrid. Lund: Department of Sociology.

Korpi, W. 1978: *The Working Class in Welfare Capitalism*. London: Routledge & Kegan Paul.

Korpi, W. 1983 *The Democratic Class Struggle*. London: Routledge & Kegan Paul.

Kuuse, J. 1986: *Strukturomvandlingen och arbetsmarknadens organisering*. Stockholm: SAF.

Landell, E. and Victorsson, J. 1991: *Långt kvar till kunskapssamhället*. Stockholm: SIND.

Lash, S. 1985: The End of Neo-Corporatism?: The Breakdown of Centralised Bargaining in Sweden. *British Journal of Industrial Relations*, 23, 2, 215–39.

Lash, S. and Urry, J. 1987: *The End of Organized Capitalism*. Cambridge: Polity Press.

Levie, H. and Sandberg, Å. 1991: Trade Unions and Workplace Technical Change in Europe. *Economic and Industrial Democracy*, 12, 2, 231–58.

Levinson, K. 1991: *Medbestämmande i strategiska beslutsprocesser. Facklig medverkan och inflytande i koncerner*. Department of Business Studies, University of Uppsala.

LO 1987: *Fackliga studier i framtiden*. Stockholm: LO.

LO 1989a: *Röster om facket och jobbet*. Stockholm: LO.

LO 1989b: *Vad gör facket?* Stockholm: LO.

LO 1990a: *Demokrati och inflytande i arbetslivet - 13 praktikfall*. Stockholm: LO/Tiden 1990.

LO 1990b: *Verksamhetsberättelse 1989*. Stockholm: LO.

LO 1991a: *Det utvecklande arbetet. En rapport till LO-kongressen 1991*. Stockholm: LO.

LO 1991b: *Rättvisa i vågskålen*. Stockholm: LO.

Mahon, R. 1991: From Solidaristic Wages to Solidaristic Work: A Post-Fordist Historical Compromise for Sweden? *Economic and Industrial Democracy*, 12, 3, 295–325.

Martin, A. 1985: Trade Unions in Sweden: Strategic Responses to Change and Crisis. In P. Gourevitch et al.(eds), *Unions and Economic Crisis: Britain, West Germany and Sweden*, London: Allen & Unwin.

Martin, A. 1987: The End of the Swedish Model? Recent Developments in Swedish Industrial Relations. *Bulletin of Comparative Labour Relations*, 16, 93–128.

Meidner, R. 1974: *Samordning och solidarisk lönepolitik*. Stockholm: Prisma/LO.

Metall 1985: *Det goda arbetet*. Stockholm: Metall.

Metall 1987: *Rewarding Work*. Stockholm: Metall.

Metall 1989: *Solidarisk arbetspolitik för det goda arbetet*. Stockholm: Metall.

Metall 1992: *En rapport om Lönesystem inom Metall*. Stockholm: Metalls löneprojekt, Svenska Metallindustriarbetareförbundet.

Molin, R. 1991: *Organisationen inom facket*. Stockholm: Carlssons.

Nilsson, T. 1990: *Bonus för industritjänstemän - lönar det sig?* Stockholm: SIF.

Nilsson, T. and Sandberg, Å. 1988: *Rörelse över gränser. Teknisk förändring och facklig organisering*. Lund: Arkiv.

Nordens Fackliga Samorganisation 1988: *Solidarisk lönepolitik i framtiden*. Stockholm: Nordens Fackliga Samorganisation.

Olsson, A. S. 1991: *The Swedish Wage Negotiation System*. Aldershot: Dartmouth.

Panitch, L. 1981: The Limits of Corporatism. *New Left Review*, 125, January–February, 21–44.

Petersson, O., Westholm, A. and Blomberg, G. 1989: *Medborgarnas makt*. Stockholm: Carlssons.

Produktivitetsdelegationen 1991a: *Drivkrafter för produktivitet och välstånd*. Produktivitetsdelegationen Stockholm: SOU 1991:82 Allmänna Förlaget.

Produktivitetsdelegationen 1991b: *Internationalisering och produktivitet*. Expertrapport 8. Produktivitetsdelegationen Stockholm: Allmänna Förlaget.

Przeworski, A. 1985: *Capitalism and Social Democracy*. Cambridge: Cambridge University Press.

Rehn, G. and Viklund, B. 1990: Changes in the Swedish Model. In G. Baglioni and C. Crouch (eds), *European Industrial Relations. The Challenge of Flexibility*, London: Sage, 300–25.

Rothstein, B. 1986: *Den socialdemokratiska staten*. Lund: Arkiv.

Rothstein, B. 1988a: *Sociala klasser och politiska institutioner. Den svenska korporatismens rötter*. Arkiv, 40, 27–46.

Rothstein, B. 1988b: State and Capital in Sweden. The Importance of Corporatist Arrangements. *Scandinavian Political Studies*, 3, 235–60.

SAF 1984: *Löneformsundersökning 1983*. Stockholm: SAF.

SAF 1985: *Löneformsundersökning 1985*. Stockholm: SAF.

SAF 1991: *Farväl till korporatismen!* Stockholm: SAF.

Sandberg, Å. (ed.) 1984: *Framtidsfrågor på arbetsplatsen. Om fackligt arbete med teknik, arbetsorganisation och produktion i fyra fallstudier*. Stockholm: Front-projektet, Arbetslivscentrum.

Sandberg, Å. (ed.) 1989: *Ledning för alla? Om perspektivbrytningar i företagsledning*. Stockholm: Arbetslivscentrum.

Sandberg, Å. et al. 1992: *Technological Change and Co-determination in Sweden*. Philadelphia: Temple University Press (forthcoming).

Schiller, B. 1988a: *Samarbete eller konflikt*. Stockholm: Allmänna Förlaget.

Schiller, B. 1988b: *Det förödande 70-talet. SAF och medbestämmandet 1965–82*. Stockholm: Allmänna Förlaget.

Shorter, E. & Tilly, C. 1974: *Strikes in France 1830–1968*. London/Cambridge: Cambridge University Press.

Simonson, B. 1989: *Arbetarmakt och näringspolitik. LO och inflytandefrågorna 1961–82*. Stockholm: Allmänna Förlaget.

Sisson, K. 1987: *The Management of Collective Bargaining. An International Comparison*. Oxford: Basil Blackwell.

SOU 1991: *Spelreglerna på arbetsmarknaden*. Stockholm: SOU 1991:13.

Steen, R. 1991: ABB Distribution. In *Arbetsorganisation och produktivitet*. Exportrapport 5. Stockholm: Produktivitetsdelegationen/Allmänna Förlaget.

Stephens, J. 1979: *The Transition from Capitalism to Socialism*. London: Macmillan.

Svensson, A. and Svensson, R. 1991: SAAB i Trollhättan. In *Arbetsorganisation och produktivitet*. Expertrapport 5. Stockholm: Produktivitetsdelegationen/Allmänna Förlaget.

Svensson, L. 1984: *Arbetarkollektivet och facket - en lokal kamp för företagsdemokrati*. Lund: Department of Sociology.

Söderpalm, S. A. 1976: *Direktörsklubben*. Stockholm: Zenit/Rabén & Sjögren.

Söderpalm, S. A. 1980: *Arbetsgivarna och Saltsjöbadspolitiken*. Stockholm: SAF.

Therborn, G. 1983: Why Some Classes Are More Successful Than Others. *New Left Review*, 138, March–April, 37–56.

Therborn, G. 1984: The Coming of Swedish Social Democracy. *Annali della Fondazione Giangiacomo Feltrinelli*, 1983/84, 527–93.

Trade Union Institute for Economic Research 1986: *Förhandlad inkomstpolitik?* Stockholm: Trade Union Institute for Economic Research.

Utbult, M. (ed.) 1991: *Nytt liv i facket. Att möta 90-talets arbetsgivare*. Stockholm: Arbetslivscentrum.

Vos, C. E. 1988: Förhandlingsformer i Sverige. In Elvander (ed.) *Förhandlingssystem, inkomstpolitik och arbetskonflikter i Norden*, Stockholm: Norstedts.

Åmark, K. 1986: *Facklig makt och fackligt medlemskap*. Lund: Arkiv.

Åsard, E. 1978: *LO och löntagarfondsfrågan*. Uppsala: Rabén & Sjögren.

Östman, L. 1987: *Lönepolitik - företagets och chefens styrinstrument*. Stockholm: SAF.

4

Norway: The 'Norwegian Model' in Transition

Jon Erik Dølvik and Dag Stokland

Introduction

The Norwegian system of industrial relations is facing sustained pressure for change as a result of the growing internationalization of the economy, changing industrial structure and patterns of employment, and tensions within the political system. So far, however, the main institutions remain intact.

As a small, open economy based on natural resources, Norway is increasingly dependent on international economic development and integration. This has encouraged a consensual industrial relations system, historically characterized by relatively close tripartite collaboration based on both collective agreements and legislation, centrally concerted but resting on local and workplace activity. The system is a variant of the broader 'Nordic model' in which political consensus has been maintained through generous public welfare services, labour market intervention, ambitious regional policies, and state transfers to individuals, firms and sectors.

A long-standing hegemonic alliance between the Labour Party and the trade unions has allowed the labour movement to maintain a successful class compromise with the employer organizations. This has been based on trade-offs between economic growth, restructuring, moderate social redistribution and generous transfers to the rural primary sectors. The trade unions have traditionally followed a solidaristic wage policy, while the state has guaranteed full employment by means of active labour market intervention, counter-cyclical management of the economy, and the promotion of structural change. This system has been made possible partly by the relative weakness of national capital, and its stability and flexibility have been underpinned by the revenues from exports of raw materials, shipping and oil.

From the mid-1970s the stability of the 'Norwegian Model' has been gradually weakened by structural changes in the economy and society, reflected in shifting political alliances and power relations. International economic problems and the 1970s oil crises, unstable growth, changes in the class structure, and the development of Norway into an oil economy in the first half of the 1970s all generated new challenges to the pattern of industrial cooperation. The question of European Community membership (rejected in a referendum in 1972) precipitated deep national cleavages and split the unions. Traditional Keynesian remedies proved less effective. Growing trade deficits, debt problems, structural economic imbalances, and loss of competitiveness paved the way for significant changes. In 1978 the Labour Party imposed a statutory wage and price freeze and implemented deflationary economic policies. In the early 1980s the Conservative government swept away key elements of economic regulation such as controls over credit and the housing market.

During the 1980s Norway experienced wild economic and political fluctuations, with deregulation succeeded by credit booms, oil crises, and stagnating production. Unemployment increased. Pay determination veered between decentralized bargaining rounds and centralized state regulation. The so-called 'negotiative economy' proved less manageable at national level. Growing dependence on oil and the backwardness of the manufacturing sector increased sensitivity to international economic fluctuations. With sectional interest groups competing for public transfers and politicians reacting uncertainly to fluctuating oil prices, the once stable system was in danger of veering out of control.

Nevertheless, the traditional characteristics of the industrial relations system remain stable. The question for the 1990s is how the Norwegian model will adapt to these ongoing external and internal pressures. This chapter addresses the following questions: first, what are the central features of the Norwegian model of industrial relations; who are the main actors? Second, what are the national peculiarities of the Norwegian system compared to other Scandinavian and European countries, and what features does it have in common with them? Is there a process of convergence between Norwegian and other models? Third, what are the elements of change, in the structure and mechanisms and in the 'outputs' of the model? What is 'new', and what is merely cyclical change within a pattern of stability over the past thirty years?

The following section describes the main characteristics of the industrial relations actors and institutions. The historical background to the Norwegian model and its post-war evolution are then explored in some detail. The remainder of the chapter is concerned with recent trends, and with the prospects for change and stability. Will the Norwegian model, as several analysts have argued, be fatally disrupted by the internationalization of the economy, or will there be pressure for a renewal of the model as a basis for international comparative advantage? Finally, do Norwegian industrial relations retain their distinctiveness or are they converging towards more 'continental' models?

An Overview of Industrial Relations Institutions and Actors

Norwegian industrial relations are fairly centralized. Although the central organizations have played a dominant role, the organizational pattern is more differentiated than in Sweden and Denmark, with increasing competition between LO and the independent federations, YS (Confederation of Vocational Organizations) and AF (Federation of Norwegian Professional Associations).

Since the Second World War the trade unions and employer organizations have channelled their political influence through a growing number of institutionalized corporate bodies and committees, especially on industrial relations and labour market questions. The LO and the main employers' confederation, NAF (Norwegian Employers' Association – reorganized and renamed Confederation of Norwegian Business and Trade, NHO, in 1987) have a long tradition of peaceful cooperation in the promotion of economic growth through productivity improvements and the introduction of new technology at firm level. In addition, the state has been an active participant in collective bargaining. These features have led Hernes (1978) to describe the Norwegian system as a 'negotiative economy and combined administration' (*forhandlingsøkonomi og blandingsadministrasjon*). Strong sectoral and regional 'iron triangles' between employers, unions and public authorities have often had an important influence on industrial as well as labour market policies. As a result, class conflict and industrial disputes are less widespread than in the other Nordic countries (see table 4.1). Peaceful collaboration emerged in the 1930s with the signing of the Basic Agreement which provided a detailed framework for the conduct of industrial relations and the settlement of disputes, and has been periodically revised. It can be regarded as a peace treaty: as long as the agreement is in force any strikes over the content of the agreement are regarded as illegal.

The pragmatic industrial cooperation that has developed since the 1930s does not imply that conflicting interests are absent, but that major areas of conflict have been transferred to the political arena where they have been manifested as disputes between the Labour Party and the Conservatives (as in the battles over codetermination and workers' participation, economic democracy and bank democratization, welfare contributions, legislation on the working environment, and so on).

Union Density and Organization

Total union density of 57 per cent is significantly lower than in other Scandinavian countries. The Norwegian Confederation of Trade Unions

Table 4.1   Strikes in Norway 1950–90

Year	Total number of work stoppages	Wage earners involved	Total working days lost
1950	30	4,399	42,310
1960	12	656	2,417
1970	15	3,133	47,204
1971	10	2,519	9,105
1972	9	1,185	12,402
1973	12	2,380	11,382
1974	13	22,149	318,433
1975	22	3,282	12,473
1976	35	21,586	137,651
1977	15	2,429	25,049
1978	14	4,459	62,888
1979	10	2,773	7,010
1980	35	18,752	103,807
1981	17	4,294	28,257
1982	12	24,581	281,183
1983	9	1,018	5,897
1984	20	30,635	104,349
1985	11	6,557	66,473
1986	16	165,742	1,030,928
1987	10	2,462	12,905
1988	15	8,332	83,254
1989	14	11,287	16,880
1990	15	60,674	139,047

Source: Central Bureau of Statistics, Norway. Labour Market Statistics.

(LO) is still the dominant union force in Norway, although its relative position is declining. It covers 60 per cent of unionized workers, and 34 per cent of all employees. LO consists of 29 different unions and had a total membership of 785,000 in 1990. Of these, 600,000 are in employment: 100,000 in the state sector, 160,000 in the municipal sector, and 340,000 in the private sector. The main competing organizations, AF and YS, have 208,000 and 184,000 members respectively. Unions outside LO together represent 23 per cent of employees. About two-thirds of the members of AF and YS are employed in the growing public sector, compared with about 40 per cent of LO members.

LO-affiliated unions are largely organized on a sectoral basis, but there are also some occupational unions. LO has, both formally and in practice, strong central authority, and has a major role in determining the unions' bargaining strategy. Historically this reflects the confederation's responsibility for reaching collective agreements and renegotiating the Basic Agreement. Strong central authority in Norwegian unions is combined with significant decentralization of some functions. First, local bargaining at workplace level is integrated into the collective bargaining system. Second, the outcome of central negotiations has to be approved in a ballot of all union members. In other words, tight central bargaining coordination is counterbalanced by a grassroots right of veto. Thus union structure is both more centralized and more decentralized than is the case in other European countries (Kjellberg 1983).

The Employers

Norway is still a sparsely industrialized country. Manufacturing industry accounts for about 16 per cent of GNP, and around 12–13 per cent of employment. Within the OECD, only Greek industry accounts for a lower share of GNP. Exports amount to about 40 per cent of GNP; two-thirds of them go to the EC. Traditional industry acounts for just under 40 per cent of export earnings, and oil and gas for about 30 per cent. Corporate structure in Norway is characterized by a relatively high level of state ownership of industry, extensive foreign ownership, and a preponderance of small and medium-sized firms. State ownership has been particularly important in the energy sector. More recently, the state has been forced to extend its role in the banking sector. In 1991 it took over the two leading private banks to save them from bankruptcy and prevent chaos in the financial system. The dominant firms are found within the export-oriented and the import-competing industries. They are big by Norwegian standards, but rather small in an international context. The two largest, Norsk Hydro (now majority state-owned) and Aker, employ about 40,000 and 16,500 respectively.

Like most European countries, Norway has experienced structural change in production and employment patterns. The primary sector has declined from 26 per cent of the labour force in 1950 to 6.5 per cent in 1989, while the public and private service sectors have increased from 30 per cent in 1962 to more than 70 per cent. Manufacturing and mining employment increased up to 1974 (28 per cent), but has since declined to 15 per cent of employment.

Private sector employers are represented by several multi-industry confederations, of which NHO (the Confederation of Norwegian Business and Industry) and HHS (the Federation of Norwegian Commercial and Service Enterprises) are the largest, covering firms with 370,000 and 60,000 employees respectively. NHO is the product of a merger in 1988 between NAF, two other umbrella organizations, and several industry organizations. It is the most influential of the employer organizations in the private sector, and is the counterpart of the LO, with which it renegotiates the Basic Agreement every four years. The different confederal organizations are composed of industry branch federations (*landsforeninger*) to which individual firms are affiliated. Most of the confederal bodies and industry federations combine the roles of employers' association and industrial interest organization. In 1989, 36 per cent of private sector enterprises belonged to an employers' organization. Membership density increases with firm size, and organized enterprises cover 67 per cent of total private sector employment.

In the public sector, there are separate organizations for state and local government. The government is formally the employer in the state sector, and pay negotiations, covering around 270,000 workers, are the responsibility of the Ministry of Labour. The outcome of negotiations requires formal approval in parliament. The local government sector is covered by the Norwegian Association of Local Authorities (KS), which is partly an employers' association, partly a lobby organization on behalf of the interests of the municipalities with the central political authorities. Pay negotiations conducted by KS cover 320,000 employees. Negotiations in the state and local government sectors are conducted separately, but are coordinated by a joint committee of KS and the Ministry of Labour. For both sectors, pay negotiations are regulated by law (*Tjenestetvistloven* and *Arbeidstvistloven*).

Collective Bargaining

Collective bargaining takes place at both national and local or workplace levels. Different models have been used over the past thirty years. While settlements during the 1950s were generally at industry level, they became more coordinated and centralized during the 1960s. The high point of centralized bargaining was reached with the so-called 'combined' settlements of 1973–6. For the first time it was agreed that the main negotiations between LO and NAF should be conducted in direct cooperation with the Labour government. The government helped the parties come to a settlement by agreeing to tax concessions, reduced employee pension contributions and price subsidies. Real pay increased in the period 1974–7 by an average of 5 per cent per annum, a figure not achieved before or since (Mjøset 1986). The greater extent of state intervention in collective bargaining compared with Sweden or Denmark reflects the relative weakness of Norwegian capital and the small size of firms. Although the state has used its influence to facilitate agreement, as with the 'combined' settlements, it has also frequently intervened to impose solutions through compulsory arbitration and wage freezes, as may be seen in table 4.2 below. Finally, it may be noted that all negotiations in which the government has played an active and direct part have been conducted under a Labour government. Only in one case was there direct intervention by a Conservative government, in the form of a wage law at the time of the main negotiations in 1966.

There has been a significant tendency for Norwegian industrial relations to oscillate between central and local negotiations and between state regulation and autonomy. The relationship between the oscillations and the economic cycle makes it tempting to see the collective bargaining system as an integrated element of the system of macroeconomic concertation. Thus periods of economic expansion with uncontrolled local wage drift have been followed by periods of deflationary policies, as under the Labour government both in the late 1970s

Table 4.2 History of LO–NAF/NHO bargaining

Year	Level of bargaining	Government	Comments
1946	LO-NAF-Industry	Labour	Wage law; main neg.
1949	LO-NAF-Industry	Labour	Wage law; reneg.[1]
1952	Industry	Labour	Wage law; main neg.
1954	LO-NAF-Industry	Labour	
1956	Industry	Labour	
1958	LO-NAF	Labour	Wage law; reneg.
1961	Industry	Labour	
1963	LO-NAF	Labour	
1964	LO-NAF	Labour	Wage law; main neg.
1966	LO-NAF	Conservative	Wage law; main neg.
1968	LO-NAF	Conservative	
1970	LO-NAF	Conservative	
1972	LO-NAF	Labour	Lab. party government tax deal under 1973 renegns.
1974	Industry	Labour	Government intervention in 1975; tax/subsidy deal
1976	LO-NAF-Government	Labour	Tax reductions
1978	LO-NAF-Government	Labour	Wage law and wage freeze; main neg.
1980	LO-NAF-Government	Labour	Wage law; reneg.
1982	Industry	Conservative	
1984	Industry	Conservative	
1986	Industry	Conservative	Agreement after lockout
1988	LO-NHO-Government	Labour	Wage law; limited wage increase
1990	LO-NHO	Conservative	

[1] 'Renegotiation' refers to bargained adjustments, in response to inflation etc., within the framework of an existing agreement.

and the 1980s. Central 'deals' with the social partners played a vital role in securing moderation and winning commitment to statutory wage regulation. The coordination of the central-local swings of collective bargaining with 'stop-go' macro-economic policy suggests that there is strong central control of the bargaining process within the unions (see below).

Industrial Democracy and Codetermination

Industrial democracy and codetermination rest on the Basic Agreement, covering 230,000 employees in the private sector, and on legislation (the Working Environment Act and the Joint Stock Companies Act), and comprise a number of elements.

First, for LO members the Basic Agreement outlines the rights and duties of shop stewards including the right to organize, the right and obligation to negotiate, and the procedures for electing stewards. For shop stewards outside LO, rights and duties are specified in different collective agreements. Second, the system of codetermination was extended during the 1960s and 1970s, leading to the Cooperation Agreement of 1966 (part of the Basic Agreement) and the establishment of cooperation committees, or works councils. The committees have consultative status and are made up of plant management and shop stewards inside and outside LO. Topics discussed include the financial situation of the enterprise, investment, changes in production systems, and questions relating to the product market.

A third element of industrial democracy is board-level participation, established under the Joint Stock Company Act of 1973. The legislation provides for a two-tier system of representation, with employees holding one-third of the seats at each level (from 1989, the threshold was lowered from companies with more than fifty employees to those with more than thirty). Employee representatives have the same rights and obligations as other board members. Fourth, the Work Environment Act of 1977 provides for employee participation through the working environment committees and safety delegates. Employers have legal responsibility for informing and consulting employee representatives on all matters relating to health and safety.

Unlike the unions in other Nordic countries, those in Norway have not historically given priority to the extension of economic democracy through ownership, wage-earner funds, profit-sharing and so on. Neither have they followed through their initial strategy of building up their own pension funds and unemployment insurance schemes, as in Denmark and Sweden. In the 1960s and 1970s they chose to rely on government to make universal public provision for welfare needs. In spite of the success of this strategy, it has left the unions and their members dependent on political and economic developments, making them vulnerable to changing government policies at times of economic recession.

Historical Background

The main institutional framework of the post-war model of industrial relations developed during the 1950s and 1960s. As we shall see, one important political condition was the high degree of national consensus after the Second World War, while the decisive economic condition was stable international economic growth. But the origin of the Norwegian model in the post-war period must be sought at the beginning of the twentieth century.

The Economic and Political Basis of the Model

Until the industrial revolution of the nineteenth century, the Norwegian economy was based on fisheries, agriculture, shipping, and the export of wood. As a semi-autonomous Danish colony, Norway developed no real aristocracy that could later form the basis for an independent national bourgeoisie. Nor, unlike the other Nordic countries, did it develop a feudal landowner class.

The 'second industrial revolution' around the turn of the century brought hydro-electricity into Norwegian industry (Cappelen et al. 1991). The state and the peripheral, small-scale Norwegian capitalist class had neither the technological competence nor the capital to cope with the requirements of the emerging electrical, metal, chemical and wood-processing industries. As a result, the modernization of Norwegian industry was to a large extent driven by investments and technology from abroad. For example, Swedish banks owned by Wallenberg worked with French and German capital to develop Norsk Hydro, the leading Norwegian manufacturing multinational (Lange 1988). As an industrial latecomer Norway experienced rapid and strong economic growth based on the export enclave – comprising shipping, forestry, semi-finished metals and chemicals – established by these foreign investments. This model of development influenced the pattern of class forces and political relations that emerged. In particular, foreign industrialization hindered the development of a strong, independent national capitalist class and of a private financial system, and gave the state a central role in economic and industrial development.

Distrust of foreign control led to laws to restrict foreign ownership (*Konsesjonslovene* of 1909 and 1918) and to control the developments of trusts (*Antitrustlovene* of 1925 and 1926). Foreign ownership is again becoming a major issue in the context of the debate on EC integration.

This background was vital for the relative political strength of the labour movement. The conservative parties lacked not only a strong economic and class basis, but also a foothold in the state. Moreover, a key segment of the Norwegian capitalist class has been historically linked to the shipping industry and thus has not been centrally affected by national policies and industrial relations.

Oil-related industry emerged as a new pillar of Norwegian industry in the early 1970s. This reinforced the existing industrial structure based on the strength of the export enclave. As the export sector has weak linkages with the rest of the domestic economy, this structure has facilitated macro-economic stabilization policies (Mjøset 1986), another significant feature of the Norwegian model. The vital role in the export economy of primary production based on natural resources distinguishes Norway from the other Scandinavian countries (especially Sweden) which export a higher proportion of finished products.

Given the limited nature of industrialization in Norway, a 'Fordist' mode of production has never been dominant. International trade, shipping, and revenue from different natural resources have laid the foundation both for the sheltered, small-scale domestic manufacturing industries and for the development of a specific industrial relations model.

The Political-Institutional Setting

As pointed out above, the lack of an independent national bourgeoisie opened up a space for political manoeuvring that the Labour Party was able to exploit. From 1814 until 1905 Norway was part of a union with Sweden. Thus the initial phase of parliamentary democratization at the end of the nineteenth century was dominated by the question of national independence. The leading parties had weak and mixed class linkages. The Labour Party and the unions were strengthened by rapid industrialization and benefited from the weakness of their opponents. Following a short period of revolutionary ferment and divisions, the labour movement reunited (except for a small communist party) on a reformist platform in the 1920s. In 1928 the first Labour government was formed. A turbulent period of widespread strikes and lockouts throughout the 1920s and early 1930s culminated in the unions' defeat in the lockout of 1932. Together with mass unemployment, this consolidated the reformist and nationalist currents in the labour movement and initiated a long period of peaceful cooperation beginning with the signing of the Basic Agreement by LO and NAF in 1935.

Cooperation was made possible by the forging of a broad class alliance between the rural petty bourgeoisie of independent peasants, fishermen and forestry workers and the emerging working class, between centre and periphery. This has been reinforced by the national policy of maintaining the regional spread of population through regional subsidies, credit arrangements (through agriculture and fisheries banks), and support for public services; and by the fact that the leading manufacturing centres have been located close to sources of energy and raw materials. The second Labour government was formed as a result of an agreement with the Peasant party in 1935; its slogan was 'by og land, hand i hand' (town and country, hand in hand).

During the 1930s the Labour Party advocated Keynesian policies. The state was no longer seen as an instrument of capital but as a tool for social-democratic reforms. The party gained 43 per cent of the vote in 1936, which was an inter-war peak.

In short, therefore, the transformation of Labour into a reformist party, the class compromise between labour and capital, and the political alliances between labour and agrarian forces were important preconditions for the evolution of the Norwegian model and its industrial relations system after the Second World War. In a comparative perspective, Norway is distinguished by its low degree of open class conflict from the 1930s to the present.

The Labour Party and Postwar National Reconstruction

The consolidation of the Norwegian model in the two decades after the Second World War was closely linked to political reconciliation and the wartime consensus on the strategy for rebuilding the Norwegian economy. The Labour Party, with an absolute parliamentary majority from 1945 until 1963, played a leading role, supported by the trade unions.

The 1950s – the Phase of State Regulation

The Norwegian model was not the product of some grand strategic vision, but emerged out of pragmatic step-by-step policies. Policy objectives in the 1950s were high and stable growth, full employment, stable prices, equitable wage distribution and trade balance, under the political slogan of 'reconstruction and stabilization'. The Labour Party stressed the continued modernization of the export enclave sectors. The strategy of regulation rested on a wage freeze and low consumption, combined with massive investments in the means of production (Mjøset 1986).

In the absence of a strong private financial sector (Lange 1988) the state developed a leading role in channelling capital to industry, to a large extent from foreign sources. Later, the state itself became a leading accumulator of capital, through its stake in the oil industry. In the face of the challenges of intensified international competition in the 1990s, this feature of the Norwegian model has become crucial in public debate.

The strategy of reconstruction narrowed the scope for collective bargaining and the programme met with resistance. But in general, its implementation was made possible by the close links between the Labour Party and the unions. The unions accepted that 'national reconstruction' had to have priority over wage increases. This led them to forswear strike action as a means of improving standards of living: 'the Trade Union will not object if the Government asks Parliament for the authority to settle conflicts between employers and workers by means of a committee on wages and prices in those cases where it is feared that a conflict will damage reconstruction' (Decision of LO Congress, 1946).

The 1960s – Welfare Reforms and Industrial Democracy

Norwegian unions have been relatively uninterested in economic democracy. In contrast to the Swedish and Danish cases, they rejected ownership as a means of achieving economic democracy throughout the 1960s and 1970s. According to Langeland (1985) this can be explained partly by the weak structure of capitalism, and thus by the stronger influence of state politics in the Norwegian model. At the beginning of the 1960s, industrial democracy was mainly seen as workplace democracy developing from below, while economic democracy was regarded as something to be implemented by the state from above, by means of economic transfers (Vennesland 1990).

The history of codetermination at board level highlights at least three central features of Norwegian industrial relations and the development of industrial democracy. First, it was the Labour Party, not the trade unions, that first put the question of board representation on the agenda, and it took twenty years from the original proposal in 1952 until final parliamentary approval. Second, despite its parliamentary majority in the 1950s, the Labour Party withdrew the proposal, partly in response to union scepticism. The reason for the lack of union support for the measure was the strong resistance from the employers' organizations and the perception that legislation would damage the centralized wage-bargaining climate in future rounds (Halvorsen 1990). This illustrates the mechanisms within the Norwegian industrial relations system encouraging the parties to adopt a consensual strategy. Third, the case of board participation also illustrates the shifts between legislative and negotiating strategies. From the mid-1950s to the late 1960s the unions unsuccessfully tried to institutionalize board participation by agreement, finally ending up with a legislative settlement. They have in practice followed a pragmatic line, combining legislation and agreements.

The so-called 'Cooperation Project' from the beginning of the 1960s until the early 1970s has attracted considerable attention in relation to the development of Norwegian industrial democracy. It was a tripartite project, financed by the two main confederations and, in the final phase, by the state. The aim was to reduce the alienation of workers by introducing forms of autonomous group working and promoting democracy at the workplace, as well as to improve economic performance. The project was based on the Tavistock Institute's 'socio-technical' approach (Emery 1959). The emphasis on local, workplace-oriented industrial democracy met with union scepticism; from the end of the 1960s it was clear that the unions' main strategy for industrial democracy was through the extension of collective agreements and legislation.

The direct effects of the project on work organization and industrial democracy seem to have been limited, partly because it was initiated from 'above' without sufficient motivation at the workplace. The indirect influence is, however, important. There is a direct line from the socio-technical approach to the Work Environment Act of 1977, with its focus on employee participation and workplace control over health and safety questions.

During the 1960s and early 1970s important welfare reforms were accomplished. The educational system was radically extended. Different pension schemes, among them the unions' unemployment insurance system, were integrated into a comprehensive public pension system (1974). The welfare state expanded rapidly, especially within the municipal sector. These developments are often seen as the peak period of the labour movement in Norway. In retrospect they also marked the beginning of the end of the traditional social-democratic hegemony.

Recent Trends

In the early 1990s one can identify several pressures for change in the Norwegian system of industrial relations. Increased internationalization, changes in the international trade regime (through the GATT negotiations), and Norwegian participation in the EC internal market will influence the economic context of state policy-making and affect the space for collective bargaining in several sectors. Possible EC membership may further constrain the options for the economic, industrial and employment policies that have been a key precondition for tripartite industrial cooperation. At the political level, the interplay between these factors and independent developments in the economy and polity may lead to important changes in the balance of power between the main industrial relations actors. Tougher international competition, growing unemployment, and unsolved structural imbalances in the national economy are likely to reinforce the political trend towards more restrictive welfare and wage policies. This may influence the strategies of the bargaining partners, provoking conflicts that may lead to changes in the model of industrial relations.

Macro-cooperation and the State

From the late 1970s, the Labour government began to move away from the counter-cyclical policies for maintaining full employment that had been a central feature of Norwegian macro-cooperation. For example, the policy of maintaining low interest rates, almost a trademark of the traditional Norwegian model, was relaxed. The change was partly a response to growing foreign debt and increased trade deficits. The first half of the 1980s saw a radical ideological shift away from post-war macro-cooperation with the election of a conservative minority government in 1981. The government used liberal tax and credit policies to stimulate investment, producing a boom in consumer spending and speculation. As a result, employment in the private service sector expanded. With mounting inflation and trade deficits, the boom collapsed in 1986: oil prices fell sharply and the employers initiated the collective bargaining round with a lockout, following internal splits (see below). The neo-liberal party was over.

This paved the way for a new period of Labour Party government and close macro-cooperation. The minority Labour government pursued a programme of national 'emergency', but its options had been narrowed by the failure of the experiment with full-blooded Keynesianism in the mid-1970s, and by the subsequent liberalization of credit markets and the abandonment of state-regulated interest rates. The overheating of the economy had to be brought under control by deflationary policies and pay restraint, but at the cost of rapidly increasing unemployment. From 1986 to 1989 there was a revival of centralized corporatism, with the leaders of the labour movement temporarily abjuring class politics in the interests of national economic responsibility.

The parallels with the post-war national reconstruction programme are striking. In the absence of a competent bourgeoisie, the labour movement takes responsibility for handling a national crisis and demonstrates its ability to rule, manage the economy, and generate loyalty. However, in the 1980s the state's role changed. The scope for state-led centralized corporatism has been much reduced.

A key question is how long the alliance of the Labour Party and the unions will withstand unemployment rates of 6–7 per cent. Traditionally, the macro-level relationship between the state and the labour movement has been based on a trade-off of frequent legal intervention in pay in return for full employment; as long as unemployment is at an acceptably low level, the basic structures of the industrial relations system remain in place. But the current combination of economic instability and increased unemployment, together with the loss of several important policy instruments over the past ten or fifteen years, suggests that the unions have less to gain from collective bargaining with state participation, either in the way of direct state contributions or in terms of policy that can sustain economic growth and full employment. Conversely, of course, the Labour Party has less to lose from relaxing its close links with LO. With an increasing proportion of the work force organized within AF and YS (or not organized at all), the traditional Labour Party – LO alliance has become a less appropriate basis for securing loyalty and votes.

Whether these developments herald a fundamental transformation of the model, or merely illustrate the system's capacity for pragmatic and flexible response to conflicting pressures, remains to be seen.

Employment and the Labour Market

The weight of export-oriented and import-competing sectors fell from 23 per cent of total employment at the beginning of the 1960s to less than 13 per cent at the end of the 1980s. An increasing number of trade union members work within the sheltered sector of the economy. This makes the policy of general pay restraint on behalf of the export-oriented and import-competing sectors a much more complex issue for the labour movement today compared with the 1950s and 1960s.

For much of the post-war period until the mid-1980s unemployment was about 2–3 per cent, while the working population steadily increased to 2.1 million, some 70 per cent of the population of working age. The increased participation of women in the labour market (59 per cent in 1990), many of them on part-time contracts, reflects the expansion of the public sector, both state and local authorities, during the 1970s and the 1980s.

The last five years have seen a dramatic increase by Norwegian standards in the numbers out of work. Unemployment stood at 6 per cent in 1991, a post-war peak. This reflects more fundamental problems in the Norwegian model, calling into question the legitimacy of the relatively centralized collective bargaining system, as well as the close connection between the LO and the Labour Party (see below).

Labour and Unions

Long-term transformations in the economy and the labour market are posing new challenges for LO. Industrial restructuring and the growth of more complex forms of enterprise ownership and work organization place new constraints on the development of formalized workplace democracy, while the processes of economic internationalization and European integration are likely to change the nationally-oriented assumptions underlying union strategies towards the state and the employers' organizations. At the same time, structural changes in the labour market have called into question the traditional basis for union recruitment, and have affected the relative strength of LO and competing union organizations. In addition, labour market developments have led to more diversified patterns in the organization of everyday life and have increased female work participation, creating new lines of division between the interests and priorities of groups of union members. At the political level, the declining hegemony of the Labour Party has tended to erode the unions' political influence, while political pressure for public sector cuts and privatization challenges the state-oriented welfare policies of the unions, opening the way for the expansion of labour-market-based welfare arrangements.

In short, these tendencies have sharpened union debates on organizational reforms, bargaining strategies and priorities, new areas of union policy, and new forms of union action. For example, the question of economic democracy is again being discussed by the unions and the Labour Party as a means of assisting the process of structural adjustment.

Changing Rates of Organization and Intensified Membership Competition

Over the past two or three decades, union density has been fairly stable in Norway. However, aggregate figures hide significant changes in density patterns. LO's share of the organized workforce has fallen substantially, from 79 per cent in 1962 to about 60 per cent in 1989 (Stokke 1991). While LO's absolute membership figures have remained stable for the last fifteen years, YS and AF have absorbed the net growth in union members. This is mainly due to the growth of more highly qualified groups in public employment. If this trend continues the competitors will together be of the same size as LO within the next decade (Fennefoss 1988).

Within LO, private sector unions lost close on 60,000 members, while public-sector unions increased their membership by nearly 90,000 in the 1980s. The main components of this change are the decline in membership of the dominant manufacturing union (*Fellesforbundet*) and the growth of the municipal workers' union (*Kommuneforbundet*). The latter is now the biggest LO union, accounting for one-third of LO-organized employees. Although the confederation organizes clerical, retail and other non-manual employees, it is generally weak in the private service sector.

The decline of LO's share of organized employees is related to structural changes in industrial and employment patterns. The decline of manufacturing and the growth of public employment and private services during the 1970s and 1980s have reduced the relative market shares of LO unions, to the benefit of YS and AF. Moreover, changes in the educational composition of the labour force and new career patterns have accelerated mobility and union turnover. Confronted with the decline in young people entering the labour market over the coming decades, the LO unions are facing not only a recruitment problem, but a major challenge to keep members in the union over their occupational life-cycle (Stokke 1991).

The decline in LO's coverage is only partly explained by direct competition from the other unions. In addition, the number of non-unionized workers has been growing, especially in private services. In this connection the example of close links between the Swedish LO and TCO has led LO to consider ways of improving relations with unions belonging to YS, AF and the teachers' union, and has raised the possibility of future mergers.

Changes in Political Loyalty

Changes in political consciousness and alliances have led to a renewed debate about the institutionalized relations between LO and the Labour Party. The political behaviour of workers is becoming less predictable and less shaped by social background. The Labour Party has lost its political hegemony over the working class. While 76 per cent of workers voted for the party in 1957, only 47 per cent did so in 1989. Twelve per cent voted for the socialist left party, and 41 per cent voted for non-socialist parties. In 1989, 33 per cent of LO-organized workers voted for non-socialist parties.

Many employees reject LO membership because of the mutual dependency between the Labour Party and LO (a 1992 poll indicates that fewer than 30 per cent of LO members are in favour of this dependency relationship continuing). The party is trying to adapt by developing more class-independent strategies, seeking alliances both with centrist parties and with non-LO organizations, while the LO unions are searching for a broader and more politically independent approach.

Organizational Change in the Unions

Changes in industrial and occupational structure have made organizational reform a central issue within LO. Historically, the question of whether industry, occupation or sector should form the basis of organizational structure has never been brought to a decisive conclusion. In practice, different criteria coexist, although the last decade has brought strengthened moves towards mergers and cartelization at a sectoral level. In the public sector different unions cooperate through a cartel. A single LO union dominates the local government sector. The strengthening of public sector unions encouraged unions in the manufacturing sector to merge, leading to the creation of a new union, *Fellesforbundet*, in 1988. In the private service sector, several smaller unions have embarked on moves towards closer collaboration. These developments may well sharpen sectoral divisions and rivalry, and further undermine the dominant role of LO.

In 1989, LO set up a high-level working group to prepare a comprehensive package of organizational reforms to be decided upon by the next congress in 1993. The aim of reorganization is to decentralize resources, activities and responsibilities, to clarify the division of tasks and responsibilities between LO, the cartels and the unions, and to provide more flexible arrangements that could attract new groups of members.

In addition to the option of retaining the present structure based on a mix of industry, sector and occupational unions, four possible models are under consideration: a structure based on industrial unionism; a radical reduction in the number of unions; the grouping together of existing unions in cartels; and the dissolution of individual unions and the conversion of LO into sections organized on occupational and sectoral criteria. A common objective of the different alternatives is to facilitate horizontal integration at a decentralized level, and to strengthen vertical integration through concentration in fewer unions, cartels or sections.

A key question will be the division of responsibilities and tasks between LO and cartels and/or sectoral or occupational sections. In a cartel-based model, the influence of the cartels would grow at the expense of the industrial unions and of the central organization itself, although local units might find more space for autonomous action. Thus such a reform would entail complex changes in patterns of influence and responsibility: a degree of decentralization from LO to cartel level; an upward shift of power from individual unions to cartel level; and decentralization from industrial union level to local units.

A major issue in the debate so far is how to balance particular occupational and industrial interests against the need for increasing concentration in cartels, sections or merged unions. It is argued that more differentiation along occupational lines is needed to attract new groups, while sectoral integration is necessary to avoid fragmentation. Several unions have argued for the adoption of a hybrid model based on a variety of different solutions, on the grounds that the challenges vary between sectors and industries. Powerful voices within central unions have signalled that they are prepared to block any organizational reform in order to safeguard their own position; the current deadlock in Danish unions over the creation of cartels may be an indication of likely Norwegian developments as well.

The outcome of the process will depend not least on how seriously the LO-affiliated unions treat the problem of coping with the new educated middle-class sections of the labour force. Should LO limit its ambitions to remaining the major organization for traditional groups of workers and for weaker groups in the service sector, or should it also attempt to win new, more highly qualified, social groups? If the latter, LO would have to develop strategies for recruiting in new areas, and forge cooperative alliances (and perhaps take-overs) with external professional or semi-professional organizations. It would also have to consider how the 'market' should be strategically divided up with the other union organizations. Some participants in the debate argue that the cartel model is best suited for recruiting external semi-professional organizations because it would allow them to retain their occupational identity and to keep their distance from LO while taking advantage of its large-scale bargaining capacity.

Developments in Collective Bargaining

As we have seen, the centralized bargaining structure came under pressure during the 1980s. With the Conservative government distancing itself from collective bargaining in the early 1980s, bargaining rounds were organized at industry level.

The 1986 bargaining round, taking place against the background of deregulation and the consumer boom, signalled a dramatic departure from the tradition of peaceful bargaining. The employers pursued a strategy of confrontation. They rejected the claims made by the unions in central negotiations (for example, for employees' working hours to be brought into line with those of civil servants) and insisted that only local, market-related, wage increases should be awarded. The negotiations quickly reached deadlock, and the employers imposed a general lockout in the private sector, to which the unions responded with strike action. However, the employers were organizationally and politically unprepared for a large-scale conflict and their strategy for decentralization and increased wage flexibility suffered a major defeat. With subsequent arbitration awards going in favour of the unions, the employers' organizations were split and their political legitimacy severely impaired.

In the following coordinated bargaining round in 1988, LO and the employers reached an agreement at central level. The unions pursued a strategy of central pay moderation, on condition that no other groups should undermine the agreement by gaining better settlements. Acting in cooperation with LO and NHO, the social-democratic government introduced a statutory pay freeze. The strategy of cooperative moderation was continued in the renegotiations the following year and again in 1990 when LO and NHO agreed centrally on a limited across-the-board pay increase with certain measures to help the low paid. Within this framework, local and industry-level bargaining was allowed within fixed time limits. LO members finally voted for the agreement, following an initial rejection in response to obstruction of negotiations by local employers. Thus the 1990 pay round introduced the notion of coordinated multi-level bargaining, combining traditional central control with limited decentralization aimed at achieving greater flexibility.

In retrospect it is difficult to identify any clear trend in the development of collective bargaining in the last decade. On the one hand, there are clear elements of continuity. The swings between local and centrally-coordinated bargaining are a recurring feature of Norwegian industrial relations (see table 4.1), as are the actors' responsiveness towards national macro-economic interests, and their close cooperation with the (social-democratic) government. On the other hand, the 1986 dispute and the problems of internal opposition and unrest on both sides during the period of statutory pay restraint reflect growing tensions and contradictions within the model of centralized bargaining.

The 1991 bargaining round brought renewed attempts by employers to decentralize bargaining in order to relate pay more to labour market conditions. NHO tried unsuccessfully to break LO's commitment to flat-rate settlements and minimum earnings clauses in the sectoral agreements. On the union side, the policy of pay moderation has come under fire at both central and local levels. For five years LO pursued 'responsible' bargaining in the name of the fight against unemployment, but was frustrated by the rise in private sector profits, wage drift for groups outside LO, and the continuous growth of unemployment. Centralization has also blocked necessary adjustments in pay structures and systems. Industrial restructuring and work reorganization require the development of new skills and strategies of worker participation, often linked to more differentiated rewards systems. The spread of profit sharing, employee ownership and calls for restructuring funds necessitate a more flexible bargaining system. Both employer and union leaderships, faced with the erosion of their internal legitimacy, have increasing misgivings about the wisdom of the strategy of centralized cooperation.

It is still too early to conclude whether these developments signal the beginning of the end for the centralized bargaining model. One possible outcome is a return to the former pattern of fluctuating bargaining procedures. Another is the consolidation of a multi-level bargaining model allowing for greater flexibility through a combination of central control and local initiative. Preparations for the main 1992 bargaining round suggest that the latter is the more likely outcome.

Employers

In the 1980s, both conservative and social-democratic governments moved away from an industrial policy based on protectionism and state subsidies. Although privatization was not a major policy tool, subsidies were withdrawn and publicly-owned enterprises forced to adapt to market pressures. Reduced state intervention coincided with increasing concentration of ownership and a rise in foreign investment. The twenty largest industrial corporations, most of them found within the export enclave, increased their share of employment in industry and mining from 25 per cent in 1977 to 49 per cent in 1989, or from 5 to 8 per cent of total employment. This concentration is partly due to mergers and acquisitions, in which Swedish corporations have been especially active. In the last part of the 1980s, Norwegian corporate investments in the US and the EC were almost double the amount invested by US and EC companies in Norway (Hippe 1990).

Increased internationalization and concentration means that a growing number of trade union members find themselves employed in a national or multinational corporate structure. This in turn has increased the need for cooperation among workers' representatives within companies, or for corporate works councils to complement traditional company-based workplace democracy. NHO has taken a comparatively 'liberal' position on the issue. At the last renegotiation of the Basic Agreement it agreed to the establishment of works councils for the provision of information to the work force, although so far they have been set up only in large corporations (Stokland 1991; Myrvang 1990).

Against the background of growing concentration and international competition, a central issue of management strategy has been the introduction of new forms of work organization and flexibility. It is difficult to generalize about the extent of 'new forms of work organization'. Unlike work reform in the 1950s and 1960s (production committees, the Cooperation Project, codetermination, and so on) which was mainly initiated and carried through by the Labour Party and the unions, new forms of work organization in the 1980s and 1990s have largely resulted from management initiative. The implementation process has tended to bypass the unions, focusing more on relations between management and the individual employee. Recent Norwegian research indicates the increased diffusion of different forms of flexibility in the use of labour and working time in certain industries. Thus Karlsen (1989) found a growing use of flexible and production-oriented working-time arrangements in the engineering industry following the working time reduction of 1987. Olsen (1991) found similar trends, as well as the use of subcontracting, in the food industry. In the service sector, Olberg (1990) and Torp and Petersen (1989) have documented the widespread use of working- time flexibility, part-time working, etc., to meet fluctuations in customer demand. Finally, in construction, there was a growing proportion of subcontracted and self-employed workers during the the 1980s (Stokland 1989). However, it is not clear from the literature whether these trends are due to new management strategies in the 1980s or can be better explained as the outcome of structural changes and business cycles.

The picture is clearer for employer strategies on collective bargaining and codetermination. Trends in corporate structure, with increased diversification and the decentralization of management responsibility within tight central financial control, have coincided with a push by the employers for a closer link between pay systems and the profitability of the individual firm. NHO has recently announced a policy of getting rid of the guaranteed minimum wage, a key element in the Norwegian model. (This ensures that no worker is paid less than 80 per cent of the average wage in the industry concerned; the minimum wage system is organized through a low wage fund, jointly financed by employers and employees.) NHO has also signalled its possible withdrawal from the wide range of corporatist public bodies.

Although it is difficult to quantify trends towards more performance-based pay, recent research gives a fairly clear idea of the current situation.

In almost 50 per cent of private enterprises, pay is determined by collective agreements; in the remainder (covering one- third of the work force) it is regulated through individual contracts alone. Performance-related pay, bonuses and profit-sharing – all buzz words of the 1980s – are slowly pushing their way into firms, although 91 per cent of all employees are still covered by traditional time-based pay systems. Within the private sector, 13 per cent had some sort of bonus or piecework arrangement instead of or as a complement to time-based pay.

Tendencies towards more performance-related and individualistic pay arrangements have often been associated with an employers' strategy of replacing traditional union-based channels of employee participation with more direct and individual forms (Sandberg 1987). It is hard to say how widespread this strategy is among Norwegian employers. NHO still takes part in the centrally initiated programmes and agreements on technology and productivity (*Hovedavtalens Fellestiltak for Bedriftsutvikling*). The spread of 'quality circles' at enterprise level is rather limited, and it appears that workers' participation still takes place largely within the traditional institutions of industrial relations.

Employers and the European Community

The advent of the single European market looms large in discussions of the future of Norwegian industrial relations. European integration has implications for issues such as the quality of working life, pay levels, and industrial policies. The increasing numbers of mergers and acquisitions in the last part of the 1980s must be seen as part of the employers' strategy for adapting to the internal market. NHO is currently lobbying for Norwegian membership of the EC, as it did in the 1972 campaign. The need to maintain Norway's international competitiveness in the face of the internal market and the increasing internationalization of the economy is used as an argument for moderation in pay settlements and for reductions in corporate taxation.

Norwegian managers believe that membership of the EC is one of the most important prerequisites for securing the future of Norwegian enterprises and attracting foreign investment. The general acceptance of the need for EC membership conceals tensions between different enterprises and sectors. Whereas the export-oriented sector has already adapted to an internationalized competitive environment, the sheltered industries and parts of the import-competing sector have a more ambivalent approach towards Norwegian integration in the internal market. Research also suggests that two-thirds of Norwegian enterprises have no strategy for coping with the internal market. For those firms that do have strategies, two predominate: the extension of the geographical market through mergers or acquisitions, and specialization through improving products and technology in areas where they are already competent. Such strategies are, if adopted, likely to strengthen the trend towards new forms of work organization referred to above. The challenge of European integration has also led managers of leading companies to establish closer ties with the Labour government, and to disscuss ways of strengthening national ownership structures and of resisting foreign competition and takeovers.

Prospects for Change and Stability

Pressures for Change in Industrial Relations

We have argued that the Norwegian industrial relations model, based on close tripartite cooperation, has come under pressure from different but interconnected directions. The political and economic sources of tension may be summarized as follows.

At the political level, the decline of social-democratic hegemony and the trend towards market-oriented policies have restricted the state's contribution to centralized bargaining. The abandonment of controls over credit and capital markets and the linking of the Norwegian krone to the ECU have limited the options for macro-economic concertation. EC integration and economic internationalization may further restrict the scope of the state's industrial policies. In short, the state is less able to deliver the goods of economic growth, social reform and full employment that have been a precondition for class compromise and central bargaining cooperation. At the same time, transformation of the social and industrial structure has been changing the composition of interests within the labour movement, challenging the traditional compromise between sheltered and exposed sectors of the economy.

These underlying strains are manifested within the industrial relations model in employer demands for more differentiated pay structures, and demands from sectoral and occupational groups of employees for more market-related pay determination. Dissatisfaction with the existing system at grassroots level has also fuelled opposition among the leadership of central unions, despite the general desire to retain a solidaristic pay policy. At the beginning of the 1990s, with unemployment at 6–7 per cent, unions seem less willing to play the role of generators of national loyalty.

It is hard to say whether these stresses will lead to a fragmentation and dismantling of the centralized bargaining model or whether the two sides will be able to maintain their cooperation within a renewed multi-level bargaining structure. The outcome will depend partly on developments within unions and employers – a recent change of leadership in NHO may lead the employers to adopt a 'modernized', politically tougher and less cooperative line – and on the strength of the logic of mutual cooperation. It will also depend on how the process of internationalization evolves and on how the question of Norwegian integration in the internal market is resolved. There are signs that internationalization is reinforcing joint strategies of employers and unions for achieving national competitiveness. The maintenance of central bargaining may be to the employers' advantage, by restricting wage drift, facilitating cooperative restructuring of production, and increasing employers' influence on state industrial and economic policies.

Unions and European Integration

The 1972 referendum which rejected Norwegian membership of the EC left the unions seriously split. The LO leadership played an active role, devoting huge resources to a campaign in favour of EC membership. Twenty years later, the wounds of this struggle have still not healed. Anxious not to provoke a repetition of the 1972 battle, LO is currently following a very cautious strategy. Following a 1989 congress decision that EC membership would not be on the agenda during the congress period 1989–93, the leadership has played down the debate in favour of discussion over the treaty on the European Economic Space (EES). However, with the debate on the EC gaining strength both within the unions and among the public, and with a majority of union members opposed to membership (58 per cent of LO members according to recent polls), this strategy is now confronting serious problems. By tying its position so tightly to the EFTA-track EES, the union leadership has been accused of blocking the debate, and at the same time of giving ammunition to the opponents of EC membership.

The issue of European integration may accentuate serious inter-union cleavages based on conflicting short-term sectoral interests. A majority of union members in sheltered and domestically oriented sectors oppose further integration, while the picture in export-dependent sectors is more varied. Integration into the internal market might also further undermine the system of regional alliances that has been such an important element in the Norwegian model.

In this situation the unions' options may be constrained by their political dependency on the Labour Party. The party is attempting to modernize its electoral base by developing a more class-independent approach and presenting itself as the administrator of the national interest. This has left it increasingly dependent on compromises with centrist parties. A plausible scenario is that the LO leadership – while favouring the application for EC membership which is likely to be submitted in 1992 – will leave it to the Labour Party to initiate the political debate. By maintaining a far more neutral stance than in 1972, LO hopes to reduce internal conflict and avoid loss of membership.

Three Strategies

The unions' need for increased autonomy from the party opens the way for a variety of sometimes contradictory responses. One significant response has come from forces wishing to re-establish 'orthodox social democracy'. Thus public sector and sheltered sector unions are likely to define themselves as the true defenders of the 'Norwegian model', and to express a growing protectionist scepticism towards further European integration.

Another smaller but more aggressive opposition group may develop among leftist rank-and-file elements in the private core industries, calling for a 'back-to-basics' traditionalist militancy centred on class policies and mobilization at the workplace.

A third tendency is the 'modernist technocratic' current in the core manufacturing unions and within LO. Supporting moderate and differentiated pay policies and economic modernization in alliance with state-dependent and 'friendly' fractions of capital (large parts of the energy and raw-material-based export industries), it may be expected to cooperate pragmatically with the Labour government on moves towards closer ties with the EC. This tendency is rooted in a private sector rationale, less willing to defend the burden of the welfare state, and predominantly interested in improving the competitiveness and employment prospects of private industry. One possibility is that opposition to the EC will form the basis of an alliance between the two 'traditionalist' tendencies against the pragmatic and relatively internationalist orientation of the headquarters leadership. If so, the 1972 situation may be about to repeat itself.

To sum up, growing sectoral cleavages are emerging that may undermine the central grip of LO. The 'technocratic-modernist' line still appears to control the main centres of power and has the support of strong social forces both inside and outside the unions and the labour movement. But the prospects of a modernized national class compromise, coupled to industrial restructuring, to cope with external challenges and internationalization, seem less favourable. One major difference from the earlier phase of national reconstruction is that the post-war growth pact was rooted in a national political consensus defined by a strong labour movement. Paradoxically, the success of the labour movement has to a large extent undermined the basis for the continuity of the model. Internal democratization, a better-educated workforce, and the differentiation of members' interests, have led to the withering away of the movement's mechanisms for securing political-ideological loyalty. Such mechanisms might be difficult to replace in a compromise based on technocratic-economic forms of control. Finally, the post-war alliance was underpinned by a process of international growth that gave all parties a larger share of the cake. Today, the opposite outcome appears more likely.

Abbreviations

LO	*Landsorganisasjonen i Norge* – Norwegian Confederation of Trade Unions
AF	*Akademikernes Fellesorganisasjon* – Federation of Norwegian Professional Associations
YS	*Yrkesorganisasjonenes Sentralforbund* – The Confederation of Vocational Organisations
HHS	*Handelens Hovedorganisasjon* – The Federation of Norwegian Commercial and Service Enterprises

NAF   *Norges Arbeidsgiverforening* – Norwegian Employers' Association, merged in 1987 with NHO

NHO   *Næringslivets Hovedorganisasjon* – Confederation of Norwegian Business and Trade

KS   *Kommunenes Sentralforbund* – The Norwegian Association of Local Authorities

References

Bull, E: 1968: *Norsk fagbevegelse*. Oslo: Tiden Norsk Forlag.

Cappelen, Å., Fagerberg, J., Mjøset, L. and Skarstein, R. 1990: The Decline of Social-Democratic State Capitalism in Norway. *New Left Review*, 181, May – June 62–94. .

Dølvik, J.E., Olberg, D. and Stokland, D. 1990: *Fagbevegelsen og Europa. Internasjonalisering og europeisk integrasjon – utfordringer for fagbevegelsen*. Oslo: FAFO.

Emery, F. 1959: *Characteristics of Sociotechnical Systems*. London: Tavistock.

Fennefoss, A. 1988: *Lønnstaker-organisering*. Oslo: FAFO.

Fulcher, J. 1988: On the Explanation of Industrial Relations Diversity: Labour Movements, Employers and the State in Britain and Sweden. *British Journal of Industrial Relations*, 26, 2, 246–74.

Halvorsen, T. 1990: *Fern og Metall. 100 År*. Bind 2. Oslo: Tiden Norsk Forlag.

Hernes, G. 1978: *Forhandlingsøkonomi og blandingsadministrasjon*. Oslo: Universitetsforlaget.

Hernes, G. 1990: The Dilemmas of Social Democracies. The Case of Norway and Sweden. In Schmitter, P. (ed.), *Experimenting with Scale*, Cambridge: Cambridge University Press.

Hippe, I. 1990: *Det nye markedet i bedrifter. Overnasjonalt eierbytte, finansspekulasjon og fusjonskontroll*. Oslo, FAFO.

Karlsen, T. 1989: *Arbeidstid og fleksibilitet i arbeidslivet*. Oslo: FAFO.

Kjellberg, A. 1983: *Facklig organisering i tolv länder*. Lund: Arkiv.

Lange, E. 1988: *Kapitaltilgangen til norsk næringsliv – hva kan vi lære av historien*. Oslo: Bedriftsøkonomisk Institut.

Langeland, O. 1985: *Økonomisk demokrati og politisk økonomi. En sammenlignende analyse av arbeiderbevegelse og økonomisk demokrati i Norge og Sverige*. Hovedoppgave, Universitetet i Oslo.

Mjøset, L. (ed.) 1986: *Norden dagen derpå*. Oslo: Universitetsforlaget.

Myrvang, G. 1990: *Konsernfaglig samarbeid i Norden – erfaringer og perspektiver*. Oslo: Stiftelsen for industriutvikling i Norden.

Olberg, D. 1990: *Fleksibilitet og Fagorganisering*. Oslo: FAFO.

Olsen, T. 1989: *Det kom som et sjokk*. Oslo: FAFO.

Olsen, T. 1991: *Bedriftsstrategier i nærings og nytelsesmiddelindustrien*. Oslo: FAFO.

Stokke, Aavaag, T. 1991: *Medlemsbevegelser i LO*. Oslo: FAFO.

Stokland, D. 1989: *Over stokk og stein*. Oslo: FAFO.

Stokland, D. 1991: *Konsernfaglig samarbeid – nasjonalt og tverrnasjonalt*. Oslo: FAFO.

Sandberg, Å. 1987: *Ledning før alla*. Stockholm: Arbetslivscentrum.

Torp, H. and Petersen, S. 1989: *Markedet for Korttidsarbeid*. Rapport 89: 6. Oslo: ISF.

Vennesland, K. 1990: Industrielt demokrati i Norden. Redegjørelse for det norske delprosjektet. In Flemming, D. (ed.), *Industrielt demokrati i Norden*, Lund: Arkiv.

5

Denmark: Return to Decentralization

Steen Scheuer

Introduction

'Decentralization' and 'flexibility' have been the industrial relations catch-words of the 1980s. Denmark is no exception to the general trend to decentralization of pay bargaining. But this has involved a move from national, multi-industry bargaining to national single-industry bargaining, rather than from national, industry-wide to single-employer bargaining, as in many other countries.

Many observers regard decentralization as a symptom of a serious crisis in the Scandinavian model of industrial relations, particularly in Sweden but also in Denmark (e.g. Amoroso 1990). But is decentralization in Denmark really new, or are the actors merely rediscovering 'lost patterns' from the period before the strong centralization of bargaining in the 1960s and especially the 1970s? It is also necessary to look at the impact of bargaining changes on the institutional framework that is an important part of the 'Scandinavian model'. Has this framework been dismantled since the end of the centralized bargaining and incomes policies of the 1970s, or has it been revitalized?

Industrial relations actors have faced other challenges in the 1980s. Their strength (in the sense of their ability to carry out their policies) is partly a reflection of their membership density. Denmark, like Sweden, experienced high and increasing union densities in the 1980s. As in other Scandinavian countries, however, the dominant position of the major union confederation, LO, has been undermined, with growing numbers of employees joining unions outside LO. This poses a serious challenge to the Scandinavian model and to the ability of LO unions to make their influence felt.

Government policies have a profound impact on the vitality of the Scandinavian model. Have the conservative-liberal governments in Denmark in the 1980s been trying to dismantle the model, or have they been pursuing reform within the existing framework? How successful have their initiatives been?

The answers to these questions will give clues to the future direction of Danish industrial relations and the fate of the broader Scandinavian model. The next section sets the scene by outlining the nature of the Danish economy and labour market. The origins of Danish industrial relations in the historic agreement of 1899 are then described, and the key institutional dynamics of the system examined. This section also summarizes the main features of union structure. The fourth section turns to developments in the last couple of decades. It deals with the impact of the 1970s crises in the world economy on the development of Danish industrial relations, looking in turn at the evolution of union density, organization and strategies, the changing policies of the conservative-liberal governments of the 1980s, and the trend towards decentralization in bargaining. In particular, it assesses the role of unemployment insurance funds in explaining the persistence of high union density in the 1980s. The section also examines the strategies of employers in the 1980s in the face of the challenge of flexibility. The conclusion speculates on what current trends are likely to mean for the future of the Danish model.

The Danish Economy and the Labour Market

Denmark is a small, open, exporting economy. It is thus very dependent on fluctuations in the world economy and has an interest in minimizing customs and trade barriers in the world market. Thirty-eight per cent of industrial production is exported, the major exports being agricultural (butter, bacon, canned ham) and related products, such as agricultural machinery, beer, and even insulin (until recently made from pigs' pancreases).

Though there is some large-scale industry (B&O radio & TV factory, Lego, B&W shipyard, Monberg & Thorsen) and important transport and shipping firms (such as Maersk or ØK), Denmark has a large proportion of small and medium-sized enterprises. Between 1978 and 1989, there was a marked shift of employment from large to small and medium firms. Little more than a fifth of employees in Danish industry are today employed in firms with 500 employees or more – a similar proportion to Portugal – compared with over a quarter in 1978. Half of all employees in industry work for firms with between 50 and 500 employees, and a further quarter in firms of between 10 and 50 employees (*Statistical Ten-Year Review*, 1989 and 1991).

Important changes have been taking place in the structure of firms since the late 1980s, with a number of significant company mergers over the last few years. For example, the two large Danish travel agents (Spies and Tjæreborg) have merged to form the largest travel agent in the Nordic countries; in the pharmaceutical industry, Novo and Nordisk Gentofte combined to form the new Novo Nordisk, controlling almost half the world market in insulin; De Danske Spritfabrikker (Danish strong spirits), Danske Sukkerfabrikker (sugar industry) and Danisco have merged to become the largest food-processing company in Denmark (no small achievement) while several acquisitions have left the re-christened MD Foods in a dominant position in the dairy industry; and two new 'mega-banks' have been created, Den Danske Bank and UniBank Danmark. These mergers are indications of a process of concentration among the very largest Danish firms. Between 1974 and 1987, the thirty largest manufacturing companies increased their share of manufacturing employment from 21 to 27 per cent, although this was far below the comparable figures for the other Nordic countries (Pestoff 1991: 31–2).

Some observers consider the rather small size of Danish firms a weakness. Small firms tend to spend relatively less on R&D, and there is evidence that Denmark spends less in this field than comparable competitors. The fear is, therefore, that it will become progressively more difficult for Danish firms to maintain their international position in areas where research efforts are an important part of competitiveness, in high-tech industries and in biotechnology, for example.

Since small and medium-sized firms form the backbone of the Danish economy, laws regulating the labour market have to a large extent aimed to facilitate employment mobility, providing generous unemployment benefits, rather than imposing rigid job security rules on the individual firm (Jensen et al. 1987). With high and stable unemployment in the 1970s and 1980s, this system has come under increasing pressure, however, since the burden it places on public expenditure (and the taxpayers) is substantial. Almost 6 per cent of GDP was spent on these measures in 1989, by far the highest level in Europe and more than double that of Britain, France, Germany, and the other Nordic countries (OECD *Employment Outlook* 1991: 240–8). Countries with comparable levels of unemployment (Germany, Britain) spend far less, 2.2 and 1.5 per cent of GDP respectively; and the Swedish level is also far lower. Unemployment has been increasing since the middle of the 1970s, reaching 10 per cent of the dependent work force in 1983, and decreasing slightly since then. Average unemployment for the period was 8 per cent.

Denmark has a labour force of 2.7 million, of whom almost 90 per cent are employees. The labour force has grown significantly faster than the population as a whole, mainly because of higher labour force participation by women. For every 100 men in the labour force there were 48 women in 1958, compared with 84 today. This trend is common to all western countries, but nowhere so marked as in Scandinavia. Thus, while labour force participation has been declining somewhat for men, it has increased for women from 39 per cent in 1960, to 71 per cent in 1980 and 76 per cent in 1987 (Brünniche-Olsen 1990: 35). The category of housewife has virtually disappeared in Denmark. In 1965, 66 per cent of mothers with children up to 6 years of age were full-time housewives; in 1987 the figure was 7 per cent (Christoffersen 1988).

A related development has been the growth of the tertiary sector: accounting for just under half the labour force in 1960, it now employs two-thirds. Two areas of employment stand out in this growth: private financial services and public services. Both sectors have more than doubled their employment

Table 5.1 The relative distribution of the labour force in Denmark by sector 1960–87 (%)

Year	Primary sector	Secondary sector	Tertiary sector
1960	21	33	46
1970	11	34	54
1980	8	27	65
1987	6	27	67

Source: Brünniche-Olsen (1990: 31).

Table 5.2 Share of work force in public services, 1958–87

Year	Percentage in public services
1958	13.7
1961	14.1
1964	15.7
1967	19.2
1970	21.3
1973	25.7
1976	28.9
1979	31.9
1982	36.0
1985	34.1
1987	33.5

Source: Statistical ten-year review (1989: 10).

in the period, finance going from 3.6 to 8.6 per cent of the total labour force, and public services from 11.7 to 29.4 per cent (see tables 5.1 and 5.2).

The public sector has thus been the main field of employment expansion, and also the area where most women currently in employment have found work. Private services other than finance have not shown the same growth: their work force has grown in absolute but not relative terms. In Denmark, the transition from industrial society to the so-called 'service society' has to a very great extent been a transition to a 'public service society'. This has had clear implications for industrial relations and for the unions.

The Basic Features of Danish Industrial Relations

The Making of the Institutional Setting

The origins of the Danish industrial relations system can be traced back to the 'September Compromise' of 1899. This followed a bitter conflict, subsequently known as the 'Hundred Days' War', between the newly formed Employers' Association (DA) and the union confederation, LO (then DsF), both established in 1898.[1] Following a series of minor strikes, the employers launched an all-out confrontation in an attempt to impose a permanent framework of industrial relations. Their aims included a greater centralization of the bargaining process and union recognition of management prerogative. They also wanted the unions and DsF to accept the principle that collective bargaining agreements should be observed until they expired (usually after two years): in effect, a 'peace obligation'.

The employers achieved many of their aims, but the unions imposed a price which proved to have important advantages for them. Managerial prerogative was recognized, and written into the agreement. Some saw this as a major sell-out, but others believed that this merely formalized an issue that the unions had never really contested. Indeed, some observers have regarded the concession as a figleaf for the employers. The unions also accepted responsibility for enforcing collective agreements – with the centralization of bargaining that that implied. However, it was the national unions, rather than the union confederation DsF, that became responsible for agreements, since DsF was not in general the bargaining partner.

It is important to note that collective responsibility for policing agreements was two-way. Individual employers who did not observe agreements (on e.g. agreed pay levels, notice of dismissal, etc.) would also be held to account. In subsequent decades this became, and remains, a major source of union power, since unions were able to enforce agreements even if their members in a specific area were unwilling or unable to fight for their implementation. Thus the formal working of the system made union power to a large extent independent of membership militancy and much less sensitive to unemployment.

An important element of the September compromise was the recognition by each party of the other's right to organize. The recognition of unions as legitimate bargaining partners was no small matter in the Denmark of 1899, some two years before the introduction of parliamentary democracy. The agreement established an industrial court and arbitration tribunals, where anti-union activities of individual employers were repeatedly challenged. (In Sweden, by contrast, workers only gained these rights in the 1930s.) As a consequence of these arrangements, union membership grew significantly over the following years.

In the years after 1899, employers and unions called on parliament to give legal backing to the industrial court system (*Arbejdsretten*), together with the various arbitration arrangements and the procedures for the renegotiation of expiring agreements. The system has been written into law (generally on the basis of the joint proposals of the two parties) and is also codified in the so-called Main Agreement (*Hovedaftalen*). This agreement has since been revised in 1960, in 1973 and most recently in 1987, introducing rules on the protection of the union shopfloor representative (the *tillidsmand*), cooperative committees in the enterprise (*Samarbejdsudvalg*), the working environment, and the introduction of new technology. However, its basic planks are essentially those established in 1899, and in the main, the workings of the Danish system of industrial relations (and to a great extent the Swedish,

Norwegian and Finnish systems as well) date back to this compromise (Skogh 1984; Bruun 1991).

In general, the early emergence of relatively strong collective actors has meant that several areas of working life, which in other countries would be governed by legislation, are regulated by collective bargaining. Thus collective agreements determine rules on overtime, shift work, notice of redundancy or lay-offs, and maximum and minimum working hours (for example, the agreements for some groups of manual workers prohibit part-time working). Minimum wage rates have also been regulated by collective bargaining; in 1977, however, a statutory minimum wage was introduced.

This traditional pattern of limited legal intervention in the Danish system may be affected by developments at the European level: if EC directives in the context of moves to the single market are implemented through legislation, rather than by collective bargaining, several important aspects of industrial relations and working life in Denmark are likely to be taken out of the hands of the traditional industrial relations actors.

A key issue in Danish industrial relations is the problem of reaching a new settlement when existing agreements expire. Given the synchronized and coordinated nature of bargaining, industrial action on a very large scale may occur if negotiations break down. In such cases, a tradition has developed in Denmark (and Norway, cf. Elvander 1989) that parliament intervenes to end the conflict, usually by extending the expiring agreements with minor changes.

The tradition of parliamentary intervention to resolve a deadlock in collective bargaining dates back to 1933. In the wake of the worldwide economic crisis, Danish employers threatened a general lockout to impose substantial pay reductions. The social-democratic government intervened through parliament, prolonging existing agreements with some minor modifications, and also devalued the Danish krone, causing some reduction in real pay. Since the war, there has been a series of interventions, most of them when special groups outside the scope of LO-DA negotiations have been unable to reach agreement. It has generally been considered unacceptable for such groups to engage in conflict with major repercussions for the rest of the labour market, when all other groups have reached a settlement. Such 'lagging' behaviour is seen as an attempt to hold the rest of the labour market to ransom, and great efforts are made (especially by the state mediator – see below) to make potential 'laggards' fall into line (Scheuer 1991).

But there have also been interventions in general bargaining, as for example in the 1956 round, when a ballot of union members rejected the negotiated settlement which was then enforced by parliament, and again in the 1963 round, when parliament created the so-called 'aggregate solution' (*Helhedsløsningen*), and prolonged existing agreements – in effect an early attempt at incomes policy (see Auken and Buksti 1964). In Denmark, the existence of a bargaining agreement is crucial for industrial peace. This is because the peace obligation on the parties (including individual employees and unions, but not LO) ceases to exist when agreements run out. Both employers and unions have a strong tradition of threatening industrial action (in accordance with the procedural rules) when expiry approaches, and strikes and lockouts commonly occur in the context of contract renewal.

The state mediator has an important role in avoiding open conflict by calling upon the parties to take part in bargaining, and by exercising the power to postpone conflicts (if there is hope of agreement) twice for a fortnight. The mediator may also put forward his or her own proposal for a new agreement, and require the parties to hold a ballot on this proposal. But these attempts – though often successful – may also fail.

It is in this situation that parliament can intervene through a law creating a new collective 'agreement'. Parliament may prolong existing agreements for a two-year period unchanged, or it may adopt the state mediator's proposal after it has been rejected by negotiators or by a ballot of the membership. Alternatively, parliament may devise its own new agreement, usually on the basis of existing agreements and possibly incorporating proposals from the state mediator. In all cases the effect is to introduce a new and binding collective 'agreement' for the following two years, together with a built-in peace obligation on the parties.

The positive side of such intervention (and the rationale for it) is that in the short run, industrial peace is secured and major conflict avoided. There is, however, also a negative side: the peace obligation in collective agreements has generally been justified by trade union leaders (especially when confronted with left-wing criticism) on the grounds that agreements are subject to endorsement by the membership in union ballots. This legitimacy is lost if settlements are repeatedly imposed by parliament. Thus, from a long-term perspective, intervention by parliament in collective bargaining must be minimized if the system is to work.

Trade Union Structure

In international comparative terms, Danish union structure is often seen as among the most heavily influenced by craft unionism (e.g. Visser 1990; Kjellberg 1983). The structure is sometimes simply described as being 'predominantly based on crafts' (Amoroso 1990: 78). The latter statement is, however, an exaggeration: only 12 per cent of the dependent work force are skilled workers, comprising 15 per cent of aggregate union membership in 1989. Thus, well over 80 per cent of union members are in unions not 'based on crafts'. The following types of unions are to be found:
Craft and General Unions. A distinction is usually made between countries in which unionism is demarcated along industrial lines (industrial unionism), and countries which have craft and general unionism. Sweden, Norway and Germany are examples of the former, Denmark and Britain of the latter. The development of general unionism in countries like Denmark and Britain may be seen as a response by unskilled workers to a craft unionism that has nothing to offer them. General unions, once established, often stand in the way of subsequent attempts to create industrial unionism. General unions are often more 'open' along both industrial and status lines (cf. Turner 1962),

whereas craft unions are 'closed' to all but those who possess certain formal qualifications.

In Denmark, the establishment of general unions followed a very distinct pattern. Unskilled workers reacted to the creation of unions for skilled workers by attempting to form their own local unions; the first was established in 1873. But it was not until 1897 that a national general workers' union, *Dansk Arbejdsmandsforbund*, was formed (Lund 1972: 39). Excluded from what was eventually to become the *Special- arbejderforbundet*, SiD, unskilled female workers were forced to create their own women-only union, KAD (Union of Female Workers in Denmark). This union still exists and has 98,000 members, all of them women. Chief among the general unions is the white-collar union, HK (Union of Commercial and Clerical Employees). With more than 300,000 members, it is today the biggest single Danish union. HK organizes 'across the board', in the private as well as the public sector. Most craft and general unions are members of LO.

Industrial Unions – Vertical and Non-Vertical. Not all Danish unions are craft or general. In some industries, for example food processing and wood, industrial unionism has been established. Some industrial unions are not comprehensive in their recruitment; those mentioned above do not organize supervisors or other salaried employees. Others do recruit members from the bottom to the very top of the organizational hierarchy. Such comprehensive industrial unions exist in the finance sector and for civil servants in the traditional occupations of the public sector. Blue-collar industrial unions are members of LO, while the comprehensive ones are mostly members of FTF (Central Confederation of Salaried Employees).

Professional Unions. Associations of professional groups have increasingly adopted union-like behaviour and must today be counted as unions. This category includes all unions of professionals, but also a whole range of semi-professional groups, such as schoolteachers, nurses, librarians and social workers. University graduates' unions are members of AC (Central Confederation of Professional Associations), whereas the semi-professionals' unions are mostly members of FTF.

Status Unions. Finally, there are bodies that could be labelled 'service' or 'status' unions. These are unions for groups attempting to defend their position in the face of strong unions of the groups mentioned above. One example is the Supervisors' Union, defending not only supervisors' pay differentials, but also the 'status differential' of those who have risen from the shopfloor either into management (as supervisors) or into technical jobs (e.g. in the drawing office). The resulting typology is shown in table 5.3.

Professional and craft unions together account for a third of Danish union members. General unions command 36 per cent of aggregate membership, and industrial unions cover roughly a quarter. Finally, status unionism has a little less than 10 per cent of union membership.

Summing up, the 'craft and general' nature of Danish union structure is substantial and undeniable. However, with the decentralized bargaining of the 1980s (and the 1940s and 1950s) taking place mainly along industrial lines, there is an apparent contradiction between 'membership structure',

Table 5.3   Typology of unions in Denmark, with estimates of membership, 1989

Type of union	Total membership (000s)	Share of union members %
Craft	300	15
General	722	36
Professional	280	14
Industrial:		
vertical	191	9
non-vertical	338	17
Status	174	9
Religious	22	1
Aggregate membership	2,027	101

Source: Estimated from Statistical Yearbook of Denmark (1990).

which is craft and general, and 'bargaining structure', which is in the main industrial (Scheuer 1990a: 44–77). Some of these problems have been addressed in LO's plans for structural change, considered below.

Despite the complexity of union structure in Denmark, demarcation disputes and poaching are relatively rare. This is because the recruitment boundaries of union unemployment insurance funds (closely related to union membership) have to be approved by the Ministry of Labour, and thus a union cannot recruit members in what is clearly another union's domain without risking the withdrawal of official recognition for its UIF.

The Crises: Intervention in the 1970s, 'De-intervention' in the 1980s

With its high degree of dependence on exports and foreign trade, Denmark was hard hit by the oil crises. After a period (lasting from 1959 to 1973) of virtually full employment, unemployment rose to 7–10 per cent of the dependent work force. Inflation rose, balance of payments deficits grew, and the problems of public expenditure worsened. These factors were interrelated: for example, public employment was used to stem the rise in unemployment, exacerbating the problem of public sector deficits already under strain from the burden of rising unemployment benefit payments. (The rate of unemployment benefit had been increased substantially in the days of full employment.) Such developments created pressures for change, not only in the political arena, but in industrial relations as well. There were moves towards new patterns of negotiation and industrial relations problem-solving. These new patterns have not proved durable, however, and they were partly reversed in the 1980s.

Implications of the Crises (I): Union Densities and Unemployment Insurance

Union strength – whether measured by membership numbers or by union density – had increased slightly in the 1950s. With the substantial rise in labour force participation in the 1960s, density stagnated, although absolute numbers of members increased. But the period from 1973 to the beginning of the 1980s was marked by a very substantial increase both in the number of union members and in union density. Aggregate union membership rose from 932,000 in 1960 to 1.1 million in 1970, and to 1.7 million in 1980; density was constant at 61 per cent in the period from 1960 to 1970, but increased to 78 per cent in 1980, rising by almost three percentage points every year (see tables 5.4 and 5.5). Membership and density have also been increasing since 1980, but much more slowly. The number of members reached 2 million in 1989 – having doubled over the previous twenty-five years, and density reached 80.7 per cent in 1985. Since then, there has been a small drop in density although absolute membership numbers are still increasing (cf. Visser 1991).

Table 5.4 Aggregate union membership, number of employees in labour force and union densities in Denmark 1960–86

Year	Number of union members (a) (000s)	Number of employees (b) (000s)	Union density (c: a/b) (%)
1960	932.5	1,533.5	60.8
1965	1,061.5	1,714.3	61.9
1970	1,140.2	1,856.1	61.4
1975	1,303.5	2,052.7	63.5
1980	1,747.1	2,245.8	77.8
1985	1,963.7	2,434.0	80.7
1989	2,066.4	2,601.0	79.4

Source: Statistical Yearbook of Denmark, cf. also Visser (1989).

Table 5.5 Average yearly increases in union membership and in union densities in Denmark 1960–86

Period	Yearly changes in membership (000s)	Yearly changes in union densities (%)
1960–65	25.8	0.22
1965–70	15.7	−0.10
1970–75	32.7	0.42
1975–80	88.7	2.86
1980–85	43.3	0.58
1985–89	25.7	−0.33

Source: Table 5.4.

One consequence is that traditional variations in union organization have virtually disappeared in Denmark. It is no longer true that blue-collar workers are significantly better organized than white-collar employees, men than women, public-sector employees than private sector employees, employees from large enterprises than employees from small enterprises, and so on. This is borne out by available survey evidence (see table 5.6). Virtually the only really significant difference remaining is in density among manual men and women (94 per cent and 87 per cent respectively in 1987, cf. Scheuer 1989a: 37–8).

The implications of this are, first, that no groups can today claim unions as their own 'special' form of expression (even though traditional groups in the LO still carry great weight); and second, that Denmark has more unionized salaried employees than manual workers – even in LO, 40 per cent of members are salaried employees.

Why is it that union density in Denmark has risen with rising unemployment, when the opposite is the case in many other Western market economies? Two major strands of the Danish debate on the issue will be reviewed: the 'unemployment insurance' argument and the 'union services' argument.

Table 5.6   Union densities of male and female, and of manual and non-manual employees according to omnibus survey data. Percentage of employees in union. Denmark 1966–87

Year	Male	Employees Female	Manual	Non-manual	All
1966	79	53	77	67	71
1972	77	53	72	62	67
1976	81	65	78	71	74
1979	85	75	84	77	80
1982	89	84	88	85	86
1985	89	88	90	87	88
1987	89	87	91	87	88

Source: Omnibus surveys by the Danish National Institute of Social Research, and Scheuer (1989a, 1989b).

The Role of Unemployment Insurance and of Individual Services

Some writers have argued that the way in which unemployment insurance is organized in Denmark amounts to a state-financed system of union recruitment (e.g. Pedersen 1978, 1979, 1982, 1988, 1989; Neumann et al. 1991). From the early days of Danish trade unionism, unemployment insurance funds (UIFs) were established alongside the union, together with strike funds, sickness insurance funds, etc. UIFs have increasingly been financed by the state and as a result have formally become financially and legally separated from the unions. In practice, however, a close link remains, since virtually every LO union has its own UIF, and the elected officials are mostly union leaders. With increasing unemployment in the 1970s, many white-collar and professional unions established their own UIFs. Formally, one may be a UIF member without being a union member. In practice this is difficult, especially in manual unions where norms of solidarity with the unemployed are dominant and the funds are seen as an integral part of union organization. Unemployment benefit rates were higher than in many other western European countries in the 1970s (about 70 per cent of a manual worker's mean annual wage), while members' contributions were moderate. The state bore almost 90 per cent of the costs of unemployment benefit.

The argument that UIFs encourage union membership finds support in the early-retirement scheme – the so-called 'post-employment wage' – introduced by the social-democratic and liberal coalition government in 1979. Designed to make room for more young people in the work force, it provided pensions from the age of 60 (normal age of retirement in Denmark is 67) for workers who had been UIF members for five of the last ten years (amended in 1980 to ten of the last fifteen years). The programme was a great success, in terms of the number of those eligible who took early retirement. For the unions, this scheme had the advantage of deterring older members from leaving the union (and the UIF), since it would disqualify them from the scheme. It was in effect an early retirement scheme for union members only (or more strictly, for UIF members only).[2]

The role of the UIF system in encouraging union membership has, however, been questioned (e.g. Scheuer 1984, 1989a; Darmer 1990). Assumptions about the system that seemed obvious ten years ago seem doubtful today. From 1982 onwards, compensation levels were cut in real terms and employees' contributions tripled. But even though unemployment insurance is formally voluntary in Denmark (like Sweden but unlike most other European countries), these changes had absolutely no effect on union densities (Arbejdsministeriet et al. 1989: 87; Scheuer 1989a: 34–5); membership of UIFs actually increased slightly, from 66 per cent of the labour force in 1982 to almost 70 in 1990 *(Statistical Ten-Year Review 1991).*

Government policies towards UIFs have reflected two objectives. One was to reduce unemployment, which had been high in Denmark since the mid-1970s. There was indeed some fall in unemployment in the early years of the new government, but from 1986 the figure rose again; in 1991 it surpassed the peak reached under the former social-democratic government. The other objective was to reduce the substantial financial burden on the state budget, and the government had some success in shifting the costs of unemployment benefit to the labour market actors. The tripling of employees' contributions and quadrupling of those of employers reduced the share financed by the state from 88 per cent in 1982 to 65 per cent in 1989 (Arbejdsministeriet (Ministry of Labour) et al. 1989). At the same time, the value of unemployment benefit fell from 71 per cent of mean annual income in 1982 to 64 per cent in 1988, primarily as a result of the government's decision to freeze the level of benefit.

Government policy has also aimed to solve more 'structural' problems of the Danish labour market which are seen as closely bound up with the system of unemployment insurance. Major reforms of the system have been proposed, but they have yet to materialize.

A detailed description and analysis of the problems have been given in a Ministry of Labour 'White Paper' (Arbejdsministeriet et al. 1989).[3] The present system has been criticized on a number of grounds. First, the benefit level is still considered too high for some groups of employees (the present maximum applies to all groups, producing relatively high compensation levels for unskilled workers). Second, there is said to be a persistent 'unintended' use of unemployment benefit by both employers and employees, as compensation for temporary lay-offs (e.g. breaks in employment caused by lack of raw materials in the fish-processing industry). Such 'unintended' uses are estimated to account for 40 per cent of all spells of unemployment and for 16 per cent of aggregate unemployment (Jensen and Westergård-Nielsen 1989: 6). Third, the emphasis on income maintenance in the Danish system means that people can remain unemployed for long periods of time, thus eroding labour market qualifications. Finally, the close connection between UIFs and unions means that the potential labour market for the individual unemployed member of a UIF is in the main restricted to the associated union's field of recruitment.

However, the system also has advantages. First, its formally voluntary character makes contributions by employees more acceptable. Second, the cost of the collection of membership contributions and the administration of benefits is borne by the UIFs and the unions themselves (Arbejdsministeriet et al. 1989). Third, the system ensures that the unemployed retain some contact with their union, in some cases facilitating a return to employment, and possibly also increasing the attentiveness of unions to the situation of the unemployed (Scheuer 1986).

Despite the high priority given to resolving the structural problems of the labour market and to developing new models of employment insurance, little has been achieved. One reason is that the government has tried to pursue its programme through some degree of consensus with the unions, rather than through confrontation or unilateral imposition; this partly reflects the Danish government's relatively weak parliamentary position as a minority government, compared with say the 1980s Conservative governments in Britain. A second reason for the absence of reform is the position of the unions. Until 1982, no non-social-democratic government had survived for more than one election period. Thus when the first Schlüter government took power in 1982, union leaders thought they could stall changes in labour market legislation until the social democrats returned to power. Several general elections later, Poul Schlüter remained in office, and it was slowly dawning on union leaders that if they wanted change before they themselves reached pension age, they would have to achieve it under a conservative-liberal government. However, the unions' desire for a compromise with the government has been thwarted by the continuing resistance to reform on the part a number of unions, particularly SiD (the General Workers' Union).

Union Services

Whether or not unions can grow in a weak labour market partly depends on the range of services on offer to potential members. Some of the specific traits of Danish industrial relations seem to assist unions in this respect. The first can be called bargaining implementation. As mentioned earlier, collective bargaining agreements are binding on the parties: unions can be fined if their members break the rules, but this goes for individual employers and their associations as well. Thus employers who try to exploit high unemployment to pay below the contract rates (or who dismiss employees without observing notice periods) can be taken to the Industrial Court and fined. In this way, unions do not have to rely on membership militancy to enforce agreements. This is particularly important in times of unemployment. The rights of the employees under collective agreements are collective rights, so that complaints can only be taken to the Industrial Court by the union (or rather, the union confederation, LO). In other words, the unions have a monopoly in defending workers' rights through the Industrial Court, a power that they exercise effectively. As a result, union membership is imperative for workers needing help in protecting their rights under collective agreements.

In the 1980s, there has been a slight tendency for these principles to be eroded. Civil courts have increasingly allowed individual employees who are not union members to bring cases on legally regulated matters of employment protection. But these are exceptions, and even for groups of employees, the cost of access to the civil courts (for example on matters of equal pay) is prohibitive.

The unions provide other important services to members. For example, many manual unions operate their own labour exchange. Formally, this service should be provided for all members of a UIF, even if they are not union members, but in practice such 'yellow' members are not normally catered for. Another service is the system of vocational training, financed by the state but run jointly by unions and employers' associations, for union members only. This system reflects the importance of craft unions in Denmark. By offering union members the chance to obtain job qualifications, it encourages the most able sections of the workforce to remain within unions.

Taken together, these services help explain why Danish unions experience membership stability in times of low unemployment, and high recruitment in times of high unemployment.

Structural Change in Unions and Employers' Associations

An important feature of union membership in the 1980s was the changing balance between individual unions and union confederations. It is not surprising that unions with a mainly blue-collar membership have been gradually losing ground. Table 5.7 shows the overall pattern of union membership by union confederation. LO unions have been able to recruit many of the new white-collar groups, especially lower-level salaried employees; nevertheless, they are losing out, especially to unions within the FTF (middle-level sala-

Table 5.7 The development of union confederations' share of union members (%)

Year	LO	FTF	AC	FR	Outside
1945	96	*	*	†	4
1950	95	*	*	†	5
1955	81	10	*	2	5
1960	79	12	*	3	5
1965	79	12	*	3	5
1970	78	14	*	3	4
1975	73	16	3	2	5
1980	72	16	4	1	7
1985	71	16	4	1	8
1989	69	16	5	3	6

* Union confederation not in existence.
† Data not available.
Source: Statistical Yearbook of Denmark, various years.

ried employees and semi-professional groups, mainly in the public and in the finance sectors) and also to some independent unions. Sixty-nine per cent of all union members are today in LO unions, compared with 78 per cent in 1970, and LO is thus gradually losing its prerogative as 'sole representative' of the employee side of industrial relations (although the rate of decline has slowed since the 1970s).

But in addition the LO itself is changing character. In 1970, just over 200,000 or 23 per cent of the LO membership were salaried employees; by 1986 this figure had grown to around 559,000 or 40 per cent. In LO, the General Workers' Union, SiD, had almost 40 per cent of the membership in the late 1940s, but this share has been declining sharply, and today SiD has little more than a fifth of LO membership (see Table 5.8). At the same time, HK – the main LO union for white-collar employees, which affiliated in 1932 – has increased its share significantly, from under 10 per cent in the 1940s and 1950s, to 23 per cent today, making it the biggest LO union. It organizes lower-level clerical employees in both private and public sectors (unlike the situation in Norway and Sweden, where clerical employees are mostly unionized outside LO). The largely white-collar Union of Municipal Workers, DKA, has also increased its share of LO membership, and is now the fourth largest member union after the blue-collar Dansk Metal.

Although LO has succeeded in expanding its organizational territory well beyond the traditional blue-collar sectors, major groups like intermediate technicians and semi-professionals still seem out of reach. The LO's ability to halt the downward trend of its share of union membership will depend on the strategies of cooperation or competition that it pursues with regard to FTF and its member unions, or with unions outside the union confederations. It is noteworthy, however, that LO's share of unionized employees was higher in 1985 (at 70 per cent) than the Norwegian or the

Table 5.8   Membership figures of two major unions since 1945 and their shares of LO aggregate membership

Year	Union membership:			Share of LO membership by:	
	LO	SiD	HK	SiD	HK
		(000s)		(%)	
1945	579.4	228.8	42.1	39	7
1950	635.8	240.1	50.0	38	8
1955	693.2	247.9	59.8	36	9
1960	739.5	249.6	79.5	34	11
1965	834.0	258.0	104.9	31	13
1970	894.4	258.9	136.4	29	15
1975	953.3	258.4	155.7	27	16
1980	1,249.6	311.9	273.3	25	22
1985	1,399.1	316.7	309.5	23	22
1990	1,423.0	313.2	323.0	22	23

Source: Statistical Yearbook of Denmark, various years.

Swedish LOs (who had 67 and 60 per cent of unionized employees respectively); thus the Danish LO may have been more successful in recruiting among lower and middle groups of non-manual employees than its Scandinavian counterparts.

Membership in the employers' association, DA, has been stable through the 1980s, when measured by the number of employees in firms which are members of the DA. As table 5.9 shows, DA's share of manual employees is between 25 and 29 per cent. It must be noted, however, that despite its modest share of the manual work force, the DA has maintained a dominant role as the 'trend setter' for pay development in the private and (therefore also) in the public sector.

Inside DA there has been a major restructuring of the member associations. Until recently, DA had both individual firms and industrial or local employers' associations as members. The number of affiliated organizations remained stable at around 150 for some years. As a result of extensive restructuring and mergers between smaller units, the number of member organizations has now been reduced to 51, and the process is continuing (DA 1990: 10). One of the more important mergers was between the employers' associations in the metal industry, JA, and in general manufacturing. The resulting association, Employers in Industry, IA, covers almost half of all employees employed by DA members, and it therefore presents an implicit threat to the central authority of DA. There is no doubt that these organizational changes have reinforced the decentralizing trend in collective bargaining. In 1991, IA merged with Industrirådet, the Council of Industry, creating Dansk Industri. This development will eliminate problems of 'dual membership' of employers' associations and trade organizations, although some member firms in Industrirådet will have to

Table 5.9   Number of manual workers employed by member firms of the DA (The Federation of Danish Employers) and DA manual workers as share of total manual work force 1979–87

Year	Manual workers: in DA firms (000s)	in dependent work force	DA share of manual work force %
1979	308	1,140	27
1983	274	1,113	25
1987	312	1,072	29

Source: Statistical ten-year review 1989.

decide whether to join an employers' association. This is particularly the case in the chemical and pharmaceutical industries where firms have traditionally remained aloof from such bodies.

On the union side, the rationalization of LO's membership structure has been a priority for many years. Mergers reduced the 72 member unions in LO in 1946 to 57 by 1971 and to 24 by 1987. However, eight new unions had joined LO in this period, making a total of 32 member unions (LO 1989).

The pressures of the single European market, whether real or not, are used as a legitimization by those who advocate change in union structure. At the 1989 LO congress at which change was debated, more than 80 per cent of the participants voted in favour of a 'new structure' proposed by the organization committee. The basis of the new structure is the creation of five broad sectoral 'cartels' from existing member unions. The cartels, covering manufacturing industry, construction, transport and services, local government and the central state sector, would deal mainly with collective bargaining and vocational training issues. An overview of the proposal is given in table 5.10.

Cartels – that is, groupings of unions in the same industry – already exist in some form in construction and in the state and local authority sectors. Amongst public employees, cartels also include unions not in LO, but this is unlikely to hinder the process of creating the new cartels.

More serious problems have arisen with the industry cartel. It presupposes the absorption of the traditionally powerful CO Metal cartel, which has always played a leading role in bargaining rounds (see table 5.12). The cartel is dominated by the skilled workers' union, Dansk Metal. In addition it comprises SiD, KAD, and some smaller craft unions (electricians, plumbers, etc.). Most supporters of the cartels see them as evolving in practice into broad sector-level unions, to which existing unions would transfer their competences in collective bargaining and other matters. SiD, as a large general union, has been vehemently opposed to the cartel proposal since it fears the emergence of powerful sector-specific unions, but it has been outmanoeuvred in LO's decision-making processes and finds itself increasingly isolated. At its 1991 congress, LO abandoned attempts to reach a

Table 5.10   Proposed LO cartel structure and estimated membership

Cartel for:	Number of: Unions	Members
Building and construction	9	215,000
Industry	19	472,000
Services, trade and transport	10	294,000
Private sector total membership		981,000
Local authorities	16	332,000
State	19	107,000
Public sector total membership		439,000
Grand total	32	1,420,000

Source: LO 1989, and *Fagbladet* (SiD journal) 31, 8 September 1989.

compromise on cartels. As a result, the trend towards broad sectoral union-ism, which already appears unstoppable, will continue at the initiative of individual unions. CO Metal will probably evolve into a cartel for the whole of manufacturing, forming the basis of a future sector union. The emergence of sector unions in Denmark would entail a radical change in the role and organization of LO.

Both in the employers' associations and the unions, current structural change may be seen as a process of re-centralization under which LO and DA respectively plan and carry out changes in their membership structures. However, the outcome may be to accelerate a limited process of vertical decentralization. As in the case of the IA, new structures may in practice weaken the authority of the central confederations and increase the empha-sis on industry-level bargaining in the 1990s. If this is the case, it will keep Denmark in step with developments in neighbouring countries (especially Germany and Sweden), and thus enhance the possibilities for international coordination and imitation between unions or cartels in individual sectors.

In the Danish finance sector – outside the scope of LO and DA – the move to industry bargaining has been encouraged by mergers on both the em-ployer and union sides. The previously separate employers' associations for clearing and savings banks have merged, and the four minor unions for employees in clearing and savings banks, insurance companies and property institutions, agreed to amalgamate into a single finance union which held its first congress in November 1991.

Implications of the Crises (II): Centralization and Decentralization of Collective Bargaining

Before the 1970s, collective bargaining in Denmark normally resulted in voluntary biennial agreements. Only exceptionally did deadlock require parliamentary intervention in negotiations between the major actors, as in the 1956 and 1963 bargaining rounds referred to earlier. In most cases, both sides endorsed the negotiated agreements in their respective ballots.

In 1973, the first signs of change appeared. The breakdown of bargaining led to a major conflict with three weeks of strikes and lockouts before the parties finally reached an agreement; two more weeks were necessary to complete the voting procedures. The next three bargaining rounds (1975, 1977 and 1979) all ended without agreement. So the norm of one in five 'going wrong' in the 1950s and 1960s became four in five 'going wrong' in the 1970s. In the 1980s, the earlier pattern was restored.

Intervention, Concertation, Centralization and Inflation

Why did collective bargaining go so wrong in the 1970s? In part, because of international factors such as the oil crisis and the need for low inflation. The government was probably influenced by attempts in countries such as Britain or West Germany to find 'tripartite solutions' in which pay increases were determined by concertation between government, unions, and employers at the national level.

There were also more specific Danish factors involved. From the end of the 1950s, there had been an increasing tendency for (mainly social-democratic) governments and top politicians to take a close interest in bargaining rounds, reflecting a concern with macro-economic stability. Increasingly, other policy aims also became important: for example, the 'solidaristic wages policy', and the reduction of pay inequalities between men and women and between skilled and unskilled workers. This led to the increasing centralization and politicization of collective bargaining, the right to negotiate becoming vested respectively in the major union or the union cartel, and the employers' associations (see table 5.11).

Bargaining at this level is called 'decentralized', in the sense that it is limited to particular industries or sectors. Unions and cartels can, however, transfer bargaining rights to LO, which then bargains centrally with the employers' confederation, DA. This became increasingly common in the 1960s and reached a peak in the 1970s, in the context of the tripartite search for a fair basis for incomes policies (Scheuer 1990a: 44–57).

There were several reasons for the failure of policies of central 'concertation', some of which can be related to similar trends in other Western European countries. First, Denmark suffered from a version of the 'British disease': LO was willing, but in practice unable, to control pay developments, especially wage drift in the individual unions and cartels. Power and control in the Danish union structure are, to a much greater extent than in Norway and Sweden, located within the individual national unions and their branches. Added to this, the absence of comprehensive industrial

Table 5.11 Major agreements in 1991 collective bargaining in Denmark

Industry	Union side	Employer side	Number of employees
Metal industry	CO Metal	IA	100,000
Other industry	SiD + KAD	IA	25,000
Textile industry	Bekl. & Teks-arbejd.	Beklaednings-arb. givere	10,000
Shops and offices	HK	BKA	100,000
State employees	Minister of CFU cartel	Finance	270,000
Municipal employees	KTO cartel	KL, ARF	485,000

Note: See list of abbreviations.

unionism in Denmark implies that unions to some extent compete for members and for their share of wage drift (Calmfors 1990).

Second, the vast increase in membership meant that most individual unions did not feel under pressure to hold back pay in response to economic crisis and mounting unemployment. Rather, the reverse was happening: increasing unemployment made individual employees more dependent on the unions, which thus had a decreasing incentive to fall into line with LO. Many new unions were gaining ground, and there was a general feeling that individual unions could stand on their own feet.

Third, repeated parliamentary interventions eroded the legitimacy of settlements, since opposing them was no longer opposing the majority of union members, but government and parliament. Thus the demarcation between parliamentary politics and industrial bargaining was becoming blurred, much to the frustration of union leaders and probably also of the politicians. All three interventions in the 1970s took place under social-democratic minority governments, and there is no doubt that many union members saw these interventions (and the policies of a government facing a non-socialist majority in parliament) as an expression of the policies of union leaders as well. Local union officials felt little commitment to pay settlements implemented in this way, especially if they were not social-democrats themselves, but from the Communist or the Socialist People's Party.[4]

Thus the incomes policies of the 1970s were not very successful. Inflation was not contained but was consistently above the average of Denmark's major trading partners. As a result, by the end of the 1970s there was strong pressure on union leaders as well as on politicians to devise new arrangements. It was clearly necessary to restore the bargaining system's legitimacy, and to 'de-couple' collective bargaining from the sphere of party politics and parliament. The social-democratic government was also under increasing strain, unable to cope with the great economic problems of inflation, balance of payments deficits and – perhaps most important in this connection – unemployment.

An expression of these problems may be seen in the level of industrial conflict in the 1970s. This was not high by international standards, but was rising, and a significant proportion was political in nature. For example, there were protest strikes against the liberal Hartling government in 1974, against the implementation of anti-inflationary measures aimed at restricting pay increases to 6 per cent (in 1976), and against the repeated parliamentary interventions in collective bargaining.

Collective Bargaining in the 1980s

Denmark's entry into the European Community in 1973 had little impact on industrial relations in the 1970s and 1980s. In these two decades, it was very much 'business as usual', and neither the employers' associations nor the unions appear to have ascribed any role in collective bargaining to decision makers in Brussels. The only major change caused by membership of the EC appears to have been that bargaining over state support for agriculture, which traditionally was closely tied to collective bargaining in the food-processing industry, now took place within the broader European context.

This 'business as usual' attitude disappeared with the passing of the Single European Act (following a referendum in Denmark in 1986) and the prospect of the single European market. Major companies, unions, and employers' associations are now gearing up their policies and their organizational structures for 1993. Thus the 1980s may be seen as the last decade of 'untainted' Danish industrial relations. This view is confirmed in a roundabout way by the fact that in some respects the 1980s had brought a return to the traditional post-war pattern of collective bargaining.

In 1982, the social-democratic minority government of Anker Jørgensen was replaced by the four-party, conservative-liberal government of Poul Schlüter, and the political climate turned less union-friendly. The new government introduced labour market policies clearly aimed at diminishing union influence and membership. Union leaders lost their close contacts with ministers, and the real value of unemployment insurance was lowered by the government's suspension of the price indexation of pay – a measure long demanded by DA – and of public transfers (except old age pensions). However, as discussed earlier, these measures failed to have any impact on union density and even if some individual unions have had slightly declining membership, nowhere has it been on the scale experienced in the UK and elsewhere in Europe (Visser 1991).

Unexpectedly perhaps, the suspension of price indexation seems to have helped the unions, because collective bargaining regained the prominence in pay determination that it had lost in the 1970s. High inflation and frequent parliamentary intervention had meant that wage drift and price indexation, rather than national bargaining agreements, had become the major factors in pay determination. Following the suspension of indexation in 1982, however, collective bargaining again became the major factor in pay increases, accounting for well over half the total in some years (OECD 1990: 78; Ibsen 1990: 173). This was a striking recovery in the influence of union bargainers, helped – albeit unintentionally – by the conservative-liberal government.

The desire to avoid the deadlocks and political intervention of the 1970s led to decentralized bargaining in 1981, but in 1983 there was a return to centralization following lack of industry-level agreement. In 1985, parliament had to break the deadlock again. This was partly due to the increased politicization of collective bargaining since some major unions, especially SiD, saw industrial confrontation as a way of bringing down the Schlüter government. This was not, however, the strategy of most unions and union leaders, and in 1987 a major breakthrough was achieved. A four-year contract (with a provision for possible adjustments after two years if prices should rise more than expected) was agreed in decentralized negotiations. This helped confirm the move to single-industry bargaining. An overview of the general bargaining rounds and their degree of centralization is shown in table 5.12.

Collective bargaining and bargainers thus regained their significance in the 1980s, and it became possible to resolve problems without resorting to politicians and parliament. The 1987 solution stands out, not only because it was agreed much faster than expected, but also because it provided significant increases in pay and a phased reduction of the working week from 39 to 37 hours, which is now standard in Denmark. (The 39-hour week had been introduced by parliamentary intervention in 1985.) The 1987 agreement was reached in a series of negotiations between major unions or cartels, with the CO Metal cartel and the employers' association for the metal industry, JA, making the initial breakthrough.

Although the 1987 negotiations were ostensibly decentralized (within the general LO-DA framework), the CO Metal-JA settlement was virtually 'carbon copied' by the other bargaining units. This highlights several important aspects of Danish collective bargaining. First, collective bargaining is highly synchronized. It takes place every second year, over a relatively limited period of time, roughly from December until March. Thus for the rest of the two-year period, agreements are implemented, not bargained over. There may of course be local adjustments, but such bargaining takes place under the peace obligation.

Second, some unions (and employers) seem to be able to 'set the pace' and establish the pattern for increases in pay, reductions in working hours and so on for all employees, private or public. No substantial differences in bargaining outcomes between sectors are normally tolerated, even though trends in actual earnings may be quite different from pay rates agreed upon in

Table 5.12   Summary of collective bargaining rounds in Denmark since 1945

Year	Degree of centralization	Main actor[1]
1946	Decentralized	CO Metal & JA
1948	Decentralized	CO Metal & JA
1950	Centralized	LO & DA[2]
1952	Decentralized	CO Metal & JA
1954	Decentralized	HK & BKA
1956	Intervention	Parliament
1958	Decentralized	CO Metal & JA
1961	Intervention	Parliament
1963	Intervention	Parliament
1965	Centralized	LO & DA
1967	Centralized	LO & DA
1969	Centralized	LO & DA
1971	Centralized	LO & DA
1973	Centralized	LO (5 weeks official conflict)
1975	Intervention	Parliament
1977	Intervention	Parliament
1979	Intervention	Parliament
1981	Decentralized	Textile Industry
1983	Centralized	LO & DA
1985	Intervention	Parliament
1987	Decentralized	CO Metal & JA
1989	Decentralized	HK & BKA
1991	Decentralized	State sector

[1] 'Main actors' are the 'leaders' in collective bargaining rounds, i.e. the bargaining unit where the breakthrough for the final agreement was made that year. Some parliamentary interventions overruled a rejection of a compromise solution on the side of the Danish Employers' Association, the DA.
[2] LO, DA etc.: See list of abbreviations
Source: *Avisårbogen* 1945 to 1987, cf. Scheuer (1990a).

collective bargaining. So not only do employers outside DA follow agreements and pay levels agreed upon by LO and DA or their members, but the results of decentralized bargaining are also standardized. When one talks of decentralized solutions in Danish collective bargaining, it is decentralization of processes rather than of outcomes.

In some instances, this has created irritation among leaders of those unions or cartels that are the first to reach a settlement. They seem to feel that other groups, especially within the public sector, are 'piggy-backing' on the efforts of the private export-oriented sector. On the other hand, this state of affairs is probably preferable to an even more decentralized type of bargaining, where those reaching early agreements run the risk of losing out (on this question in relation to Finland cf. Ahonen 1990). In a small country like Denmark, however, there is not much room for wide variations between settlements. If it is impossible to exclude public employees from the gains of employees in the export industries, it is also much more difficult for any group to 'free-ride' in the sense of remaining completely outside the union movement. The very high union densities are testimony to this.

In 1983 the first finance minister of the Schlüter governments, Henning Christoffersen (now Danish member of the European Commission), called for the public sector to 'go first' and set the bench-mark in national collective bargaining rounds. It seemed an exotic proposal at the time, but became a reality in 1991 when for the first time public sector negotiations opened the bargaining round, signalling a continuation of the low-inflation trend of the late 1980s. This was the culmination of the sector's increasingly prominent role in industrial relations (see e.g. Mikkelsen 1992; Due and Madsen 1988, 1990), reflected for example in rising conflict during the 1980s, and in changing patterns of collective bargaining.

From the end of the 1970s, bargaining cartels were established for groups of public employees. Today two cartels exist, the CFU – for 270,000 state employees – and the KTO – for 485,000 employees in local government and institutions. The remarkable thing about these cartels is that they have been able to cross several boundaries that earlier seemed unsurmountable: they represent both civil servants and the majority of employees on normal contracts of employment (i.e. without special pension rights, and with normal conditions of termination of employment). They also represent groups of manual workers, and include LO unions as well as members of FTF and AC. Thus between them they cover virtually all public employees, accounting for a third of the total Danish work force. The cartels are able to coordinate their bargaining efforts very closely. They are, therefore, heavy-weight participants in the general bargaining process. Public employees have secured for themselves a share in any private sector wage drift through a regulation mechanism which gives them 80 per cent of private sector pay increases above the agreed levels.

The leading role of the public sector was demonstrated in the 1989 round which provided the first general employment-related pension schemes for lower-paid employees in the public sector, semi-professionals and academics having enjoyed such schemes for many years. This was a major breakthrough, and was followed in the 1991 round by the establishment of similar pension schemes in significant parts of the private sector, including the engineering industry. This may be considered a step towards European integration, since it is similar to the earnings-related pension schemes that exist in continental Europe, and thus a step away from the traditional Scandinavian model in which pensions were financed out of general taxation and did not depend on former labour market status (a step which Denmark is the last of the Scandinavian countries to take, see Andersen 1991: 13).

The establishment of strong bargaining cartels in the public sector and the willingness of the conservative-liberal government as employer to negotiate at this level has strengthened the move towards decentralization. By including non-LO unions, these cartels have probably weakened the power of the central LO leadership to determine bargaining outcomes. In general, the role of bargainers at industry or sector level has been reinforced, while the influence of the national level leaderships of DA and LO has been reduced.

Increasing Flexibility

There have been profound changes in the framework of rules governing bargaining over pay and working time at different levels of the system. Rules have become more flexible. One aspect of this is the regulation of working hours and of overtime. Earlier agreements laid down very precisely the number of working hours per week, overtime rates, and, in many cases, the maximum overtime allowable. The rules have been undermined by local practices, and have been formally relaxed. For example, the 1987 agreements merely prescribe average monthly or even yearly working hours. In building and construction, working hours may thus be shorter in winter and longer in summer, without employers having to pay overtime. Thus the details of the working time of the individual employee are today settled at the workplace, and central regulations have been reduced to a minimum. Other areas of employment regulation have been similarly affected.

On the other hand employers have tightened their grip on wage drift. Traditionally, local negotiations over pay adjustments (formally related to productivity increases) took place several times a year. This system allowed for substantial pay increases outside the central bargaining system. In the 1983 round, however, a 'wage regulation mechanism' was introduced, limiting the number of times local pay bargaining could take place. It permitted employers' associations for the first time to set a ceiling on local productivity-related pay increases. This arrangement continued in 1985, and was tightened in 1987 as part of the price the union side had to pay for the reduction of the working week. The change has had two important effects. First, it has effectively reduced wage drift, contributing significantly to lower inflation in Denmark in the 1980s. Second, it seems to have been effective in putting a stop to competition between different groups of employees, which had contributed to the inflationary problems of the 1960s and 1970s. As a result, it has probably helped reduce industrial conflict, which to a large degree stemmed from this local bargaining. This wage regulation mechanism has in some respects counteracted the decentralization of bargaining, since it has restricted workplace negotiation and increased the control of industry-level employers' associations over wage drift.

Summing Up: Re-establishing the 'Relative Autonomy' of Industrial Relations

While the 1970s saw an increased politicization of industrial relations, in the 1980s collective bargaining regained much of the institutional legitimacy it had lost. Senior negotiators from the unions and employers' associations were back on stage, setting the agenda, although some of the key actors had changed. In the 1960s and 1970s, the 'top echelon' on the union side were the LO president, and those of SiD and of Dansk Metal (Auken 1970). By the end of the 1980s, the core group was composed of the presidents of Dansk Metal (in his capacity as president of the metal industry bargaining cartel, 'CO Metal'), of the Industry Group in SiD (who is also the vice-president of the CO Metal cartel) and of HK, who made the breakthrough in the 1989 negotiations. LO now occupies a much more marginal position than in the past.

Thus the policies of both union and employer bargainers, as well as the government, have resulted in a return to the more decentralized forms of bargaining which were common in Denmark in the 1950s. Since the basic framework of procedural rules governing the bargaining system remains largely unchanged, the result has not been inflation and leap-frogging, but highly synchronized, decentralized bargaining rounds. Less centralized bargaining reduces the scope for politicians to intervene, and it minimizes the emphasis on pay relativities. The suspension of indexation 'gave back' to the unions the role of bargaining over pay that they had virtually lost in the late 1970s, and thus the industrial relations actors regained their traditional autonomy.

Despite the suggestion of Amoroso (1990: 91) that decentralization has led to a narrowing of the bargaining agenda, issues other than pay were prominent in 1980s bargaining – the reduction of working hours which was handled successfully in a decentralized setting; (unsuccessful) union demands for better notice in case of lay-offs; and the introduction of pensions for lower non-manual and for manual employees.

Conclusions

The Danish economy suffered from continuing imbalances in the 1980s which governments were unable to correct. These problems were partly connected to structural and institutional aspects of the labour market, placing a heavy burden on industrial relations actors. Some problems have been alleviated, but there is general agreement that basic flaws remain. The 1980s saw a weakening of the corporatist system of consultation following the change of government in 1982. But Denmark still has a system with strong corporatist traits. For example, representatives of major organizations continue to sit on important public committees.

Important changes have been taking place in collective bargaining procedures and in the structures of the industrial relations actors, mostly in the direction of a slow decentralization. These developments accelerated towards the end of the 1980s. This has not weakened the 'Scandinavian model'. On the contrary, the 'Scandinavian way' of handling industrial conflict and collective bargaining in a highly institutionalized manner has been strengthened in Denmark. Attempts in the 1970s to establish a model closer to the Swedish pattern – based on high-trust relationships between leaders of (social-democratic) governments, LO and the employers' confederation, acting partly independently of their 'constituencies' – have failed utterly in Denmark. This is not lamented by this author.

Industrial conflict has been falling, although public employees have become more prominent in conflict as they have in collective bargaining. The 1980s, unlike the 1970s, saw no political strikes with the exception of protests against the 1985 parliamentary intervention in collective bargaining.

Danish unions and employers face great changes in the 1990s. How should they handle the risk that they will be increasingly marginalized, and the growing role of non-manual employees in collective bargaining? For the employers, the question can be posed in the following manner. DA is restructuring extensively, but its legitimacy is constrained by competition from employers' associations in agriculture and in the finance sector, and from a great number of individual employers who stand outside any association. For DA, the problem is how to improve relations with other employers' associations, and – most importantly – how to increase its membership 'density' so as to become comparable with its generally stronger Scandinavian counterparts.

LO has had some success in enticing minor unions away from FTF. It is now trying to make its structure more 'industrial', via the new cartel proposal. However, LO might also try to exploit the strength of craft-based unionism (and of its white-collar professional counterpart) by giving greater emphasis to professional qualifications and training in the 1990s. Such a strategy would probably require closer cooperation between LO and non-LO unions, something that is already taking place in the public sector. Formal cooperation, including mergers, would probably require LO to play down its affiliation to social democracy, perhaps introducing the kind of 'political levy' system which exists in Britain, where members have a formal right to opt out. If this were done, the justification for staying outside LO would disappear, and for many of the smaller status and professional unions, closer cooperation would become possible. LO may have considered such cooperation unnecessary in the past, but the prospects of the single European market may lead senior LO strategists to contemplate it more seriously. If the Scandinavian way is to survive, it probably requires that Danish unions move away from the present fragmentation.

Notes

1   For information about the conflict itself, see e.g. Nielsen 1978; for an excellent, if somewhat outdated English description of the conflict and the ensuing system, see Galenson (1952/1955); see also Ibsen and Jørgensen 1979.

2   For an English description and analysis, see Pedersen and Smith (1991).

3   A summary of the analysis may be found in OECD 1990: 57–93. English language descriptions of the system can be found in e.g. Jensen and Westergård-Nielsen (1989: 24–6) and in Jensen et al. (1987).

4   The Socialistisk Folkeparti, Socialist People's Party, is a left reformist party that originated as a splinter from the Communist Party following the Hungarian uprising of 1956. It

developed a distinctive policy and gained a substantial share of parliamentary seats (over 10 per cent in the 1980s), but it never achieved much influence in parliament. It has some limited support among unions.

Abbreviations

AC	*Akademikernes Centralorganisation* – Central Confederation of Professional Associations
ARF	*Amtsrådsforeningen* – Associations of Regional Authorities in Denmark (Employers)
BKA	*Butiks- og Kontorfagenes Arbejdsgiverforening* – Federation of Employers in Commercial and Clerical Industries
CFU	*Centralorganisationernes Forhandlingudvalg* – The bargaining committee of the central organizations (for unions of state employees and civil servants)
CO Metal	*Centralorganisationen af Metalarbejdere* – Federation of workers in Metal Industry, memberships from Dansk Metal, SiD, KAD and others
DA	*Dansk Arbejdsgiverforening* – Danish Employers' Federation
Dansk Metal	*Dansk Metalarbejderforbund* – Union of Danish Metal Workers
FR	*Hovedorganisationen for Arbejdsleder- og tekniske Funktionserforeninger i Danmark* – Association of Foremen and Technical Employees.
FTF	*Funktionærernes og Tjenestemændenes Fællesråd* – Central Confederation of salaried employees
HK	*Handels– og Kontorfunktionærernes Forbund i Danmark* – Union of Commercial and Clerical Employees in Denmark
IA	(before 1990) *Industrifagenes Arbejdsgiverforening* – Federation of Employers in [other] Industry
IA	(from 1990) *Industriens Arbejdsgivere* – Employers in Industry (merger of former IA with JA)
JA	*Jernets Arbejdsgiverforening* – Federation of Employers in Metal Industry
KAD	*Kvindeligt Arbejderforbund i Danmark* – Union of Female Workers in Denmark
KL	*Kommunernes Landsforening* – Association of Local Authorities in Denmark (Employers)
KTO	*Kommunale Tjenestemænd og Overenskomstansatte* – Civil servants and salaried employees in local administration and institutions (Union bargaining cartel)
LO	*Landsorganisationen i Danmark* – Danish Federation of Trade Unions
SiD	*Specialarbejderforbundet i Danmark* – Union of General Workers in Denmark
TCO	*Tjänstmännens Centralorganisation* – Central organization of salaried employees (in Sweden)
TL	*Teknisk Landsforbund* – Union of Technicians
UIF	Unemployment Insurance Fund

References

Ahonen, G. 1990: Spelöppningen. Om kollektivavtalsprocessen i Finland på 1980-talet. *Politeia*, no. 1, 1990, 1–133. Institutionen för Ekonomisk Politologi, Svenska Handelshögskolen.

Amoroso, B. 1990: Development and Crisis of the Scandinavian Model of Labour Relations in Denmark. In G. Baglioni and C. Crouch (eds), *European Industrial Relations – The Challenge of Flexibility*, London: Sage, 71–96.

Andersen, B. R. 1991: Den danske model i EF's indre marked. *Samfundsøkonomen*, 1, 13–23, Copenhagen.

196 *Industrial Relations in the New Europe*

Arbejdsministeriet et al. 1989: *Hvidbog om arbejdsmarkedets strukturproblemer*. Copenhagen: Arbejdsministeriet.

Auken, S. 1970: Tilrettelæggelsen af dansk fagbevægelses politik i overenskomsforhandlingerne på det private arbejdsmarked. *Økonomiog Politik*, 44, no. 2, 117–142.

Auken, S. and Buksti, J. 1975: Den Indkomst-politiske Problematik i Danmark. *Økonomi og Politik*, 49, 3, 241–74.

Bruun, N. 1991: *Law and Society in the Global Village – Toward Collaboration and Comparative Research* (Working Paper). Helsinki: Swedish School of Economics and Business Administration.

Brünniche-Olsen, P. 1990: *Arbejdsmarkedspolitik*. Copenhagen: Handelshøjskolens Forlag.

Calmfors, L. (ed.) 1990: *Wage Formation and Macro-Economic Policy in the Nordic Countries*. Stockholm/Oxford: OUP.

Christoffersen, M. N 1988: Myter om familien. *Samfundsøkonomen*, no 4 Copenhagen: DJØFs Forlag.

DA 1990: *Årsberetning 1989–90*. Copenhagen: Dansk Arbejdsgiverforening.

Darmer, M. 1990: Arbejdslshedsforsikringen og dens betydning for organisationsgraden. *Økonomi og Politik*, 63, 4, 52–61.

Due, J. and Madsen, J. S. 1980: *Overenskomstsystemets sammenbrud*. Copenhagen: Akademisk Forlag.

Due, J. and Madsen, J. S. 1988: *Når der slås søm i. Overenskomstforhandlinger og organisationskultur*. Copenhagen: Jurist- og Økonomforbundets Forlag.

Due, J. and Madsen, J. S. 1990: Centraliseret decentralisering. Overenskomstforhandlinger på det offentlige område i 1970'erne og 1980'erne. In *Årbog for Arbejderbevægelsens Historie*, vol. 20, Copenhagen: Selskabet til Forskning i Arbejderbevægelsens Historie.

Elvander, N. 1988a: *Den svenska modellen. Löneförhandlingar och inkomstpolitik*. Stockholm: Almänne Förlaget.

Elvander, N. (ed.) 1988b: *Förhandlingssystem, inkomstpolitik och arbetskonflikter i Norden*. Stockholm: Norstedts.

Elvander, N. 1989: Bargaining Systems, Incomes Policies and Conflict in the Nordic Countries *(Current Approaches to Collective Bargaining)*. Geneva: International Labour Office.

Freeman, R. B. and Medoff, J. L. 1984: *What do Unions do?* New York: Basic Books.

Galenson, W. 1955: *Arbejder og arbejdsgiver i Danmark*. Copenhagen: Det danske forlag (English original: 1952).

Ibsen, F. 1990: Lokale lønforhandlinger, omfang, muligheder og problemer. In *Årbog for Arbejderbevægelsens Historie*, vol. 20, Copenhagen: Selskabet til Forskning i Arbejderbevægelsens Historie.

Ibsen, F. and Jørgensen, H. 1979: *Fagbevægelse og stat*, vols. 1, 2. Copenhagen: Nyt Nordisk Forlag.

Jensen, P. H. Larsen, J. E. and Olofsson, G. 1987: Labour Movement and Unemployment Policies. In Lund, R., Pedersen P. J. and Schmidt-Sørensen, J. B. (eds), *Studies in Unemployment*, Copenhagen: New Social Science Monographs.

Jensen, P. and Westergård-Nielsen, N. 1989: *Temporary lay-offs* (Studies in Labour Market Dynamics, Working Paper 89-2). Århus: Labour Economics Group, University of Århus and Århus School of Business.

Kjellberg, A. 1983: *Facklig organisering i tolv länder*. Lund: Arkiv.

Kjellberg, A. 1985: Facklig radikalism i Danmark. *ARKIV för studier i arbetarrörelsens historia*, 31-2, 35–58.

LO 1989: *Oplæg til beslutninger om fagbevægelsens fremtidige struktur*. Copenhagen: LO.

Lund, R. 1972: *Sammenslutningen og Centralorganisationen. Tilblivelse og udvikling*. Copenhagen: Socialforskningsinstituttet.

Lyck, L. (ed.) 1990: *The Nordic Countries and the Internal Market of the EEC*. Copenhagen: Handelshøjskolens Forlag.

Mikkelsen, F. 1991 (forthcoming): *Protest og konflikt blandt offentligt ansatte*. Copenhagen.

Mikkelsen, F. 1992: *Arbejdskonflikter i Skandinavien 1848–1980.* Doctoral thesis, Copenhagen.
Neumann, G. P., Pedersen, P. J. and Westergård-Nielsen, N. 1991: Long-run International Trends in Aggregate Unionization. *European Journal of Political Economy*, 7, 3, 249–74.
Nielsen, C. 1978: *100 dages krigen.* Copenhagen: Gyldendal.
OECD 1990: *Denmark*, OECD Economic Surveys. Paris: OECD.
OECD 1991: *Employment Outlook*, July. Paris: OECD.
Pedersen, P. J. 1978: Union Growth and the Business Cycle: A Note on the Bain- Elsheik Model. *British Journal of Industrial Relations*, 16, 3, 373–7.
Pedersen, P. J. 1979: *Aspekter af fagbevægelsens vækst i Danmark*, 1911–1976. Mimeo 1979–5 Økonomisk Institut, Århus Universitet.
Pedersen, P. J. 1982: Union Growth in Denmark, 1911–39. *Scandinavian Journal of Economics*, 84, 4, 583–92.
Pedersen, P. J. 1988: *Arbejdsløshedsforsikringen 1911–1985.* Mimeo: Århus.
Pedersen, P. J. 1989: Langsigtede internationale tendenser i den faglige organisering og i den politiske venstrefløj. *Økonomi og Politik*, 62, 2,
Pedersen, P. J. 1990: Arbejdsmarkedet og det indre marked. *Ledelse og erhvervsøkonomi*, 1, 1990. Copenhagen: Civil Økonomernes Forlag.
Pedersen, P. J. and Smith, N. 1991: *Early Exit in the Danish Labour Market – A Time Series Approach.* Working paper 91–2, Centre for Labour Economics, University of Århus School of Business.
Pestoff, V. 1991: The demise of the Swedish Model and the resurgence of organized business as a major political actor. University of Stockholm, Department of Business Administration. (Paper presented to 10th EGOS Colloquium, Vienna, 15–17 July 1991.)
Price, R. J. 1989: The Decline and Fall of the Status Divide? In Sisson, K. (ed.), *Personnel Management in Britain*, Oxford: Blackwell, 271–95.
Scheuer, S. 1984: *Hvorfor stiger den faglige organisering?* Copenhagen: Nyt fra Samfundsvidenskaberne.
Scheuer, S. 1986: *Fagforeninger mellem kollektiv og profession*, Copenhagen: Nyt fra Samfundsvidenskaberne.
Scheuer, S. 1987a: Arbejdstid og beskæftigelse – fagbevægelsens mobiliseringsproblemer. *Samfundsøkonomen*, 2, 4–10.
Scheuer, S. 1987b: Den korteste arbejdstid i Europa, *Samfunds, kønomen*, 5, 23–32.
Scheuer, S. 1989a: Faglig organisering 1966 til 1987 – Del 1: Betydningen af a-kasser og af kvindernes stigende erhvervsdeltagelse. *Økonomi og Politik*, 62, 1, 33–40.
Scheuer, S. 1989b: Faglig organisering 1966 til 1987 – Del 2: Væksten i funktionær- og servicesektoren og i særlige grupper med lav faglig organisering. *Økonomi politik*, 62, 3, 20–8.
Scheuer, S. 1990a: Struktur og forhandling. Aspekter af fagbevægelsens strukturudvikling i efterkrigstiden: Ekstern struktur, medlemstal samt strukturen i de kollektive overenskomstforhandlinger. In *Årbog for Arbejderbevægelsens Historie*, 20, 17–79. Copenhagen: Selskabet til Forskning i Arbejderbevægelsens Historie.
Scheuer, S. 1990b: Hvem er de gule? *Samfundsøkonomen*, 8, 5–10.
Scheuer, S. 1991: Leaders and laggards: Who goes First in Bargaining Rounds?, *Warwick Papers in Industrial Relations*. Coventry: University of Warwick.
Skogh, G. 1984: Employers associations in Sweden. In Windmuller, J. P. and A. (eds.) Gladstone: *Employers Associations and Industrial Relations*. Oxford: Clarendon.
Turner, H. A. 1962: *Trade Union Growth, Structure and Policy.* London: Allen & Unwin.
Udvalget om større fleksibilitet i det offentlige aftale- og overenskomstsystem 1988: *90'ernes aftaler og overenskomster.* Betænkning 1150 Copenhagen.
Visser, J. 1989: *European Trade Unions in Figures.* Deventer: Kluwer.
Visser, J. 1990: In Search of Inclusive Unionism. In *Bulletin of Comparative Labour Relations*, 18. Boston: Kluwer (Institute of Labour Relations, Catholic University of Leuven).
Visser, J. 1991: Trends in Trade Union Membership. In *OECD Employment Outlook*, Paris, July.

6

Finland: No Longer the Nordic Exception

Kari Lilja

Introduction

This chapter presents an overview of the Finnish industrial relations system from a comparative perspective.[1] The most immediate point of comparison is the Scandinavian model of industrial relations (summarized by Kjellberg in chapter 3). The Finnish case has come to resemble the Scandinavian model, primarily since the end of the 1960s. But its earlier history was markedly different from that of other Nordic countries.

The Finnish system of industrial relations has lacked long-term consistency, and has been marked by sharp discontinuities. The changes in the level of collective bargaining are, perhaps, its most notable feature. In the other Nordic countries the tradition of industry-level collective bargaining was established at the beginning of the twentieth century. The Finnish system got stuck at the formative phase: from 1909, and especially during the 1920s and 1930s, the employers' federation refused to participate in collective bargaining. Only in 1944, after the end of the war between Finland and the Soviet Union, did industry-level collective bargaining start to become established. This occurred under statutory control of wage increases until 1955. The relaxation of statutory wage controls, and an upsurge in inflation, led to a general strike in 1956. The manual workers' federation, SAK, split into three blocks, and a competing federation was established in 1960. How was it possible to transform the collective bargaining system from a state of complete disintegration into a Scandinavian-type model within a decade?

The historical evolution of Finnish industrial relations reflects the economic infrastructure and the cleavages and compromises of the political system (cf. Ingham 1974; Jackson and Sisson 1976). Thus the concept of the industrial relations system is somewhat misleading in the Finnish case, because it implies some kind of autonomy from the economic and political systems and a development induced endogenously by the actions of employers, employees and the state. In the Finnish case the evolution of the industrial relations system has to be seen as the consequence of the multi-dimensional transformation of Finnish society. From an economic point of view it has changed from a peripheral agricultural and raw-material-producing country to one whose forest industry enterprises are important players at the European level (Senghaas 1985), and whose national economy has been one of the fastest-growing in Europe during the 1980s. From a political point of view it has moved from a condition of intense class conflict to an exceptionally consensual polity.

Finnish *economic infrastructure* is extremely simple. The engine of the Finnish economy has been the forest sector: the value-added chain starting from growing trees to the sale of forest products and pulp and paper machinery all over the world. Paper has been the pattern-setting industry for many of the characteristics of the industrial relations system.

Since the declaration of independence in 1917, the Finnish *political system* has gone through a set of intense conflicts, starting with a civil war in 1918. The class-based cleavages have, however, been moderated by 'historic compromises'. These have been both procedural and substantive: the widening of political representation from various class-based constituencies, and the gradual development of a welfare state. This has meant rapid social mobility, access to education being the main mechanism for a levelling of opportunities. Thus in the course of three generations it has been possible to heal the social and political wounds of the civil war and create a political system which is exceptionally stable and consensual. The widening of representation and several reforms in the welfare system have also been achieved through the mechanism of collective bargaining.

The structure of the chapter is as follows: in the next section the main institutional features of Finnish industrial relations are examined from the point of view of the situation since the late 1960s. The four following sections take up specific issues:
- Why did Finland converge with the Scandinavian model at such a late stage?
- Why was the collective bargaining system successful?
- What explains the high propensity to strike?
- What explains the persistence of the centralized system despite internal strains?

The last section identifies issues which are important catalysts for change in the Finnish industrial relations system.

A Scandinavian model

Since the late 1960s the Finnish industrial relations system has come to resemble the Scandinavian model. The similarity can be recognized in the following dimensions: union structure and density; the structure and membership density of employers' organizations; the degree of centralization of collective bargaining; and institutional reforms encouraging workplace-level representation of the employees. What remains different however is the high rate of strikes.

Union Structure and Density

The largest and most influential federation is the Central Organization of Finnish Trade Unions, SAK (see table 6.1). It covers the manufacturing, construction and transport unions, and several large unions representing public sector (state and local authority) workers. The principle of organization has long been industrial unionism. There are no significant craft unions left. The last such union of note was the electrical workers' union, which has now become primarily an industrial union in energy and electrical construction. The proportion of white-collar workers in SAK is about 30 per cent. The second largest federation, the Confederation of Salaried Employees (TVK), comprises unions which represent only white-collar workers. Most members are female, employed in the public sector or in private services. There are two other federations: one for professionals, the Confederation of Unions for Academic Professionals in Finland (AKAVA), which is mainly organized according to members' educational background, and the other for supervisors and technical specialists, the Confederation of Technical Employees' Organizations in Finland (STTK). This structure is similar to the other Nordic countries. Relatively distinctive is the STTK, though it has a Danish counterpart (Kauppinen 1989: 334); it reflects a relatively strong gender-based segregation in Finnish labour markets.

What is distinctive about Finland is the sudden jump in the number of unionized workers since the end of the 1960s. From around 40 per cent of the employed population in the mid-1960s, density had leapt to 80 per cent at the end of the 1970s (see table 6.2; Yli-Pietilä et al. 1990: 57–8).

Table 6.1   Membership of Finnish union federations 1944–90

Year	SAK	SAJ	TVK	STTK	AKAVA	All Unionized Employees
1944	106,000		25,800			167,200
1945	299,600		70,300			371,300
1950	269,100		70,800	8,500	12,000	381,900
1955	269,400		780,000	11,800	19,000	405,500
1960	228,500	53,500	114,400	11,300	22,400	468,000
1965	248,000	105,400	152,200	16,100	28,700	642,900
1970	650,200		210,800	27,200	42,400	946,300
1975	920,600		286,000	83,700	103,500	
1980	1,032,100		324,600	105,400	162,200	1,646,000
1985	1,054,900		369,800	130,100	213,900	1,783,900
1988	1,092,400		365,200	144,100	247,800	1,865,900

Source: Yli-Pietilä et al. (1990: 38–41; 54–5); *Statistical Yearbook of Finland*, vol. 86, 376–7.

Table 6.2   Union density in Finland 1944–88

Year	All Employees (%)
1944	17
1945	37
1950	35
1955	33
1960	34
1965	42
1970	57
1975	74
1980	82
1985	81*
1988	86*

* figure not comparable with earlier computations.
Source: Yli-Pietilä et al. (1990: 57–8).

The reasons for this dramatic change are discussed below. Density has not altered significantly in the 1980s; according to a survey conducted in 1988 it was still 78 per cent (Melin 1991). It should also be noted that since the 1930s, density has been, on average, higher among white-collar workers, technical staff and professionals than among manual workers.

The Structure and Membership Density of Employers' Organizations

There are currently three main groups of employers' organizations: the federation of associations representing manufacturing, construction and transport industries (STK), the federation of associations in commerce and service industries (LTK), and the public sector employers, organized into two central associations: one for state administration (VTML) and one for local authorities (KT).

One peculiarity in the structure of Finnish employers' associations compared to other Nordic countries is that there are two federations in the private sector. This is because pay levels are relatively low in the service sector, represented by LTK, which employs mainly female workers. As a result, service employers have not wished to be in the same federation as manufacturers.

There is a functional division between trade associations and employers' associations. In the metal industry, however, both types of interest organization have merged. A similar change will occur in the peak organizations in 1993. But the network of associations representing the interests of capital will remain complex because chambers of commerce have an important role both nationally and especially regionally. For small business there is also a federation (SYKL) which competes with the representative organization of big business.

Large and medium-sized firms (with 100 or more employees) are with few exceptions members of employers' associations. The member firms of the STK had 580,000 employees in 1989, or 75 per cent of all employees in manufacturing and construction. In the LTK the figure is 320,000, or about 40 per cent of employment in service industries (Kauppinen et al. 1990: 19). State-owned manufacturing firms have a relatively high percentage, 14 per cent of all employees in manufacturing (p.14), and all belong to the STK. This differs from the Italian case where the proportion of state-owned companies is also large but they have an independent employers' association. Public sector employers make agreements covering all their employees, of whom 460,000 are in local government and 210,000 in state administration (Kauppinen 1989: 113). The number and role of foreign-owned companies is small in Finland, and they operate mainly in the distribution sector. Without exception they have conformed to Finnish institutional arrangements.

A Centralized System of Collective Bargaining Linked to a Neo-Corporatist Political Regime

The high density of unions and employers' associations has made it possible to centralize collective bargaining. The peak organizations of both employers and employees negotiate package deals with the government, a tradition established in 1968, with some earlier precedents. At first, the main partners in the centralized agreement were STK from the employers' side and SAK from the workers' side. But since the mid-1970s, the other federations have become officially incorporated into the centralized system of negotiations. Since 1968 only four negotiating rounds (in 1973, 1980, 1983 and 1988) have completely failed to produce a centrally-agreed contract or guidelines (see e.g. Ahonen 1990: 30; Kauppinen 1989: 26–7).

In practice, however, the centralized agreements at the level of federations and the state have become diluted. For instance, in SAK contracts are not binding on member unions: they have two weeks in which to accept or reject the negotiated agreement. In the course of every negotiating round a number of unions withdraw to try to get a better agreement at industry level. In many cases this is possible only by resorting to a strike. Thus the peaks in the statistics for days lost in strikes are due to unions breaking away from the centralized agreements.

Such neo-corporatist arrangements are dependent on political ties between the unions and the political parties in government. In Finland since 1966 this linkage has been with the Social Democratic Party, but it has not been in such a hegemonic position as its Swedish counterpart. The Communist Party has also been important in the trade union and cooperative movements, in parliament and even in coalition governments (cf. Kjellberg in this volume). Another important condition for the package deals has been the informal personal ties of the top leaders of the four power blocs: employers, farmers, unions and the government. In general, this has meant that macro-economic planning and social reforms have been closely linked to collective bargaining.

Workplace and Company-Level Participation

One of the main areas of reform included in incomes policy agreements has been workers' participation. The approach which was finally adopted in 1979 (the Law of Cooperation within Companies) was based on strengthening the position of shop stewards. Thus negotiating rights have been extended from wages and conditions of work to issues of managerial prerogative. Though the right of final decision rests with management, the new generation of professional managers has involved workers' representatives in planning and other areas of management. This development will be strengthened by a new law in 1991 which introduces board-room participation in firms with more than 150 employees. A related reform makes it possible to establish employee funds. Firms can pay bonuses to the company-specific funds according to jointly agreed rules. The rules emphasise economic performance indicators, and the intention is to motivate employees by providing a stake in improved company performance.

Reforms relating to employee participation have clearly lagged behind the Swedish precedent. Finnish managers in Swedish companies tend to complain at the delays in decision-making caused by the extended negotiating procedure.

High Strike Propensity

There is one distinctive feature in the Finnish system: the high level of industrial disputes (for earlier comparisons, see Korpi and Shalev 1980; Poole 1986). The number of strikes increased sharply at the end of the 1960s (see table 6.3). The peak year was 1976, when the number of industrial disputes reached 3,200. While the number of strikes also increased in Sweden during the 1970s, and in Denmark especially in the 1980s, the Finnish case is still qualitatively different. In Sweden the number of strikes has not been more than 250 and in Denmark the peak figure has been about 850 (Yli-Pietilä et al. 1990: 141). In Finland there is thus a positive correlation between the centralization of the system of collective bargaining and the increase in strikes.

Finland as a Late-comer to the Scandinavian Model

Why was Finland a late-comer to the Scandinavian model? We must first note the long-lasting effect of the civil war in 1918, and the dominance of forest industry companies in the economy and in the company towns and villages. These two factors explain why the employers' federation refused to participate in collective bargaining, and expelled industry associations which breached this rule. Second, the political situation changed completely in Finland after the Second World War. A popular front government

Table 6.3　Strikes in Finland 1945–91

Year	Frequency	Number of employees involved (000s)	Working days lost (000s)
1945	102	37	358
1950	78	118	4,644
1955	72	42	344
1960	44	19	96
1965	29	7	16
1970	240	202	233
1971*	838	403	2,711
1972	849	240	473
1973	1,009	678	2,497
1974	1,788	371	435
1975	1,530	215	284
1976	3,282	513	1,326
1977	1,673	744	2,375
1978	1,237	165	132
1979	1,753	229	243
1980	2,238	413	1,606
1981	1,612	493	659
1982	1,240	168	208
1983	1,940	422	720
1984	1,710	562	1,527
1985	848	171	174
1986	1,225	603	2,788
1987	802	99	131
1988	1,353	244	180
1989	629	158	204
1990	455	244	935
1991	251	160	457

* Since the statistical method has been revised, the figures from 1971 onwards are not comparable with those for earlier years,.
Source: Yli Pietilä et al. (1990: 140–7); *Labour Disputes 1990 and 1991*. Central Statistical Office of Finland.

was formed in 1944, and workers rushed to join unions. But the internal struggles within the labour movement led to a split in the centralized union federation.

In 1905, Finland experienced a national awakening. Within the new political culture, both employers and workers formed their loose federations in 1907. The initiative for the union federation came from the Social Democratic Party. For a short time the employers had a cautious but positive attitude towards collective bargaining at industry level. But wage claims and strikes in 1908–12 led to a rejection of collective bargaining. During the First World War strikes were forbidden and unrest was suppressed; but the Social Democratic Party began to gain wide support and won a parliamentary majority in 1916. In the summer of 1917 parliament was dismissed by the interim government of Russia, which called new elections in the autumn. The bourgeois parties won these elections. Working-class mobilization intensified and political cleavages in the country deepened. The October revolution in Russia hastened the declaration of Finnish independence on 6 December 1917. But the regime's lack of legitimacy led to a civil war which was won by the Whites. The Red troops consisted of trade unionists and tenant farmers. The whole working-class movement was viewed with suspicion by the victors of the civil war, and the employers' federation decided not to engage in collective bargaining. The unions and their federation were dominated by left-wing socialists, and the federation was suspected of having contacts with the Finnish Communist Party, established in 1918. The party was banned and had to work underground. Because the situation was defined as revolutionary, for several years after the civil war there was also a disinclination within the trade unions to engage in collective bargaining. For their part, employers lent their support to a strike-breaking organization, which recruited in the countryside. Thus during the 1920s the relatively few strikes were long and bitter.

The backbone of the employers' federation was the association of forest industries. It was strong enough to dominate policy-making in the whole federation. Policy towards trade unionism and collective bargaining can be derived from the interests and experiences of the owners of pulp and paper mills during and after the civil war (see Kettunen 1990). Tarmo Koskinen (1987: 102) has characterized Finland as an archipelago of forest communities. This captures the essence of community formation in Finland since industrialization, which until the 1950s was exclusively based on forest industry. Because the saw-mills, pulp and paper mills were located alongside rapids and waterways it was geography which determined the selection of mill sites and the consequent concentrations of population. Within forest industry the pulp and paper mills constitute the paradigm. Their social dynamics differ considerably from the saw-mills and other mechanical wood-working factories.

The employers had to create a community infrastructure in the remote areas, and to a large extent they owned the land around the mill and the village. The employees were recruited from the countryside without prior experience of wage labour in factories. Employers had the power to exclude all autonomous working-class activities from their own territory. This meant that trade union activities were very marginal until the end of the Second World War. (The experience was, for a long time, similar in Swedish paper industry communities (Karlbom 1945); but because of the importance of other sectors, especially the metalworking and engineering industry, the working-class movement developed different characteristics in Sweden.)

During the 1920s and 1930s the employers received considerable help from the right, which was eager to attack all forms of working-class organization. These pressures led to a law banning the left-wing domi-nated trade union federation in 1930. The social democrats established a new federation and renewed their demands for negotiating rights, but the STK was rigid in its policy of non-negotiation. Even the Swedish employ-ers tried to persuade their Finnish counterpart to enter into collective agreements (see Mansner 1981). This time their refusal was officially supported by the argument that unions were not representative enough (Savola 1968): union density was very low during this period (see table 6.2). The one notable exception was in the printing industry, whose employers' organization was expelled from the federation for engaging in collective bargaining. There were also local contracts for the construction trades.

After the Second World War the internal political situation changed substantially. The Communist Party was legalized. A new front organ-ization called the People's Democratic League (SKDL) was established under the leadership of the communists. This league won a landslide victory in the parliamentary elections of 1945, gaining a quarter of the seats. A popular front government was formed, including the now legal-ized communists who acted under the banner of the SKDL. The political climate was, for the first time in Finnish history, favourable to the trade union movement. The unions were rapidly re-established, members flooded in, and shop stewards were elected on a massive scale, especially in manufacturing workplaces. Under this new political regime the em-ployers had limited room for manoeuvre. Thus, they entered into negotiations with the trade unions, and the pulp and paper industry was the first to sign an industry-level contract in December 1944. A new era in the history of Finnish collective bargaining began.

After the war, social democrats and communists fought for leadership of the labour movement. The PDL lost the parliamentary elections and in 1948 were excluded from the government. By 1951 they had also lost ground in the trade union federation. After their victory in the various institutions of the labour movement, the social democrats underwent an internal power struggle which by the end of the 1950s had led to a split in the party, in the trade union federation and in the workers' sports federa-tion as well. Within the union movement, the breakaway unions established a competing federation, SAJ, in 1960. SAJ had a structure that closely paralleled that of SAK. Few unions escaped the split. Some did so by leaving SAK but remaining outside SAJ. For trade union leaders this meant that they had to turn their attention to internal organizational problems. The main implication of the split in the trade union movement for collective bargaining was that negotiations became very complicated (see Urmas 1975): unions competed for workers' support, outbidding each other in their negotiating demands, and resorting to strikes in order to get a better settlement than that achieved by the rival union. This jungle war in the trade union movement meant that by the end of the 1960s collective bargaining took place under conditions totally different from other Nordic countries.

The development of the system of collective bargaining was thus retarded by the intensity of class conflict between 1916 and 1944, and the internal struggles in the labour movement between 1944 and 1968. The most surprising event in the history of Finnish industrial relations was the fact that a new architecture emerged from the fragmented elements of the trade union movement and practically the whole working population became unionized during the 1970s.

Why was the Centralization of the Collective Bargaining System Successful?

The centralization of the collective bargaining system at the end of the 1960s was made possible by three developments. First, there was increasing external pressure towards macro-economic planning and regulation as Finland became more integrated into the western economy, and an incomes policy became necessary. Second, a new federation of labour unions was formed in 1969 which was able to reintegrate the competing unions and the two ideologically competing political forces, the social democrats and the communists. At the same time these two parties also won representation in the Finnish government. Third, the employers' federations were interested in a historic compromise with the newly formed trade union federation and the political parties of the left. The compromise was implemented in a series of incomes policy agreements, encouraged by the government, in 1968, 1969 and 1970.

In the early 1960s, ideas of macro-economic planning found their way to Finland. One set of concerns involved wage increases, labour costs and the relative rate of inflation. Finland had started to liberalize its trade at the end of the 1950s and entered EFTA in 1961. Until the 1950s it had been possible to support the price competitiveness of exports, mainly forest products, by devaluations of the Finnish mark. When the economy became more integrated into the western economies in the 1960s, a more sophisticated macro-economic regulation became necessary.

The system of industrial relations had, however, disintegrated because of the split in the SAK and the Social Democratic Party at the end of the 1950s. The larger part of the party was also outside the government. For these reasons the first three attempts to introduce incomes policy agreements, by bourgeois governments, in 1963, 1964, and 1966, were not successful. But conditions were to change.

First, the Social Democratic Party won the parliamentary elections of 1966. The communists also joined the government. This diminished competition between the two political groupings of the working class, and opened the way for centralized agreements involving both wings of the trade union movement. While the social-democratic movement started to regain its political unity, the communist movement split in 1969, largely as a result of disagreements over participation in government and over incomes policy. The preparations for the unification of the trade union movement and for the first incomes policy agreements were conducted in parallel. The other main federation of workers' unions (SAJ) started to lose ground, especially after 1967. A new unified federation was formed in 1969.

It is noteworthy that the employers' federation was committed to the unification of the trade union movement. This was encouraged by favouring SAK in collective bargaining during the 1960s, and especially in the breakthrough to the first incomes policy agreement in 1968. The architect of the employers' policies, Päiviö Hetemäki, wanted to see an end to the constant inter-union rivalry, and to push the union movement to a level of centralization that would allow national incomes policies on the Swedish model. This was also in the mind of President Kekkonen, who in the early 1970s was reaching the peak of his exceptional power in Finnish politics.

The first two incomes policy agreements (in 1968 and 1969) were a 'historic compromise' whereby both the employers and the state recognized the legitimacy of the (unified) trade union movement. The employers agreed to operate a check-off system, while a new law made union subscriptions tax-deductible. This was a strong signal to employees that trade unionism was now legitimate. For the union movement this meant that a steady income flow was assured for the first time in its history. The movement became unified union by union during the early 1970s. This eased the conflicting pressures felt by the workers at the workplace and a massive increase in union membership began, spreading to the public sector and to white-collar occupations and professionals (see table 6.2). At the same time, the economy and the public sector were growing rapidly. All reserves of labour were drawn in to the labour market. For instance, the proportion of women employees rose from 43 per cent in 1970 to 47 per cent by 1980 and 50 per cent in 1987 (R. Lilja et al. 1990: 72). These factors helped stimulate the exceptionally high union density in Finland. The employers found a centralized bargaining partner, and the incomes policy agreements provided them with a channel for influencing the government and parliament.

Causes of the High Strike Propensity

In international comparisons Finland displays a high propensity to strike. In this respect it differs from the other Nordic countries. What accounts for this phenomenon?

Firstly, traditional management attitudes provoked conflict. By the end of the 1960s the employers' federation had made a rapid and radical re-evaluation of its policies and accepted union representatives as negotiating partners even on the shopfloor. But managers at enterprise level were slower to adapt. They were dominated by an older generation whose style was very authoritarian, and who were hostile to demands for industrial democracy and hesitant to enter into workplace bargaining. The leaders of the employers' federations, recognizing the resistance to the new approach at company level, threw their weight behind a managerial reform movement whose purpose was to introduce modern personnel management into Finnish firms. With a labour shortage from 1970 to 1974, the reform movement was very successful: hundreds of personnel departments were established and several hundreds of personnel specialists were hired (see Lilja 1983: 124; 1987). Thus there rapidly developed a dual management culture with respect to employees and workplace industrial relations. But it took another fifteen years before the predominant leadership style became more participative, following a generation shift in management. By the 1980s the post-war generation had taken over the top management posts, and had started to apply the pluralistic institutional machinery for workplace industrial relations established during the 1970s. Before this gradual change in managerial style occurred, the rigid attitudes of foremen and managers in the workplace had provoked hundreds of local conflicts.

But strikes at workplace and industry levels must also be understood from the point of view of the labour movement. Behind the strike waves of the 1970s lay the following factors: first, the emergence of a shop steward movement with strongholds in large manufacturing workplaces; second, political rivalry within the trade union movement among the political parties of the left; third, inter-federation, inter-union and reference group competition in the market for union membership and economic rewards.

The Shop Steward Movement

The procedural reforms of the 1970s met long-standing demands for security for shop stewards and other workplace representatives. The shop stewards provided leadership for an independent workers' organization at the workplace. In large workplaces the senior shop stewards are engaged full-time in negotiations and related trade union business. They are paid by the employer, enjoy employment security and have good facilities.

The incomes policy agreements opened a space for local action, because the centrally agreed wage increases did not reflect the productivity increases in the largest workplaces. When workplace representatives recognized the opportunities for local bargaining they started to apply pressure for local wage increases. This activity was the main cause of wage drift on the one hand, and strike waves on the other. The peak in the number of strikes was in 1976 and 1977, when the employers launched a concerted attack on wage drift.

A small number of workplaces account for the majority of workplace strikes. Metalworking is by far the most strike-prone industry. The ten most strike-prone workplaces have on average about 20 per cent of all strikes in Finland and about 30 per cent of strikes in the metal industry. At the top of the list are three large shipyards; the other workplaces among the ten are in the engineering and vehicle industry (Kohtanen and

Kauppinen 1988: 77–80). The uneven distribution of strikes is even more pronounced in the pulp and paper industry where one workplace, the cardboard mill Tako in Tampere, accounted for 20 per cent of all strikes in the industry in the years 1972–84 (Kohtanen and Kauppinen 1989: 120–1). In these cases shopfloor organizations have turned workplace industrial relations into a pattern which Fox (1974: 310–13) called continuous challenge: the legitimacy of management and managerial decisions is constantly contested and every situation in which bargaining power shifts in favour of the workers is exploited. Most of the very strike-prone workplaces are also bastions of left-wing radicalism.

Political Rivalry in the Trade Union Movement

In SAK there has been competition since the 1960s between social democrats and communists, and among the communists themselves who from 1969 were split into two factions. In the white-collar federations even more political groupings compete with each other, because the bourgeois parties are strongly represented in the union leadership. The political divisions within the trade union movement have made it relatively difficult to control it from above.

Strike action has always been multi-functional (see Hyman 1984: 120–32). Strike activity increases when elections take place at the workplace and within the trade unions. Competition between communists and social democrats for union office, and particularly for shop steward positions, encourages a militant stance in collective bargaining rounds. The approach of elections increases the probability that a union will break away from the centralized agreement and try to get better terms by threatening a strike. The communist-led unions have been the most active in this respect, but pressures to show militant leadership before union elections also affect the social democrats. On average, there are about six industry-level strikes after every centralized negotiating round. This helps explain why participation rates in Finnish strikes have been among the highest in the world (see e.g. Poole 1986: 128–33).

Inter-Federation and Inter-Union Competition and Reference Group Comparisons

The frequency of industry-wide strikes also reflects inter-federation and inter-union competition, and the way that comparisons are used in wage bargaining. The main confederations of employers and workers – STK and SAK – were the initiators of the centralized collective bargaining system. The other federations have from time to time tried to raise their profile in order to gain recognition for their own priorities. Strikes have mainly been called by individual unions refusing to be bound by the centrally agreed contracts. STK became the first federation outside SAK to call on its unions to strike, in 1973 and 1977. The unions in TVK and AKAVA followed suit during the 1980s. But in 1986 even SAK had to resort to strike action because employers had first reached a centralized agreement with the white-collar federations. After a 58-hour strike by 240,000 workers, STK agreed to negotiate a new centralized contract with SAK, thus emphasizing its leading role among the union federations (Kauppinen 1989: 46–50, 98).

One of the reasons given in Finland for the high level of conflict is the effect of reference group comparisons. It is common for negotiators to argue that their members' wages or salaries have fallen below those of other occupational groups with similar qualifications or which undertake similar work. Such comparisons have been typical between private- and public-sector groups, and between male- and female-dominated industries. During the 1980s a new feature has been the incidence of white-collar strikes, especially in industries which are dominated by women employees. These strikes started with a clerical workers' strike in 1980 and have been followed by strikes of such groups as health-care workers, school-teachers, kindergarten teachers, librarians, social workers and bank employees.

It is therefore clear that the centralization of collective bargaining has not diminished the strike-proneness of Finnish working life. On the contrary, it has brought new sectors and new socio-economic groups into unions. These groups have had to establish their own position in negotiations and in the hierarchy of wages and salaries. The system of industrial relations has been changing ever since the beginning of centralized bargaining at the end of the 1960s. Thus the continuity of the centralized system has been under constant pressure.

The Continuity of the Centralized System of Collective Bargaining

The occasional collapse of centralized agreements and frequent breakaway movements, wage drift and strike waves have provoked continuous debate on the feasibility of a centralized incomes policy in Finland. However, several underlying factors have contributed to the continuity of the centralized system.

First, Finnish economic performance in the last two decades has been good by European standards, and has unquestionably increased the relative standard of living in Finland. The critical phase was immediately after the structural recession of the middle of the 1970s. Manufacturing industry recovered very quickly, largely as a result of bilateral trade with the Soviet Union; the rise in oil prices created new opportunities for Finnish firms to export goods to the Soviet Union. In most other countries the oil crisis had only negative consequences, aggravating the decline in basic industries. In Finland employment in manufacturing did not fall as it did in the other Nordic countries and in almost the whole of Western Europe. In the 1980s, economic growth accelerated, and the last part of the decade was one of the most vigorous phases in Finnish economic history. The main reason for the boom was the high price of pulp and the heavy demand for writing and printing papers, in which many Finnish firms specialize.

Second, economic growth has provided the material basis for social reforms. This created the opportunity for political exchanges between the governments and the trade union movement. Reforms have served to improve conditions of employment. The role of the Social Democratic Party, with its key position both in the government and in unions, has been crucial. Political exchanges have reinforced its power position. It has remained the largest party in parliament and the backbone of government. It also won the presidency for the first time when Mauno Koivisto was elected in 1981. On the other hand, the political position of the SKDL, representing the communists and the radical left, has weakened both in parliament and in the unions. Thus the social democrats have come closer to a hegemony in the labour movement, as in the other Nordic countries.

After the elections of 1987, the social democrats and the conservatives formed a coalition government. The Centre Party was left in opposition, after fifty years in government. In order to legitimate the partnership with the Conservative Party, the social democrats wanted to give clear signals to the workers that the party was not moving to the right. Thus a programme for the reform of working life was launched. Although the Conservative Party's willingness to go along with the social democrats' demands caused some astonishment in the business community, it is less surprising if one bears in mind that the Finnish Conservative Party has considerable support amongst unionized white-collar and professional employees, in contrast to the Centre Party, whose main support comes from farmers and rural communities. The new laws implementing working life reform were formulated in state committees on which interest organizations were represented, and their terms were endorsed in the incomes policy agreements. The main reforms have been the introduction of employee representation on boards of directors, and the law on employee funds which provides a framework for employers to establish voluntary, company-specific funds.

The third reason for the continuity of corporatist practices in collective bargaining and macro-economic policy-making is that centralization is much more important for the unions than for the employers' federations. Firms can pursue their macro-economic interests through their sectoral interest organizations, independently of the system of collective bargaining. Large corporations are well able to handle collective bargaining for themselves, and the employers' associations have been willing to change to a more consultative role. But the role of unions and their federations in collective bargaining and centralized incomes policy is essential if they are to retain their power positions in the labour movement and in the political system. As a result, they remain strongly committed to centralized negotiations, and have proposed and implemented new organizational structures in order to maintain the system.

The main proposed change involves a new organizational model for the most influential union federation, SAK. Its new chairman has recommended a divisional structure, with unions divided into sectoral groups for manufacturing, private services and public services. If the reform succeeds it will sustain the centralized system of collective bargaining. The sectoral chairmen would function as mediators between the unions and the federation. In this way there could be collective bargaining agreements at sectoral level, reflecting federation guidelines but taking into account the differences in the competitive situation of firms and employers in each sector. This proposal is also a reaction to the emerging trend in the white-collar federations to form bargaining cartels among unions representing different occupational groups (and belonging to different federations) within the same sector. If SAK does not respond to this challenge, some unions in SAK will be tempted to join the white-collar workers' cartels. This would undermine the dominant role of SAK in national negotiations, because the combined strength of the white-collar workers' federations has been increasing steadily since the middle of the 1970s. The experiment carried out by the employers in 1986 of negotiating the opening contract with the white-collar federations was a sharp reminder to the SAK that white-collar and professional employees together outnumber the manual workers in manufacturing and construction.

Finally, the continuity of centralized bargaining has been helped by institutional innovations which allow leeway for deviant behaviour. In every bargaining round there are difficulties in getting the unions and employer federations to commit themselves to a centralized agreement. It has thus become customary for a mediator to propose the final settlement terms. The mediator is typically a well-respected senior civil servant, political figure or former employers' association leader. The mediator enables the conflicting parties to make their final moves towards agreement.

Though the federations negotiate and sign the central collective bargaining contracts there are several institutional practices which give flexibility to the system. Several federations on both sides allow sectoral adjustments to the agreements. In the 1980s LTK was able to deviate from the common policies of the employers' side by entering into collective agreements lasting longer (three to four years) than most other agreements, and which thus expire at different dates.

The possibility of a breakaway from the federation contract is the next form of flexibility. In manufacturing, the application of industry agreements means, at least in large workplaces, a further chance to negotiate better wages. The paper-workers' union has been able to develop a system of productivity bargaining which gives it considerable autonomy from the central collective bargaining system (Koistinen and Lilja 1988: 169). Wage increases based on productivity bargaining are negotiated at the workplace, and can double the increase agreed at industry level. Because technological change has been very rapid in the Finnish pulp and paper industry since the end of the 1960s, workers in this industry have emerged as the labour aristocracy in Finland (Lilja et al. 1992).

The Future of the Finnish Industrial Relations System

The stability of Finnish industrial relations since the end of the 1960s would suggest that in the immediate future the key actors will be able to maintain the system through adaptations along lines developed over the last twenty years. The consolidating features are linked to the increase in the relative power position of the Social Democratic Party. The Communist Party and the People's Democratic League have dissolved and turned into a new party called the Left Wing League. The role of the communists and their successors in trade union leaderships has diminished. This makes it easier for the social democrats to pursue centralized agreements. The fines for illegal strikes were increased tenfold in 1985 which means that rank-and-file activism at the workplace is also likely to decline. These trends accentuate the pressures towards stabilization.

In Finland economic recessions have stimulated governments to pursue an active role in incomes policies (cf. Elvander 1974). Consensus has been reached on incomes policy because the economic signals have been clear to all interest groups. This contingency is again relevant because after a long period of economic growth and prosperity the Finnish economy has fallen into deep recession. The new centre-right government which came to power in spring 1991 faced a very difficult economic environment. Inflation had raised labour costs above those of competing countries. High loan-financed investment by firms in the forest and engineering industries was imposing intolerable financial burdens. The collapse in Soviet trade as the Soviet Union disintegrated and recession in the most important customer countries had slowed demand: the wheels of manufacturing and construction were grinding to a halt. Rumours of a devaluation of the Finnish mark started to circulate. New peaks in unemployment were being reached almost every month, leading to a serious fall in tax revenues. The government made a plea for a social contract that would lower wages and salaries, but, with the social democrats in opposition, this proved difficult to accomplish. Many influential trade union leaders felt that it would be easier to accept a devaluation than a wage cut. Thus negotiations on a centralized incomes policy agreement progressed slowly. As a final resort, a mediator was called for in November 1991, but at the same time, the new government was forced to devalue the currency by 14 per cent. Negotiations on incomes policy were then rapidly completed and an agreement was signed at the end of November. Labour costs were reduced but nominal wages were not cut. The moral of the story is that a macro-economic crisis in an economy as open as Finland's generates support for incomes policy agreements from which no party dares withdraw.

There remains, however, a long-standing mistrust in the business community towards centralized collective bargaining agreements. The employers' argument is that centralized agreements take no account of the competitive situation at the level of the firm. If the employers withdraw from centralized negotiations it is possible that a new type of corporatism at the level of the enterprise or the business unit – productivity coalitions – will emerge in the industrial relations system (cf. Andersson 1989: 387; Windolf 1989: 1–4). The building blocks could be the enthusiasm for new human resource management methods (extensive training, management by results, performance appraisal), intensive use of the negotiating procedure provided by the Law on Cooperation in Companies, board-level participation and employee funds. A critical step towards micro-level corporatism would be the introduction of transnational corporate consultation mechanisms, which is one of the key demands of the Nordic trade union movement.

At present it is not possible to foresee the future of Finnish industrial relations. There are two apparently conflicting trends: one for the consolidation of the centralized system of bargaining by sectoral cartels, and the other a tendency towards a decentralization through the widening of participation and bargaining rights at the company and business unit. Perhaps these are not alternatives. It is also possible that a division of labour and increasing specialization can be established for the different levels. This would accommodate much of the tension which has recently accumulated in the industrial relations system.

Notes

[1] I am indebted to Tuomo Alasoini, Anthony Ferner, Richard Hyman, Pauli Kettunen and Stephen Wood for their comments on the earlier versions of this paper.

Earlier English language discussions of Finnish industrial relations include Knoellinger (1960), Kauhanen and Laaksonen (1981), Koskimies (1981), Lilja (1983, Suviranta (1987), Kauppinen et al. (1990).

Abbreviations

AKAVA	*Akateeminen Yhteisvaltuuskunta* – Confederation of Unions For Academic Professionals in Finland
KT	*Kunnallinen työmarkkinalaitos* – Commission for Local Authority Employers
LTK	*Liiketyönantajain Keskusliitto* – Employers' Confederation of Service Industries
SAJ	*Suomen Ammattijärjestö (1960-1969)* – Finnish Trade Union Federation
SAK	*Suomen Ammattiliittojen Keskusjärjestö* – Central Organization of Finnish Trade Unions
SKDL	*Suomen Kansan Demokraattinen Liitto* – People's Democratic League
STK	*Suomen Työnantajain Keskusliitto* – Finnish Employers' Con-federation
STTK	*Suomen Teknisten Toimihenkilöiden Keskusliitto* – Confederation of Technical Employee Organizations in Finland
SYKL	*Suomen Yrittäjäin Keskusliitto* – Finnish Confederation of Entrepreneurs
TVK	*Toimihenkilö - ja Virkamiesjärjestöjen Keskusliitto* – Confederation of Salaried Employees
VTML	*Valtion työmarkkinalaitos* – Department of Public Personnel Management

References

Ahonen, G. 1990: Spelöppningen. Om Kollektivavtalsprocess i Finland på 1980-talet. Department of Political Science, Swedish School of Economics, Helsingfors.

Andersson, J. O. 1989: Controlled Restructuring in Finland. *Scandinavian Political Studies*, 12, 4, 373–89.

Elvander, N. 1974: Collective Bargaining and Industrial Relations in the Nordic countries: A Comparative Analysis. *British Journal of Industrial Relations*, 12, 3, 417–37.

Fox, A. 1974: *Beyond Contract: Work, Power and Trust Relations.* London: Faber & Faber.

Hyman, R. 1984: *Strikes.* 3rd edition. Aylesbury: Fontana.

Ingham, G.K. 1974: *Strikes and Industrial Conflict.* London: Macmillan.

Jackson, P. and Sisson, K. 1976: Employers' Confederations in Sweden and in the UK and the Significance of Industrial Infrastructure. *British Journal of Industrial Relations*, 14, 3, 306–23.

Karlbom, T. 1945: *Pappersindustriarbetarnas fackliga organisationshistoria.* Stockholm: Tiden.

Kauhanen, J. and Laaksonen, O. 1981: The Finnish Industrial Relations System. In IDE, *European Industrial Relations,* Oxford: Clarendon Press.

Kauppinen, T. 1989: Työelämän suhteet markkinatalousmaissa. *Työelämän suhteiden neuvottelukunta* 1/1989. Helsinki: Valtion painatuskeskus.

Kauppinen, T. et al. (eds), 1990: *Labour Relations in Finland.* Helsinki: Ministry of Labour.

Kettunen, P. 1990: Hur legitimerades arbetsgivarnas politik i 'första republikens' Finland. In D. Fleming (ed.) *Industriel demokrati i Norden,* Lund: Arkiv Förlag.

Knoellinger, C. E. 1960: *Labor in Finland.* Cambridge, Mass.: Harvard University Press.

Kohtanen, Jukka, Kauppinen, Timo 1988: Työtaistelut Suomessa vuosina 1971-1984. *Työelämän suhteiden neuvottelukunta* 3/1988. Helsinki.

Kohtanen, J. and Kauppinen, T. 1989: Työtaistelut ja neuvottelusuhteet paperiteollisudessa vuosina 1971–1984. *Työelämän suhteiden neuvottelukunta* 2/1989. Helsinki.

Koistinen, P. Lilja, K. 1988: Consensual Adaptation to New Technology: The Finnish Case. In R. Hyman, and W. Streeck, (eds), *New Technology and Industrial Relations,* Oxford: Basil Blackwell, 263–71.

Korpi, W., and Shalev, M. 1980: Strikes, Power and Politics in the Western Nations, 1900-1976. *Political Power and Social Theory,* 1, 301–34.

Koskimies, J. 1981: Finland. In A.A. Blum (ed.), *International Handbook of Industrial Relations,* London: Aldwych Press.

Koskinen, T. 1987: Herruutta, hallintaa vai vuorovaikutusta? Tehdasyhd-yskuntien muotoja ja vaiheita Suomessa. *Hallinnon tutkimus,* 6, 2, 102–6.

Lilja, K. 1983: *Workers' Workplace Organisations.* Helsinki: HSE, A:39.

Lilja, K. 1987: Henkilöstöhallinnon ammattikäytänmön kehityspiirteitä Suomessa. *Hallinnon tutkimus,* 6, 3, 185–94.

Lilja, K., Räsänen, K. and Tainio, R. 1992: The Forest Sector Business Recipe in Finland and its Domination of the National Business System. In R. Whitley (ed.), *The Social Structuring of Enterprise: Europe in Comparative Perspective,* London: Sage.

Lilja, R., Santamäki-Vuori, T. and Standing, G. 1990: *Unemployment and Labour Market Flexibility: Finland.* Geneva: ILO.

Mansner, M. 1981: *Suomalaista yhteiskuntaa rakentamassa. Suomen Työnantajain Keskusliitto 1907–1940.* Jyväskylä: Teollisuuden Kustannus Oy.

Melin, Harri 1991: Personal communication based on a survey conducted in the project '1980-luvun yhteiskuntarakenne'. University of Tampere.

Poole, M. 1986: *Industrial Relations.* London: Routledge.

Savola, M. 1968: *Lakko yhteiskunnan ristiriitana.* Porvoo: WSOY.

Senghaas, D. 1985: *The European Experience.* Leamington Spa: Berg Publishers.

Sisson, K. 1987: *The Management of Collective Bargaining. An International Comparison.* Oxford: Blackwell.

Suviranta, A. J. 1987: *Labour Law and Industrial Relations in Finland.* Deventer: Kluwer.

Urmas, H. 1975: *Työrauhajärjestelmä yhteiskunnan osajärjestelmänä.* Helsinki: HSE, A:12.

Windolf, P. 1989: Productivity Coalitions and the Future of European Corporatism. *Industrial Relations,* 28, 1, 1–20.

Yli-Pietilä, P., Alasoini, T., Kauppinen, and T. and Mikola-Lahnalammi, T. 1990: *Työelämän suhteet. Aikasarjoja 1907–1988.* Helsinki. Työministeriö.

7

Germany: Codetermining the Future?

Otto Jacobi, Berndt Keller and Walther Müller-Jentsch

Introduction: Continuity and Challenges in the 'German Model'

Industrial relations systems differ not only in their institutions and procedures but also in their capacity for conflict resolution. The German industrial relations system, through its containment of industrial conflict, has been regarded as a basic element in the virtuous circle of Germany's prosperous economy.

The 'German model' is based upon four principles. The most important is the dual structure of interest representation, originating in the early years of the Weimar Republic, in which workers' representation at establishment and workplace levels is separated from the collective bargaining system. The dual system means that structural conflicts between labour and capital can be broken down and dealt with in two arenas separated according to interests, actors and modes of enforcement. In collective bargaining, interests are generalized and quantitative (especially wages and hours); in the workplace they are specialized and more qualitative. Unions and employers' associations are responsible for collective bargaining; works councils and managements for relations at company level. Strikes and lockouts are a legitimate means of applying pressure in collective bargaining, but not in the exercise of codetermination, consultation and information rights in the workplace, where only peaceful negotiations and labour court proceedings are permitted.

Within this dual system of interest representation both sets of actors are, in strictly legal or formal terms, independent. In reality, however, they are mutually dependent, have a close and stable division of labour, and are reliable partners within a network of stable cooperation. Unions train members of the works councils, and provide them with information and legal advice; while works councillors are in most cases union members (or even union officials) and often recruit members for their union.

Employers and management, too, see advantages in being relieved of some of their responsibilities by employers' associations which, for example, take wages out of competition.

A second notable feature of German industrial relations is their extensive juridification. The dual system has a legal basis in the forms of free collective bargaining (*Tarifautonomie*) and works constitution (*Betriebsverfassung*), and there is detailed legal regulation of labour conflicts and industrial relations at the workplace. The works council has no right to strike; and extensive juridification helps to channel and depoliticize industrial conflict and also encourages the professionalization of conflict management. Since the penalties for breaching legal regulations are severe, legal experts, especially on the workers' side, gain importance and influence.

Of special importance for German industrial relations is the degree to which the institutions of collective representation encompass their constituencies. The institutions of worker representation, unions and works councils, can make decisions in the name of the entire work force, with little formal obligation to seek endorsement. The claim that German unions do represent the interests of all employees, and not just those of their members, is supported by law. The works council, too, is an institution representing the entire work force, not subject to any mandate from its constituency (save for the need to seek re-election every four years). Employers' associations also effectively represent all employers in their industry, or even (in the case of the peak confederation) the whole economy, not by law but by virtue of their strength of organization.

A final characteristic is the relative centralization of collective bargaining and the coordinated policies of the bargaining parties at sectoral level. Towards the end of the nineteenth century unions adopted the principle of central authority rather than local autonomy, and later they chose industrial unionism in preference to craft or occupational organization. After 1945 the unions' former political divisions were replaced by the principle of unitary trade unions (*Einheitsgewerkschaften*). Since then, the main German unions have faced little organizational competition. The employers also tended to organize in central confederations from an early date. Each side promoted the concentration and centralization of the other; the result was a centralized bargaining system with large bargaining territories.

There have been political debates on the consequences of the dual system for union policy and workers' collective orientation. During the 1960s and early 1970s academic socialists and union activists condemned the German industrial relations system for stifling industrial militancy and suppressing class conflict. They argued for an increased role for shop-floor union delegates and for a shop-floor bargaining system as ways of strengthening the rank and file and reducing the control of union officials. However, unionists and academic experts of the political mainstream of social democracy viewed the 'dual system' much more positively, arguing that it provided benefits for both unions and works councils.

This controversy has now died down as a result of the defeats suffered by unions in neighbouring countries during the 1980s. Economic crisis and the strategies of conservative governments, and the resulting decline elsewhere in union membership and bargaining power, have made the advantages of the German dual system self-evident. It is now almost universally agreed that the system allows flexible adjustment to change, without weakening the representational strength of unions.

Economic and Legal Framework

Basic Framework of Economic Conditions

Since its establishment in 1949, the Federal Republic of Germany (BRD) has achieved consistent economic success. Export performance, based on competitive prices and advanced technology, has brought it a dominant position in world trade, with high employment at home, and the leading economic role within the EC. The BRD has long since left behind the material devastation and moral bankruptcy of the Nazi dictatorship and subsequent military defeat. The establishment of a stable democratic order is also an element of this (West) German success story; an order based on the model of the 'social market economy' underpinned by legal regulation, free collective bargaining and co-determination. Whether the accession of the former German Democratic Republic (DDR) will interrupt or accelerate this favourable socio-economic development is as yet uncertain.

The development of the BRD can be divided into five main phases, corresponding to the decades since the foundation of the Republic. The 1950s were marked by the reconstruction of the productive base as well as public administration and infrastructure. Gross national product doubled in real terms; inflation was kept to an annual rate of 2 per cent. At the same time, the number of wage- and salary-earners rose to 20 million. By the middle of the decade, unemployment was virtually eliminated in the main industrial centres. Total employment income tripled, but the sustained influx of workers from the east inhibited the trade unions from adopting an aggressive wage policy. Nevertheless, the unions were able to improve real wages; and arguably, higher wage costs forced employers to invest in modernization. This innovatory dynamic remains the decisive pillar of German economic strength and performance.

A phase of stabilization ensued at the beginning of the 1960s, characterized not by stagnation but by the continuation of the previous trends. Industrial production, exports and investment continued to increase rapidly, and the value of the Deutsche Mark (DM) rose in relation to foreign currencies. The most important innovation in economic policy was the Promotion of Stability and Growth Act of 1967, which provided a Keynesian instrument for managing the economy, including tripartite consultation (*Konzertierte Aktion*) over economic policy and wage negotiation. This change in part reflected a major political shift: the Christian

Democrats (CDU/CSU), who had governed (usually in coalition with the Free Democrats, FDP) since the formation of the BRD, lost ground electorally and in 1966 brought the Social Democrats (SPD) into a 'grand coalition', with an SPD Economics Minister. Employment remained high until the recession of 1967 served as a warning to the unions. But towards the end of the decade there was a new boom which the unions were able to exploit, forcing significant wage improvements.

After 1969 the SPD became the largest party and governed in coalition with the FDP. But economic circumstances soon conspired against the social democrats. A phase of stagnation and structural change was ushered in by the collapse of the Bretton Woods system of fixed exchange rates and intensified by the oil price rises imposed by the cartel of oil-producing countries. The troughs of this phase were the recessions of 1974–5 and 1981–2. Most visible was the fall in investment and the steep rise in unemployment. Another indicator of the worsening economic situation was the rapid increase in public debt. Keynesian-based efforts to stimulate growth and employment proved futile in the face of the policy of the *Bundesbank*: the bank's constitutional autonomy from the political authorities allows it to pursue tight monetary policies that can negate the expansionary preferences of governments. The unions were put on the defensive and were unable to maintain workers' share of national income. Foreign trade continued to expand, however.

The shock of both recessions triggered a wave of modernization for which the Council of Economic Advisers (*Sachverständigenrat*), the government's most influential advisory body, had already indicated a line of approach in 1981:

The improvement of competitiveness must be achieved through the introduction of new products, i.e. those whose production requires special technical knowledge available only to a few suppliers. Such products are competitive not because they are particularly cheap, but because of their utility to those who use them; in short, because they are particularly expensive. In other words: in a dynamic economy, competitiveness is the ability to develop new speciality products and new technical solutions to an extent that permits rising incomes under conditions of high employment even though competitors gradually acquire the necessary technical knowledge and organizing abilities to manufacture those products as well. A high-wage country cannot afford to fall back on second-hand innovation.

The modernization of industry, services and public administration was recognized by all affected interests as an essential response to changed conditions. The unions opposed only certain measures for implementing the modernization process, in particular the government's supply-side economics and the *Bundesbank*'s tight money policy; for these policies implied the deliberate creation of unemployment to penalize wage increases which were considered excessive.

The SPD lost office in 1982, when their coalition partners switched support to the CDU. Labour's share of national income, which had been stable at around 68 to 71 per cent in the 1970s, declined more or less continuously from the early 1980s: from 70 per cent in 1981 to 66 per cent in 1985 and 62 per cent in 1990 (Bispinck 1991c). At the same time, real wages fell continuously in the first half of the 1980s, before starting to rise once more from 1986. However, deregulation and cuts in social services were limited; and during the 1980s there was a new phase of growth, based again on industrial production and exports, which increased to 38 per cent of GNP in 1990 compared with 28 per cent at the beginning of the decade.

A broad consensus exists that the German economy depends on success within a prosperous and expanding world economy. This export orientation explains the interest of government and business in the completion of the single European market and the development of EC monetary and political union. European integration has sparked a wave of capital concentration in which German enterprises have been leading participants. A series of spectacular mergers and takeovers has resulted in powerful transnational firms in the manufacturing sector (table 7.1). Multinational concerns have also developed in banking and insurance: for example, Deutsche Bank with approximately 70,000 employees and Allianzversicherung with about 50,000 (1990 figures). It is not only the large transnationals, but many medium-sized enterprises as well which have seen a rising volume of direct foreign investment since the early 1970s.

Another aspect of modernization in the 1980s was the increase in employment, which in 1990 reached a record level of 25.5 million in the original BRD (see table 7.2). Demand for labour was high, with shortages of skilled workers. The unions found themselves in a strong position to push for wage increases, sometimes through special additional earnings in areas where labour was especially scarce. The *Bundesbank* reacted with

Table 7.1   The largest German private employers (1989)

Firm	Branch	Employees world	Employees BRD
Daimler-Benz	vehicles/technology	380,000	300,000
Siemens	elec./engineering	370,000	230,000
Volkswagen	vehicles	250,000	160,000
Bosch	electrical	175,000	115,000
Bayer	chemicals	170,000	90,000
Hoechst	chemicals	170,000	90,000
BASF	chemicals	135,000	90,000
Thyssen	steel	135,000	110,000
Mannesmann	steel/engineering	125,000	85,000
Ruhrkohle	coal	125,000	125,000

Table 7.2 Dependent labour force in Western Germany 1950–90

Year	Employed[a] (000s)	Unemployed[b] (registered) (000s)	Unemployed[c] (%)	'Hidden' unemployed[d] (000s)
1950	13,674	1,580	10.4	
1955	16,840	928	5.2	
1960	20,257	271	1.3	
1965	21,757	147	0.7	
1970	22,246	149	0.7	0.03
1975	22,467	1,074	4.6	0.43
1980	23,897	889	3.6	0.62
1985	23,559	2,304	8.9	1.29
1990	25,550	1,883	6.9	

[a]Employed wage and salary earners, including civil servants (*Beamte*).
[b]Officially registered unemployed.
[c]Unemployed persons in relation to the entire dependent labour force (employed + unemployed)
[d]Persons available for work but not registered unemployed.
Source: *Sachverständigenrat*.

a tight money policy and announced it was willing to run the risk of higher unemployment.

Despite labour shortages in areas of economic growth, unemployment remains relatively high in certain regions and in declining industrial sectors; women are disproportionately unemployed. Nearly three-quarters of all unemployed workers have only basic education. Special employment measures have been unable to correct structural unemployment characterized by excess demand for skilled workers and a surplus of those with few if any qualifications.

As in other countries, the restructuring of employment was a feature of the German economy in the 1980s. Part-time work increased to some 14 per cent of the labour force, and other 'atypical' forms of work also expanded. White-collar employment has risen consistently, overtaking the manual labour force in 1986 (see table 7.3). The service sector has continued to increase in importance. Such trends have been encouraged by the CDU-led government which came to power in 1982. The centres of economic activity are shifting to high-tech regions such as the Munich and Stuttgart areas, or to service-oriented metropoles such as Frankfurt. Nevertheless, it should be noted that 'de-industrialization' has been far less a feature of Germany than of other European economies. Manufacturing continues to employ a far higher proportion of the labour force than in the other major EC countries (see tables 7.4 and 7.5).

In stark contrast to the economic dynamism of western Germany, the former Deutsche Demokratische Republik (DDR) was marked by technological backwardness and low productivity, antiquated infrastructure, inefficient administration and ecological damage. The full extent of eco-

Table 7.3 Composition of dependent labour force
(% of wage- and salary-earners), 1950–90

Year	Manual	White-collar	Beamte	Women
1950	70.9	23.0	6.1	
1955	68.7	24.9	6.4	
1960	62.3	30.4	7.2	33.6
1965	59.7	32.1	8.2	33.8
1970	56.2	35.1	8.7	34.0
1975	50.1	39.9	10.0	36.1
1980	48.0	41.9	10.1	37.0
1985	45.2	44.0	10.8	38.2
1990	43.0	46.5	10.5	39.0

Source: Statistisches Bundesamt (Federal Office of Statistics);
Bundesanstalt für Arbeit (Federal Institute of Labour).

nomic (and political, social and moral) self-destruction only became apparent with the DDR's accession to the BRD in 1990. The human problems associated with unification are immense. The people of eastern Germany were subjugated for nearly sixty years while those in western Germany successfully seized the opportunity for an early and speedy recovery after the war. The national-socialist dictatorship left behind a country destroyed by war; the communist dictatorship, a ravaged economy.

Unification meant a complete change of system. The governmental, economic and social structures of the east were adapted to the West German model, transforming a command economy into a social market economy (Kromphardt and Bruno-Latocha 1991; SVR 1990, 1991). A modernization process which required several decades for completion in the BRD is currently being compressed into a few years in eastern Germany. This involves the modernization of production technology and infrastructure, changes in the organization of the labour process and industrial relations, and the development of the service sector.

Table 7.4 GNP by sector (%)

Year	Agriculture energy, construction	Manufacturing	Services
1960	17.1	33.6	49.3
1965	15.7	35.3	49.0
1970	14.0	37.0	49.0
1975	12.7	34.7	52.6
1980	12.3	33.7	54.0
1985	10.9	32.6	56.5
1990	10.3	31.3	58.4

Source: Sachverständigenrat.

Table 7.5 Employment by sectors (% of dependent labour force) 1960–90

Year	Agriculture energy, construction	Manufacturing	Services
1960	15.7	44.1	40.2
1965	15.0	43.6	41.4
1970	13.2	43.3	43.5
1975	11.5	38.7	49.8
1980	11.3	36.6	52.1
1985	10.3	34.5	55.2
1990	9.5	33.7	56.8

Source: Sachverständigenrat.

When political unification was accomplished on 3 October 1990, according to Paragraph 23 of the Basic Law, the entire West German state and constitutional system was extended into eastern Germany. The same is true for the legal, institutional and organizational framework of industrial relations. Unions and employers' organizations have extended their jurisdiction into eastern Germany and introduced free collective bargaining in a short period of time. The trade unions were very anxious to avoid being identified as the successors of the completely discredited communist trade unions. The employers, by contrast, had the advantage of being able to start from scratch since there were no employer interest associations under the communist system.

Unlike many other eastern European countries, eastern Germany is far from being a Third World country. Nonetheless, revitalization will not be possible without massive support from the BRD. DM 140 billion in public subsidies was transferred to the five new eastern federal states (*Bundesländer*) in 1991 alone, and a similar level of subsidy is expected to continue. The objectives are to stimulate investment, establish modern infrastructure and administration, and support social measures to help the victims of labour market policy.

The introduction of the Deutsche Mark into the area of what was the DDR symbolized the political downfall of the communist regime and triggered economic consequences which are still being felt (Deutsche Bundesbank 1991a, 1991b). The free convertibility of the two German currencies, and the removal of state subsidies, made east German products uncompetitive in the west. There was a similar collapse in the eastern European markets to which the East German economy had been oriented, because currency shortages in those countries led to drastic reductions in imports. The economic consequences were concentrated in what was once the backbone of the DDR's economy – the industrial sector. In autumn 1991, the volume of east German production had fallen to 30 per cent of its previous level. Entire branches, such as motor vehicles, collapsed because the products no longer found buyers on the market. In the chemical industry, which was additionally burdened by environmental catastrophes, the number of jobs had fallen from 330,000 to 100,000 and is expected to halve again in 1992. Expansion is taking place only in those sectors which were neglected by the old government: construction, printing, banking and insurance.

This transformation crisis has been accompanied by a massive decline in jobs. Statistics for 1989 put the number of employed at 9.5 million; at the end of 1991 the figure dropped to 6.5 million. A further decline is projected for 1992. At the end of 1991 there were one million people registered as unemployed in east Germany and 1.1 million *Kurzarbeiter* (short-time workers). A further 1.3 million people are currently affected by various labour market policy measures such as job creation, training and pre-retirement programmes. There are 500,000 commuters who live in east Germany and work in the west, thereby easing the burden on the east German labour market. In total, 3.4 million persons in the east depend on unemployment benefits (Kühl 1991).

Despite broad consensus between government and opposition parties, as well as employers' associations and trade unions, on the integration of the *neue Bundesländer* within the western system, there are disputes over the speed and the extent to which market forces should prevail. Significant conflicts between government, employers and unions have been triggered by the privatization of East German operations which were formerly owned and operated by the state. The *Treuhand* institute was set up to undertake this task after economic union in July 1990. Altogether 8,500 companies with approximately four million employees were covered, and by the end of 1991 more than 4,000 enterprises employing more than 2.5 million workers had been sold, transferred to local authorities or closed. *Treuhand* has followed a policy of selling off companies which can be restructured and made viable, and shutting down those which it considers unsalvageable. IG Metall by contrast called for government finance to rescue many of the threatened companies, and called for a Swedish-style fund to enable workers collectively to own shares as a supplement to their wages.

A similar controversy – discussed below – has developed over the question of wage levels. While government officials and many economic experts would like to preserve eastern Germany's character as a low-wage region, the unions wish to turn it into a high-wage area as quickly as possible. Nevertheless, an unspoken understanding seems to exist between employers and unions to use high wages and social services (far beyond what is justified by economic performance) as a vehicle for rationalization and modernization. The old firms are supposed to die off as quickly as possible and be replaced by companies which will be made competitive through the introduction of the most modern technology and organization of the labour process.

Despite these economic and social problems, observers (including the unions) agree that the standard of living has actually risen. First, the favourable conversion of east German savings into western Marks made it possible for east Germans to acquire higher-value consumer goods. Second, the infusion of money from the *Bundesanstalt für Arbeit* (Federal Institute of Labour) has meant that workers in eastern Germany who lost their jobs have been able to maintain their standard of living. Finally, the wage increases negotiated by the unions have improved the living standards of those workers who still have jobs.

Whether the decline in employment and output turns out to be a temporary, transitional phenomenon remains to be seen. It is conceivable that east Germany will become a zone of economic backwardness, a sort of German *Mezzogiorno*. Other experts do not rule out the possibility of an economic reunification boom, arguing that the economic integration of the east will act as a challenge to Germany's innovative powers and facilitate the emergence of a united and modern German economy which will dominate the eastern European market. Hence, it is argued, the short-run economic costs of unification will lead to substantial long-run benefits (Jürgensen 1991). According to IG Metall, Daimler-Benz, Opel and Volkswagen are building Europe's most modern automobile plants in eastern Germany. Most commentators agree, however, that the costs of reconstructing the east German economy will be higher, and the process more protracted, than was widely imagined in the euphoric days of the collapse of the Berlin Wall and the old DDR regime. As we write in 1992, the social costs in the east of the rapid introduction of a market economy, and the financial costs in the west of cushioning this transition, indeed threaten a dual crisis in both politics and industrial relations.

The Legal Framework: The State and Law

The high degree of juridification of German industrial relations has already been emphasized. The Works Constitution Act (*BetrVG*) requires the appointment by the work force of a works council (*Betriebsrat*), elected by and from all employees. The law defines precisely the questions on which councils possess rights of information, consultation and codetermination. There is provision for combined works councils (*Gesamt-* or *Konzernbetriebsräte*) in multi-plant companies. The operation of this pivotal institution is discussed in detail in a later section. The Act applies only in the private sector. There is parallel legislation in the public sector, the Federal Staff Representation Act (*BPersVG*) with supplementary acts in the various *Länder*. These provide for staff councils with somewhat fewer powers than works councils. Their operation is also examined below.

The other main level of employee representation is on company boards. German firms have a two-tier structure: a small management board which reports to and is appointed by the supervisory board. There are three different types of legal provision. The *BetrVG* (1952) provided for one-third employee representation on the supervisory boards of all companies with over 500 employees. The Codetermination Act (*MitbG*)

(1976) provides notional parity in firms with more than 2,000 employees; though in practice the shareholders' representatives retain a majority in the event of disagreement. Finally, there is a special Codetermination Act for the Coal and Steel Industry (*MontanMitbG*) (1951, amended several times). This provides genuine parity on the supervisory board; and the employee representatives have a veto over the appointment of the labour director (*Arbeitsdirektor*) who acts as de facto representative of the employees and their interests on the management board. The *MontanMitbG* guarantees the most far-reaching opportunities for codetermination ever established in Germany and is therefore of enormous symbolic significance. Nowadays it is only of limited practical importance because of the decline of the coal and steel industries: only about thirty establishments operate under the Act.

Perhaps surprisingly, collective bargaining is not subject to detailed legal regulation. The Collective Agreement Act (*TVG*) (1949, amended 1969) guarantees free collective bargaining: the right of the parties involved to negotiate pay and other working conditions without state intervention. There are no special acts governing the contents of collective agreements (*Tarifverträge*). Collective agreements are in reality, though not in legal terms, generally applicable to all employees and not just to union members. As in most other countries there is a strict peace obligation during the currency of a collective agreement. Under the *TVG* a declaration of general applicability can be made by the federal or *Land* Minister of Labour if either party so requests. This provision is rarely used, since most employers are members of the associations which negotiate on their behalf, and those that are not usually observe the terms of collective agreements.

Union recognition is rarely a problem in Germany, and there is no legislation directly related to the issue; although in practice, as will be shown below, the Acts already discussed provide very strong support for collective representation. Nor is there legislation regulating the internal affairs of trade unions: the unions determine their own rules and constitutions.

As well as the dense network of statute law, German industrial relations are subject to a considerable body of case law. In particular, the conduct of strikes and lockouts (which as noted above, can legally be called only between the expiry of an existing agreement and the conclusion of a new one) is regulated by a series of judgments of the Federal Labour Court. Two key principles enunciated by the Court are 'proportionality' and 'social adequacy': a strike or lockout is legitimate only if the cause is appropriate and the action is not excessive in comparison to the issue provoking it. Only trade unions can call strikes; 'wildcat' action is illegal. Strikes must relate to the agenda of collective bargaining – hence political strikes are illegal – and be called only after the breakdown of bargaining. Industrial disputes suspend, rather than terminate, contracts of employment. Lockouts have been judged lawful – a contentious issue –

but only in response to a (selective) strike; and the numbers locked out must not substantially exceed those on strike.

There is a clear legal distinction between conflicts of rights over the interpretation of existing collective agreements, and conflicts of interest concerning the terms of new agreements. The former must be settled by peaceful means: if no negotiated resolution is possible, through the conciliation committees specified in the *BetrVG*, or else by reference to the labour courts. Only conflicts of interest can be resolved by industrial action, if mediation procedures fail.

As in other European countries, many employment-related conditions and benefits (retirement pensions, health insurance, maternity benefits, maximum hours of work, minimum holiday periods, unemployment insurance) are the subject of legislation. This reduces the issues in collective bargaining which can lead to conflict.

The Work Promotion Act (*AFG*, 1969) introduced an 'active and preventive' labour market policy, and has become increasingly important since the mid-1970s when unemployment started to rise dramatically. The *AFG* provides a variety of instruments: information and consultation, promotion of vocational training, integration of disabled persons, job preservation and creation. The Act has not been effective in preventing or curing large-scale unemployment, although expenditure on labour market intervention has increased considerably. Most of its instruments were designed for a context of full employment, and are difficult to adapt to a completely changed situation.

Germany is exceptional in having a formal national system of vocational training with a long, sometimes controversial, history. Nowadays this system is generally valued by employers, unions and governments, and the general public as well; its characteristic feature is its tripartite organization, including unions. All school-leavers, even those who do not enter the vocational training system, have to attend vocational schools until the age of 18. The system eases the transition from school to labour market, prevents youth unemployment and guarantees the acquisition of standardized and intensive qualifications which are both practical and theoretical. This dual system successfully blends general training (in specialized, independent public vocational schools) with specific training (within the individual establishment). The system creates opportunities for internal mobility and functional flexibility, reduces the significance of job demarcations, and avoids over-specialization (Sengenberger 1987). From a macro perspective it encourages adaptability of qualifications and job content to changed structural conditions and guarantees a comparatively high standard of education for the national work force. There exist more than 400 detailed training plans. In recent years, many of these have been adapted through tripartite negotiations to new technological requirements and to introduce new 'key qualifications'. It is often argued that this system of vocational training creates a competitive advantage for German industry (Timmermann 1990).

Up to the 1970s it was common to criticize the high degree of juridification of German industrial relations (Erd 1978, 1979); but in the 1980s the positive effects have become more evident. It now seems that the tendency to legalization works not so much as a restriction on collective action, but rather as a relatively effective institutional buffer against attempts drastically to change the system. This comparatively stable institutional framework places a brake on two possible strategies: on aggressive moves by employers when capital has the upper hand; and on major changes initiated by conservative or liberal governments (cf. Katzenstein 1989).

There is a clear legal distinction between the establishment and the sectoral levels; the differences in the real world are less clear, and the actors at both levels cooperate closely. All these rules create a legal, institutionalized framework for the voluntary interaction of the actors at different levels. Individual and collective actions and their consequences can be predicted by the other side, leading to an iterated game of mutual interdependence and compromise.

Trade Unions

Before the Nazis crushed trade unionism in 1933, craft and industrial unions existed side by side and were also divided by party alignment. The biggest movement, affiliated to the Social Democratic Party, was the General Federation of German Trade Unions (*Allgemeiner Deutscher Gewerkschaftsbund*) with about five million members; the Christian and Liberal trade unions covered about two million more. When trade unionism was rebuilt after 1945, former divisions were transcended. Not only were the various ideological factions united in a single organizational structure, but so were workers of different social status: blue- and white-collar workers, and civil servants.

The new peak association, the German Trade Union Federation (*Deutscher Gewerkschaftsbund*, DGB) originally had sixteen affiliated unions, each responsible for one industry or economic sector. In 1978 the formerly independent Police Union joined as the seventeenth affiliate; and in 1989 the printers' union amalgamated with some smaller organizations, reducing the number of affiliated unions to 16 again (see table 7.6). Otherwise the structure has remained unaltered since the DGB was founded in 1949.

The corollary of a 'unitary' trade union movement is that post-war German unions have not been formally affiliated to any political party. Nevertheless, the DGB maintains close links with the SDP, most full-time union officials are party members, and the majority of union members vote for the social democrats. However, the DGB, and almost all industry unions, reserve a minority of executive seats for CDU members. Traditional patterns of political alignment have been weakened in the last decade or so by the rise of new social movements on the left, and in particular the emergence of the Green Party.

There are two other main union confederations: the German Salaried Employees' Union (DAG) and the German Civil Servants' Federation (DBB). In the early 1990s, there has been a rapprochement between the DAG and the DGB-affiliated Union of Employees in Commerce, Banking and Insurance (HBV); a merger is currently possible. In contrast to the position during the Weimar Republic – and in other European countries today – these two rival confederations represent fewer white-collar employees and civil servants than does the DGB; one can justifiably speak of the achievement of unitary and industrial unionism in Germany. A fourth confederation, the Christian Federation of Trade Unions (CGB), has fewer than 300,000 members. More than 80 per cent of all union members belong to the DGB.

German unification has brought a considerable increase in union membership; but because of the unstable employment situation in the east, membership is in constant flux, and exact numbers are not available at the time of writing. However, it can be said that density in the east is higher than in the west. IG Metall, for example, has gained about 900,000 new members. Membership fluctuation is accentuated by the common practice of poaching members from organizational domains whose previous demarcation lines were different from those in the west. These demarcation disputes have given rise to discussions on mergers and a far-reaching reorganization of the DGB. Most notably, IG Chemie (Chemicals) and IG Bergbau (Mining and Energy) are likely to amalgamate in the near future.

Table 7.6   *Deutscher Gewerkschaftsbund* (DGB) membership (000s) 1990

Sector	Manual	White-collar	Beamte	Women	Total
Metal industry	2,315	412	–	433	2,727
Public service	586	584	82	431	1,252
Chemicals	541	135	–	132	676
Posts	151	43	285	164	479
Construction	423	39	–	37	463
Commerce, banking, insurance	54	351	–	246	405
Mining and energy	278	45	–	7	323
Rail	148	11	153	31	312
Food, drink, tobacco	221	54	–	97	275
Textile, clothing	220	30	–	144	250
Education, science		51	138	104	189
Media	123	62	–	50	185
Police	9	17	136	17	163
Wood, plastics	142	11	–	22	153
Agriculture	38	3	3	8	44
Leather	40	3	–	17	43
Total DGB	5,289	1,851	798	1,940	7,938

Source: DGB.

Table 7.7 Union membership and density (BRD) 1950–90

Year	DGB (000s)	DGB density (%)	DBB (000s)	DAG (000s)	CGB (000s)	All Confederations (DGB, DBB, DAG, CGB) (000s)	All Confederations density (%)	Potential membership (employed and unemployed) (000s)
1950	5,450	35.7	234[a]	344[a]	–	6,028	39.5	15,254
1955	6,105	34.4	517	421	–	7,043	39.7	17,768
1960	6,379	31.0	650	450	200	7,679	37.4	20,528
1965	6,574	30.0	703	476	235[b]	7,988	36.5	21,904
1970	6,713	30.0	721	461	199[c]	8,094	36.1	22,395
1975	7,365	31.3	727	470	224	8,786	37.3	23,541
1980	7,883	31.8	821	495	288	9,487	38.3	24,786
1985	7,719	29.8	796	500	307	9,322	36.0	25,863
1990	7,938	29.0	799	573	309	9,619	35.2	27,364

[a]1951
[b]1964
[c]1972

Source: Union figures.

The following analysis perforce excludes from consideration the former DDR. In the forty years from 1950 to 1990, DGB membership increased by almost 2.5 million, with the greatest increases in the early 1950s and the 1970s. Social scientists and industrial relations experts (Treu 1978; Herkommer et al. 1979; Streeck 1981; Müller-Jentsch 1981; Brandt et al. 1982) have offered a number of explanations for the growth wave of the 1970s. First, the accession of the social democrats to government and the development of 'neo-corporatist' concertation increased the unions' political legitimacy. Second, the 1972 amendments to the *BetrVG* strengthened their workplace presence. Third, unions were successful in rationalizing their recruitment methods and internal administration. Fourth, changes in workers' consciousness resulting from economic recession made them aware of the need for union representation. Finally, there was an increase in union militancy in response to members' heightened expectations, unofficial strike waves and other pressures from the rank and file.

In the early 1980s membership decreased slightly, by 300,000, a loss that had been fully recouped by 1990. Trends in union density have been uneven: from 1950 to 1960 it fell from 35.7 to 31.0 per cent, then stagnated at around 30 per cent during the 1960s; it rose to about 32 per cent in the 1970s before falling back once more to 29 per cent in the 1980s (see table 7.7).

The DGB does not seem to be strong when measured by density. But since the groups with high density rates (blue-collar workers in the strong manufacturing sector and employees in the public sector) occupy strategic positions, the unions are in a position to negotiate pace-setting agreements. In addition, the system of industrial unionism and sectoral collective bargaining leaves hardly any room for a non-union sector. Only very small employers could pay below union rates without provoking their employees to join a union. Union density is also an inadequate measure of union strength because it tells us nothing about the intensity and quality of the membership bond. A large membership – perhaps recruited on the basis of individual incentives – may not provide real collective strength. Smaller numbers, but a greater commitment to collective interests, may make for stronger unionism. In this respect the German unions, despite relatively low density, have from time to time demonstrated their ability to mobilize their members in disciplined, protracted and effective strike action.

In the past twenty years important changes have taken place in the composition of DGB membership. These include the shift from industry to the service sector, and from blue-collar to white-collar work. Between 1950 and 1990, the percentage of blue-collar workers in DGB unions fell from 83 to 67, while that of white-collar staff rose from 11 to 23 and of *Beamte* (see below) from 6 to 10.

Although white-collar and female employees constitute an increasing proportion of union membership, their unionization has not kept pace with their growing numbers in the labour force. Membership composition of 1990 is more in line with the labour force composition of 1950 than that of today. Unions have two main strongholds: male manual workers and public employees. More than 60 per cent of the former and more than 50 per cent of the latter are organized in unions affiliated to the DGB. The groups with low density rates are white-collar (18 per cent), female (20 per cent), and younger workers (22 per cent). Foreign workers are fairly well organized (36 per cent) (see Table 7.8).

Union democracy is based on a delegate system with representative and executive bodies at local, regional and national levels. Ordinary members are directly involved – apart from elections for local representatives – only when ballots on industrial action are held. Such ballots are called by national executive committees, and require a 75 per cent vote before a strike can be declared, according to the unions' own rules. On the same principle, a strike can be ended by a vote of 25 per cent. The logic behind these rules is that strikes need to have the support of a large majority of members to be effective.

The national trade union conference is the most important policy-making body. As a rule, it takes place every four years (though in the past, conferences were held more frequently) and elects the national executive committee, which is the most important body for policy implementation.

The segmentation of the labour market into relatively privileged and underprivileged groups is clearly reflected in unions' representational structures. Male skilled or professional employees are generally over-represented. There are also clear tendencies towards professionalized representation: most elected bodies have a high proportion of full-time officers. There have been parallel tendencies towards bureaucratic structures, centralization of decision-making and concentration of control over personnel and financial resources in the national executive committee that coordinates wage policy, selects full-time officers and controls the union press. Restrictions on the influence of the rank and file are an expression of oligarchical tendencies in labour organizations, present since before the First World War, as shown in Michels' famous study (1911). More contemporary analyses by Witjes (1976) and Wilke (1979) have underlined the continuing prevalence of oligarchical structures. Some authors (Weitbrecht 1969; Bergmann et al. 1975; Müller-Jentsch 1985) have argued that the neutralization of direct member influence on union policy is a prerequisite for the unions to perform their functions of negotiating and dealing with employers and the state in a cooperative and authoritative way.

In the course of its history, the DGB has formulated three basic programmes: the Munich Programme of 1949, the first Düsseldorf Programme of 1963 and the second Düsseldorf Programme of 1981. The programme formulated at the founding congress was anti-capitalist, arguing for the 'reorganization of the economy and society' with the socialization of key industries, economic planning, and codetermination. The second programme (1963) revised the anti-capitalist goals and followed the neo-Keynesian line of the 1959 Godesberg Programme of the SPD. The third programme (1981) is primarily an extension of the second. Full

Table 7.8   Union density[a] (DGB only) by category of worker (%)

Group/Sector	1960	1970	1980	1990
Men	39.3	38.7	42.6	39.6
Women	16.8	13.6	17.5	18.8
Blue-collar workers	40.7	40.7	47.3	48.0
Male	48.1	49.4	56.0	55.0
Female	22.5	18.7	25.7	30.0
White-collar workers	11.7	12.6	16.3	15.4
Male	15.6	17.4	21.7	18.9
Female	7.7	7.7	11.5	12.6
Civil servants	35.0	32.8	36.2	32.3
Male	35.4	32.6	37.4	33.0
Female	31.1	34.5	30.7	30.1
Foreign workers		25.0[b]	30.6	33.9
Young workers[c]		21.1	21.6	20.9
Private sector	26.7	26.0	28.4	27.0
Public sector	58.9	51.3	53.3	51.3

[a]DGB members as proportion of dependent labour force (excluding unemployed).
[b]1974.
[c]Up to the age of 25.

employment is now the first priority; economic growth is regarded as an important, but not necessarily essential means to this end. An equitable distribution of income and property is advocated, but what this means is not defined. The *Montan* model of codetermination in coal and steel remains the objective for all large establishments. The programme also calls for bilateral Social Councils at national and regional levels, as instruments for the control of economic planning. The programme combines socialist rhetoric with pragmatic accommodation to capitalism: offering, in effect, a compromise between the right and left wings of the DGB.

In the late 1980s and early 1990s, unions initiated an open debate on their role in a changing economic and social environment. The microelectronic revolution and the globalization of economic relations, the death of traditional working-class cultures and the decline of socialist ideology, the crisis of the Keynesian welfare state and the 'silent revolution' of value systems, the increasing tertiarization and feminization of the occupational structure, the political cleavages caused by the emergence of new social movements and parties, all these challenges and their consequences for unionism determine the agenda of union conferences and workshops. In response to these pressures, the DGB has recently established a working party to draft a new basic programme.

German unification has intensified the debate on union strategy for the 1990s. German unions had hardly begun to discuss their future role in a 'post-Fordist' society when they were confronted with social problems inherited from an earlier stage of industrialism. Unification of the two German states – and of unionism in east and west – presents unprecedented and contradictory challenges. In the west, the unions are expected to respond to the challenges of advanced industrialism; in the east, they have to cope with the social heritage of a centrally planned and industrially backward society faced by the problems of sudden transformation into a market economy. These issues are discussed in a later section.

The Representation of Business Interests

German employers are very highly organized and extremely loyal to their associations. All establishments, from small one-man companies to transnationals, have been integrated into structures organized along functional, sectoral and geographical lines. Three basic types of organization can be distinguished: chambers of industry and commerce, business associations and employers' associations. The Joint Committee of German Business (*Gemeinschaftsausschuß der Deutschen Gewerblichen Wirtschaft*) has been appointed by the three central organizations to coordinate their activities.

The chamber system represents the general economic interests of firms, whatever their sector of operation. The chambers of industry and commerce are the local units of organization; they enjoy a formal legal status which makes membership compulsory for all eligible firms. The chambers perform a variety of public or semi-governmental tasks: licensing and regulating trade practices, and occupational training programmes, in particular apprenticeship training. They also offer a broad range of market-related services, including advice on current business issues. Their national organization, the German Association of Chambers of Commerce (DIHT), represents about 100 regional and local chambers. The DIHT concentrates on questions of economic policy and foreign trade. In the GATT negotiations, the DIHT has argued against the official policy of the EC and the German government; the DIHT favours further trade liberalization to enhance export opportunities, and pressed for massive cuts in agricultural subsidies.

Business (or trade) associations are organized by industry, in local associations affiliated to sectoral peak organizations. They are concerned with such matters as technology, production, marketing and research. The Association of German Machine and System Builders (VDMA) provides a good example of the structure and functioning of these business organizations. The VDMA, with approximately 2,500 member companies, represents nearly 60 per cent of the eligible firms and 80 per cent of the sales in one of the key German industries. It has separate *Länder* associations, and sub-divisions for mechanical engineering, printing equipment and other specialist products.

The main economy-wide peak association is the Federation of German Industries (BDI), which comprises the business associations of the entire industrial sector. In 1985 it consisted of 35 business associations with around 150 regional subdivisions and some 350 specialized industrial sub-units. The BDI acts as a central coordinating body and represents German industry to the general public and government bodies. Any overlap of functions between business associations and chambers is accommodated by coordination between the two sets of organizations.

Employers' associations are the third type, responsible for promoting employers' interests in the areas of wages, working hours and other working conditions. They are exclusively responsible for negotiating collective agreements, with the responsible union; agreements affecting the vast majority of employees are sectoral and multi-employer in character. It is legally possible for a single employer to negotiate a collective agreement, and Volkswagen is a well-known example of this; but it is very much an exception to the general rule of multi-employer bargaining. Though in most industries bargaining takes place at regional (*Bundesland*) level, the national employers' associations exercise tight coordination and control over the process. The Federation of Employers' Associations of the Metalworking Industry (*Gesamtmetall*) far exceeds all others in influence, representing employers in the motor, machine-tool and electrical industries. It is a multi-sectoral federation of employers' associations, which – like its union counterpart, IG Metall – has to reconcile diverse interests as well as handling collective bargaining for four million workers.

The sectoral employers' associations are combined in the Confederation of German Employers' Associations (BDA). This central body, like the DGB, plays no direct role in collective bargaining, but has a coordinating and mediating function. The BDA represents German employers in the field of social policy and industrial relations to the government, the public and international organizations. The BDA is an association of associations and, unlike the BDI, extends far beyond manufacturing industry, covering almost all private-sector employers' associations. The Employers' Association of the Iron and Steel Industry is the only significant organization outside the BDA network. In 1985 the BDA consisted of 46 national industry associations (with nearly 400 local affiliates) and 12 state (*Land*) associations (now increased to 17 with the establishment of organization in the *neue Bundesländer*); altogether, there are approximately 200 different employers' associations at the regional and sectoral level. It is estimated that around 80 per cent of employees in the private sector are covered by the BDA's member associations. Precise figures are available for associations representing particular industrial branches. *Gesamtmetall* (with 8,300 member companies) covered 55 per cent of eligible firms in 1985; these companies employ nearly three million workers, about 75 per cent of the labour force in the metalworking industries. In some other sectors – the chemical industry or the financial services sector, for example – the degree of representation is higher, and occasionally reaches 100 per cent. The sectoral peak associations such as *Gesamtmetall* have substantial financial resources, and have set up dispute funds to support member companies that are the target of strikes.

The BDA and its member associations are governed by an executive board and a management board. These are elected by member firms with votes proportional to company size; hence the leadership and the policy of the employers' associations are determined by the largest firms. Positions on the management board are filled by full-time BDA staff; the presidium is the central policy-making body and is composed of senior representatives of the member companies. Great importance is attached to about 20 committees and working groups which deal with such questions as wage policy, labour law, training programmes, the single European market, and overall policy coordination.

In order to understand the internal mechanisms of German industrial relations it is important to see that on the employers' side institutions and spheres of jurisdiction parallel those of the unions. The exercise of free collective bargaining, including the right to conclude agreements on wages, working time and other working conditions or to initiate strikes or lock-outs, is the province of the individual unions and employers' associations within their particular industry. On the employers' side, the BDA has an important coordinating role; bargaining policy, however, is determined and implemented by the industry associations. Member companies may not independently conclude company agreements and must observe collective agreements reached by their employers' association; breach of these principles is grounds for expulsion.

Because multi-employer bargaining guarantees industrial peace during the currency of the industry-wide agreement, large firms have a strong incentive to join their employers' association and observe its disciplines. Small firms, however, may see less need for membership, and act as 'free riders'. Just how highly the employers prize this system was revealed when the east German *Länder* joined the BRD. With no tradition of free collective bargaining, it seemed possible for a time that a distinctive model of industrial relations might be established – based, for example, on single-employer bargaining. But in fact, West German unions and employers' associations worked together to transplant their own organizational structures and collective bargaining arrangements to the east (Bispinck 1991a). The principle of sectoral agreements is being strictly observed. The advantages for the employers of orderly industrial relations have outweighed any potential gains from a strategy of deregulation.

The State

Moderate Macrocorporatism in the 1960s and 1970's

As in other western market economies, the state in Germany has played a gradually increasing role in industrial relations. In the 1960s its previously conservative economic policies shifted towards Keynesian macro-economic management, an approach which was extremely successful when first applied by the Grand Coalition between the Christian-democrat CDU and the social-democrat SPD. In this period, two initiatives were taken which remain important.

First, the Council of Economic Advisers (*Sachverständigenrat*) was created in 1963. Its role is to report regularly on the state of the economy and likely developments; it is not, however, authorized to offer detailed recommendations for public policy. Although it has no formal powers, the informal influence of the Council – which usually supports some form of wage restraint – has been considerable. Second, the Act on the Promotion of Stability and Growth of 1967 obliges the state and *Bundesländer* to adopt economic and financial policies consistent with such macro-economic goals as price stability, full employment, foreign trade balance and economic growth.

In the late 1960s and 1970s tripartite concertation between the state and national leaderships of unions and employers' associations was an important feature of German industrial relations, when active labour market policies and macro-economic strategies designed to stabilize growth and fight unemployment were part of the political agenda. Unions became a powerful partner and their role was recognized within a system of voluntary political exchange with governments led by the SPD (joined by the Free Democrats) between 1969 and 1982.

An essential part of the German version of corporatism was the *Konzertierte Aktion* (concerted action) which resulted from the Act on the Promotion of Stability and Growth. This trilateral cooperation, which lasted from 1967 to 1977, was intended to achieve relative stability of prices and of income distribution, including some sort of voluntary wage restraint by unions, and steady economic growth. The participants were intended to de-politicize and neutralize their differing interests by exchanging information about macro-economic processes. While the results of their more or less informal meetings were – in contrast to other countries – not binding, they had an important function in public discussion and influenced the internal and external decision-making processes of the parties involved. Expected benefits for the unions from bargained corporatism included increased organizational strength, improved rights of codetermination and participation, expansion of the welfare state and more influence within the political process. But union leaders faced enormous difficulties: they could not vigorously pursue their members' immediate economic interests because of the constraints of consensual wage policies. Thus *Konzertierte Aktion* came under heavy pressure from the rank and file, who could see no positive benefits in exchange for their voluntary wage restraint. At the same time, the government was unable to control other important macro-economic variables. *Konzertierte Aktion* came to an official end in 1977 after the employers' associations raised a constitutional challenge to the legality of the new Codetermination Act; the unions took the opportunity to withdraw from formal concertation. The outcome of the experiment was disappointing, and it is unlikely to be repeated.

Moderate Deregulation in the 1980s

The political preconditions for concertation changed to some degree in the 1980s with the formation of the neo-conservative CDU/CSU/FDP government in 1982, and its orientation (already initiated in the latter stages of the SDP-led government) to supply-side monetarist strategies. Yet there has not been a complete or abrupt change as in other western countries. Political regulation has only partially been replaced by market forces; in practice, continuities in economic, social and industrial relations policies can be clearly observed.

There have indeed been some efforts by the conservative government to deregulate aspects of social and labour law. A highly contentious change was contained in Paragraph 116 of the Work Promotion Act of 1986. This ended the former entitlement to unemployment and short-time working benefit for employees whose jobs are indirectly affected by industrial action in the same industry, but in another bargaining district. Such payments had been a valuable resource for the unions in the past. Since in most industries negotiations – and hence also strikes – are normally conducted at regional level it was possible to choose strike tactics which affected an industry across the whole economy, thus intensifying the pressure on employers to settle, while the union involved had only to give financial support to workers striking or laid off in a single district.

The consequences of this legal change have not yet been empirically tested. But it is probable that the traditional, and successful, policy of regionalized but centrally coordinated bargaining and selective strike action – developed to a fine art by IG Metall – has been made more difficult.

The Employment Promotion Act of 1985, extended in 1989, dilutes previous protective labour legislation. Important parts of individual labour law, giving protection against dismissal, were abolished. For new recruits, fixed-term contracts for up to eighteen months (the previous maximum was six months) were legalized. While the law did not initiate the trend towards precarious employment, the empirical evidence is that it accelerated this trend, without however achieving the government's proclaimed aim of a significant increase in employment. The law has made a minimal impact on employment levels, but it has had a significant structural effect, increasing labour market segmentation (Büchtemann and Höland 1989). By comparison with other countries, however, this might be considered a moderate form of labour market deregulation.

The 1989 amendment to the Works Constitution Act brought various detailed changes. Most were fairly technical, but the main contentious innovations were the creation of special representative bodies for managerial staff, and the strengthening of representation rights for other minority groups. By fragmenting interest representation, this may conceivably weaken the works council as a unitary representative of all employees. A new Working Time Act has been under discussion since

1987, to replace an Act of 1938. This would allow greater flexibility in determining daily and weekly working-time, ending the principle of the normal working day. Further proposals would facilitate night and Sunday working.

These changes cannot plausibly be viewed as the outcome of a coherent long-term political strategy. Nevertheless, important consequences may result from the accumulation of individual measures of procedural and substantive deregulation, and the elimination of individual protective rights. Current employer moves towards more flexibility coincide with high unemployment, which has significantly reduced the bargaining power of the unions. The danger of a more severe segmentation of the labour market cannot be dismissed. It is probable, however, that attempts at deregulation will have only limited effects in Germany; they are more important as an expression of conservative political ideology than in practice. Existing institutions, formal and informal mechanisms of regulation and strategies of the actors function as important stabilizers.

Why has deregulation in Germany been so half-hearted? One important factor is the role of Christian-democrat trade unionists, who exercise a two-way mediating role in German industrial relations. One of the bases of the post-war construction of a unitary trade union movement was the guarantee of institutionalized representation (albeit as a small minority) for Christian democrats in the unions' governing bodies –inhibiting too unqualified a commitment by the unions to the SPD. But conversely, important CDU politicians possess a strong trade union identity, and are organized in a long-established 'social committee' within the party. This group has strongly opposed deregulation, and Paragraph 116 was passed only against its vehement opposition, causing friction in the CDU. The influence of this fraction should not be exaggerated, but it has undoubtedly placed a brake on deregulation. In addition, it should be noted that it is the FDP – the minority governing party – which is most committed to deregulation rather than the CDU/CSU majority. The recent legislation therefore reflects complex bargaining within the coalition government. The FDP strongly advocated the separate representative committees for management staff, though the CDU was unenthusiastic. On the other hand, the CDU (and in particular its union fraction) wished to preserve the special Codeter-mination Act for coal and steel which was about to expire, while the FDP was strongly opposed. The eventual shape of the legislation thus reflected behind-the-scenes negotiations within the government itself.

Another important explanation of the limited extent of deregulation in Germany is that German employers' associations, in contrast to their counterparts in other countries, are not seeking the deregulation of the collective bargaining system or the destruction of institutions of workers' representation. The amendment to the Works Constitution Act was strongly opposed not only by the unions but also by the employers' associations, which were not interested in any fragmentation of the works council system. Their interest in deregulation is limited and specific.

Workplace Institutions and Relations

Works Councils

Works councils are by law formally independent of the unions and represent the entire workforce of an establishment, not only union members. There are no official statistics on the coverage of works councils, but the DGB collects data for all establishments where DGB-affiliated unions are represented, and these are regarded by Ministry of Labour officials as a fairly accurate picture of the overall situation. The DGB figures for 1990 cover more than 33,000 establishments with works councils, in which some 180,000 councillors were elected (table 7.9).

There are no statistics on the number of establishments – with five or more employees – where workers have a legal right to elect a works council. Most estimates put the figure somewhere above 40,000; in other words, works councils exist in 70–80 per cent of eligible workplaces. Since it is mainly in the smaller firms that works councils do not operate, a higher proportion of German employees is represented by councils.

Works councillors are elected for a four-year term of office (increased from three years in 1989). The size of works councils varies according to the number of employees. In larger establishments – with more than 300 employees – one or more works councillors can act as full-time employee representatives. The works council cannot be mandated by the work force, but is required to call a quarterly works meeting of all employees, when it reports on its activities. All costs arising out of the activities of the works council have to be paid by the employer. According to an employers' survey (Niedenhoff 1987), the average annual cost of the system is DM 440 per employee. The bulk of this sum – which is almost certainly an exaggeration – is for the day-to-day activities of the works councils; in large establishments they have their own offices and secretaries.

The participation rights of the works council are linked to the legal obligation to work with management 'in a spirit of mutual trust for the good of the employees and of the establishment'. The works council is required to negotiate 'with a serious desire to reach agreement'; 'acts of industrial warfare' as well as 'activities that interfere with operations or imperil the peace of the establishment' are prohibited. There is also a secrecy obligation: information defined by the employer as business secrets may not be shared with the work force.

The statutory rights of the works council are prescribed in detail. Codetermination rights exist on 'social' matters, such as principles of remuneration and the introduction of new payment methods, bonus rates and performance-related pay, daily and weekly work schedules, regulation of overtime and short-time working, holiday arrangements and the use of technical devices to monitor employees' performance. Codetermination also applies to personnel matters, such as policies for recruitment, transfer, regrading and dismissal. In specific circumstances there is a right of veto over individual cases of hiring, grading, transfer and dis-

Table 7.9   Works council elections: Number of establishments and composition of works councils 1965–90

Year	No. of establish-ments	Councillors elected	Female (%)	Foreign (%)	DGB (%)	DAG & others (%)	Non-union (%)
				Members of works councils			
1965	23,813	142,672	11.0		82.7	4.3	13.1
1968	24,902	142,412	11.4		83.1	3.5	13.4
1972	29,298	173,670	13.5	2.2	77.6	3.5	18.9
1975	34,059	191,015	15.7	2.6	77.5	3.5	18.8
1978	35,294	194,455	17.1	3.1	78.1	3.8	18.1
1981	36,307	199,125	19.3	3.3	77.5	3.9	18.6
1984	35,343	190,193	20.0	3.1	77.4	3.6	19.0
1987	34,807	189,292	20.5	4.5	76.6	3.4	20.0
1990	33,012	183,680	23.5	4.6	76.3	3.1	20.6

Sources: Deutscher Gewerkschaftsbund, Institut der Deutschen Wirtschaft

missal. Information and consultation rights apply to personnel planning and changes in work processes, the working environment, and job content. The information and consultation rights concerning the introduction of new technology were extended in 1989. Finally, there is a right to information on financial matters. A standing committee of the works council, the economic committee, must be informed by the employer 'in full and good time of the financial affairs of the establishment'; the same applies in case of planned changes 'which may significantly disadvantage employees'.

In general, works councils' participation rights are strong in relation to social policy; weaker in the case of personnel issues; and weaker still in financial and economic matters. In other words, the potential for works council intervention in managerial decision-making decreases the more closely it impinges on business policy.

Most works councillors are loyal unionists with close ties to their union. Unions and works councils are mutually dependent: the union supplies the council with information and expertise through educational courses or direct advice by full-time officials; while works councillors usually sustain union organization by recruiting new members and in general functioning – despite the legal distinction between the two institutions – as the arm of the union in the workplace. This dependence of the unions on the works councils gives the latter significant autonomy in relation to union officialdom; their power is, however, constrained by the fact that election and re-election usually depend on being nominated on an official union list.

In the 1960s and 1970s it was common in large establishments for works councils to negotiate informally with management for additional wage increases after the settlement of the industry-wide wage agreement. Technically this practice was usually illegal, since matters which form part of the agenda of collective bargaining can be regulated by works agreements only if the collective agreement authorizes this step by a so-called opening clause. In the 1970s some important collective agreements on working conditions and new technology introduced such a clause and prescribed supplementary works agreements to permit the flexible implementation of general rules. This move towards negotiation at establishment level, as a complement to union collective bargaining at industry level, has been strengthened in the 1980s with agreements on flexible working time. Thus more than 10,000 works agreements were negotiated in the engineering industry after the 1984 strike for the shorter working week (see below). Today, some works councils complain about the burden of negotiating now imposed on them.

The stable coalition between works councils and the union apparatus that has developed requires that a sufficient number of loyal unionists are elected as works councillors. For this reason the results of works council elections are of primary importance for unions. Challenges are possible, first from competing unions and unorganized groups mobilizing protest votes, and second from oppositional groups within the union itself demanding a more militant policy of interest representation.

DGB-affiliated unions have been fairly successful in warding off the first type of competition (see table 7.9 above); according to union sources more than three-quarters, and according to employers more than two-thirds of all elected works councillors belong to DGB unions. Hence union dominance in the councils is far in excess of union density among the work force. The exception to this pattern are the management staff committees set up under the 1988 legislation: 80 per cent of those elected in the first elections, held in 1990, were non-unionists.

The second type of challenge comes from active union delegates (*Vertrauensleute*) or militant dissenters in large companies. They usually seek either to break with social partnership or to achieve more democratic grass-roots procedures for nominating works councillors. Since the early seventies, challenges of this kind have emerged in the motor, steel, shipbuilding and chemical industries. In several cases, oppositional unionists have submitted their own list, sometimes with spectacular success. In a few establishments, foreign workers also challenged the official union lists following complaints about under-representation. Overall, however, such oppositional initiatives in works council elections have been very exceptional.

Union Delegates

Most – though not all – German unions have their own representatives alongside the works council, the *Vertrauensleute*. These are union stewards, each of whom usually represents between thirty and fifty workers and is elected by union members in a department or group. Their functions are limited, but include recruitment of members, distribution of union material and serving as a channel of information. They are also expected to support the (unionized) works councillors in fulfilling their tasks. In many cases, *Vertrauensleute* are both messengers of the works council and the mouthpiece of their work groups. In the event of open conflict, such as token or unofficial strikes, they function as informal organizers of industrial action.

Conflict may sometimes arise between *Vertrauensleute* and works councils. Rivalry was fostered in the late 1960s and early 1970s, when IG Metall and some other unions adopted the aim of increasing the powers and functions of the *Vertrauensleute* to make them a counterweight to the works councils. Some activist union delegates adopted an explicit oppositional stance, especially in IG Metall and IG Chemie: rank-and-file activists organized unofficial strikes, challenged established works councillors, and became the mouthpiece of discontented groups among the membership. The rivalry between *Vertrauensleute* and *Betriebsräte* ended in victory for the works councillors, a reflection of the legally established position of the works councils and their strategic role in recruiting union members. Today *Vertrauensleute* are expected to support rather than control the works councils' activities. Most unions have made the unionized works councillors *ex officio* members of the *Vertrauensleute* organization, which in most establishments they are able to dominate.

Quality Circles and Teamworking

As in several other countries, new forms of employee involvement have been introduced as part of a human resource management policy by many German companies. However, the German style of HRM differs from the Anglo-Saxon pattern. In Germany 'participatory management', the term preferred to HRM, is intended to complement institutionalized employee representation rather than to displace it. Quality circles and teamwork are the two main models of employee participation (Malsch 1989; Beisheim et al. 1991).

Some unions and works councils at first rejected such participation initiatives, especially quality circles, but in most cases they have now accepted them, and some representatives of the unions and works councils regard them as a first step towards 'codetermination at the workplace'. Since the mid-1980s several works agreements have been signed in individual establishments regulating the formation and functioning of quality circles and guaranteeing works council participation in the process. Such works agreements mainly cover large companies in the motor and chemical industries (Breisig 1991). In some other firms, circles have been unilaterally established by management. Estimates suggest that quality circles have expanded greatly in recent years. Before the 1980s they were almost unknown in Germany; by the latter part of the decade there were well over a thousand and more than half of the hundred largest companies have now introduced them. The latest trend is to move on to establishing procedures of total quality management.

Teamworking has been introduced principally in car firms, as part of a process of restructuring production and work organization stimulated by evidence (Womack et al. 1990) of the large productivity lead of Japanese and even American car producers. The most ambitious is Opel (a subsidiary of GM), which has started the restructuring of the production process and plans to involve all employees in teamwork by the end of 1992. Mercedes-Benz aims to restructure production work more gradually and to introduce teamwork for roughly half of the direct work force by the mid-1990s. Volkswagen, which has an extended network of quality circles, has introduced semi-autonomous groups in some smaller establishments, and is on the brink of introducing this type of work organization for one of the six lines of Golf production in its main plant at Wolfsburg. In most companies, management and works councils have signed works agreements on teamworking, providing for extra time for team discussions, the right to elect team leaders, and better pay for the more integrated and flexible work tasks. There are some anxieties on the union side that it may be more difficult to integrate the lower-level employee representatives within the unions' own policy process than has been possible with the works councils. Whether they can achieve this will become apparent in the next few years, as the unions attempt to integrate team-leader positions within the *Vertrauensleute* system.

Recent Developments in Labour–Management Relations

Recent studies (Kern and Schumann 1984; Eberwein and Tholen 1990; Kotthoff 1990) have shown that employers have increasingly accepted works councils and their functions after the uncertainties and reservations which accompanied the substantial amendment of the Works Constitution Act in 1972. A recent survey of 30 engineering companies (Kreikebaum and Herbert 1990) shows that over 90 per cent of works councillors and over three-quarters of managers are satisfied with the sections of the 1972 Act which stipulate information and consultation rights on changes in work processes, the work environment and job design. Although these are not strong participation rights, their practical impact is appreciated by both sides, even though works council representatives would prefer full codetermination rights on these matters.

Managers quite frequently take advantage of the works councils' authority over the work force to make them share responsibility not only for awkward personnel matters but also for more strategic goals. In general, works councils positively support management policies for modernization and rationalization of the production system, if they are convinced that the establishment's economic position will benefit, and providing two preconditions are met: no dismissals and no drop in wages for employees transferred to other jobs. There is also a broad understanding that work reorganization serves a dual goal: increased productivity and product quality on the one hand and humanization of work on the other.

Industry-wide collective bargaining does not entail a common pattern of labour relations at company and workplace levels within one industry. Although sectoral multi-employer bargaining still prevails, the scope of negotiations between management and works councils has increased.

There is a large sector of small and medium-sized establishments with less formalized labour relations. Many are sweat-shops, but the more dynamic establishments work on the basis of an implicit reciprocity and a kind of 'tacit participation' by the work force, mostly without an elected works council (Hilbert and Sperling 1990). At the other extreme, there are large enterprises with company-specific patterns of labour relations. For example, the biggest European company in the media industry, Bertelsmann, established a far-reaching participative culture long before 'corporate identity' came into vogue. The scheme of employee participation, introduced in cooperation with the works council, includes semi-autonomous groups, quality circles, employee reviews of their supervisors and profit-sharing. The Media Union (IG Medien), which initially opposed this management-sponsored participation, is very poorly represented among the work force (about 12 per cent), and its influence on the central works councils is severely limited. Although the terms of the collective agreements for the printing and media industries are binding for Bertelsmann, they do not have a great impact on labour relations in practice.

Another case is Volkswagen, which is not a member of the employers' association and bargains directly with IG Metall, generating company collective agreements and a host of works agreements. The union's bargaining committee is almost entirely composed of works councillors. A very high union density rate among blue- and white-collar workers, and the close collaboration between the union and works council, allows IG Metall to use Volkswagen to pioneer socially progressive policies. While the origins of this special case lie in the history of Volkswagen as a nationalized company, the relationship has continued since the partial privatization of the corporation. The agreement to establish a European Works Council, which first met in March 1992, is an example of innovatory industrial relations.

Collective Bargaining and Industrial Disputes

Types and Mechanisms of Agreement

According to the Collective Agreement Act (TVG) the parties to a collective agreement must be unions on the workers' side and single employers or employers' associations on the other. In practice, bargaining takes place at regional (metalworking, chemicals) or national (public sector) levels between the union and the corresponding employers' association. Company collective agreements are mainly found in smaller firms (Volkswagen is the obvious exception) and cover only a small minority of employees. Industry-wide or sectoral agreements contribute to a high degree of standardization of wages and other working conditions, as does state regulation. Though in many cases sectoral collective bargaining is formally undertaken at regional level, it is centrally directed by the sectoral peak organizations on both sides. So-called pilot agreements reached in key areas of the engineering industry (usually Baden-Württemberg) are the model for the rest of this sector and exert influence on all other industries as well. This creates a specific German form of 'pattern bargaining' with IG Metall as pace-setter. In general, other industries settle wage increases within 1 per cent of the engineering agreement.

Such a centralized system needs mechanisms for adapting the general conditions of collective agreements to the circumstances of individual establishments. Works agreements, negotiated between works councils and management, are not allowed to violate or contradict the provisions of the industry-wide collective agreement but are important supplements to it. Large establishments have hundreds of works agreements which are sometimes extensive documents regulating details of wage systems, working conditions etc. In general the subjects of workplace agreements are restricted to 'social' and 'personnel' questions on which codetermination rights exist. A 1982 study (Knuth 1982) showed that written works agreements existed in four-fifths of firms with over 200 employees. They are less common in small firms with weaker works councils.

Three different kinds of collective agreements are commonly distinguished: wage agreements (*Lohn- und Gehaltstarifverträge*) fix the level of wages and periodic alterations; framework agreements (*Rahmentarifverträge*) specify wage-payment systems; and 'umbrella' agreements (*Manteltarifverträge*) regulate all other conditions of employment (working time, overtime, holidays, dismissals).

The collective bargaining process follows a characteristic sequence. A more or less extended period of negotiations leads to agreement in the majority of cases; but if negotiations fail, both parties try to resolve the conflict through mediation procedures. These procedures are established by voluntary union-employer agreement, not by government intervention – in clear contrast to the Weimar Republic, when compulsory state arbitration existed. In the vast majority of cases mediation proves successful. However, if it fails, a collective labour conflict becomes possible, in the form of a strike and possibly also a lockout.

Despite occasional major conflicts (recently on a four- or five-year cycle), Germany is notable for its low level of industrial disputes. Co-operative conflict management has been encouraged by favourable economic conditions with high rates of growth and low levels of unemployment, and governments relatively sympathetic to labour and to the principle of macro-economic management. Within the collective bargaining system, both parties have been able to change priorities from 'quantitative' to 'qualitative' issues, and to adapt their collectively created institutions and regulatory methods. Unions in particular have had to adapt to new circumstances. Since the 1970s, with severely reduced scope for real wage increases, pay has had a lower priority and non-wage issues have received enhanced attention. In the late 1970s, bargaining in many industries focused on protection against rationalization. Later, collective agreements on working time were reached in different industries, in response to union demands for the 35-hour week, and management pursuit of increased flexibility (see below). Working-time arrangements have dominated 'qualitative' union demands since the mid-1980s, in part as a strategy for job-creation. Perhaps surprisingly, most studies suggest that the effect of shorter hours – as the unions claimed, and employers disputed – has indeed been to increase employment (Keller 1991).

In 1992, conflict over wages has returned to the agenda. The costs of German unification have led the government, and the *Bundesbank*, to press for rigid pay restraint. Union efforts to protect real earnings have led to a bank employees' dispute and the first national public sector strike for eighteen years; and as we write, a major stoppage in engineering seem imminent.

Collective Bargaining Outcomes

Collective Agreements in Western Germany

Collective agreements now regulate a vast and complex range of issues affecting wages, working time and working conditions, and both of the negotiating parties must employ large staffs of experts to keep abreast of collective agreements within the branches they represent. A recent survey (Bispinck 1991c) found that in 1990, 2,982 agreements were negotiated at sector level in the (pre-unification) BRD, and 1,931 at enterprise level. The total number of agreements in force at the end of the year was 24,695 at sector level and 8,754 at enterprise level. These figures exclude works agreements negotiated between managements and works councils.

With the exception of a few companies – such as Volkswagen and the large oil companies – which have often negotiated innovative and progressive single-employer agreements with their trade union counterparts, company-level agreements follow those for their sector with only slight modifications.

The majority of agreements cover pay, since these usually have only a twelve- to fifteen-month lifespan. Agreements on non-pay questions are normally of longer duration; they comprise the majority of agreements currently in force. Collective agreements signed by DGB-affiliated unions and in force at the end of 1990 covered nearly 19 million manual and white-collar workers. Not included in this figure are those contracts which cover less than 1,000 employees, almost exclusively involving single-employer agreements. The 1.85 million civil servants (*Beamte*) are also excluded. As indicated below, their conditions of employment are set not by collective bargaining but by legislation, though after consultation with the relevant unions.

Agreements involving the two largest unions – IGM and ÖTV – cover the largest number of workers, though HBV, with a smaller membership, covers almost as many as ÖTV. This indicates an important feature of German industrial relations: the scope of collective regulation is not closely related to union membership. Roughly 90 per cent of all employees are covered by a collective agreement – almost three times the number of union members.

In 1990 average earnings per employee rose by 5.0 per cent to around DM 42,000; the increase was significantly more than that in overall productivity (1.9 per cent), continuing the trend of the late 1980s to rising unit labour costs. In much of the private sector, actual wages are higher than the contractually agreed pay-scales. Multi-employer agreements are based on the economic situation of the average enterprise; in more profitable companies, the works council may succeed in securing higher wages through a works agreement. This gap between the contractually agreed wage and actual rates differs greatly from sector to sector and from region to region as a result of varying conditions in product and labour markets. Earnings drift, which has been important in some countries, was not a significant phenomenon in Germany in the 1980s.

Collective bargaining seems to have had only a limited impact on income differentials. German unions have not regarded egalitarian pay policies as a priority. The 1970s did indeed see a narrowing of differentials, but these widened again in the 1980s. Pay differentials are greater for white-collar than for manual employees, though the gap between the median rates for the two groups has been closing – a trend which has encouraged the development of common pay scales. Geographical differences in pay have increased recently. It should also be noted that women tend to be concentrated in the lowest pay grades.

From the founding of the BRD until well into the 1950s the working week was contractually fixed at 48 hours. This was followed by a long phase of step-by-step reductions, leading to the 40-hour week in printing in 1965, followed by metalworking in 1967, chemicals in 1970 and the public sector in 1974.

The 40-hour week was in force until 1984 when IG Metall conducted a successful strike, defeating the employers' 'taboo' against a shorter week. Since then there has been a rapid movement towards reduced working hours. At the end of 1990, only 9 per cent of the labour force still worked a 40-hour week. Many of the others – as in metalworking – were covered by agreements providing for the introduction of the 35-hour week during the 1990s. Annual holidays have increased progressively, from two weeks in the early 1950s to six weeks in 1990. As in many other areas of collective bargaining, there were pace-setting agreements which then stimulated a wave of matching settlements in other sectors of the economy. The most notable example is IG Metall's strike in the steel industry in 1979 which led the way to the general introduction of the six-week holiday.

The price which the trade unions had to pay for their successes in working-time policy was the flexible regulation of working time, with a diversity of models in different sectors and companies. Some trend-setting agreements were negotiated by unions and employers' associations, but many others by works councils and managements under so-called opening clauses which authorize them to conclude enterprise-level working-time agreements. Trade unions' earlier fears of losing control over this sphere of labour relations have given way to the view that flexible working hours serve not only the employers but also the unions themselves, by satisfying employee demands for individual variability of working time. For example, a large retail chain reached agreement with its employees on the total number of hours to be worked each year, allowing individual employees an important say in determining their own work schedules. In Baden-Württemberg, IG Metall has negotiated a contract making it possible for some individual workers to choose their working week within the range of 35 to 40 hours. In the financial services sector, with nearly one million employees, the unions are demanding such a high degree of individual working-time variability that the employers are resisting.

'Umbrella' or general framework agreements have undergone significant changes. The unions' earlier preoccupation with defensive, protective measures has given way to a more active attempt to shape the bargaining agenda on such issues as job descriptions and working conditions. Altogether it can be said that the number of general framework agreements and the particular areas that they cover have grown, as trade union demands have become broader and more diverse.

Several types of non-monetary agreements deserve special attention. The first relates pay to the individual's training and qualifications, rather than to the job currently performed. The company Voegele was expelled from the employers' association for concluding such a contract with IG Metall. Second, there are collective agreements which regulate and promote vocational training and education. IG Metall, for example, has managed to achieve a more closely defined regulation of continuing education within the metal industry of Baden-Württemberg. The construction union, to give another example, has developed the occupational profile of a 'high-tech' construction worker in order to protect skilled workers from competition from low-paid immigrant workers from Eastern Europe. Third, some collective agreements provide for a common pay structure for blue- and white-collar workers. Innovations in technology and the organization of the labour process have blurred the differences between the two categories and have led the unions to demand unified wage and salary scales. Fourth, unions also seek to extend collective bargaining to include questions of work organization (group work) and to cover all employees with the exception of senior executives. One aspect is the inclusion in collective agreements of the precariously employed as well as those in more secure and highly paid occupations: for example, a recent agreement in construction covers building cleaners, a group of poorly paid temporary employees who are usually unskilled women or foreign workers.

Bargaining Outcomes in Eastern Germany

The key feature of labour relations in eastern Germany is the continuing adaptation of wages, working time and working conditions to western German standards. In the first six months after the German–German economic union (July to December 1990) over 700 wage contracts were concluded; a development which has proceeded at an accelerating pace. At the end of 1991, average wages in eastern Germany stood at about 60 per cent of those in western Germany. Wage differences range from 43 per cent in the clothing industry to parity in the east Berlin construction industry; but in most sectors, wage levels in the east are between 50 and 60 per cent of those in the west. In many sectors, for example engineering, it has been agreed that pay parity should be achieved by the middle of the 1990s.

Weekly working hours and annual holidays are also being adjusted. By the end of 1991 the average working week was forty hours and average holiday time was twenty-one days. In a few large sectors such as construction, however, working conditions in the east are already equal to those in the west. More generally, the target of parity in the mid-1990s has been agreed.

Similarly, for many areas regulated by framework or umbrella agreements (pay classification schemes, overtime or shiftwork bonuses, paid leave, protection against dismissal, and vocational training, re-training and further training programmes), the standard provisions of the west have now been introduced, or will be applied over the coming years.

Such agreements, however, are purely 'political agreements' between the bargaining parties, which the employers have signed in the 'interest of social peace'; they have nothing to do with the economic realities facing companies in eastern Germany. The vast majority are uncompetitive; technology and work organization are so outdated and productivity is so low that economic survival is problematic even at the old levels of pay and working conditions.

As mentioned above, economic and currency unification and restructuring have involved a massive loss of jobs. Relatively generous unemployment benefits, early retirement allowances and financial grants for re-training and further occupational training have been made available; and following trade union pressure, publicly subsidized employment agencies have been created to train or upgrade unemployed workers.

After initial consensus on wage policy, conflict broke out in the autumn of 1991 over how quickly east German workers should be brought up to the level of their western counterparts. In their desire for a slower tempo, the government and the employers have been supported by the reports and recommendations of the *Bundesbank* and the *Sachverständigenrat*. They have argued that wages are already too high, given the level of productivity. The trade unions, on the other hand, insist on the fastest possible closing of the gap between the workers in the east and west, to guarantee social peace and prevent the growth of political radicalization. The fact that prices are quickly rising to the western German level also tends to support the union position. In addition, the labour markets are fusing into a single whole, and workers from eastern Germany are able to look for employment in the west. At present, these considerations in practice take precedence over the 'supply-side' arguments; and a high proportion of east German workers recognise the new unions as representatives of their interests.

Industrial Disputes: Strikes and Lockouts

On any international comparison, Germany has a very low level of industrial conflict. There are few strikes; and while there is a pattern of major disputes every few years, the aggregate economic impact is small. Until recently at least, strikes were simply not perceived as a problem. There are, however, significant trends which can be identified in the post-war decades.

The 1950s, a decade of reconstruction and economic growth, saw a relatively high intensity of conflict because collective bargaining mechanisms had to be re-institutionalized (table 7.10). Institutional stability and political confusion made the early and mid-1960s years of low conflict. The period was marked by cooperative wage policies within the by now established centralized collective bargaining system. In the late 1960s and early 1970s, a period of full employment after the first, short post-war recession of 1966–7, conflict rose to unprecedented levels (at least for modern Germany). There were waves of wildcat and spontaneous strikes in a period of general political unrest. Working conditions, as well as pay, were central issues. The mid- and late 1970s were a phase of comparatively high and rather intense conflict, mainly about new 'qualitative' demands (protection against rationalization, introduction of new technologies and new forms of work organization) even though unemployment had reached levels not experienced for several decades. The 1980s were a period of economic modernization, accompanied by mass unemployment despite considerable growth of employment. There was a marked decline in conflict, with the exception of the protracted disputes over the shortening of the working week in the metalworking and printing industries in 1984. This development of 'high-trust, low-conflict relations' matched international trends towards fewer disputes. In the 1990s, however, there are signs of a more confrontational climate of industrial relations.

The sectoral distribution of strikes has undergone significant changes since the 1950s, when the wage round and the principle of wage leadership did not yet exist. The diminishing importance of certain sectors (mining, textiles, iron and steel, construction) is mirrored in their decreasing strike activity, whereas the significance of engineering, and also printing and paper, has consistently increased (table 7.11). The concentration of strikes in a few industries – and the existence of a large number of almost strike-free industries – is a notable feature. And even in strike-prone industries, as noted above, the system of 'pilot agreements' means that disputes are concentrated in particular bargaining districts.

Since the mid 1970s there has been a change in strike strategies initiated by IG Metall. The so-called 'new mobility' (*neue Beweglichkeit*) replaces the one big, expensive strike of indefinite length *after* negotiations have failed by a series of more or less unexpected smaller, shorter, and therefore inexpensive walk-outs in different establishments *during* the negotiations. These increase the pressure on employers and accelerate the negotiations. These so-called warning-strikes (*Warnstreiks*) were legalized by a decision of the Federal Labour Court in 1976; their legality was confirmed in 1984 and 1985.

A related, rather sophisticated strategy is use of the 'pinpoint strike' (*Schwerpunktstreik*) which hits a selected number of suppliers whose products are of crucial importance for the production process of a whole industry (notably the car industry, as in the 1984 strike). This comparatively new form is very effective because of the increasing interdependence between different establishments and their suppliers (particularly those using the kanban system of just-in-time production); this was the reason for the change in paragraph 116 of the *AFG*, discussed earlier. Wildcat strikes are illegal because of the unions' strike monopoly but have occurred throughout the history of the Federal Republic. Especially in the late 1960s and early 1970s, spontaneous walk-outs were frequent and caused public concern. Nevertheless, such strikes are far less significant in Germany than in many other countries.

Lockouts are more frequent than in most other western nations because of favourable legal conditions for employers. In other industrialized countries lockouts are either illegal or – within decentralized bargaining systems – insignificant in practice. Major lockouts have taken place in a number of German industries and have been more intensively used since the 1970s: the key instances have been in metalworking (1963, 1971, 1978, 1984);

Table 7.10   Strikes and lockouts (annual average) 1950–89

Years	establishments affected	Strikes workers involved	days lost	Strikes and lockouts workers involved	days lost
1950–54	1,467	100,843	1,098,126	100,843	1,098,126
1955–59	552	178,392	868,089	178,392	868,089
1960–64	113	44,755	289,733	87,864	483,333
1965–69	218	75,321	147,924	75,329	148,117
1970–74	486	195,376	874,600	235,768	1,251,466
1975–79	376	109,798	691,414	160,788	1,078,085
1980–84	321	166,403	632,799	193,962	1,172,065
1985–89	123	85,222	47,617	85,222	47,617

Note: German official statistics do not indicate the number of strikes.
Source: Own calculations based on official figures of *Statistisches Bundesamt* and *Bundesanstalt für Arbeit*.

printing (1976, 1978); and steel (1978–9). Lockouts affect more employees than strikes, and their intensity and duration exceed those of strikes, because their main purpose is to increase the financial pressure on the union which has to pay strike benefits to its locked-out members. Lockouts are almost without exception defensive, occurring after the start of a strike; they are the means by which employers' associations respond to selective strikes (Kalbitz 1979). On both sides, those affected by disputes are financially supported from funds maintained if necessary by special levies.

Unions have long demanded the prohibition of lockouts, which they consider unconstitutional and which considerably reduce their bargaining power (Kittner 1974). Employers' associations have argued that the 'parity of weapons' is necessary in order to preserve the balance of bargaining power. No statutory change to the present legal position is conceivable in any foreseeable political situation.

Table 7.11 Distribution of strikes by sector 1950–89

Sector	*1950–59*	*1960–69*	*1970–79*	*1980–89*
		Workers involved (%)		
Mining	40.2	23.6	0.4	0.0
Construction	5.1	1.5	0.6	0.2
Textiles	4.0	2.5	0.5	1.0
Engineering	28.1	50.5	61.2	77.8
Iron & Steel	11.7	15.4	10.5	3.1
Printing & Paper	4.3	1.2	8.0	10.9
Chemicals	0.1	3.5	3.2	0.4
Public sercices	3.3	0.4	14.3	5.1
Others	3.2	1.3	1.2	1.5
		Working days lost (%)		
Mining	6.2	15.6	0.2	0.0
Construction	7.8	14.3	1.3	1.1
Textiles	9.2	2.9	0.3	0.1
Engineering	61.7	44.0	62.0	78.4
Iron & Steel	5.4	7.9	18.2	0.5
Printing & Paper	2.7	5.5	6.0	13.7
Chemicals	0.2	7.4	3.4	1.4
Public Sector	2.5	0.1	7.6	4.0
Others	4.2	2.3	0.9	0.8
	100	100	100	100

Source: Deutscher Gewerkschaftsbund, Institut der Deutschen Wirtschaft.

Public-Sector Labour Relations

Trends and Structure of Public Employment

Public agencies (federal, *Land*, and local governments) employ about 4.6 million workers; this includes the postal service with 426,000 and the railways with about 270,000, the only area where employment has fallen significantly in recent decades. In international terms, Germany has a medium-sized public sector. Employment expanded steadily until the end of the 1970s; but the rate of increase slowed in the early 1980s, and came to a virtual standstill in the late 1980s. The slight increase in the 1980s was mainly caused by a steady rise in the number of part-time jobs (now more than 800,000) offsetting a reduction in full-time jobs (now about 3.8 million). In other words, increased public employment in the 1980s has been a statistical effect of the shift between full-time and part-time employment. The number of fixed-term contracts has also increased within a system of otherwise stable employment conditions; they now cover more than 10 per cent of public employees (mostly in education and the postal service). These developments may be expected to continue. Thus differences in the labour market behaviour of public and private employers are diminishing as both pursue greater flexibility; public employers are no longer 'model' employers guaranteeing stable and life-long employment.

Within the German political system there is a clear and stable division of responsibilities between federal, *Land* and local authorities influencing, among other things, the number and qualifications of personnel. The *Länder* do not differ significantly in their public employment legislation, despite some variations in practices. Some public employers have tried to increase the number and proportion of their *Beamte* in order to bypass collective bargaining and prevent strikes. But, again, this has not been a general trend. Employment policies are neither horizontally nor vertically coordinated between different employers. Public employers intensify general labour market conditions and problems by acting in a pro-cyclical fashion.

Of fundamental significance is the differing legal status of the three employee groups: the conventional contractual position of salaried employees (*Angestellte*) and wage-earners (*Arbeiter*) as against the public law employment status of 'civil servants' (*Beamte*). This division goes back at least to the Bismarck Constitution. The so-called 'customary principle of officialdom', laid down in the Basic Law establishing the modern Federal Republic, applies such rules as employment for life to a wide range of public employees (mainly skilled or professional) such as teachers and train-drivers, as well as civil servants narrowly defined. This special status can hardly be justified on functional grounds in a modern democratic state. There are many contexts (including the postal service or education) where salaried employees and *Beamte* perform exactly the same jobs. It is notable that the changing nature of public employment in recent times has brought a decline in the proportion of *Arbeiter* (now just over 20 per cent) and a corresponding increase in *Angestellte* (to about 37 per cent); yet the proportion of *Beamte*, at about 40 per cent, has remained almost unchanged.

Two Related Systems of Regulation

The system of labour relations in the public sector has a comparatively long history which can be traced back to the early days of the Weimar Republic. All public employees have the same right as private-sector workers to join unions or other interest organizations. The degree of organization is fairly high (about 75 per cent) and significantly higher than in private industry (about 40 per cent). In both sectors, unions have similar difficulties in organizing such categories as women, part-time employees and young workers.

For historical reasons (which have often been questioned), employee participation in decision-making in the public sector is governed by a distinct body of legislation. At 'establishment' level the Federal Staff Representation Act (1955, 1974, 1989) and supplementary legislation in each of the *Länder* correspond to the *BetrVG* in private industry. The functional equivalent of the works council is the staff council (*Personalrat*), on which the different employment groups (blue- and white-collar workers and *Beamte*) have proportional representation. Government departments and staff councils work together, 'in a spirit of mutual trust', according to the Act, 'for the benefit of the employees and in fulfilment of the obligatory functions of the government departments'. Like their counterparts in private industry they have a whole range of precisely defined rights, from strict codetermination and veto power to mere consultation and information. In general, the allocation of rights – which most staff councils exercise actively – is on the same basis as in the private sector: codetermination over 'social' issues, consultation over personnel policy. However, there is no equivalent to the (weak) private-sector right to information on 'economic' questions.

At sectoral level two systems of regulation co-exist. The legal basis for the collective bargaining system is the *TVG* of 1949, which guarantees free collective bargaining throughout the economy. Unions and employers' associations negotiate for wage-earners and salaried employees; there are no special restrictions on industrial conflict. Thus the law does not differentiate between the private and the public sectors.

The most important union is the Union for Public Services, Transport and Communication (ÖTV). The ÖTV, Germany's second largest union, has more than 1.2 million members in the old federal states, and claims 800,000 in the east. There are several other, smaller public sector unions which unlike ÖTV are occupationally specific but are also affiliated with the DGB. The most important are the German Railway Union, the German Postal Union, and the Police Union. The DAG also organizes in the public sector. National employers' associations exist for the municipalities and

Länder: the Federation of Local Government Employers Associations and the Bargaining Association of German *Länder* (Keller 1987a, 1987b). At federal level the Minister of the Interior is responsible for matters affecting public employees, coordinates the interests of all public employers, and leads all negotiations on their behalf.

Collective bargaining rights apply to *Arbeiter* and *Angestellte* only. *Beamte* are covered by special legislation. According to statute and legal opinion *Beamte* have no rights to collective bargaining or to strike: the principle of *Tarifautonomie* does not apply to this group. While such rights are restricted in other western countries for categories of public employment, the German peculiarity is that the restriction is defined by the collective status of *Beamte* and not by the performance of particular essential jobs. Furthermore, it applies at every level, from local authority to federal government. The lack of strike and bargaining rights does not mean that the organizations representing *Beamte* are ineffectual. Pay and conditions are determined by specific parliamentary legislation; but the laws defining the special status of *Beamte* also specify that their representative associations must be consulted during the parliamentary process.

Collective organization is divided almost equally between two confederations. The DGB has seven member unions recruiting in the public sector which together represent over 800,000 *Beamte*. The DBB, which almost exclusively covers *Beamte*, has just under 800,000 members in its 40 associations.

As well as their formal rights of consultation, these associations are adept at parliamentary lobbying. The 40 per cent of members of parliament at federal and *Land* levels who are themselves *Beamte* are susceptible to appeals for *Beamte* to be treated no less favourably than groups which bargain collectively. The senior civil servants who help draft the legislation on conditions of employment are, of course, *Beamte*. If necessary, campaigns can be organized to win public sympathy, and the threat to mobilize the votes of *Beamte* and their families against unsympathetic legislators can also prove potent. Hence the restricted rights of *Beamte* are not necessarily a handicap (Keller 1983).

Both forms of interest representation usually lead to identical results which are implemented simultaneously. Thus the legal differences in employment status and models of interest representation do not lead to significant differences in pay or other working conditions.

The centralization of collective bargaining which is a general feature of German industrial relations is particularly marked in the public sector; normally a single set of negotiations covers all wage-earners and salaried employees in federal, *Land*, and local government. Even though there may be conflicts of interest between public employers at different levels (for example local authorities, with a high proportion of low-paid workers, find flat-rate pay settlements particularly expensive), all public employers know that it is in their own long-term interest to maintain their coalition. The informal nature of the co-ordination which takes place during all phases of collective bargaining increases the flexibility of the system. The only major exceptions to the general pattern of centralization are independent negotiations for special groups of employees such as nurses and police.

Centralization leads to uniform regulations and procedures as well as to an increasing standardization of pay and working conditions for the different groups of employees. This avoids problems which occur in some other countries, such as the definition of bargaining units. Collective bargaining in the public sector – over both wages and other conditions of employment – tends to follow the pattern of settlements in private industry. In particular, the agreements negotiated by IG Metall normally serve as a model. Only twice in recent decades – as long ago as 1971 and 1974 – have public-sector bargainers taken the lead in the negotiating round.

Strikes and Arbitration Procedures

Though public employees (apart from *Beamte*) enjoy the same right to strike as their private-sector counterparts, disputes are very rare. Until 1992, only one significant strike had occurred in the history of the BRD, in 1974. The growth of public-sector militancy in other European countries in the 1980s was not replicated in Germany. This may be attributed to the continuing efficacy of disciplined, centralized bargaining procedures. When strikes do occur in public services it is normally at local level. Bargaining pressure is directed selectively by strikes of groups – such as refuse collectors or public transport staff – whose action will achieve an immediate impact. Such tactics can be very effective in winning gains for the groups involved; and because of the centralized bargaining system the improvements in pay and other working conditions achieved by these groups are automatically extended to all other groups. This pattern has been evident in a whole series of bargaining rounds since the mid-1950s. Strikes in the public sector are on average shorter than those in private industry, and protracted stoppages never occur. Employers are strike-sensitive and are therefore usually prepared to make quick concessions, above all because of their limited experience in responding to strikes. The national dispute which began in April 1992 reflects an exceptional conjuncture of economic and political forces; whether it indicates a pattern for the future it is too early to say.

More common than strikes have been such actions as go-slows by wage-earners and salaried employees and working-to-rule by *Beamte*. These protests are limited to a few departments and are shorter than strikes, but can be just as effective.

Because conflict is rare, there is no elaborate system for dispute resolution in the public sector. Only after the 1974 strike were mediation procedures introduced. In contrast to many other countries, arbitration is never used in the German public sector if the parties to collective bargaining fail to reach agreement.

Privatization

Privatization has been on the political agenda since the 1970s, when employers' representatives and conservatives started to demand a reduction in publicly provided services. Some moves in this direction have been made at local level (privatizing refuse collection, slaughterhouses, public transport, cleaning of public buildings), but hardly any at *Land* and federal levels. The overall impact of privatization has, in contrast to some other countries, been insignificant because this strategy has not been pressed strongly by public authorities against the explicit opposition of the unions. The ideological demand to 'roll back the state' has always been part of conservative rhetoric, but hardly of political reality.

Why have German governments given privatization such low priority? The SPD, in power (with the FDP) until 1982, resisted privatization on grounds of political principle. Within the CDU–FDP coalition which replaced it, many different interests and political positions are represented; this makes any radical shift of policy difficult to accomplish. Moreover, the federal constitution gives considerable autonomy to the *Länder*, most of which are controlled by the SPD. In contrast to Britain, it is impossible for central government to impose a general policy of privatization (König 1988). There are other practical obstacles to privatization. All public-sector unions and major interest organizations have offered strong and coordinated resistance, and a more vigorous strategy of privatization would cause social conflicts. Moreover, the German public sector contains few easily disposable units. The majority of public-sector jobs created in the late 1960s and early 1970s are in areas which are unsuitable for privatization (education, social services, health care, police). Substantial reductions in public personnel in the period of high unemployment since the mid-1970s would have created additional labour market problems and incurred serious political costs for the government. Finally, the limited exercises in privatization which have been undertaken have not been clearly successful in reducing costs or improving the quality of service (Sturm 1990).

The federal railway (*Deutsche Bundesbahn*) is the only part of the public sector where employment has steadily declined in recent decades. Political attempts to achieve economies and to reduce its large deficits have included various rationalization measures, including job cuts. Only recently have plans for privatization reached the agenda. The Basic Law defines both the railway and the postal service as special federal assets; to change the law to permit privatization is politically difficult.

In the public sector as in private industry, managements are seeking more flexibility and adaptability. A frequent complaint has been that the rigidity of the *Beamte* status prevents urgently needed numerical and functional flexibility. In line with this argument, the postal service was recently split into three independent parts (posts, telecommunications and banking) and parts of the telecommunications system have indeed been privatized. The main 'benefit' of the change so far, however, has been higher charges for consumers. In any event, it is unclear why flexibility cannot be achieved under public ownership.

The cautious attempts to privatize limited parts of the public sector in the west cannot be compared with the wholesale privatization of the east German economy that was started after unification in October 1990 (see below). In the latter case, privatization means an abrupt switch from socialist to capitalist principles of production, from central planning to a market economy, a complete restructuring of the national economy from scratch. Nevertheless, a substantial public sector will obviously remain in the *neue Bundesländer*.

Future Perspectives

After the completion of unification the reorganization of the public sector of the former DDR will be a long-term political and administrative problem. Dismissals for such reasons as political identification with the old communist regime, or the dissolution or privatization of former public agencies, are the main short-term means of cutting public employment (over two million at the time of unification) and re-modelling it on the West German pattern. The cautious introduction of *Beamte* status, previously unknown in the east, is a highly contentious political step, since it will create the well-known dualism of employment status within the public sector. Reproducing in the east the administrative structure of the BRD requires the drafting-in of western personnel. To attract the necessary staff, special bonuses are paid to western officials who agree to a period of service in the east. This is proving expensive.

New unions (for all public employees) and interest associations (for *Beamte*) were founded, with organizational support from their west German counterparts, after the old communist mass trade unions had dissolved. They have now merged into unified organizations. New employers' associations in the public sector were also formed on the west German model. The first collective agreements attempt to adjust wages and all other conditions of employment by stages to west German standards; in 1991 pay levels were set at 60 per cent of those in the west. The aim is to prevent a further mass exodus from the territory of the former DDR and to create 'equal living conditions' in both parts of the country.

The completion of the European single market is also likely to have important implications for public sector labour relations. The principle, embodied in the changes to the EC treaty, that many areas of public sector employment in member states should be open to all Community citizens will, for example, force a change in the German law on *Beamte* status. Under present law, *Beamte* must (with few exceptions) be German nationals; in the future, legal obstacles to other EC nationals becoming *Beamte* will have to be removed. In practice, however, such a change need not drastically affect either the status of *Beamte* or the actual recruitment practices of public employers. Given financial stringencies, the number of new *Beamte* appointments in the foreseeable future will be limited; language competence will be a legitimate basis for rejecting foreign applicants; and almost inevitably, informal discrimination will occur (Keller and Henneberger 1992). Hence it seems very unlikely that the process of European integration will have an input in the German public sector analogous to that in private industry.

The Future of Industrial Relations

Trends to Decentralization – and their Limits

As has been seen, moves towards employment deregulation by the German state have been relatively modest. However, employers and their associations have pursued flexibility in other ways. A central priority has been to increase productivity by detaching individual working time from the operating hours of the establishment (through shift systems, for example) so that production time can increase even as the individual working week is reduced. The typical 'exchange' between unions and employers' associations during the mid- and late 1980s has been a staged reduction of the working week (from 40 in the early 1980s towards 35 hours per week, to be finally achieved from 1995) in return for more flexibility in the organization of working time (sometimes including regular Saturday or weekend work).

The union goal of a shorter working week will have been accomplished by the mid- or late 1990s once the 35-hour week takes effect. The unions have already begun to address more systematically other problems, such as training, re-training and skill enhancement. This will reinforce the trend towards decentralization, because the general policies on training agreed in multi-employer bargaining will have to be adapted to company-specific requirements in negotiations between management and the works council.

There is no necessary interconnection between deregulation (initiated by neo-conservative governments) and flexibility (pursued by assertive employers); but in practice they coincide and both contribute to an obvious process of decentralization of labour relations. The actors at plant level, works council and management, gain in importance whereas the actors at sectoral level, unions and employers' associations, lose some of their former power. Within this general shift of competence and influence a new institutionalized balance of power will have to be found. The new role of associations on both sides will need to include the provision of new kinds of services to their constituents at establishment level. This is illustrated by current negotiations over working time: all general regulations negotiated between unions and employers' associations have to be adapted to the special circumstances of each establishment. Hence they must be renegotiated between management and works council in a very specific German variant of 'company-level bargaining'.

Micro-corporatist arrangements or productivity coalitions have gained in importance in the 1980s (Streeck 1984; Windolf 1989). Relatively stable alliances have developed at establishment level between works councils and management which further the complementary interests of both sides, although often to the disadvantage of those outside the firm's internal labour market. For example, works councils often agree to over-time working, which enhances the earnings of their constituents while allowing the company to increase production without the long-term commitments involved in taking on new workers. This contradicts the policy to which the unions are strongly committed, that the works councils should restrict overtime and encourage additional recruitment in order to reduce unemployment. The goal of these 'high trust – low conflict relations' is, above all, a stabilization of the companies' product and labour markets and an internalization of advantages – accompanied by strong tendencies towards increasing labour market segmentation.

Both unions and employers' associations have an obvious interest in retaining the centralized collective bargaining system, even though opinions to the contrary are sometimes voiced on both sides. The 'atomization' (or in the current jargon 'Japanization') of bargaining without any multi-employer regulatory structure would create dangerous unpredictability for both parties, making strategic planning in the labour market virtually impossible. What is sometimes criticized as the rigidity and inflexibility of German employment law and centralized collective bargaining is, in practice, recognized as a source of order and stability which assists economic performance.

Decentralization is inevitable; the question is whether it will involve the displacement of state and institutional control by market forces, or whether new regulatory structures will emerge that are compatible with the increased autonomy at lower levels of the system. German traditions clearly point to the second option. The same is as true in the *neue Bundesländer* of the east, it may be added, as it is in the west; the radical changes occurring in the former DDR also constitute a form of re-regulation rather than deregulation.

European Integration

Unions and employers are in broad agreement on the need for rapid European integration. They endorse the current schedule for completing the single European market, argue for the rapid establishment of European monetary union, and support further and irreversible steps towards European political union. There is also agreement that the single market should encompass the EFTA countries, that economic co-operation should be fostered with the eastern European countries, and that EC membership should be enlarged.

German employers view the single European market and monetary union as necessary responses to intensified competition with the US and Japan. The interests of the German economy, which is dependent on a flourishing world market to a greater degree than that of any other large country, make it impossible for German employers and their associations to support parochial nationalistic positions.

As influential as German capital is in the sphere of the European economy and technology, the employers find themselves in the minority in the political arena. Indeed, German employers are critical of the social orientation and pro-union attitude of EC bodies. The Economic and Social Committee, the EC Commission and especially the broad consensus on social policy between the large Socialist and Christian-Democratic blocs in the European Parliament are singled out for criticism.

The employers have repeatedly confirmed their qualified commitment to a social Europe, but object to what they regard as excessive social intervention and bureaucratic over-regulation. They accept the Social Charter, which is a 'solemn declaration without legal effect'; but the Action Programme and the Commission's initiatives come in for heavy criticism. Against the Commission's 'far-reaching policy of social regulation', they insist that priority must be given to the principle of subsidiarity at the national level and to agreements between the two parties involved in collective bargaining. Many of the Commission's (draft) directives are viewed by German employers as violations of the principle of subsidiarity and rejected on that basis. The best example is the proposal to establish European Works Councils (EWCs) in transnational firms. A joint statement by the BDA and the BDI emphasizes the contrast between EWCs as centralized, supra-national bodies and the decentralized German works councils. They emphasize that the proposed EWCs are not obliged to exercise a policy of 'trustful cooperation' and fear that they will unduly restrict managerial decisions.

Unlike the employers, the trade unions failed to recognize the new dynamic of European integration which began to take hold in the mid-1980s and long underestimated the powerful economic thrust and political attractiveness of the EC's single European market project. Two concerns have, however, forced them to take European integration seriously. First, leading union representatives have recognized that German industrial relations are much more stable than in many other European countries. The German trade unions and the German system of works constitution, codetermination and collective bargaining autonomy, enjoy growing prestige in other countries. In addition, the unions' self-confidence and their readiness to assume greater responsibility for Europe's social dimension has increased. Second, the strengthened social and political initiatives of the EC Parliament and Commission have inspired trade union involvement in European affairs.

The European Social Charter, the social dialogue and most of the draft directives have been welcomed by the unions as steps in the right direction. Despite criticisms that the planned measures fall short of union expectations, German trade unions increasingly accept the Commission's strategy: that rather than pursuing ambitious regulations at Community level, they should use Euro-legislation only to secure basic minimum conditions, with superior provisions negotiated by the bargaining parties themselves. The conviction is growing that the construction of a social Europe is a trade union task and that negotiations with the employers' associations are an appropriate means to shape industrial relations at the European level. The joint opinions within the framework of the ongoing social dialogue, and especially the agreement reached by the ETUC, UNICE and CEEP at the end of 1991 on the revision of Article 118 of the EC Treaty, have been greeted as milestones on the road to the Europeanization of labour relations. The understanding reached at the Maastricht summit, enabling the United Kingdom to opt out of the social chapter, is in part regretted, but it is also seen as removing an obstacle to progress on the social dimension.

The German unions attach great importance to agreements with transnational firms on the establishment of EWCs. Such agreements, with rights to consultation and information clearly below the standards of codetermination under the Works Constitution Act, have already been concluded with Volkswagen and Mannesmann. A comparable pact has been concluded with some of the large transnational firms in the chemical sector.

Conclusions

It was common in the past to regard German industrial relations as rigid, formalistic and over-legalized. Perhaps surprisingly, then, in recent decades the system has proved markedly adaptable. Trade unions and works councils as well as employers and their associations have had to cope with economic fluctuations, political changes and socio-economic developments. Supported by the political and legal framework they have managed to overcome these challenges, while retaining remarkable stability in their institutions and organizations.

In short, the German model of industrial relations has proved to be one of the most stable and adaptable in the western world. We cannot conclude from the successful management of past challenges that those of the future will also be overcome, although some optimism seems justified since the actors' learning capacities have clearly increased. Nevertheless the response to the following three major challenges will determine the future of the German model of industrial relations.

First, the demands arising from German unification have put the established system under considerable stress. It is true that the transfer of institutions and the extension of organizational domains from the West to the East proceeded with less friction than expected. But industrial relations *practice* cannot be so easily transferred; it requires a long learning process. The handling of industrial disputes (in terms of the development of case law and conflict management) demands experience and skills which were rarely able to develop under the authoritarian communist regime. The 'social partners' have played a major role in the transition from a command economy to a social market economy, but the social problems to be solved are beyond their capacities. Hence they are permanently tempted to abandon their common understanding and replace the corporatist approach with traditional adversarial strategies. In the spring of 1992, the social and economic costs of unification have contributed to severe political uncertainties and a new instability in industrial relations.

Moreover, while the old 'workplace trade union leadership' in east German firms has been replaced by works councils, their main activities differ greatly from those of their colleagues in the western part of the country. Works councils in the east act as co-managers in their firm's struggle for economic survival, in collaboration with a management that has still to learn the appropriate behaviour.

One may be confident that, in the long run, the outcome of the 'open experiment' taking place in the east will approximate the pattern of the west. Nevertheless, it will not be a mere copy, nor will it leave the original untouched. Thus the debate on the organizational reform of the DGB has been fuelled by the demarcation disputes following the expansion of the unions' organizational domains from the west to the east.

The second challenge – of the productivity gap between Japanese and German manufacturing – is probably more serious. The turbulence caused by fierce global competition in manufacturing industries has put the whole production system under strain. Anxious managers seek radical changes in the organization of production and look for allies among the works councillors. A complete redesign of the labour process is on the agenda. 'New production concepts', 'flexible specialization', 'lean production' are the catch-phrases of the restructuring process, linked to notions of 'human resource management' or 'participatory management'.

If these changes in the production system and the labour process were widely implemented, their repercussions on the German model of industrial relations would be profound. A highly formalized and representative system of trade unions and works councils is experiencing the emergence of new actors – work-groups and production teams. Up to now participation, codetermination and collective bargaining were exclusively the business of representative labour institutions. Although the DGB passed a motion in 1984 in favour of codetermination 'at the point of production', it had no effect whatever on industrial relations practice. However, works councils and trade unions have now accepted managements' initiatives on direct worker participation as first steps towards *Mitbestimmung am Arbeitsplatz*.

The centrifugal consequences for the German model will probably intensify. There will be scope for greater decentralization and more actors, for a wider variety of patterns and coalitions. The works councils will have to extend their participation in the procedural regulation of day-to-day activities and job performance, and in doing so they will inevitably develop a co-management role. The unions will be forced to adjust their traditional structures and policies to these decentralizing tendencies; they will certainly have to increase their organizational knowledge and technical competence and – above all – improve their services to the works councils.

Sooner or later the structural characteristics of the German model outlined in the introductory section may be modified: the dual system may give way to a triple system of interest representation with sectoral bargaining between trade unions and employers' associations, enterprise negotiations between work councils and management, and direct participation by work-groups with elected team leaders. This implies that the highly formalized and strongly representative model will be modified. And there is no guarantee that the integration of the formal and representative institutions with the emerging decentralized and informal structures will succeed.

The final challenge is the single European market. The broadest possible spectrum of opinion is to be found, ranging from Euro-pessimism to Euro-optimism. Some argue that the domestic German system will be weakened by 'the creeping intrusion of a more voluntary and "flexible" industrial relations regime' (Streeck 1991: 347). Others expect the displacement of sectoral bargaining by enterprise bargaining, especially in transnational companies. A third group suggests that some elements of the strong German model may be exported, most notably in the case of the European Works Council (although with a different legal status from the German works council).

It seems likely that the consequences of European integration will be uneven. German industrial relations are becoming more decentralized, and employers require the commitment of their employees more than ever before. One can therefore expect that the emergent patterns of industrial relations will depend on local, regional and sectoral circumstances on the one hand, and on the level of aspirations and expectations of the labour force on the other. The future remains uncertain; but German workers and their representative institutions may play an important role in its codetermination.

Terms and Abbreviations

Angestellter	salaried employee
Arbeiter	wage earner
Arbeitsgericht	Labour Court
AFG	*Arbeitsförderungsgesetz* – Work Promotion Act
Aufsichtsrat	supervisory board
Beamter	public employee with special status
BFG	*Beschäftigungsförderungsgesetz* – Employment Promotion Act
Betriebsrat	works council
BetrVG	*Betriebsverfassungsgesetz* – Works Constitution Act
Bundesbank	Federal Bank
Bundesland	See *Land*
BPersVG	*Bundespersonalvertretungsgesetz* – Federal Staff Representation

BDA	*Bundesvereinigung der Deutschen Arbeitgeberverbände* – Confederation of German Employers' Associations
CDU (/CSU)	*Christlich-Demokratische Union* (*/Christlich-Soziale Union*) – Christian Democratic Union (/Christian Social Union)
CGB	*Christlicher Gewerkschaftsbund* – Christian Federation of Trade Unions
DAG	*Deutsche Angestelltengewerkschaft* – German Salaried Employees' Union
DDR	*Deutsche Demokratische Republik* – German Democratic Republic
DBB	*Deutscher Beamtenbund* – German Civil Servants' Federation
DGB	*Deutscher Gewerkschaftsbund* – German Trade Union Federation
DIHT	*Deutscher Industrie und Handelstag* – German Association of Chambers of Commerce
FDP	*Freie Demokratische Partei* – Free Democratic Party
Friedenspflicht	peace obligation
Gesamt-/Konzern betriebsrat	company or group works council
Gesamtmetall	*Gesamtverband der metallindustriellen Arbeitgeberverbände* – Federation of Metal Industry Employers' Associations
IG	*Industriegewerkschaft* – Industrial Union
Konzertierte Aktion	Concerted Action
Land	Regional/provincial unit of the BRD
Leitende Angestellte	Senior Staff
MitbG	*Mitbestimmungsgesetz* – Co-determination Act
MontanMitbG	special Co-Determination Act for the Coal and Steel Industries
ÖTV	*Gewerkschaft Öffentliche Dienste, Transport und Verkehr* – Union for Public Services, Transport and Communication
SPD	*Sozialdemokratische Partei Deutschlands* – Social-Democratic Party
Tarifautonomie	free collective bargaining
Tarifvertrag	collective agreement
TVG	*Tarifvertragsgesetz* – Collective Agreement Act
Verrechtlichung	juridification
Vertrauensleute	union workplace representatives

References

Beisheim, M., von Eckardstein, D. and Müller, M. 1991: Partizipative Organisationsformen und industrielle Beziehungen. In W. Müller-Jentsch (ed.) *Konfliktpartnerschaft: Akteure und Institutionen der industriellen Beziehungen*, Munich: Hampp, 123–38.

Bergmann, J., Jacobi, O. and Müller-Jentsch, W. 1975: *Gewerkschaften in der Bundesrepublik*. Vol 1: *Gewerkschaftliche Lohnpolitik zwischen Mitgliederinteressen und ökonomischen Systemzwängen*. Frankfurt: Campus.

Bispinck, R. 1991a: Auf dem Weg zur Tarifunion. *WSI-Mitteilungen*, 44, 3, 87–98.

Bispinck, R. 1991b: Die Gratwanderung – Tarifpolitik in den neuen Bundesländern. *Gewerkschaftliche Monatshefte*, 42, 12, 744–55.

Bispinck, R. 1991c: *Tarifpolitisches Taschenbuch*. Cologne: Bund.

Bollinger, D., Cornetz, W. and Pfau-Effinger, B. 1991: Atypische Beschäftigung – Betriebliche Kalküle und Arbeitnehmerinteressen. In K.Semlinger (ed.) *Flexibilisierung des Arbeitsmarktes. Interessen, Wirkungen, Perspektiven*, Frankfurt Campus, 177–99.

Brandt, G., Jacobi, O. and Müller-Jentsch, W. 1982: *Anpassung an die Krise: Gewerkschaften in den siebziger Jahren*. Frankfurt: Campus.

Breisig, T. 1991: Betriebsvereinbarungen zu Qualitätszirkeln – Eine Inhaltsanalyse. *Die Betriebswirtschaft*, 51, 1, 65–77.

Büchtemann, C. F. with A. Höland 1989: *Befristete Arbeitsverträge nach dem Beschäftigungsförderungsgesetz (BeschFG 1985). Ergebnisse einer empirischen Untersuchung im Auftrag des Bundesministers für Arbeit und Sozialordnung.* Bonn: Bundesminister für Arbeit und Sozialordnung.

Bundesvereinigung der Deutschen Arbeitgeberverbände (BDA) 1990: *Jahresbericht 1990.* Cologne.

Bunn, R. F. 1984: Employers' Associations in the Federal Republic of Germany. In J.P. Windmuller and A. Gladstone (eds), *Employers' Associations and Industrial Relations* Oxford: Clarendon Press, 169–201.

Dabrowski, H., Jacobi, O., Schudlich, E. and Teschner, E. (eds) 1989: *Tarifpolitische Interessen der Arbeitgeber und neue Managementstrategien.* Düsseldorf: Hans-Böckler-Stiftung.

Deutsche Bundesbank 1991a: *Report for the Year 1990.* Frankfurt.

Deutsche Bundesbank 1991b: *Monthly Reports 1991.* Frankfurt.

Eberwein, W. and Tholen, J. 1990: *Managermentalität.* Frankfurt: FAZ.

Endruweit, G. et al. (eds) 1985: *Handbuch der Arbeitsbeziehungen. Deutschland – Österreich – Schweiz.* Berlin: de Gruyter.

Erd, R. 1978: *Verrechtlichung industrieller Konflikte. Normative Rahmenbedingungen des dualen Systems der Interessenvertretung.* Frankfurt: Suhrkamp.

Erd, R. 1979: Verrechtlichte Gewerkschaftspolitik. Bedingungen ihrer Entwicklung und Veränderung. In J. Bergmann (ed.), *Beiträge zur Soziologie der Gewerkschaften,* Frankfurt: Suhrkamp, 143–82.

Erdmann, E. 1991: *Arbeitsverfassung und Tarifpolitik im vereinten Deutschland.* Cologne: BDA.

Hagelstange, T. 1979: *Der Einfluß der ökonomischen Konjunktur auf die Streiktätigkeit und die Mitgliederstärke der Gewerkschaften in der BRD von 1950 bis 1975.* Stuttgart: Hochschulverlag.

Herkommer, S., Bischoff, P., Lohauß, P., Maldaner, K.H. and Steinfeld, F. 1979: Organisationsgrad und Bewußtsein. *Gewerkschaftliche Monatshefte,* 30, 709–20.

Hilbert, J. and Sperling, H.J. 1990: *Die kleine Fabrik.* Munich: Hampp.

Jacobi, O. 1990: Elements of a European Community of the future: A trade union view. In C. Crouch and D. Marquand (eds), *The Politics of 1992,* Oxford: Blackwell.

Jacobi, O. and Müller-Jentsch, W. 1990: West Germany: Continuity and structural change. In G. Baglioni and C. Crouch (eds), *European Industrial Relations,* London: Sage.

Jürgensen, H. 1991: Die Bundesrepublik Deutschland zwischen Wiedervereinigung und Binnenmarkt 1993. *Volkswirtschaftliche Korrespondenz der Adolf-Weber-Stiftung,* 30, 10, 1–4.

Kalbitz, R. 1979: *Aussperrungen. Die vergessenen Konflikte.* Frankfurt: EVA.

Katzenstein, P. 1989: Industry in a changing West Germany. In P. Katzenstein (ed.) *Industry and Politics in West Germany.* Ithaca: Cornell University Press, 3–29.

Keller, B. 1983: *Arbeitsbeziehungen im öffentlichen Dienst. Tarifpolitik der Gewerkschaften und Interessenpolitik der Beamtenverbände.* Frankfurt: Campus.

Keller, B. 1987a: Kommunale Arbeitgeber und ihre Verbände – zur sozialwissenschaftlichen Analyse einer 'Forschungslücke'. *Zeitschrift für öffentliche und gemeinwirtschaftliche Unternehmen,* 10, 3, 262–77.

Keller, B. 1987b: Interessenaggregation und -transformation in Verbänden öffentlicher Arbeitgeber. In A. Windhoff-Héritier (ed.), *Verwaltung und ihre Umwelt. Festschrift für Thomas Ellwein,* Opladen: Westdeutscher Verlag, 258–76.

Keller, B. 1991: *Einführung in die Arbeitspolitik. Arbeitsbeziehungen und Arbeitsmarkt in sozialwissenschaftlicher Perspektive.* 2nd edn. Munich/Vienna: Oldenbourg.

Keller, B. and Henneberger, F. 1992: Europäische Einigung und nationaler öffentlicher Dienst. *WSI-Mitteilungen,* 45, 1, 18–23.

Kern, H., and Schumann, M. 1984: *Das Ende der Arbeitsteilung?* Munich: Beck.

Kittner, M. (ed.) 1974: *Streik und Aussperrung.* Frankfurt: EVA.

8

Austria: Still the Country of Corporatism

Franz Traxler

Introduction

According to international comparative studies (e.g. Schmitter 1981), Austria's political system is among the most corporatist of all western countries. In this system of 'social partnership' *(Sozialpartnerschaft)*, based on close cooperation between the state, capital and labour, industrial relations play a key role. Capital and labour are represented by the 'big four' interest associations: the Federal Chamber of Business, BWK, the Peak of the Chambers of Agriculture, the Austrian Trade Union Federation, ÖGB, and the Austrian Central Chamber of Labour, ÖAKT. Although the membership and leadership of the ÖGB and ÖAKT largely overlap and the two bodies cooperate closely, there is a division of labour between them. While collective bargaining is the ÖGB's exclusive domain, the ÖAKT works as a brains trust for the ÖGB, and is entitled to advise the authorities on all matters affecting workers' interests. Hence the ÖGB and ÖAKT co-represent labour *vis-à-vis* government. Their complementarity is manifested in the fact that the ÖAKT's organizational structure is territorial, while that of the ÖGB is mainly sectoral.

Social partnership arrangements reconcile collective bargaining with state economic policy, and in turn subject all economic and social policy matters to the influence of the principal interest associations of labour and capital. As well as being consulted on the drafting of policy regulations, the peak organizations also perform regulatory functions.

Austria's industrial relations system is exceptional, not only in its extremely corporatist form but also in its stability: it has apparently been immune to the pressures which have weakened corporatism elsewhere in Europe over the past decade. The chapter's analytical focus is, therefore, on explaining this stability. It argues that stability rests on a unique configuration of power relations, institutional (i.e. associational and legal) arrangements and cultural patterns. The chapter concludes with some hypotheses on the recent challenges posed to this configuration by a changing environment and on the related prospects for the future of 'social partnership'.

Social Partnership: Origins and Properties

Although it may appear paradoxical at first glance, the same enduring properties of Austrian society gave rise both to violent class struggle in the inter-war period, culminating in the civil war of 1934, and to intimate cooperation after the Second World War. Compared with other European countries, Austria is notable for the relative weakness of capital and strength of labour (Traxler 1987): the product of relatively late industrialization, the negative effects of which were magnified by a political alliance between the great feudal landowners and the petty bourgeoisie during the Habsburg Empire. By protecting the agricultural and handicraft sectors from competitive pressures at the cost of big business, this alliance helped to preserve small establishments as the dominant form of production. Large enterprises were hard hit by the loss of a good part of their former home markets following the fall of the Habsburg Empire in 1918. Politically, capital was confronted by an insurgent working class, which could be pacified only by extending welfare legislation and by a legal framework granting representational and organizational rights to the labour organizations.

Though unfavourable conditions of accumulation hampered improvements in living standards, they nevertheless strengthened the labour movement organizationally. After the repeal of measures outlawing the labour movement and social democracy, unions enjoyed a rapid growth in the late nineteenth century. Most importantly, social democracy succeeded in forming a cohesive network of organizations covering all aspects of workers' interests. In addition, the predominance of small firms in the Austrian economy encouraged the development of unions. In all European countries for which data is available, unionization and multi-employer collective bargaining first spread through the skilled trades, which were dispersed among a multiplicity of small and medium-sized firms (Sisson 1979, Traxler 1985). There are two main reasons for this. First, such firms tended to employ a high proportion of skilled workers, whose strong labour market position facilitated collective organization. Second, small firms found multi-employer collective bargaining a useful means of taking wages out of competition (Traxler 1990a). In contrast, highly concentrated sectors such as heavy industry were much more hostile to unionization and collective bargaining.

Before the First World War, unions were at best tolerated by the state. But relations began to change when the state needed the assistance of the associations of capital and labour in implementing its wartime command economy. In exchange, the associations were granted a corporate legal status and organizational security, and their role in the formulation of aspects of public policy was formally recognized. During the brief post-war revolutionary republic, the legal status of unions and employers' associations was reinforced; and this juridification *(Verrechtlichung)* persisted. In 1920, the law on collective bargaining made collective agreements legally enforceable. The Works Constitution Act, passed in 1919, established works councils as the legal representatives of workers' interests within companies, at the same time restricting their activities in a well-ordered system of industrial relations. In 1920, parliament passed a law on the formation of chambers of labour. Based on compulsory membership, the chambers were granted the right to consultation on all matters of economic and social policy. The aim of the legislation was to create an equivalent to the chambers of business which had already been established at the time of the bourgeois revolution of 1848.

For all these reasons, Austrian social democracy developed into a fully-fledged political camp opposed to that of the Christian-conservative bourgeoisie after the First World War, and became the strongest and most well-organized labour movement outside the Soviet Union in the interwar period. Ideologically integrated by Austro-Marxism, the social democrats (then called the Social Democratic Party of Labour, SDAP) remained unchallenged at the political level; communism was unable to establish itself in Austria. Although the union movement was politically and ideologically fragmented, the social democrats maintained their dominant role, representing more than 70 per cent of total union membership (Traxler 1982).

In its manifesto of 1926, the SDAP claimed that it would transform capitalism into socialism by attaining a majority in parliament, whereas the bourgeois camp intended to remove the achievements that labour had gained in the peaceful revolution of 1918–19. The conflict ended with the bourgeoisie's victory in the civil war of 1934 and the outlawing of social-democratic organizations. But the outcome was short-lived: Austria was occupied by Nazi Germany in 1938.

With the elites of both political camps exposed to persecution during the Nazi regime, the occupation of Austria was the turning point in their relationship. They unanimously perceived occupation as the consequence of the bitter conflict between them, exacerbated by a permanent economic crisis culminating in one of the highest unemployment rates in Europe. Thus with the defeat of the Nazis, both camps were determined to replace class struggle with cooperation. Concerted, consociational policy-making became the guiding principle and the promotion of economic growth and employment became the predominant goals of Austria's social partnership.

Why has corporatism been so pervasive and stable in Austria? Its strength derives, first, from specific *institutional* preconditions: favourable labour legislation, close ties between the state, the political parties and the 'big four', and encompassing and centralized associational structures. Second, corporatism has a *material* base: it rests on the unique properties of the Austrian economy, most notably the persistent weakness of private capital.

This structural weakness of capital, most obviously demonstrated by the country's relatively large public sector and small firm size, forces capitalists confronted with a strong labour movement to cooperate on labour-market questions. In addition to this imperative, which applies to all sectors of Austrian capital, inter-class cooperation is also required to assure the specific product-market interests of the export-oriented sector (Traxler 1987).

Since small firms tend to orient their activities towards the domestic economy, protectionist interests prevail among Austrian employers, given the weight of small firms. It is estimated that 50 per cent of domestic consumption is supplied by the sheltered sector, while this sector covers only 15 per cent in the EC (Polt 1988). As internal decision-making is based on the 'one person, one vote' principle in Austria's main business association, the BWK, small capital is in a strong position to pursue business interests through political and associational action. As a consequence, not only has large, export-oriented industry been forced to set up a trade association of its own, but it is also extremely dependent on the support of labour's peak associations to defend its product-market interests in the face of the protectionist demands of small firms.

The predominance of protectionist interests among capitalists is also the key reason for the state's greater willingness than in any other western country to share its economic and social governance responsibilities with the associations. Capital's weakness poses a persistent threat to the international competitiveness of the Austrian economy. This problem is indicated by Austrian per capita exports which are only about 70 per cent of those of comparable small countries (Kramer 1984). Hence Austria faces a unique dilemma: on the one hand, as a small country, its economic prosperity is particularly dependent on foreign trade and international competitiveness; on the other hand, maintaining competitiveness through economic modernization is very difficult because of capital's weakness. This task cannot therefore be left to the free play of market forces but must be *politically* guided. The state's interests in achieving economic modernization and maintaining competitiveness can only be achieved if allies can be found against protectionism.

In this respect, organized labour plays a key role, given the inherent 'organizability' problems of employers: business associations are less capable than unions of unifying members' interests in pursuit of collective goals (Traxler 1989). Austrian business associations have thus had greater difficulty in overcoming small-firm protectionism and in adopting a policy appropriate for international competitiveness. Furthermore, the ÖGB, the central labour representative, tends to support the export-oriented sector as a result of its own internal balance of power. Since union density is above average in large industrial firms, the ÖGB's policies – in stark contrast to those of the BWK – are structurally biased in favour of large firms whose interests are generally anti-protectionist. Together with the Central Chamber of Labour, ÖAKT, the ÖGB also sees itself as the consumers' representative, advocating an anti-protectionist policy in order to keep down consumer prices.

State and Law

The state plays four main roles in Austria's industrial relations, although these roles tend to overlap in practice, especially in the public sector: first, it lays down substantive rules governing working conditions; second, it defines procedural rules establishing the formal framework of industrial relations; third, it is an employer in its own right; and fourth, it is the sponsor of corporatist macro-economic management.

The Legislative Framework

Industrial relations are highly regulated by law. But there is no unified statute covering all legal dimensions of the employment relationship. Instead, there is a variety of laws, each of which regulates a specific aspect of employment (for example, vocational training, working hours) or the employment rights of specific groups of employees. The law makes a fundamental distinction between 'public' employment by state authorities and 'private' employment by other employers; and in the latter, between blue- and white-collar workers. Employment in nationalized enterprises is private from a legal point of view unless enterprises are organized as state authorities (as is the case with Austrian railways). While individual employment relations are based on freedom of contract, they are regulated by legal norms, which define such matters as methods of payment, working hours and dismissal.

A special Works Constitution Act (*Arbeitsverfassungsgesetz* – ArbVG) governs collective labour relations in the private sector (Strasser 1984). As in Germany, this law distinguishes between collective employment relations within the firm and at multi-firm (i.e. associational) level. The works council is constituted as the main employee representative within the firm. In every establishment with five or more employees, a works council must be set up if the work force so requests. Councils are elected by proportional representation for a period of four years. In multi-plant companies, each works council is entitled to elect a number of its members to a central (enterprise) works council. The works councils' role in representing employees *vis-à-vis* management is precisely defined. Works councils, like their German counterparts, must act in a cooperative manner.

Works councils' rights extend from information and consultation to codetermination, including the opportunity to conclude a formal plant agreement (*Betriebsvereinbarung*) with management. While information and consultation rights apply to all matters affecting the establishment's employees, codetermination is legally limited to a narrow range of social and personnel matters. Management decisions are dependent on the works council's approval for matters such as the introduction of control systems that affect human dignity, for the introduction of performance-related payment schemes, and for internal transfers that downgrade the position of employees within the firm. The scope of matters subject to settlement by plant agreement is also specified by law, while collective agreements at multi-employer level may also delegate matters for regulation by plant agreement. Plant agreements on matters such as working-time schedules, and provisions for coping with the impact of major changes within the firm (the *Sozialplan*), are legally enforceable, as are those of higher-level collective agreements. In firms with a supervisory board, one-third of the board's seats are reserved for the works council. Overall, the system of employee representation resembles the German model, the main difference being that works councils in Austria have fewer rights than in Germany.

Although based on the principle of free collective bargaining, labour relations at the multi-firm level are also governed by the ArbVG, which regulates the bargaining parties and the scope and legal effects of agreements. One of the most notable features of Austria's labour law is that it authorizes only associations (employers' associations and unions at multi-employer level) to conclude collective agreements. In order to be licensed to conclude collective agreements, an association must be independent from its bargaining counterpart. Agreements at this level may cover all aspects of the employment relationship as well as the relationship between the bargaining parties themselves. Closed and union shop agreements are prohibited. Agreements bind not only the bargaining parties' members but also non-members within these parties' associational domain. Bargaining parties are subject to a peace obligation as long as an agreement is in force.

Despite the comprehensive regulation of other industrial relations issues, the law does not cover industrial disputes or internal union affairs. There are so few strikes in Austria that the issue has never troubled the legislature or the courts. Nevertheless, the ArbVG provides voluntary public mediation or arbitration procedures for disputes over the content of collective agreements. In contrast, the resolution of disputes over rights enacted in the ArbVG can be legally enforced by either party. Depending on issues, the labour courts or special public arbitration boards are responsible for judgments on such disputes.

Overall, the ArbVG defines a highly ordered system of industrial relations in terms of both procedural rules and regulatory levels. Different types of regulation (statutes, collective agreements, plant agreements, employment contracts) generally follow the principle that the provision most favourable to labour overrides others on the same issue. The ordering of regulatory levels establishes a clear predominance of the actors at the multi-employer level over those below. The exclusive right of employers' associations to conclude collective agreements is notable given that in other countries employers' associations regularly have trouble obtaining such authority from their members. Unions are superior to works councils, as almost all industrial relations issues may be subject to collective bargaining by unions at multi-employer level, while the works councils' competence embraces only a narrow range of issues. Most importantly, this implies that only unions are empowered to conclude legally enforceable agreements on wage rates.

The State as Employer

In the public sector, which accounted for about 28 per cent of all employment in Austria in 1989, employee representation in the workplace is analogous to that laid down in the ArbVG. Rules vary somewhat for different public employers. Similarly, individual employment relations in the public sector are variable, with group-specific differences in legal employment status and in the employing authorities. In collective employment relations, this is reflected in patterns of union representation: one union organizes the employees of the *Bund* (federal state) and *Länder* (provincial governments); a second covers local authorities; another organizes railways; and yet another the postal service.

Only a minority of public employees have employment conditions determined through collective agreements; the conditions of the majority are fixed by law. In practice, however, they are not determined unilaterally by the state but by regular bargaining rounds between the four public employees' unions and the authorities. Agreements reached are formally embodied in legislation.

In contrast to other countries (for example, Britain and Sweden) where the militancy of public employees posed a particular threat to incomes policies (Lash and Urry 1987), wage increases in the Austrian public sector were significantly lower than in the private sector during the 1980s, furthering government efforts to reduce public deficits. The main reason for the moderation of the public sector unions is their close links with the political parties of the two main camps. Despite these cooperative tendencies, the union of federal and provincial state employees accounted for the highest strike share of all unions, with 58 per cent of workers involved and 60 per cent of working hours lost in the 1980s.

Macro-level Concertation and the State

Macro-corporatist concertation allows the integration of industrial relations into overall economic and social policy-making. Two main arenas of concertation can be distinguished. First, incomes policy is implemented by the Parity Commission for Wages and Prices. All wages and certain retail prices are subject to its control. The Commission is also a forum for developing future economic and social policy. It is composed of the 'big four' and those ministers responsible for economic and social matters. Since decisions are made exclusively by the 'big four' and ministers have only an advisory vote, incomes policy is formulated on a voluntary and autonomous basis. The Commission's aim is to avoid wage-price spirals and thus to enhance economic competitiveness in the short term. Other economic and social policy issues are the formal responsibility of the state, with the big four's influence resting on devolution by the state of advisory and regulatory powers. This state-licensed cooperation is aimed at increasing long-term competitiveness through economic restructuring.

Concertation in policy arenas is coupled with a symbiotic relationship between the actors, relying on complex interlocking leaderships and political exchange according to informal rules, in contrast to the high juridification of industrial relations. Thus cooperative incomes policy may be seen as an exchange in which organized capital gains some control over wages in return for conceding to labour some influence on prices. The integration of each of the 'big four' with their associated political parties strengthens their authority over their members and guarantees representation in parliament and government, thus making cooperation between the 'big four' and the state largely insensitive to changes in government.

Labour

Union Structure

The ÖGB was founded in 1945, after the overthrow of the Nazi regime and before sectoral unions were set up. Completely new union structures were then reconstructed from the top down, in line with the political aim of preventing inter-union rivalry.

Austrian unionism is the most centralized in Western Europe, and, uniquely from a comparative perspective (Visser 1984), the ÖGB encompasses the whole of the country's union membership. It consists of fourteen member unions which cover the whole economy. Though each has a distinct jurisdiction, industrial unionism (in the strict sense of one plant, one union) is not fully established. In the private sector, blue-collar workers are organized separately from white-collar employees: while there are eight sectoral unions of blue-collar workers, nearly all the private sector's white-collar workers are in a single union. In addition, one union recruits both white- and blue-collar workers in the arts and the media. Between them, these unions cover the whole private sector. The remaining four member unions each organize distinct parts of the public sector, as outlined above.

Experience has shown that the advantages of separating blue- from white-collar workers tend to outweigh the disadvantages. One disadvantage is that employers are given the opportunity to play the unions off against each other. Moreover, the distinction between white- and blue-collar workers has recently become much less clear than in the past. For example, employers seeking to increase employee involvement may classify workers performing manual tasks as white-collar employees, a status privileged by labour law. This threatens to undermine the membership domain of manual unions. The problem is further exacerbated by the expansion of white-collar employment in the service sector (see tables 8.1 and 8.2); since 1974, the white-collar union has been the ÖGB's largest member (Traxler 1982). In response, some manual unions have called for a stricter application of the principle of industrial unionism: in effect restricting white-collar unions to the service sector, with industrial unions embracing all types of employee in their sector of organization. But this is not a credible proposal, since no union wishes to provoke a conflict between ÖGB members. Moreover, it is accepted that the separate organization of white-collar workers is necessary to prevent the formation of an autonomous white-collar union outside the ÖGB, as happened in Sweden and to a lesser extent in Germany. Thus the principle of industrial unionism is moderated for the sake of unity.

Before examining the character and preconditions of Austria's unitary unionism, attention should be paid to the relationship between the ÖGB and its member unions. The power relations between a federation and its affiliates are broadly determined by three resources: control over finance and over full-time officials, and the allocation of representative functions. According to its constitution, the ÖGB exercises control over the entire system of union finances. Members' dues are collected by the unions for the ÖGB, which then returns a certain percentage to the unions. The lion's share is kept by the ÖGB: in the 1980s, only 16 per cent was paid back to the unions. The ÖGB also sets the level of subscriptions (currently 1 per cent of an employee's gross income). Control over personnel is regulated in a similar fashion: the ÖGB appoints not only its own staff but those of its member unions, although only a minority (about 16 per cent in 1980) work in its office.

The ÖGB is responsible for representing interests common to all employees, and member unions are responsible for matters affecting their own membership. In practice, the ÖGB is pre-eminent in formulating long-term union goals as well as in representing labour in government. Union representatives in corporatist policy-making are nominated by the ÖGB, considerably strengthening its position in relation to the unions. Their autonomy is greatest in collective bargaining, since each union carries out its own negotiations for employees within its domain. However, these negotiations are coordinated by the ÖGB via informal discussions between union leaders and ÖGB officials. In addition, the ÖGB itself negotiates 'general' collective agreements covering all sections of the labour force. Overall, authority is extremely centralized. According to the ÖGB constitution, member unions are not independent associations but subdivisions of the ÖGB; hence, they are not entitled to make binding agreements with external interlocutors. Collective agreements must therefore be concluded by them on behalf of the ÖGB.

This centralization of union power is supplemented by organizational unity. Since there is no union outside its umbrella, the ÖGB enjoys a *de facto* monopoly of representation. Given the politicization of Austrian society, entrenched in political camps since the late nineteenth century, this unitary structure can only be sustained by the systematic internalization of political cleavages. Seven political factions exist within the unions. Although they are not explicitly recognized under the union's constitu-

Table 8.1 Average employment in Austria by gender and status (% total employees) 1955–59 to 1985–89

	1955–59	1960–64	1965–69	1970–74	1975–79	1980–84	1985–89
Male employees	65.1	63.6	63.1	62.5	60.6	59.6	59.0
Female employees	34.9	36.4	36.9	37.5	39.4	40.4	41.0
Blue-collar workers	65.5*	63.1	59.4	55.9	50.9	48.3	46.2
White-collar workers	34.5*	36.9	40.6	44.1	49.1	51.7	53.9
Foreign workers				7.1	6.6	5.7	5.4
Total number of employees	2,167,115	2,330,090	2,364,924	2,524,310	2,722,175	2,766,576	2,799,598

* 1957–9 only
Source: Österreichisches Institut für Wirtschaftsforschung.

Table 8.2 Average employment by sectors (% of total employees), 1955–59 to 1985–89

	1955–59	1960–64	1965–69	1970–74	1975–79	1980–84	1985–89
Agriculture	7.34	4.51	3.05	2.02	1.52	1.24	1.04
Mining	1.51	1.23	1.00	0.76	0.59	0.49	0.42
Manufacturing	37.61	37.12	35.78	36.04	33.42	29.24	28.93
Electricity, gas and water	1.01	1.07	1.18	1.19	1.16	1.17	1.19
Construction	10.65	10.70	10.71	10.10	9.42	8.44	7.71
Trade, restaurants and hotels	10.91	12.83	14.06	14.86	16.31	17.08	17.71
Transport and communication	8.21	8.11	8.09	7.56	7.36	7.39	7.53
Finance, insurance, business services	4.08	4.37	4.82	5.66	6.45	7.06	7.52
Other activities	18.69	20.06	21.32	21.81	23.77	27.89	27.95
All activities	100.00	100.00	100.00	100.00	100.00	100.00	100.00

Source: Österreichisches Institut für Wirtschaftsforschung.

tion, they have achieved a quasi-official status, and about 1 per cent of the ÖGB's revenues is allotted to them each year. As a result of these political affiliations, since 1945 union representatives have continuously held not only parliamentary seats, but also ministerial posts. Especially close ties exist with the Social Democratic Party (SPÖ), within which the union faction has formed a highly influential group. Conversely, the unions are clearly dominated by the social democrats.

The strength of political factions and representation on union bodies at all levels up to the top of the ÖGB is determined by the results of works councils elections. By nominating separate lists of candidates for these elections, the factions compete for employees' support. The social-democratic faction usually receives 65–70 per cent of votes, and the Christian faction and 'independent' groups 15–20 per cent each.

This electoral system is unorthodox in that the works council is formally independent of the unions. It is questionable whether the system is truly representative (Traxler 1982). Those unionists working in plants without a works council are inevitably excluded from union elections. Conversely, employees who are not unionized can influence intra-union delegations since all employees have the right to vote in the works council election. Nevertheless, unions prefer this system for three reasons. First, it is said that it ensures a higher turnout than conventional union elections in other countries, thus providing great plebiscitary legitimacy for union representatives (Lachs 1976). Second, the system gives the two main political camps some degree of freedom in distributing seats on representative bodies, because of the impossibility of ascertaining the ideological affiliation of all the works councillors elected. 'Independent' works councillors are not normally accepted as members of the unions' representative bodies. Third, the issues discussed in the context of a works council election are related to the specific problems of the establishment in which it takes place. The formulation of more general union policies can thus be separated to a considerable extent from controversial debates among union members and employees (Traxler 1982).

However, the central precondition for using works councils elections for the purpose of intra-union representation is the integration of works councils with the unions. More than 90 per cent of works councillors are estimated to be union members. Many are also union officials, and they predominate in the unions' representative bodies. Some unions have a formal rule that their representative bodies should consist exclusively of works councillors. Most importantly, the works councils perform union representative functions on the shopfloor: alternative channels of union workplace representation such as shop stewards do not exist. What makes the devolution of shopfloor representation especially attractive to the unions is that, in performing functions on the unions' behalf, works councils can make use of their legally privileged position, and their protection from discriminatory treatment by the employer. Works councils are the backbone of the unions, providing them with organizational essentials such as collecting dues, explaining union policy, and supplying union officials with information on employees' opinions and morale. Above all, works councils play a key role in recruiting members: as a rule, density is notably higher in establishments which have a works council than in those which do not.

Thus there are two basic structural channels through which interests are processed and unified. The formalized one is a modified industrial unionism. According to their sectoral and occupational affiliation, employees are grouped in ÖGB unions. These in turn send delegates to the ÖGB federal congress and its general executive committee. The second, informal channel, based on political differentiation by factions, cross-cuts the first one by pre-determining policy formation in the ÖGB and its member unions. In addition to this doubly structured interest aggregation, there is some scope for articulating interests that are neither sectoral/occupational nor ideological. Thus interests of women and young people are institutionalized through specific organizational arrangements and participation rights (for example, sending delegates to representative bodies) in the ÖGB and in most unions. The unions' concern with these groups reflects their difficulties in recruiting them: while union density for male workers was 67 per cent in 1989, only 43 per cent of women workers were unionized.

Citizenship is criterion that, unlike gender and age, has not found an institutional expression in unions. This particularly affects the position of foreign workers. A discriminatory provision allows foreign workers to vote in works council elections, but not to be nominated as candidates; this results in their complete exclusion from representation on union bodies.

Union Policy and Legitimation Patterns

Austria's unions are unusual not only in their structure, but also their policy. They have adopted an extremely consistent position based on long-term cooperation with capital. The ÖGB's main goal has always been to preserve employment by promoting economic growth. Economic growth also allows for increases in incomes without generating conflict with capital over income redistribution. Accordingly, productivity is the guiding principle of Austria's wage policy. Over the last three decades, real wages and total productivity both increased by 3.5 per cent a year on average (Guger 1990a). Employment problems in the 1980s were reflected in increases in real wages slightly below the rate of growth of total productivity, causing a shift in income distribution in favour of capital (see table 8.3). By giving employment priority over wage increases, the ÖGB succeeded in keeping unemployment lower than in most other countries, but it failed to realize its distributional goal of a solidaristic wage policy. Wages differ more between sectors than in other countries (Guger 1990b).

Despite considerable continuity, union policy has responded to changes in the balance of political power. The single-party social-democratic government in the 1970s shared the unions' primary commitment to full

Table 8.3 Main indicators of Austrian economic development 1955–89

	Real GDP	Inflation[1,2]	Unemployment[3]	Real per capita income of employees[1]	Labour's share in total national income[4]
1955	11.5	0.8	5.4	6.6	68.6
1956	6.2	3.5	5.1	5.3	68.6
1957	5.8	2.2	4.7	5.1	67.8
1958	3.7	2.3	5.1	2.3	67.7
1959	3.1	1.1	4.6	3.9	67.6
1960	8.6	1.9	3.5	5.6	65.4
1961	5.3	3.6	2.7	5.0	65.5
1962	2.4	4.4	2.7	3.9	66.6
1963	4.1	2.7	2.9	5.2	66.4
1964	6.0	3.8	2.7	4.4	66.4
1965	3.0	5.0	2.7	2.6	66.6
1966	5.1	2.2	2.5	6.7	66.8
1967	2.8	4.0	2.7	5.1	67.7
1968	4.1	2.8	2.9	4.1	67.2
1969	5.5	3.1	2.8	3.0	66.1
1970	6.4	4.4	2.4	2.3	64.0
1971	5.1	4.7	2.1	7.6	65.4
19722	6.2	6.3	1.9	3.7	64.6
1973	4.9	7.6	1.6	6.0	65.9
1974	3.9	9.5	1.5	2.5	65.8
1975	−0.4	8.4	2.0	4.7	68.6
1976	4.6	7.3	2.0	0.1	67.4
1977	4.5	5.5	1.8	1.1	67.9
1978	0.1	3.6	2.1	−0.4	69.6
1979	4.7	3.7	2.0	1.9	67.6
1980	2.9	6.4	1.9	−0.4	67.3
1981	−0.3	6.8	2.4	−0.4	68.9
1982	1.1	5.4	3.7	0.5	67.2
1983	2.0	3.3	4.5	1.1	66.2
1984	1.4	5.6	4.5	−2.4	66.0
1985	2.5	3.2	4.8	0.6	65.6
1986	1.1	1.7	5.2	3.5	65.4
1987	1.9	1.4	5.6	3.4	65.5
1988	4.2	2.0	5.3	-	-
1989	3.8	2.5	5.0	-	-

[1] percentage change per year
[2] consumer prices
[3] percentage of total labour force
[4] adjusted for the change in dependent employment to total employment (1970=100)
Source: Österreichisches Institut für Wirtschaftsforschung.

employment. Thus the ÖGB could turn to the government to achieve its employment goals (as well as other improvements in workers' living standards). Since 1983, when the social democrats lost their absolute majority and were forced to form a multi-party government, the ÖGB's influence on policy has decreased. At the same time, the coalition governments placed a lower priority on full employment. The unions have concentrated on negotiating shorter working hours as a way of combating growing unemployment. With agreements reached in several sectors, the ÖGB has been calling for a general agreement on the 35-hour week.

All in all, its cooperation with capital and the state has strongly oriented the ÖGB towards quantitative, macro-economic goals. By comparison, qualitative goals relating to workplace problems are clearly of secondary importance. Job control scarcely figures on the collective bargaining agenda in Austria. There is only one collective agreement, in printing, regulating the introduction of new technology. When the ÖGB addresses the question of new technology, it does so mainly with reference to industrial policy and international competitiveness rather than to its workplace implications (Traxler 1988). There are several reasons for this. Qualitative demands are more likely to provoke conflict with employers; while centralized unionism and collective bargaining is remote from employees' experience in the workplace.

It would be no exaggeration to say that a 'cooperative bias' is built into unionism. Three structural elements foster inter-class cooperation. First, representational monopoly and unity make it nearly impossible to externalize the costs (for example, of increased inflation and unemployment) of a conflict-oriented policy; and the absence of competition for members facilitates union restraint. Second, internal political differentiation exposes decision-making to strong pressures for consensus. Generally, this works in favour of cooperative policies. Third, the establishment of the works council as the union representative in the workplace has also encouraged cooperation.

All these structures support the formulation, but not necessarily the implementation, of cooperative policies. The most serious implementation problems arise over securing employee commitment to union goals (i.e. joining the union and complying with its policies). The more centralized policy-making becomes, the fewer the opportunities for participation; and the more union policy is oriented toward the technocratic requirements of macro-economic management, the less it can be related to the immediate interests of workers.

Nevertheless, Austrian unions achieve a high degree of membership conformity, as several indicators demonstrate. Above all, they have enjoyed a high membership density throughout the post-war period (see table 8.4). In terms of class consciousness, Austrian workers rank very high according to an international comparison in the 1960s and early 1970s (Lane and Ersson 1987). Class consciousness was, however, well-attuned to union policy: in contrast to many other countries, such as

Table 8.4 Selected data on unionism in Austria 1955–89

	Total membership[1]	Density ratio[2]
1955	1,398,446	67.5
1956	1,427,301	66.8
1957	1,438,755	65.8
1958	1,458,310	66.2
1959	1,474,929	66.0
1960	1,501,047	65.8
1961	1,518,004	65.4
1962	1,518,096	64.9
1963	1,531,695	65.4
1964	1,539,586	65.1
1965	1,542,813	64.8
1966	1,542,979	64.6
1967	1,512,405	65.1
1968	1,514,016	64.7
1969	1,517,124	64.4
1970	1,520,259	63.6
1971	1,526,364	62.2
1972	1,542,042	61.4
1973	1,559,513	59.8
1974	1,580,357	59.5
1975	1,587,500	59.8
1976	1,604,668	59.7
1977	1,619,103	59.2
1978	1,628,803	59.1
1979	1,641,475	59.2
1980	1,660,985	59.6
1981	1,677,265	59.9
1982	1,672,509	60.5
1983	1,660,453	60.7
1984	1,672,820	61.0
1985	1,671,381	60.6
1986	1,671,217	60.1
1987	1,652,839	59.3
1988	1,677,265	59.7
1989	1,644,408	57.5

[1] at end of year
[2] percentage of all employees
Source: *Tätigkeitsberichte des ÖGB*, Traxler (1982; 1988).

Germany, widespread waves of worker militancy and unofficial strikes did not occur in Austria during the late 1960s and early 1970s.

Austrian unions have several means of securing employee conformity. For the reasons already mentioned, the highly 'pillarized' political culture helps to legitimize union policy. Unions are also able to encourage employee conformity by offering selective goods: financial benefits (e.g. for strikes, accidents and unemployment), representation in labour court proceedings, individual advice, and training courses. But such benefits are of secondary importance compared with union security and organizational privileges guaranteed by the state and employers; for example, the encouragement of union membership through the recruitment activities of works councils, check-off arrangements for the payment of subscriptions (which are tax-deductible), and the pre-eminent role of unions in collective pay determination. In consequence, employees' support for unions seems to be somewhat decoupled from their interests. According to a study on foreign workers (BMfSV n. d.) 56 per cent of these workers were unionized in 1983 but 66 per cent said that the unions were not representing their interests or that they did not know what the unions were doing for them. Finally, the unions seldom organize strikes since they pursue their goals through centralized negotiations with employers and the state. Thus they only rarely need their members' active support.

Employers

The Structure of Capital and the Organization of Employers' Associations

In terms of performance and ownership, Austria's economy displays great contrasts. Those industrial sectors that are highly integrated into the world market achieved the same level of productivity as their West German counterparts in 1990; in the 1970s their productivity had been only 40 per cent of the Germans'. However, the productivity of the sheltered sectors is still only two-thirds of the German level.

A very large public sector comprises state authorities and nationalized enterprises. In 1978 about 29 per cent of employees in Austrian industry worked in enterprises where the state held a majority share; for financial institutions, the figure was 47 per cent (see tables 8.5 and 8.6). The relative weakness and fragmentation of domestic private capital is underscored by the fact that nationalized enterprises are the largest firms in Austria and that, in contrast to other small countries, no multinational enterprise has its home base in Austria.

Generally, Austrian firms are very small. In 1983, the average firm size in the manufacturing sector was 12 employees. In 1973, establishments employing 1,000 or more accounted for 27.6 per cent of total employment in Austrian industry, compared with 38.7 per cent in West Germany (Aiginger and Tichy 1982: 11); there is a lack of satisfactory comparative data for more recent years.

With their large size and their subordination to government and the 'big four' (especially the ÖGB), public enterprises have dominated industrial relations and have long set the pace for improving pay and working conditions. In the 1970s, nationalized enterprises played an important role in maintaining full employment by hoarding excess labour (e.g.

Table 8.5   The Austrian economy by type of ownership (%). Plants with 20 or more employees 1978

Majority of capital	Share of employees			
	Industry	Finance	Insurance	Trade
Private domestic	33.8	50.4	20.0	73.0
Private foreign	22.5	2.0	49.2	23.7
Public	28.4	47.2	30.3	2.4
Others	15.3	0.4	0.5	0.9
Total	100.0	100.0	100.0	100.0

Source: Ederer et al. (1985).

Andrlik 1984). During the 1980s, they were increasingly beset by economic problems, which made massive state subsidies necessary for their survival. Although restructuring since the late 1980s seems to have been successful, the large nationalized enterprises have lost their pace-setting role in industrial relations. Job losses and privatization have reduced nationalized industry's share of employment (table 8.6).

The fragmentation and relative weakness of capital contrasts sharply with the unique degree of unity and organizational strength of the central employers' association. According to data from an international comparative study on business associations (OBI 1985), the BWK is Europe's most comprehensive, well-resourced and politically influential association. It has more resources relative not only to country size, but also in absolute terms. For instance, in 1980 the BWK's office staff (4,665 employees) was 58 times higher and its total revenues (AS3.6 billion) about 36 times higher than the principal West German employers' association, the BDA.

The co-existence of weak and fragmented capital and a strong, unified business association is no coincidence. The high degree of *associational* concentration and centralization compensates politically for the low degree of *economic* concentration and centralization; small firms, more than large ones, need both the collective interest representation and individual consultancy provided by associations. The centralization of business organization in Austria may also be seen as a development stimulated by the extraordinarily comprehensive and centralized character of Austrian unions.

As the BWK and its subunits negotiate on behalf of nearly all sections of employers, it is worth dealing in more detail with the BWK's constituency, structures and policy. The BWK has a public status insofar as it is

Table 8.6   Austria's 100 largest industrial enterprises by type of ownership (%)

Type of ownership	Number of enterprises		Share in employment	
	1979	*1988*	*1979*	*1988*
Private domestic	39	39	17.4	25.7
Private foreign	29	30	19.4	25.8
Public	27	26	62.2	47.4
Cooperative	5	5	1,0	1.1
Total	100	100	100.0	100.0

Source: Karazman-Morawetz (1991).

established by a special law that regulates its coverage, organizational structure and tasks. All firms in the BWK's domain are legally required to be members. Thus it embraces all privately and publicly owned firms in industry, the artisan sector, commerce, banking and insurance, transport and tourism; agriculture and the non-trading public sector are the main parts of the economy outside the BWK's domain. In 1983, the organization had 256,700 member firms which together employed 65.5 per cent of all Austrian employees.

The BWK is the peak of a complex chamber system with a two-dimensional, matrix organization (Traxler 1986). The first dimension is based on Austria's territorial differentiation. For each of the nine *Länder* of the Austrian federal state, a special territorial chamber exists. The second dimension focuses on sectors and branches. BWK members are grouped by product market, which allows them to form subunits for different subsectors of activity. They are incorporated into the territorial chambers as well as into the BWK. Within the BWK nationally there are more than 130 sectoral subunits, and more than 1,200 such subunits exist within the territorial chambers. The regional organizations are the basic units of the whole chamber system, articulating and aggregating territorial as well as sectoral interests. In addition, it is in these subunits that member firms directly participate.

Members elect the representatives of their respective territorial sector subunit. Other representatives are not elected directly by members but are appointed in a hierarchical process beginning with the territorial sector subunits and continuing up to leadership positions in the BWK. Lists of candidates are mainly presented by political parties; thus elections serve as the link connecting the chamber with the party system. About 70–85 per cent of the representatives directly elected by members are affiliated to the conservative party, and 8–15 per cent to the SPÖ.

Given the high degree of internal differentiation, the division of responsibilities is especially important for coordinated collective action. The chamber system follows the principle of *Subsidiarität*, that matters should be dealt with at a level as close to the members as possible. However, this principle is qualified insofar as a unit is autonomous only in dealing with matters exclusively affecting the interests of its own members. If members of other units are affected, responsibility must be transferred to the higher-level body whose domain covers all members involved. As a result of the highly centralized mode of public policy and industrial relations in Austria, many responsibilities are concentrated at the top level of the BWK.

The BWK is both a trade association and an employers' organization, as it represents business interests in the product as well as the labour market. This is one important precondition for macro-corporatist concertation, which deals with product-market and labour-market interests in an integrated way. The BWK enjoys a legally guaranteed right to be consulted by government on all economic and social matters. This privileged position is further strengthened by the authorities' preference for dealing with the BWK rather than with other business associations.

The BWK also comes close to having a representational monopoly in collective bargaining. About 95 per cent of all collective agreements are signed on behalf of business under the umbrella of the BWK. Here too, the division of labour between the BWK and its subunits is based on the principle of *Subsidiarität*. This means that the BWK itself negotiates collective agreements only when they have generalized coverage. Other collective bargaining is left to the sectoral subunits within the chamber. They sign agreements partly on behalf of particular subgroups of members, partly on behalf of their membership as a whole, and they sometimes form a common bargaining committee with other closely related sectoral subunits. Collective bargaining is conducted on behalf of both public and private firms in the same sector. Nationalized industry's pace-setting role in industrial relations derived from the granting of additional concessions through intra-firm bargaining.

Although subunits have collective bargaining autonomy on matters relating to their specific domain, their activities are coordinated by the BWK by means of a continuous exchange of information. Vertical coordination by the BWK is supplemented by horizontal coordinating efforts among sectoral subunits negotiating separately on behalf of contiguous business groups, in order to prevent business groups from being played off against each other.

The agreements concluded by the BWK and its subunits do not cover all their members, some 4–5 per cent of whom remain outside these agreements. The chamber acts on behalf of these members only as a trade association. Historically, their labour-market interests have been represented by specialized employers' associations based on voluntary membership. Since the chamber is the representative of nearly all employers, special inter-associational coordination is not necessary. The other employers' organizations tend to base their policies on the collective agreements concluded by the chamber.

Employers' Strategies and Intra-Firm Labour Management

Individual employers generally have a free hand in personnel management: unions are little concerned with qualitative, workplace-related issues for the reasons outlined above. Successful firms also have considerable autonomy on pay and working hours, since unions' quantitative demands are geared to the productivity performance of a sector or of the economy as a whole. This autonomy, which is upheld by labour law, is reflected in pay drift; for example, actual earnings for blue-collar workers were 26 per cent above pay rates in 1988 (BWK 1989). Research (Traxler 1991) suggests that the ArbVG exerts a downward 'ratchet effect' on interest representation by the works council. On the one hand, the law confines works council activities to narrowly defined issues, which must be dealt with in a cooperative manner. On the other, the works council's ability to exploit its rights depends significantly on union strength, and particularly on a high union density in the enterprise.

Given this room for manoeuvre, it is not surprising that some multinationals use their Austrian subsidiaries as a site for testing strategic approaches to human resource management and the restructuring of work organization. A notable example was General Motors' introduction of a new form of work organization based on integrated working teams in its plant in Aspern in the 1980s (Streeck 1987). While an anti-unionist objective often underlies human resource management approaches, in this case the metalworking union was able to enforce the right to be fully involved in the project through its unionized works councillors. In general, multinationals have been in the forefront of introducing human resource management in Austria, with domestic firms following suit. Cooperation with the works council is also the norm. Companies have placed special emphasis on establishing quality circles, granting white-collar status to all employees, setting up internal training programmes and introducing performance-related pay.

In recent bargaining rounds, employers have called for increases in basic rates to be split into a fixed and a flexible (performance-related) component. This has been rejected by the unions, and wage flexibility remains an issue to be dealt with at the level of the individual enterprise. There is a strong tendency among larger firms to distribute additional remuneration (in excess of collectively negotiated rates) according to performance-related criteria. This has increasingly affected white-collar employees (Gewerkschaft der Privatangestellten 1990), eroding seniority as the main criterion of pay differentiation.

A long-term approach to industrial relations is the exception rather than the rule among Austrian companies. Given the small size of most firms, scarcity of resources constrains strategic planning. The high degree of juridification and the representational monopoly of the ÖGB further reduce the scope for firms to make strategic choices in industrial relations. However, although employers may not be able to affect the institutional framework of industrial relations, they can decisively influence its practical application within the firm. Employers have formal and informal ways of influencing the establishment and subsequent operation of the works council. Informally, management can attempt to prevent employees from setting up a works council. Formally, companies can avoid the legislation by dividing themselves into subunits with fewer than five employees: this has been the strategy adopted by some large retail firms. Nevertheless, as industrial relations are highly cooperative, most firms (especially large ones in the core industrial sectors) have learned to value unions and works councils as guarantors of social peace. One expression of this is management assistance in the collection of union subscriptions.

In the past, employers have never publicly questioned the basic structure of Austrian industrial relations. However, in recent years, some have called for deregulation and increased flexibility of employment relations, echoing the international trend. These demands focus on flexible pay and working hours, the easing of regulations protecting young people at work, and the removal of restrictions in the domestic labour market.

Employers' interests are by no means unequivocal. For example, the majority of small retail firms are opposed to more flexible business hours. There is also evidence that employers fail to take advantage of the opportunities for increased flexibility that already exist. An investigation (Traxler 1990b) in printing and engineering showed that firms have hardly used the scope for more flexible working hours provided in recent sectoral agreements but prefer conventional, rigid working-time arrangements. Empirical studies also indicate that Austrian firms fail to exploit the potential of new electronic office technology, tending to apply it in ways that reproduce conventional patterns of work organization (e.g. Aichholzer et al. 1987).

The 'conventional' approach to personnel management in Austrian firms reflects the properties of the Austrian economy described above. First, small firms often do not have the skills and resources to apply flexibility options effectively. In any case, they are generally less bureaucratic and more adaptable than large ones. Consequently, small firms are likely to be less dependent than large firms on a formalized strategy for achieving flexibility. Second, the fact that large parts of the economy are sheltered from international competition diminishes the need to follow the world-wide trend towards deregulation and flexibility.

However, the process of European integration, especially the completion of the single European market in 1992, is likely to reduce the insulation of Austrian employers from international trends. In 1989, the Austrian government formally applied for EC membership. This issue has renewed the division between export-oriented and protectionist business interests. As Austrian industry has been in full competition with EC firms since the 1972 free trade agreement, the export and import-competing sectors have long since paid the price for achieving international competitiveness, and the business association representing export interests was one of the first bodies to call for Austria to apply for Community membership. The clash between this group and the powerful sheltered sector, which will come under increased pressure if Austria joins the EC, has once again led the export-oriented groups to seek the support of organized labour for their policy objectives (Traxler 1990c).

Main Patterns of Industrial Relations

The well-tuned institutional framework has given rise to highly ordered industrial relations. Incomes are regulated by the Parity Commission setting the limits for collective bargaining. Unions and employers' associations have jointly to apply for the Commission's approval before renegotiating collective agreements. The Commission thus controls the timing of bargaining rounds, but does not influence their agenda or outcome. Given that the ÖGB and the BWK are the Commission's key members and that nearly all bargaining associations are under the umbrella of either the ÖGB or BWK, the Commission's governance capacities ultimately rest on the ability of the two peak organizations to control their affiliates.

Economy-wide bargaining is conducted by the ÖGB and BWK themselves; their agreements regulate especially important issues, and cover almost all private employment outside agriculture. Customarily, collective bargaining takes place at the 'meso-level' of branches and sectors. Agreements cover either the entire country or specific regions. Very few collective agreements are fixed on behalf of a single enterprise.

Bargaining in the different sectors is spread over the whole year, and separate negotiations for blue- and white-collar workers in the same sector are generally synchronized. Agreements reached in the metalworking industry set the pace for bargaining rounds in other sectors.

Collectively agreed employment conditions cover nearly all employees. In the private sector, 90 per cent of employees are within the scope of a collective agreement. Working conditions in the public sector are generally determined by negotiations between unions and state authorities.

As a rule, the bargaining process is peaceful: Austria has very few strikes or lockouts (see table 8.7). Even short demonstration strikes in the context of bargaining rounds are unusual. This reflects the bargaining associations' commitment to a productivity-oriented wage policy and their strong internal discipline.

Over and above what is agreed in national and sectoral collective bargaining, prosperous firms are able to grant their employees better working conditions than are fixed by standard rates. These extra benefits

Table 8.7 Industrial disputes in Austria 1955–89

| | Workers involved | | | Share of non-union |
	Total	per 1000 employees	Work hours lost	strikes in work hours lost
1955	26,011	12.5	464,167	15.6
1956	43,249	20.2	1,227,292	0.8
1957	19,555	9.0	364,841	4.5
1958	28,745	13.1	349,811	4.7
1959	47,007	21.0	404,290	41.1
1960	30,654	13.4	550,582	26.3
1961	38,338	16.5	911,025	9.9
1962	207,459	88.6	5,181,762	0.1
1963	16,501	7.1	272,134	-
1964	40,843	17.3	283,588	22.1
1965	146,009	61.3	3,387,787	0.3
1966	120,922	50.7	570,846	8.7
1967	7,496	3.2	131,285	0.6
1968	3,129	1.3	53,365	6.3
1969	17,449	7.4	148,139	3.1
1970	7,547	3.2	212,928	22.1
1971	2,431	1.0	29,614	74.5
1972	7,096	2.8	120,832	17.8
1973	78,251	30.0	794,119	12.1
1974	7,295	2.8	57,948	77.9
1975	3,783	1.4	44,098	5.9
1976	2,352	0.9	4,711	45.3
1977	43	0.0	86	0.0
1978	699	0.3	81,778	0.6
1979	786	0.3	6,111	13.3
1980	24,181	8.7	135,684	0.0
1981	17,115	6.1	32,188	1.4
1982	91	0.0	2,755	1.1
1983	208	0.1	4,115	0.6
1984	268	0.1	4,349	0.0
1985	35,531	9.8	182,019	0.0
1986	3,222	1.2	26,023	0.0
1987	7,203	2.6	38,575	0.0
1988	24,252	8.6	68,335	8.0
1989	3,715	1.3	23,887	0.0

Source: Tätigkeitsberichte des ÖGB, Traxler (1982; 1988).

are conceded either unilaterally by management, or settled in negotiations where an effective works council exists. In large enterprises, a second bargaining round often occurs, customarily resulting in a plant agreement. Since works councils are not formally authorized to negotiate on wage increases, they can only conclude informal (i.e. legally unenforceable) plant agreements on this issue (Traxler 1982). This is tolerated by the associations since it permits a flexible adaptation of wages to the business cycle and to company performance. Other informal arrangements most frequently concern the introduction of flexible working time and performance-related pay schemes.

This divergence between formal and informal procedures arises from two phenomena: 'plant egoism' (implying a conflict between the plant-specific interests of employees and supra-plant arrangements); and the 'ratchet effect' of codetermination outlined above, in which a works council is typically forced to tolerate a lax enforcement of the legal rules in exchange for other rights or informal concessions (Traxler 1991). Even this form of political exchange demonstrates how much informal procedures are bound to the formal framework defined by the ArbVG, since the works council's ultimate power resource is the legal enforceability of its rights. To create informal opportunities for bargaining, a works council can deliberately refrain from enforcing *certain* rules only to the extent that this does not generally endanger compliance with labour law as its basic power resource. Hence, the room for informal negotiations is rather limited.

Prospects and Conclusions

The Austrian industrial relations system has faced far fewer challenges than most other European countries. Just as workers' militancy was absent in the 1960s and 1970s, so were anti-union strategies in the 1980s. No attempt to redesign the system has been made by the state, employers or unions.

It would be misleading to see this stability as evidence of institutional rigidity: there are good reasons to suppose that a system survives in the long term only if it can adapt to changes in its environment. An indication of the Austrian system's adaptability is the smooth management of the restructuring of nationalized industry, largely through early retirement schemes. There are several important elements of flexibility in the Austrian model. First, there is a cooperative policy orientation. Governments and employers attempted to restructure industrial relations in the 1980s mainly in those countries where the system was seen as an obstacle to competitiveness; but in Austria, the actors have consistently oriented their policies towards economic performance. Second, the autonomy of employers in the management of labour enables them to respond flexibly to increased competition. Thus there is little incentive to change the system. It is no accident that even multinational enterprises are well integrated into this system since – together with the relatively high skill level of the labour force – social peace is one of the main reasons that they invest in Austria (Glatz and Moser 1989). In addition, capital's relative weakness would make any attempt to restructure the system in its own favour a high risk strategy.

The system's persistence has until now been based on a specific distribution of interests and of power. The unusual strength of both capital and labour at the supra-plant, associational level is combined with the weakness of capital in the economy and of labour representatives in the workplace. The system's future continuity, however, will depend not only on its adaptability, but also on the scale of the challenges that confront it. Several potential sources of instability may be identified.

First, the easing of labour market regulation in 1990 has made entry to the labour market easier for foreign workers who are now entering Austria in large numbers from former Eastern bloc countries. Second, since the mid-1980s, there have been a number of sectoral collective agreements combining flexibility and a reduction in weekly working hours. Unprecedented responsibilities for specific arrangements for working hours have been devolved by the bargaining associations to management and works councils; such decentralization is likely to continue in future. Third, the crisis of the nationalized industries has prompted a change in ownership: minority stakes have been sold to private investors, and the government now plans to sell the majority of stock in all state-owned enterprises. The effect will be to reduce the economic stabilizing role traditionally played by Austria's public enterprises. Fourth, trends and pressures in the international economy are reducing the freedom of manoeuvre of both the state and the associations. In line with world-wide trends, cutting the public deficit has become an increasingly important government priority, even at the cost of full employment. This has resulted in rising unemployment since the early 1980s; in recent years, employment levels have been stabilized only in years of high economic growth (see table 8.3 above). Import penetration has undermined the Parity Commission's ability to control prices. The internationalization of product markets is the major factor behind Austria's application for EC membership.

Finally, there are also sources of uncertainty in the political system. An erosion of the main political camps in response to shifts in the occupational structure, particularly the growth of white-collar employment and the service sector, has paved the way for the 'individualization' of values. The trend is most clearly seen in the dramatic rise in the proportion of floating voters in elections, accompanied by the formation of a more competitive party system in which populist and green parties confront the two traditional political camps. Through their political affiliation to the two camps the 'big four' are affected by these developments (Traxler 1990b). Externally, state support and thus continuity in political exchange has become much more uncertain for them. Internally, the main parties' contribution to legitimizing associational policies has been qualified. Even more importantly, individualization is likely to pose a future threat to compulsory membership of the chambers and is also making it more difficult for the unions to recruit (especially young workers, women and white-collar employees in the private sector).

All these tendencies inevitably strain the governance capacity of macro-corporatism in general and the power of the unions in particular. However, each kind of challenge differs in its destabilizing potential. Deregulation and decentralization seem to be of secondary importance: deregulation of barriers to labour market entry in favour of foreign workers was enacted on the basis of a macro-corporatist accord; while the decentralization of the regulation of working hours was managed within a binding framework established by the bargaining parties (Maurer et al. 1990). The other challenges are more serious. In the face of surveys showing that 66 per cent of Austria's population are opposed to compulsory membership (*Der Standard*, 17 September 1990), political competition may force the parties to heed the populist call for the abolition of the principle of compulsion. This would immediately change the 'rules of the game'. Internationalization poses a rather more long-term threat to the system's stability, regardless of whether Austria becomes an EC member. The more Austria's markets are opened up to international competition, the more capital's power position *vis-à-vis* labour will be strengthened and 'normalized' relative to other European countries. As table 8.6 shows, large privately-owned companies have continuously increased their economic weight over the last decade. Mergers and take-overs in advance of the single market, as well as further privatization, will accentuate the dominance of large firms. This development will make Austrian firms as independent as those in other countries of labour's support in advancing their interests; thus the central prerequisite for Austria's macro-corporatism and for labour's key role in the system may be eroded.

Abbreviations

ArbVG	*Arbeitsverfassungsgesetz* – Labour Constitution Law
BDA	*Bundesvereinigung der Deutschen Arbeitgeberverbände* – Federal Confederation of the German Employers' Associations
BWK	*Bundeskammer der gewerblichen Wirtschaft* – Federal Chamber of Business
EC	European Community
ÖAKT	*Österreichischer Arbeiterkammertag* – Austrian Central Chamber of Labour
ÖGB	*Österreichischer Gewerkschaftsbund* – Austrian Trade Union Federation
SPÖ	*Sozialdemokratische Partei Österreichs* – Austrian Social Democratic Party.

References

Aichholzer, G., Flecker, J. and Schienstock, G. 1987: *Informationstechnologien im Angestelltenbereich*. Vienna: Studie im Auftrag des Bundesministeriums für Wissenschaft und Forschung.

Aiginger, K. and Tichy, G. 1982: Entwicklungstendenzen der Klein- und Mittelbetriebe in den achtziger Jahren. Sonderheft *Politische Studien*, 5–123.

Andrlik, E. 1984: Die Sozialpartnerschaft in der Wirtschaftskrise: Der Fall VEW (1975–1984). *Journal für Sozialforschung*, 24, 4, 395–421.

BMfSV (ed.) n. d.: *Ausländische Arbeitnehmer in Österreich*. Vienna: BMfSV.

BWK 1989: *Jahrbuch der österreichischen Wirtschaft 1988*. Vienna: BWK.

Ederer, B., Goldmann, W., Reiterlechner, C., Reitzner, R. N. and Wehsely, H. 1985: Eigentumsverhältnisse der österreichischen Wirtschaft. Sonderheft *Wirtschaft und Gesellschaft*.

Gewerkschaft der Privatangestellten (ed.) 1990: *Leistung ohne Seniorität?* Regensburg: Transfer Verlag.

Glatz, H. and Moser, H. 1989: Ausländische Direktinvestitionen und Industriepolitik. *Wirtschaft und Gesellschaft*, 15, 1, 33–61.

Guger, A. 1990a: Einkommens- und Produktivitätsgefälle gegenüber Westeuropa verringert. *Monatsberichte*, 63, 2, 74–8.

Guger, A. 1990b: Verteilungspolitik als Strukturpolitik. In Beigewum/Memorandum-Gruppe (eds.), *Steuerungsprobleme der Wirtschaftspolitik*, Vienna, Bremen: Eigenverlag, 93–104.

Karazman-Morawetz, I. 1991: Wirtschaftsmacht und politischer Einfluß (mit einem Exkurs von G. Pleschiutschnig). In H. Dachs et al. (eds.), *Handbuch des Politischen Systems Österreichs*, Vienna: Manz, 377–89.

Kramer, H. 1984: Ansatzpunkte für eine Steigerung der österreichischen Exportquote. Paper prepared for the Volkswirtschaftliche Tagung der Österreichischen Nationalbank in Baden bei Wien.

Lane, J.-E. and Ersson, S. 1987: *Politics and Society in Western Europe*. London: Sage.

Lachs, T. 1976: *Wirtschaftspartnerschaft in Österreich*. Vienna: ÖGB.

Lash, S. and Urry, J. 1987: *The End of Organized Capitalism*. Oxford: Polity Press.

Maurer, A., Moser, U., Perchinig, B., Pirker, R. and Traxler, F. 1990: *Arbeitszeit zwischen Verkürzung und Flexibilisierung*. Vienna: BMfAS.

OBI 1985: Data-Set of the 'Organization of Business Interests' Project (MRDF). Berlin/Florence.

Polt, W. 1988: 'Einige kritische Thesen zur EG-Integration Österreichs. *Kurswechsel*, 3, 8–11.

Schmitter, P. 1981: Interest Intermediation and Regime Governability in contemporary Western Europe and North America. In S. Berger (ed.), *Organizing Interests in Western Europe*, Cambridge: Cambridge University Press, 287–327.

Sisson, K. 1979: The Organisation of Employers' Associations in Five European Countries: Some Comments on their Origins and Development. Paper prepared for the International Institute of Management Workshop on 'Employers' Associations as Organisations', Berlin, 14–16 November 1979.

Streeck, W. 1987: Neue Formen der Arbeitsorganisation im internationalen Vergleich. *Wirtschaft und Gesellschaft*, 13, 3, 317–335.

Traxler, F. 1982: *Evolution gewerkschaftlicher Interessenvertretung. Entwicklungslogik und Organisationsdynamik gewerkschaftlichen Handelns am Beispiel Österreich*. Frankfurt/Vienna: Braumüller/Campus.

Traxler, F. 1985: Arbeitgeberverbände. In G.Endruweit, E.Gaugler, W.H. Staehle and B. Wilpert (eds), *Handbuch der Arbeitsbeziehungen*, Berlin, New York: De Gruyter, 51–64.

Traxler, F. 1986: *Interessenverbände der Unternehmer*. Frankfurt/New York: Campus.

Traxler, F. 1987: Klassenstruktur, Korporatismus und Krise. *Politische Vierteljahresschrift*, 28, 59–79.

Traxler, F. 1988: Von der Hegemonie in die Defensive. Österreichs Gewerkschaften im System der Sozialpartnerschaft. In W. Müller-Jentsch (ed.) *Zukunft der Gewerkschaften. Ein internationaler Vergleich*, Frankfurt/New York: Campus, 45–69.

Traxler, F. 1989: Business Associations and Labor Unions in Comparison. Theoretical Perspectives and Empirical Findings on Social Class, Collective Action and Associational Organizability. Unpublished Paper.

Traxler, F. 1990a: Political Exchange, Collective Action and Interest Governance. Towards a Theory of the Genesis of Industrial Relations and Corporatism. In B. Marin (ed.), *Governance and Generalized Exchange. Self-Organizing Policy Networks in Action*, Frankfurt/Boulder: Campus-Westview, 37–67.

Traxler, F. 1990b: Sectoral Working Time Policy and its Implementation at Firm Level. Paper prepared for the third Conference of the 'International Symposium on Working Time (ISWT),' Vienna, 12–15 December 1989.

Traxler, F. 1990c: Interests, Politics, and European Integration. Forthcoming in *European Journal for Political Research*.

Traxler, F. 1991: Mitbestimmung und ökonomisch-technischer Strukturwandel. In H. Diefenbacher and H. G. Nutzinger (eds), *Mitbestimmung in Europa*, Heidelberg: FEST, 131–58.

Visser, J. 1984: The Position of Central Confederations in the National Union Movement. A Ten-Country Comparison. European University Institute Working Paper no. 102.

9

Switzerland: Still as Smooth as Clockwork?

Beat Hotz-Hart[1]

Introduction

Switzerland is one of the smaller European countries (though third largest of the seven EFTA members). A stable democracy, neutral in both world wars, its institutions – including those of industrial relations – have displayed relatively few radical changes during the present century. Internal pluralism is symbolized by the confederal political system, with the 26 cantons and sub-cantons enjoying considerable autonomy. German, French and Italian are all official languages; but German is spoken by over two-thirds of the population, and in this chapter Swiss institutions are therefore referred to only in that language.

Maintaining social and political unity despite diversity has depended on a complex pluralistic system of interest accommodation. This has certainly been true of industrial relations. In contrast to the unitary representational models of Germany and Austria, Switzerland is characterized by inter-organizational competition. Nevertheless, differences both within and between the two sides of industry are normally resolved peacefully; industrial conflict is almost non-existent.

The Swiss system of industrial relations is characterized by a structure of social partnership, which dates from the 1937 'peace accord' in the engineering industry. Neither freedom of association nor the right to strike (and, as a counterpart, the right to lockout) are explicitly enshrined in the Swiss constitution or legal system. Conditions of employment in the private sector are settled by negotiation between employers' associations and trade unions or employee associations. Voluntarism has been practised in Switzerland in an exemplary way and with a high sense of responsibility.

The Economic Background

Swiss prosperity is based primarily on technological know-how and skills. By international standards manufacturing remains relatively central to the Swiss economy, accounting for 25 per cent of total (and 30 per cent of male) employment in 1990. What is notable, however, is that Swiss industry has never rested on the mass production of a narrow range of products; and it still reflects its origins in craft traditions, remaining heterogeneous and diversified, and therefore more broadly based than, for instance, Swedish manufacturing. Most products are small-batch, customer-oriented specialized items of high quality and reliability, supported by prompt delivery and excellent after-sales service. The Swiss economy is to a very high extent internationalized and focused on foreign trade, but primarily oriented to market niches not as yet penetrated by large enterprises.

In percentage terms the Swiss economy is one of the most research-intensive in the world, yet in absolute terms the amounts spent on R&D are relatively modest: comparable with the budgets of IBM or GM. Switzerland is therefore unable either to instigate technological developments or to achieve a leading position simultaneously in a number of key technologies. Its competitive edge lies in the role of 'first user', the intelligent first application of new technologies. It is therefore in its interest at least to have a presence in key technologies in order to spot new developments at an early stage and to make use of their potential.

A particular strength of the Swiss economy is a work force which is skilled but not academically qualified, technicians with considerable specialist knowledge as well as craftsmen. The associated industrial-commercial culture sustains a high degree of work discipline and morale, quality awareness, reliability and accumulated expertise. These qualities are geographically fixed and are difficult for other countries to imitate. The so-called 'skill-based' economic activities, dependent on such qualifications, represent an important competitive advantage for Switzerland.

The economic structure is dominated by small and medium-sized enterprises. Ninety-eight per cent of all Swiss undertakings, employing about 72 per cent of the labour force, have fewer than 500 employees. These are not a homogeneous group; there is a great variety of enterprises, diversified by size and also by sector.

Two main areas of the economy can be distinguished. The traditionally strong export sector, in particular chemicals and pharmaceuticals, consists of a few big multinational companies and a multitude of medium-sized and small enterprises. Science-based and capital intensive, these firms reflect the typical characteristics and strengths of Swiss manufacturing.

Other parts of export manufacturing, such as clothing and textiles, were formerly successful but have recently become less competitive, and are losing market shares. Pursuing cost rather than quality competitiveness, and failing to develop new technologies and skills, they are losing their position in the advancing international division of labour. The mechanical and electrical engineering industries, to some extent also watch-making, are in an intermediate position. They too are structurally at risk.

In order to withstand international competition, export-oriented firms pursue a number of different strategies. These can involve changes in product line – abandoning products which face declining markets; adoption of newer technologies; and mergers and joint ventures – for example, ABB and Ascom (a merger of all the main Swiss telecommunications companies).

In the second sector of the economy, by contrast, activities oriented to the domestic market are to a large extent privately regulated and protected from foreign competition. This sector consists of *Gewerbe* (small businesses and self-employed tradespeople), the retail trade, to some extent construction, and banking, as well as the part of the economy regulated by the state: the post office, telecommunications, railways, electricity.

The service sector is heterogeneous. In terms of contribution to GNP the most important sector is commercial, and in particular financial, services (banking and insurance). Finance and insurance are of considerable and increasing importance. Tourism is, by international standards, also of particular significance. But services are not universally strong in Switzerland. Instances of less competitive areas are software production, technical planning and advisory services.

Services and manufacturing are interdependent and often complementary. Many services, such as engineering or planning, are found within manufacturing: a quarter to a third of people employed in manufacturing are engaged in such services. This reflects the complexity of many manufacturing projects: what is sold is no longer just machines or instruments but fully installed factories or hospitals or projects such as the electrification of a whole town. In a highly developed economy such as Switzerland's a separation of sectoral activities has become practically untenable. Today there is a servo-manufacturing area in which services are no longer merely supportive, but have become a principal ingredient of competitiveness. Also crucial is the ability of the servo-manufacturing system to find solutions to complex problems and to put them into practice.

To sum up: the Swiss economy is characterized by a mature manufacturing sector coupled with a dynamic service sector. It operates principally by applying new technologies in traditional markets which world-wide are stagnant or even shrinking. Examples are textile machinery and machine tools, textiles, organic chemicals. Of central importance is the creative combination of high, middle and low technologies. Switzerland's strength lies in its ability to use new technologies for numerous made-to-measure solutions of a high standard, and to combine well-known products and processes with new developments. In new, technologically dynamic markets, by contrast, Swiss firms are not well represented.

Overall, the Swiss economy has proved extremely successful. Per capita GNP is among the highest in the world. Employment levels are high and stable; and though unemployment rose sharply after 1990, the rate is still little more than 1 per cent. Inflation rates have long been among the lowest in the world.

The Labour Market

Employment in Switzerland reflects the general economic structure, described above. Manufacturing and related activities still employ over a third of the labour force; private services cover the largest sector of workers; while public services and public administration are relatively underdeveloped (see table 9.1).

All western industrialized countries are experiencing a rise in the ratio of old people to the total population. This is particularly true of Switzerland and Germany. In Switzerland the number of young people entering the labour market is declining annually. Between 1980 and 1990 the age group 15–19 has diminished by about 100,000 (some 20 per cent). This 'demographic time bomb', which has serious long- and medium-term implications, is already reflected in labour shortages.

Participation rates (in terms of full-time employment), which in most countries have been steadily increasing, have not done so in Switzerland. In 1960 the employment ratio reached a peak of almost 50 per cent. During the 1970s the activity rate declined, but is now again about 50 per cent. The participation rate for men (62 per cent in 1990 compared with 67 per cent in 1950) is above the average, but has clearly declined over time. By contrast, the participation rate for women in full-time employment has steadily increased (from 26 per cent in 1950 to 37.5 per cent in 1990). Between 1960 and 1990 employment of middle-aged women noticeably increased while that of younger and older females declined. This is partly

Table 9.1 Employment by sector 1990

Sector	Numbers employed (000s)	%
Agriculture	197.5	5.5
Industry	1,245.2	34.9
Energy, water, mining	24.9	0.7
Manufacturing	880.6	24.7
Building and civil engineering	339.7	9.5
Services	2,120.3	59.5
Hotels, catering, distribution	817.8	23.0
Transport, communications	216.7	6.1
Banking, insurance, consultancy	443.9	12.5
Other services	512.9	14.4
Public administration	129.0	3.6
Total	3,563.2	100.0

Source: Statistiches Jahrbuch der Schweiz.

due to the lowering of the retirement age (or the disinclination to continue work after reaching retirement age) and partly to a change of attitude among young women towards training and education. Although female participation in terms of full-time employment remains among the lowest in Europe there is now a high rate of part-time female employment, so that the overall participation rate for women was 54 per cent in 1991.

Despite these trends in demography and labour force participation, employment has been increasing consistently since 1976 (the end of the recession caused by the oil crisis), reaching a record level of 3.5 million in 1990. The main source of this expansion has been the availability of foreign labour. After the Second World War Switzerland became a country of high immigration, which reached a peak in the 1960s. The annual increase in foreign residents rose to nearly 50,000, about 1 per cent of the total population. The 1980s saw another rise in the numbers of foreign workers. Switzerland has the highest proportion of foreign workers in Europe: in 1990, in a labour force of 3,563,000, there were 955,000 foreigners. Foreign workers with their families constituted 16.4 per cent of the population, as against a European average of 4 per cent.

Employment of foreign workers is concentrated in particular sectors, though the dispersion has become greater in recent years. Engineering, construction, retail distribution, hotels and catering and the health services are the major employers (Seghezzi and Lenzlinger 1991: 33). While formerly most migrant workers came from neighbouring countries (Italy, France, Germany, Austria), the proportion from such countries as Spain and Yugoslavia has been steadily increasing.

Right-wing campaigns against immigration have been influential since the 1960s. Restrictions were imposed in 1963, and since 1970 have taken the form of a national ceiling on immigration, set annually by the government. Quotas are set for different forms of work permit, all temporary – with in most cases a maximum period of nine months. Immigration is linked to social divisions within the Swiss labour force, reinforced by these legal regulations. Less skilled, unpleasant and heavy work is increasingly undertaken by foreign workers, in Switzerland on a temporary basis and without political rights. They are weakly placed to improve their working conditions. The availability of a vulnerable temporary work force lowers labour costs artificially. Certain industries, in particular construction and tourism, whose value added per employee is clearly below the Swiss average, can rely on a relatively secure source of cheap labour.

If Switzerland is to participate in the economic integration of Europe it will not be possible to maintain restrictions on the cross-border mobility of workers. Improvements in the statute covering seasonal workers, or its replacement by new forms of short-term permit, are imminent. Repeal of the statute will result in rising wage levels since foreign workers will be able to choose their jobs freely. This will increasingly force employers to adapt their production techniques and will lead to structural improvements in the economy. Not surprisingly, representatives of the building industry, tourism, and other trades benefiting from the seasonal worker status campaign vehemently for the retention of the statute and are extremely sceptical, if not hostile, towards European integration.

The Political System and Industrial Relations

Switzerland possesses a stable political system in which divisions of class, religion and language are accommodated. There is a bicameral parliament, with an upper chamber of two members from each canton (a system which benefits the right) and a federal assembly elected by proportional representation. Four parties have traditionally dominated: the Liberal Democrats (FDP), Christian People's Party (CVP), Social Democrats (SPS) and Swiss People's Party (SVP). Government is by a seven-member federal council, which for the past century has involved a cross-party coalition. Since 1959 the so-called 'magic formula' has prevailed, with two seats each for the three largest parties and one for the SVP. By convention, two or three members are French or Italian speakers.

This stability has recently been challenged by increased support for a number of minor parties of both left and right, notably the Greens and National Conservatives (who each won 15 of the 200 assembly seats in 1991). The four coalition parties won only three-quarters of the seats, an all-time low – though the bias in the election system for the upper chamber allowed them to increase their joint control to 89 per cent of seats. Nevertheless, the complex network of checks and balances normally makes for cautious (and often conservative) public policy.

Politics in Switzerland (as in Austria) relies on the mobilization of social consensus through a system of democratic corporatism. It has the following aspects (Katzenstein 1984: 27): an ideology of social partnership at national level, despite often intense political arguments within the individual interest groups; a relatively centralized and concentrated system of interest groups; and voluntary and informal accommodation of interests through continuous political bargaining between interest groups, the state and the political parties (a 'collaborative policy process'). This corporatism permits the combination of political stability and economic flexibility. It is linked to liberal capitalism based on strong, export-oriented enterprises, strong conservative political parties, few centralized political institutions, and a policy of global adaptation and private profit.

The political system's emphasis on consensus and compromise is furthered by the mechanisms of direct democracy, the initiative and the referendum. Opponents of any act of parliament need obtain only 50,000 signatures in order for a referendum to be held. By such means, radical economic policy initiatives are likely to end in defeat; hence moderate solutions are the rule. Consultations and negotiations between the administration and influential interest groups play a crucial role in the preparation of legislation.

Another distinctive constitutional provision is the right to initiate legislative reforms (*Initiativrecht*). On the basis of 100,000 signatures, a referendum may be demanded on any constitutional proposal. This enables new ideas and claims to be put forward. Almost without exception, measures proposed by this mechanism – regularly used in recent years – have been defeated. Yet where an initiative reveals substantial public support for reform, government and parliament have typically responded by introducing compromise legislation. Hence the consensual nature of politics is sustained.

Trade unions play a minor role within the social coalition in Switzerland, because of the structure of the Swiss economy and the unions' own political choices. The strength of the trade union movement has been hampered by the decentralized industrial structure, the small size of enterprises, and the growing number of employees transferring from manufacturing to the service sector. The trade union movement has also been weakened over recent decades by economic prosperity and full employment (Katzenstein 1984: 101).

In addition the unions are politically divided. There is a considerable difference between the moderate engineering workers and the more militant public service trade unions or the industrial unions of the printers, the building workers and the woodworkers, or the chemicals, textiles and paper union.

There is also a difference in approach between the trade unions and the Social Democratic Party (SPS). The unions tend towards private solutions to their problems while the social democrats look for solutions via the state. An example was the discussion of the regulation of old-age pension schemes, with the trade unions (together with the bourgeois parties) supporting the existing private insurance schemes and the social democrats pleading for a national pension plan.

As for the relationship between trade unions and the political parties, the literature talks of a Dutch-style 'pillarization' (*Versäulung*) (Steiner 1970; Höpflinger 1976: 200). There are institutionalized links between unions of differing tendencies and their respective parties, from informal contacts between members of staff to an overlap of functions or mutual consultations up to formal election pacts. But in principle the unions are legally and financially independent of political parties. Traditionally there are close links between the Swiss Trade Union Confederation (SGB) and the SPS and between the National Federation of Christian Trade Unions (CNG) and the Christian People's Party (CVP). These links tend to prevent state interference in the affairs of the unions or the federations and thus guarantee free collective bargaining (*Lohnautonomie*).

In the case of government measures which affect their interests, trade unions and employers participate at all levels of the so-called pre-parliamentary process. The ability of an interest group to threaten a referendum on the statute in question strengthens its position in the consultation process. In this way inequalities of power between employers and unions are reduced, though not eliminated.

The institutionalized goal of consensus also has an effect on collective bargaining. Employers prefer regulation of working conditions by negotiation rather than by uniform and inflexible legislation. In general, negotiated solutions are faster, more progressive and more detailed than is the law. Trade unions and employees as well as employers adhere to the principle of subsidiarity: state intervention is accepted only if labour market or social policy problems can no longer be resolved by direct agreement between the parties. The principle of free collective bargaining applies in particular to wage determination: incomes policy has so far had no role in Switzerland (Höpflinger 1976: 195).

Federalism, the Trade Union Movement and Industrial Relations

Unions and employers in Switzerland possess organizations at local, cantonal, regional and national level. The Swiss principle of federalism finds expression in the trade union movement and industrial relations: for example, in the delegation of functions to individual unions and the relatively weak position of the national confederations.

The main confederation, SGB, itself possesses separate units in each canton. This is not true, however, of all affiliated unions. For example, the structure of the engineering union (SMUV) reflects the country's industrial geography, with a number of branches in cantons where the industry is concentrated, but branches spanning several cantons where there is little employment in the industry. Organization by territory is stronger and institutional federalism important in sectors with a high degree of legal regulation. Teachers' pay, for instance, is settled separately in each canton; whereas in engineering, pay is determined in a nationally applicable agreement.

Industrial relations are indirectly affected by the federal structure of the state in a number of ways. First, there exist separate conciliation and mediation services in each canton. Second, quotas of foreign workers are allocated by canton, and in some cantons (for example, Geneva) are subject to joint negotiation between employers and unions. Third, the cantons are heavily engaged in vocational training.

The peak level of unions and employers' associations comprises central or umbrella confederations. These deal with the federal government and attempt to influence its economic and social policies to their advantage. Companies do not affiliate directly to their national confederation (although in isolated cases individual large enterprises also exert an influence on the state) but through membership of sectoral associations. Similarly, workers become members of the national confederations through specific industrial or occupational unions. Thus the national confederations are organizations of organizations. It is these sectoral associations which are primarily and directly concerned with labour market regulation.

Trade Unions

Trade unions are divided by religion, ideology and status. Taking the membership of all Swiss trade unions together (and this calculation is not straightforward, since a number of employee organizations cannot be unproblematically classified as unions), aggregate union density is currently about 27 per cent. While well above the level in France or Spain, this is one of the lowest rates of unionization in Europe.

Swiss unions can be grouped into four categories. First, the SGB is a socialist-oriented federation which traditionally dominated Swiss trade unionism and still comprises about half the total union membership. Its highest membership in relation to the labour force – 16 per cent – was achieved in 1960. In absolute numbers it reached its peak in 1976; thereafter membership declined, though this has stabilized since the mid-1980s and in 1990 there was a slight increase. However, the 1990 membership of 444,000 represents only 13 per cent of Swiss employment. Its affiliated unions cover mainly manual workers in the private sector, and both manual and white-collar public employees.

Competing across roughly the same constituency is the Catholic CNG, which has a membership only about a quarter of that of the SGB. Another general confederation, the LFSA – associated with the Liberal Democrats – is even smaller, with little more than 20,000 members.

The third main organization is the federation of white-collar workers (VSA), represented mainly in catering, commerce, banking and insurance, and among white-collar workers in manufacturing and in the public services. In contrast to other trade unions, VSA benefits from an expanding recruitment base, and its membership now exceeds that of CNG.

Finally, there exist a variety of occupational and professional associations, particularly in the public sector, which are affiliated neither to VSA nor to the general confederations. The largest of these is the national and local government union, ZV.

Although the structure of plants and enterprises is less concentrated in Switzerland than in most comparable industrial countries, this is not necessarily a disadvantage for trade union organization, which often extends to SMEs and artisan establishments. Nor is the urban/rural divide of significance for the degree of organization. There are instances where trade unions in medium-sized enterprises in rural environments have been in existence for a longer period and have stronger roots than in large towns and cities; while in conurbations such as Zürich there is often a surfeit of rhetoric and paperwork.

The structure of Swiss unions is complex, with occupational and status divisions compounding those of ideology. In practice, the political-religious differences between SGB and CNG do not prevent cooperative working relationships. But the separation between manual and white-collar workers, and public and private sectors, is less easily bridged; while principles of craft identity compete with those of industrial unionism. Moreover, the central confederations have only limited powers to transcend this fragmentation: for example, the interrelationship between SGB and SMUV is far weaker than the parallel relationship between DGB and IG Metall in Germany.

Recently SGB unions have declared in favour of 'industrial trade unionism', that is, the organization of the entire work force in each sector, including white-collar employees, in the same trade union. Nevertheless the organization of employees, as compared with that of employers, is still considerably fragmented (Katzenstein 1984: 114).

Sectoral Organization

The distribution of union membership by broad sector, the density within each sector, and the relative shares of each group of unions are shown in table 9.2.

The SGB has just over half its membership in two of the 16 affiliated unions: the building and construction union GBH, and the engineering union SMUV, with respectively 125,000 and 111,000 members in 1990.

GBH has succeeded in recruiting the expanding labour force of the construction industry, and has grown in membership by 24 per cent since 1970. Its density rate is roughly 40 per cent. In transport and communications, SGB unions are even more strongly entrenched, with a density of 46 per cent.

In manufacturing, SGB also has a high and improving density: some 35 per cent in 1988. However, economic restructuring and technological

Table 9.2 Distribution of union membership by sector and organization (%) 1986

Sector	Degree of organization	Sector share	Share of Membership			Independent unions
			SGB	CNG	VSA	
Industrial sector	**32.0**	**49.3**	**61.4**	**16.4**	**16.2**	**5.9**
Construction	61.1	17.4	72.5	19.5	5.9	2.2
Machine/metal/watch	31.2	19.4	61.2	11.2	25.7	2.0
Chemicals	19.4	1.8	57.0	21.0	18.0	4.0
Textile	16.9	1.6	43.0	36.0	11.0	10.0
Printing	46.3	3.5	70.5	13.5	1.0	14.9
Public service sector	**37.9**	**34.6**	**43.0**	**6.8**	**3.5**	**46.7**
Public administration	79.1	11.1	26.4	3.7	9.2	60.7
Postal services	71.6	5.9	79.5	19.2	0.0	1.4
Public transport	69.8	7.0	77.5	8.5	0.0	14.0
Private service sector	**8.7**	**11.6**	**14.9**	**2.2**	**56.7**	**26.2**
Trade/hotel/restaurant	7.7	5.8	19.0	1.4	72.0	7.6
Bank/insurance/other commercial services	15.1	5.5	0.9	0.0	42.8	56.4
Total	**24.6**	**100.0**	**48.6**	**11.6**	**17.0**	**22.8**

Source: Fluder (1991).

change currently present serious challenges. SMUV has recently suffered a slight decline in membership, a reflection of the crisis in engineering. In textiles and clothing, contraction has hit trade union membership; and in paper and printing – another traditional stronghold – membership has fallen in the face of radical technical change.

In the key areas of employment growth – retail distribution, catering and finance – which today account for 35 per cent of the labour force, unionism is extremely weak. SGB and CNG together have a density of at most 2 per cent in these categories; and though VSA and independent unions have a stronger position, union density overall in private services is less than 10 per cent.

In the public sector, SGB is strong in posts and telecommunications (where CNG also has a significant membership) and on the railways. In public administration more generally, however, the relevant SGB union is weak and losing ground. But in a number of areas there exists a relatively high degree of organization in the form of vocational or professional associations, for instance among doctors, nurses, teachers, police and civil servants. To some extent these organizations also bargain over issues such as working hours or vocational training and enter into binding agreements with employers. Thus they carry out functions which were originally considered to be those of trade unions, and hence function as trade unions. If they are included, then employees in the public service sector are highly organized.

The employment relationship in the public sector differs from that in private industry. It is based on the public law concept of *Beamtenrecht*, analogous to that in Germany. An appointment as *Beamter* is in practice permanent, and dismissal is possible only on proof of misconduct, established under a protracted procedure. Conversely, *Beamte* are (at least in theory) totally at the disposal of the employer; their obligations are not contractually limited, as in the case of an ordinary employment relationship. The rights and obligations are legally defined in the federal *Beamtengesetz*, with additional local regulations for cantonal and municipal personnel. With very few exceptions, *Beamte* are under a no-strike obligation. Their social security is particularly well consolidated.

The sectoral imbalance in membership represents a serious problem for SGB, and for Swiss trade unionism as a whole. In general, membership is strongest in sectors where employment is declining, or at least static; it is far weaker in the areas of employment growth. Though this is indeed a problem for unions in most of Europe, in Switzerland the disparities are particularly great.

One aspect of organizational unevenness is the weak unionization of women, who comprise only 12 per cent of SGB membership. In no other major confederation in Europe (apart from Spain) is female representation so low. By contrast, women constitute 37 per cent of total employment. It is true that female employment is concentrated in white-collar occupations and the service sector, where SGB is weak; and women constitute 26 per cent of VSA membership and 31 per cent in independent unions

(Fluder et al. 1991: 59). But the overall proportion of women in Swiss unions – 18.6 per cent in 1986 – is only half their proportion of the labour force.

The particular location of women's employment, and such factors as part-time work, present special obstacles for unionization. But women's marginal position in trade unions may also reflect their traditional subordination in Swiss society: women obtained the vote in national elections only in 1971, and in every canton and municipality only in 1990.

The SGB has been pressing recently for an improvement in the situation of women workers. In June 1991 – the tenth anniversary of equal rights legislation in Switzerland – it organized a day of strikes and demonstrations, calling for more speedy and decisive action to remedy social and economic inequalities. It was estimated that over half a million women participated in the day of action – far more than the organizers themselves anticipated.

Young workers and apprentices, too, are under-represented in trade unions. Unions are thus in danger of becoming ageing institutions. By contrast, in most unions foreigners are now fairly well represented. In recent years, unions have become active in support of the rights of foreign workers.

In conclusion, it may be argued that SGB has failed to respond adequately to the challenges of recent decades. It has concentrated too long on traditional strongholds where employment is now contracting. Its member unions have failed to pursue the opportunity to organize among the growing numbers of white-collar and professional groups. In consequence, membership decline threatens both its financial viability and its representative status.

Arguably, the commitment to collectivism which was characteristic of the traditional skilled manual worker has given way to more individualistic career paths and employment identities. To compete successfully for the allegiance of the new types of worker, unions would need to offer selective individual incentives. To some extent, the benefit payments which unions traditionally provided performed this function; but state provision of welfare benefits – as well as legal and advisory services – displaces unions' role here. Thus it is not clear that Swiss unions will be able to resist a process of secular decline.

Workplace Representation

The main vehicle for representing employee interests at company level is the works committee (*Betriebskommission*). In marked contrast to Germany or Austria, Switzerland has no legal framework requiring the establishment of such committees; those that exist are voluntary institutions set up under the terms of collective agreements, and probably cover only a third of the Swiss labour force. In the 1970s the SGB pressed strongly for legislation making works committees compulsory, but in 1976 both its proposals and an alternative version drawn up by parliament were defeated in a referendum. Since then the issue has been allowed to drop, and indeed some unions – for example, the watchmakers' union in the French-speaking part of Switzerland – oppose the formation of committees as a potential threat to their own status as employee representatives.

Where works committees exist, their constitution and functions vary according to the precise terms of the collective agreement. A committee is typically established on the initiative of the work force, confirmed by a ballot of employees. Normally all workers, unionized or otherwise, can vote and stand for election. Unions – and specifically, those belonging to the SGB – attempt to control the committees, presenting lists of candidates. In most cases the unions win a majority of positions, but it is also common for some non-unionists to be elected.

Employee participation on the basis of collective agreements is well established in enterprises with more than 50 employees and in 1990 was probably available to about 50 per cent of all employees in such firms. There are considerable variations in the extent and intensity of participation between one sector and another as well as within industries. It is most advanced in engineering and in retail chains such as Migros and the Coop. Codetermination is most institutionalized in large enterprises with more than 1,000 employees. They also offer more social institutions such as company housing, elaborate canteen provisions, personnel commissions, etc. Representation of employee interests at the level of the multi-plant corporation is practically non-existent (Jans 1991).

As in Germany, the existence of works committees gives rise to a 'dual system' of interest representation: the union is responsible for collective bargaining above the level of the company, while the committee has jurisdiction over workplace issues. The latter is meant to be accountable to the employees rather than the union, though in practice the unionized members of the committees usually maintain close contact with the local branches and officials. Unions such as SMUV attempt to ensure their influence over the committees, holding special meetings and conferences and running training courses for committee members (Fluder et al. 1991: 367–8).

In general the committees possess information and consultation rights; provision for codetermination rights is not normal (Sonderegger 1979: 132–3; Wagner 1985). The agreement in the engineering industry is exceptional in providing for the committees to act as bargaining agents within the workplace, though the resulting agreements do not have the formal status of collective contracts.

A study in 1981 (Wagner 1985) found that consultation was strongest in the area of 'organization of working time', followed by issues concerned with dismissal. Between 5 and 30 per cent of employees had co-decision rights on different types of personnel and workplace issues. There were hardly any co-decision rights on strategic business policy (1.5 per cent). Around one-third of enterprises had co-decision rights in the administration of their pension funds. Since then facilities have been significantly enlarged at workplace and plant level, but hardly at all at enterprise level. Compared with Germany the degree of genuine codetermination in Switzerland is low. If one considers the collective agreement in engineering, then German works councillors have considerably more authority than their Swiss counterparts. The rights of Swiss works committees are similar to those in France. Only in relation to general enterprise policies, and because of their power to call in external experts, can French representatives be considered to be in a stronger position.

In the public sector, parallel arrangements exist. The *Beamtengesetz* authorizes the election of staff committees (*Personalausschüsse*), with consultative functions. In cantonal and municipal employment there are a variety of arrangements, reflecting the different requirements of local *Beamten* regulations. In public enterprises such as posts and telecommunications, and the railways, more extensive participation rights apply.

Employers' Organizations

ZSAO has as members only employers' associations, not individual companies; it deals only indirectly with individual firms. The federation does not conclude legally binding agreements. The affiliation of associations to ZSAO is purely voluntary. Thirty-six industry-wide employers' associations and the same number of local or regional associations are currently affiliated. The division between industry-wide and regional associations reflects Switzerland's federal structure and the differences within its economy. Industry-wide employers' associations cover the whole country and represent interests in the manufacturing sector, small businesses and the service sector. The local and regional associations cover a number of different trades and protect their local or regional interests.

Organizational density is higher among employers than it is among unions, but their structure is much more heterogeneous. Frequently trade unions have to bargain with a great number of regional or trade-specific employers' associations (Höpflinger 1976:208). There are considerable differences between one industry and another.

ZSAO was formed in 1908 as a defence organization, in particular against strikes. But the 1937 peace agreement in the metal industry and subsequent collective agreements in other industries explicitly preclude industrial action. Thus the main purpose of the federation has shifted. Today its main tasks are: the coordination of employment and social policies of the affiliated associations and their members; discussions with public authorities and representation on standing commissions; and discussions with employee organizations, including joint committees for issues concerning white-collar staff.

While ZSAO concentrates on collective bargaining and social policy, the Swiss Federation of Commerce and Industry (SHIV) is the central body for Swiss industry and is responsible for questions of economic policy. These two central organizations collaborate with each other.

The largest, and a particularly active member of ZSAO is the engineering employers' association (ASM). It also maintains direct contact with other employers' associations. Its membership consists of firms in the machine, electrical and metal industries in all parts of the country. In 1991 around 580 firms were ASM members with some 200,000 employees in firms with more than 20 employees. Smaller, artisan-type firms are organized in a separate association. The ASM is concerned with personnel policy, labour law, social insurance, training and further vocational education as well as relations between employees and employers. There also exists a trade association for the metal and engineering industries which deals with other aspects of economic policy, paralleling the division of labour at the higher level.

Towards the end of the 1980s, ASM experienced a slight decline in membership. The small, newly established firms in the high-tech growth sectors, in particular, remained outside. Though they appreciated the advantages of industrial peace, they balked at the costs of collective agreements and organizational administration. The ASM is currently concerned whether legal changes may be desirable to prevent such 'free-riding'.

Legislation versus Voluntary Regulation

As a matter of principle the state does not intervene directly in the relationships between unions and employers. Rather, it defines the framework for free collective bargaining. The parties' rights and obligations are laid down in the legislation on employment contracts (*Arbeitsvertragsrecht*). Collective agreements have to comply with the requirements of statute law.

The Federal Employment Act (*Eidgenössisches Arbeitsgesetz* – EAG) contains provisions on accident prevention and health care, working and rest time, special protection for women and young workers. These are minimum provisions which complement regulation by collective agreement. For example, working hours are determined by agreement within the framework provided by law. Absolute limits in the public interest are laid down by legislation; within the legal requirements, detailed regulations are specified by collective agreement; subject to these provisions, working hours are determined in each employee's individual contract of employment.

In principle, matters arising between employers and employees can be regulated by statute or by contract, in the form of multi-employer collective agreements or arrangements between the two parties at company level. The Swiss system of industrial relations is based on both these forms of regulation.

Prevailing opinion in Switzerland is that industrial peace can best be maintained by collective agreements. Thus the system of Swiss industrial relations is characterized by the maxim 'agreement in preference to law'. State intervention is avoided except in exceptional circumstances; hence labour law is loose and flexible. Proposals for legislative or constitutional regulation of employment issues have frequently been rejected by referendum (as with initiatives on working hours and codetermination), or else have become stalled in the parliamentary process. But the two legal forms, contract and legislation, are not necessarily in conflict, rather they can complement each other.

Collective bargaining covers a broad spectrum of issues, including, for instance, welfare (such as child benefits) which in other countries are regulated by law. Trade unions are not only collective bargaining agents but also social partners; thus in their negotiations with employers they also regulate issues other than working conditions.

State social welfare measures are weaker in Switzerland than in Germany and many other European countries. On the other hand, the social insurance scheme of SMUV, for instance, is more extensive and generous than that of the German Metalworkers. Particularly striking is the superior position of benefits in respect of unemployment, pensions, accidents and sickness. In this way trade unions have gained a status in Swiss politics which they value and defend. They are therefore opposed to policies which would displace collective agreements by legislation. In particular they are opposed to incomes policy which would infringe free collective bargaining. They participate actively in private social welfare arrangements.

Negotiated arrangements are considered superior to state provision because they offer solutions which are decentralized, flexible and capable of adjustment to local conditions. Rapid decision-making is possible. The speedy adaptability of the Swiss system of industrial relations is its strength and advantage.

Collective Agreements and Individual Contracts

The law provides a background regulatory function for industrial relations. The individual contract of employment between workers and employers defines the legal rights and obligations of each. Since 1912, however, the law has prescribed that individual contracts may not contradict the provisions of any collective agreement (*Gesamtarbeitsvertrag* or GAV). The latter, as in Germany and Austria, is binding not only on the negotiating parties – unions and employers' associations – but also on the firms and workers who are their members. The terms of collective agreements are thus incorporated in individual contracts of employment. Technically, the terms of a GAV do not apply to non-union workers or non-federated firms. The law does permit the extension of the terms of an agreement to all firms and employees within its jurisdiction (*Allgemeinverbindlichkeitserklärung* –AVE); but as in Germany, this provision is rarely utilized. An AVE is issued only under strict legal conditions. Agreements have to take account of minority interests and regional differences and have to safeguard basic rights and the public interest. The result is that overall applicability cannot be declared in precisely those cases where government support is most needed. In 1989 only eleven GAVs had been declared generally applicable at federal level and eight at canton level, covering 44,600 employers and 336,000 employees. In practice, the GAV sets the basic terms of employment throughout the sector concerned, without the need for legal enforcement.

Since the path-breaking engineering agreement of 1937, it has become the norm for GAVs to include an absolute peace obligation. This entails not only – as in many other countries – that disputes over the application and interpretation of existing agreements should be resolved peacefully, but also that disagreements on questions not covered in agreements must be settled in similar fashion. Some four-fifths of Swiss workers are covered by such provisions, which specify procedures for mediation and if necessary arbitration over any differences during the currency of a GAV; most employers refuse to conclude any agreement which does not include the absolute peace obligation. However, in some sectors – chemicals, construction, textiles and printing, for example – the peace obligation applies only to issues included in the terms of the agreement, not to disputes over other issues.

The 1937 agreement was originally a purely procedural agreement. As it was renewed and extended, more important substantive rules were added and it became a comprehensive collective agreement. A recent example of contractually regulated issues is the phased introduction of the 40-hour week. Despite the relatively favourable nature of employment conditions in Switzerland, working hours are still longer than in most comparable countries. In 1982, average annual hours worked were 2,044, similar to Japan with 2,101. In Germany the figure was 1,773, in the USA 1,904, and in Belgium 1,756. The standard week in Switzerland is longer, and holidays shorter, than in most of western Europe. Other substantive issues dealt with include vocational training and further education; equal pay for women; the establishment of works committees; and the question of job security (Beer 1990: 17).

In recognition of the unions' law-and-order role, collective agreements often contain the right to collect dues from non-unionists (Katzenstein 1984: 145).

The contractual regulation of employment relationships by collective agreements has become the norm in Switzerland. At the beginning of the 1960s around 55 per cent of all employees were covered by a GAV or a similar arrangement (Gallati 1976). At the beginning of the 1990s around 1,000 to 1,500 GAV are in force. They form a close network in the shape of national, regional, local and company agreements in almost all economic areas, coupled with a high density of coverage.

Plant-Level Application of Agreements

Collective agreements concluded at industry level have to be applied and interpreted at plant level. The national association is involved in dealing with ensuing problems. Under the terms of the peace obligation, agreements provide for the associations to mediate and, if need be, settle any disagreements in individual companies.

There is considerable variation in collective bargaining structures between different sectors. In some, collective bargaining is conducted centrally, in others at a number of levels: national, regional and canton level. Industry-wide agreements frequently contain merely procedural rules and statements of principle, and leave the substantive regulation of wages etc. to subsequent decentralized negotiations. They lay down minimum conditions which can be exceeded at company level. It is in individual companies that the majority of agreements are nowadays concluded.

This highly decentralized structure has been a crucial reason for the generally satisfactory functioning of the Swiss labour market. Since 1970 there has however been a tendency towards centralization and uniformity of agreements.

Agreements concluded at national level regulate all conditions of employment with the exception of wages. These are negotiated at lower levels, between individual employers and works councils, for an indeterminate period of time which does not necessarily coincide with the term of the national agreement. In addition, supplementary agreements may be made for a sub-section of an industry (for example, watchmaking), for periods of time independent of the national agreement. Another variation is the agreement of additional clauses between employer and employee organizations at canton or regional level (as in construction).

Since the early 1970s trade unions have demanded the extension of their collective agreements to cover white-collar workers. This was eventually achieved with the 1988 uniform collective agreement in the engineering industry.

Special attention is paid to the enforcement of agreements. Frequently this is entrusted to a joint committee (*paritätische Kommission*) established jointly by the unions and employers' associations. Dispute settlement often involves a special tribunal. In general there is a three-level procedure: plant-level mediation, discussions between the parties to the agreement, and, as a last resort, arbitration. Independent arbitration at canton or national level is legally available but rarely used.

Strikes and Industrial Peace

The 1937 peace agreement in engineering represented a commitment to the peaceful settlement of conflicts on the basis of clear and agreed procedures. It provided the model for a system of relations between the social partners in Switzerland which are stable and informed by a climate of mutual trust. Their behaviour is characterized by a high degree of pragmatism and realism. Social peace is a tradition, industrial conflicts are of little significance, and in the context of the agreements and arrangements prevalent in Switzerland the strike is no longer a legitimate weapon. In general the mentality of Swiss employees is consensual and trusting, certainly not confrontational. Ideologically there exists a far-reaching integration of employees into the enterprise: workers identify with the firm and the employer. At times this is skilfully exploited by employers.

Strike statistics show that the union-employer commitment to industrial peace is indeed effective. In many years, no strikes whatever are recorded. When strikes do occur, their economic impact is usually negligible. As table 9.3 indicates, the Swiss strike record in recent years is remarkably low.

Table 9.3   Strikes in Switzerland 1971–90

Year	Number of strikes	Workers involved (000)	Days Lost (000)
1971	11	2.3	7.5
1972	5	0.5	2.0
1973	0	0	0
1974	3	0.3	2.8
1975	6	0.3	1.7
1976	19	2.4	19.6
1977	9	1.4	4.6
1978	10	1.2	5.3
1979	8	0.5	2.3
1980	5	3.6	5.7
1981	1	0.02	0.2
1982	1	0.06	0.6
1983	5	1.0	4.4
1984	2	0.05	0.7
1985	3	0.4	0.7
1986	1	0.04	0.07
1987	0	0	0
1988	4	0.1	0.9
1989	2	0.02	0.3
1990	2	0.6	4.1

Source: Statistiches Jahrbuch der Schweiz.

Recent Developments and Prospects

Decentralization and the Challenge to Employers' Associations

Two problems in particular are of current significance for industrial relations in Switzerland: the growing independence of individual enterprises and hence the possible displacement of collective bargaining between unions and employers' associations; and the effects of economic and technological restructuring on the representation of employee and employer interests. Both developments tend to weaken the position and significance of collective agreements.

Some employers want to bring about necessary structural change without being constrained by industry-wide regulation. More and more firms are critical of collective agreements and prepared to abandon them. In 1991 three printing and publishing firms withdrew from the current GAV; and Swissair gave notice to terminate the collective agreement with its ground staff. The number of plants covered by collective agreements is steadily decreasing.

Secession from industry-wide collective regulation may be seen also as a reflection of structural change in production and the adaptation of corporate strategy to a more competitive environment. In the last few years, more and more Swiss companies have become general contractors who purchase components and assemble them, rather than manufacturers. Components and sub-assemblies previously produced by the enterprise are increasingly obtained from outside firms and stocks are drastically reduced ('just-in-time'): a major example of this development is the firm of Landis & Gyr. Within this system of competitive production neither main contractor nor subcontractors have much sympathy with trade unions, and the delays in decision-making and cost increases which they cause. Companies want a free hand. At the same time, organizing the representation of union interests becomes much more difficult in this complex network of numerous semi-autonomous units. Under the pressure of economic transformation, and in particular the single European market, a number of firms are also in favour of abolishing or weakening the employers' associations so as to make restructuring easier.

In 1991, a number of individual firms left their employers' association. Examples are to be found in the watch industry, in clothing, and – as indicated – in printing. Some of these firms argue that independence from the employers' association makes restructuring or mergers easier to accomplish. Others complain that the associations are no longer willing to fight, that they are indecisive and unnecessarily ready to compromise, in particular on political issues. Another argument by some large employers is that the associations are dominated by smaller firms which are in the majority.

The recent defections from the newspaper publishers' association have raised the question of whether current developments signal a weakening of social partnership: the printing industry has traditionally played a leading role in the development of cooperative industrial relations in Switzerland. An important condition for industrial peace may be lost if employers attempt to regulate the employment relationship on the basis of individual contracts rather than collective agreements. The associations themselves are firmly committed to social partnership and condemn the rigorous pursuit of individual enterprise interests. They are conscious of the fact that a climate of confrontational social policies would significantly weaken Switzerland's international competitiveness. They will have to solve sensitive problems within their own ranks.

The attitude of the construction industry, for instance, is different. There the aim is improved quality, to be achieved by higher wages and shorter working hours: not least because of the knowledge that in future it will be more difficult to obtain seasonal workers.

The engineering employers, like those in many other industries, have always opposed the regulation of wages at association level, and favour the devolution of wage determination to enterprise level. In their view, this enables individual enterprises to adjust flexibly to economic conditions. Under pressure of recent developments they have taken the initiative for change towards the 'individualization of working conditions' and therefore the 'individualization of agreements' at plant level. Wages are to be related to individual workers' performance. Individual wage increases are to be granted. Significant, too, is a greater trend towards individual arrangements on working hours.

In the view of employers, and in particular ASM, collective agreements deal too extensively with substantive issues, and regulate them in excessive detail. In future they would like to exclude from the collective agreement and devolve to plant level the determination not only of wages but of other substantive issues such as holidays, hours of work and vocational training. At the plant level employers are normally more powerful than employee representatives. The collective agreement would be reduced to procedural rules such as no-strike and no-lockout clauses.

The unions have reacted critically. They had previously supported the extension of collective bargaining to issues such as cooperation, health, training and retraining. They would also like to secure participation and co-determination rights in new collective agreements. But the introduction of new areas should not be at the expense of the exclusion from collective agreements of issues such as sickness, working hours, and holidays.

So far the traditional issues of collective bargaining - wages, working hours, holidays, social security - have remained central, and non-wage issues such as co-determination, humanization of working conditions, or health and safety, have been less important. The rapid application of new technologies and their effects on the work environment have led to greater concentration in collective agreements on retraining. Again they generally contain framework provisions only. Further specification is left to individual employment contracts at plant level (Beer 1980: 18).

The trend is towards a transfer of negotiations to the plant level. But too highly differentiated plant-level regulations become remote from the basic character of collective agreements. It will be important to find a practicable division of roles, with well defined areas of responsibility, between the negotiators at industry level and those at plant level.

Challenges for Trade Unions

A major problem for SGB and CNG is the increasing discrepancy between developments in the structure of employment and the unions' organizational structures. SGB is weak in the expanding tertiary sector and among white-collar workers. By contrast VSA, as the white-collar umbrella organization with strong representation in the tertiary sector, is in a more favourable position. The unions aim to extend their organizational base vertically into the white-collar sector and horizontally into the tertiary sector.

Another potential threat to the unions is loss of contact with the plant. There is a danger of the creation of house or company associations, initiated and supported by management, which would bargain over substantive issues at plant level and conclude plant agreements. This is a threat to the sectoral unions: the umbrella organizations SGB and CNG would be able to carry on with their national and economic policy activities as before, though with diminished authority.

Employee organizations are fragmented and to a certain extent have lost their sense of direction. The trend is towards a decrease in union membership coupled with a marked structural shift within the trade union movement. The unions are particularly weak in the ideological or conceptual field. The majority of them (particularly SMUV) are inflexible and conservative. Their concern is to maintain the status quo; they are unable to develop an identity that transcends the boundaries of industry categories, and their members, too, appear to have an interest in preserving existing demarcations. The unions lack a new programme to match changed circumstances such as changes at the workplace, greater autonomy at work, higher average qualifications of potential members, effects of European integration, and environmental problems.

Proposals have recently been made for one union in a region to act on behalf of employees in another industry who are not organized in the locality. The locally strong organization would represent employees in trades other than its own. It is conceivable that in future a kind of SGB trade union may act on behalf of all industries and bring about some local coordination; but by today's standards this is for many unions a frightening scenario rather than a desirable goal.

There has been progress in the relationship between white-collar and blue-collar workers. The novel collective agreement concluded in the summer of 1991 between SMUV and ASM removed the distinction between blue- and white-collar workers in the engineering industry: there is now only one category of employees. This is of pioneering significance for collective agreements in Switzerland. In other industries the issue is not so dramatic. The distinction has also been abandoned in the public sector – on the railways, for instance, some time ago. The collective agreement in construction continues to make the distinction.

In general the organization of white-collar workers is beset by problems of mentality. A bank employee, for instance, is greatly concerned with his or her career prospects and does not want to endanger them by any activity in a white-collar union. To be able to appeal to and mobilize broader groups of employees, the trade union has to alter its blue-collar image and its identity. Thus SMUV has recently attempted to present itself more as a vocational organization and to offer a wider spectrum of services, for example, further training and education. The SGB associations are today in favour of the principle of 'industrial trade unionism', i.e. the organization of all employees in an industry, including white-collar workers, in one trade union. There is a development towards a policy of more qualitative, rather than quantitative, demands.

New Personnel Strategies?

In general Swiss managements are conservative; they are hardly ever innovators in the field of personnel policies. On the employee side, too, there is hardly any interest in significant new ideas. This complacency means that there are hardly any attempts at applying new personnel strategies. For Swiss enterprises, 'corporate identity' is hardly a problem requiring new personnel strategies. There are admittedly some experiments, for instance with quality circles or team working, but they are insignificant.

Controversies over personnel policy issues have arisen in current negotiations over a partial revision of the EAG, intended to make working conditions more flexible, particularly the regulation of working time, without removing the protection of socially disadvantaged groups. In sectors with high capital investment, employers are keen to maximize the use of expensive machinery. In principle this could be done by employing men. But they are difficult to obtain and are more expensive than women. It is therefore proposed, particularly by employers, to repeal the existing legal ban on night and Sunday working by women, enabling companies to employ women, for instance on night shifts in the production of integrated circuits. In February 1992 Switzerland gave notice to terminate the relevant international ILO convention. However, there is opposition to such a change and the outcome remains in the balance.

European Integration and Swiss Industrial Relations

It is almost certain that Switzerland will become a member of the European Community in the 1990s, and that before then the Swiss economy will become increasingly aligned with that of the EC. The principle of the 'free movement of labour' will certainly have important implications for Switzerland. Current restrictions on migrant workers will have to be removed, at least as far as citizens of EC countries are concerned. The markedly favourable labour market position may not survive a relaxation. Liberalization of access to employment would cover white-collar occupations, in the past largely barred to foreigners. This could have important implications for white-collar organizations such as VSA. To the extent that artificial protections for the Swiss labour market are removed, and employment becomes less secure, one foundation of consensual industrial relations may be undermined.

The broad agenda of the EC 'social dimension' is unlikely to have a major impact in Switzerland, though some changes will doubtless be necessary. Given that Swiss law provides an extensive basis of minimum individual employee rights, it already complies with many of the requirements of the emergent EC social policy. On the issue of employee participation, as has been seen, Switzerland differs from most EC countries through the absence of any statutory system. But it is not the only exception, and current EC proposals involve a choice among three alternative models, one of which is the system of works committees established by collective bargaining which already exists in Switzerland.

The principle of subsidiarity within EC decision-making allows member states to retain the majority of their traditional arrangements in industrial relations. Employers, unions and governments in Switzerland should be able to continue on their established basis of free collective bargaining, preferring voluntary agreement to statutory regulation. It is clear that, at least for the present, they are still committed to this principle.

Note

[1] I wish to thank Annemarie Flanders for her speedy and efficient translation of this chapter.

Abbreviations

ASM	*Arbeitgeberverband Schweizerischer Maschinen- und Metallindustrieller* – Swiss Metal and Engineering Employers' Association
AVE	*Allgemeinverbindlichkeitserklärung* – declaration of general application (of a collective agreement)
CNG	*Christlich Nationaler Gewerkschaftsbund* – Christian National Trade Union Confederation
CVP	*Christlich Demokratische Volkspartei* – Christian Democratic People's Party
EAG	*Eidgenössisches Arbeitsgesetz* – Federal Employment Act
FDP	*Freisinnig-demokratische Partei* – Liberal Democratic Party
GAV	*Gesamtarbeitsvertrag* – collective agreement (contract)
GBH	*Gewerkschaft Bau und Holz* – Building and Woodworkers' Union
LFSA	*Landesverband Freier Schweizer Arbeitnehmer* – National Association of Free Swiss Workers
SGB	*Schweizerischer Gewerkschaftsbund* – Swiss Trade Union Confederation
SHIV	*Schweizerischer Handels- und Industrieverein* – Swiss Federation of Commerce and Industry
SMUV	*Schweizerischer Metall- und Uhrenarbeiterverband* – Swiss Metal and Watch Workers' Association
SPS	*Sozialdemokratische Partei der Schweiz* – Swiss Social-Democratic Party
SVP	*Schweizerische Volkspartei* – Swiss People's Party
VSA	*Vereinigung Schweizerischer Angestelltenverbände* – Federation of Swiss White-Collar Associations
VSM	*Verband Schweizerischer Maschinenindustrieller* – Swiss Association of Ma-

chinery Manufacturers

ZSAO   *Zentralverband Schweizerischer Arbeitgeber-Organizationen* – Central Association of Swiss Employers' Organizations

ZV   *Zentralverband des Staats- und Gemeindepersonals* – Central Association of National and Local Government Staff

References

Anderegg, H. 1991: Migliederentwicklung der Schweizer Gewerkschaften im Jahre 1990. *Gewerkschaftliche Rundschau*, 3/4, 108-24.

Beer, M. 1990: System und Bedeutung der Sozialpartnerbeziehungen: Entwicklungstendenzen. *Die Volkswirtschaft*, 1, 17-19.

Bundesamt für Statistik 1990: *Statistisches Jahrbuch der Schweiz*, Bern: Erwerbsleber.

Evers-Koelman, I., Fischer, M. and Nijkamp, P. 1987: Cross-national Comparison of Regional Labour Markets. In Fischer, M. and Nijkamp, P. (eds), *Regional Labour Markets*. Amsterdam: North-Holland.

Fluder, R. 1990: Stability under Pluralist Conditions. Trade Unions and Collective Bargaining in Switzerland. Paper presented to the 12th World Congress of Sociology, Madrid.

Fluder, R., Ruf, H., Schöni, W. and Wicki, M. 1991: *Gewerkschaften und Angestelltenverbände in der schweizerischen Privatwirtschaft*. Zürich: Seismo.

Höpflinger, F. 1976: *Industriegewerkschaften in der Schweiz: Eine soziologische Untersuchung*. Zürich: Limmat.

Jans, A. 1991: Die Mitbestimmung in der Schweiz und die europäische Herausforderung. *Gewerkschaftliche Rundschau*, 3/4, 58-107.

Katzenstein, P. 1984: *Corporatism and Change. Austria, Switzerland and the Politics of Industry*. Ithaca: Cornell University Press.

Schmidt, M.-G. 1985: *Der schweizerische Weg zur Vollbeschäftigung*. Frankfurt: Campus.

Seghezzi, H. and Lenzlinger, K. 1991: *Industriestandort Schweiz, Chancen und Risiken für die Wettbewerbsfähigkeit des Industriesektors*. St. Gallen: Schweizerische Akademie für technische Wissenschaften.

Siegenthaler, J. 1968: *Die Politik der Gewerkschaften. Eine Untersuchung der öffentlichen Funktionen schweizerischer Gewerkschaften nach dem zweiten Weltkrieg*. Bern: Francke.

Sonderegger, A. 1979: *Mitbestimmung als Gewerkschaftsforderung*. Diessenhofen: Ruegger.

Steiner, J. 1970: *Gewaltlose Politik und kulturelle Vielfalt*. Bern: Haupt.

Wagner, A. 1985: *Wohlfahrtsstaat Schweiz*. Bern: Haupt.

Zanetti, B. 1981: Gesamtarbeitsvertrag und Friedenspflicht. *Wirtschaft und Recht*, 2, 30-9.

10

The Netherlands:
The End of an Era and the
End of a System

Jelle Visser[1]

Introduction

'The central task of a theory of industrial relations is to explain why particular rules are established in particular industrial relations systems and how and why they change in response to changes affecting the system' (Dunlop 1958: ix). It could be argued that growing international interdependence – in Europe symbolized by the EC single market, and by the growing influence of transnational corporations – signals a decisive reduction in the role of the nation-state and in the distinctive character of national systems of labour relations. Nevertheless, homogeneity in European industrial relations still seems far away; and in the case of The Netherlands, unique national features remain – though their significance is indeed diminishing.

The main theme of this chapter is that the Dutch system of labour relations is losing its national identity as a distinct configuration of interest-group organization and consensual policy-making. Distinctness was probably greatest in the 1950s – the pinnacle of a cross-class coalition which helped to implement a successful policy of industrialization and welfare state development, based on a legally enforced strategy of lower wage costs than foreign competitors. The policy was destroyed in the 1960s and proved impossible to re-establish in the 1970s. As a national strategy it was undermined by the forces unleashed by the internationalization and concentration of the Dutch economy. Its return was made impossible by increased demands for participation in organizations and society, the sharply decreased autonomy of the state, a process of fragmentation and polarization of interest group elites; and technological changes eroding the foundations and rationality of a centralized labour relations model (ter Hoeven 1972; Peper 1973; Teulings 1973; Akkermans and Grootings 1978; and Peper 1980).

1980 proved another turning point in Dutch labour relations. Unemployment rose to much higher levels than in comparable (small, European) countries (Therborn 1986), and union membership decline was among the most severe in the OECD area (Visser 1988; 1991). There was a sharp reassessment of the role of the state and public policies in labour relations and economic policy (Visser 1990a). With the completion of the EC's internal market and growing international competition, wage moderation again became important for Dutch business; though this time the balance of power in industrial relations had shifted in favour of the employers (Reynaerts 1985), and pay restraint could be imposed through the market rather than negotiated through 'political exchange'. For the first time since 1945, decentralization of bargaining and consultation practices proceeded without resistance, increasing the variation in conditions across industries and firms.

Why did unemployment assume such massive proportions in the mid-1980s? Why did Dutch trade unions suffer such a large decline in density? Before addressing these questions I will outline some broad historical patterns and themes in Dutch labour relations. The Netherlands is a small country (currently 15 million inhabitants) with a relatively weak industrial base (only about 20 per cent of the total labour force) and a large presence of multinational firms (employing half the industrial work force). The government is dominated by Christian-democratic parties (who have been in every cabinet since 1901), and the labour movement divided between socialist and Christian unions and parties. By international standards, The Netherlands has one of the most developed welfare states. We must comprehend such features if we are to understand the present dilemmas in Dutch labour relations, and the ways in which they may be resolved.

The Foundations of the Post-War Settlement

In most western European countries one can identify a post-war settlement with four main features: a government commitment to full employment; acceptance by all political parties, left and right, of welfare provision for all citizens; the participation of trade unions in the development and application of national social and economic policies; and a role for central union leadership in a responsible wage policy designed to combine price stability with full employment (Crouch 1977). In The Netherlands such a settlement was initiated as early as 1943, in illegal meetings during the war-time occupation, when leaders of the central organizations of employers and unions agreed a new approach to labour relations. Henceforth they would negotiate through a joint body, the Foundation of Labour (SvdA). Founded within a fortnight of the liberation in May 1945, the SvdA was recognized by the government as its top advisory body in matters of socio-economic policy-making.

According to Windmuller (1969: 432–8) three features characterized the post-war Dutch system of labour relations. First and foremost there was an unusual degree of government influence. In the decades after the war this was manifested in the centralized wage policy under a government-appointed Board of Mediators; from 1963 to 1982 in recurrent *ad hoc* regulation of wage settlements. Second, the system relied heavily on government consultation (*overleg*) with organized interest groups before decision-making in nearly all policy domains. Representation and consultation were highly institutionalized in a plethora of rules and boards. In addition to the SvdA, a tripartite Social-Economic Council (SER), with equal representation of central employers' organizations, union confederations and government-appointed experts, was founded in 1950. The SER was given extensive advisory and executive power in the domain of socio-economic policy-making. Mandatory neo-corporatist structures at the level of sectors and product-groups were also inaugurated, but proved ineffective outside agriculture and the retailing of basic foodstuffs. Centralization is the third basic feature of the Dutch system; in the first decade after the war it approached 'the outermost limits permissible in a non-authoritarian society' (Windmuller 1969:438). Consultation was limited to the leaders of central organizations. Collective bargaining took the form of national wage rounds and was conducted by a handful of officials, their advisers, the Board and the Minister. Individual employers had only limited discretion over the pricing of their products and how to reward labour. Regional or local union officials, let alone lay members, had no say. Democratic procedures to ensure the accountability of leaders or to ratify collective agreements were weak if not entirely absent. Structures of participation and consultation at the level of firms were either absent or vehicles for downward communication in tune with the paternalism of the time.

National Recovery

The centrally directed wage policy embodied a national economic strategy based on low wage costs compared to foreign competitors. The choice of this strategy and its initial acceptance are usually explained with reference to the disastrous state of the country after the war, the memory of the deep recession and high unemployment of the 1930s, and the need to revive a process of industrialization which had halted in the 1920s and 1930s, leaving The Netherlands as an economy based mainly on agriculture and trade. Low wage costs were considered a necessary condition for export-led industrial growth which would lay the foundations for increased welfare. The loss of the colonies (notably Indonesia) added urgency to the search for a strategy of national recovery.

It is not clear whether full employment was ever a policy objective in its own right, as was the case with economic growth, low wage costs, price stability and a favourable balance of payments. The prevalent view appears to have been that the favourable effects of the centrally guided wage policy, combined with counter-cyclical fiscal measures, would be such that no further instruments were needed. Unemployment rates were in fact low during most of the 1950s and 1960s (see table 10.1) and this is likely to have reinforced the assumption that employment policies were unnecessary. A specific unemployment or labour market policy never existed; in the late 1960s the lack of a regional manpower policy attracted for the first time international criticism from the OECD (OECD 1967; Veltman et al. 1968).

Table 10.1   Unemployment in The Netherlands (% of total labour force) 1950–90

1950	2.2
1960	1.2
1965	0.8
1970	1.2
1975	5.2
1980	6.0
1981	8.5
1982	11.4
1983	12.0
1984	11.8
1985	10.6
1986	9.9
1987	9.6
1988	9.2
1989	8.3
1990	7.5

Workers' Acquiescence

Steady income growth and increased social security, in addition to full employment, seem plausible reasons for worker support of wage moderation. It was not until the Second World War that a comprehensive statutory system of social security developed in The Netherlands. Before 1940 social security was a patchwork of voluntary and compulsory insurance and privately organized, mainly Christian and municipal poor-relief funds (van Loo 1981). Unemployment insurance had been a union affair, supplemented with public and municipal subsidies. This provision proved grossly inadequate during the 1930s recession when unemployment affected more than 20 per cent of the labour force (de Vries 1988). 'Against all economic logic and purely for the sake of prestige' (Klein 1980:5), The Netherlands had been among the very last countries to abandon the gold standard, with disastrous effects on employment and wages. During the war, the occupying Germans had started to reform the labour relations and social security systems as part of their attempt to 'nazify' political and social relations (Asselberghs 1982). Some of these reforms – e.g. the Board of Mediators, compulsory insurance against unemployment, public employment services, and limitations on dismissals – stayed after the war, and it was hard to deny that they were improvements compared to the previous laissez-faire. In 1947 the government – a Christian-socialist coalition which remained in office from 1945 to 1958 – introduced old age pensions, made permanent in 1956. In 1952 compulsory unemployment insurance was introduced, fixing benefits at the unprecedented level of 80 per cent of the daily wage for 'bread-winners', 70 per cent for other married persons, and 60 per cent for juveniles living at home. Employers, workers and the state each incurred one-third of the cost.

There is no evidence that union members rejected wage moderation. Between 1948 and 1957 union membership increased by 4.4 per cent per year, a rate of growth never matched before or since over such a long period in time. It was not until the austerity measures of 1957 that members began to 'vote with their feet'. Membership turnover increased markedly between 1957 and 1962, especially in the socialist unions (van de Vall 1964). The incidence of strikes, already low by international comparison before the war, decreased even further and was comparable only to the post-war low strike records in Switzerland, Austria, Sweden and Germany (Ross and Hartman 1960; Korpi 1983) (see table 10.2). Official strikes became rare; unofficial strikes, which are of course a better indicator of discontent over wage moderation, did take place but attracted few participants once the wave of Communist-led protests over the military policy in Indonesia (1946–9) and Marshall aid had subsided.

Table 10.2 Working days lost per 10,000 employees (yearly average) 1945–89

1945–9	1,148
1950–4	250
1955–9	260
1960–4	603
1965–9	59
1970–4	559
1975–9	266
1980–4	196
1984–9	91
1980	125
1981	53
1982	478
1983	260
1984	63
1985	188
1986	81
1987	117
1988	18
1989	50

Between 1948 and 1968 there was no significant opposition to the left of the official unions.

The conjunctural explanation of the centrally directed wage policy has the advantage that it also explains the gradual erosion of support when conditions improved and the memory of recession and war receded. Yet it does not explain why worker support continued over such a long period of time. The policy began to falter by the early 1960s, but Windmuller (1969: 392) is right to remind us that 'no other system of administered wage determination has done well for an equally long period of time'. Why did union leaders continue to support a policy which placed very strict limits on what is often regarded as their *raison d'être*? The consent of employers needs explanation as well, especially given their traditional opposition to state intervention in the domain of labour relations (van Waarden 1985).

Pillarization

Dutch trade unions used to be divided into three main currents and two fringes: a socialist movement and a Catholic and Protestant centre; a liberal fringe to the right, mainly attracting civil servants and clerical staff, and a syndicalist-communist opposition to the left with support in the rural north and in the two main urban centres, Amsterdam and Rotterdam. In the 1970s the socialist and Catholic movements merged, a process which was formally completed with the foundation of the Dutch Federation of Trade Unions (FNV) in 1981. Some non-affiliated Catholic civil servants' unions joined the Christian Union Federation (CNV), the old Protestant centre which finally realized its historical claim to be an all-Christian organization. The upsurge in unionization of clerical and managerial staff led to the foundation of a new Federation of White-Collar Staff Organizations (MHP). The syndicalist-communist opposition disappeared, or was re-absorbed into the FNV unions, when the tensions of the cold war eased and the anti-communist clauses in most socialist unions were abolished. FNV unions represent about 60 per cent of all union members, CNV unions 20 per cent, and MHP unions 7–8 per cent. FNV, CNV and MHP are represented in the SER and the SvdA and most other fora. A new federation of mainly (semi-) public employee unions (ACV), which represents also 7–8 per cent of all union members in the country, was founded in 1990 and is now demanding official recognition, which the SER has refused.

The development of the trade union movement fitted neatly in the 'pillarized' (*verzuilde*) organization of Dutch society between 1900 and 1970. The image of 'pillars' refers to the segmented organization of social, cultural and political activities and services – from nurseries to funeral parlours, and everything in between: schools, hospitals, insurance, sports clubs, cultural associations, women's leagues, unions, employers' associations, newspapers and broadcasting companies. Rigid separation of membership, supporters, clients or interest categories was combined with a high degree of elite control within each of these segments. Between these pillars, elites cooperated through interlocking directorates (see, among others, Daalder 1966, and Lijphart 1968). Most authors recognize two complete pillars (Catholic and Protestant) and two incomplete ones: socialist (without, for instance, an employers' federation, socialist schools or the 'cement' of a church) and liberal (with a weak union component and without a church). This system emerged around the turn of the century as the result of the competition between a Catholic emancipation movement, a petty-bourgeois and mainly Protestant reaction against early industrialization and the spirit of nineteenth century liberalism, and the emerging socialist labour movement. Not until the late 1960s did the pillar system begin to crumble (see also table 10.3).

Table 10.3 Union membership by religious and ideological affiliation (% of total membership)

Year	Catholic	Protestant	Socialist	Syndical Communist	Other
1909	14.1	7.8	21.9	3.4	52.8
1919	23.0	11.9	36.5	7.4	21.2
1939	26.9	16.9	39.8	1.5	14.9
1945	27.5	13.7	29.9	20.3	8.6
1955	34.0	17.8	37.1	3.7	7.5
1965	34.0	18.0	36.1	1.3	10.6
1975	27.2	15.6	40.8	1.2	15.2

Note: Membership in Catholic, Protestant, socialist etc. trade unions, i.e. unions which according to their rulebooks adhere to Catholic, Protestant, socialist principles.
Source: J. Visser (Dues database).

The Emergence of Economic Policy Unionism

The seeds of 'economic policy unionism' (Barbash and Barbash 1972) were planted early. In The Netherlands, trade unions did not make their breakthrough in the industrial work force until the decade before the outbreak of the First World War, at a time when only half of adult males had the vote (Daalder 1985: 320–1). Industrial take-off had only just started (de Jonge 1968). Unionization was negligible at the turn of the century, but rose to 17 per cent by 1913 (see table 10.4) – a higher proportion than in most European countries. The coincidence of the formation of the Dutch union movement with the struggle for universal suffrage and the mobilization of Dutch society into 'pillars' was not without consequences. Trade unions received their organizational imprint and ideological programme from mobilizing political movements, before industrial take-off had created large concentrations of workers subject to industrial discipline and living in large urban centres. Dutch trade unions were created by socialist organizers,

Table 10.4 Union density in The Netherlands 1910–89

1910	13.1
1920	35.8
1930	30.1
1940	29.4
1950	42.2
1960	39.4
1970	36.5
1980	31.5
1981	29.6
1982	27.9
1983	26.2
1984	24.8
1985	24.1
1986	23.5
1987	23.4
1988	23.2
1989	23.4

Note: There is a break in the data from 1952, when the Communist federation EVC stopped reporting membership figures.
Source: Visser (DUES database).

Catholic priests and Protestant ministers, not craftsmen or factory workers (Rüter 1946). This explains the early dominance of confederations and the preference for political action.

Not only did Dutch trade unions originate outside the workplace, there also were no significant craft traditions. Hence the questions of union presence in the workplace and control over the labour process never appeared relevant to organization until the 1970s. The orientations of Dutch unions to organization above plant level also reflects a power balance in favour of employers. Since 'employers were almost invariably strong enough to prevail in any contest of wills over these issues, ... the neglect of the plant as a place of activity was also very much the result of a sober appraisal of the power distribution between management and labour' (Windmuller 1969: 402). The dominant course of action of Dutch unions, socialist and non-socialist alike, was to seek protection of workers' rights through rules and institutions, negotiated and defended outside the workplace, preferably guaranteed and extended by the law. The ballot box, legal protection and, if necessary, well-organized strikes would bring the rights and benefits which workers would never achieve through the market.

The orientation towards the state and political action was reinforced by the need of socialist unions to distance themselves from their syndicalist progenitors, and by misgivings over the strike weapon in Christian union circles. Until the turn of the century syndicalism was still the most popular blend of unionism. Its fluid principles of organization and direct approach to action had a natural appeal to the common labourers of the pre-industrial era: seasonal workers in agriculture, peat-diggers, navvies digging canals and waterways, unskilled labourers in construction, ports and warehouses, who generally lived and worked in appalling conditions (Harmsen and Reinalda 1975). The alliance between syndicalism and socialism as a political movement (the Social-Democratic Labour Party was founded in 1894, the syndicalist union federation a year earlier) was inevitably unstable and ended with the 1903 general railway strike. The strike was lost; large numbers of workers were sacked and a liberal-Christian government responded with a 'Strangulation Law' – as the socialists called it – which prohibited strikes by public employees. After the strike, Protestant and Catholic workers were mobilized against the ideas and methods of class struggle on a much wider scale than before and placed their confidence in 'corporatist' alternatives based on coop-eration with employers. Socialist union organizers decided to break with syndicalism and to build their unions on the principles of strong leader-ship, well-paid officials, central strike funds, membership discipline and substantial contributions and benefits. This 'strategic choice' was influ-enced by the success story of the Amsterdam diamond workers who had succeeded in organizing all occupations within the same union and achieved an unusual degree of solidarity as well as much higher wages and benefits than workers in comparable industries. The leader of this union, Henri Polak, was to become the founder and long-term president of the socialist union federation (1905). Having worked in Britain and translated the Webbs' *History of Trade Unionism*, Polak was convinced of the 'new union' model but combined with the advantages of German-style industrial unionism.

Institutionalization

The 'most striking' feature of Dutch trade unions, according to Windmuller, was 'their underlying sense of responsibility for the welfare of the nation as a whole ... showing itself after the war in many different ways – wage restraint, participation in innumerable public and semi-public institutions, an exceedingly low rate of conflict, acceptance of stringent economic con-trols, and the imposition of discipline in labour's own ranks'. Following Lester (1953), Dunlop (1958) and Ross and Hartman (1960), he emphasized the post-war maturation of the trade unions and the elevated role of national union leaders as explanations of industrial peace.

Continuing a process which had started in 1919 when they had been invited to take part in a newly created High Council of Labour, union leaders became part of the most prestigious advisory councils of the country. They had become social partners and took part in an ever-increasing number of boards and committees. This had a profound effect on the professionalization of trade unions. The ratio of paid officials to members increased three-fold, the number of paid staff ten-fold. The supremacy of national and confederal headquarters was further strengthened. There was a constant rise in the salaries and prestige of expert staff and consultants, especially economists and lawyers. Lay members disappeared from the national executives of most unions. By international standards, Dutch union confederations have one of the highest staff-membership ratios (Visser 1990b: 168), which can be seen as a legacy of a sustained period of central wage policies (Windmuller 1975).

Under the guise of the centrally imposed wage standards, collective bargaining became established as the main regulatory device for employment relations. Before 1940, collective agreements had applied to less than 20 per cent of workers. Bargaining coverage had actually declined during the 1930s recession when employers started to force wages down. By 1951, coverage had risen to 40 per cent of workers in the private sector; in 1956 to 70 per cent and in 1960 to 73 per cent, about the same percentage as today. Blue-collar workers are almost 100 per cent covered, except in very small firms, while bargaining coverage of white-collar employees has expanded steadily in the 1960s and 1970s. Owing to a high degree of employer organization (see below) and the system of legal reinforcement, especially under the Collective Agreement Extension Act of 1937,[2] twice as many workers are covered by bargaining as are in trade unions, compared to only two-thirds before the war. The centrally directed wage policy also helped establish the national industry-level multi-employer agreement as the dominant form of labour contract. Before the war only 10 per cent of all private-sector employees were covered by national agreements, by the mid-1950s the proportion had risen to 60 per cent. Regional, local and single-employer agreements declined in number and importance. Salaries and other terms of employment in the public sector were determined by government order, after a prescribed round of consultations with recognized cartels of public employee unions belonging to FNV, CNV, MHP and ACV. Between 1962 and 1982, salary increases were pegged to private-sector pay rises; since 1982 the public sector has been slowly evolving towards true collective bargaining.

The institutionalization of the advisory and bargaining tasks of trade unions, though limited to a role outside the firm or workplace, increased union security. Recognition of unions affiliated to the main confederations was automatic, their representation in bargaining committees and advisory boards assured. Security at first translated into steady growth. As in many European countries, union membership had peaked at the end of the First World War (in which The Netherlands remained neutral) when expectations of a new social and political order were high. One worker in three was in a union, against one in six before 1913. Disappointment followed when the post-war boom ended in recession, unemployment rose sharply, many social and political aspirations remained unfulfilled, and the unions lost a quarter of their members. After the Second World War, during the phase of centralized wage policy, union density rose to almost 40 per cent – lower than in the Scandinavian countries, but almost as high as in Britain or Belgium, higher than in Germany and much higher than in France. Density among blue-collar workers averaged 60, among private-sector white-collar workers 15, and among public employees 70 per cent (Visser 1990b (see table 10.4). Membership continued to grow until the 1980s, though at a slower rate than employment. Unions could expect income to increase as a result of higher wages and more members; new functions and services were added to old ones; little foresight was necessary in what seemed a placid environment; organizational inertia did not threaten survival.

Employers: Power or Profits?

Employers in The Netherlands are well organized (van Voorden 1981; Nobelen 1983; van Waarden 1985). Nearly all firms with a hundred or more employees are members of an association. In the small-firm sector, employers are less organized but there are some well-staffed federations of small and medium-sized employers whose capacity for lobbying and political pressure, especially via the Christian and liberal parties, is considerable. Like trade unions, Dutch employers used to follow the pattern of religious segmentation. Another characteristic was the distinction between business and employers' associations. However, in 1968 the two functions were merged in the Federation of Dutch Enterprises (VNO). Two years later the Catholic and Protestant federations joined forces in the Christian Employers' Federation (NCW). The latter organization is an employers' federation only. Both NCW and VNO are politically well-connected, the NCW through the Christian Democratic Party, the VNO through the Christian and Liberal Parties. These peak associations encompass strong industry associations, e.g. in engineering, construction, printing and banking. Some of these are members of both VNO and NCW, for instance the powerful Engineering Federation (FME), and the General Employers' Federation (AWV) which straddles several industries and has most large multinational corporations (Shell, AKZO, DSM) among its members.[3] Philips is a member of the FME and is represented on the executive councils of both VNO and NCW. Like most multinational firms, however, Philips negotiates separately with the unions and signs its own collective agreements.

While the unions sought the attention of the state, Dutch employers organized against state intervention. The first major association was formed in 1899 to resist a proposal for mandatory compensation for work-related accidents. Christian employers' associations gave no support to social and labour legislation, corporatist ideology and the encouragement of church leaders notwithstanding. Employer opposition prevented comprehensive legislation on unemployment insurance before 1940. A platform of employers' associations managed to delay a law on collective agreements until 1927. Ten years later the Collective Agreement Extension Act would probably not have seen the light of day without a prior, successful, lobby of employers for legal protection of price cartels during the recession of the 1930s. Having gained important oligopolistic benefits, it became difficult to resist the application of the same principle to the labour contract: the cartel legislation of 1935 prepared the ground for the Act of 1937. Both laws introduced the notion of a 'public interest', superior to the will of free contracting parties and ultimately only safe in the hands of a popularly elected government. It was a small step towards a statutory wage policy.

The initial cooperation of employers with a statutory wage and price policy is perhaps best explained by 'their disarray after the war' (Peper 1980: 128). The country was in ruins; the government-in-exile wished to avoid a return to pre-war political and industrial conditions; individual employers were looking for leadership, and their leaders had decided that the world had changed and intensive cooperation with unions was needed for an orderly reconstruction of a capitalist economy. Trade unions accepted the capitalist foundations of the economy and the authority of employers to manage their firms, in exchange for what they considered a greater gain: social and economic benefits for their members and a role as co-manager in the nation's economy. Yet employers never became ardent supporters of the mandatory wage policy while it existed. The policy brought important benefits, of which low wage costs were probably the most tangible. While high economic growth guaranteed more welfare to everybody, labour's share of national income actually fell between 1950 and 1960, from 72 to 68 per cent. The fact that the policy helped to keep wages down and gave Dutch companies a significant cost advantage over foreign competitors was 'not altogether overlooked by the employers, but strangely enough it was overruled by more ideological arguments' (Pen 1973: 261). According to one insightful author, Dutch employers tend to place 'power above profits' (Nobelen 1983). Large employers soon complained that the policy was too rigid and prevented expanding firms, regions and industries from attracting additional labour.

The Development of a Passive Welfare State

In the years after 1958, following the Treaty of Rome and the formation of the European Economic Community, The Netherlands was sometimes accused of 'social dumping' (Pen 1963: 218; Terpstra 1973). Dutch wages were 20–25 per cent below those in Germany or Belgium; working hours were significantly longer than in either country (Visser 1989a). In border areas, workers crossed into Belgium and Germany to find better-paid jobs. In 1961 a paper entitled 'The Netherlands – A Social Paradise?' aroused considerable debate, questioning post-war moral and social progress and comparing the Dutch unfavourably with the more militant unions in Belgium and France (Hoefnagels 1961). A television broadcast in 1963 shocked the nation with evidence of blue-collar poverty. Only two decades later The Netherlands figured among the leading welfare states. In terms of public expenditure it is second only to Sweden. In 1982 one-third of GDP was spent on social security (compared to 23 per cent in the UK). 'If somewhere must be found to ride out the recession, Holland must be the nicest, comfiest place to choose', wrote *The Economist* in its issue of 30 January, 1982, adding that 'Dutch thinking and debate ... in particular on public finance and on the long-term effects of keeping more than a million people supported by the welfare state – is still cloudy and lacking in realism'. Schmidt (1982: 219) has classified The Netherlands among the passive social-democratic welfare states: a combination of a generous income support system and the absence of a coherent and active labour market policy. The Dutch name for welfare state, *verzorgingsstaat* (literally: 'caring state') expresses this rather well.

How do we explain this development? Economic theories of welfare state development (Cutright 1965; Pryor 1968; Wilensky 1975) emphasize economic growth. In the Dutch case this thesis has plausibility: the second stage of the welfare state revolution took off in the booming 1960s (see table 10.5 for some main social and economic indicators of the post-war years). In 1964 unions and employers agreed on a minimum wage which was made statutory four years later. In the same year the old Poor Law of 1854 was replaced by the General Relief Act, a safety-net for those not entitled to other benefits. Probably the outstanding innovation was the disability insurance for employees under the General Disability Act of 1967, which guaranteed 80 per cent of the last wage received until the age of 65. In 1965 the principle of automatic price indexation was introduced

Table 10.5   Main economic and labour relations indicators

	1950–63	1964–73	1974–9	1980–4	1985–9
National income[a]	4.3	5.6	1.5	0.5	2.7
Labour productivity[a]	3.5	4.6	2.4	1.7	1.4
Employment growth[a]	1.3	0.7	0.3	−1.2	1.5
Inflation (CPI)[a]	3.4	5.8	7.4	5.0	1.0
Real wage growth[a]	3.8	6.4	2.8	−1.7	1.1
labour's share[b]	0.1	5.4	6.6	−4.2	−5.0
unemployment[c]	1.8	1.5	4.9	9.9	9.5
working hours[d]	−13	−20	−20	−11	−18
union members[a]	2.9	1.2	1.0	−2.5	1.1
union density[c]	39.1	36.8	34.4	28.0	23.5
strikes[d]	68	42	36	13	35
strike involvement[e]	298	317	227	196	91

[a]=annual average change in percentage
[b]=change in percentage of net national income, per period
[c]=average per period
[d]=average number per year (annual contractual workingtime; strikes)
[e]=annual average of days lost per 10,000 workers in employment

Source: Own calculations from CBS (1990), CPB (1992), Visser (1989b) and DUES database.

in the triennial collective agreement at Philips, which like other large firms preferred the security of long-term planning of wage costs. In 1969 the SER accepted the principle of price indexation, soon applied in nearly all collective agreements. In 1974 the minimum wage, and with it all social benefits, was indexed to wage increases in the private sector.

However, the economic explanation cannot account for the leadership of The Netherlands among modern welfare states, nor for the continuous expansion of the welfare state after 1973 under conditions of faltering economic growth. The concurrent *Politics Does Matter* approach (Cameron 1978; Castles 1981; Schmidt 1982; Flora and Alber 1981; Korpi 1983; and Esping-Andersen 1985) stresses the impact of a strong union movement, the strength of social democracy, a centralized political system, and an export-oriented open economy in explaining high levels of welfare spending. But The Netherlands, with rather weak unions, a divided union movement and the minority position of social democracy, is an awkward case. During the years of welfare state expansion (1960s and 1970s), the Labour Party (PvdA) was in office for only five years (1965–6; 1973–7), always as a coalition partner of Christian parties and with a maximum vote of only one- third of the electorate. Our indicators of union density, union fragmentation, unity and militancy do not suggest that the Dutch union movement became stronger during this period, rather the reverse. Alternative explanations have stressed the competition between the PvdA and the Catholic People's Party (KVP) for the vote of Catholic workers, leading Christian democracy to do what in Scandinavia or Britain was done by social democracy. The Dutch welfare state is very much a product of Christian-democratic policies and ideologies, especially in its organizational reliance on, and support for, private institutions (Albeda 1982). Decisions over levels of insurance and welfare spending are often left to private organizations representing particular interests, while the costs must be met elsewhere or are reinsured through the public purse. This is supposed to have made political readjustments under adverse economic conditions during the latter half of the 1970s and early 1980s more difficult ('institutional sclerosis').

International Pressure and Economic Restructuring

It began with international pressure. The opening of international markets with the formation of the EEC and the tight labour market after 1958, in particular in the populous western part of the country, would pull the large and expanding employers out of centralized wage determination and ultimately destroy it. In international circles, Dutch wage policy drew the criticism that it 'operated as a bounty on exports and as protection against foreign competition' (Windmuller 1969: 392). Perhaps defensible as an instrument of rapid industrialization after the war, the policy was not in fashion with the European Common Market and the new free trade initiatives of the early 1960s.

In 1959 the government, for the first time since 1945 without the participation of the PvdA, conceded a small differentiation of wages by industry based on productivity. However, since reliable productivity statistics were hard to come by and labour shortages also existed in low productivity sectors, the new system led to frustrations and encouraged evasion. Employers with full order books in tight labour markets had no choice but to offer 'black' wages, far above those negotiated between their representatives, the unions and the government. The unions were in a very difficult position: in 1964 they claimed an increase of 10 per cent, but a wage 'explosion' brought rises of 15 per cent, against an original prediction by the Central Planning Office of 2.6 per cent. For some observers this demonstrated the need, for others the impossibility or even undesirability, of centrally regulated wages. During the 1960s unions and employers tried voluntary central coordination, with limited success. Towards the end of the decade the government was again seeking statutory instruments of wage control. Wage levels in The Netherlands were now on a par with West Germany, Belgium or France. Labour's share in national income rose to 79 per cent in 1970 and to 83 per cent in 1973. The unions had little reason to regret the demise of the centrally guided wage policy, but employers often showed 'nostalgia' (Albeda 1987: 274). They became in fact the 'belated supporters of a centralised policy which no longer worked' (Pen 1973: 261; Windmuller 1969: 363).

Deregulating wage developments in the private sector after 1963 led to a sharp increase in wage costs, which shocked the economy into a process of restructuring. Labour-intensive industries, no longer protected by a wage-cost advantage, were forced to modernize and invest in labour-saving techniques, move abroad, or shut down. Plant closures and take-overs by larger corporations were the result. By 1970, 53 per cent of all industrial employment was concentrated in 30 corporations, including the multinationals Philips, Shell, AKZO and Unilever. In 1980 Philips, Shell, AKZO, Unilever and the fertilizer and chemical company DSM employed around one million people world-wide, one-sixth of these in The Netherlands (a reduction by half compared to 1967). In the 1980s these firms further reduced their staff; currently Philips is cutting employment from 70,000 to 45,000 in The Netherlands.

At first, displaced workers were easily absorbed by expanding firms and sectors. Union officials routinely limited their role to negotiating a 'social plan' including severance payments for older workers. Within the major employers' federations there were conflicts between large and small firms; on occasion the suspicion was voiced that large firms used trade union pressure to force a concentration process upon Dutch industry. The fact is that employers' organizations were not very effective in maintaining collective discipline under pressure; paradoxically, years of statutory wage controls had 'disarmed' them. Before 1940 most associations had imposed fines on deviant members (Windmuller 1969; van Waarden 1985); after 1945 they shifted their attention like unions to representative and advisory functions, and concentrated on technical assistance to firms in the context of collective bargaining, in particular the introduction of 'rational' job classification and payment systems. The old 'resistance funds' were in many cases discontinued – unions were no longer a threat and it was now the task of the state to uphold order. Of course, dissident members could be threatened with expulsion, but this was hardly an effective sanction against large firms and was rarely used; the threat to withhold services was only effective in the case of small and medium-sized firms which did not have their own 'labour relations' departments. Hence, it did not discourage large firms from 'going it alone'. Employers' federations are more dependent on the resources of large firms (membership contributions are based on the total wage bill), than large firms are on associations' resources (information, political access, legitimacy). Nearly all large multinational firms in The Netherlands, while remaining prominent members in employers' associations, negotiate outside sectoral agreements. They began to experiment with 'progressive' personnel policies in the 1960s in order to attract more highly skilled and better motivated workers. Following the concentration process in Dutch industry, these single-firm agreements increased in number and size during the 1970s. Agreements in small firms tended to disappear (Huiskamp 1983).

In the 1970s, following the merger and reorganization of VNO and NCW, employers' organizations professionalized. The VNO elected its first full-time president in 1973; decision-making was centralized, and the staff greatly increased. Today about three times as many officials and staff members work in employers' associations as in trade unions. In response to strikes in 1972 and 1973, the FME reinstated a mutual resistance fund to which member firms had to pledge a contribution which they would forfeit if they yielded to union pressure on an 'off-limits' issue; the VNO introduced a similar fund. In the Council of Employers' Organizations (RCO), VNO and NCW coordinated their policies with organizations of small and medium-sized firms and federations representing agricultural interests. Some authors have claimed that these changes express the increased power of large firms (Teulings et al. 1978: 273; Frenkel et al. 1980: 125). Kendall (1977: 253) writes that Philips, Shell and Unilever have a 'disproportionate influence on employers' attitudes and policies'. They pay the bill; they have guaranteed seats on executive councils, and votes are cast on the basis of contributions (though it must be added that formal voting in the executive councils of employers' federations is a rare event) (Nobelen 1983: 57–8).

Polarization

Around 1970, relations between unions and the government, and between employers and unions, deteriorated. This was followed by a period in which employers went into opposition against the Den Uyl government (1973–7), the only Dutch government dominated by social democrats and other left parties. The struggle over the Wage Bill, introduced in 1968 in order to replace the old statute of 1945, reflected the changing ideological and political climate in the union movement. In the new bill the Board of

Mediators was abolished and replaced by a set of powers in the hands of the Minister of Social Affairs, to be applied only after advice from the SER. Under the act, a statutory wage freeze would be possible in the event of an economic emergency, and collective agreements could be abrogated if considered harmful to the economy. The latter provision caused a storm of union protest: socialist union leaders called it the private-sector version of the 'Strangulation Law' (Pen 1973). Unions organized protest strikes when the proposal came up for debate in parliament, and the socialist and Catholic union federations suspended their participation in the SER. The government won but only after it promised never to apply the offending clause, which was deleted from the law in 1974. This episode can only be understood against the background of an ideological radicalization in the union leadership against statutory wage controls. It was a right-centre government which had proposed the bill. Union leaders, who had risked so much in supporting the policy in the past and had felt cheated by evasion on the part of employers, were in no mood to try again. Moreover, warnings by economists that wage and price rises would cause unemployment were not borne out by events – until 1971–2 the unemployment rate stayed near 1 per cent.

Other events which marked the transition to a less consensual era in industrial relations were the unofficial strike wave of 1970 in the Rotterdam port, which challenged a stultified union leadership and signalled the re-emergence of a radical Marxist left; the successful opposition in 1972 to a plant closure in the AKZO corporation by means of a factory occupation, which drew widespread support from church leaders, local and national union leaders, students and news-papers; leadership clashes between the newly-formed *Industriebond* NVV (a merger of unions in metal and electrical engineering, chemicals, textiles, clothing and leather, mining and miscellaneous industries) and its (socialist) confederation over wage moderation, causing the resignation of the confederation's president; highly publicized strikes in engineering in the spring of 1973 over a wage package including income redistribution clauses, which angered employers and led to the restoration of the FME's mutual resistance fund, and provoked managerial staffs to establish company staff unions.

De-Pillarization and Democratization

The radicalization of labour relations reflected deep changes in Dutch society which accompanied the de-pillarization process. These changes include a decline in religious identity and allegiance, looser ties between religion and organization, anti-leadership sentiments, demands for participation, and growing insecurity of authority. Fewer people identified with Protestant, Catholic or socialist sports clubs, newspapers, youth associations, unions, etc. This tendency was most pronounced in the political arena and in the Catholic constituency; in the elections of 1967 the Christian parties lost the majority which they had held since 1917, while the Catholic

People's Party lost almost half its electoral support between 1963 and 1972. The Catholic union movement, also in decline (see table 10.3), began to radicalize and pursued trade union unity, eventually merging with the social-democrat unions (FNV).

The crisis of authority and an increased demand for participation in the name of 'self-actualization', 'equality', 'humanization of work', or other lofty goals, spread from universities, schools, churches and political parties to companies and trade unions (Lammers 1973; Daalder 1974). Negative experiences with the merger waves of the 1960s and a number of painful plant closures had drawn sharp criticism from union members who felt abandoned by union officials. Unions had no status within the plant, and lay-off terms were negotiated by union full-time officials. The mandatory works council, introduced in 1950, was first and foremost a paternalist body, chaired by the employer as 'head of the enterprise' and at best serving as a channel for consultation between employer and workers under the auspices of the former. In 1950, trade unions had accepted the works council because they attached little strategic importance to the enterprise and had conceded the workplace to the employer – real power would be located outside the firm. In the course of the 1960s, following unrest over plant closures and restructuring, unions were forced to revise this view. Union representatives on the works council began in some cases to meet separately from the employer (Teulings 1981). This innovation was later sanctioned in the new Works Council Act of 1971, which kept the employer in the chair but stressed representation in addition to consultation tasks. The new Act also increased the number of issues on which the council's consent was needed, strengthened the rights of council members, and for the first time laid down legal penalties in the case of non-cooperation by employers.

The compromise of a dual council left almost everybody dissatisfied. Employers suddenly discovered the virtues of consultation (although before the Act less than 40 per cent of all firms of 50 and more employees had actually established a council) and had difficulties in accepting the increased independence of 'their' council. Unions could not be sure whether they could trust the council. Radical unions such as the *Industriebond* saw no place for the council and began to organize union plant committees (*bedrijfsledengroepen*), but found it very hard to make them effective (a report in 1989 showed that only a quarter of the committees functioned satisfactorily). In 1979 the law was again revised and the works council finally became a representative body, elected from and by the firm's employees, but with the obligation to meet management at least six times a year. Works councils are mandatory in firms with 100 or more employees, and with more limited tasks and rights in firms with 35 to 99 employees. They actually exist in 80–90 per cent of all firms with 100 or more employees, and in at least 50 per cent of the smaller firms (Looise 1989). In a recent survey just over 80 per cent of all employees in the private sector, working in firms with 35 or more employees, reported the existence of a works council. Only 21 per cent of these employees report a union plant committee (van den Putte et al. 1991).

Windmuller observed that 'Dutch union leaders have the same tendency to deal with their members in a spirit of benevolent authoritarianism or high-handed paternalism which they want employers to abandon in dealing with their employees' (1969: 223). According to Pen (1973: 223), this 'went unnoticed for a long time [but] now draws attention from critics in and outside the union movement'. The 1970s witnessed a new generation of union leaders and officials, looser ties between unions and parties (until the early 1970s top union officials were represented in parliament and on party executive committees), the decline in anti-communism, and a more open style of handling conflicts. Union rulebooks were generally revised to allow for more membership participation, strengthening 'representative' over 'administrative' rationality.

The Left Conjuncture

Social changes in the 1960s weakened government authority and respect for the law. Students challenged educational policies; women defied the ban on abortion; environmentalists resisted urban development; workers fought to defend their jobs; civil servants defied the prohibition on strikes. The government's response was to increase participatory schemes, advisory boards, tripartism, in short, co-optation of groups which might otherwise obstruct the implementation of its policies. In 1973, this 'left conjuncture' enabled the formation of a government dominated by PvdA and other left-wing democrats, supported by the KVP under pressure of its union wing, and one of the Protestant parties. The new government had a rough ride since it was barely tolerated by the right wing in the Christian parties who held the balance of power in parliament. Nevertheless, it embarked upon an ambitious programme of reforms (including new legislation on works councils, and wage-earner funds), but it lost office after failing to win a parliamentary majority in 1977.

The Den Uyl government was almost immediately faced with the sobering consequences of the 1973-4 oil crisis. It responded with mandatory wage controls. Since it saw the support of its trade union allies rather than the cooperation of employers as the key to success, these controls were packaged in policies aiming at income redistribution, expansion and individualization of the family-based social security system and job-creation programme. Employers felt under attack; in an unprecedented open letter to the prime minister and Labour leader, the presidents of the nine largest multinational corporations complained about anti-employer policies allegedly undermining confidence in the market and the investment climate. More worrying than this vote of no-confidence was the declining willingness to invest in Dutch firms and the increased investment by Dutch companies overseas. Net domestic investment declined from an average of 7 per cent of GDP before 1973 to 4.6 per cent after 1973, and to a mere 1.2 per cent in the early 1980s. Reviving a long tradition – interrupted only in the 1940s and 1950s – The Netherlands became again a major capital exporter and Dutch investments abroad, particularly in the United States, reached an all-time high.

Wage Moderation and the Incomes Policy Failure

In the second half of the 1970s economic conditions deteriorated, leading in the early 1980s to the worst economic recession since 1945 (see table 10.5). After 1973 national income and labour productivity increased at half their previous rates; in the early 1980s national income actually declined. Until 1982 wages increased in real terms, though only by small amounts; after 1982 real wages fell. Inflation was also higher, but fell sharply in the 1980s following a series of austerity measures. Unemployment jumped from around 100,000 to 200,000 after the first oil crisis, and soared to 800,000 or 14 per cent of the labour force after the second. The number of beneficiaries under the disability insurance scheme – initially estimated to grow to a maximum of 200,000 people – had risen to 400,000 by 1978, and rose further to 900,000 in the course of the 1980s. Currently, less than one-third of the male population aged 55 to 65 is in the labour force; two-thirds are disabled or in early retirement. Costs soared as well; taxes and social security charges, as a percentage of national income, rose from 32.2 in 1968 to 52.2 in 1980. In 1960 eight employees paid for the benefit of one inactive (unemployed, disabled, sick) person; in 1983 this proportion was 2.2 to 1 (Douben 1984: 50).

The government, faced with the increased costs of an expanding social security system linked to private-sector wage growth, intervened on many occasions with wage freezes, ceilings and other measures. Almost inevitably, this had a standardizing and levelling impact: inter-industry wage relativities remained constant despite diverging productivity and labour market trends; intra-industry wage differentials contracted somewhat (de Wolff 1983). Employers and the government's macro-economic advisers, in particular the central bank and the finance ministry, voiced dissatisfaction. Flanagan et al. (1983: 131), who reviewed the final years of Dutch incomes policy, concluded that there was 'a limited responsiveness of the bargaining system to the problems emanating from both an appreciating currency and an expansive welfare policy'. Wage moderation could not prevent unit labour costs rising more in the 1970s than in West Germany, by far the largest export market for the Dutch economy.

The long-term instability of an egalitarian wage restraint policy, as analysed by Svensen (1989) for the case of Sweden, applies also to The Netherlands. Without a compensatory active labour market policy and some mechanism for redeploying excess profits, relatively high increases in the low-pay sector and relatively low increases in the high-pay sector produce wage drift in the latter and structural unemployment in the former. Ultimately this weakens the independent bargaining power of unions in the low-pay sector and reduces the employers' need for central wage bargaining. Unemployment and union weakness make a centralized wage policy not only economically but also, rather surprisingly, politically dispensable. Wage moderation could be achieved without a political price; and in the 1980s a centre-right government was still able to gain a parliamentary majority despite soaring unemployment and the condemnation of its policies by the entire union movement, Christian unions included.

Wil Albeda, who served as Minister of Social Affairs in the centre-right coalition (1977–81) which replaced the Den Uyl government and was the author of many incomes policy measures, later argued that the 'collapse of the centralized wage policy produced a kind of trauma in labour relations in the Netherlands' (1985: 254). It was above all a government (not an employer or union) priority, because any government since the welfare revolution of the 1960s 'felt deprived of political controls over wages on which it had come to rely'. Successive governments tried to convince trade unions to accept less private income for more public expenditure and solidarity with unemployed and disabled workers. Dutch unions had not been deaf to this plea, but they were divided, failed to convince their membership, or asked for side-payments and reforms which employers refused to pay. The failed campaign of FNV unions in 1977–8 for decentralized job-guarantee planning agreements (*Arbeidsplaatsen-overeenkomsten*) was an example of the latter. A year later the members of some FNV unions rejected a central agreement which confederal leaders and employers had almost signed, trading a wage standstill for a halt in public spending cuts and the maintenance of benefit levels. Three years and half a million unemployed later, in 1982, a central agreement was reached, the first in a decade, proposing a freeze in price indexation in exchange for a working-time reduction on condition that it would not increase costs. Unions and employers agreed on the need to restore profits as a means to keep jobs in The Netherlands and in the meantime to share existing jobs between a growing number of people in order to contain the rise in unemployment.

Crisis and Realignment

The need to improve the industrial base and to restore private sector profitability was expressed in two major policy documents which appeared in the midst of the 1980s recession. The first report, written by an expert committee chaired by a Labour Party technocrat, advocated public policies to improve the structure and management of Dutch industry, and to stimulate growth sectors – adopting an approach not unlike MITI in Japan – but also stressed the need to reduce welfare spending and subsidies to ailing firms and industries. The second report, written by a committee chaired by Shell's president, preferred an American (or British) to a Japanese approach. No government interference with the market, except for general tax rebates and investment premia, and a reduction in public spending were presented as the best remedies to restore business confidence and profits. Other recommendations included continued wage moderation, the abolition of automatic cost-of-living adjustments in collective agreements, a reduction in the minimum wage and social security benefits, wider wage differentials reflecting skill and productivity, and the abandonment of incomes policy. These measures were more or less implemented by the 'no nonsense' government of Ruud Lubbers, a coalition between Christian and liberal parties (1982–6; 1986–9), although the government only managed to meet its austerity targets for public expenditure through the sale of public assets.

Austerity and the End of Income Redistribution

Salaries and benefits in the public sector were frozen in 1982, and incomes lowered by 3 per cent in 1983, causing a major conflict with public service unions. Salaries remained frozen in subsequent years, in part compensated by a two-hour reduction in the average working week. The same measures applied to the minimum wage and the social benefits tied to it. In 1987 major changes in the system of social security came into effect. The old unemployment provisions have been consolidated in a new Unemployment Act, the main difference being a lower benefit level (70 per cent instead of 80) and a shorter period of entitlement. For a further year the unemployed may receive 70 per cent of the minimum wage (the so-called 'social minimum' below which no income is supposed to fall). When this benefit ends they must rely on social assistance. In the case of disability, benefits remain at 70 per cent until the retirement age of 65. All benefits, including old age pensions (also based on the 'social minimum') have been individualized. The impact of these measures has been a slight reduction in total costs despite the increase in benefit recipients. The return of the PvdA to the government coalition, in September 1989, was accompanied by the restoration of some degree of linkage between pay increases and social benefit adjustments, though this was made conditional upon continued wage moderation and austerity measures affecting social security. Coalition partners have promised each other to give a high priority to a further reduction of the public deficit (in order to meet the conditions for entry to the new European currency regime in 1996) and allow no further rises in taxes and social charges.

In the market sector, 1982 to 1986 was a period of wage moderation – a standstill in real terms with very low inflation rates (see table 10.5). Following the recommendations of the central agreement of 1982, cost-of-living adjustment clauses were frozen or abolished; very few still exist. Labour's share, which had risen from 83 to 91 per cent of the national income in the course of the 1970s fell to 80 per cent in 1986 and is expected to remain at that level in the early 1990s (CPB 1992). Over the full ten-year period 1977–87 unit labour costs rose by an annual average of 2.5 per cent, the lowest rate of increase in the European Community (Germany: 2.9; France: 4.1; Belgium: 4.6; Britain: 8.0; EC average: 7.2). This mainly reflects lower wage costs achieved between 1982 and 1987. From 1987 to 1990 the wage cost and unit labour cost increases in The Netherlands slowly approached German levels but remained far below the EC average (OECD 1991, table 1.5). In 1991, The Netherlands was mildly reprimanded by the International Monetary Fund for its excessive emphasis on wage moderation. The IMF argued that more emphasis should be placed on reducing government spending on social security and investing more in training and other infrastructural needs. The OECD has voiced similar recommendations in its recent survey of the Dutch economy.

The economic recession, continued wage moderation and the government's austerity measures have ended redistributive income policies. The long-term movement, from the early 1960s until early 1982, towards smaller differences between capital incomes and wage earners, and between wage earners and benefit recipients, was reversed after 1982. There is evidence of larger inter-firm differences in wages, between skilled and unskilled workers (CBS 1991), increased differences between post-tax wages and social benefits (Visser 1990a), and a more unequal distribution of wealth (Wilterdink 1991). The policy objectives of employers and the intention of the Lubbers government, expressed in 1982, that profits should be increased and income differences widened, have by and large been realized. Following the 1982 Central Agreement, price indexation clauses were first frozen and later removed from most collective agreements. In recent years a new debate has started on whether the minimum wage should be further lowered, by 30 per cent in order to create more low-paid jobs. The pressure to reduce benefit levels and increase the difference between wages and benefits is still mounting. Finally, proposals abound to replace the present comprehensive welfare state system by a so-called mini-system in which compulsory insurance provides only a basic minimum level of income maintenance, leaving it to individual choice to insure privately for higher benefits.

Causes and Consequences of Unemployment

Among the smaller European countries, The Netherlands had one of the worst unemployment records of the 1980s. After 1987 unemployment fell, but the current rate of 7.5 per cent (1991) is not comparable because official Dutch statistics have removed about a third of the unemployed from the official count on the ground that they are not immediately available for work. If one considers disguised forms of unemployment, especially those classified as disabled, there remains a very serious problem. The Netherlands has one of the lowest labour force participation rates in the OECD.

Various explanations for the extraordinary rise in unemployment during the early 1980s have been suggested, including the structure of wage policies, rising wages and unit labour costs, declining profits and investment rates, minimum wage levels which squeeze low productivity jobs out of the market, too generous social benefits, and a comparatively high rate of labour force growth. Birth-rates were higher and decreased later than in many neighbouring countries. In the 1970s changing life-style, marriage, birth-rate and child-rearing patterns caused a large influx of women into the labour market, where they stayed for longer periods than before: historically, few women stayed in the labour force after marriage, the result of a deliberate policy of discouragement by Christian-democratic governments, employers and unions (Blok 1978), reflected in a family-based tax and social security system. Only recently did this begin to change, partly through international pressure following the European directives on Equal Pay and Equal Opportunity.

Therborn (1986) has shown that, from a comparative perspective, these factors are insufficient to explain the size and depth of unemployment in The Netherlands. In his view mass unemployment on this scale can be explained only by the absence of an institutionalized commitment to full employment. As mentioned earlier, full employment was never an autonomous policy goal under the post-war settlement, but always dependent on the attainment of other goals, such as export growth and a stable currency rate (Fortuyn 1980: 80). In the 1970s it was overshadowed by the goal of income maintenance (Braun 1988): in 1983, 95 per cent of all the money spent on labour market policy went to income maintenance, compared to 80 per cent in Austria, 50 per cent in Norway and only 20 per cent in Sweden (Allaart 1988). Currently, the proportion spent on income maintenance is still 75 per cent. As early as 1977, the OECD wrote in its survey *The Dutch Economy in 1976* that in spite of the sharp increase in unemployment 'public concern had been less than what one would have expected only a few years ago'. The organization attributed this to the 'highly sophisticated system of social security and income guarantees' (OECD 1977: 11). Elsewhere I have argued that the diversion of surplus labour into channels other than overt unemployment (disability pensions, extended schooling, early retirement) has demobilized public attitudes to the unemployment problem; not until 1982 were trade unions mobilized on the issue (Visser 1987; 1989a: 234–5). The transfer of surplus workers to the disability system, rather than unemployment, was attractive to workers (who received generous benefits until retirement age while they did not have to be available for work), to employers (who bought off worker resistance for restructuring and lay-offs while the costs could be externalized) and trade unions (who despite the lack of bargaining power in declining industries often bargained more generous benefits, up to 100 per cent of final wages). The austerity measures of 1987 were not enough to halt this rise, and the number receiving disability pensions rose towards the million mark. In the summer of 1991 the government announced new austerity measures, shortening the length of benefits and lowering levels in a desperate attempt to regain control. A major conflict between the unions and the PvdA in particular resulted; and opinion polls suggest that in an election the party would receive only half the seats it did at the 1989 elections, clear evidence of public sensitivity on this issue.

A few years ago I wrote that continuous high unemployment combined with barriers to entry triggers processes which enlarge the area of the economy outside the scope of collective representation and bargaining (Visser 1990b: 237). Recent examples are the proposals to lower the minimum wage by 30 per cent in order to absorb more unskilled workers with low marginal productivity; by the Central Planning Office to abrogate the Collective Agreement Extension Act of 1937, ending public protection for collective agreements against non-organized employers; and by liberal and Christian-democratic politicians to replace the comprehensive welfare state by a minimal system. The philosophy puts the priority on increasing the comparatively low labour force participation rate in order to create a larger social and fiscal basis for welfare benefits for growing numbers of older people. The minimum-wage proposal would also affect benefits and bring many more people below the 'social minimum' level. Already three out of four benefit recipients have an income on or near the minimum. Of full-time employed workers only about 2 or 3 per cent actually earn the minimum wage, though the great majority receive wages not much higher, specified in collective agreements which are extended to non-unionized employers. The proposed reduction of the minimum wage would presumably create a wider range of lower wages – if unions and employers could be prevented from agreeing basic rates at their present levels. Hence, the public support for collective agreements which prevent wage- and cost-cutting would have to be overcome before the strategy could succeed.

There is little support for these proposals from employers, who seem to doubt whether lower wages would attract more people to accept jobs. A study by the research institute associated with the federation of small- and medium-sized employers shows that in retailing it is already difficult to fill jobs at the present minimum wage level (EIM 1991). Employers call instead for lower taxes and social security contributions, to reduce the gap between gross and net wages, and a wider differential between wages and benefits in order to increase the incentive to work. The proposal to dismantle the comprehensive welfare state, to restrict compulsory insurance to income maintenance at the level of the 'social minimum' and to encourage workers to take voluntary insurance for additional risks and benefits has more appeal to employers.

Trade unions, preoccupied with a debate about their own future, have not yet made up their mind. The decline in unionization in the past decade has encouraged the search for new (or very old?) ways to attract members. Should unions remain true to their 'inclusive' past, giving equal attention to those with and without jobs, and to members and non-members? Some unions seem attracted by the possibility of introducing selective benefits: collective agreements and additional benefits restricted to members, and membership-related insurance schemes. Others warn that the withdrawal of public protection for collective agreements may increase the incentive for employers to do away with unions and collective agreements, in line with the American scenario (Blanchflower and Freeman 1990). Similarly, a system of minimum social security is likely to cause a fatal underestimation (and hence underinsurance) of future risks by workers, leading to the emergence of a large social underclass. Interestingly, a recent representative survey among Dutch citizens shows a full appreciation of these dangers and clear-cut rejection, across the political spectrum, of the mini-system.

Union Decline

Unemployment was one of the main causes of union decline. The largest losses were incurred by unions in industry; factory closures and redundancies in engineering, shipyards, textiles and clothing cost them tens of thousands of members every year. The largest union in the market sector, the *Industriebond FNV*, lost more than 100,000 (or one-third) of its members between 1977 and 1987. Moreover, the collapse of the youth labour market led to a much smaller 'intake' of young members. An ageing membership and growing numbers of pensioners, disabled and unemployed, who maintained their membership card, resulted in an increasing proportion of 'inactive' members – up to 18 per cent overall, and 25 per cent of the FNV and CNV unions. Finally, unemployment also eroded confidence in union policies and bargaining power, leading to lower entry and higher exit rates of people with jobs. This lack of confidence and market power was demonstrated in a defensive campaign on working-time reduction and a decline in real wage rates between 1982 and 1986.

Unions did not have the strength to control the process of working-time reduction (Visser 1989a). The campaign was wholly defensive, intended to share out jobs ('old for young'; 'full-time for part-time') while many firms were busy scaling-down the size of their (blue-collar) work force in order to reduce costs and increase their competitiveness in a depressed market. Between 1983 and 1986 the average working week was reduced from 40 to 38 hours, but this was associated with few employment gains, and heavier workloads for those remaining in employment. Working-time reductions have led to a major reorganization in work schedules, accelerating the decline of the standard labour contract based on a normal week's work. It is through part-time jobs, many of which are *less* than half-time and of a flexible nature (such as 'on call' jobs), that the growing supply of female labour is accommodated.

In 1987 unions began to shift their bargaining objectives, from work redistribution to wage increases. The campaign for shorter working hours came, as expected, to a standstill. Given the sharp rise in profits and in work intensity, unions had to seek compensation for members' dissatisfaction and discovered that they could win members by pressing wage claims instead. After 1987 union membership started to increase again; 1990 in particular was a very promising year for unions, though still not enough to lift union density above 25 per cent. Most union growth was in the public sector and the proportion of 'inactive' members continues to increase as the membership grows older.

Table 10.4 shows that the decline in unionization began in the 1960s, continued in the 1970s and was particularly sharp in the 1980s. A time-series analysis on the basis of the Bain-Elsheikh model showed a strong correlation between membership growth and inflation, but little with

Table 10.6   Union density by federation, sex, employment and sector

Year	1970	1980	1990
FNV	23.6	21.0	14.8
CNV	5.6	6.1	4.6
MHP	-	2.3	1.7
other	7.8	5.9	3.9
male	43.7	44.2	35.2
female	13.9	18.0	13.0
market	29.4	26.2	20.3
manual workers	40.1	38.0	n.a.
non-manual workers	16.5	15.1	n.a.
government	64.4	59.7	49.0
manufacturing, mining and utilities	41.0	42.0	25.0
construction	48.0	44.0	40.0
transport and communications	52.0	49.0	33.0
trade, commerce and restaurants	10.0	10.0	6.0
financial and business services	8.0	8.0	9.0
social, communal and personal services	44.0	44.0	32.0

Note: Standardized density rates (without retired members).
Source: Own calculation from Visser 1989b; 1991.

changing levels of unemployment (Hendriks 1986; Visser 1987). The decline in density was general and affected all sectors of the economy (table 10.6), but the sharp fall in aggregate density was accelerated by the shift in employment from industry to services (Visser 1991: 115). Finally, unionization of women and young workers is particularly low in The Netherlands. Research suggests job instability, part-time work, and an employment bias towards ill-organized services and smaller firms as probable causes (van Rij et al. 1990; Visser et al. 1991). Controlling for these factors, the statistics of some FNV unions suggest that females have a higher propensity to unionize than males (Kaspers and Visser 1991). Currently, one-third of all jobs in The Netherlands are part-time, the highest percentage in the OECD, and more than 70 per cent of these jobs are held by females (OECD 1991: 46). It is not yet clear whether the membership decline of the 1980s represents a cultural shift as well and a lower propensity of youth to join permanent organizations rather than support temporary campaigns – support for and even membership in social movements such as Greenpeace has flourished during these years and is comparatively high in The Netherlands.

Dutch trade unions have not had an easy time. Density has fallen to its lowest point since the 1920s; private sector unions in particular have suffered a large decline in income, resources and staff. They are more divided among themselves than at any time since 1945: by political affiliation, between private and public sector unions, especially between rich and poor unions, and between 'inclusive' and 'exclusive' strategies. In the main confederation a programme for reorganizing union structures and recruitment activities foundered in the late 1980s because of opposition by the larger and richer unions; unions in the poorly organized service sector (less than 10 per cent organized), and the confederation itself (fewer resources and no bargaining partners), are the main losers. Dutch unions are still ambivalent towards the works councils. Are they rivals or allies? This old question is still unresolved as far as the unions are concerned. Recently they have tried to work out a deal with central employers' associations to reduce the bargaining role of the councils, but nothing has come of it. A large majority (about 70 per cent) of all works councillors are union members, but that has never guaranteed union control over the councils. The Dutch situation is characterized by multi-unionism, strengthening shop-floor autonomy; a union would have few if any sanctions against works council members who followed their own policies. Except where they offer (and could withhold) adequate professional services to the councils, which they scarcely do, and run a strong and well-organized union representative committee in the plant, Dutch unions have no control over works councils. Research shows that the most active councils are those which draw support from a union plant committee or union official; thus by offering positive rather than negative sanctions, unions may increase their influence over the councils, helping both workers and themselves. But at present only one in four works councils reports a regular contact with a union plant committee. The organizational and departmental structure of unions (and confederations) is still to a large extent shaped by their role in rather centralized bargaining settings and based upon their presence in hundreds of joint advisory committees. Services to members or member groups are poor.

Decentralization and Divergence

But for the changes in technology and company organization, it would be possible to believe that the current decentralization process in Dutch labour relations is a temporary phenomenon. In the 1980s virtually all Dutch organizations have undergone a process of restructuring of activities, often accompanied by heavy cutbacks in employment. The first motive was to restore cost-efficiency and profitability; later the generalized demand for working-time reductions necessitated new solutions to the organization of teams and rosters. In addition, new ideas about leaner organization and human resources management encouraged flatter hierarchies; reintegration of staff and line functions; market-like transactions between organization units; employee involvement; and productivity- and quality-related reward structures. From being championed for its own sake, worker participation becomes a means to improve productivity and product quality; in the words of a major Dutch sociologist of organizations, participation is promoted for functional rather than structural reasons (Lammers 1973).

It is not yet possible to estimate the full impact of these changes, but undoubtedly labour relations have been decentralized below the level of industries. This does not mean that (multi-employer) industry agreements have disappeared; where they existed (metal and engineering, construction, printing, dairies, banking, insurance, hospitals and health-care institutions, and agriculture, to name only the most important) they still do. But there is a tendency to make the application of these agreements more flexible and allow tailoring to the needs of individual firms and workers. Company agreements have increased in number and scope and today affect about one-third of all workers. Industry agreements in The Netherlands tend to determine minimum rather than standard terms, but differences are often trifling. Unions, in particular the *Industriebond-FNV* seem attracted to a 'second stage' in the negotiating process after framework agreements at the level of the industry, but employers' federations like the FME reject this view, arguing that two bargaining rounds are two pay rounds. The AWV, which is much less involved in industry bargaining and instead assists individual firms, is better disposed. Both FME and AWV agree that collective agreements still have a function, but they should be streamlined, that is, reduced in coverage (allowing more individual contracting), and scope (reversing the trend to add on new subjects such as training, health, job security, facilities).

However, Dutch employers are unready to concede local union representatives or works councils a greater bargaining role. Public pleas, for instance by the Minister of Social Affairs when still parliamentary leader of the CDA, for a greater role of works councils in wage bargaining have not received their support. The general position of employers' associations, and the actual behaviour of employers, is to keep works councils out of wage bargaining, as is required by current law unless unions and employers explicitly agree otherwise. According to a survey by Huiskamp and Risseuw (1988), only 6 per cent of works councils are involved in wage bargaining: employers prefer to leave wage bargaining in the hands of trade union leaders. This is true for employers' federations negotiating industry agreements and for companies negotiating their own agreement. The union, in The Netherlands, generally means an appointed union district official or, if the company is a very large multi-plant corporation, a national official. Employers appreciate continuous wage moderation, union acceptance of corporate restructuring and a low incidence of strikes.

Conclusions

In my view the current deconstruction of the post-war model of labour relations in The Netherlands is irreversible. Technological and organizational changes have rehabilitated the firm as the central theatre of operations in labour relations. Employers rather than trade unions have the initiative and power to seek new directions in labour relations, and they do so mainly in relation to a model in which internal, community-based commitments are stressed over and against the external, class- or status-based bonds on which trade unions of the European type are built. There are of course many people to whom the community model will never apply or appeal – those without work or holding marginal jobs; people employed in old-fashioned bureaucracies or in traditional occupational job markets. In this sense, labour relations tend to fall into at least three quite different types: a *terra nova* of large and small firms, connected to the international market and engaged in innovating their organizational and labour relations practices; an eroding *mainland* of firms, producing for the national market or in some way protected from foreign competition (agriculture, construction), which continue to employ rather traditional methods of labour management; and a *commons* (the semi-public sector) where things have become less cosy compared to the past but the impact of legal statutes and union protection is still very much felt (Visser 1992).

Dutch employers have no reason to return to central multi-industry bargaining. Neither do they expect benefits from a further weakening of trade unions – it could only lead to unpredictable and unwieldy conflicts. Hence Dutch employers are in no mood to de-recognize unions, to discontinue multi-employer bargaining or to disengage from joint institutions; but they are happy to attach less and less normative importance to all this. Employers' associations stress their role in assisting individual firms in conducting personnel policies and helping employers to comply with a far greater array of legal regulations (on works councils, health and safety, equal pay and equal opportunity, quotas for disabled workers, tax subsidies for jobless youth or training, etc.). Founded long before the first consulting firms and engaged in many consulting activities, especially during the centrally directed wage policy (for instance, on how the policy should apply, how a job classification system or measured work payment system – the two fads of the 1950s – were to operate), Dutch employers' associations are well-placed for a role in human resource management.

It must be feared that trade unions are among the conservative organizations of our time. Once they have adapted to a particular organizational mode of operation, usually very early in their history, they tend to stick to it. Dutch unions originated outside the firm, in industrial and open markets and in a highly politically charged environment. Success derived from tactical pressure on vulnerable employers and a calculated use of the strike weapon; and from gaining external control over the fruits of labour by influencing parties and governments through votes and alliances. Both methods require and favour a centralized and bureaucratic, because stable and predictable organization. Given the divisions in the labour movement at both political and industrial level, Dutch unions were remarkably successful. The development of the post-war full employment economy and welfare state was no small accomplishment. But once the national and international preconditions of the model on which union influence rested were destroyed, unions seemed blinded by their own specialization. Employers' associations seem to have found compensation in the thriving consulting business. Trade unions may yet have to find a new role.

Notes

1   The first draft of this chapter was written during a stay at Stanford University; I thank Philippe Schmitter and the Center for European Studies for their hospitality. Unknown to Philippe, perhaps, one of our conversations put me on the track of the main question of this chapter. I want to express my gratitude to the University of Amsterdam for granting me leave of absence and to The Netherlands–America Commission for Educational Exchange for funding my stay in the United States with a Fulbright scholarship. Finally, I owe Richard Hyman my thanks for requiring me to explain the demise of Dutch corporatism and for his patience.

2   This legal instrument, meant to protect the collective agreement against the competition of non-organized employers, was only applied four times before the outbreak of the war. In the first year of the occupation the law was 'discovered' by the new administration and applied 21 times; after the war extension became standard practice. The final decision is made by the Minister of Social Affairs and Employment.

3   This is a small minority of all firms. Of 234,000 private firms with employees in The Netherlands in January 1989, only 4,354 (less than 2 per cent) had 100 or more employees; 39,364 firms (16.8 per cent) had between 10 and 99 employees (information from the VNO, *Ecostat*, 29 November 1989). The importance of the small-firm sector (less than 99 employees) is also underscored by the fact that 45 per cent of all employees work in such firms, less than the EC average (55 per cent), but more than in Britain or Germany. In 1990 the small-firm sector produced 45 per cent of total output and 50 per cent of the value added of all private businesses (EIM 1990).

Abbreviations

ACV	*Algemene Vakcentrale* – General Federation of Trade Unions
AWV	*Algemene Werkgeversvereniging* – General Employers' Federation
CDA	*Christen Democratisch Appèl* – Christian-Democratic Appeal
CNV	*Christelijk Nationaal Vakverbond* – Christian Union Federation
CvR	*College van Rijksbemiddelaars* – Board of Mediators
FME	*Federatie van Werkgevers in de Metaal- en Electrotechnische Industrie* – Engineering Employers' Federation
FNV	*Federatie Nederlandse Vakbeweging* – Dutch Federation of Trade Unions
HRvdA	*Hoge Raad van de Arbeid* – High Council of Labour
IB-FNV	*Industriebond-FNV* – FNV Industrial Union
KVP	*Katholieke Volkspartij* – Catholic People's Party
MHP	*Centrale voor Middelbaar en Hoger Personeel* – Federation of White-Collar Staff Organizations
NCW	*Nederlandse Christelijke Werkgeversorganisatie* – Christian Employers' Federation
PvdA	*Partij van de Arbeid* – Labour Party
RCO	*Raad van Centrale Ondernemersorganisaties* – Council of Central Employers' Organizations
SER	*Sociaal-Economische Raad* – Social-Economic Council
SvdA	*Stichting van de Arbeid* – Foundation of Labour

VNO   *Verbond van Nederlandse Ondernemers* – Federation of Dutch Enteprises

References

Akkermans, M. and Grootings, P. 1978: From Corporatism to Polarisation: Elements of the Development of Dutch Industrial Relations. In C. Crouch and A. Pizzorno (eds), *The Resurgence of Class Conflict in Western Europe Since 1968*, vol. I, *National Studies*, London: Macmillan, 159-90.

Albeda, W. 1982: Christendemokratie en de ideologie van de verzorgingsstaat. *Beleid en Maatschappij*, 7, 2, 58-64.

Albeda, W. 1987: Recent Trends in Collective Bargaining in The Netherlands. In J.P. Windmuller et al., *Collective Bargaining In Industrialised Market Economies: A Reappraisal*, Geneva: ILO, 253-64.

Allaart, P. (ed.) 1988: *The Labour Market in Five Small European Countries*. The Hague: Organisatie voor Strategisch Arbeidsmarktonderzoek.

Asselberghs, K. 1982: De sociale verzekering tijdens de bezetting. *Sociologisch Tijdschrift*, 9, 1, 5-40.

Barbash, J. and Barbash, K. 1972: *Trade Unions and National Economic Policy*. Baltimore: Johns Hopkins U.P.

Blanchflower, D.G. and Freeman, R.B. 1990: Going Different Ways: Unionism in the US and Other Advanced OECD Countries. Discussion Paper no. 5. London School of Economics, Centre for Economic Performance.

Blok, E. 1978: *Loonarbeid van vrouwen in Nederland 1945-55*. Nijmegen: SUN.

Braun, D. 1988: *Der niederländische Weg in die Massenarbeidslosigkeit (1973-1981). Ein politisch-institutionelle Analyse*. Dissertation, Amsterdam.

Cameron, D.R. 1978: The Expansion of the Public Economy: A Comparative Analysis. *American Political Science Review*, 72, 4, 1243-61.

Castles, F.G. 1981: How Does Politics Matter? Structure and Agency in the Determination of Public Policy Outcomes. *European Journal of Political Research*, 9, 1, 119-32.

Child, J., Loveridge, R. and Warner, M. 1973: Towards an Organisational Study of Trade Unions. *Sociology*, 7, 1.

CPB 1992: *De Nederlandse economie in 1992*. The Hague: Central Planning Office.

Crouch, C. 1977: *The Politics of Industrial Relations*. London and Basingstoke: Penguin.

Cutright, P. 1965: Political Structure, Economic Development, and National Security Programs. *American Journal of Sociology*, 70, 2, 537-50.

Daalder, H. 1966: The Netherlands: Opposition in a Segmented Society. In R.A. Dahl (ed.), *Political Oppositions in Western Europe*, New Haven, Conn.: Yale U.P., 188-236.

Daalder, H. 1974: *Politisering en lijdelijkheid in de Nederlandse politiek*. Assen: van Gorcum.

Daalder, H. 1985: Politieke instellingen en politieke partijen. In F.L. van Holthoorn (ed.), *De Nederlandse samenleving sinds 1815. Wording en Samenhang*, Assen/Masstricht: van Gorcum, 305-40.

Douben, N.H. 1984: Sociale zekerheid. Een economische benadering. Leyden/Antwerp: Stenfert Kroese.

Dunlop, J.T. 1958: *Industrial Relations Systems*. New York: Holt.

EIM 1991: *The State of Small Business in The Netherlands*. Zoetermeer: Economisch Onderzoeksinstituut van het Midden- en Kleinbedrijf, September, revised edition.

Esping-Andersen, G. 1985: *Politics Against Markets. The Social Democratic Road to Power*. Princeton N.J.: Princeton U.P.

Flora, P. and Alber, J. 1981: Modernization, Democratization, and the Development of Welfare States in Western Europe. In P. Flora and A.J. Heidenheimer (eds), *The Development of Welfare States in Europe and America*, New Brunswick N.J.: Transaction Books.

Flanagan, R.J., Soskice, D.W. and Ulman, L. 1983: *Unionism, Economic Stabilisation and Incomes*

Policies: European Experience. Washington D.C.: The Brookings Institution.

Fortuyn, W.S.P. 1980: *Sociaal-economische politiek in Nederland 1945-1949.* Dissertation, Groningen.

Frenkel, B.S., Jacobs, T. and Niewstraten-Driessen, E. 1980: *De structuur van het CAO-overleg.* Alphen a/d Rijn: Samson.

Harmsen, G. and Reinalda, B. 1975. *Voor de brevrijding van de arbeid.* Nijmegen: SUN.

Hendriks, J. 1986: *De conjunctuur en de ontwikkeling van de nederlandse vakbeweging. Een tijdreeksanalyse.* MA thesis, Universiteit van Amsterdam.

ter Hoeven, P.J. 1972: *Breukvlakken in het arbeidsbestel.* Alphen a/d Rijn: Samson.

Hoefnagels, H. 1961: Nederland een sociaal paradijs? *Sociologisch Gids,* 8, 6, 274-89.

Huiskamp, M. and Risseeuw, P. 1988: Ondernemingsraad en arbeidsvoorwaarden. Een onderzoek naar de rol van de OR bij het tot stand komen van primaire arbeidsvoorwaarden. VU/ESI report, Amsterdam.

Huiskamp, R. 1983: De CAO-structuur in de Nederlandse industrie. *Economische-Statistische Berichten,* 72.

de Jonge, J. 1968. *De industrialisatie van Nederlands tussen 1850 en 1914.* Amsterdam.

Kaspers, P. and Visser, J. 1991: FNV-statistiek. Rapportages over de ABVA-KABO, de Vervoersbond en de Dienstenbond-FNV. Report UvA/FNV onderzoek, Amsterdam.

Kendall, W. 1977: *Gewerkschaften in Europa.* Hamburg: Hoffmann & Campe.

Klein, P. 1980: The Foundations of Dutch Prosperity. In R. Griffiths (ed.), *The Economy and Politics of The Netherlands Since 1945,* The Hague: Martinus Nijhoff, 1-13.

de Kleijn, H., van der Stadt, H. and van der Werf, R. 1991: Inkomensontwikkelingen 1977-1990. *Economisch-Statistische Berichten,* 27, 1189-91.

Korpi, W. 1983: *The Democratic Class Struggle.* London: Routledge & Kegan Paul.

Lammers, C. 1973: Self-Management and Participation: Two Conceptions of Democratisation in Organisations. *Organisation and Administration Sciences,* 5, 4, 17-33.

Lester, R. 1953: *As Unions Mature.* New York: Basic Books.

van Loo, L. 1981: 'Den arme gegeven....' *Een beschrijving van armoede, armenzorg en sociale zekerheid in Nederland. 1784-1965.* Meppel: Boom.

Looise, J. 1989: The Recent Growth in Employees' Representation in The Netherlands: Defying the Times? In C.J. Lammers and G. Széll (eds), *International Handbook of Participation in Organisations,* vol. 1: *Organisational Democracy. Taking Stock,* Oxford: OUP, 268-84.

Lijphart, J. 1986: *The Politics of Accommodation. Pluralism and Democracy in The Netherlands.* Berkeley: University of California Press.

Nobelen, P. 1983: *Ondernemersorganisaties in beweging.* Deventer: Kluwer.

OECD 1967: *Manpower and Social Policy in The Netherlands.* Paris: OECD.

OECD 1977: *The Dutch Economy in 1976.* Paris: OECD.

OECD 1991: *Employment Outlook,* July. Paris: OECD.

Pen, J. 1963: The Strange Adventures of Dutch Wage Policies. *British Journal of Industrial Relations,* 1, 3, 318-30.

Pen, J. 1973: Trade Union Attitudes Toward Central Wage Policy: Remarks on the Dutch Experience. In A. Sturmthal and J.G. Scoville (eds), *The International Labor Movement in Transition. Essays on Africa, Asia, Europe and South America,* Urbana: University of Illinois Press, 259-82.

Peper, A. 1973: De overgangsjaren van de Nederlandse arbeidsverhoudingen. In A. Peper (ed.), *De Nederlandse arbeidsverhoudingen: continuïteit en verandering,* Rotterdam: Universitaire Pers Rotterdam, 15-34.

Peper, A. 1980: The Netherlands: From an Ordered Harmony to a Bargained Relationship. In S. Barkin (ed.), *Worker Militancy and its Consequences, 1965-1975,* New York: Praeger, 113-53.

van den Putte, B., van Rij, C. and Visser, J. 1991: Het vakbond in het bedrijf. Report Universiteit van Amsterdam-FNV onderzoek, Amsterdam.

Pryor, F. 1968: *Public Expenditure in Capitalist and Communist Nations.* Homewood Ill.: Irwin.

van Rij, C., Kersten, A., Saris, W. and Visser, J. 1990: Age and Trade Union Membership. Amsterdam Working Papers in Sociology 90/1. Amsterdam: Universiteit van Amsterdam.

Reynaerts, W. 1985: Kantelende posities. Arbeidsverhoudingen in een keertijd. In *Bespiegelingen over de toekomst van de sociale partners*, OSA-voorstudie no. 4, The Hague.

Ross, A. and Hartman, P. 1960: *Changing Patterns of Industrial Conflict*. New York: Wiley.

Rüter, A. 1946: De Nederlandse trekken der Nederlandse arbeidersbeweging. In J. Bartstra and W. Banning (es), *Nederland tussen de natiën*, vol. 1, Amsterdam: Ploegsma, 184-221.

Schmidt, M. 1982: *Wohlfahrtsstaatliche Politik unter bürgerlichen und sozialdemokratischen Regierungen. Ein internationaler Vergleich*. Frankfurt: Campus.

Svensen, P. 1989: *Fair Shares. Unions, Pay, and Politics in Sweden and West Germany*. Ithaca N.Y.: Cornell U.P.

Terpstra, G. 1973: De verhoudingen tussen werkgevers en werknemers in Nederland. *Europese dokumentatie*, 73/2.

Teulings, A. 1973: Gewerkschaften und Arbeitskämpfe in den Niederlanden. In O. Jacobi et al. (eds), *Gewerskchaften und Klassenkampf: Kritisches Jahrbuch '73*, Frankfurt: Fischer, 242-57.

Teulings, A. 1981: *Ondernemingsraadpolitiek in Nederland*. Amsterdam: van Gennep.

Teulings, Leijnse, F. and van Waarden, F. 1978: *De nieuwe vakbondsstrategie*. Alphen a/d Rijn: Samson.

Therborn, G. 1986: *Why Some People Are More Unemployed Than Others*. London: Verso.

van de Vall, M. 1964: *De vakbeweging in de welvaartsstaat*. Meppel: Boom (translated as *Labor Organizations*, Cambridge Mass.: CUP).

Visser, J. 1987: In Search of Inclusive Unionism. A Comparative Analysis. Dissertation. Amsterdam: Universiteit van Amsterdam.

Visser, J. 1988: Trade Unions in Western Europe: Present Situations and Prospects. *Labour and Society*, 13, 2, 125-82.

Visser, J. 1989a: Working-Time Arrangements in The Netherlands. In A. Gladstone et al. (eds), *Current Issues in Industrial Relations: An International Perspective*, Berlin: de Gruyter, 29-51.

Visser, J. 1989b: *European Trade Unions in Figures, 1913-1985*. Deventer: Kluwer.

Visser, J. 1990a: *In Search of Inclusive Unionism*. Deventer: Kluwer (*Bulletin of Comparative Labour Relations*, 18).

Visser, J. 1990b: Continuity and Change in Dutch Industrial Relations. In G. Baglioni and C. Crouch (eds), *European Industrial Relations. The Challenge of Flexibility*, London: Sage, 199-242.

Visser, J. 1991: Trends in Trade Union Membership. *OECD Employment Outlook*, Paris: OECD: 97-134.

Visser, J. 1992: The Coming Divergence in Dutch Industrial Relations. In A. Gladstone et al. (eds), *Labour Relations in a Changing Environment*, Berlin/New York: de Gruyter, 251-66.

Visser, J., Kersten, A., van Rij, C. and Saris, W. 1991: Waarom zijn weinig vrouwen lid van de vakbeweging. In C. Bouw et al. (eds), *Macht en onbehagen. Veranderingen in de verhouding tussen mannen en vrouwen*, Amsterdam: SUA, 167-82.

van Voorden, W. 1981: Werkgeversorganisaties: een poging tot plaatsbepaling. In W. Voorden (ed.), *Arbeidsverhoudingen uit model*, Alphen a/d Rijn: Samson, 66-88.

de Vries, J. 1988: Het economisch leven in Nederland 1918-1940. In J. Boogman et al., *Geschiedenis van het moderne Nederland*, Bussum: de Haan, 360-97.

Wilensky, H. 1975: *The Welfare State and Equality. Structural and Ideological Roots of Public Expenditure*. Berkeley: University of California Press.

Windmuller, J. 1969: *Labor Relations in The Netherlands*. Ithaca N.Y.: Cornell U.P.

van Waarden, F. 1985: Regulering en belangenorganisaties van ondernemers. In F. van Holthoor (ed.) *De Nederlandse samenleving sinds 1815. Wording en Samenhang*, Assen/Maastricht: van Gorcum, 227-60.

Wilterdink, N. 1991: Vermogensverhoudingen in Nederland: Recente ontwikkelingen. Amsterdam Working Papers in Sociology, 91/3.

de Wolff, P. 1983: Incomes Policy Developments in The Netherlands. *Industrial Relations*, 22, 2, 203-23.

11

Belgium: A New Stability in Industrial Relations?

Jacques Vilrokx and Jim Van Leemput[1]

Introduction

Although the Belgian case is generally under-represented in comparative social analysis, some excellent accounts of Belgian industrial relations are available for the English reader. Articles by Spineux (1990) and Beaupain (1983) offer useful and detailed pictures of the complex collective bargaining situation, while Blanpain (1984) provides a broad survey of the dynamics of the industrial relations system. Given the availability of these sources, what is the distinctive contribution of the present chapter?

First, our account takes the story to the end of 1991. The authors cited (even Spineux's overview was written in 1986, before national inter-industry bargaining between social partners could successfully be resumed) all questioned the ability of the existing industrial relations system to survive. They covered a period when the system of national inter-industry agreements, which had been at the very heart of Belgian industrial relations since 1960, had broken down. The absence of these agreements was seen as a threat to the bargaining system itself, and to the trade unions as social actors. Only at the end of 1986, after ten years of fruitless attempts and authoritarian government regulation, did a modest two-year national inter-industry agreement revive the tradition. Subsequent agreements have been signed every two years since 1986, and their scope has progressively increased. Thus our hypothesis is that industrial relations in Belgium have entered a new period of relative balance after the restructuring of the (world) economy in the 1970s and the 1980s.

A second feature obvious today but neglected in the past is the regional (or 'community') aspect of national life. So important has regionalism become that it is likely to have a profound influence on industrial relations in Belgium; it is even conceivable that the Belgian model will be supplanted by Walloon and Flemish (and perhaps Brussels?) models. What is certain, however, is that in recent years the growing number of regional collective bargaining bodies has increased the complexity of Belgian industrial relations. While some attention has been paid to differences between industrial relations practices and values in the southern (Walloon) and northern (Flemish) parts of the country, this has not been done systematically. Now that each region has its own bargaining arrangements, it will become even more necessary than before to take the regional dimension into account as an independent variable.

The third difference from earlier assessments of Belgian industrial relations is related. The regional divide is one of the three major 'cleavages' by which Belgian society is characterized. The others are the opposition between Catholics and non-Catholics, and between capital and labour. Together with the ideological 'pillar' structure (socialist, Christian-democratic and liberal) the cleavages are the most important influences on Belgian social structure, shaping all cultural, political and socio-economic activities. Nevertheless, the study of industrial relations has in general been concerned with one of the cleavages (capital–labour), isolating it from this broader pillar/cleavage configuration. In this chapter we take into account the pillar/cleavage environment without which, in our view, Belgian industrial relations cannot be understood.

We first summarize the nineteenth-century developments that laid the foundations of the power relations governing the Belgian industrial relations system. The year 1886 represents a turning point: no social legislation existed before that date and labour relations were based on '*le débat individuel*' (Chlepner 1972: 50). From 1886 a pre-institutional situation emerged, making way for more collective forms of bargaining supported by a rapid growth in legislation.

In the following section, this period, which ends with the Second World War, is analysed in terms of two 'incorporation tendencies'. We argue that the creation of employers' and workers' organizations from the end of the nineteenth century followed existing lines of division (and hence involved an ideological incorporation of the actors); on the other hand, it also established the preconditions for a highly regulated bargaining system that was to be fully implemented after the Second World War (and hence provided an institutional dimension of incorporation). The third section offers an exposition of theoretical perspectives on the collective bargaining environment in Belgium; the pluralist, neo-corporatist and 'compensation-democratic' approaches are reviewed. Next, the main actors and institutional arrangements in the bargaining process are examined, as is one of the more important outcomes of industrial relations practices, the pattern of industrial disputes in Belgium. This is followed by an analysis of recent developments in collective bargaining. We have chosen three main themes to illustrate these changes: technological innovation; the organization of change in working patterns; and the involvement of the state in pay determination.

The Emergence of Collective Action

Belgium was the first country in continental Europe to industrialize. From the beginning of the nineteenth century, the steel and metal-working industries developed rapidly in the Walloon Liège and Charleroi regions (where the most important coalmining centres were concentrated). Other more traditional industries such as wool and cotton textiles had been located in Flanders, mostly in the Ghent region, for centuries. At this time, Antwerp was developing as a service metropole rather than as an industrial centre.

The first half of the nineteenth century saw a dynamic of industrial expansion and crises. In 1822 the Société Générale was founded by William I of Holland (Belgium was under Dutch rule for fifteen years until its independence in 1830). From 1840 it developed from a financial institution into a holding company, continuing to control large parts of Belgian industry until it was sold to the French group Suez in 1988, by which time it represented approximately a third of national capital. The first king of independent Belgium continued to intervene in the economy; in 1835, for example, he ordered at the Cockerill Works (at that time the world's largest factory) the material needed to build Europe's first railway, and he also initiated programmes for the development of other forms of transport infrastructure such as canals. These investments were financed by loans from the Société Générale, which also acted as a national bank (Cottenier et al. 1989: 18). Financial, economic and political power were thereafter closely interwoven.

With the process of capital accumulation, industry became less dependent on state intervention. By 1886 an economic liberalism '*le plus dur, le plus absolu*' (Chlepner 1972: 46) had become consolidated. At the same time, a labour movement was emerging. Workers' protest against appalling working conditions focussed on issues of working time and legislative reform.

Early Working-Class Organization

The first expressions of workers' organization in the face of harsh working and living conditions were the *mutualités*: associations of mutual help in the event of accidents and sickness (Michielsen 1976: 14). They developed in Belgium from around 1840 and engendered the first trade unions. It was in the textile industry in the Ghent region, rather than in the new industrial centres of Wallonia, that an organized workers' movement emerged. For centuries a form of guild organization had existed in the traditional craft industries and it was in this environment that an 'aristocracy of labour' created the first trade unions, both to provide health insurance and to preserve skilled workers' occupational status in the face of widespread automation. The weavers' association founded in Ghent in 1857 is generally considered the first of these 'real' trade unions. It was followed, from around 1860, by attempts to construct industry-wide organizations.

The issue of the reduction of working time provided the impetus for a more socio-cultural emancipation of the working class. The problem of long working hours for women and children was highlighted by a parliamentary commission and the writings of socially engaged authors (Ducpétiaux, Delavaleye, Visschers, etc.). Reform was, however, blocked by employers, who saw cheap and unrestricted child and female labour as a means of keeping men's wages low as well. The Catholic church was also opposed to reform, since proposals to restrict children's working hours were linked to demands for a public education system – and this threatened the church's monopoly of educational provision. Thus it was not until 1884 that legislation on children's work (and then only in the mining industry) proved possible, and in the form of a Royal Decree rather than an act of parliament.

The other main subject of protest was the legal inferiority of workers compared to employers. As in France (the *loi le Chapelier*) or Britain (the Combination Acts), Belgian law prescribed penalties against workers' combinations, and privileged the employers' account in court proceedings. This legal discrimination was modified in 1866 but not finally abolished until 1921.

1886: The Turning Point

Far from being merely formal, these arrangements had a profound impact on everyday (working) life, and 'misbehaviour' was systematically and severely repressed. For these reasons, among others, Marx characterized Belgium as the 'paradise and hunting ground for landowners, capitalists and priests. In the same way as the earth yearly circles around the sun, one can be sure that the Belgian government will organize its yearly massacre of the workers' (cited by Cottenier et al. 1989: 34).

This long-standing status of inferiority of workers as wage-earners, as socio-cultural beings and as citizens only began to be transformed in 1886. In the so-called 'Black Year', strike and protest movements created an explosive situation, and politicians turned to reform as a means of defusing the crisis. Legislation was passed on working conditions and the legal status of trade unions. Demands for democratic political rights gathered pace, spearheaded by the Belgian Workers' Party formed in 1885. Universal male suffrage was eventually achieved in 1919, coincidentally the year that the first bipartite collective bargaining commission was established.

Two Dimensions of the Incorporation of the Labour Movement

Towards the end of the nineteenth century Belgian industrial relations began to display the centralization which was to characterize its later development. Employers had previously felt no need to organize nationally; but in 1886, when the first social laws were enacted, existing local associations of employers (mostly organized on the model of chambers of commerce) began to act as pressure groups in order to influence legislation. In 1895 the first centralized employers' organization was founded under the name of Central Committee for Industrial Labour, the forerunner of the current Federation of Belgian Enterprises (VBO/FEB), which now also includes the service sector.

The same period saw moves towards centralization in the fragmented labour movement. The Belgian Workers' Party established a Trade Union Committee in 1898, and until 1937 the socialist unions continued to function as an arm of the party. In 1945 the socialist trade union united with three other unions: communist, anarcho-syndicalist, and a left-wing public sector organization. The Catholic workers' organization at first participated in the unity discussions, but soon withdrew, arguing for 'unity in action but pluralism in organization'. Centralization occurred more slowly in the Catholic labour movement, which developed nationally after the 1891 papal encyclical, *Rerum Novarum*. A General Secretariat of Professional Christian Unions of Belgium was established in 1904, but the Walloon and Flemish organizations continued to function autonomously. The first national congress of the Catholic labour movement took place in 1912, and in 1923 the current name, General Christian Trade Union Federation (ACV/CSC), was adopted. The smaller liberal trade union originated in 1891 out of the *mutualités* of Flemish craftsmen. The present title, General Confederation of Liberal Trade Unions of Belgium (ACLVB/CGSLB), was adopted in 1930.

Ideological Incorporation

From this short overview, one of the two dimensions of the incorporation of the labour movement in Belgium is already apparent, namely its strong links with the three dominant ideological currents (or 'pillars'). In The Netherlands a similar evolution can be observed (along Catholic, Protestant and socialist lines), but in the Dutch case the incorporation of the labour movement in the pillar structure is less encompassing than in Belgium.

Pillars are institutionalized socio-cultural, economic and political mechanisms for the defence of specific interests. Each ideological pillar provides a comprehensive package of services for its members, and all important societal functions and needs may be met within it. The pillar structure has three essential characteristics: it forms a framework for socio-cultural, economic and political exchanges; it defines the frontiers of competitive, but not antagonistic, power domains; and it provides formal and informal social control mechanisms which regulate exchanges within and between pillars, sustaining the legitimacy and stability of the system. The structure is crossed by three cleavages: between capital and labour, Catholics and non-Catholics, and the Walloon (French-speaking) and Flemish (Dutch-speaking) communities, each with their own institutional arrangements.

Most conflicts in Belgium originate from or interconnect with tensions arising from different institutional interests in the pillar/cleavage structure. The incorporation of the labour movement in this network of conflicting interests is a central feature of Belgian industrial relations. It means, for example, that questions not normally associated with trade unionism may affect the labour movement and that, conversely, trade union matters can rarely be isolated from broader interest conflicts (see Spineux 1990); '*tout est dans tout*', it is often said in Belgium.

Institutional Incorporation

The second feature of Belgian industrial relations, institutional incorporation, is a consequence of the formalization of the pillar/cleavage configuration. But it also reflects a specific social-democratic dynamic that has favoured the participation of the labour movement at virtually every possible level of local, regional and national decision-making, ranging from the production and marketing of nuclear energy to more conventional industrial relations questions.

In the industrial relations field, an early impetus to collective bargaining was provided in 1919 by the state-initiated Committee for the Study of the Diminution of Working Time in the Metalworking Industry. More committees were established in other sectors, eventually developing into Joint Committees, the current bilateral bargaining institutions at the sectoral level. Different forms of bargaining also began to emerge. Collective bargaining was initially informal and not legally regulated, but from the Second World War, Belgium adopted one of the most formalized participation structures in Europe. The corner-stone was the Draft Agreement on Social Solidarity (generally called the 'Social Pact') concluded in 1944 by representatives of the workers' and employers' organizations. This agreement led to a multitude of legal and voluntary arrangements, bilateral and trilateral, at almost every level of activity.

A key measure was the Law on the Organization of the Economy (1948) which required the formation of works councils and established the Central Economic Council (CRB/CCE). The latter provided the government with regular economic advice on such questions as the competitiveness of Belgian industry. After a period of relative insignificance, this Council has in recent years regained considerable importance. The foundation of the National Labour Council (NAR/CNT) in 1952 – in which the parties now have powers to sign national inter-industry agreements applicable to all workers – was also a significant initiative.

In the recent history of Belgian labour relations, bilateral union-employer negotiation has been of primary importance. The state has tended to intervene less and less as a partner in a trilateral bargaining process and more and more as an autonomous regulator of bilateral negotiations. This was not always the case. For example, the National Labour Conferences, first convened in 1936, previously resulted in agreements which regulated many of the issues that might otherwise have provoked strikes or lockouts; thus the 1945 Conference introduced an automatic link between wages and the prices of consumer goods. The principle of the trade union 'delegation' (a body composed of trade union workplace representatives authorized to sign collective agreements with the employer) was agreed by the National Labour Conference in 1947.

Another key event of the early post-war years was the Productivity Agreement of 1954; it ensured that the rise in productivity resulting from the wave of technological and organizational innovation in the 1950s benefited workers and consumers as well as employers. Together with the Social Pact of 1944, the Productivity Agreement is often considered the 'basic compromise' which lays down the principles of Belgian labour relations. These principles reaffirm exclusive managerial prerogative over financial decision-making, while obliging employers to negotiate with or consult workers' representatives on social and work-related matters.

Although the 'basic compromise' is of the utmost importance for the structuring of labour relations in Belgium, it cannot fully explain the specificity of the Belgian situation: in other countries such as The Netherlands and France, similar agreements were reached at the end of the war. The Belgian version of the social-democratic compromise familiar elsewhere in Europe must be understood as the result of the pillar/cleavage configuration outlined above.

Political and Socio-Economic Relations in Belgium and the Role of the State in Collective Bargaining

It is impossible to understand Belgian industrial relations without taking into account the highly complex and interdependent web of relations of the pillar/cleavage configuration. We therefore explore the collective bargaining process as a subsystem of this pillar/cleavage network.

The parties involved in the network are both conflict initiators and problem-solvers. They 'divide Belgian society and they give it a relative cohesion, on condition, however, that divisions are not superimposed, but that the parties seek *ad hoc* alliances according to the specific conflict at hand' (Arcq and Marques-Pereira 1991: 165). The 'pluralist' approach argues that the extremely subtle arrangements needed in such a situation have led to the very elaborate system of political and socio-economic bargaining in Belgium. On the other hand, 'neo-corporatist' theorists stress the role of the state in structuring the bargaining system. The pluralism / neo-corporatism debate provides the main organizing device in this section. We shall propose the concept of 'compensation democracy' as a way of understanding Belgian social relations more fully.

Pluralism vs Neo-corporatism

The most significant contributions to the study of the pillar/cleavage configuration are by Van Den Brande (e.g. 1987) and Huyse (e.g. 1980). Despite important differences, both recognize pillarization ('*verzuiling*' is the Dutch word often used in the international literature) and cleavages as fundamental aspects of the Belgian system. In this they follow those authors who have studied the specific functioning of the 'small democracies in the Low Countries' (cf. Lorwin 1979). Despite the evident importance of such an approach, however, there have been few attempts to examine industrial relations in Belgium from the point of view of the pillar/ cleavage configuration. (Exceptions include Bundervoet (1981) and Vilrokx (1981a); the latter highlights the importance of investment decision-making by industrial-financial groups in the structuring of power relationships within the pillar/cleavage configuration.)

The role of the state is, in the numerous varieties of neo-corporatism, understood in different ways: as actor, guarantor of the national interest, regulator etc. It is clear that the state in Belgium has been far more than an onlooker; indeed, it has acquired unusually broad powers of intervention in industrial relations. In collective bargaining, this is manifested in the distinction between bipartite (capital–labour) and tripartite (capital–labour–state) levels of bargaining. While at first sight the bipartite level is the most 'active' and institutionalized, it is always possible for public authorities to intervene. Below we cite several cases in which limitations have been put on the cherished principle of 'free collective bargaining'.

In addition to imposing formal regulations, the government uses its power in an indirect way. In March 1991, for example, the bipartite Central Economic Council issued its half-yearly report on the state of the economy. Its rather pessimistic analysis blamed Belgian competitive weakness on wage costs in particular. The government asked the unions and employers' organizations to reach an agreement on wage restraint; had they failed to do so, it would have used its powers of intervention under the legislation, for example by altering the indexation system. Although unions and employers were unable to reach an agreement within the time-limit set by the government, it refrained from intervention on the grounds that favourable movements in exchange rates made it unnecessary. (Some commentators, however, suggest that intervention would have proved unpopular and could have damaged the governing coalition, particularly the Christian democrats and socialists, in the forthcoming general election.) However, the state does often intervene in collective bargaining, usually to issue warnings or impose guidelines within which the social partners should negotiate.

Thus the state is not the neutral agent that the pluralist perspective on collective bargaining would have us believe. Arcq and Marques-Pereira cite Vanderstraeten (1988) as a representative of a neo-corporatist approach. Vanderstraeten compares tripartite socio-economic concertation with the political system of parliamentary democracy. The two mechanisms of negotiation are complementary, the state performing the role of setting the rules of the game in both cases. However, an institutional approach does not reveal the whole picture, since the state does not necessarily intervene within the framework of bipartite or tripartite bargaining structures. The great complexity of institutional arrangements makes it increasingly easy for the government to short-circuit formal bargaining procedures and to intervene in an informal, and at times authoritarian, fashion.

Positive-sum vs Zero-sum Functioning of Compensation Democracy

Arcq and Marques-Pereira (1991) question whether the 'basic compromise' could really be labelled neo-corporatist. They emphasize the fundamental ambiguities of the 1944 Social Pact, the 1948 legislation on the 'Organisation of the Economy' and the 1954 Productivity Agreement, the three main corner-stones of the Belgian industrial relations system. The consensual character of the neo-corporatist frame of reference, they argue, makes it unable to explain situations of conflict and the genesis and transformation of the system. They maintain, as against Vanderstraeten and Van Den Brande, that from the beginning of the 1980s, industrial relations have profoundly changed the post-war social-democratic compromise. As Bleeckx (1985) has forcefully argued, the whole basis of wage settlement changed in the 1980s: the key consideration was no longer the distribution of the gains from constantly increasing productivity and national income, but accommodation to intensified international competition.

A 'compensation-democratic' perspective offers a means of synthesizing the insights and concepts of the pluralist and neo-corporatist points of view. The reality of the Belgian situation is that the social partners are represented in virtually all socio-economic organizations and committees. There they are confronted with competing cleavage-based parties and representatives of the other ideological pillars. In this complex network of relations and political and socio-economic exchanges, ubiquitous interest conflicts have to be regulated.

In our view, the process of reaching a consensus in such situations is not (as most accounts of the Belgian situation assume) an end in itself, but rather a means. More fundamental is the underlying objective of the opposing parties in situations of conflict: the consolidation of power or influence within the pillar/cleavage configuration. The ability to manipulate the system of cross-cutting interests so that every party concerned in a conflict gets more resources, is characteristic of the Belgian situation. This is what has changed in the last fifteen years; not because the abilities of the negotiators involved in these exchanges have diminished, but rather because the financial means to sustain the pillar/cleavage configuration have dried up.

In the past, the demands of one interest group could be satisfied because the opposing group was almost automatically compensated. If the Flemish community needed resources to modernize the ports, it would be granted them on condition, say, that Wallonia got a more or less equivalent amount of money for road-building. The compensation principle was accepted by the pillar/cleavage elites and public opinion, particularly at the level of these kinds of large-scale public investment, since the balance of power was preserved and each party could increase its resources. The consolidation of the parties could be achieved within an exchange system in which conflicts and power struggles were neutralized through material compensation. The state financed these positive-sum consequences of the pillar/cleavage divisions. The major failure of the process of reciprocal compensation at the end of 1991 – when benefits for Flanders were demanded as the price for authorizing Walloon arms sales to Arab countries – precipitated a government crisis still unresolved at the time of writing.

Far from being a neutral party, the state thus actively shaped neo-corporatist arrangements in Belgium. It was *able* to do so because it had the resources – after the Second World War Belgium was a rich, prosperous country and a colonial power; and it was *forced* to do so because the strongly developed pillar and cleavage organizations were relatively autonomous centres of power capable of destabilizing the state should the underlying principles of the system come under pressure (as happened with the 'Royal Question' in the first half of the 1950s, the General Strike of 1960–1, and the regional problems of the late 1960s).

Paradoxically, the state's role in organizing this 'compensation democracy' legitimized its much more restrictive role when the conditions for maintaining positive-sum outcomes disappeared. This happened when the restructuring of the world economy in the 1970s began to affect the Belgian economy, initiating a period of tight state control of collective bargaining. The state assumed the new role of active participant and legislator in the field of industrial relations, as we analyse below.

The Actors and the Institutions

The Unions

The Structure of Belgian Unionism and Unions

The structure of Belgian unionism reflects the major cleavages of Belgian society. A separate union confederation exists for each of the three most important ideological tendencies: the socialist General Belgian Trade

Union Federation (ABVV/FGTB), the Catholic General Christian Trade Union Federation (ACV/CSC), and the smaller liberal General Confederation of Liberal Trade Unions of Belgium (ACLVB/CGSLB).

All unions are affected by the division between Dutch-speaking Flanders and French-speaking Wallonia, together with the bilingual Brussels region. The Catholic ACV/CSC, with the somewhat larger membership, is predominantly based in the more populous Flanders region. By contrast, the ABVV/FGTB has its membership evenly divided between the two main regions; while heavily outnumbered by its rival in Flanders, it is correspondingly dominant in Wallonia (see table 11.1).

In recent decades, Belgian union structures have adapted to the growing importance of regional identities. Within the socialist ABVV/FGTB, three regional federations established in 1963 have gained increasing autonomy and power. The Christian ACV/CSC also reacted to regionalization, although somewhat later. In 1978 three regional committees were set up, and the constitution of 1984 confirmed this new structure. As table 11.1 shows, the CSC is relatively weak in Wallonia and is therefore obliged to work together with the much stronger FGTB. But ideologically too the CSC is closer to FGTB than the Flemish ACV is to the Flemish ABVV. Cooperation in the form of a 'common front' is a generally accepted trade union strategy in Wallonia, but not in Flanders.

Differences connected with regional developments partly explain why the ACV/CSC has over the years become the strongest union. The ACV was already larger in Flanders before the Second World War. In the 1950s and 1960s, economic power (and employment) shifted from Wallonia to the newly developed Flanders. The expansion of the number of white-collar workers also favoured the ACV/CSC, which even between the wars had focused less than the ABVV/FGTB on blue-collar workers.

In addition to the three larger unions, there are numerous small independent trade unions. They cannot, however, represent workers in the institutions of social concertation, where the 'representative' trade unions have a monopoly of worker representation. The 'representative' unions also have the sole right to conclude legally enforceable collective agreements. In order to be considered representative a union must organize across industries and occupations, be established at the national level, be represented on the National Labour Council (NAR/CNT) and the Central Economic Council (CRB/CCE) and have at least 50,000 members. There is one exception to the rule: the National Confederation of Middle Management (NCK/CNC) is not a representative union but has gained the right to present candidates at works council elections.

Although there is a strong similarity in structure between the Christian and socialist trade unions, the division of power within each is essentially different. Both have a dual industrial and geographical structure. The socialist ABVV/FGTB is divided into eleven trade unions ('centrals'): one for all white-collar workers, one for all civil servants

Table 11.1   Regional membership distribution of the two main Belgian unions

	Flanders		Wallonia		Brussels		Belgium	
	1985	1990	1985	1990	1985	1990	1985	1990
ABVV/FGTB	470,561	454,397	468,256	418,204	158,777	141,464	1,097,594	1,014,065
ACV/CSC	934,220	984,719	271,847	290,638	161,325	155,214	1,367,589	1,430,571
Subtotal	1,404,781	1,439,116	740,103	708,842	320,102	296,678	2,465,183	2,444,636
ACLVB/CGSLB							210,936	213,098
Total							2,676,119	2,657,734

Source: 1985 ABVV/FGTB and ACV/CSC Arcq and Blaise 1986; ACLVB/CGSLB figure provided by the union; 1990 figures provided by the unions.

and nine organized by sector of industry. Within the ABVV/FGTB the centrals have considerable autonomy and power. They have their own strike funds, and in most cases are separately represented on the various national statutory bodies. Each central has company-level and sub-regional sections. Geographically, these industrial unions combine in twenty-five sub-regional bodies, grouped in turn into three regional organizations (Inter-Regionals), for Flanders, Wallonia and Brussels. The national organization of the ABVV/FGTB has coordinating and administrative functions. The national confederation represents the union in national collective bargaining, the regional federations do the same at regional level.

The Christian ACV/CSC has a similar structure: 16 centrals with regional federations, 32 sub-regional federations and 3 regional committees. But the ACV/CSC is more centralized than its socialist counterpart: the national confederation and the regional federations are more powerful, and there is one single national strike fund.

The organization of the much smaller liberal trade union (ACLVB/CGSLB) is the most centralized. It has no industrial federations and no separate organizations for white- and blue-collar workers. Only since 1989 has its administrative structure been reluctantly adapted to regionalism, and it does not publish a regional membership breakdown.

Ideology

There is a striking divergence between the formal goals of Belgian unions and their practical behaviour. The programme of the socialist ABVV/FGTB still refers to class struggle and a classless society. State initiative is preferred to private enterprise, and workers' control rather than participation is the aim of trade union action. In practice however a more pragmatic policy is followed. Workers' control goes hand in hand with a 'responsible' approach 'where necessary' (National Congress of 1954), which leads more often to participation than to control.

The philosophy of the ACV/CSC, founded on Christian values, is based on the idea of a 'community of labour' and the necessity of an 'open and sincere dialogue' between the social partners. At the 1971 Congress self-management became the official goal. During the late 1960s and early 1970s the ACV/CSC actively supported wildcat strikes and factory occupations (in a number of instances combined with production under self-management), as in the case of Prestige (De Coninck and Vilrokx 1977). This largely ineffective strategy was quickly abandoned for a more prudent approach, though it remained true that 'the CSC, through its affiliation to the ETUC, put its name to more radical statements at the international level than it had generally done at the national level' (Beaupain 1983: 152).

The liberal ACLVB/CGSLB states that cooperation between workers and employers has to rest on the basic liberal principles of liberty, progress, justice and social peace. Liberal trade unionism has, however, often been considered incompatible with the demands of collective solidarity, one of the reasons why in 1991 the ACLVB/CGSLB was once again refused membership of ETUC.

Membership and Influence

Statistics of trade union membership in Belgium have often been criticized. Most commentators suggest that density is 70 per cent or more. However, Visser (1991) argues that excluding union members who are retired or unemployed, density is only 53 per cent. But in any event, Belgium has very high union density compared to most other EC countries. The main reasons for this are the following: first, collective agreements provide for a 'union premium' (roughly equal to trade union dues, though much higher in some sectors) to be paid by the employers to union members; second, the unemployed continue to be members (some 25–30 per cent of total membership), because the unions play an intermediary role in distributing unemployment benefits (and much more efficiently than the public authorities); third, the unions provide a wide range of services to members, from help with filling in tax returns to advice on housing and matrimonial problems.

Although the ABVV/FGTB became formally independent of the Socialist Party (SP/PS) in 1945, the ties with the party remain very strong. Union leaders have seats on the party executive bureau, party and union leaders meet regularly, together with the other components of the socialist movement, in what is called the Socialist Common Action, and the union supports the party in general elections.

The situation is more complicated within the Catholic pillar. The Christian Democratic Party (CVP/PSC) is a multi-class organization with labour, agriculture and business wings. As each wing gets a share of cabinet seats, and as the party has been in office almost continuously since the Second World War, the union has significant political influence. The crucial role of the labour movement within the Christian pillar and its influence on the country's destiny in the post-war period are highlighted by the now famous secret Poupehan meetings, which only became public knowledge at the beginning of 1991. Involving the Christian democrat prime minister, the (Christian democrat) president of the National Bank, the president of the Christian bank and the senior Christian trade union leader, these meetings were an attempt to formulate an agreed national recovery programme in the first half of the 1980s. It has to be stressed, however, that there have been differences of approach between the Flemish ACV, which has been fairly uncritical of CVP policies, and its Walloon counterpart which has tended to take a more independent standpoint with regard to the PSC.

While the political power of the trade unions derives from their links with the political components of the pillars, those same links tend to weaken the unions in periods of economic crisis and force them to comply with 'higher economic interests' embodied by the political parties.

Recently, the power of the unions in Belgium has diminished, as in most European countries. Yet there has been no significant decline in union membership. The number of unionized white-collar workers has grown, although not proportionally to their numbers in the labour force. Maintaining solidarity amongst this more heterogeneous membership is a problem. However, the fear that the declining number of members in the traditionally most active sectors would lead to a reduction in union activism seems contradicted by growing mobilization among white-collar workers.

Somewhat hesitantly, the unions are defining a new role for themselves. Services to members have become a priority. Both major unions claim to regard the environment as an issue as important as economic growth or full employment. Questions such as housing, child care and education have been accorded the same status as pay and working time. In general the quality of working life in its broadest sense seems to be at the forefront of union strategy.

The Employers' Associations

There are three main groups of employers' organizations in Belgium: the national, regional and sectoral organizations of the main employers in industry and commerce; specialist organizations for small business; and those for agriculture.

The Federation of Belgian Enterprises (VBO/FEB) is a confederation of employers' federations in the private sector. It maintains a strong 'unitary' (Belgian) orientation, and undertakes economy-wide bargaining with the national trade union organizations. As regional industrial relations develop, employers' organizations at this level (to which individual firms are directly affiliated) are increasing their influence. The Flemish Economic Union (VEV), established in 1926, is the oldest. Less influential are the newer Walloon Union of Enterprises (UWE) founded in 1968, and the Union of Brussels Enterprises (VOB/UEB) established in 1971.

From the start, the VEV has promoted a regional perspective, mostly in reaction to the French-speaking capitalist elite that concentrated its investment in traditional industrial sectors in the Walloon part of the country. Its strong distaste for the old Belgian financial-industrial establishment, with its preference for a consensual approach to industrial relations, prompted the VEV to adopt a more radical stance.

In this environment, jurisdictional conflicts have arisen as to what should be handled at national and what at regional level, since the demarcation is often unclear. For example, the social partners in the National Labour Council recently issued a Collective Agreement on 'outplacement' (that is on measures to help redundant workers find other employment), on the grounds that it falls within the sphere of labour legislation, which is a national responsibility; but the regional Minister of Employment and Labour in Flanders is currently preparing his own regulations, claiming that outplacement is an employment-related issue, for which responsibility has been transferred to the regions. The policy of all four employers' organizations is that collective bargaining should take place as far as possible at plant level and without state interference, but with state-imposed restraints on union demands if necessary. The classic strategy of global agreements based on 'give-and-take' with the trade unions (De Koster and Van Holm 1989: 47) has thus been replaced by more direct bargaining with the unions at workplace level or even with individual workers.

Smaller firms are under-represented within the employers' sectoral federations and thus within the VBO/FEB. Hence small and medium-sized enterprises are often affiliated to specialist organizations, of which the National Christian Traders' Union (NCMV) in Flanders and its Walloon counterpart UCM are among the most important. Employers' interests in agriculture are defended by the Belgian Farmers' Union (BB), the Walloon National Federation of Unions of Agricultural Professionals (UAP) and the Belgian Agriculture Alliance (AAB). The BB is the strongest of the three organizations and is politically influential, forming the agricultural wing of the Christian Democratic Party.

The Institutions

The Formal Participation Structure in the Private Sector

A distinction must be made between bipartite concertation in which only workers' and employers' organizations take part, and tripartite concertation in which the government participates. There is also a distinction between 'institutionalized' concertation and non-institutionalized, more *ad hoc*, discussions between workers' and employers' organizations. In bipartite concertation, institutions where social issues are discussed may be distinguished from those for handling economic issues; some bodies deal with both. This corresponds exactly to the ideas underlying the 1944 Social Pact, the 1948 Law on the Organization of the Economy and the 1954 Productivity Agreement already mentioned. A final important variable is the level at which concertation takes place: national, regional, sectoral or company. Figure 11.1 depicts the various types of concertation machinery, grouped according to these criteria.

In 1936 the first of a series of National Labour Conferences (NAC/CNT) was held. Issues such as paid holidays, wage indexation, and the establishment of trade union representation at company level were negotiated. Many of the functions of the NAC/CNT were taken over by the Central Economic Council (CRB/CCE) and the National Labour Council (NAR/CNT), established in 1948. However, the conferences are still convened from time to time, under different names, to discuss such problems as the rise in unemployment.

The Central Economic Council (CRB/CCE) is an advisory board, composed of an equal number of representatives of employers' and workers' organizations, complemented by experts from the world of

Figure 11.1 Bargaining, concertation and consultation in the private sector

| | | Tripartite | | Bipartite | | |
| | | institutional | non-institutional | institutional | | non-institutional |
		social and economic matters	social and economic matters	social matters	economic matters	social matters
national		NCEE* CNEE	NAC CNT	NAR CNT	CRB CCE	(IPA) (AIP)
regional	W		TABLE RONDE	CESRW		
	B	ESRBG CESRB				
	FL	VESOC		SERV		
sectoral	Reg				SERV**	
	Nat	OC OC		PC CP	BRC CCS	
company				OR/CVGV CE/CSHE		SD DS

* Although the NCEE/CNEE still formally exists, it has not been active since 1970.
** Since May 1990, SERV has had five sectoral committees.

science and technology. Its advice on economic policy can be compared to that of NAR/CNT on social policy. Recently, the CRB/CCE seems to have increased in importance (see below). The periodic reports of the CRB/CCE and its sectoral committees (Special Advisory Commissions: figure 11.1 BRC/CCS) on economic development are an important source of information.

The creation of the National Labour Council (NAR/CNT) in 1952 gave legal status to a general joint council with an advisory role, established in the concertation agreement of 1944. The NAR/CNT advises the government and parliament on labour law, social security, general social issues and international labour regulations. Since 1968 the parties in the MAR/CNT have also had the right to conclude inter-industry collective agreements which can be declared binding by Royal Decree – as has occurred with all but one of the forty-nine agreements reached up to the end of 1991. This right is a specific feature of Belgian industrial relations. Some of these agreements not only apply to the active working population but also to the unemployed, retired workers or special interest groups. This quasi-legislative power makes the NAR/CNT the most important of the concertation institutions, certainly at national level.

The necessity for tripartite as well as bipartite concertation was recognized in all three regions, although the dynamics of the process were different in each case. Flanders has made most progress in creating a 'new' bargaining structure. The bipartite Social and Economic Council of Flanders (SERV) is an example. It advises on social and economic issues concerning Flanders and takes positions on socio-economic questions. Tripartite concertation, concerning all social-economic policy issues within the competence of the Flemish community, takes place in the Flemish Economic and Social Concertation Committee (VESOC). The Flemish government has agreed to implement all proposals on which an agreement is reached within VESOC. Recently there have been proposals to integrate the functions of the two bodies. The role played by SERV at regional level may be seen as increasingly similar to that of the National Labour Council and the Central Economic Council nationally. In Wallonia, institutional concertation is not as developed as in Flanders; there is no formal tripartite concertation. But unions, employers' organizations and the Walloon government meet monthly at the so-called Round Table talks to consult on social and economic policy. The bipartite Economic and Social Council of the Walloon Region (CESRW) advises national and regional bodies on economic and social matters concerning Wallonia. In Brussels, where regionalization is less well developed, the bipartite Economic and Social Council for the Brussels Region (ESRBG/CESRB) also functions provisionally as a tripartite forum.

Other important institutions are the Joint Committees (PC/CP). They originated in 1919 out of the Commission for the Study of Working Time in the Metal Industry and soon proliferated in other branches of industry, taking on increasingly broad functions. In 1935 there were 26 Joint Commissions, as they were now called. After the national strike of 1936, government, employers and workers agreed to reinforce the role of the Joint Commissions, and their number increased to 47 in 1939. In June 1945, they acquired legal status; in particular, collective agreements made in the Joint Committees (their new title) could be ratified by the minister and become binding for the sector – a procedure which thereafter became normal practice. Since 1969, a second crucial role of the PCs has been the organization of conciliation and mediation procedures in industrial disputes.

A further dimension of the bargaining system is the company level. Works councils (OR/CE) were established as bipartite bodies within the enterprise by the 1948 Law on the Organization of the Economy. The employer is obliged to provide them with regular information on the economic, financial, organizational and investment situation and future policy of the company. A further role of the works council is monitoring the application of welfare legislation. Its decision-making power is limited, mainly covering the determination of holiday dates; and it may also organize so-called social funds (extra-legal pension schemes, etc.) which are, however, subject to the ultimate control of management.

A second company-level institution is the bipartite Committee for Safety, Health and Improvement of the Workplace (CVGV/CSHE). These committees were established by law in 1952. As their name suggests, they are mainly concerned with physical working conditions.

While management directly appoints its own nominees to these two institutions, the workers' representatives are chosen every four years by all employees in the company in the so-called social elections. Until recently, only the representative workers' organizations could nominate candidates, although in 1987 the National Confederation of Middle Management also won this right. Social elections for the works council have to be held in companies with more than 100 employees, while for the health and safety committees, the number of employees is 50. These social elections are generally seen as the key indicator of the relative power of the unions.

Table 11.2 Percentage of votes for works councils 1954–91

	ABVV/FGTB	*ACV/CSC*	*ACLVB/CGSLB*	*NCK/CNC*
1954	59.0	37.0	3.5	
1958	55.0	41.0	4.0	
1963	51.1	43.8	5.1	
1967	51.5	42.5	6.0	
1971	48.7	45.5	5.8	
1975	46.1	47.7	6.2	
1979	42.6	50.1	7.3	
1983	43.4	48.6	7.9	
1987	40.8	47.9	7.5	3.8
1991	37.9	51.5	7.5	3.1

Source: Ministry of Employment and Labour.

More than one million workers were entitled to vote in 1991. The actual participation rate, though declining, is still around 70 per cent. The result of these workplace elections influences the power of the unions within the political party to which they are affiliated, their power in relation to each other, and the relative power of the various sectoral federations within each union (see EIRR 215, December 1991: 16–20).

As can be seen in table 11.2, the ABVV/FGTB won the highest level of support in social elections up to the early 1970s; from the 1975 elections, it was overtaken by the ACV/CSC as the largest vote-winner. In terms of numbers of seats won, the difference is even more marked: the ACV/CSC has won the largest number of seats at every electoral round since 1967. This is largely a reflection of the union's strength in smaller companies, where there are relatively more seats per employee. In the

Table 11.3   Percentage of seats won in works councils 1991*

	ABVV/FGTB	*ACV/CSC*	*ACLVB/CGSLB*	*NCK/CNC etc.*
Overall	33.7	59.1	4.2	3.1
Sector				
Market sector	39.5	52.2	4.6	3.8
Non-market sector	15.1	81.1	3.0	0.8
Region				
Flanders	25.8 (31.8)	68.2 (60.9)	4.0 (4.9)	2.0 (2.5)
Wallonia	46.0 (55.7)	48.1 (38.1)	2.7 (2.2)	3.1 (3.9)
Brussels	41.4 (43.3)	45.8 (43.2)	6.7 (6.3)	6.1 (7.1)
Category				
Blue-collar	41.8 (44.1)	54.5 (52.0)	3.8 (3.9)	
White-collar	28.6 (38.4)	66.7 (55.7)	4.7 (5.9)	
Youngsters	34.8 (37.8)	62.1 (59.0)	3.1 (3.2)	
Middle management	14.9 (15.3)	32.5 (29.9)	5.0 (4.8)	47.6 (50.0)

* figures in brackets are for the market sector only
Source: Ministerie van Tewerkstelling en Arbeid 1992.

1991 elections, the ACV/CSC overtook the ABVV/FGTB as the strongest union among blue-collar workers and is now the most important union for all categories of workers (manual, white-collar, young workers, and middle management). Its strength is greatest among the growing number of white-collar employees. The fall in the ABVV/FGTB's vote among manual workers can be ascribed to the decline of its traditional strongholds such as steel and metalworking.

As might be expected, there are major regional differences in the election results (see table 11.3). Support for the ACV/CSC is growing in all three regions. It has a large majority in Flanders (68 per cent of seats, compared with 26 per cent for the ABVV). In Wallonia the FGTB has a majority in the market sector, but not overall. The CSC has won the majority of seats for the first time. The ACV/CSC also has the larger support in Brussels. In the non-market sector, the dominance of the ACV/CSC is particularly pronounced in all regions, owing to the strength of the Catholic pillar in this sector: as well as health and welfare, the sector covers 'free' (i.e. non-state) education, which is largely Catholic. In Catholic Flanders, the ACV/CSC receives 92 per cent of the non-market sector votes, but even in the more socialist Wallonia it gets 70 per cent of the votes.

The reasons for these electoral trends must be sought in the superior organizational power of the Catholic pillar, providing the ACV/CSC with more resources. This enables it to employ more – and more active – officials than its rival, to provide better training and support for its representatives, and to deliver better services to members (Hancké and Wijgaerts 1989: 189). The ABVV/FGTB, on the other hand, has been losing votes both among its more radical supporters, who see its behaviour as too moderate, and among more moderate workers put off by its radical image.

The workplace Trade Union Delegation (SD/DS), is older than the OR/CE and the CVGV/CSHE. It is not a true concertation body but the bargaining partner of management in workplace negotiations; it, rather than the works council, is entitled to conclude agreements. The union delegation monitors the application of collective agreements and social legislation, and has the right to negotiate over all personnel matters such as pay, working time, and conditions of work.

Bargaining in the Private Sector: A Pyramid of Collective Agreements

At the top of the collective bargaining pyramid are the national Inter-Industry Agreements (IPA/AIPs). These agreements establish the general arrangements for all workers in the private sector. The latest IPA/AIP, concluded in November 1990, not only contains important agreements on wage rises and extra holidays but also covers early retirement and the unemployed. These arrangements form the basis for, and are put into practice by, the economy-wide collective agreements concluded in the National Labour Council.

Central agreements made in the NAR/CNT are later implemented by the several hundred collective agreements concluded annually in the Joint Committees at sectoral level (see table 11.4), the principle being that agreements at lower levels are always bound by the provisions of higher-level agreements. These sectoral agreements are presented to the Minister of Employment for ratification, thus making them legally binding for the whole sector. This normally occurs automatically, though the minister refused to sign on several occasions in the 1970s and 1980s when agreements breached the limits of government pay policy.

Sectoral agreements often require detailed elaboration at company level, in bargaining between the union delegation and management. In most cases the union side is assisted or led by local or regional officials; the SD/DS normally functions as an extension of the union within the company. Although a collective agreement signed between one representative union and the employer is legally binding for all employees,

Table 11.4   Number of collective agreements registered by the Department for Collective Industrial Relations 1970–91

Year	in NAR/CNT	in PC/CP	Others (mainly company level)
1970	4	392	38
1971	4	453	69
1972	2	637	54
1973	5	556	50
1974	3	728	66
1975	12	500	51
1976	5	401	44
1977	4	518	46
1978	5	501	120
1979	5	400	225
1980	2	442	341
1981	10	243	480
1982	2	185	624
1983	7	227	1,862
1984	6	199	910
1985	3	346	3,253
1986	7	192	1,443
1987	3	512	1,989
1988	4	257	1,851
1989	11	767	2,258
1990	1	241	1,093
1991	20	879	2,218

Note: Royal Decree 181 (30 December 1982) made registration of enterprise-level agreements obligatory in practice.

Source: Ministry of Employment and Labour, Department of Collective Industrial Relations.

the different unions almost always draw up a joint list of demands, and bargain and sign together.

There is little information on how bargaining is typically conducted in multi-plant companies. In some cases, agreements cover all plants; sometimes, each subsidiary has its own agreement; in other cases, there are separate agreements but bargaining is closely coordinated. The collective agreement on the union delegation applies only to larger companies. The size threshold is from 20 to 50, according to sector. In recent years, there have been discussions on extending the provision to smaller firms; but the issue has been referred to sectoral negotiation.

Collective Bargaining in the Public Sector

About 20 per cent of the active population is employed in the public sector, where individual labour relations are regulated by statute (see Janvier and Rigaux 1987). Collective bargaining in the public sector is as complex as in the private sector, and is more or less similar in structure. This means that agreements comparable to IPA/AIPs are concluded for all workers in the sector. Framework agreements provide minimum guidelines for bargaining at national and regional levels and within 'sectors' such as finance, education or postal services.

The right to belong to a union is guaranteed for all workers in Belgium, including civil servants (with restrictions on the exercise of certain trade union rights for some categories). Although public authorities are obliged to bargain, they are not legally bound by the outcome; the government retains the right to determine unilaterally the labour conditions of its employees. Civil servants depend on their union power (public sector unionization is relatively high in Belgium) to hold the government to its agreements.

Recent years have seen a convergence in labour conditions in the public and private sectors. Civil servants have been the chief victims of the austerity policies of successive governments, and they have lost many of their prerogatives (such as life-time employment and favourable pension schemes). This has prompted patterns of conflict analogous to those in the private sector. Moreover, public agencies have been required to become more 'business-like', taking into account principles of 'rational' management and productivity. This has led, as in the private sector, to a growing differentiation in the pay and other labour conditions of civil servants in different regions, sectors and even within departments.

Given this convergence between the two sectors, it is conceivable that in the future there will be one collective agreement for private workers and civil servants alike, at least at regional level.

Strikes since the 1960s

Industrial conflict in Belgium has proved very sensitive to economic conditions. Strike activity was low in the 1960s, perhaps because of the defeat suffered by the unions in the national conflict of 1960–1, and the rise in workers' living standards in a period of economic growth. In the 1970s, the number of strikes increased as the economic crisis developed. Only after economic restructuring during the 1980s had helped to contain the crisis did the number of strikes decrease dramatically (see table 11.5).

Table 11.5   Strike frequency in the private sector 1963–90

| | NIS | | ACV/CSC | | |
| | | | TESA/VUB | | |
Year	Belgium	Flanders	Wallonia	Brussels	Belgium
1963	48				
1964	41				
1965	43				
1966	74				
1967	58				
1968	71				
1969	88				
1970	151				
1971	184				
1972	191				
1973	172				
1974	235				
1975	243				
1976	281	74	209	25	308
1977	220	75	175	14	264
1978	195	80	283	16	379
1979	215	101	170	12	283
1980	132	133	176	7	316
1981		74	164	14	252
1982		48	106	13	167
1983		26	99	6	131
1984		29	75	3	107
1985	65	53	123	5	181
1986		47	22	9	82*
1987		72	15	16	106*
1988	64				
1989	83				
1990	30				

* Figures for 1986 include four national strikes, and for 1987 three.
Source: NIS – National Institute for Statistics, *Sociale Statistieken*
         ACV/CSC – for 1976–8: Piret et al 1985; Hertogs and Piret 1986
         TESA/VUB – for 1986–7: Boogaerts 1990.

With the growing importance of public sector disputes, official statistics – which cover only the private sector – have become increasingly unreliable as an indicator of strike trends.[2] For example, figures compiled by Boogaerts (1990) from media reports indicated 130 strikes in the public sector during 1986–7, as against 185 in the private sector. This is further evidence of the growing similarity in organization and managerial practice of state and private sectors. Traditionally, low pay in the public sector was supposedly compensated by almost complete job security. However, new managerial policies in some services, such as telephones or airports, have challenged this job security. Performance-related pay for groups such as tax collectors has been an additional cause of discontent and conflict, by disturbing customary relativities.

In the private sector there has been an increase in conflicts at company or even plant level – a reflection of the growing autonomy of lower levels of organization (see below). A similar shift is apparent in the

Table 11.6   Number of working days lost by region (000s) 1963–90

Year	Flanders	Wallonia	Brussels	Total
1963				247
1964	376	56	12	444
1965	35	28	7	70
1966	86	433	14	533
1967	106	50	16	181
1968	180	182	2	364
1969	115	44	3	162
1970	1,133	229	70	1,432
1971	432	809	1	1,242
1972	157	174	23	354
1973	271	593	7	866
1974	304	274	2	580
1975	304	285	19	610
1976	395	498	4	896
1977	275	385	4	659
1978	613	378	11	1,002
1979	247	368	0	622
1980	83	127	7	222
1981	-	-	-	-
1982	-	-	-	-
1983	-	-	-	-
1984	-	-	-	-
1985	-	-	-	127
1986	-	-	-	-
1987	-	-	-	-
1988	-	-	-	194
1989	-	-	-	133
1990	-	-	-	101

Source: National Institute for Statistics, *Sociale Statistieken*, 1970–1991.

public sector, with the growing importance of sectional demands: hospital personnel in Belgium, as in France or the Netherlands, have a long-standing tradition of collective action. In public transport there have been a number of instances of action in support of local demands. Other disputes have involved local authority workers, including local police and fire services.

International comparative studies have always found it difficult to explain the Belgian strike pattern. We believe that the main reason for this is the difference in strike behaviour between Flanders and Wallonia. Though regional figures are available only for a limited period (and do not include the public sector), they indicate a continuing contrast (see tables 11.5 and 11.6).

Despite its smaller work force, the number of working days lost is consistently higher in Wallonia than in Flanders. Over the whole period 1964–80 an annual average of about 240 working days per 1000 workers were lost in Flanders, compared with 330 in Wallonia. The figures are distorted in individual years by the effects of large strikes: for example, the protracted disputes in the Flanders metalworking industry in 1964 and in the mines in 1970; and the 1971 steel strike in Wallonia. More recently, the 1988 figures are again influenced by a miners' strike in Flanders.

From the figures on strike frequency, it is clear that Walloon workers have been much more strike-prone than their Flemish counterparts. Except in 1979 and 1980, the absolute number of strikes in Wallonia was at least double that of Flanders, and – taking into account Wallonia's smaller working population – relative strike frequency was higher still. However, the figures for 1986–7 compiled by Boogaerts (1990: 406, 416), while not directly comparable with the official statistics for previous years, show a completely different pattern: 119 strikes in Flanders as against only 37 in Wallonia and 25 in Brussels. It is impossible to know whether this means that there has been a real reversal of strike-proneness between the two regions.

A major factor in explaining the contrast in strike behaviour is the difference in economic structure between the two regions. In the post-war decades, Flanders developed modern, productive and prosperous industrial and service sectors, whereas Wallonia remained based on

Table 11.7 Unemployment in Belgium (% of the labour force)

	1970	1975	1980	1985	1990*
Flanders	1.4	4.0	7.3	11.5	8.8
Wallonia	2.7	5.3	9.0	15.5	14.9
Brussels	1.0	3.6	7.0	12.6	10.7
Belgium	1.8	4.3	7.8	12.8	10.8

* estimate

Source: *Weekberichten* Kredietbank, 15 September 1989.

ageing, uncompetitive industries such as mining and steel. Whether or not one accepts the hypotheses of Kerr and Siegel (1954), it is evident that these industries are traditionally strike prone. In addition, industrial decline in Wallonia has meant that unemployment was considerably higher than in Flanders (see table 11.7). And as Paldam and Pedersen (1982: 511) have noted, Belgium is one of the countries with a historically positive correlation between unemployment and strike frequency.

The early industrialization of Wallonia, its working-class culture and the leading role of the more combative FGTB, combined to create a tradition of industrial conflict, but also of conflict regulation and resolution. This has led to a pattern of frequent short conflicts. In Flanders, on the other hand, there are fewer conflicts, partly reflecting a strong rural background and the dominant position of the ACV with its Catholic ideology of cooperation. But if disputes do occur, the structure of ownership – often involving foreign multinationals – makes resolution more difficult; hence strikes are often large and protracted.

Another important factor is political. Korpi and Shalev (1979) argue that the number of strikes decreases when labour parties are in power for an extended period, and increases when these parties alternate between government and opposition. Belgium does not fit their categories; but distinguishing between Flanders and Wallonia again helps. In Flanders the CVP is the largest party and has been in power almost continuously since the end of the war. Although it is certainly not a labour party in the true sense, it represents the majority of Flemish workers through its labour wing. Flemish workers may therefore feel continuously represented in government. Walloon workers on the other hand are represented predominantly by the PS, which has been in power only intermittently.

Recent Developments in Collective Bargaining: Processes and Issues

In the following discussion we assess the changes that have taken place in the industrial relations environment. A key element of transformation is the increasing importance of lower-level units within global organizations. This tendency towards enhanced responsibility for smaller organizational units, groups or even individuals co-exists with trends to greater interdependence; hence we use the term 'relative autonomization' (see Vilrokx 1987). Reflections of this process within the sphere of industrial relations are the shift of centralized bargaining towards sectors and enterprises (and individuals), and the trend from traditional labour contracts to a variety of atypical employment relationships.

The notion of relative autonomization is particularly useful for the analysis of Belgian industrial relations, by characterizing how collective bargaining fits within global framework agreements. The employer strategy of concluding company agreements has been consolidated over the years (see above, table 11.4), even though employers' organizations have continued to insist on reaching national inter-industry agreements. We examine below the two themes of technological innovation and employment flexibility as a way of illuminating the dynamics of Belgian industrial relations from this analytical perspective.

Collective Bargaining and Technological Change

One of the most significant features of Belgian industrial relations was the breakdown in national inter-industry bargaining between 1976 and 1986. The nominal agreement of 1981 may be discounted, since it was imposed by the government and did little more than endorse the government's two-year pay freeze. Similarly, it could be argued that the 1986 accord (covering 1987–8) was not a fully-fledged national agreement, since it merely stipulated that negotiations could be organized at lower bargaining levels on non-wage matters. However, the 1986 agreement was important in re-establishing the practice of bilateral national inter-industry bargaining relatively free from government pressure.

It would be wrong to draw conclusions about the state of national bargaining only on the basis of the number of agreements of this kind. Much national inter-industry bargaining takes place, as we have seen above, within the institutionalized framework of the National Labour Council. Some of the more important collective agreements of recent years fall in this category, including the 1983 Collective Labour Agreement (CLA) 39 concerning the introduction of new technology.

In the face of economic restructuring from the 1970s, unions in Belgium developed a hostile attitude to technological innovation as a threat to jobs and to the quality of work. This opposition conflicted with government support for economic rationalization as a way of improving the competitiveness of the Belgian economy.

In this situation the government pressed unions and employers' associations to sign an agreement on the introduction of new technology. From early 1982 it gave clear indications that it wanted the matter resolved in a national agreement. The government intervened whenever the bargaining process stalled, ultimately threatening to legislate if negotiations failed. Unions and employers finally reached an agreement, just as the government's deadline was about to expire, in December 1983.

The agreement was, understandably, bland and imprecise. Applying to private sector firms with more than 50 employees, Collective Labour Agreement (CLA) 39 stipulated that at least three months before the planned introduction of new technologies with important collective consequences, the employer must inform the works council about the timing of the planned changes, their economic and technological justification, and their social consequences (for work organization, working conditions, skills, training, etc.). The unions are given a role in the handling of these social consequences of technological change. The agreement barely addresses the issue of enforcement, despite the unions' demands, and consequently has never had much impact on the actual introduction of new technologies within enterprises.

Yet this does not mean that CLA 39 was of no importance. The government's purpose in pressing for a technology agreement was to create a more innovation-friendly climate by influencing the rather negative and inflexible position of the trade unions. This has been achieved, although the time needed to reach the agreement (almost two years) indicates that it was far from easy. Moreover by the time the national agreement was signed, several sectoral and enterprise-level agreements had already been negotiated: indicating that attitudes 'in the field' were less dogmatic than the official position of the unions at national level.

The unions were also influenced by the growing intervention of the government in socio-economic affairs (wages, working time, flexibility, etc.). It seemed preferable for them to sign an agreement with the employers rather than once again leave the initiative to the government. In CLA 39 the unions therefore recognized their inability to exercise more than a marginal influence on the innovation process and its consequences.

Does history repeat itself? The government had taken the initiative in 1950 in establishing a national tripartite commission for the promotion of productivity, and subsequently a bipartite Belgian Bureau for the Increase of Productivity (BDOP/OBAP) was created. Government officials, trade union representatives, employers and academics went to study automation processes in the USA, particularly in the motor industry, as they were later to visit Japan at the time of the information technology revolution. Unlike CLA 39, the 1954 Productivity Declaration was considered an important achievement, constituting a necessary step in the institutionalization of industrial relations in Belgium. But the leaders of the labour movement were soon bitterly disappointed by the unions' inability to influence the process of change at enterprise level (see Van Der Hallen and Huys 1986: 8).

Despite evident differences between the 1954 and 1983 agreements on industrial innovation there are some striking similarities. The role of the state was decisive in both cases, reflecting government perceptions of the need to modernize Belgian industry. (Though the Socialist Party was not in government on either occasion, there is no reason to assume that it would have acted differently.) It is also notable that in both cases the labour movement failed to develop a strategy towards technological change, attempting only to influence the 'social consequences'.

Collective Bargaining and Employment Flexibility

Since the mid-1970s, unemployment has been a key feature of the industrial relations environment, with the official rate increasing by an average of 20 per cent a year between 1974 and 1984. By 1980, with nearly 400,000 out of work, it was possible to speak of a generally recognized crisis of unemployment (Vilrokx 1981b: xii). By 1983 official unemployment had reached 500,000 or some 12–13 per cent of the labour force. In 1984 the figure reached 14 per cent, exceeded only by Ireland and Spain among OECD countries (Hughes 1989: 70–1). Some argued that official statistics gravely understated the problem; adding to the unemployed those involved in special employment programmes, early retirement schemes, short-time working, etc., the proportion excluded from 'normal' employment was perhaps as high as 25 per cent (Vranken 1985: 140).

Governments responded to the crisis in the labour market, and the associated spate of bankruptcies, with a series of Recovery Acts and Royal Decrees designed to improve business competitiveness. Central to this policy were proposals to uncouple working time from production time, influenced by the arguments of academics advocating extended shift-working to enhance the profitability of capital. In particular, the proposals of Tamas Palasthy for a 12–hour production system of twin 6–hour shifts were regarded as a potential means of increasing employment while improving productivity, and influenced the 'Hansenne experiments' (named after the then Minister of Employment and Labour) implemented by Royal Decree 179 of 1982. This decree authorized experiments in working-time reorganization, providing they enabled new workers to be recruited; normally, such experiments would have been prohibited by collective agreement or the 1971 Labour Law. More flexibility would be allowed for weekend work, or abnormal patterns of working days. Such initiatives required the agreement of the employer and unions at company level, and the approval of the Minister of Employment and Labour. The minister's consent was in turn conditional on a '5–3–3' agreement: a working time reduction of 5 per cent, a 3 per cent cut in wages, and 3 per cent extra employment.

If an enterprise did not sign such an agreement, and was not covered by a sectoral agreement, compensation had to be paid into the Employment Fund. Although 33,000 supplementary jobs were created under the scheme in the first year, total employment in the private sector still fell by 26,000 in 1983. In the Recovery Law of 1985 the 5–3–3 scheme was renewed.

The 1985 Recovery Law extended the deregulation of the labour market, providing for more flexibility in employment contracts, redundancy regulations, and probationary periods, as well as in working time: 'Who knows which working time regulation now applies in which situation', one commentator was driven to enquire (Vanachter 1985: 68). Indeed, according to Vanachter (1987: 19), the complexity of the regulations meant that they were not always applied in practice.

The Law of 1987 added few new elements of flexibility to the Recovery Laws of 1983 and 1985. The Hansenne experiments (Royal Decree 179 and subsequent laws) allowed for virtually every possible working time arrangement. But the Royal Decree had been a temporary experiment, whereas the 1987 Law permitted new working regulations to be introduced for an unlimited period. More significantly, though, the 1987 Law was the result of the National Labour Council's CLA 42 of 23 April 1986: the trade unions evidently preferred a negotiated solution to the unilateral imposition of working-time flexibility. The main significance of the Agreement and the Law is thus their emphasis on bilateral bargaining and employee consultation in the process of work reorganization.

Government Intervention in Pay Determination

The various Recovery Acts enabled the government to intervene in wage determination, for example by interfering with the 'cost-of-living' system of wage indexation, and by imposing special restrictions on public employees. From 1982, when the Belgian franc was devalued by 8.5 per cent, wages were compensated for only a part of the increase in the price index. This long-anticipated attack on the indexation system was carried through despite strong protests by the labour movement. Further modifications of the wage–price linkage were to follow.[3]

Other examples of direct intervention in wage determination were the 10 per cent reduction imposed in industries in economic difficulties, and the 1983 injunction that labour costs should not rise faster than those of Belgium's seven most important trading partners. Indeed, between 1982 and 1986, wages were frozen. Only from 1987 were the restrictions relaxed, while from 1988 a government-supervised increase was allowed.

The Law on the Protection of Competitiveness (1989) provides renewed powers for government intervention in response to adverse trends in key economic indicators. If these show a deterioration relative to the seven most important trading countries, negotiations must take place in the bipartite Central Economic Council. In an emergency the Law permits the government to take immediate action, for example by freezing collective agreements or reviewing automatic indexation.

All this means that the state has consolidated its powers of legal intervention in pay determination. It now has the statutory means to determine almost completely the scope for renewed bilateral bargaining, and to overrule the outcome of negotiations.

Conclusions

This chapter has argued that the character of Belgian industrial relations reflects a distinctive ideological, cultural and socio-economic structure which is shaped by the cleavage/pillar configurations. One cannot understand the standpoints and actions of the parties to industrial relations – and in particular the unions – unless these contextual influences are taken into account.

Like a Russian doll, the institutions of Belgian society at different levels have a common form but distinctive features. At national level we can speak of a Belgian model of industrial relations – with a key role for inter-industry agreements, automatic wage indexation, very high union density, and quasi-legislative powers wielded by the organizations of workers and employers. At regional level while many of the national patterns are replicated, there are also important variations. These too can be attributed to the contrasting ways in which the cleavage/pillar structure results in a different balance of power in each region.

Because the nature of Belgian labour relations is deeply embedded in the social structure, the crisis of trade unionism and industrial relations which has affected many European countries in recent years has been overcome more easily here. Aggregate union membership has remained relatively stable throughout the last two decades. For a ten-year period the practice of economy-wide agreements was indeed interrupted; but, in a context where the bargaining agenda was often set by government, the same functions of stabilization were met by agreements at sectoral, regional and company levels. An important feature of Belgian society is that the parties to collective bargaining also meet in a variety of other institutional settings, creating a high degree of 'conviviality'. Even when the bargaining process in one forum encounters obstacles, the incentives and the opportunities to reach consensual outcomes on other issues in other parts of the institutional machinery of industrial relations are very great.

This reflects the multiple linkages between the different pillars and cleavage organizations. Trade unions, for example, are each connected with a particular political party, finance and insurance organizations, newspapers, etc. associated with their pillar; often there is an interchange of moral, material and personnel resources. Horizontal inter-organizational solidarity is particularly strong within the Christian pillar: thus if members of the Christian trade unions retain their membership after retirement they automatically became members also of the Chritsian pensioners' organizations. Analogies exist within every pillar. Similarly, there is strong integration between different levels of organization: thus workplace trade union organization is not detached from the national structure. This has meant that Belgian trade unions are well adapted to dealing with decentralized negotiations over such issues as technological change.

The state has become increasingly central to Belgian industrial relations. A four-stage development can be identified. From 1945 to 1959, the main role of the state was to encourage the institutionalization of collective bargaining. Employers and unions were then free to develop their bargaining relationship; and in the second phase, between 1960 and 1973, governments normally abstained from direct intervention. The years 1974–88 were a period of major economic restructuring. The state imposed many restrictions on collective bargaining, forced unions and employers to address new issues, and took unilateral action to impose new forms of labour market flexibility. This led to a new phase dating from 1989: the state now possesses a powerful set of mechanisms to monitor and intervene in Belgian economic performance and, if necessary, in industrial relations; but this also permits a more detached relationship ('collective bargaining under house arrest') so long as the parties themselves observe a sufficient degree of self-restraint.

Accordingly, institutional stability has been sustained and can be expected to survive any future devolution of functions from the central state to the regions. The Belgian model is not an endangered species. In the 1980s, unions at first reacted passively and defensively in the face of extensive technological and organizational innovation; later, the institutional mechanisms established in the 1980s enabled the challenge of flexibility to be handled consensually. Moreover, following the phase of major restructuring and innovation, the industrial relations agenda has once again shifted back to the familiar territory of labour market issues. While the EC single market, and the broader issues of adaptation to economic (product- and labour-market) integration across the whole of Europe, will inevitably create problems for Belgian industrial relations, the parties have already learned to cope with such issues.

Notes

1 The authors would like to Thérèse Beaupain for constructive comments on a draft of this chapter.
2 Official strike statistics in Belgium, collected by the National Institute for Statistics (NIS), show the same deficiencies as in other countries but with the additional problem that the figures are missing for some years (1981–4 and 1986–7), and do not cover conflicts in the public sector. Other organizations (ACV; TESA–VUB) have collected data for these periods but they are not comparable to the NIS figures. Our analysis is based mainly on the NIS data.
3 Normally, an automatic 2 per cent rise in wages would be triggered for each 2 per cent rise in the cost-of-living index, and so on for each subsequent 2 per cent rise. On several occasions since 1982, one 2 per cent increment has been discounted, so that it took a 4 per cent rise in prices to trigger a 2 per cent rise in wages.

Abbreviations

Note: in this list, and in the text, first Flemish and then French titles and initials are given - except for organizations which exist in only one region.

AAB	*Alliance Agriculture Belge* – Belgian Agriculture Alliance
ABVV	*Algemeen Belgisch Vakverbond*
FGTB	*Fédération des Travailleurs de Belgique* – General Belgian Trade Union Federation
ACLVB	*Algemene Centrale der Liberale Vakbonden va België*
CGSLB	*Confédération Générale des Syndicats Libéraux de Belgique* – General Confederation of Liberal Trade Unions of Belgium
ACV	*Algemeen Christelijk Vakverbond*
CSC	*Confédération des Syndicats Chrétiens* – General Christian Trade Union Federation
BB	*Belgische Boerenbond* – Belgian Farmers' Union
BDOP	*Belgische Dienst voor de Opvoering van de Produktiviteit*

OBAP	*Office Belge pour l'Accroissement de la Productivité* – Belgian Bureau for the Increase of Productivity
BRC	*Bijzondere Raadgevende Commissies*
CCS	*Commissions Consultatives Spéciales* – Special Advisory Commissions
CAO	*Collectieve Arbeidsovereenkomst*
CCT	*Convention collective de travail* – collective agreement
CESRB	*Conseil Economique et Social de la Region Bruxelloise* – Economic and Social Council for the Brussels Region
CESRW	*Conseil Economique et Social de la Region Wallonne* – Economic and Social Council of the Walloon Region
CRB	*Centrale Raad voor het Bedrijfsleven*
CCE	*Conseil Centrale de l'Economie* – Central Economic Council
CVGV	*Comité voor Veiligheid, Gezondheid en Verfraaiing van de werkplaatsen*
CSHE	*Comité de Sécurité, Hygiène et d'Embellissement des lieux de travail* – Committee for Safety, Health and Improvement of the Workplace
CVP	*Christelijke Volkspartij*
PSC	*Parti Social Chrétien* – Christian Democratic Party
ESRBG	*Economische en Sociale Raad voor het Brussels Gewest* – Economic and Social Council for the Brussels Region
IPA	*Interprofessioneel Akkoord*
AIP	*Accord Interprofessionnel* – Multi-industry/Agreement
NAC	*Nationale Arbeidsconferentie*
CNT	*Conférence Nationale du Travail* – National Conferences of Labour
NAR	*Nationale Arbeidsraad*
CNT	*Conseil National du Travail* – National Labour Council
NCEE	*Nationaal Comité voor Economische Expansie*
CNEE	*Comité Nationale d'Expansion Economique* – National Committee for Economic Expansion
NCK	*Nationale Confederatie van Kaderleden*
CNC	*Confédération Nationale des Cadres* – National Confederation of Middle Management
NCMV	*Nationaal Christelijk Middenstandsverbond* – National Christian Traders' Union
OC	*Overlegcomités*
CC	*Comités de Concertation* – Concertation Committees
OR	*Ondernemingsraad*
CE	*Conseil d'Entreprise* – Works Council
PC	*Paritaire Comités*
CP	*Commission Paritaires* – Joint Committees
SD	*Syndicale Delegatie*
DS	*Délégation Syndicale* – Trade Union Delegation
SERV	*Sociaal-Economische Raad van Vlaanderen* – Social Economic Council of Flanders
SP	*Socialistische Partij*
PS	*Parti Socialiste* – Socialist Party
TR	*Table Ronde* – Round Table
UAP	*Unions des Agriculteurs Professionels* – Unions of Agricultural Professionals
UCM	*Union des Classes Moyennes* – Union of Traders
UWE	*Union Wallonne des Entreprises* – Walloon Union of Enterprises
VBO	*Verbond van Belgische Ondernemingen*
FEB	*Fédération des Entreprises de Belgique* – Federation of Belgian Enterprises

VESOC   *Vlaams Economisch Sociaal Overlegcomité* – Flemish Economic and Social
        Concertation Committee
VEV   *Vlaams Economisch Verbond* – Flemish Economic Union
VOB   *Verbond van Ondernemingen van Brussel*
UEB   *Union des Entreprises de Bruxelles* – Union of Brussels' Enterprises

References

Arcq, E. and Blaise, P. 1986: Les Organisations syndicales en Belgique. *Dossier du Crisp*, 23, 1–24.

Arcq, E. and Marques-Pereira, B. 1991: Néo-corporatisme et concertation sociale en Belgique. *Politiques et management public*, 9, 3, September, 160–79.

Beaupain, T. 1983: Belgium: Collective Bargaining and Concertation System Inhibited by Economic Crisis and Government. In S. Barkin, *Worker Militancy and its Consequences: The Changing Climate of Western Industrial Relations.* New York: Praeger.

Beaupain, T. 1989: La Négociation collective: niveaux et contenus. In T. Beaupain et al. *50 jaararbeidsverhoudingen.* Brugge: Die Keure, 231–51.

Beaupain, T. et al. 1989: *50 jaar arbeidsverhoudingen.* Brugge: Die Keure.

Blanpain, R. 1984: Recent Trends in Collective Bargaining in Belgium. *International Labour Review*, 123, 3, May-June, 319–32.

Bleeckx, F. 1985: *La Négociation collective en Belgique: repères et enjeux.* Louvain-la Neuve, UCL, Institut des Sciences du Travail.

Boogaerts, R. 1990: *Arbeidsconflicten in België in de periode 1986–1987.* Brussels: Licentiaatsverhandeling, VUB.

Bundervoet, J. 1981: Kapitaalstrategieën en regionalisering in België: enkele vragen en bedenkingen. *Tijdschrift voor Sociologie*, 2, 3-4, 261–300.

Chlepner, B.-S. 1972: *Cent ans d'histoire sociale en Belgique.* Brussels: ULB, Institut de Sociologie.

Cottenier, J. et al. 1989: *De Generale, 1822–1992.* Berchem: EPO.

Cressey, P. et al. 1988: *La Participation. Synthèse des études de la Fondation sur la participation.* Luxembourg: Fondation européenne pour l'amélioration des conditions de vie et de travail, Office des publications officielles des Communautés européennes.

De Broeck, G. 1989: De overheid en het sociaal overleg. In Beaupain, T. et al., *50 jaar arbeidsverhoudingen.* Brugge: Die Keure, 49–70.

De Coninck, P. and Vilrokx, J. 1977: Een bedrijfsbezetting: Prestige-Tessenderlo. *De Nieuwe Maand*, 20, 10, December, 608–18.

EIRR, 1991: The 1991 workplace elections. *European Industrial Relations Review*, 215, December, 16–20.

Hancké, B. and Wijgaerts, D. 1989: Belgian Unionism and Self-Management. In G. Szell et al. (eds.), *The State, Trade Unions and Self-Mangement: Issues of Competence and Control*, Berlin: de Gruyter.

Hertogs, B. and Piret, C. 1986: *De stakingen in 1985.* Brussels: ACV.

Hughes, J.J. 1989: Unemployment. In R. Bean (ed.), *International Labour Statistics. A Handbook, Guide and Recent Trends*, London: Routledge, 50–76.

Huyse, L. 1980: *De gewapende vrede. De Belgische politiek na 1945.* Leuven: Kritak.

Janvier, R. and Rigaux, M. 1987: Individuele en collectieve arbeidsverhoudingen in de publieke en particuliere sector; Een beknopte juridische vergelijking. In P. Gevers (ed.), *Ambtenarenbeleid en arbeidsverhoudingen.* Brugge: Die Keure, 37–139.

Kendall, W. 1975: Belgium. In A. Lane (ed.), *The Labour Movement in Europe*, London: Allen Lane, 209–41.

Kerr, C. and Siegel, A. 1954: The Interindustry Propensity to Strike. An International Comparison. In A. Kornhauser et al. *Industrial conflict*, New York: McGraw-Hill, 189–212.

Korpi, W. and Shalev, M. 1979: Strikes, Industrial Relations and Class Conflict in Capitalist Societies. *British Journal of Sociology*, 30, 2, June, 164–87.

Kredietbank, 1989: Economisch profiel van België. *Kredietbank Weekberichten,* 44, 28, 15 September, p.7.

Lorwin, V. 1979: Segmented Pluralism: Ideological Cleavages and Political Cohesion in Smaller European Democracies. *Comparative Politics,* 2, January, 141–75

Michielsen, L. 1976: *Geschiedenis van de Europese arbeidsbeweging. Deel I: tot 1914.* Brussels: Fans Masereelfonds.

Ministerie van Tewerkstelling en Arbeid 1992: *Resultaten van de sociale verkiezingen 1991.* Brussels: Ministerie van Tewerkstelling en Arbeid.

Nationaal Instituut voor de Statistiek 1970–1991: *Sociale statistieken.* Brussels.

Paldam, M. and Pedersen, P.J. 1982: The Macroeconomic Strike Model: A Study of Seventeen Countries, 1948–1975. *Industrial and Labor Relations Review,* 35, 4, July, 504–21.

Piret, C. et al. 1985: *De stakingen in 1983 en 1984.* Brussels: ACV.

Spineux, A. 1990: Trade Unionism in Belgium: The Difficulties of a Major Renovation. In G. Baglioni and C. Crouch (eds.), *European Industrial Relations: The Challenge of Flexibility,* London: Sage, 42–70.

Stroobant, M. 1989: De overheid en het collectief overleg in België tijdens de sociaal economische crisis 1970–1988. In T. Beaupain et al. *50 jaar arbeidsverhoudingen.* Bruges: Die Keure, 71–115.

Vanachter, O. 1985: De grenzen van de arbeidstijd. In M. Vranken (ed.) *Arbeidsrecht en flexibiliteit. De Sociale Herstelwet 1985.* Antwerp: Kluwer rechtwetenschappen, 67–97.

Vanachter, O. 1987: Arbeidsduur – arbeidsorganisatie en flexibiliteit. Recente ontwikkelingen in België. In C. Engels (ed.) *Invoering van nieuwe arbeidsregelingen in de ondernemingen. De Wet van 17 maart 1987.* Antwerp: Kluwer rechtswetenschappen, 18–33.

Van den Brande, A. 1987: Neo-corporatism and Functional-Integral Power in Belgium. In I. Scholten (ed.), *Political Stability and Neo-corporatism,* London: Sage, 95–119.

Van Der Hallen, P. and Huys, J. 1986: *Les Accords de technologie en Belgique.* Luxembourg: Commission des Communautés Européennes.

Vanderstraeten, A. 1988: Neo-corporatisme en het Belgisch sociaal-economisch overlegsysteem. *Res Publica,* 28, 4, 671–88.

Vilrokx, J. 1981a: Sociaal-economische verhoudingen in het twee-ledige België: een interactionele en multidimensionele benadering. *Tijdschrift voor Sociologie,* 2, 3–4, 22–158.

Vilrokx, J. 1981b: *Werknemers in onzekerheid: sociaal bewustzijn in krisisbeleving in een bedeigde onderneming.* Gent: Masereelfonds.

Vilrokx, J. 1987: *Self-Employment in Europe as a Form of Relative Autonomy: Significance and Prospects.* Brussels: EC-FAST.

Vilrokx, J. and Van Leemput, J. 1989: De evolutie van stakingen en bezettingen sinds de jaren '60. In T. Beaupain et al. *50 jaar arbeidsverhoudingen.,* 279–313 Bruges: Die Keure.

Visser, J. 1991: Tendances de la syndicalisation. In OECD, *Perspectives de l'emploi.* Paris: OECD, chapter 4.

Vranken, M. 1985: Flexibiliteit van arbeidsovereenkomsten en -voorwaarden. In Vranken, M. (ed.) *Arbeidsrecht en flexibiliteit. De Sociale Herstelwet 1985.* Antwerp: Kluwer, 26–8.

Witte E. and Craeybeckx, J. 1981: *Politieke geschiedenis van België sinds 1830; Spanningen in een burgerlijke democratie.* Antwerp: Standaard wetenschappelijke uitgeverij.

Ysebaert, C. and Asselberghs, L. 1988: *Instellingen zakboekje 1989.* Antwerp: Kluwer.

Ysebaert, C. and De Boeck, J. 1988: *Politiek zakboekje, Martens VIII 1988.* Antwerp: Kluwer.

12

Luxembourg: An Island of Stability

Gary Tunsch

Introduction

The Grand-Duchy of Luxembourg is the smallest member country of the EC, with an area of 1,000 square miles and a population of 380,000. There are three national languages: French (used for governmental business), German and Lëtzebuergesch.

Luxembourg is a constitutional monarchy with three main political parties: the *Parti Chrétien Social* (PCS – Social Christian Party), *Parti Ouvrier Socialiste Luxembourgeois* (POSL – Luxembourg Workers' Socialist Party) and *Parti Démocratique* (PD – Democratic Party). Government is normally by a coalition between the PCS and one of the other parties, currently the POSL; at present these two parties share two-thirds of the seats in parliament. Also represented in parliament are two green parties, the communist party, and a single-issue party (Action 5/6) which calls for the system of public-sector pensions (based on five-sixths of final salary) to be extended to the private sector.

Total employment at the end of 1991 was 182,000. This includes a high proportion of migrant labour (primarily Portuguese and Italian), which constitutes 27.5 per cent of the population and a larger share of the labour force. Of growing significance are the cross-frontier commuters whose numbers have more than doubled in the last five years and stand at roughly 40,000 (about half of whom work in services). This reflects the fact that employment is buoyant, despite the international recession, increasing at an annual rate of 5 per cent in recent years. The rate of unemployment, for many years among the lowest in Europe, has fallen to 1.3 per cent of the domestic labour force – far below the rest of the EC.

The Luxembourg economy – which is heavily dependent on that of Germany – traditionally rested on the steel industry. Despite a considerable contraction in recent decades, it still employs over 10,000 workers;

and the main company, ARBED is, with over 9,000 employees, by far the largest private firm in the country. Since the economic crisis of the early 1970s, Luxembourg has pursued economic diversification, encouraging such industries as tyres (Goodyear is the second largest private firm) and plastics. The main growth of employment, however, is in services, and in particular banking (see table 12.1). Today 187 banks operate in Luxembourg, compared with 37 in 1970; three of the seven largest employers are banks. This sectoral shift has brought some increase in female labour force participation – for much of the 1980s, the third lowest in western Europe – but the proportion is still well below the EC average. Part-time employment has also increased rapidly in recent years, but is still low by EC standards.

Table 12.1   Employment by Sector (September 1991)

	Number (000s)	%
Agriculture	1.54	0.8
Mining and Manufacturing	35.99	19.7
Building and Civil Engineering	18.90	10.4
Energy and Water	1.42	0.8
Marketable Service	97.29	53.4
Non-Market Services	27.20	14.9

Source: STATEC, *Note de Conjoncture*, 4/1991.

Trade Unions

Trade unionism in Luxembourg (as in neighbouring Belgium) is marked by structural pluralism and high membership density (roughly 50 per cent).

Unions have existed since the 1860s, initially based in traditional crafts, and emerging in heavy industry after the turn of the century. Schoolteachers unionized in the late nineteenth century followed by other groups of public employees and by white-collar staff in private industry.

Before the First World War the level of union membership was very low and the structure of organization extremely fragmented. A phase of organizational consolidation then occurred, with the growth of unionization in the main industrial sectors, and the polarization of unions between socialist and catholic federations. After the suppression of trade unionism during German wartime occupation, an effort was made in 1944 to establish a unified movement; but the following year there was a communist breakaway, followed by the catholics; and in 1948 a 'neutral' occupationally-based federation was also established. In the 1960s the communist federation re-joined the socialists, but appeals for broader unification were rebuffed. Subsequent decades saw a complex pattern of alignments as individual unions switched allegiances or opted for independence from the main confederations.

Today there exist two trade union confederations with national representative status for blue- and white-collar staff. The larger, the *Onofhängege Gewerkschafts-Bond Lëtzebuerg* (OGB-L, or Independent Trade Union Confederation of Luxembourg) comprises 14 sectoral federations with both manual and white-collar membership. While socialist in origin and orientation, OGB-L is not organizationally attached to the POSL and still aspires to unity with the other sections of the movement.

The *Lëtzebuerger Chrëstleche Gewerkschafts-Bond* (LCGB – Luxembourg Confederation of Christian Trade Unions) is closely linked to the PCS, though it too is formally independent. LCGB strongly supports the principle of trade union pluralism. It contains 13 federations covering specific industries and economic sectors.

A third organization, the *Fédération des Employés Privés/Fédération Indépendante des Travailleurs et Cadres* (FEP/FITC – Federation of Private-Sector Staffs/Independent Federation of Workers and Managers), has national representative status on behalf of private-sector white-collar staff. Its membership is almost exclusively drawn from this group, and it is politically neutral. FEP/FITC has suffered severely in the last dozen years with breakaways by a number of sectoral associations, some joining one or other of the two main confederations and others (notably the banking and insurance union ALEBA) opting for independence. More recently an internal split, initiated by the employee committee of Goodyear, has resulted in the formation of a rival federation, SNEP-R.

A variety of other unions are confined to specific sectors of the economy. The *Neutral Gewerkschaft Lëtzebuerg* (NGL – Neutral Trade Union of Luxembourg) inherits some of the traditions of craft unionism, and is associated with the 'Action 5/6' party. The oldest Luxembourg trade union, the *Fédération Luxembourgeoise des Travailleurs du Livre* (FLTL), covers printing workers, and there are two rival unions of transport workers (FNCTTFEL and FCPT). In the public sector, the *Confédération Générale de la Fonction Publique* (CGFP) and the *Fédération Générale des Fonctionnaires Communaux* (FGFC) cover national and local government respectively.

Two of these organizations, FLTL and FNCTTFEL, are linked in a loose confederation with OGB-L; while FCPT is similarly associated with LCGB. The rival confederations have no negotiating functions, but serve as vehicles for political pressure and international affiliation.

Employers' Organizations

The dominant representative of Luxembourg employers is the *Fédération des Industriels Luxembourgeois* (FEDIL – Federation of Luxembourg Industrialists), founded in 1917. It covers virtually every manufacturing enterprise, regardless of size, and a growing number of firms from the service sector.

Currently some 350 firms are directly affiliated, as well as eleven sectoral employers' associations. FEDIL is not directly involved in collective bargaining but assists member firms, particularly in cases before the National Conciliation Office (see below).

Artisan industries are represented by a national confederation established in 1905, which comprises 50 trade-based federations and occupational associations. Affiliated membership covers 3,600 firms, or 90 per cent of all registered artisan enterprises.

The first collective organization in the commercial sector was formed in 1909. After various mergers and changes of name it is now known as the *Confédération du Commerce Luxembourgeois* (CCL – Luxembourg Confederation of Commerce).

The hotel and restaurant trade is separately organized, and for a long time was split between three rival associations. Since 1970, however, there has been a single organization, the *Fédération Nationale des Hôteliers, Restaurateurs et Cafetiers du Grand-Duché de Luxembourg* (HORESCA – National Federation of Luxembourg Hotels, Restaurants and Cafés). So far no collective agreements exist in this sector, but HORESCA is currently negotiating with the relevant unions.

In banking, the *Association des Banques et Banquiers Luxembourg* (ABBL – Luxembourg Association of Banks and Bankers) was founded in 1939. It has 158 members, covering virtually the whole of the sector. Among other functions it represents its members in collective bargaining. In the insurance sector, the *Association des Compagnies d'Assurances Agréées au Grand-Duché de Luxembourg* (ACA – Luxembourg Association of Chartered Insurance Companies), founded in 1956, covers most eligible firms; it also represents its membership in collective bargaining.

In agriculture there are two rival organizations, the *Centrale Paysanne* (CP – Central Farmers' Organization) founded in 1944, and the *Fédération Libre des Agriculteurs du Luxembourg* (FLB – Free Federation of Luxembourg Agriculture) created in 1979. The split reflected the dissatisfaction of a section of farmers with the working of the cooperative system run by the CP.

Collective Agreements

Though collective agreements have been negotiated since the 1870s, they were rare before the 1930s. Greater coordination on the trade union side during that decade was followed by the appointment of a government arbitration committee (*Conseil National du Travail* – CNT) in 1936.

The current legal framework is defined in the 1965 law on collective agreements. A valid agreement must be signed between an employer or employers' association and a union or unions with representative status. This status (currently enjoyed, as indicated above, by two general confederations and one white-collar federation) is confirmed – or refused – by the Ministry of Labour when agreements are submitted for official registration. The law specifies issues which should be covered in collective agreements, and requires in particular rules for money payments for night work and dangerous or uncongenial working conditions, for avoiding sex discrimination in pay, and for the indexation of wages to the cost of living. All workers within a company must be covered by a single agreement. There is no obligation on employers to reach an agreement, but if so requested by employee representatives, they must enter into negotiations.

Most sectors of employment in Luxembourg are currently covered by collective agreements. In wholesale and retail distribution, no general agreement has been negotiated for several years; but the provisions of the previous agreements have been maintained through enterprise-level bargaining. The main gap in the coverage of collective agreements is in hotels and catering, though recently the unions and HORESCA have been negotiating to introduce an agreement.

Industry-level bargaining is not particularly common in Luxembourg, though where sectoral agreements exist they can be made obligatory throughout the industry. Sectors covered by multi-employer agreements include building and civil engineering, banking and insurance, petrol distribution, and road haulage. In hospitals and breweries there are also multi-employer agreements, though these have not been made generally enforceable. Elsewhere, company negotiations are the norm.

Disputes over the interpretation of collective agreements are determined by the Labour Tribunal, consisting of a judge with employer and union assessors. The Tribunal, which was established in 1989, also handles individual employment disputes.

The National Conciliation Office

Established in 1945, the *Office National de Conciliation* (ONC) has replaced the CNT of 1936 and is charged with the peaceful resolution of disagreements between the parties to collective bargaining.

Mediation by the ONC is obligatory in the case of breakdown in negotiations, and must precede any resort to a strike or lockout. A joint conciliation committee exists, chaired by a senior civil servant and with three representatives each of employers and workers. In 1991 the committee met 20 times to consider 22 disputes, 20 of which were resolved. If conciliation fails, either party may call for the establishment of an arbitration panel chaired by a government nominee with union and employer representatives. If approved by the parties, an arbitration award acquires the status of a collective agreement. In the case of the two unresolved disputes in 1991 – in banking and insurance – there was no resort to arbitration, but after token strikes a settlement was negotiated.

The jurisdiction of the ONC does not extend to the public sector. However, there exist analogous procedures for conciliation and mediation.

Strikes and Lockouts

The right to strike, in the private sector, is implied in the constitution and was explicitly recognized in an interpretative motion adopted by parliament in the 1950s. In the following decade, the right to lockout was also implicitly recognized. However, neither action may be undertaken or threatened during the currency of an agreement, or before conciliation procedures have been exhausted. In the public sector the right to strike was conceded in a law of 1979, though with the exclusion of such categories as higher civil servants, senior managers, police, and various medical and security personnel.

Strikes in Luxembourg are exceptional; the level of conflict, relative to the size of the work force, is the lowest in the EC. In the past decade there have been only four disputes involving more than 50 workers: tilelayers in 1984–5, secondary teachers in 1988, postal workers in 1990, and the token strike in banking and insurance in 1991.

Individual Employment Rights

Legislation in 1989 provided for the first time an equivalent status for manual and white-collar employees, though some special conditions still apply to non-manual staff in the private sector. Every employee has the right to a written contract of employment including a job description, a statement of normal hours and pay, and any probationary period.

Employment contracts should normally be permanent; fixed-term contracts are permitted only when the work to be undertaken is temporary. The law lays down detailed procedures governing dismissal, redundancy and company closure or takeover.

The legal minimum wage sets a floor to every employment contract. Every employee (except in case of physical or mental disability) is entitled to a 'minimum social wage', linked to the cost-of-living index. The level of the minimum social wage is fixed by law. Every two years, the government submits to parliament a report on the evolution of general economic conditions and salaries. If necessary, this report is accompanied by proposals to increase the minimum social wage. Skilled workers are entitled to a minimum 20 per cent above that for unskilled, and lower rates are prescribed for juveniles.

The principle of indexation applies to all wages. Since 1963, public-sector pay has been index-linked, and this principle was legally extended to the whole of the private sector in 1975.

The working week is legally prescribed, and has been set at 40 hours since 1970. The law also provides for annual leave with pay of 25 working days for all employees, with an additional 6 days for disabled workers, and for those whose work requires unsocial shift patterns. Other special leave entitlements are defined by law; while collective agreements often provide for additional days of leave. There are also ten public holidays each year.

Workplace Representation

Every employer – private or public – with 15 or more workers must provide for the election of a *délégation du personnel* (employee committee). If there are 100 or more employees, separate elections must be held for manual and white-collar delegates. The number of delegates varies according to the size of the firm: only one if there are 25 employees or fewer, up to 25 or more if there are over 5,000.

Delegates can be nominated by those unions nationally recognized as representative, or by groups of workers comprising at least 5 per cent of the labour force. Election is by secret ballot, normally on the basis of proportional representation.

The function of the *délégation* is to protect employees' working conditions, job security and social rights. One delegate is designated to take specific responsibility for health and safety issues. The *délégation* has rights of information on the economic situation of the company, and of consultation over matters directly affecting employees.

In large private firms – with at least 150 employees – there also exists a *comité mixte d'entreprise* (joint works committee) composed of equal numbers of employer and employee representatives. The latter are elected by the *délégation*. Either side can nominate advisers (in practice, officials of trade unions or employers' associations) to participate in committee proceedings in a consultative role.

The joint committee has co-determination rights over the use of equipment to monitor employee performance; questions of health and safety; policies concerning recruitment, promotion, transfer and dismissal; employee appraisal; and company rules. Management must inform and consult the committee in advance of decisions on technical changes, working methods and the working environment, current and forecast demand for labour, and vocational education and training. Management must also provide a half-yearly written report on the economic and financial position of the company.

Finally, the law of 1974 which established joint committees also provided for employee representation on the boards of companies with 1,000 or more employees. In such companies the *délégation* elects one-third of the members of the board, who enjoy the same status as other directors.

Statutory National Institutions

Under legislation dating from 1924 there exists a system of chambers of labour and trade (*chambres professionnelles*) with compulsory membership, with the function of representing the interests of their constituencies, and the right to submit proposals for legislation. The members of each chamber are elected by and from their constituents.

Three chambers exist for employees, catering respectively for manual workers, private-sector white-collar staff, and public officials. Each chamber has between 20 and 30 members, elected on the basis of the different industries and services which they cover. On the employers' side there are also three chambers, for industrial and commercial firms, artisan firms, and agriculture.

The *Conseil Économique et Social* (CES – Economic and Social Council) is a consultative body charged with oversight of national economic, financial and social developments. It produces an annual report, and can also be asked for advice – which is normally presented unanimously – on issues of current concern, or on questions on which the *chambres professionnelles* have submitted conflicting proposals. The government is also required to consult the CES before initiating legislation on general matters of social or economic concern. The CES has 35 members, representing the two sides of industry and the different economic sectors, together with a number of independent experts.

The *Comité de Coordination Tripartite* (CCT – Tripartite Coordination Committee) is the product of a series of meetings in 1977 between government, employers and unions in response to the economic crisis which threatened to disrupt the Luxembourg labour market. These tripartite meetings expressed unanimous support for the goals of economic growth and full employment, and legislation was enacted to establish the CCT.

The committee, with four members from each of the three parties, is convened when the numbers unemployed (or under notice of dismissal) exceed a specified threshold, or when other important issues relating to the labour market arise. Thus meetings have recently been held to discuss the single European market and immigration policy.

The *Comité de Conjoncture* (CC – Economic Committee) is a similar tripartite body, created in 1975, to advise on measures to avoid dismissals caused by temporary economic fluctuations. It meets monthly, monitors developments in the economy and the labour market, and advises on job protection measures in industries threatened by job losses.

The *Commission Nationale de l'Emploi* (CNE – National Employment Commission) is a tripartite advisory body, established in 1976, when the official employment department was set up. It oversees the administration of government employment policy and advises the Minister on issues related to labour market organization and the employment services.

Prospects for Industrial Relations in Luxembourg

A key issue for current industrial relations is the regulation of 'atypical' work, which has not previously been governed by special legislation. Two proposals are at present under discussion. One is to remove disincentives to part-time work by providing for the first time a legal framework for such work, covering such issues as employment contracts, overtime and unemployment benefits. The other concerns temporary employees, and is intended to ensure adequate social protection for such workers without unduly restricting the ability of firms to react flexibly to fluctuations in demand. This proposal is the more contentious, and is unlikely to be resolved during 1992.

Other legislative changes in prospect are a reform of the procedures of the ONC, and a modification to the law on *chambres professionnelles* to permit the election of foreign nationals.

In the collective bargaining arena, the worsening economic environment is likely to cause increasing difficulties. Several major companies have proposed a wage freeze in the current bargaining round. The more difficult climate is evident from the growing number of disputes referred to the ONC.

The commitment to industrial peace and social consensus remains strong in Luxembourg. Nevertheless, the tensions in the system were demonstrated by the decision of both the OGB-L and the LCGB to call a national day of action for April 1992, with demonstrations and a general strike, against a proposed amendment to the sickness insurance system. This was the first time for many years that the two confederations had taken joint action over an issue of social policy, reflecting their common belief that the government's economy measures threatened to initiate a two-class social security system. Opposition to the amendment was also voiced by employers' organizations and the doctors' professional association. However, the tradition of consensual problem-solving was maintained by a last-minute agreement between the government and the organizations opposed to the changes, allowing the day of action to be called off.

In 1993 the next elections will take place for the *chambres professionnelles* and *délégations du personnel*. These may well consolidate the position of the OGB-L and LCGB; while the FEP/FITC is likely to suffer badly as a result of its recent internal divisions.

Employers are strongly affected by the harsher economic environment. At its meeting in January 1992, the FEDIL reported a serious decline in activity in 1991 and saw few prospects of recovery. Its board of directors has stressed the need for the government to pursue cautious economic and social policies to improve competitiveness.

This gloomy assessment receives some support from the latest economic report of STATEC, the government economics service. However, it sees some prospect for modest improvement in 1992. In any event, the Luxembourg economy remains far healthier than in most other countries of western Europe. Though circumstances will doubtless generate new pressures in industrial relations, the strong traditions of consensual problem-solving are likely to remain effective.

Abbreviations

ABBL	*Association des Banques et Banquiers Luxembourg* – (Luxembourg Association of Banks and Bankers)
ACA	*Association des Compagnies d'Assurances Agréées* – Luxembourg Association of Chartered Insurance Companies
ALEBA	*Association Luxembourgeoise des Employés de Banques et d'Assurances* – Luxembourg Banking and Insurance Workers' Union
BMIAV	*Berg - Metall - und Industriearbeiterverband* – Union of Miners, Metalworkers and Industrial Workers
CC	*Comité de Conjoncture* – Economic Committee
CCL	*Confédération du Commerce Luxembourgeois* – Confederation of Luxembourg Commerce
CCT	*Comité de Coordination Tripartite* – Tripartite Cordination Committee
CES	*Conseil Économique et Social* – Economic and Social Council
CGFP	*Confédération Générale de la Fonction Publique* – Civil Service Union
CGT	*Confédération Générale du Travail* – General Confederation of Labour
CME	*comité mixte d'Entreprise* – joint works committee
CNT	*Conseil National du Travail* – National Arbitration Committee
CP	*Centrale Paysanne / Baurenzentral* – Farmers' Central Organization
FCPT	*Fédération Chrétienne du Personnel du Transport* – Christian Transport Workers' Union
FEDIL	*Fédération des Industriels Luxembourgeois* – Federation of Luxembourg Industrialists
FEP/FITC	*Fédération des Employés Privés/Fedération Indépendante des Travailleurs et Cadres* – Federation of Private-Sector Staffs Independent Federation of Workers and Managers
FGFC	*Fédération Générale des Fonctionnaires Communaux* – Local Authority Workers' Union
FLA	*Freie Lëtzebuerger Arbechter-Verband* – Free Federation of Luxembourg Workers
FLB	*Fédération Libre des Agriculteurs du Luxembourg / Freie Letzebuerger Baurenverband* – Free Federation of Luxembourg Farmers
FLTL	*Fédération Luxembourgeoise des Travailleurs du Livre* – Luxembourg Printing Workers' Federation
FNCTTFEL	*Fédération Nationale des Cheminots, Travailleurs du Transport, Fonctionnaires et Employés Luxembourgeois* – National Federation of Railway and Transport Workers, Civil Servants and White-Collar Workers
HORESCA	*Fédération Nationale des Hôteliers, Restaurateurs et Cafetiers* – National Federation of Hotel, Restaurant and Café Employers
LAV	*Lëtzebuerger Arbechterverband* – Luxembourg Workers' Union
LCGB	*Lëtzeburger Chrëstleche Gewerkschafts-Bond* – Luxembourg Confederation of Christian Trade Unions
NGL	*Neutral Gewerkschaft Lëtzebuerg* – Independent Union of Luxembourg Workers
NHV	*Neutralen Handwierker Verband* – Craftworkers' Association
OGB-L	*Onofhängege Gewerkschafts-Bond Lëtzebuerg* – Confederation of Independent Trade Unions
ONC	*Office National de Conciliation* – National Conciliation Office

PCS	*Parti Chrétien Social* – Social Christian Party
PD	*Parti Démocratique* – Democratic Party
POSL	*Parti Ouvrier Socialiste Luxembourgeois* – Luxembourg Workers' Socialist Party
SNEP-R	*Syndicat National des Employés Privés - Rénovateurs* – Reconstructed National Union of White-Collar Workers

13

France: The Industrial Relations System at a Turning Point?

Janine Goetschy and Patrick Rozenblatt

Introduction: The 'Exceptionalism' of the French?

Scholars have depicted the French system of industrial relations as atypical in several respects. First, industrial conflict and legal intervention, rather than collective bargaining, have been the traditional modes of 'rule-making' in the sphere of employment relations. Second, both unions and employers have been strongly driven by ideological considerations, and characterized by organizational weakness. Third, in recent years the French labour movement has undergone a more catastrophic decline in membership strength and influence than any other European union movement.

Explanations of the French 'anomaly' have often been sought in the ambiguous history of the links between political parties and unions. The northern European model in which a strong social-democratic party is closely linked to a strong union, with a fairly clear division of labour between the two, has been absent in France, where the links between parties, unions and politics have always been complex and their respective functions have overlapped. Thus commentators (e.g. Lange et al. 1982) argue that post-war French labour relations were indelibly marked by the existence of a strong communist party which attempted to use the trade union movement to mobilize a mass base. The result was an ideological fragmentation of the labour movement and a continuing ambivalence in party–union ties: was the union to concentrate on economic issues, or was it to be a disguised 'transmission belt', used to further the party's political objectives? Given the Communist Party's long exclusion from political power, its close relationship with a major component of the union movement inevitably entailed the marginalization of the latter as well.

Historically, the role of the French state in industrial relations has been threefold. Already by the turn of the century the state was trying to reverse the emerging logic of industrial relations by encouraging some form of social dialogue between capital and labour at national level. The failure of this 'inter-class' project to gain the support of either employers or unions reflected both their ideological divisions and their organizational fragility. But the state has continued to play the role of midwife to a national dialogue between employers and unions, with rather more success in recent years. Second, since the birth of the fifth republic in 1958 and especially since the social and political upheavals of May 1968, it has attempted to incorporate unions by treating them as a partner, albeit often in an advisory capacity, in the formulation of important social policy decisions, particularly on welfare issues. Third, the state has used legal intervention to compensate the unions for their organizational weaknesses. However, by granting individual rights and benefits directly to employees (for example, through the *erga omnes* provisions allowing collective agreements to be extended to employees in non-signatory firms), the state undermined the unions' role in industrial relations, and the unions' response to state intervention was thus ambivalent. Indeed, some authors (e.g. Sellier and Sylvestre 1986) have argued that the unions' weakness is state-created.

The role of historical, political, ideological and legal factors in shaping the organizational arrangements and strategic choices of French social actors, and consequently in moulding the evolution of the industrial relations system, has been analysed at length by scholars such as Mouriaux (1983) and Rosanvallon (1988). But the impact of processes of industrial and economic development since the nineteenth century on unions and employers has been much less thoroughly investigated. The historical legacy – of a productive structure highly oriented to the domestic economy, low industrial concentration, and a high proportion of the highly mobile labour force dividing its time between factory and farm – has been seen as hindering the emergence of strong and centralized unions and employers' associations (Charle 1991).

In the post-war period, the relationship between the evolution of the economy and the industrial relations system has been better grasped, notably by the French regulationist school. Regulationists such as Boyer (1985) argue that from the end of the Second World War until the 1960s, an implicit 'Fordist' compromise characterized relations between capital, labour and the state: unions were content to leave to management issues relating to the sphere of production – work norms, job content, work organization and so on; in return, the unions were guaranteed their share of the fruits of economic progress in the sphere of distribution, as rising productivity brought higher wages. The Fordist compromise began to break down as a result of the well-known combination of economic, social and political pressures that made up the crisis of the early 1970s. The specificity of the problems faced by the French economy, and the solutions to them, have been widely analysed (e.g. Petit 1985; Lipietz 1991).

In this context, and in contrast to other European labour movements, French unions 'had very few ideas about new policies which might make

French capitalism more successful in changing international economic circumstances. Instead, they advocated a radical new economic order to be installed through political change' (Lange et al. 1982: 10). Hopes for the implementation of this project were dashed by the bitter defeat of the Left in 1978, only to be resuscitated by the election victory of the socialists in 1981. The scope for the implementation of a new order was, however, severely constrained as economic crisis forced the socialists to abandon their attempted break with conventional economic management. None the less, the socialists further strengthened the institutional framework of voluntary industrial relations; this, together with the processes of rationalization, restructuring and technological innovation in French industry from the late 1970s, encouraged the unions to turn their attention away from politics and back to the sphere of production – just as their capacity for action was being constrained by a severe drop in membership and influence.

One of the major aims of the chapter will be to assess how far the new political context of the 1980s, with the Left in power for most of the period, has transformed French industrial relations. To what extent have unions and employers been persuaded – or bullied – to adopt new bargaining practices, and more generally towards 'normalizing' a system of relations hitherto based on a lack of mutual recognition. In short, has the system of industrial relations in France been 'catching up' with long-standing patterns in other European countries?

The chapter begins by looking at French unions in historical perspective, stressing the ideological divisions of the union movement, and the growing crisis of membership and influence occurring, paradoxically, in parallel with increasing institutional support. The following section examines the characteristics of French employers. It argues that industrial relations in French firms have been coloured by factors such as the importance of small and medium-sized enterprise, the role of state ownership, and the peculiarities of French 'industrial culture'. The section also examines the structure and strategies of French employers' organizations, and ends with an assessment of changing personnel and industrial relations policies of French firms as they pursue greater 'flexibility' in the workplace.

The French state's place in industrial relations is then considered: its role as an employer, both in the government sector and in nationalized industry; its intervention in the regulation of the labour market and in pay determination; and its role in creating an institutional framework of industrial relations and collective bargaining. The processes and outcomes of collective bargaining under the regulatory framework provided by the Auroux laws of the early 1980s are the subject of the following section. The importance of different bargaining levels and the changing relationship between them are examined in some detail. The next two sections consider current developments in company-level employee representation and in industrial conflict. Finally, the conclusion assesses the overall impact of attempts to modernize and 'normalize' the structures of French industrial relations in recent years.

Trade Unions

The French labour movement has traditionally been marked by trade-union pluralism and fragmentation, inter-union rivalry, low union density, and a paucity of financial and organizational resources. Since the late 1970s these structural weaknesses have become increasingly prominent. At the start of the 1990s, the French labour movement is one of the weakest in western Europe in membership terms, with barely a tenth of the work force in unions. Some argue that 'the weakness of unionism in France is largely a state-created weakness' (Sellier and Sylvestre 1986). At first sight, the assertion appears paradoxical, since union power has been underpinned by the state in periods of social and political change – in 1936, 1945, 1968, and 1982, usually when the Left was in power. The state has compensated for the unions' organizational weaknesses in three ways. First, it has granted special legal rights enabling unions to represent the interests of all employees and not only those of their limited membership. A good example is the quasi-monopoly given to the five national confederations (CGT, CFDT, CGT-FO, CFTC, CGC) in collective bargaining matters at all levels, independent of their actual membership strength. Such measures were intended to bolster unions but in practice have often proved detrimental by removing the incentive for individuals to join unions, and have created a vicious circle, encouraging further dependence on state support (e.g. Ross 1982). Second, social legislation has provided workers directly with benefits which unions have been unable to obtain through collective bargaining. This has done little to encourage unions to rely on their own resources and has been a further disincentive for wage earners to unionize. Third, the state has attempted to compensate for the unions' organizational deficiencies and to increase their social and political influence by granting them a substantial role in public bodies. This has tempted the unions to ground their legitimacy on playing some sort of 'public service' role, defending the wider interests of employees and participating in the running of the welfare state system.

Thus French unions have more political and social influence than their organizational weaknesses imply. Their role as 'a public service agency' seems to be on the increase, and while they play an important role in collective bargaining, their effectiveness in representing employees' interests at plant level has been seriously challenged in recent years (Rosanvallon 1988).

As the section on the legacy of history (see below) will show, the solutions adopted by the state fitted fairly well the unions' own early ideological preferences and organizational choices. They also suited employer organizations which, in comparison with other European countries, were reluctant to recognize unions and to engage in collective bargaining, even with the more moderate unions. Though legalized in 1884, unions would have to wait until 1968 for the legally guaranteed right to establish union branches at enterprise level.

The Legacy of History

The oldest trade union confederation is the marxist CGT (*Confédération générale du travail*), set up in 1895. In its founding document, the Charter of Amiens of 1906, it adopted an anarcho-syndicalist stance, proclaiming its autonomy *vis-à-vis* political parties and the state. The union rejected the opportunities proffered by the state for an enhanced role within the system. For example, it turned down the proposal made by the Minister of Industry, Millerand, in 1900 to strengthen the union movement by integrating it within state structures. Embracing the anarcho-syndicalist doctrine that real power lay in the hands of those who produced national wealth, and that the workers' direct involvement in struggle at the point of production was the path to their self-emancipation, the CGT favoured militant action and strikes at enterprise level. From the beginning, the CGT's aim was to promote a unionism based on the strength of militancy rather than on a mass membership. This implied the early choice of a rather loose, decentralized organizational structure (and as a corollary fairly low union dues) with a minimal degree of individual coercion and internal discipline. In 1908 the socialist leader Jaurès unsuccessfully pressed for the union's power to be legitimated, and strikes to be sanctioned, through work force ballots. At the time, union leaders considered that the union's strength was as a community of militants united by cultural and social values, and that this might be jeopardized by the holding of elections, which would have implied a different model of interest representation.

The CGT's anarcho-syndicalist stance has proved vulnerable to the challenges of domestic and international political events as well as to social developments. Already in 1921, the CGT had experienced a major split between the reformist majority and the more revolutionary minority group (CGTU) over whether the union should support French participation in the First World War and over its reaction to the Russian Revolution. The changing relationship between the union and the state was at the heart of the debate. The CGT majority turned to the state for social reforms such as social security benefits and family allowances which it won in the 1930s. Party politics were also to influence the union's trajectory, and the strategy of union autonomy began to be challenged. Despite the fairly reformist position of the CGT at this time, French employers failed to take the opportunity to engage in collective bargaining.

The two wings of the union reunited under the Left government of the Popular Front in 1936. This was marked by a massive spontaneous strike movement leading to labour law reforms such as the introduction of employee delegates at plant-level, industry-level collective agreements, paid holidays, and the forty-hour week. The state played an important mediating role in the Matignon agreement which ended the strike and in most of the industry collective agreements.

A new split occurred in 1939 following the Nazi–Soviet pact. Existing unions were dissolved by the Vichy government under the Nazi occupation in 1940, but underground leaders of the CGT and CGTU agreed to the formation of a united confederation, facilitated by the spirit of the Liberation and the advent of a tripartite government including communists, socialists and centrists. In 1947–8, there was yet another split: the CGT–FO (including socialist, reformist and anarcho-syndicalist elements) broke off from a CGT in which the Communist Party had become increasingly dominant, taking over most official posts within the union apparatus. The immediate cause of the secession was the ousting of communist ministers from the government and a wave of communist-led strikes in late 1947. Two further sources of division were the Marshall Plan (the CGT denounced US economic aid to Europe whereas the CGT–FO favoured it) and the onset of the cold war. The major reason for the split was, however, the CGT–FO belief that the CGT had been betraying the Charter of Amiens principle of independence from political parties; the division was to prove permanent.

The CGT has remained strikingly faithful to the ideology of class struggle. But it has proved less faithful to the ambitious aim of the early days of remaining independent from party politics. Between 1947 and 1952, it based its policy on explicit political objectives, pronouncing itself in favour of nationalizations and against the European plan of Schuman. In general, it has been acutely sensitive to political factors and, in practice, has been an exponent of the Leninist conception of the union as transmission belt between the party and the workers. The Communist Party has retained its dominance over the CGT, although it does not hold undivided power. Indeed, an unwritten rule says that of the 18 members of the confederal bureau (the effective ruling body) half should be communists and half non-communists. In 1985, the executive committee comprised 30 non-communists and 95 communists. But nearly all the leaders of the departmental unions and industrial federations are Communist Party members.

Generally speaking, economic factors and fluctuations in membership have exerted fairly little influence on the CGT's marxist frame of analysis; if anything they have strengthened it (see Mouriaux 1986). The political history of the Left (i.e. of the communist and socialist parties) has been the crucial determinant of the CGT's strategies, even more so from 1968. At the union's 1978 congress, a less sectarian and more democratic approach was advocated. But the phase of self-criticism was short-lived, and the CGT's attitude to Mitterrand's election in 1980 and to the socialist government was highly ambiguous. Though it gave its conditional support to the government of the Left, it has been very resistant to the socialist government's policy of 'employment flexibility', especially following the withdrawal of the communists from office. At its 1989 congress it reaffirmed the need to stick to the traditional confrontational model, in which

strike action remains crucial and collective bargaining represents a pragmatic tactic for testing the balance of power between labour and capital at
a given time. According to the CGT, 'the experience of the 1980s illustrates the extent to which certain types of collective agreement are likely
to lead to the dismantling of social legislation and social progress' (CGT
Congress, 1989).

The CGT's membership has passed through four phases since the
1940s. From a peak in 1947, it declined until 1958; it grew between 1959
and 1975, and declined again from the mid-1970s. Indeed, membership
fell from over two million in the late 1970s to about 1.5 million in 1983 and
1 million in 1987; and excluding retired members, there was a 50 per cent
fall in membership in the 1980s alone.

Like the other confederations, the CGT is organized in industry federations, and in geographically based local unions. It draws its main strength
from skilled manual workers, and in engineering, local government and
health, construction, and the chemical industry. The CGT has an important technical, managerial and professional staff section, the UGICT *(Union
générale des ingénieurs, cadres et techniciens)*.

FO *(Force ouvrière)*, set up in 1948 in reaction to communist involvement
in the CGT, claims to be the true heir of the CGT's old policy of political
independence, and is staunchly anti-communist. From the very beginning, its basic weakness has been the diversity of its component groups –
which include revolutionaries, anarcho-syndicalists and trotskyists, as
well as conservatives – impeding the development of an efficient organizational structure and hampering recruitment. Despite its internal
fragmentation, FO has played a major role in collective bargaining, which
it sees as the main element of union action, and has secured significant
benefits for its members. Though it accepts the legitimacy of state action
in the public sector, it opposes state intervention in private sector bargaining, and thus rejects 'social compromises' involving wage restraint. It
emphasizes the importance of the union's role in representing workers'
interests, and distrusts direct forms of employee representation and participation such as mass meetings on the grounds that they may lead to the
manipulation of the work force by the employer.

Socialist in its inspiration, FO has nevertheless kept its distance from
the socialist party and government. Its approach is essentially pragmatic
and its overall strategy sufficiently general to appeal to its different
components. Its 1989 Congress, however, marked a shift of emphasis
towards a more confrontational strategy, and FO has since hardened its
position in multi-industry negotiations, and in its key stronghold in the
public sector; for example, it adopted a tougher attitude in recent public
sector strikes and in subsequent negotiations on job grading. The union
has also become more anti-European in recent years. Thus there has been
a degree of convergence with the approach of the CGT, and this has led to
some internal turmoil in FO.

FO has, however, been gaining ground. By the mid-1980s, it claimed to
be the second largest confederation, with nearly one million members.[1] Its

membership rose until 1981, stagnated in 1982 and then decreased slightly again. The union is strongest among white-collar workers, technical and professional groups in the public sector, but has also been growing in the private sector. By 1979, it claimed that as many as 55 per cent of its members were from the private sector. The FO has also a small cadre section, the UCI *(Union des cadres et ingénieurs)*.

Confessional unionism began in 1919 with the formation of the CFTC *(Confédération française des travailleurs chrétiens)*. Its main objective was to promote peaceful collaboration between capital and labour, in line with the social doctrine of the Catholic church. Two of its major principles were union share ownership and employee profit-sharing, but its plans found little favour with employers.

In 1944, the CFTC and the CGT formed an inter-confederal liaison committee, but the CFTC rejected CGT proposals for a merger after the war. Largely composed of white-collar employees in the early years, its membership shifted increasingly towards manual workers in engineering, chemicals and construction. Recruitment was no longer limited to traditional Catholic regions. The changing social composition of the membership was reflected in challenges to the traditional principles of the union. After the war, a fraction known as the *'minoritaires'*, grouped around the journal *Reconstruction,* argued for the union to abandon its strict religious affiliation and compete directly with the CGT and FO. The *minoritaires* advocated a more open, independent and democratic, though still Christian-influenced, socialist position. In its first post-war congress, the CFTC affirmed that political office was incompatible with trade union office, and in 1947, it weakened its link with the Catholic church by giving up its reference to papal encyclicals. In the 1950s, the union advocated a flexible economic system based on 'democratic planning'. By 1964 the reformists were in the majority, and the union split. The minority group retained the religious orientation and kept the name CFTC, while the majority severed the Catholic connection and became the CFDT *(Confédération française démocratique du travail).*

The CFTC currently has around 250,000 members. Membership grew slightly in the 1970s, stagnated between 1982 and 1985 and decreased somewhat from 1986. The unions' power base includes miners, Christian schoolteachers and health workers, and it has a tiny cadre section, the UGICA *(Union générale des cadres).* It emphasizes the primacy of the individual and the defence of the family, rejects class struggle and the politicization of unions, and supports the development of collective bargaining. Its priorities for the future include an active recruitment policy, the fight against night and Sunday working, vocational training and the development of Social Europe.

The CFDT was the second-largest union confederation in the mid-1970s, its membership having nearly doubled between 1948 (as the old CFTC) and 1976 to over 800,000 members; but it declined from 1977 onwards and was estimated to be around 600,000 at the end of the 1980s. The confederation is strongest in engineering, the health sector, oil, chemicals, banking and insurance. It has a small cadre section, the UCC *(Union confédérale des ingénieurs et cadres)*; however, UCC membership is restricted to 'senior' *cadres* (that is, professional and managerial staff), which partly explains why it is smaller than the *cadre* sections of the other unions.

Following its split from the CFTC, the CFDT was radicalized by its leading role in the industrial unrest accompanying the social and political crisis of 1968. At its 1970 congress, it pronounced itself in favour of class struggle and advocated a form of workers' control or self-management *(socialisme autogestionnaire)*. The radicalization of its ideology put it in closer competition with the CGT. Since 1978, however, the CFDT has played down its former ideological emphasis. It undertook a process of *'resyndicalisation'* (emphasizing closely defined trade union issues) and *'recentrage'* (return to the centre), giving priority to union adaptation to economic change. This approach had been criticized by a minority as 'pragmatism without a programme'. However, Edmond Maire, the leading force behind the pragmatic approach, was re-elected for a further three-year term as secretary general at the 40th congress in 1985. Maire's replacement as leader in 1988 partly reflected growing grassroots dissatisfaction over the close link between the leader and the socialist government of Michel Rocard, as expressed in the strike wave of 1988.

The CFDT's industrial relations priorities in the 1980s included the reduction of working hours; collective agreements on new technology; better opportunities for the young; equal rights for women and reduction of gender inequalities; and the transformation of hierarchical relationships in the workplace. Despite the pressure of federations such as the Clothing and Textile Federation, the Finance Employees Federation (grouping government employees), and some regional federations for greater use of the strike weapon, the new general secretary, J. Kaspar continued his predecessor's strategy, arguing at the 1988 congress that 'unionism must demonstrate its usefulness to individuals, enterprises and society by its capacity to put forward relevant proposals and practices'.

The CGC *(Confédération générale des cadres)* was formed in 1944. Its 1976 membership of around 325,000 (engineers, executives, sales representatives, supervisors, technicians) had dropped by a third to about 240,000 by 1986. It is strongest in the engineering and chemical industries and among sales representatives. The confederation's priorities are to win greater participation for *cadres*, maximize their pay differentials, and protect their interests on tax and social security matters. It claims not to be party-political.

With the exception of the CGC, unions from all five confederations recruit across all industries and trades and across all categories of employee. They thus compete with each other, although they each have specific sectors, occupational groups and regions in which they are traditionally represented. All five confederations are known as 'representative unions' at national level. This is a legal attribute granted on the basis of five criteria (the most important being the ability to prove that the union is totally independent from the employer) and which confers exclusive rights, for instance in collective bargaining, in the nomination of candidates in the system of employee representation within the firm (see below) and in representation on government consultative bodies.

Another important specialist union, the FEN (*Fédération de l'éducation nationale*) also has 'representative' status, but only on the sectoral level, i.e. within education. The FEN decided to remain independent at the time of the CGT split. It recruits staff in most types of state educational institutions and had slightly less than 400,000 members in 1988, considerably below its 1970s peak. Measured by membership density in its own sector, the FEN is nevertheless one of the strongest French unions.

There are several other 'autonomous' unions in specific sectors (for example, the automobile industry); among certain groups of employees such as lorry drivers and journalists; and in the public sector among air traffic controllers, train drivers, tax collectors and the police.

French Unions in Crisis

Following Caire (1990), one may identify a 'crisis of membership, a crisis of influence and a crisis of militancy' in French unions from the late 1970s (see also Bibes and Mouriaux 1990).

The Membership Crisis

Union density has traditionally been low in France. It fell from around 20 per cent in the mid 1970s (Adam 1983) to 15 per cent between 1975 and 1985 (Mouriaux 1986), and dropped as low as 9 per cent in the late 1980s (Rosanvallon 1988). These figures are estimates provided by researchers, as accurate data are unobtainable: membership figures reported by union confederations are inflated as they include members who do not pay their monthly dues regularly; there is no equivalent of the British check-off system, which is outlawed in France. But even official union figures show an overall decline in membership during the 1980s (see *Liaisons Sociales* 1988) (see table 13.1).[2]

Low union membership compounds other weaknesses such as the lack of financial and organizational resources. Dues are low (on average less than 1 per cent of the wage), and are paid irregularly – the average member pays six monthly dues per year, out of the twelve (Mouriaux 1983). The formal structure of French unions is underdeveloped in comparison with other European unions, with few full-time officers.

The Crisis of Influence

Trade union support or influence (*audience*) can also be assessed on the basis of the results of 'social' elections for representatives on bodies such as works councils (*comités d'entreprise*) (see below) and industrial tribunals (*Prud'hommes*).[3] In industrial tribunal elections (see table 13.2), support for the CGT declined sharply from 1979 to 1987, although it retains the highest

Table 13.1   Official membership figures of the six major French unions

	1976	1983	1986–88
CGT	2,074,072	1,622,095	1,030,843
FO	926,324	1,150,000	1,108,000
CFDT	829,024	681,300	600,000*
FEN**	525,860	492,900	394,389
CFE-CGC	325,469	307,383	240,870
CFTC	223,100	260,000	250,000

* estimate
**FEN is only 'representative' in the education sector, whereas the other unions are 'representative' at national level.
Source: Bibes and Mouriaux (1990).

Table 13.2   Elections for Industrial Tribunals (% of the vote)

	CGT	CFDT	FO	CFTC	CGC	Others
1979	42.3	23.2	17.3	7.2	5.2	4.8
1982	37.0	23.5	17.7	8.5	9.6	3.7
1987	36.5	23.0	20.4	8.3	7.4	4.5

Source: Bibes and Mouriaux (1990).

level of support. The percentage vote for the CFDT remained stable, while FO increased its share.

In works council elections, the five representative unions together obtained around 70 per cent of the votes (see table 13.3). Thus the unions have a much higher degree of support in 'social' elections than might be inferred from their low membership.

None the less, the trend in works council election results indicates that the unions have been suffering a crisis of support in the 1980s. Between 1977 and 1989 there was a significant increase in the vote for non-union representatives, a trend shown even more starkly by the results in terms of seats (e.g. in 1987 non-union representatives won 23.9 per cent of the votes and 43.6 per cent of the seats, cf. table 13.4). The disparity between votes and seats reflects not only the peculiarities of the electoral system, but also the large proportion of non-unionized small firms.

Work force participation in works council elections remains fairly high, although its has been declining (70.5 per cent in 1977, 65.4 per cent in 1989). As table 13.3 shows, the support obtained by the CGT (as a proportion of the votes) declined from 37.4 per cent in 1977 to 25.1 per cent in 1989. In 1989, for the first time, the CGT came second in terms of votes, behind non-union representatives. The CFDT seems to have stabilized its position after a continuous decrease between 1981 and 1985. FO and the CFTC have slowly increased their share of the vote over the last fifteen years, although the former's share in works council elections has increased by less than its membership. The CGC remained fairly stable, with a slight decrease in votes from 1987 onwards.

As regards employee delegates, a study by the Ministry of Labour (1990) shows a decline in CGT's share of the vote in the 43 per cent of firms with one delegate or more (see table 13.5).

The level of trade union representation in French firms continues to decline. Between 1987 and 1989, the proportion of workplaces with 50 or more employees where there was at least one union delegate, fell from 55 per cent to 50.7 per cent (Report of the Ministry of Labour 1990)

Table 13.3a   Results of works committee elections (%) 1977–89

	CGT	CFDT	FO	CFTC	CGC	Others	Non-union
1977	37.4	20.2	9.0	3.0	5.4	5.7	18.8
1979	34.4	20.5	9.7	3.1	5.8	4.8	21.2
1981	32.0	22.3	9.9	2.9	6.1	4.1	22.2
1983	28.5	21.9	11.1	4.0	6.5	4.7	22.8
1985	27.7	21.2	12.6	5.0	6.2	5.8	21.5
1987	26.8	21.3	11.3	4.8	5.9	6.0	23.9
1989	25.1	21.0	11.2	4.6	5.5	6.3	26.4

Source: Liaisons Sociales (25 July 1990).

Table 13.3b   Results of works committee elections (as a % of the vote) 1982–90

	CGT	CFDT	FO	CFTC	CFE-CGC	Others	Non-union
1982	32.3	22.8	11.7	2.9	7.0	4.4	18.4
1984	29.3	21.0	13.9	3.8	7.1	4.8	19.7
1986	27.1	21.2	14.4	3.8	7.5	5.0	21.1
1988	26.7	20.7	13.7	3.7	6.8	4.8	23.5
1990	24.9	19.9	12.8	3.6	6.5	5.6	26.6

Note: Elections for works committees take place every two years, with some companies holding them in odd years and the remainder in even years. Thus the evolution of voting patterns in a particular population of companies may be seen by following the results of either odd or even years.
Source: EIRR 211 (August 1991: 5).

Table 13.4   Results of works committee elections as a % of seats obtained 1987

CGT	CFDT	FO	CFTC	CGC	Others	Non-unions
18.3	15.9	9.1	3.6	5.1	4.6	43.6

Source: Liaisons Sociales 23 February 1989.

Table 13.5   Employee delegate elections – % of seats obtained

	CGT	CFDT	FO	CFTC	CGC	Others	Non-union
1988	22.7	16.4	10.9	2.8	5.4	4.5	36.4
1985	24.8	15.5	10.1	2.5	5.1	3.4	38.6

Source: Liaisons Sociales (28 November 1990, table 5).

The Crisis of Militancy and Institutional Participation

A number of studies have claimed to identify a crisis of militancy in French unionism, an assessment possibly inspired by a certain degree of nostalgia for the old anarcho-syndicalist traditions. Rosanvallon (1988) argues that whereas to be a union member at the beginning of the century was automatically to be an active militant as part of the 'social community', union membership now implies very varying degrees of involvement in union activities. Support for unions may range from non-membership through voting for union candidates in social elections, to being a union sympathizer, being a regular dues-paying member, and being a *militant*. Both Rosanvallon (1988) and Adam (1983) have argued that the unions' power is essentially institutional, based on their presence and participation in state bodies rather than on their membership.

Neo-corporatist arrangements have on the whole been limited in France. Aspects of the French industrial relations system such as inter-union rivalry and the lack of internal union discipline over members (for example, the lack of formal union control over the right of individuals to strike) have reduced the attractiveness of neo-corporatist solutions for the state. None the less, the integration and institutionalization of unions has been occurring through their participation in around one hundred public bodies (Rosanvallon 1988), notably the Economic and Social Council, a sort of corporatist institution advising the government on important policy issues, either at the request of the government or at its own initiative. For example, it provides analyses of the social and economic consequences of new technologies. Each union is entitled to add its own point of view to the majority report. At the regional level similar committees exist. Unions have access to economic information, within the framework of the commissions preparing five-year modernization plans. They have the opportunity to express their opinion, although their influence on decisions is limited. Unions also participate in numerous other official institutions at national and local levels, including the national commissions on collective bargaining, vocational training, improvement of working conditions, social security funds, and unemployment funds. About 30,000 union representatives are occupied in these functions.

Explanations for Low Union Density

Structural Factors

Low union density in France may be explained by a number of traditional features of French unions and industrial relations. First, as a legacy of their anarcho-syndicalist origins, the unions have traditionally put more emphasis on building an active core of 'militant' organizers, rather than on recruiting a stable mass membership. This also explains why they have rarely built up bureaucratic organizations on the scale of German unions, for example. This early ideological choice meant that militants have tended to see their role as the fostering of strikes and political action, rather than engaging in collective bargaining with employers; this made it difficult to obtain concrete benefits for their members from bargaining. Second, the ideological and political fragmentation of unions has hampered the recruitment and retention of members. Third, the ability of unions to organize has been affected by employer opposition to any extension of union influence, and paternalist practices were long paramount, particularly in small firms. Union organization in the workplace was especially weak, and it was only in 1968 that unions obtained the legal right to establish workplace branches. Fourth, the legal framework has also constrained unionization. The closed shop is illegal in France, on the grounds of the freedom of the individual to decide whether or not to join a union (though there are *de facto* closed shops in some sectors such as the docks and printing). Moreover, the incentive for union membership is reduced by the extension of collective agreements to all employees, whether unionized or not. Finally, unlike Scandinavian countries, for example, no specific welfare benefits accrue to union members (Armingeon et al. 1981).

Reasons for Union Decline in the 1980s

It is a paradox of recent French industrial relations that the unions experienced a drastic decline in membership and influence in the 1980s, just when the political environment provided by the socialist governments of the 1980s was apparently most favourable. A rise in membership might have been expected, as had been the case in 1936 and 1945. The weakness of the unions reflects, first, the impact of major changes in the French economy: industrial restructuring away from traditionally well-organized industrial sectors (coal, steel, engineering, shipbuilding) to new sectors such as electronics; the shift of jobs from industry to the service sector; the increasing weight of small firms. All these changes meant a loss of union members (Bridgford 1990; Goetschy and Linhart 1990; Visser 1990).

Second, major changes in the labour market were detrimental to unionization: unemployment rose from 6.4 per cent (of the active population) in 1980 to 10.4 per cent in 1988. Changes in employment contracts and employment practices led to an increase in part-time and fixed-contract workers, groups which are difficult to unionize. The rise in these 'precarious' forms of employment contract (see below) may be one reason why

418 *Industrial Relations in the New Europe*

the decline in union density among women workers has been higher than that of men. The development of schemes for youth training and employment such as TUC (*Travail d'utilité collective*) and SVIP (*stage d'initiation à la vie professionnelle*) also hindered union attempts to organize the workforce.

Third, there has been a shift in social attitudes towards trade unions. Young people have expressed increasing scepticism about the efficiency of union action and put more faith in their own individual capacity for negotiating over work matters with the employer (Linhart and Malan 1988).

Fourth, changes in employers' personnel policies since 1977, particularly the use of direct forms of communication and participation, flexibility measures, and the increased individualization of the employment relationship (Morville 1985), have tended to weaken unions within the enterprise (see the section on employers, below).

Fifth, the unions have faced internal criticism for their failure to meet the challenges of the 1980s. The increase in union duties resulting from the Auroux laws (see below), from increasing union participation in state welfare bodies (social security, unemployment insurance, vocational training, employment bodies, administrative committees in the public sector, etc.) and from the newly developing trend towards multi-industry bargaining has overloaded the unions' administrative capacity. The 'institutionalization' of union business also appears to have increased the isolation of the top echelons from their rank and file over the last ten years (Adam 1983; Rosanvallon 1988).

Within each confederation, there have been tensions between different federations. For example, intra-confederal turmoil was apparent in December 1984 in the failure of the national multi-industry negotiations on flexibility of employment. Top negotiators in FO and CFDT had been ready to accept the package deal, but they faced bitter opposition from lower levels and certain federations within their respective organizations. But the unions' representation crisis was particularly highlighted by a new strike wave in the late 1980s, in which the rank and file set up organizations (*coordinations*) outside official union structures to pursue their demands (see strikes). The membership criticized union leaders for being too political, divided and bureaucratic. Such *coordinations* (similar to the Italian *cobas*) claimed to represent all strikers and deliberately remained transitory, unstable and uninstitutionalized groupings.

Union fragmentation was exacerbated during the 1980s by increasing animosity between unions. Inter-confederal rivalry between CGT and CFDT followed the break-up of the Union of the Left in 1977. After the Left's electoral failure in 1978, the CGT and CFDT both initiated a process of self-criticism. The CFDT admitted that it had been too dogmatic and that it had been insufficiently attentive to workers' immediate concerns. The CGT was less self-critical, failing to question its fundamental strategies or the links with the declining Communist Party that had been one of the causes of its own decline. Inter-union fragmentation became even

more acute in the face of the socialist governments' austerity, modernization and flexibility policies. The CGT became increasingly isolated whereas
the CFDT continued to follow its reformist strategy of *recentrage* initiated
in 1979, and launched the idea of a merger of non-communist unions. In
early 1990, leaders of the CFDT and the FEN called for a 'labour axis'
plan, a united front between non-communist confederations. The proposal has not so far generated great enthusiasm among the other unions.
Part of the aim of such an alignment would be to counterbalance the
influence of large national groups such as the DGB or the TUC within the
unified European market. Thus the 'unity of action' of the 1970s, when
CGT and CFDT managed to agree on a range of issues, belongs to the
past.

In short, overloaded union administration, union fragmentation, the
fairly disappointing results of the CFDT's strategy of *recentrage*, and the
Left unions' strategic disarray under a Left government have all contributed to the trade unions' decline. Unions have been attempting to formulate
new strategies and roles in response to the crisis. Some have been developing more individual services for their members, for example legal
assistance, advice on tax returns, or organizing of leisure services. For
Rosanvallon (1988), such solutions are a dead end. The unions are not in a
position to offer services that would be sufficiently attractive to members.
Moreover, such services are likely to increase the individualization of the
relationship with members: for example, union involvement in the organization of members' leisure-time activities could once be rooted in
workers' feelings of belonging to the same social and cultural community,
which is no longer the case today.

Employers

Characteristics of French Employers

The French economy has, in common with other European countries,
shown a continuing shift from primary and secondary to tertiary sector
activities. In 1980, agriculture accounted for 8.8 per cent of employment,
industry (including mining, utilities and construction) for 35.9 per cent, and
services for 55.7 per cent. By the end of the 1980s, the figures were 6.4, 28.5
and 65.1 per cent respectively (OECD data).

Though traditionally small and medium firms were important in the
French economy, economic development especially since the late 1950s
has given large companies a dominant role in the industrial structure. In
1987, firms of over 500 employees accounted for 36 per cent of the
employed work force, a figure comparable to Germany, Britain and the
Netherlands (Sisson et al. 1991: 97). In manufacturing industry, 53 per
cent of workers in firms of 20 employees or more worked in firms of over
500 employees, which also accounted for 62 per cent of total manufacturing value added (Eurostat 1990: 154). While French firms are somewhat
under-represented among the very largest European firms, compared

with British and German companies, 14 of the top 100 private employers based in the European Community in 1990 were French (Sisson et al. 1991: 104–7); twenty French firms (including state enterprises) figured among the hundred largest European multinationals (Sisson et al. 1992).

Ownership, especially in smaller firms, but even in large ones, has tended to be dominated by family interests (Marceau 1989). A survey of the top 500 French firms in 1976 showed that 30 per cent were family-controlled, 35 per cent were state-owned and a mere 17 per cent were French manager-controlled (the remaining 16 per cent being multinationals) (Europa 1988: 187); in the early 1980s, nearly half the top 200 companies were majority-owned or dominated by family interests. As in Italy, there were complex interlinkages between industrial and financial capital.

The state has played a major role in the development and subsequent rationalization of French capital. A large public enterprise sector (see below) has controlled a significant proportion of industry; while state expenditure provided a secure domestic base for French capital, (notably through major public investment in telecommunications, defence, energy and transport), and a wary state policy towards foreign capital limited competition in the home market in the 1960s and 1970s. The state-regulated and extensively state-owned financial sector plays a key role in the allocation of investment funds to industry.

Prompted by concern for French industry's competitiveness within the EC the state also encouraged a further notable feature of French corporate structure, the growth in 'industrial groups' through merger and acquisition from the 1960s. These groups, unlike the Anglo-Saxon diversified multidivisional enterprise, are loose associations of companies without legal identity, held together through webs of financial participations (Thollon-Pommerol 1990) rather than by centralized management control. In the 1980s, French industry responded to economic crisis, European integration, and the growth of international competition by a process of rationalization, both in old-established industries such as steel, cars and textiles, and new more dynamic industries. Groups have concentrated on their core businesses, although a new wave of mergers, acquisitions and joint ventures, often with the participation of foreign capital, gained pace in the late 1980s to meet the impending completion of the single European market (OECD 1991: 89-90). Some of the largest and most important groups, such as Thomson, Saint Gobain, Péchiney and Rhône-Poulenc were nationalized in 1982, and state ownership was used to carry out restructuring and rationalization, bringing greater efficiency and a more commercial orientation to the unwieldy conglomerates before a number were returned to the private sector by Chirac in 1986–8 (Durupty 1988).

French employers have been characterized as paternalist and authoritarian, traditionally rejècting worker participation in decision-making and aggressively asserting managerial prerogative.[4] Such features have been ascribed to the predominance of small and medium family-owned firms in the formative phase of French industrialization, reinforced by the bureaucratic ethos fostered by the elite traditions of the *grandes écoles* and perpetuated by the practices of *pantouflage*, the interpenetration of state and corporate elites, for example through the presence of civil servants on company boards (Lane 1989: 106). Authoritarian, aggressive management has also been strengthened by the fragmentation of French unionism described above, by the ideological rejection of capitalist enterprise by a major section of the union movement, and by the unions' weakness at the workplace.

Management control is centralized and, in larger firms, bureaucratic, with limited delegation. Social relations within the firm are marked by high 'social distance' and a mutual distrust between workers and managers. As Lane (1989: 105) argues:

> To gain the necessary degree of cooperation in this context of worker disaffection, French management has adopted a two-pronged strategy: first, to limit worker discretion in task performance and to apply detailed and close supervision...secondly, to reward good performance in a highly individualistic way and to make sure that such rewards are clearly seen to be entirely within management's discretion.

One reflection of these characteristics is the high ratio of managerial, supervisory and staff employees to production workers compared with Britain or Germany (Maurice et al. 1986a: 61–5). French workers tend to have narrowly defined, firm-specific skills and operate within predefined, rigidly classified job structures, partly a reflection of the rapid expansion of industry from the late 1950s, leading to the rapid absorption of a labour force unused to factory culture (Maurice and Sellier 1979). Bureaucratic management hierarchies and rigid job structures would appear to be mutually reinforcing traits, although larger French firms have been trying to adopt new 'social' strategies since the late 1970s, an issue that is dealt with in more detail below.

A second consequence of French industrial culture was a pattern of conflictual industrial relations within the enterprise and what Batstone (1978) has called 'arms'-length bargaining'. Despite the lack of mutual recognition by employers and unions, and the absence of conventional bargaining, the work force exerted considerable influence on management 'at a distance'. Management took into account 'hints and cues' about the balance of power on the shopfloor and the power of the workforce to disrupt production, granting concessions to the work force as a way of forestalling workplace militancy, while preserving the appearance of unilateral managerial decision-taking.

Employer Organization

In contrast to the pluralism of union representation at national level, employers' organization is more unitary. The main employers' body is the CNPF, which embraces about three-quarters of all French enterprises. It is made up of some eighty industry-based organizations, many of them federations representing narrower subsectors of activity, and about 140 multi-industry groups organized into a score of regional associations. Most of the constituent bodies are trade organizations as well as employers' associations, fulfilling 'economic' interest functions as well as industrial relations ones (Sisson 1987: 56–7).

Early employers' organizations developed from the 1840s in construction, textiles, iron and coalmining. Their main objective was to oppose free trade ideas and to protect the French economy against foreign competition. Resistance to trade unionism only later became a motive for employer organization. However, owing to the relative weakness and fragmentation of local organizations, the importance of regional associations, and the predominance of the association of metal and mining industries (UIMM), the national power of employer associations remained fairly weak up to the First World War. In 1919 a national confederation, the CGPF (*Confédération générale de la production française*), came into existence largely at the prompting of the government which was looking to deal with a single employers' organization. The CGPF was dissolved in 1940, but certain prominent employers played an active role in the organizing committees set up by the Vichy regime. In 1945, the CNPF was established to coordinate the various branches of trade and industry.

The CNPF has often been accused of being dominated by the interests of large, technocratic companies, and has had to face the hostility of rival organizations of small employers. The extension of new rights to workers in small and medium-sized enterprises following the 1982 Auroux laws led the CGPME (*Confédération générale des petites et moyennes entreprises*) to distance itself from the CNPF. The two organizations have no legal or financial links but have tended to avoid open confrontation on official consultative or negotiating bodies, and have sometimes joined forces, as in the case of industrial tribunal elections. There is another, more extreme and relatively isolated organization for small business, the SNPMI (*Syndicat nationale des petites et moyennes industries*) which opposes both the state and the trade unions. The SNPMI engages in forms of direct action and does not rule out the use of violence.

Given the heterogeneity of interests among French employers, the CNPF programme has been minimalist, hindering basic change in the French model of industrial relations. While continuing to veto change on many issues, the CNPF's strategy over the years has tended towards one of enlightened capitalism, recognizing the need for dialogue with the trade unions. Since 1977, concerned that the unions should not have a monopoly on social progress, the CNPF has encouraged managements to adopt an active personnel policy at plant-level, based on direct dialogue with employees. A group of young progressive managers within CNPF has also been concerned with improving shopfloor work organization (Lane 1989: 106).

Changing Employer Strategies

The post-1973 economic crisis, European integration and the growth of international competition, and more specifically French concerns with social integration of the work force, have stimulated important changes in employers' strategies and practices over the past decade or so (Segrestin 1990).

In response to the CNPF's call for direct dialogue with employees, employers have attempted to mobilize middle management as a channel of communication with the work force, outside the formal employee representation system, and they have also experimented with more 'participative' styles of management. As a result, unions have often been by-passed. Despite the CNPF's initial fears and a degree of ideological hostility, employers have welcomed the Auroux law granting employees the right of direct expression (Goetschy 1991a). One indicator was the rise in quality circles to around 30,000, a figure higher than in any other European country. Despite the spread of quality circles, however, there is some evidence that they do not sit easily with the French management style described above. In one case observed by Barsoux and Lawrence (1990: 200–1), an initially successful experiment with a small highly motivated group subsequently foundered on the opposition of middle managers anxious to protect their professional terrain and their monopoly of information.

Despite initial attempts of the 1981 socialist government to stem the trend toward flexibility of employment, labour market regulation has been relaxed during the 1980s (see below), and employers have been able to introduce a range of measures to increase flexibility of employment contracts. Forms of employment flexibility have often responded to employees' wishes, but have had the effect of extending the individualization of social relations within the firm. Employers were all the more keen on such recruitment practices, given the difficulty of effecting mass redundancies as a way of achieving 'numerical flexibility': a 1976 law on economic redundancies, introduced by the Chirac government, required administrative authorization before redundancies could be implemented; the law was abolished ten years later, also under a Chirac government. There has been a rise in the use of temporary, fixed-term and part-time employment contracts. Part-time employment rose by half a million between 1982 and 1986, although it remained low by European standards, at about 12 per cent of the total. In 1985, the majority of entries to the labour force were on fixed-term contracts; and by 1989, there were around 600,000 people on such contracts, i.e. 70 per cent of new employment. In the same year there were around 280,000 temporary agency staff, corresponding to a rise in the use of temporary workers from about 2.5 per cent of all employment in 1977 to around 7 per cent in 1989. In recent years, there has also been a strong growth in 'training contracts' for young employees, and in subcontracting. Further flexibility has been achieved within companies through greater variations in working time, by the use of variable working weeks, annualized hours, the development of week-end work, shift-work, and flexi-time. These developments have increasingly been the subject of plant- and company-level bargaining in the 1980s and 1990s. One example is the recent introduction of a four-day working week at Peugeot's Poissy factory to increase plant utilization and expand production; the move has been seen as a response to increasingly competitive and unpredictable world markets (EIRR 204, January 1991: 16–18).

A second 'flexibility' trend of the 1980s has been the growth of pay flexibility through the use of merit-based rewards and the individualization of pay systems. The trend was reinforced by the CNPF's 1987 guidelines on promoting individual pay determination by ending the link between pay and the cost of living. Annual Ministry of Labour surveys, summarized by Dejonghe (1990), show a steady increase in individually determined pay elements in the second half of the 1980s. By 1988, about one-third of firms in the sample used some kind of individual pay system, covering about half of employees, compared with one-fifth of firms and one-third of employees in 1985. The number of firms *only* using individual forms of pay increase doubled (from 6 to 12 per cent) in the same period. These trends were especially marked in smaller firms, and affected managerial and professional staff (*cadres*) more than manual workers. In 1988, more than half of *cadres'* pay increases came from individual elements. Wage individualization became an important subject of company-level collective bargaining in the 1980s (see below).

Functional flexibility, that is changes in work organization such as team-working and multi-skilling, has been a third trend of the 1980s, although a more ambiguous one. Experiments have been carried out by employers over the last fifteen years, but they have required permanent vocational training programmes and their scope and diffusion are still difficult to evaluate. However, in the second half of the 1980s, numerous French firms were introducing innovative employment planning agreements (*accords sur la gestion prévisionelle de l'emploi*) as ways both of avoiding future redundancies and of maintaining competitiveness through technological change and the development of new work-force skills through training (Eyraud et al. 1991: 10–11, 28). One example is the insurance company, GAN, where a special contract (GAN-Avenir) involves retraining and the guarantee of a transfer to a job corresponding to the worker's new qualifications (EIRR 197, June 1990: 6–7).

Lane (1989: 188–92) has suggested that functional flexibility has been inhibited by aspects of French industrial relations and the structuring of work. The pattern of low trust relationships and narrowly defined skill areas reduces the scope for upgrading and increasing the flexibility of workers' skills. Research by Maurice et al. (1986b) suggests that the work organization problems posed by the introduction of new technology (in this case the use of numerically controlled machine tools) are solved by introducing new work roles – such as the position of *régleur* somewhere between machine programmers and operators – rather than the reorganization of the skills of existing workers, for whom close task supervision remains the rule. To an extent, therefore, the rise of flexible forms of employment contract may have provided French firms with an alternative source of flexibility given their limited progress on enhancing functional flexibility during the 1980s (Lane 1989: 192). None the less, there are signs of adaptation of job structures and skill boundaries. In 1987, for example, the Crédit Agricole Bank introduced a reclassification of jobs and grades throughout the organization, while in a large chemical company, the concept of 'function' replaced that of 'post' in a new simplified classification scheme (Eyraud et al. 1991: 13).

One of the paradoxes of the 1980s was that, despite the unions' opposition to the individualization of work relationships which they saw as reducing their own role, the reputation of private enterprise recovered, not only in public opinion but among trade unions themselves. Previously regarded with indifference if not hostility, the private sector is now seen as a major source of jobs and of the creation of wealth and welfare. Even more paradoxically, this reassessment has taken place under a socialist government; but all parties are now committed to a dynamic private sector, less reliant on state subsidies, and in 1991 the socialists also abandoned their policy of '*ni-ni*' (neither nationalization nor privatization), opening up the prospect of further partial privatizations of state assets.

The State

The State as Employer

The state's role in industrial relations is conditioned, first, by its importance as an employer. General (non-trading) government employees (central and local government, state education and health services, etc.) were nearly a quarter of the total employed work force in 1989. In addition, the state trading sector occupies a major role within the French economy. The socialist nationalization programme of 1982 which brought the major manufacturing and financial groups into public ownership increased the share of public enterprise in industrial output from 9 to 24 per cent. Employment reached a high point in the mid-1980s: in 1985, about 2.4 million people worked for public enterprises in the non-agricultural sectors (CEEP 1987: 117).

The state sector has been in the forefront of industrial relations innovations – for example, state companies such as Renault were among the first to sign company agreements in the 1950s. From the early 1970s, the public sector has also been used to further the government's aim of giving renewed impetus to collective bargaining in the French system of industrial relations. Through the example of the public sector, it intended to pave the way for the extension of collective bargaining in the private sector. Jacques Delors (at the time a social adviser to the right-wing government of Chaban-Delmas) advocated a new pay policy, linking public sector pay to productivity increases and national wealth as well as to the cost of living. Delors also proposed granting employees salaried status and the possibility of share ownership, in return for no-strike agreements. Many '*accords de progrès*' were reached in nationalized industries, although unions rejected the inclusion of peace clauses.

In the 1980s, state enterprises were expected to further government social goals as well as commercial ones; for example, the enterprises nationalized by the first socialist government, as well as existing state industries such as the railways, were initially seen as instruments for relieving the crisis of unemployment (Rand Smith 1990). In 1983, the socialists passed a law on the democratization of the public sector which granted trade unions better access to information in the more than 600 enterprises where the state held at least 50 per cent of the shares. The legislation provided for the election of worker representatives to the board, giving them up to one-third of the seats depending on the enterprise's size. In the latter part of the 1980s, French state enterprises such as Thomson, Saint Gobain, Péchiney and Rhône-Poulenc were in the forefront of developments in work-force consultation, setting up European-level information and consultation bodies (Gold and Hall 1992; Jobert 1990). In both Thomson and Bull, 'the fact that the Managing Director was a Socialist was mentioned as an explicit factor [in setting up the bodies]..., but also at Rhône-Poulenc...where his support for legislation requiring company group-level committees (*comités de groupe*) within France had led him to accept its logical extension to the European-level as well' (Gold and Hall 1992: 30).

In the civil service (the public sector employment status of *titulaire* covers state teachers as well as civil servants), pay negotiations proved particularly difficult throughout the 1980s. There was no pay agreement in 1984 and 1987, and in 1986 no negotiations at all. The Chirac government's refusal to compromise on the issue of cash limits led to major discontent and there was an upsurge in strikes in the second part of the decade. There was a loss of purchasing power of around 10 per cent between 1984 and 1988 resulting in a wave of claims for reviews of salaries, working conditions, staffing and training programmes (see strikes). The government adhered to a policy of strict pay guidelines for the public sector. In February 1990, however, it took a major step towards the renewal of public sector industrial relations with an agreement on the restructuring of the public sector pay and grading system applying to some 4.5 million *fonctionnaires* which had not been revised since its introduction in 1946. The agreement, which runs for seven years, maps out the careers of all French public servants from the moment they enter into service until they retire, and introduces a degree of flexibility into the rigid structure of job categories. However, CGT and FO refused to sign the agreement on the grounds that it would lead to performance-related pay.

The Regulation of the Labour Market

The state's main concern since the early 1980s has been with the high level of unemployment. The rate of unemployment rose from under 6 per cent in 1979 to a 1987 peak of 10.5 per cent, before falling back to around 9 per cent by 1990. Government policies have been directed to the stabilization of unemployment through special programmes for the unemployed rather than through macro-economic measures. The socialist government has launched youth employment programmes, and has used training and re-training schemes to increase the job prospects of new entrants to the labour market. Training policy has been linked to industrial restructuring both in the nationalized and private sectors (steel, coalmining, cars, shipbuilding and so on). The government has also encouraged employers and unions to negotiate 'solidarity contracts' under which shorter weekly working hours or the introduction of early retirement plans are used to give employers more scope to recruit new workers. However, government working-time policies do not seem to have been particularly effective in creating new jobs.

From 1988, the Rocard government launched an impressive series of initiatives to fight unemployment within the framework of three successive 'employment plans'. The first and most spectacular measure was the setting up of a *salaire minimum d'insertion* of 2,000 FF. The scheme guaranteed a minimum income for the poorest groups, provided that they agreed to join state-funded schemes to improve their labour market prospects. Among subsequent measures were schemes to improve the integration of immigrants, the reduction of employers' social security contributions in order to encourage recruitment, and tax credits for firms operating flexible working-time schemes with the aim of cutting overtime and encouraging multi-shift systems. Further measures were introduced to improve existing training schemes and to help the young and long-term unemployed find work. Despite the array of policy measures, the government has abandoned its expectation of the early 1980s that unemployment would disappear with economic recovery, and now believes that the existence of a significant level of unemployment is unavoidable.

The main drift of government policy was interrupted by the 1986–8 interlude of 'cohabitation' between the Mitterrand presidency and the right-wing government of Jacques Chirac: the main preoccupation of the Chirac government was to introduce more flexible labour regulation on redundancy, working time, fixed-term and part-time hiring. A 1986 law abolished the system under which all redundancies were subject to prior authorization by the Labour Inspectorate. When the socialists returned to power, however, the Rocard government chose not to repeal the legislation passed by its predecessor, but to encourage the CNPF and the unions to negotiate national enabling agreements as a way of amending the legal framework. New legislation in 1989 provided for greater information and consultation rights for works councils in redundancy matters, gave greater protection for older workers, and required companies to prepare a 'social plan' in the event of economic redundancies. But official controls over redundancies have not been restored.

The State and Pay Determination

The state has adopted a fairly interventionist stance on pay matters since the mid-1970s, both by 'setting an example' in public sector pay settlements, and by implementing wider austerity and pay restraint plans. The government also influences pay scales through adjustments to the statutory national minimum wage, the SMIC (*salaire minimum interprofessionnel de croissance*). The SMIC is automatically adjusted when the retail price index rises by 2 per cent; the government can also raise the SMIC independently whenever it wishes to do so, as it did for example in 1981 when the Left came to power. Though the SMIC should not in law affect pay scales as a whole, increases in SMIC have repercussions throughout the pay structure. In the 1980s, successive governments tended to avoid letting the SMIC rise faster than average pay, as happened in the period 1970–5. According to a Ministry of Labour survey, around 1.7 million workers were receiving the SMIC in July 1988, that is nearly 10 per cent of workers. In 1990, the CNPF and the union confederations agreed, at government prompting, to negotiate at sector level to improve the earnings of low paid workers. Between 1990 and 1991, considerable progress was achieved, according to a Ministry of Labour assessment (1991) which shows that 94 out of 164 sectors have now set basic pay rates at or above the statutory minimum.

The Framework of Industrial Relations and Collective Bargaining

Traditionally, state intervention has been important in creating and reinforcing the framework of industrial relations. In periods when the Left has been in the ascendancy, unions have pressed for new laws: in 1936 with the Popular Front, in 1945 with the Liberation, in 1968 following the May events, and in 1981 with the advent of the Socialist government.

From the late 1960s onwards, and especially in the early 1970s and late 1980s, it became usual for laws to embody the contents of negotiated agreements or the outcome of discussions between unions, employers and the state. This process was supposed to decrease state intervention in labour relations. However, the legislative step also gives the state the opportunity to modify, and sometimes to improve, the previously negotiated deal, with implications for the bargaining strategies of both employers and unions.

In the 1980s the influence of government policies on industrial relations and union strength was twofold. On the one hand, the position of the unions was on the whole reinforced by the major body of industrial relations legislation introduced between 1981 and 1986, the so-called Auroux laws whose main innovation has been to institutionalize collective bargaining within the enterprise (see below). Further planned reforms – to improve employee representation within small and medium-sized enterprises, increase employment protection for trade unionists, and foster social dialogue within companies especially over modernization programmes – may continue this trend (although the framework legislation is currently stalled).

On the other hand, macro-economic policies have tended to weaken union power. Following an initial phase of Keynesian economic policy, the socialist government adopted anti-inflationary measures including a temporary wage and price freeze in June 1982. Subsequently, the emphasis on control of inflation, pay restraint and the reduction of public expenditure has been intensified.

Collective Bargaining

The characteristics of French collective bargaining have largely been shaped by successive collective bargaining Acts (1919, 1936, 1946, 1950, 1971, 1982) (Goetschy and Rojot 1987). However, bargaining pre-dates the creation of a legal framework. At the turn of the century, around 2,000 collective agreements had been signed (Sellier 1984). Government attempts to unify the diversity of local practices had not met with great success, since employers preferred to stick to more paternalistic practices and the CGT was anxious to preserve its autonomy *vis-à-vis* the state and to avoid becoming 'institutionalized'. However, the context of the First World War enabled the government to pass the first collective bargaining Act (1919) and to begin the process of unifying local bargaining practices within industrial sectors.

The 1919 Act was deficient in many respects, and it was the 1936 Act which in effect established the basic framework for French collective bargaining. First, industry bargaining was defined as the essential bargaining level. This solution suited both employer and union organizations which preferred such bargaining for ideological as well as tactical reasons. Industry agreements cover the maximum number of employees, which is an advantage for the unions when their membership is low, and they promote the equality of treatment of workers across companies. The employers have favoured industry agreements because they establish only minimum standards for a given industrial sector, leaving individual companies with considerable leeway in setting terms and conditions, and because they spare employers from having to recognize unions at plant-level. In the French context, such preferences were also a more profound reflection of the lack of mutual recognition between unions and employers.

Second, the 1936 Act established the principle of the extension procedure which enables the Minister of Labour to make a collective agreement binding on all employers in a given industrial sector, whether or not they are members of the employers' association. Third, the Act gave the 'most representative' unions the power to make 'the law of the trade' (*la loi de la profession*). In practice, this meant that all employees, whether unionized or not, could benefit from the terms of a collective agreement. Furthermore, the Act stipulated that a collective agreement was valid even if only one representative union signed it, which reinforced union pluralism and would subsequently favour minority organizations such as the CFTC, CGC and FO. All these provisions attempted to compensate for the unions' organizational weakness and to stimulate collective bargaining in the face of the employers' reluctance.

At the Liberation, the 1946 collective bargaining Act was drawn up in the context of the move to a planned economy, and granted little autonomy to employers and unions in pay determination. The Act was short-lived and was replaced by the 1950 Act which embodied most of the principles of the 1936 Act. It continued to privilege industry bargaining, and it left little scope for plant-level or multi-industry bargaining. In any case neither social partner was keen to develop plant-level bargaining: employers were still concerned to avoid any union organization within plants and to limit the unions' function to the industry level, while the unions were weak at plant level and feared that decentralized bargaining might endanger the solidarity of interests within the labour movement.

The volume of bargaining was fairly low between 1950 and 1959: on average there were 420 collective agreements per year. The number of industry agreements increased rapidly between 1960 and 1967, with an average of 990 collective agreements per year. Over the same two periods, plant-level bargaining rose from 143 to 356 agreements per year. By the end of the 1950s, a few multi-industry agreements had been reached on unemployment and retirement benefits.

Following the social and political unrest of 1968, there were significant developments in multi-industry and plant-level bargaining, reinforced by the 1971 amendments to the 1950 Act. Innovative multi-industry bargaining dealt with issues such as job security, vocational training, the introduction of salaried status for manual workers, redundancy payments, and working conditions. Such national agreements provided a 'framework' which was aimed at encouraging collective bargaining at lower levels. At industry level, the number of agreements rose to an average of 1,560 a year in the 1970s.

An increase in the number of plant-level agreements resulted from the pressures of employees after May 1968, from renewed employers' social strategies aimed at reducing employee turnover by introducing additional company-specific benefits, and from the 1968 Statute, which legalized union delegates at plant-level and gave them a collective bargaining function. Between 1968 and 1975, more than 600 agreements were concluded annually in plant-level bargaining. Plant-level agreements were not generally innovative, but improved on higher-level agreements or adapted them to local conditions. In practice, such domestic bargaining was largely confined to larger firms.

Following the 1973 energy crisis, plant-level agreements became less numerous. Multi-industry enabling agreements were less often followed by agreements at lower levels; there were significant difficulties, for instance, in implementing the 1975 multi-industry agreement on working conditions. However, during this period, there were a number of more specific multi-industry agreements setting precise and detailed conditions rather than providing a framework for lower-level bargaining, especially on employment issues such as redundancy.

The advent of a Left government brought about a significant change in the political and legal context of collective bargaining in the 1980s. The search for a new balance between legal intervention and collective bargaining was the hallmark of the government's post-1981 strategy of social reform, with priority being given to the development of bargaining. This strategy can be traced back to the 1969–71 industrial relations policy of the then right-wing government of Chaban-Delmas (to whom, as mentioned, Jacques Delors was adviser).

A major objective of the Mitterrand government was the reform of workplace relations, as outlined in the 'Report on Workers' Rights' by the Minister of Labour, Jean Auroux. The government's proposals aimed to provide employees with real 'citizenship within the firm' and to create new opportunities for employees to 'become agents of change within the enterprise'. The Auroux report was not completely new; adopting a gradual rather than a revolutionary approach, it partly reflected the 1975 Sudreau report. Though it took union demands into account (especially those of the CGT and of the CFDT), it steered a line of its own, and it was given a mixed reception by union and employer organizations (Goetschy 1983).

The Auroux report identified a number of deficiencies in the French system of collective bargaining. First, many employees were not covered by any collective agreements, whether at industry or plant-level. Such 'excluded workers', amounting to 11 per cent of the total in firms of at least ten employees, were particularly concentrated among temporary workers, for example, in the distributive trades and in hotels and restaurants. Below industry level, the coverage of collective bargaining was even lower: only a quarter of employees were covered by a plant agreement. Second, collective agreements were highly fragmented: 40 of the 1,023 national or regional-level collective agreements covered more than half of employees. Third, low union density and the divisions between unions undermined the 'legitimacy' of agreements. Fourth, Auroux noted, many existing agreements lacked job classification structures, and there was a large gap between basic pay and actual earnings (an average of 30 per cent).

The Auroux report led to the 1982 collective bargaining Act. Most of its provisions sought to improve existing arrangements, but some were innovative. For instance, in firms with union branches, employers were obliged to open negotiations every year on pay and working hours. The employers were fiercely critical of the obligation to negotiate at company level, although their criticisms have faded away with the implementation of the law. Indeed, there is no obligation to reach an agreement and the employer has the final say. Thus, unlike the USA, there is no requirement to bargain 'in good faith'. These provisions were intended to foster collective bargaining within the firm by providing a learning process leading to 'negotiating' attitudes: employers would become more aware of their 'social responsibilities' and unions would be more attentive to economic constraints.

A further innovation allows non-signatory unions to veto a plant-level agreement, for example if an agreement contradicts one reached at a higher level. Before using a veto, the non-signatory opponents must win more than half of the votes in the works council or employee delegate elections. Granting such veto rights to the largest opposition unions (i.e. CGT and CFDT) was expected to lead to more legitimate agreements. In practice, veto rights over 'derogatory agreements' have rarely been used. In national industry agreements, the obligation to meet once a year to negotiate pay and every fifth year to discuss job classifications should bring basic pay and other conditions closer to actual practice (Eyraud et al. 1989). At both the firm and industry level, the provision that negotiators meet at stipulated intervals was intended to promote responsible negotiations and to make the parties more representative of their constituents.

The 1982 Act contains several provisions enlarging union rights to information and to expert help in the bargaining process. The Act also strengthens existing procedures under which the Minister of Labour can extend certain collective agreements to non-signatory firms. The annual report of the Minister of Labour (1990) records an average of 400 agreements per year resulting from the extension procedure. Its use is particularly important in sectors where enterprise bargaining is absent. Such agreements have also been reached for specific forms of employment in, for example, tourism, cleaning, and catering.

The attempts by the Mitterrand government to promote collective bargaining became entangled with its austerity plans of 1982 and 1983. Nevertheless, plant-level bargaining was boosted not only by the Auroux laws but also because it served employers' interests in their pursuit of increased productivity and improved quality and flexibility. Since 1987, the number of plant-level agreements has quadrupled from its 1981 level to an average of 6,000 per year. Sixty-five per cent of enterprises subject to the provisions on compulsory bargaining have conducted negotiations. There are few means of forcing the remaining 35 per cent to comply with the obligation to negotiate, and they have rarely been subject to sanctions. In the firms that do negotiate, the duration of negotiations in 60 per cent of cases is fairly short (one or two meetings) and though employees are informed, they are consulted in only 25 per cent of cases.

The issues covered by company bargaining have been those defined as compulsory by the 1982 Act. In 1989, 57 per cent of plant-level agreements, covering around 18 per cent of employees, related to wages and 35 per cent to working-time issues, a distribution which had not changed much since 1986. Other issues, relating to technological change, qualifications, training and employment have been less subject to negotiations than might have been expected.

Plant-level agreements on working time have largely been concerned with the 'classical' issues of the organization of annual holidays, bank holidays and so on, which account for 45 per cent of all clauses. Provisions on the reduction of working time have become marginal. Among provisions concerning a more flexible organization of working time, those on 'increased machine utilization time' account for 18.5 per cent of clauses, with shift work the major issue. Other provisions cover casual shift work and night work for women. Clauses which are more directly linked to seasonal and economic fluctuations amount to 21 per cent of the total and include measures on the 'modulation' of weekly working hours (that is averaging weekly hours over a multi-week period to allow for variations around the average in any particular week), flexitime, casual work contracts, part-time work and so on. The Ministry of Labour stresses that some flexibility deals, such as the modulation of weekly working hours, currently offer only limited compensating benefits to employees. It adds that 'despite their complexity, the social partners seem to understand the subtleties of such flexibility deals; however, the control of their implementation remains deficient' (*Ministère du Travail* 1991). The high density of plant-level agreements on working-time issues is all the more remarkable in that industry-level framework agreements are lacking in most cases (Jobert and Rozenblatt 1989a).

There was also an increase of the number of agreements on individualized forms of pay in the 1980s. In 1985 nearly 25 per cent of company pay agreements contained an individualization clause, rising to 33 per cent in 1988 and 31 per cent in 1990. Another striking feature has been the increasing number of profit-sharing agreements. Between 1988 and 1990, the number of French employees covered by voluntary profit-sharing schemes (*intéressement*) has doubled. In 1990, the various profit-sharing and share-ownership agreements affected about five million workers. The increase is most noticeable in smaller firms with fewer than 50 employees, although agreements are concentrated in larger companies (see EIRR 210, July 1991: 19). Profit schemes amounted to around 3.5 per cent of the paybill of companies paying out on them, although their value as a motivating device was reduced by the problem of variability from year to year, especially in periods of economic downturn.

In 1989, plant-level bargaining still covered less than a fifth of all employees, and was largely non-existent in smaller firms without unions. Firms with fewer than 50 employees account for only 6 per cent of the total number of plant-level agreements, whereas firms with 150 to 500 employees have signed 40 per cent of them. Larger firms – and not only those in the public sector – are said to play a major role in the dynamics of company bargaining by implementing innovatory agreements (as, for example, with the Renault, Peugeot and Péchiney agreements). However, while the media tend to give much publicity to such agreements their broader impact has been relatively limited.

There are also important sectoral differences in the extent of company and plant bargaining: while the percentage of plant-level agreements is relatively low in construction, it is high in sectors such as insurance, energy, and capital goods. This heterogeneity led the Ministry of Labour, in its 1989 evaluation of collective bargaining, to propose the development of specific forms of employee representation and collective bargaining for small and medium-sized enterprises, and the strengthening of the central role of industry-wide bargaining.

Even where plant-level bargaining takes place, it faces a number of obstacles. The bargaining process tends to increase in complexity due to the growing variety of employees' demands, the technical nature of the issues involved, and the increasing opacity of 'package deals' treating several items simultaneously (productivity, working time, pay, job creation, training, etc.). Such complexity often creates problems of expertise for union representatives. In some instances employers have tended to favour plant-level bargaining discussions within the framework of works councils or some form of direct dialogue, rather than with the official union delegates. Finally, plant-level bargaining creates conflicting pressures: on the one hand, it implies a greater involvement of employees and unions within the firm and the setting up of fairly durable work relations; on the other hand, however, the stability of work relations is undermined by changing employment practices, the use of more precarious forms of employment, the threat of redundancies, and so on.

Despite the growth of plant and company bargaining, collective bargaining at industry level remains essential. Industry agreements continue to set the basic framework and rules within which plant-level bargaining evolves. Most employees are covered by an industry agreement, which was one of the objectives of the Auroux laws. If the situation has been improving since 1981 when 3.5 million workers (a quarter of the private sector labour force) were not covered by an industry agreement, one million still remained unprotected in 1990, in sectors such as sports, leisure, and the media. Around 80 per cent of industry agreements reached each year concern pay. In 1989 the figure was 85 per cent. Provisions relating to increases in minimum rates of pay formed a growing proportion compared to issues such as bonuses and other exceptional payments. Long-running sectoral talks on the plight of the low-paid made progress. The talks affected 63 sectors, most of which had lowest basic rates below the SMIC.[5] According to a 1991 Ministry of Labour assessment, the great majority of sectors (49) have been bringing their basic rates into line with the SMIC.

The significance of bargaining activity at industry-level cannot be assessed merely on the basis of the number of agreements reached. Qualitative developments have also been important. Employer and union bodies have been holding discussions and conducting forecasting studies in a number of sectors on subjects such as employment and vocational training within the framework of sectoral joint bodies.

Multi-industry bargaining was revitalized at the end of the 1980s, following a slowdown in the late 1970s and the first half of the 1980s.

Some of the inter-industry agreements have been the prelude to legal reform.

National negotiations in December 1984, over the introduction of greater flexibility in labour relations and employment conditions, had ended in failure, largely as a result of divisions between and within the unions as to the possibilities for a multi-industry flexibility agreement at this juncture. The reformist FO, as well as the CGT, were against an agreement. The CFDT faced severe internal dissent: while national negotiators and the membership would have been ready to reach a flexibility deal, intermediate levels, including regional bodies and some industrial federations, were strongly opposed to an agreement. CFDT was finally forced to reject agreement and as a result no other union confederation was ready to risk signing it. Agreement was made all the harder by the fact that the proposed deal covered several issues (flexibility in hiring practices and in work organization, the legal regulations governing employee representative bodies, and legal constraints on collective redundancies) as a single package.

By the end of the 1980s, however, the CFDT was once more ready to support multi-industry bargaining, and the government and the CNPF were also favourable to a 'consensus approach' to the modernization of French enterprises. Employers and unions entered negotiations on a series of 'orientation agreements' designed to encourage bargaining on modernization at sector and company level in preparation for the single European market. Talks opened between the two rounds of the 1988 presidential elections in order to demonstrate their independence from political timetables. Subsequently, the Rocard government actively supported the strategy of enabling agreements.

In September 1988, a national orientation agreement was signed on technological change, with the objective of relaunching sectoral negotiations on the issue. The agreement strengthened the role of workplace consultation and of retraining in firms planning to introduce new technology. A similar 'consensus orientation' inspires the national framework agreement of March 1989 on the flexible organization of working time which contains broad guidelines for company negotiations and places limits on overtime and continuous working. Issues such as sexual equality (November 1989) and working conditions (October 1989) have been subject to similar multi-industry agreements. In March 1990 new rules governing fixed-term and temporary hiring were established in a further multi-industry agreement. Its provisions covered the length of contracts, end-of-contract payments, the circumstances in which different contracts could be used, and the rights of the works council to information and consultation on such issues. In the same year, discussions on occupational training were opened to update the famous 1970 agreement on vocational training. The items re-examined include individual training leave, induction training, company plans, and the financing of vocational training. In 1990, employers' statutory contributions to vocational training amounted to 1.2 per cent of the total paybill (in firms with 10 employees and more);

in practice, French companies spend around 2.7 per cent of their paybill on employee training. Throughout the 1980s, employers and unions negotiated actively and successfully at national level on training issues.

Some unions have been reluctant partners in multi-industry bargaining. The CFDT and the CGC have been the warmest supporters of such deals with the CNPF. Their increased willingness to talk at national level reflects the problems posed at company and plant level by employers' flexibility strategies during the 1980s; in particular there has been an enormous rise in overtime working, and a multiplication of the use of fixed-term and temporary contracts (see above). Despite this, the FO and CFTC have remained critical, refusing to sign some agreements; and there has been continued scepticism of the CNPF's enthusiasm for multi-industry bargaining, given the employers' reluctance to bargain at industry level in the 1980s.

Despite the continuing problems of collective bargaining, the overall objectives of the Auroux laws have on the whole been achieved. Whereas in the past collective bargaining had been closely tied in with strikes and mass mobilizations, in the 1980s and 1990s it became commonplace, a normal, regular and institutionalized social practice.

Employee Representation at Company Level

A major feature of the French system of industrial relations is the multiplicity of representative institutions, each reflecting specific social and political pressures at a particular period. Employee delegates (*délégués du personnel*) were instituted by the Popular Front in 1936 to deal with individual employee grievances and to make sure labour laws and collective agreements were enforced. Works councils (*comités d'entreprise*), set up in 1945 following the Liberation to contain the spontaneous establishment of production committees in factories, have information and consultation rights and are responsible for developing social and cultural activities. In 1968, after the events of May, workplace union branches and trade union delegates (*délégués syndicaux*) were introduced in companies to carry out union activities and to participate in plant-level bargaining. In 1982, with the Left in power, the powers of these institutions on 'economic' issues were widened and they were given additional resources. 'Group committees' were also created, enabling works councils to intervene in decision centres beyond their own enterprise.

Employee delegates and works council representatives are elected by the whole work force, reflecting the state's concern to endow these bodies with genuine legitimacy. But the state has also aimed to strengthen national unions at enterprise level by giving them a monopoly on proposing candidates in the first round of elections, and successful candidates are generally elected on a union slate (see above, tables 13.3–4).

A government-commissioned report (*rapport* Bélier) of May 1990 found that provisions for representation work poorly in smaller firms. Some 64 per cent of firms with between 11 and 49 staff do not have employee delegates. About 60 per cent of concerns with between 50–100 employees have no union delegates, and in the same size-category around 30 per cent have no company works councils. The report recommended that employee delegates, works council and safety committee be merged into a single body. However, with the government's attention focused on employment issues, intended legislation has, for the moment, been dropped.

Another major innovation of the socialists' legislation is the workers' right of expression, introduced in the Act of August 1982. The law offers employees the opportunity to express their views 'directly' and collectively on the content of work, its organization and on working conditions more generally. National union reactions were mixed. While both the CFDT and the CGT had been demanding workers' rights of expression and welcomed the new measure, FO saw it as a dangerous challenge to the primacy of the union and feared that it might lead to workers being manipulated by employers; the CGC, by contrast, thought that it was likely to encroach on the role of management and supervisory staff. In practice, such fears were largely dissipated. As framework legislation, it had to be followed by plant-level agreements laying down issues such as the number of meetings to be held per year, the size of the 'expression groups', whether they would be led by a trade unionist or by line management, and procedures for dealing with issues raised by the group. Survey evidence suggests that, where they were present, most unions signed such agreements. The signature rate was the following: CGT, 76 per cent; CFDT, 78 per cent; FO, 62 per cent; CFTC, 84 per cent; CGC, 87 per cent (Report of the French Ministry of Labour 1985). Initially very reluctant, even employers realized that there were advantages for management in the new bodies. The Ministry of Labour estimates that in 1990 between 10,000 and 12,000 enterprises employing 3.5 million people were covered by expression agreements.

The major achievement of the *groupes d'expression* lies in the improvement of working conditions and work stations. However, qualitative assessments of the actual working of the groups are fairly negative. Expression groups too often functioned in a rather formalistic way and on the whole employers failed to deal with employees' requests in a satisfactory manner, which eroded the effectiveness of the groups (for an overview, see Goetschy 1991a; Borzeix and Linhart 1988).

Strikes

Recognized since 1864, the right to strike is regarded as a fundamental right under the Constitution of 1946. The law says relatively little about the regulation of strikes and the distinction between legal and illegal strikes is essentially left to jurisprudence.

Industrial disputes tend to be unpredictable in France, as there are few, if any, no-strike provisions, procedural agreements or strike notice procedures, except for the public sector where unions have to give five days' notice before a strike. Strikes tend to be short because, as a legacy of the anarcho-syndicalist tradition, French unions have limited financial resources and do not generally grant strike pay. Moreover, France loses relatively few days due to stoppages compared with Italy and the English-speaking countries. However, strikes traditionally involved large numbers of workers, reflecting the strategy of CGT and the Communist Party of mobilizing massive national demonstration strikes over aspects of the political agenda. Strikes were, therefore, as much an aspect of politics as of collective bargaining (Shorter and Tilly 1974).

An average of 147 days per 1,000 workers per year were lost to strikes for the period 1970–88 (IW-Trends, FRG). In that period, France was slightly more strike prone than Sweden, and the number of strikes fell drastically in the 1980s. Between 1979 and 1988, the number of days lost per annum was about a third of the annual average recorded between 1970 and 1979 (1.2 million days lost on average per year in the 1980s against 3.6 million days per year for the 1970s). However, both in 1982 and 1984 there were increases in the number of working days lost, arising from industrial action over the 1982 working-hours ordinance, disputes in the car industry, and to a lesser extent incomes policy. But the most salient feature is the proportion of strikes in the public sector from 1986 onwards. In 1986, they accounted for 43.5 per cent of days lost, with strikes on the railways (SNCF), the Paris metro, and in gas and electricity. In 1987, in SNCF alone strikes amounted to a third of the total number of days lost. Other public sector groups such as schoolteachers, air traffic controllers and pilots also undertook strike action. The following year saw a spectacular strike by nurses that spread throughout the hospital sector; stoppages also occurred among prisons warders, postal workers, television employees and in SNECMA (a nationalized enterprise in the aviation sector). In 1989 there were serious stoppages in the finance ministry. Finally, in 1991, important public sector stoppages included further action by health workers and a bitter strike at Renault's Cléon factory in Normandy.

As mentioned above, a key characteristic of public sector strikes in the 1980s was the setting up of rank-and-file 'coordination groups' to organize strike action either alongside or in opposition to official union channels (as in the rail strike and the nurses' strike respectively). The *coordinations* were largely a phenomenon of the public sector. Under charismatic (often extreme left-wing) leaders, they particularly attracted younger workers and addressed their claims directly to the state. They questioned the traditional and often bureaucratic negotiating practices of the union confederations and tried to bridge what they saw as a gap between the demands of the rank and file and those put forward by official union representatives. In addition to seeking greater rank-and-file unity the *coordinations* also saw mass meetings as a way of exerting greater control over strike committees and negotiating bodies. As a result of the initiatives of the *coordinations*, unions tended to consult employees more frequently beforehand about bargaining priorities and about the conduct of strikes and negotiations. There were significant differences between the various *coordinations*: the railways, with the work force's strong sense of occupational identity and enterprise culture, high union density, and traditional industrial relations practices, contrasted sharply with the hospital sector (Visier 1990). Some sociologists have insisted that the *coordinations* are manifestations of anomie, and the erosion of a collective perspective within the French labour movement, but others saw them as part of a movement for the democratization of union practices (Rozenblatt 1991; Hassenteufel 1991). In any case, *coordinations* are a clear reflection of some of the deficiencies of French union activity in the 1980s.

While changes in the ways of organizing strikes and the occupational groups involved were fairly dramatic in the late 1980s, the number of strike days per 1,000 employees in the latter half of the 1980s was less than half that in the first half of the decade (41 days for the period 1985–9 compared to 94 days for 1980–4). In 1990 strike days fell to their lowest level since the Liberation.

On average, pay issues remained the single most important motive for strike action in the 1980s, although they amounted to less than half the total. Employment issues, particularly redundancy, accounted for about a third of the reasons for strikes. In 1988, however, the relative importance of wages increased again, reflecting the upturn in the economy. In the public sector, strikes were a combination of both classical pay claims (rates of pay were lower than those of the private sector) and also the demands of specific occupational groups, for example of railway drivers and nurses over poor working conditions, the lack of career opportunities, and more generally the absence of modern personnel policies in the public sector.

Eight out of ten strikes on average result from union action, of which four are initiated by the CGT, three by more than one union acting together, and one by the CFDT. Two out of ten strikes are launched by employees independently of the unions.

Conclusion

The striking feature of contemporary French industrial relations is the active role of successive socialist governments in fostering collective bargaining at both plant and industry level since the beginning of the 1980s. Legislation has reshaped the framework of industrial relations, encouraging greater flexibility to encourage companies to modernize and to create employment. At the same time, the government has attempted to give employees and their representatives a greater say in management decision-making.

The importance of the various bargaining levels (plant, industry and multi-industry) in this modernization process has been the subject of debate and contention among management and unions and between Left and Right. The Right and employers have favoured the decentralization of bargaining to plant level, whereas the Left and labour have been anxious to retain industry-level bargaining as well. The conflict over the most appropriate bargaining level has been prominent in discussions on working-time flexibility. In general, there was a significant trend towards decentralized bargaining in France throughout the 1980s, as in most European countries.

At the end of the decade, the Rocard government gave renewed stimulus to multi-industry agreements, with the aim of fostering 'articulated' bargaining and developing a more consensual approach to major industrial relations issues, a strategy which had the support of the CNPF. In addition, the Rocard government encouraged management and unions to revise the provisions of Chirac's employment legislation through national-level negotiations.

Over the past decade or so, a constellation of social forces, including successive socialist governments and some reformist unions – notably the CFDT – have been endeavouring, on the basis of the framework established by the Auroux laws, to institutionalize collective bargaining as the major means of regulation in the French industrial relations system. They have been supported in their efforts by an 'enlightened' fraction of French capital which has been sympathetic to the CFDT's position and accepts the need for a bargained approach to industrial restructuring and the modernization of enterprises. The group includes some French multinationals and nationalized enterprises, and has been active in the setting up of European-level works councils.

This project has had to confront considerable opposition and the industrial relations system has yet to achieve a new stability. Opponents were to be found among both employers and the unions. An ultra-liberal group of employers has seized upon continuing union decline as an opportunity to develop direct forms of communication and bargaining with the work force. Another employer fraction, while prepared to deal with union delegates within the enterprise, has been pushing for more flexible plant-level bargaining and regards industry-level bargaining as the source of too many rigidities. On the union side, the idea, prominent throughout the history of French industrial relations, that strikes are the motor of social progress and an essential accompaniment of the collective bargaining process, has been given a new lease of life by the development of new forms of conflict from 1986 onwards, as debates at recent congresses of CGT, FO and CFDT have shown.

How does this picture of French industrial relations at the beginning of the 1990s compare with other European models? If the severe decline of French unionism since the mid-1970s tends to reinforce the atypical character of the French system, the increasing intensity and scope of collective bargaining activity over the last decade contributes to the 'normalization' of the French case. France looks more like countries with strongly institutionalized bargaining practices than it did at the beginning of the 1980s (cf. Rojot 1988). At the heart of this upsurge of collective bargaining has been the socialists' modernization strategy. Paradoxically, a socialist government has presided over the progressive decline of the unions and the improvement of the image of the enterprise as job provider and wealth creator.

Although the diversity of European industrial relations systems remains high, the transformation of the French system seems likely to facilitate the convergence of future union and employer policies with other national confederations at European level. In general, however, French union confederations have been unable to mount a lively national debate on European integration and the social dimension (Goetschy 1991b). This stands in contradiction to the fact that the CFDT, with its close links with Delors' policy network, has been fairly influential in Brussels in the shaping of Social Europe, both within the ETUC and more widely within the Commission, the European Parliament and the Economic and Social Committee. The CNPF, in contrast to the traditional views that it expresses in France, seems to have adopted a fairly progressive posture at European level and has been trying to persuade UNICE to move forward on the European social dialogue, while major French multinational companies have anticipated likely developments on 'European works councils' by establishing European-level employee consultation bodies. In short, European developments may be playing their part in the erosion of the traditionally wary, authoritarian outlook of French management.

Notes

1. Membership data are based on the unions' own figures, and need to be treated with considerable caution: most unions have tended to inflate their respective membership figures. Moreover, different unions calculate their membership in different ways: for example, some include retired members, others do not.
2. In 1990, CFDT claimed 539,000 members (defined as those making regular contributions). On the same basis, it calculated that CGT membership was 682,000; FO, 416,000; CGC, 115,000; CFTC, 106,000; and FEN, 183,000.
3. There are also elections for representatives on the social welfare boards (*Sécurité Sociale*). But since only half the electorate for these boards is composed of wage earners, they will not be discussed here.
4. A very useful synthesis of research on French industrial culture and industrial relations is to be found in Lane 1989; other accounts are Maurice et al. 1986a, 1986b; Maurice and Sellier 1979; Gallie 1978; Dyas and Thanheiser 1976; d'Iribarne 1989; and Batstone 1978.
5. The apparent anomaly is explained by the fact that the SMIC includes pay premia in addition to basic pay.

Abbreviations

CFDT	*Confédération française démocratique du travail* – French Democratic Confederation of Labour
CFE-CGC	*Confédération française de l'encadrement – Confédération générale des cadres* – French Confederation of Managerial Staffs – General Confederation of Managerial Staffs

CFTC	*Confédération française des travailleurs chrétiens* – French Confederation of Christian Workers
CGC	see CFE-CGC
CGT	*Confédération générale du travail* – General Confederation of Labour
CNPF	*Conseil national du patronat français* – National Council of French Employers
FEN	*Fédération de l'éducation nationale* – Federation of National Education
FO	*Force ouvrière* – Workers' Strength
SMIC	*Salaire minimum interprofessionel de croissance* – national minimum wage.
SNPMI	*Syndicat national des petites et moyennes industries* – National Union of Small and Medium-sized Industries
TUC	*Travaux d'utilité collective* (special employment scheme for young unemployed)

References

Adam, G. 1983: *Le Pouvoir syndical en France*. Paris: Dunod.

Armingeon, K. et al. 1981: *Les Syndicats européens et la crise*. Grenoble: Presses Universitaires de Grenoble.

Barsoux, J.-L. and Lawrence, P. 1990: *Management in France*. London: Cassell.

Batstone, E. 1978: Arms' Length Bargaining: Industrial Relations in a French Company. Unpublished typescript. Coventry: Industrial Relations Research Unit.

Bibes, G. and Mouriaux, R. (eds) 1990: *Les Syndicats européens a l'épreuve*. Paris: Fondation Nationale des Sciences Politiques.

Borzeix, A. and Linhart, D. 1988: La participation: un clair-obscur. *Sociologie du Travail*, 30, 37–54.

Boyer, R. 1985: *La Flexibilité du travail en Europe*. Paris: La Découverte.

Bridgford, J. 1990: French Trade Unions: Crisis in the 1980s. *Industrial Relations Journal*, 21, 2, 126–35.

Caire, G. 1990. Syndicalisme en crise? In G. Bibes and R. Mouriaux (eds), 1990, 15–46.

CEEP (Centre européen de l'entreprise publique) 1987: *L'entreprise publique dans la communauté économique européenne*. Brussels: CEEP.

Charle, C. 1991: *Histoire sociale de la France au XIXième siècle*. Paris: Seuil.

d'Iribarne, P. 1989: *La Logique de l'Honneur. Gestion des entreprises et traditions nationales*. Paris: Seuil.

Dejonghe, V. 1990: L'Individualisation des salaires en France depuis 1985. *Rencontre européenne sur les salaires*, Paris 22–4 March 1990. Actes du colloque, vol. 4, *Les Modes de Négociation des salaires*, 49–68.

Durupty, M. 1988: *Les Privatisations en France*. Paris: La Documentation Française.

Dyas, G. and Thanheiser, H. 1976: *The Emerging European Enterprise. Strategy and Structure in French and German Industry*. London: Macmillan.

Europa 1988: *Western Europe 1989. A Political and Economic Survey*. London: Europa Publications.

Eurostat 1990: *Structure and Activity of Industry*. Brussels: Commision of the European Communities.

Eyraud, F., Jobert, A., Rozenblatt, P. and Tallard, M. 1989: *Les classifications dans l'entreprise: production des hiérarchies professionnelles et salariales*. Paris: La Documentation Française.

Eyraud, F., Shaheed, Z., Vaughan-Whitehead, D. 1991: 'Productivity and the Bargaining Process. A Comparative Perspective'. Paper for 3rd European Regional Congress of the International Industrial Relations Association, Bari 23–6 September.

Gallie, D. 1978: *In Search of the New Working Class. Automation and Integration within the Capitalist Enterprise*. Cambridge: Cambridge University Press.

Goetschy, J. 1983: A New Future for Industrial Democracy in France. *Economic and Industrial Democracy*, 4, 1, 85–103.

Goetschy, J. 1991a: An Appraisal of French Research on Direct Participation. In R. Russel and V.

Rus (eds), *International Yearbook of Participation in Organizations*, Oxford: OUP, 235–47.

Goetschy, J. 1991b: 1992 and the Social dimension. *Economic and Industrial Democracy*, 12, 2, 259–75.

Goetschy, J. and Linhart, D. 1990: *La Crise des syndicats en europe occidentale*. Paris: Documentation Française.

Goetschy, J. and Rojot, J. 1987. France. In G. Bamber and R. Lansbury (eds), *International and Comparative Industrial Relations*, London: Allen & Unwin, 142–64.

Gold, M. and Hall, M. 1992: *European-Level Information and Consultation in Multinational Companies: An Evaluation of Practice*. Dublin: European Foundation for the Improvement of Living and Working Conditions.

Hassenteufel, P. 1991: Pratiques représentatives et construction identitaire: une approche des coordinations. *Revue Française de Science Politique*, 41, 1, 5–26.

Jobert, A. 1990: La Négociation collective dans les entreprises multinationales en Europe. In G. Devin (ed.), *Dimensions internationales*, Nanterre: Erasme, 313–30.

Jobert, A. and Rozenblatt, P. 1989a: L'Entreprise au coeur de la négociation collective. In *L'État de la France*, Paris: La Découverte, 92–4.

Jobert, A. and Rozenblatt, P. 1989b: Les Syndicats de salariés. In *L'État de la France*, Paris: La Découverte, 385-9

Kesselman, M. (ed.) 1984: *The French Workers' Movement: Economic Crisis and Political Change*. London: Allen & Unwin.

Lane, C. 1989: *Management and Labour in Europe. The Industrial Enterprise in Germany, Britain and France*. Aldershot: Edward Elgar.

Lange, P., Ross, G. and Vannicelli, M. 1982: *Unions, Change and Crisis: French and Italian Union Strategy and the Political Economy*. London: Allen & Unwin.

Linhart, D. and Malan, A. 1988: Individualisme professionel des jeunes et action collective. *Travail et Emploi*, 36–7, June–September, 9–18.

Lipietz, A. 1991: Governing the Economy in the Face of International Challenge: From National Developmentalism to National Crisis. In Hollifield, J. and Ross, G. (eds), *Searching for the New France*, London: Routledge, 17–42.

Marceau, J. 1989: France. In Bottomore, T. and Brym, R. *The Capitalist Class. An International Study*, Brighton: Harvester, 46–72.

Maurice, M. and Sellier, F. 1979: Societal Analysis of Industrial Relations: A Comparison between France and West Germany. *British Journal of Industrial Relations*, 17, 3, 322–36.

Maurice, M. Sellier, F. and Silvestre, J.-J. 1986a: *The Social Foundations of Industrial Power. A Comparison of France and Germany*. London/Cambridge, Mass.: MIT.

Maurice, M. et al. 1986b: *Des Entreprises en mutation dans la crise. Apprentissage des technologies flexibles et émergence de nouveaux acteurs*. Aix: LEST.

Morville, P. 1985: *Les nouvelles politiques sociales du patronat*. Paris: La Découverte.

Mouriaux, R. 1983: *Les Syndicats dans la société française*. Paris: Fondation Nationale des Sciences Politiques.

Mouriaux, R. 1986: *Le Syndicalisme face à la crise*. Paris: La Découverte.

OECD 1991: *Economic Surveys. France 1990–1991*. Paris: OECD.

Petit, P. 1985: Heurs et malheurs face au rapport salarial: la France. In Boyer, R. (ed.), *La Flexibilité du travail en Europe*, Paris: La Déouverte, 35–65.

Rand Smith, W. 1990: Nationalization For What? Capitalist Power and Public Enterprise in Mitterrand's France. *Politics & Society*, 18, 1, 75–99.

Reynaud, J.D. 1975: *Les Syndicats en France*. Paris: Seuil.

Rojot, J. 1988: The Myth of French Exceptionalism. In. J. Barbash and K. Barbash (eds), *Theories and Concepts in Comparative Industrial Relations*, Columbia S. C.: South Carolina Press, 76–88.

Rosanvallon, P. 1988: *La Question syndicale*. Paris: Calmann-Lévy.

Ross, G. 1982: The Perils of Politics: French Unions and the Crisis of the 1970s. In P. Lange, G. Ross, and M. Vannicelli (eds), *Unions, Change and Crisis: French and Italian Union Strategy and the Political Economy, 1945–1980*, London: Allen & Unwin, 13–93.

Rozenblatt, P. 1991: La Forme coordination: une catégorie sociale révélatrice de sens. *Sociologie du Travail*, 33, 2, 239–54.

Segrestin, D. 1990: Recent Changes in France. In G. Baglioni and C. Crouch (eds), *European Industrial Relations* London: Sage, 97–126.

Sellier, F. 1984: *La Confrontation sociale en France: 1936–1981*. Paris: PUF.

Sellier, F. and Sylvestre, J.J. 1986: Unions' Policies in the Economic Crisis in France. In R. Edwards, P. Garonna and F. Tödtling (eds), *Unions in Crisis and Beyond*, London: Auburn House, 173–227.

Shorter, E. and Tilly, C. 1974: *Strikes in France 1830–1968*. Cambridge: Cambridge University Press.

Sisson, K. 1987: *The Management of Collective Bargaining. An International Comparison*. Oxford: Blackwell.

Sisson, K., Waddington, J. and Whitston, C. 1991: Company Size in the European Community. *Human Resource Management Journal*, 2, 1, 94–109.

Sisson, K., Waddington, J. and Whitston, C. 1992: The Structure of capital in the European Community: The Size of Companies and the Implications for Industrial Relations. Warwick Papers in Industrial Relations, no. 38, February. Coventry: IRRU.

Syzman, J. 1983: *Governments, Markets and Growth*. Oxford: Martin Robertson.

Thollon-Pommerol, V. 1990: Les groupes et la déformation du système productif. *Economie et Statistique*, 229, Février, 21–8.

Visier, L. 1990: A l'Épreuve des coordinations. *CFDT Aujourd'hui*, July, 97, 21–32.

Visser, J. 1990: *In Search of Inclusive Unionism*. Deventer: Kluwer.

14

Portugal: Industrial Relations Under Democracy

José Barreto

Introduction

Political and Economic Background

Major political, economic and social changes have taken place in Portugal over the last two decades. In 1974 the authoritarian, conservative and corporatist regime that had ruled the country for over forty years was overthrown. The right of free association was restored, political parties were created or emerged from the underground. Democratization was threatened by a communist-inspired revolutionary movement which led the country to the brink of violent conflict and was to have enduring consequences for Portuguese society. The largest national industrial and financial groups were nationalized in 1975, many hundreds of small and medium-sized enterprises were put under direct state control or were run by the workers and nearly one million hectares of land were collectivized after having been occupied by their workforces.

In 1975 the African colonies gained their independence. This meant the loss of Portugal's protected markets and access to resources in Africa, and led to a massive influx of white colonists. In 1975 and 1976 free elections based on universal suffrage were held for the first time in the country's history. A new constitution was approved, proclaiming the transition to socialism under a system of liberal democratic institutions, but subsequent revisions in 1982 and 1989 removed the main doctrinal references, paving the way for the current process of reprivatization. The country has been governed since 1976 by the socialists (PS, centre left) or the social democrats (PSD, centre right). The PSD has been in power since 1980: in coalition with the Christian democrats (CDS, right) until 1983, with the socialists between 1983 and 1985 and alone since then, having won an absolute majority in the 1987 and 1991 general elections. These elections confirmed a trend towards the polarization of Portuguese politics between the two centre parties, the PSD and the PS (with 50 per cent and 30 per cent of the votes respectively in 1991), and showed a sharp decline in support for the communists (PCP) (9 per cent in 1991) and the Christian democrats (4 per cent).

The revolutionary events of 1974–5 had a severe and lasting impact on the economy, compounding the consequences of the 1973–4 and 1980–1 oil shocks – devastating to a country highly dependent on oil imports – and the effects of world recession. Inflation, which had been increasing slowly from the late 1960s, jumped in 1973–4 to the highest annual rates since the First World War, and in 1984 was still near 30 per cent. Trends in productivity, private investment, unemployment, national debt, foreign debt and (since 1977) real wages also reflected a deep economic crisis from which the country did not emerge until the mid-1980s. Political instability – ten constitutional governments took office between 1976 and 1985, following six provisional governments in 1974–5 – constituted an additional source of economic uncertainty and affected the process of democratic consolidation.

In January 1986 Portugal became a member of the European Community, the final step in the long process of breaking with autarchy and integrating into the international economy. Subjected for a long period of its recent history to an isolationist and protectionist regime, oriented more towards the African colonies than to the rest of Europe, and lacking the conditions for endogenous economic growth, Portugal had basically remained a peripheral economy, unable to match the development of other European countries. Even the narrower development gap between Portugal and Spain had widened.

Nevertheless, economic structures had been undergoing profound transformation, particularly in the post-war period. Under the forty-year regime of Salazar and Caetano, a capitalist economy developed – though largely

Table 14.1　Structure of employment (1900–89) (% share of employed population)

	Primary sector	Secondary sector	Tertiary sector	Total employment (000s)	Wage & salary earners (000s)	Unemployment (000s)
1900	65.1	19.6	15.3	2,350	"	"
1911	61.2	23.4	15.4	2,386	"	"
1930	55.9	20.9	23.2	2,415	"	"
1940	52.6	21.1	26.3	2,920	(1,900)	"
1950	49.1	24.6	26.3	3,196	2,295	"
1960	43.9	29.1	27.0	3,315	2,453	"
1970	32.6	33.3	34.1	3,163	(2,500)	"
1980	27.9	35.8	36.3	3,961	2,673	340
1989	18.9	35.2	45.9	4,395	3,076	233

Source: INE-IE.

under state tutelage, in contrast to the successful liberalization pursued by the Francoist regime in Spain in the same period. Agriculture ceased to be the dominant sector and colonial trade became far less important as trade with western Europe grew.

The pace of industrialization had been very slow until the Second World War, when it began to accelerate sharply. Between 1900 and 1950 the proportion of the active population in the primary sector had fallen only from 65 per cent to 49 per cent, while employment in industry increased from 19 to 24 per cent. By the end of the 1960s, however, industry and services were the two leading sectors of employment. In 1988, agriculture still represented 20 per cent of employment but only 6 per cent of output, while the equivalent figures for industry were 35 and 38 per cent respectively, and for services, 44 and 56 per cent. Employment in the primary sector has been decreasing by almost 1 per cent of the total active population per year since 1980. (See tables 14.1–3.)

The rapid decline in agricultural employment in the 1960s and early 1970s was primarily due to massive emigration to western Europe, rather than the transfer of peasants to the industrial and service sectors within Portugal. Between 1960 and 1975 total emigration amounted to 1.5 million people, among them nearly 800,000 of working age, mainly from rural areas. By 1974 nearly a fifth of Portuguese citizens were living abroad – attracted by wages three or four times the level of those at home. Given the acceleration of economic growth in the same period (real GDP more than doubled from 1963 to 1973), emigration, together with the mobilization of soldiers for service in Africa, helped create an unprecedented labour shortage, pulling real wages up faster than ever before.

After 1974 the situation changed completely. Emigration fell abruptly as a result of host country restrictions. Steady economic growth gave way to stagnation and very slow recovery. Decolonization caused the sudden

Table 14.2 Structure of production
(1953–88) % of GDP in selected years

	Primary sector	*Secondary sector*	*Tertiary sector*
1953	33	28	39
1963	23	38	39
1966	20	43	37
1970	18	42	40
1976	15	43	42
1978	12	38	50
1980	10	40	50
1984	9	40	51
1988	6	38	56

Note: Comparability affected by a break in statistical series in 1977.
Source: INE-IE.

Table 14.3   Wage employment by main sectors (1989) % of all
wage and salary earners

Primary sector	4.8
Manufacturing industry and mining	33.6
Electricity, gas and water	1.2
Construction	9.8
Commerce, restaurants and hotels	11.0
Transportation and communications	4.7
Banking, insurance and real estate	4.6
Central and local administration	10.0
Public and private education and health services	10.5
Other services	9.8
Total	100.0

Source: INE-IE.

return of many hundreds of thousands of settlers and soldiers. These developments resulted in a labour surplus far more severe than the shortage that had preceded it. Unemployment grew to unprecedented levels (though still considerably lower than in Spain). From a merely frictional rate of 1–1.5 per cent up to the first quarter of 1974, the percentage of registered job seekers climbed to 7 per cent in 1976, and remained steady at 7–9 per cent before falling to 5 per cent in 1988–90 and 4 per cent in 1991. Simultaneously, however, the volume of employment has grown much faster than elsewhere in western Europe, partly as a result of the rapid growth in female employment, from 26 per cent of total employment in 1970 to 42 per cent in 1989. Between the beginning of the emigration boom of the 1960s and 1980, the female participation rate more than doubled to nearly 45 per cent; it has been rising ever since, and now stands at almost 60 per cent (compared with 80 per cent for males). Female employment is dominant in education and health and in some traditional labour-intensive industries – its share is 91 per cent in the strongest exporting industry, clothing, and 54 per cent in textiles, both with wage levels below the average for manufacturing industry.

Tertiarization began to intensify in the 1960s. Services became the dominant sector in terms of both employment and output during the 1970s and their relative weight is still increasing rapidly. One of the main reasons is the spectacular growth of public education, health, and social welfare services – all of which had lagged far behind those of other European countries – and of public administration in the decade following the 1974 revolution. The continuous growth of the tertiary sector is also due to the expansion of activities such as tourism, distribution, banking, insurance and related services.

Post-war industrialization was at first driven by import-substitution policies. It was concentrated in basic sectors protected from competition and it relied largely on domestic capital. In the late 1950s and early 1960s there was a shift in economic policy with Portugal's membership of EFTA (1959) and the subsequent opening up of the economy to direct foreign investment. Such investment increased significantly up to 1974 as multinationals took advantage of Portugal's strategic location and its low wages and taxes. Foreign-owned plants were generally integrated into international production and marketing networks, and dependent on component imports. In many cases, all or most of local production was destined for export. Export capacity in traditional sectors (food, textiles, clothing and footwear, and forestry-based industries) as well as new ones (machinery, transport equipment, chemicals) was thus frequently controlled by multinational companies, sometimes in association with national capital. Few complementary activities were generated locally by this pattern of investment, and it contributed little to the dissemination of advanced technology or skills.

From the late 1960s, the government and the leading national economic groups launched a highly ambitious industrialization plan, based on the promotion of new basic industries such as petrochemicals, mining, nuclear energy, basic metals, automobiles, shipbuilding and machinery, and strengthening the economic ties with the African colonies. The oil shocks and their after-effects, wide-scale industrial restructuring in Europe, and the events of 1974–5 in Portugal contributed to the failure of this massive project, although elements of it were revived by the democratic governments.

In general, Portugal's status as provider of mainly unskilled and low paid labour was consolidated. But with obsolete production methods and marketing techniques in the traditional exporting sectors, even low wages could not preserve Portugal's competitiveness in markets where the newly industrialized Asian economies were its main competitors: in 1990 wages in the Portuguese textile and clothing industries were already behind those of several non-European countries traditionally accused of 'social dumping'. EC membership and increased international competition made industrial restructuring and modernization more pressing than ever. A massive programme of investment in basic infrastructure, technological development, vocational training, and industrial innovation is currently being implemented. Since Portugal joined the EC, direct foreign investment in manufacturing industry has also increased very rapidly.

Given the probable effect of industrial restructuring on jobs, the significant fall in unemployment over the last few years is unlikely to be maintained in the 1990s, especially after 1993. The textile industry alone may have to eliminate at least 15 per cent of its work force over the next few years. The current privatization programme may have similar effects. A less favourable outlook for the black economy in the 1990s may also worsen unemployment. Likewise, the return of double-digit inflation since 1989, and the need to bring Portuguese inflation rates in line with the EC average, have led the government to adopt new deflationary policies with probable repercussions on employment growth.

Industrial Relations in Twentieth-Century Portugal

The years following the overthrow of the authoritarian regime saw radical changes in industrial relations attitudes, practices, and structures. The legal and institutional framework of the old regime was at first believed to provide a basis for the transition to a new system, and, indeed, much of the so-called 'corporative organization' was maintained, at least provisionally. But a gradual reform of the existing framework proved impossible; until the foundations of a democratic constitutional order were finally laid in 1976, social upheaval and a power struggle between opposing ideologies had a devastating effect on Portuguese industrial relations. After decades of corporatist repression, the new balance of power boosted the bargaining position of workers and unions. Wages and social security benefits improved spectacularly in 1974 and 1975. Claims, disputes and bargaining processes were increasingly politicized and subject to partisan manipulation, and deep divisions appeared in the union movement.

At the same time, and partly as a consequence of these traumatic political developments, the economic situation was rapidly worsening. Mass unemployment combined with high inflation, huge budget deficits and recession exerted overwhelming pressure on the labour market, placed heavy burdens on enterprises, and compelled successive governments to adopt deflationary economic policies and an interventionist role in labour matters.

Historical Background

The influence of these political and economic factors on the current industrial relations system must be seen against the background of earlier historical developments. The evolution of industrial relations in twentieth-century Portugal falls into three broad periods, resulting from two great divides in the country's contemporary political history: the establishment of an authoritarian corporatist regime in 1933 and the foundation of a modern democratic state after the 1974–5 revolution.

The Early Years

The first period begins in the last century and covers the liberal monarchical and republican regimes, embracing the initial stage of industrialization. Although this period saw the emergence of the first working class interest organizations and their subsequent legalization (1891), incipient industrialization did not favour the development of a strong union movement. Employers were poorly organized, mainly in multi-sector regional associations, and given to lobbying and political action. The union movement was originally linked with the relatively weak Socialist Party; however, the early decades of this century saw a decline in socialist influence within the unions in favour of the anarchists, the revolutionary trade unionists and (in the 1920s) the communists.

The triumph of French-style anarcho-syndicalism was consummated by the end of the First World War, leading to the formation of the CGT, the first well-organized Portuguese union confederation. The CGT proclaimed the self-sufficiency of trade unionism, repudiated party links and involvement in bourgeois politics, and advocated 'direct' class struggle. Its vision of society was dependent on the success of a revolutionary general strike, which never came. Inspired by changes in union structure elsewhere in Europe, where mechanization and mass production were far more widespread than in Portugal, the CGT tried to promote industry-wide unions (only white-collar employees were organized separately).

Collective bargaining was not among CGT's most valued forms of action, but some affiliated unions practised it. In reality, very few industrial agreements were concluded during the first quarter of the century. Liberal governments made no attempt to provide a legislative framework for collective bargaining (although they did introduce ineffectual legislation on disputes procedures), and only a minority of employers were interested in taking wages and other conditions out of competition. Great disparities between companies and industries also discouraged multi-employer bargaining, which small firms systematically resisted. Unions lacked the strength to impose regular bargaining on employers, or to control the supply of labour unilaterally. Moreover, workers and unions were divided by particular occupational interests and strategies. This was reflected in a controversy over the suitable structure for unions: should workers be organized along industrial or occupational lines? In the course of the century the question was to be raised repeatedly without being finally resolved.

Radicalization may have been a major factor in the decline of unionization and affiliation to the CGT after the membership peak of 1920–1, when the confederation represented no more than 80,000 workers. A communist secession in 1925 only accelerated the decay of the union movement, which was in complete disarray when in 1926 a military coup – supported by the political party of businessmen and owners, the UIE (*União dos Interesses Económicos*) – suspended liberal-democratic institutions.

The Period of Authoritarian Rule, 1926–74

The period of military rule, leading to the Salazar dictatorship (1933–68), opens the second broad phase of Portuguese industrial relations. Strikes were banned (1927), the CGT was dissolved, and the multi-party system suppressed. The existing free unions were tolerated until a new Constitution (1933) and the *Estatuto do Trabalho Nacional* (National Labour Statute), a version of its Italian namesake, introduced the compulsory framework of labour relations and interest representation for the next four decades.

The 'New State' aimed to supersede liberal democracy and class struggle. State intervention played a major role in regulating the market economy through market protection measures, licensing of new enterprises and foreign investments, provision of state finance, economic planning, and authoritarian control of prices, wages and rents. Independent trade unionism was rejected for two well-known reasons: its traditional relationship with political movements and the threat it was believed to represent to economic stability.

The corporatist regime created a system of single unions in every occupation or sector and region, the so-called *sindicatos nacionais* (national unions). Union leaders were selected for their political trustworthiness. Unionization was formally voluntary, but non-members were usually compelled to pay dues. Despite their obvious lack of autonomy, the corporatist unions succeeded in organizing more or less 'voluntarily' an increasing proportion of workers and employees: in 1973, 841,000 or 36 per cent of all wage and salary earners were members (another 25 per cent were compulsory contributors, and the remaining 39 per cent mostly belonged to the sectors such as public administration, public services, and agriculture where unionization was not permitted). Enjoying a legal monopoly of representation, the national unions were often able to take a stand in support of their members. Even the underground PCP occasionally acknowledged the efforts of some formal union leaders. From the early 1940s, already under the leadership of Alvaro Cunhal (still in charge in 1991), the communists periodically appealed to the workers to join the national unions and participate in their activities.

In theory, a prominent function of national unions should have been collective bargaining, since the regime – in marked contrast to the Franco regime in Spain – believed that it represented one of the most important features of corporatist industrial relations and the only means of achieving the goals of class cooperation enshrined in the Constitution. In practice, collective bargaining was a state-directed process. But even watered-down bargaining under strict state supervision and with cooperative unions aroused strong employer resistance. In the absence of effective pressure and of any legal obligation to bargain, the main industrial sectors (textiles, metal, construction, chemicals) escaped collective regulation until the late 1960s. In these sectors, a limited number of enterprises were occasionally prepared, at the government's request, to conclude a multi-employer agreement with the unions. Collective agreements at company level were very exceptional and not articulated with sectoral provisions. Multi-employer collective bargaining ensured that union action would not be encouraged within the enterprise and that the handling of conflicting interests would be transferred to industry-level corporatist bodies or to government departments.

The government was soon compelled to rely on direct statutory regulation of sectors and occupational groups, in order to restore basic minimum wage levels. Between the 1950s and the 1970s, statutory regulation became less frequent, but the threat of state intervention was a means of persuading employers to accept collective bargaining. Following the 1974 revolution, direct regulation was again widely used by the government to fill the gaps caused by the failure of a growing number of collective negotiations. Until 1985, when it practically disappeared, direct regulation continued as an alternative to regular bargaining.

With the national unions cast – at best – in the role of supplicants, and the Ministry of Corporations (the successor of the old Ministry of Labour) playing a decisive role in the elaboration of so-called collective agreements, it may be concluded that until the late 1960s, wages and other conditions were generally established directly or indirectly by the government or, more often, individually determined on the labour market. None the less, the corporatist regime paid particular attention to white-collar unions, partly in an attempt to ensure middle-class support but also in order to establish a model of 'constructive' unionism for the working class. Unions representing banking, insurance and office employees among others enjoyed more favourable treatment and could exert more effective influence; as a result these groups were covered by regularly amended collective agreements. The banking unions were the first to be allowed to appoint workplace delegates (*delegados sindicais*).

Until 1969 only individual grievances – not interest conflicts or industrial disputes – were admitted and regulated by law. A plan of 1934 to submit collective interest conflicts to the labour courts was abandoned as the government chose to deal itself with conflicting interests in a discretionary and unpublicized way. In practice, strikes and other forms of protest or pressure, though illegal and severely repressed, never disappeared completely and from time to time a wave of conflict reminded the government that corporatist harmony had to be maintained by force.

Under the corporatist regime employers were also supposed to create new organizations stipulated by law, the *grémios nacionais* (national guilds), but in general they did so promptly only when compelled to associate by specific government decree. In many industries or regions employers resisted corporatist association when it was merely voluntary. Several important guilds were founded only in the 1950s or the 1960s. As long as they were not formally organized, employers had a legal pretext to avoid collective bargaining. Lack of interest in or even veiled hostility towards their official organizations were quite common among industrialists, who complained of the *grémios*' lack of power, autonomy, effectiveness and leadership (Makler 1976). Similar factors lay behind workers' discontent with official unions, but the regime was far more benevolent towards employers, whose old interest associations, dating from the last century, were allowed to survive alongside the corporatist network.

The sectoral-regional unions and guilds represented workers and employers separately, but in the late 1950s the regime introduced a national level of mixed class representation, the 'corporations' (of industry, agriculture, commerce, etc.) This structure, similar to that of Francoist Spain, excluded single-class peak associations: union or employer confederations as they had existed in the past were viewed as 'classist' organizations, incompatible with corporatism.

In its final years, the authoritarian regime under its new leader Caetano (1968–74) attempted to move from state corporatism towards a system of industrial relations closer to western European patterns and more compatible with a faster pace of industrialization, economic growth and internationalization. The regime tried to foster greater union autonomy and more responsible collective bargaining: regular bargaining was seen as a way of improving productivity, encouraging better management of the labour force, and redressing the low pay levels that were seen as a main cause of mass emigration.

An early consequence of the reforms was that fairer elections led to 30 to 40 primary unions (out of 325) being taken over by elements opposed to the regime; these were mainly communists and so-called 'progressive Catholics', but a wide range of other political beliefs were also represented. The opposition forces were particularly successful in gaining control of the richer and better-organized white-collar unions. During the 1960s, the middle class had become increasingly less supportive of the regime, often for political rather than economic reasons. The relatively well-paid banking employees supplied the most active component of the emerging union movement.

In addition, collective bargaining was made legally compulsory, with fixed terms for engaging in negotiations and reaching agreement. The prohibition of strikes was not lifted, but the law finally admitted the concept of industrial dispute, and state-sponsored, in effect compulsory, conciliation and arbitration procedures were introduced. Collective bargaining was revitalized by the reforms, and from the regime's point of view became a source of considerable tension. Growing politicization turned industrial disputes into the main form of action against the regime and the government was soon forced to retreat on some crucial elements of reform. Union leaders were removed and persecuted as the fight for further union rights continued. The creation of a central coordinating body of 'representative' unions was attempted, but it was outlawed. Nevertheless, the embryo of a future union confederation (Intersindical) remained active as a semi-clandestine organization until 1974.

Authoritarian corporatism suspended for almost half a century the free development of industrial relations, which were largely dominated by the state in almost every respect. Its attempt to oversee a project of class cooperation failed completely: the mentality of workers and employers had not been transformed, at least not in the direction that the regime had hoped.

Paradoxically, however, at the end of the corporatist regime, unions and employer associations had far larger memberships than ever before. Under government supervision, the unions had gained official acknowledgement and a status and respectability not achieved in the past, particularly since the rise of the anarcho-syndicalists in the early decades of the century. Sectoral collective bargaining was finally becoming generalized, though it was still broadly state-controlled and more favourably regarded by the unions than by the employers, who often criticized the reforms for being too generous to the unions. In retrospect it might be said that state corporatism eventually succeeded in imposing union recognition and collective bargaining upon employers, although its main initial purpose had been to subjugate the unions to its authoritarian corporatist vision.

The Fall of the Authoritarian Regime and the Democratic Transition

The third and most recent period in the development of industrial relations begins with the fall of the authoritarian regime and the formal dismantling of the corporatist system. The transition was abrupt and turbulent, in contrast to the much more gradual and consensual Spanish transition to democracy. The radical course of political events influenced the evolution of industrial relations at all levels, from the workplace to industry collective bargaining and labour legislation.

The transformation of industrial relations as a consequence of the democratic transition was bound to be a difficult process for many employers accustomed to the shelter of state. The transition to democracy in Spain, for all its comparative smoothness in political terms, was also accompanied by an upsurge in labour disputes: until the end of the 1970s the level of industrial conflict in Spain was far higher than in Portugal (as had also been the case before the revolution). But in Portugal, the background to industrial conflict was, for more than a year in the mid-1970s, the construction of a socialist society, rather than the transition to liberal democracy. This made for a profound rupture in industrial relations, reflected, for example, in the widespread purges of managements by their work forces and in the use of intimidation and physical violence in collective bargaining.

Following the defeat of the revolution, its legacy continued to influence industrial relations. The state's intervention in the economy had extended well beyond the classic confines of a market economy during the revolutionary period. Labour legislation and the direct regulation of working conditions in both public and private sectors had mushroomed; but in any case there was little room for collective bargaining in the run-down and technologically antiquated private sector which was in no position to offer concessions to employees (although public enterprises could always rely on large state budget deficits to finance the cost of collective agreements).

Successive impasses at the negotiating table led the unions to demand increasing direct intervention by government. In 1978 the great majority of wage earners were covered by direct statutory regulation in individual industries. A national minimum wage was introduced by the government in 1974, and has been revised every year since then. A revolutionary law of 1975, only partially amended afterwards, made individual and collective dismissals extremely difficult. Another prohibited the reduction of working hours in individual or collective contracts without the government's consent, and the scope of collective bargaining was further reduced by other measures. Maximum rates for all statutory and collectively bargained pay increases, known as 'wage ceilings', were imposed by the government from 1977. In addition, shortly after the revolution a universal and compulsory system of social security was extended to the whole population. Thus the role of the state in industrial relations expanded considerably during the transition to democracy, even when compared to the corporatist period.

In the 1980s, the statist trend began to decline. With a significant improvement in employment and real wages from 1985 and the return of political stability – at the cost of the comprehensive defeat of the Left – industrial relations gradually became less tense and politicized. Important changes in union structures and strategies also favoured a new climate in labour-management relations and the resumption of regular collective bargaining, though industrial relations still lacked dynamism. The recent emergence of a new relationship between the peak employer and union organizations, partly as a result of institutionalized tripartite 'social concertation' since 1984, may be a further sign of increased autonomy from the state.

The Employers and their Organizations

Characteristics of Portuguese Employers

Until the nationalizations of 1975, seven large corporate groups dominated the Portuguese economy, from the financial sector to industry and colonial trade. The groups had grown up under the protection of the 'New State', forming oligopolies in sectors sheltered from external competition. The corporatist policy of *condicionamento industrial* discouraged competition between these consortia. Some economic groups had their own labour and social policies, cross-cutting the sectoral logic of corporatist representation and collective bargaining. In the final years of the regime, they promoted paternalistic representation structures within their companies, as an alternative to dialogue with the still predominantly occupation-based unions (some enterprises had to deal with as many as twenty or thirty different unions).

In the spring of 1975, the immense economic power of large capital disappeared almost overnight with the nationalization of the whole domestic financial sector and the largest industrial firms, giving the state control over the bulk of investment and credit. The exporting and competitive industries, where smaller firms predominated, were mostly spared, but the nationalization of the financial sector also gave the state control over a large number of medium-sized enterprises. The leading economic groups were depicted as the upholders and major beneficiaries of the repressive corporatist order and accused of resisting the democratic changes. In reality, the authoritarian regime had not so much entailed the control of the state by the capitalist class as the reverse. The adherence of the economic elites to the revolution in its early stages was apparently sincere; conflicts emerged later, when the democratic revolution altered course towards state socialism, but even then the decisive resistance did not initially come from big capital.

The radical nationalization process prompted a shift of private enterprise to the competitive and exporting sectors. Multinational companies were not directly affected by the nationalizations and only a few closed their Portuguese subsidiaries following the large pay rises of 1974–5. Many multinationals not only survived the revolution but were able to grow faster than before, with successive devaluations of the currency helping to boost exports.

The role of the state as employer was considerably enlarged during and after the revolution, with the emergence of over 120 new public enterprises – representing 10 per cent of all wage earners at that time – and a steady growth in public services and public administration. By the end of the 1980s, the share of the public sector in the total labour force amounted to 17 per cent (22 per cent of all wage and salary earners), having more than doubled in twenty years.

In 1989, 48 out of the 500 largest firms were still public or state controlled, 108 were foreign-based multinationals and the remainder domestic private companies, but 19 out of the 20 largest employers (including banks) were public, some controlling entire sectors. The current privatization of nationalized companies, initiated in the late 1980s, is leading to the break-up of some large enterprises even before they are sold off, as in the case of Telecom Portugal (separated from the Post Office), although a number of privatized firms are likely to look for mergers in order to compete in the single European market. The privatization process was still very far from completion in 1991. Concerns about a possible loss of domestic control over strategic sectors have been insistently expressed by Portuguese capitalists dispossessed in the so-called 'wild-cat nationalizations' of 1975 who are seeking favourable treatment from the government. But unions, particularly the communist-led Intersindical, have also voiced opposition to the loss of national economic control: up to 1986, Intersindical had fought (with the PCP) a solitary campaign against Portugal's EEC membership on the same grounds. Other Portuguese entrepreneurs, however, are showing an interest in acquiring control of privatized companies, often in partnership with foreign investors.

Private enterprises are marked by great disparities in size, technology, work-force skills and conditions of employment. There is a higher proportion of small firms than anywhere else in the EC, with 75 per cent of firms (excluding self-employed individuals and companies without waged employees) employing fewer than 10 workers (see table 14.4). Since the 1970s, domestic companies (though not multinationals) have tended to move away from large concentrations of workers in single establishments; corporate organization is increasingly characterized by greater flexibility, mobility and decentralization of production. This reflects financial problems, economic and political uncertainty and bad memories of the revolutionary period, but also strategic considerations, interna-

Table 14.4   Company size and employment in Portugal (1989)

Employees	Number of companies	% of companies	Average staff	Share of employment
1–9	99,113	75.3	4	17.3
10–19	16,227	12.3	13	10.3
20–49	10,306	7.8	30	14.7
50–99	3,359	2.6	69	10.9
100–199	1,512	1.1	138	9.8
200–499	853	0.6	298	12.0
500–	350	0.3	1,510	25.0
Total	131,720	100.0	16	100.0

Source: MESS (Quadros do Pessoal).

tional market trends, new management policies and the introduction of advanced technologies. The rebuilding of large domestic economic groups (partly the old pre-revolution groups, partly new ones) since the mid-1980s also seems to be following this pattern.

Foreign multinationals are the leading companies in several industrial sectors, notably cars, chemicals, petrochemicals, food, clothing, electrical equipment and electronics. As a rule, they can afford to offer better wages and conditions, well above the minima established by industry agreements. The national export-oriented firms, predominantly small or medium-sized, have been increasingly compelled to improve productivity, technology, management and commercial strategies, but many have so far failed to keep pace with modernization. Only low wages (especially of women workers, who were paid on average 32 per cent less than men in 1991) and the resources of the black economy – including the widespread use of child labour – have enabled these firms to go on exporting. The internal market is also becoming more competitive and over the last decade many internally oriented domestic firms have faced increasing foreign and national competition, and have had to prepare themselves for the completion of the single European market.

Since the early and mid-1980s, the restructuring of declining heavy industries such as shipbuilding and steel, and of sectors (such as textiles) facing tougher international competition, has led to large-scale redundancies and chronic unemployment, creating serious social problems in regions (such as the Setúbal Peninsula and the Ave Valley) heavily reliant on single industries.

In the public sector, the ending of state monopolies and preparations for privatization have also led to widespread job losses. The sector has often been associated with overstaffing and rigidities arising from collective bargaining (e.g. automatic wage increases, seniority-based promotion, and obstacles to job mobility). Company managements are trying to solve these problems without declaring war on the unions, and workers affected by rationalization are being compensated. However, less consensual restructurings, involving drastic cuts in the work force or the dismantling of collective bargaining, are taking place in some chronically loss-making 'dinosaurs' in heavy industry and transportation.

Ten years ago, such developments, and indeed the acceptance of the very notion of privatization by the unions, would have been inconceivable. On government instructions, state companies have used direct incentives to entice workers to accept change and this has helped soften the unions' defence of the public sector – though perhaps not as much as the repeated defeats of the left in the 1985, 1987 and 1991 general elections. The workers themselves have become increasingly aware of the requirements of competitiveness and they are also concerned by the prospects of foreign takeover. In Centralcer (the leading breweries, which once had a 70 per cent domestic market share), half of the 2,400 staff signed a petition to the government in 1990, shortly before privatization, asking for control of the company to be returned to its former owners and claiming that it should never have been nationalized in the first place. (Centralcer is now controlled by a foreign multinational.)

Employers' Organizations

The transformation of the employers' organizations began soon after the revolution of April 1974. The old *grémios* were renamed 'associations' and developed into autonomous and genuinely representative bodies, even if they lost members with the ending of compulsory affiliation. Few new primary associations were formed and the regional and sectoral domains of the existing organizations were also retained. The first significant step away from the corporatist representative structure was the creation of the CIP (the Confederation of Portuguese Industry) in June 1974, followed later by the CAP (for agriculture) and CCP (for commerce), to which the majority of the former guilds affiliated. These confederations may also be seen in some ways as the successors of the old vertical or mixed 'corporations', which had been seized by union activists and dismantled following the revolution (Gaspar 1988).

The main objectives of the employer organizations between 1974 and 1975 were to counterbalance the new political influence and bargaining power of labour, to create an entirely different image for the entrepreneurial class, to seek accommodation with the new rulers and, subsequently, to resist the revolutionary process. They largely failed in all these aims. Thousands of owners and top managers chose to leave the country and employers' organizations were compelled to adopt a strategy of mere survival until 1976.

Apart from some experience of industry bargaining in the final years of the corporatist regime, the 'national guilds' had functioned largely as official channels of communication with the government. (The large economic groups were able to influence the political system more directly, through personal contacts with different sectors of the state apparatus (Makler 1976).) As a result, the new employers' organizations and most individual employers were ill-equipped for free collective bargaining, and for dealing with a wide range of claims, strikes and new workplace organizations (the 'workers' commissions' – see below). Thus, a major aspect of the post-1974 reorganization was the development of bargaining structures in the sectoral-regional associations, under the guidance of CIP. However, the confederation was unable to impose a common bargaining strategy on employers.

Initially CIP adopted a politically neutral or even apolitical image, seeking to deflect accusations of connivance with the old regime. Its leaders were chosen for their lack of involvement with the previous order or with the main economic groups. CIP policies were conciliatory and reformist: it accepted the legalization of strikes, albeit at a time when the regulation of industrial disputes seemed the only way of controlling an unprecedented strike wave; and it supported a 'concerted economy', tripartite arrangements, 'industrial democracy' and negotiations at all levels with the unions. It also backed the introduction of a national minimum wage and accepted the unions' case for narrower wage differentials as a way of reducing social inequalities. CIP proposed an ambitious national housing programme financed by employers and the state and administered jointly with the unions, and in early 1975 it was even prepared to accept a programme of moderate nationalizations and a larger state role in the management of the economy. CIP's reformist proposals were simply ignored by Intersindical, the sole union confederation at the time. To Intersindical, closely linked to the orthodox PCP, CIP embodied the threat of a return to 'fascism' and 'monopoly capitalism'. In 1975, CIP's headquarters were destroyed in a riot and its dissolution was demanded by several labour organizations.

With the end of the revolution in November 1975 and the gradual emergence of the centre parties as the main political actors, CIP's neutral image rapidly waned. Open links with political organizations were still avoided, despite the existence of numerous personal ties with the CDS and the PSD; indeed, CIP adopted a far more unambiguous and uncompromising political stance than the parties it was associated with. Often referred to as the party of the entrepreneurial class, it was in the forefront of the struggle against surviving revolutionary measures and the economic policies of the left and centre-left democratic governments (Gaspar 1988).

From 1976, while the entrepreneurial classes began their slow recovery from the shock treatment of 1974–5, the main targets of CIP's criticism were the economic section of the new constitution, the legislation on dismissals, industrial disputes and 'workers' commissions', soaring budget deficits, 'marxist' economic planning and the inefficiency of public enterprises (not affiliated to CIP). In the early 1980s, the new CIP leadership began openly to demand the ending of state monopolies, privatization of the economy and the drawing up of a new constitution. CIP increasingly intervened in politics, for example supporting or opposing government coalitions. Although it lacked representativeness and provided few services to its members, it was none the less a powerful pressure group advocating a reduced state role in the economy and the improvement of the competitiveness of Portuguese enterprises (Pinto 1990).

Between 1977 and 1984 CIP abandoned its previous proposals for tripartite 'social contracts' and until 1990 rejected any bilateral negotiations with the union confederations. Despite their doubts over the value of concertation, the employers' confederations took their seats in the *Conselho Permanente de Concertação Social* (CPCS) set up by the PS–PSD coalition government. Two years later they signed the first agreement on incomes policy with the government and UGT, the socialist-led union confederation. The initially grudging acceptance of the CPCS gradually gave way to active support for institutionalized tripartite concertation. In 1990, a series of unprecedented bilateral meetings between the employer and union confederations took place. Although they had not resulted in any agreement by the end of 1991, they paved the way for the tripartite negotiation of a broad Economic and Social Agreement in October 1990 (see the section on social concertation below) and for additional agreements on single issues in 1991.

There are no reliable data on membership of employers' associations. Since the early 1980s, CIP has claimed to represent 35,000 private companies, nearly 75 per cent of the total. However, a recent empirical study (Cardoso et al. 1990) covering companies with at least ten employees indicates a 60 per cent rate of affiliation to the primary associations, which are not all members of the CIP; while according to union sources, overall membership density of employers' associations may be even lower than the figure of around 30 per cent for unionized workers.

After 1974, the old regional multi-sector associations, which had survived state corporatism, were retained as a parallel but functionally differentiated structure. They provide a wide range of services to member firms on technological development, sales promotion, international fairs and vocational training, and leave industrial relations functions almost entirely to the sectoral associations. The regional associations, as they are known (though the sector associations are also regionally based), have smaller memberships, but they are more locally rooted and far better organized, and have an image of political moderation and pragmatism. Over 3,000 industrial firms, including public enterprises and subsidiaries of multinationals, are directly affiliated to the largest regional association, the Lisbon-based AIP (*Associação Industrial Portuguesa*).

The existence of two separate employer structures has led to a degree of competition between them, especially in manufacturing. Divergent attitudes towards the public sector, state intervention, economic policies, European integration, international competition and privatization, as well as deep-rooted regional rivalries, are the main causes of division within and among the various associations. This also explains CIP's hitherto unsuccessful attempt to affiliate AIP and other regional associations of industrialists, and the difficulties in setting up a unified national body to represent all business interests. After two failed launches in 1975 and

1979, CNEP (National Council of Portuguese Enterprises, grouping CIP, CAP and CCP), was reactivated in 1990, just before the first bilateral summit talks with the unions took place.

The Unions

The Phase of Communist Dominance of the Labour Movement

Almost fifty years after the dissolution of the CGT and the prohibition of strikes, and 41 years after the establishment of state corporatism, the restoration of free trade unions in 1974–6 coincided with communist hegemony in the labour movement and the emergence of deep ideological and political cleavages leading, eventually, to union pluralism (Barreto 1991).

In the final years of the old regime, opposition activists led by the communists had gained control of a number of 'national unions', which subsequently came together in Intersindical, a strongly politicized coordinating body soon banned by the government. Emerging from the underground following the revolution of 1974, Intersindical sought recognition as the legitimate peak organization of the emerging union movement. The 'national unions' themselves were spared dissolution, since some of them had already withdrawn from the orbit of the old regime and communists were rapidly extending their control over the remainder. Even compulsory dues for non-members were maintained by the new government at Intersindical's request.

The socialist and social-democratic parties had at first only very limited influence in the unions. The PS, founded in 1875, virtually disappeared in the 1930s following the establishment of the authoritarian regime, and its reorganization began only in 1973. The PSD was founded shortly after the fall of the old regime. In practice, the illegal PCP alone had managed to survive as an organized opposition force. Its strategy of infiltrating the corporatist unions gave it considerable room for manoeuvre in the transition to democracy, when the unions were at the forefront of the political process. Intersindical was the first organization to demand large-scale nationalizations.

In 1974–5 two-thirds of existing unions joined Intersindical. The confederation successfully headed off attempts to form rival unions, and won a legal monopoly under the union law of 1975 which prevented the establishment of new organizations in competition with existing ones, from workplace up to confederal level. Thus the corporatist system of single unions was perpetuated by the revolutionary government. Union structure and government became highly centralized, reproducing to some extent the internal organization of the PCP. New union structures were created to coordinate local unions in each region (*distrito*), directly financed by the confederation. Intersindical also took the initiative in setting up new associations in areas where unionization had not been allowed before.

While the communists were able to secure the leadership of almost the entire union organization, real control of the rank and file turned out to be much more problematic, as the unions attempted to moderate workers' demands and channel them towards the government, in which the PCP participated. Moreover, new workplace representative bodies, the *comissões de trabalhadores* (workers' commissions) began to emerge more or less spontaneously outside union control. Competing in some areas with the unions' workplace organization, they initiated negotiations over a wide range of issues, called strikes in the face of union opposition, frequently demanded purges of management and even took over the running of hundreds of small companies.

The workers' commissions were supported by various leftist and moderate factions opposed to the PCP and for a while they were seen as an alternative to the Intersindical organization. After the revolution, the workers' commissions were recognized by the constitution and regulated by law, which confined them to the 'supervision of management' (a dead letter in practice) and to participation in the administration of welfare matters within the firm.

Only about 1,000 such commissions have been officially registered, though many thousands could have been formed under the law (one may be elected in each establishment). A recent Intersindical survey, reported at the union's National Conference of December 1991, revealed that over 60 per cent of the registered commissions are now inactive, but in the public sector and in some large private enterprises they are regularly elected and operational. The initial conflict with the unions has largely subsided, and the electoral lists for the commissions are now usually organized or influenced by the unions. The unions were given exclusive collective bargaining rights in 1976; in practice, however, workers' commissions have a role in handling grievances, presenting claims and negotiating 'informally' at company or establishment level (see the section on collective bargaining below). The commissions also have the right to be consulted before the restructuring of companies or sectors, on redundancies, decisions concerning working hours or new grading or promotion criteria, etc. In a few cases, they have signed 'social contracts' with the managements of companies in economic difficulties, in order to avoid closure.

In 1975, the communist leadership of the union movement faced bitter criticism for its active support of the increasingly radical government. The struggle against the legal monopoly of Intersindical became a central political issue for the parties opposed to the communists' revolutionary objectives and in 1975 and 1976 the moderate socialist and social-democratic factions won the elections in a series of important, mainly white-collar, unions, which had previously been strongly represented in the Intersindical leadership.

The Emergence of Parallel Unions

The new constitution (1976) removed Intersindical's monopoly and allowed the free establishment of trade unions at any level. From 1976 on, new ('parallel') unions were created in almost every sector, occupation and professional category, with the exception of banking, which continues to be unitary. In 1978, moderate tendencies led by the unions of banking, insurance and office employees founded a second union confederation, UGT (*União Geral de Trabalhadores* – General Workers' Union). This alliance had the support of the two main parties, the PS and the PSD, finding common ground in their attempt to break the hegemony of the PCP and Intersindical over the union movement. UGT started out with 30 unions and currently has 60, against 150 for Intersindical (also known since 1977 as CGTP, *Confederação Geral dos Trabalhadores Portugueses*). The new confederation failed to attract the majority of existing independent unions.

Despite numerous mergers, the number of unions has risen from the 1974 figure of 328 to the current total of 370. This reflects the rapid rise in the number of independents during the 1980s, frequently as a result of the fragmentation of larger organizations. There are now more than 150, mostly small, occupational or even grade-based independent unions among groups such as airline pilots, train drivers, dockers and civil servants. Operating either as labour market cartels or as lobbying groups or both, they are highly cohesive and effective organizations, though they do not see themselves as part of the wider union movement. They share a common desire to avoid integration in broader organizations, to defend their particular interests and to preserve their autonomy from government and from political parties and ideologies. They reject egalitarian policies, narrow wage differentials and inter-occupational solidarity. UGT and Intersindical view them largely as egocentric interest organizations serving privileged minorities.

UGT has proposed the creation of a new organizational structure with a limited number of national industrial unions on the German or Austrian model (UGT has always had close links with the union movements of central Europe and Scandinavia – though not, given the traditional social, economic and political barriers between Portugal and its Iberian neighbour, with its namesake, the Spanish UGT). However, the plan has made little real progress. Traditionally-organized UGT unions have defended existing demarcations and have resisted even the most obvious mergers in banking, insurance, services, transport, education, and fisheries. The new national industry-based UGT unions in textiles and clothing, metal, chemicals, telecommunications, construction, energy, etc. are all weaker than Intersindical's corresponding industrial federations; and, with white-collar groups and their unions resisting absorption into large sectoral organizations, they have been unable to achieve the 'vertical' integration of different groups of workers (Intersindical has faced similar problems). Other occupational and territorial divisions also persist, sometimes nourished by the rivalry between socialists and social democrats. In 1988 a new confederation of professional and managerial unions was formed, but it still lacks representativity.

Thus the strongest national trend since 1976 has been the fragmentation of labour representation, together with the maintenance of occupational and territorial divisions inherited from the pre-1974 period. Even within the more ideologically homogeneous Intersindical, significant steps towards concentration have failed to eliminate many regional or occupational boundaries and it took the confederation a long time to set up a national network of 19 sectoral federations with effective powers. Up to 1987–8, inter-union competition and open hostility between Intersindical and UGT hindered joint action in collective bargaining and dealings with government. In recent years, however, there has been something of a reconciliation between them, especially with the joint calling of a successful national general strike in March 1988 against the liberalization of dismissals. Until 1991, the emerging collaboration between UGT and Intersindical was somewhat patchy, but there are now prospects of a much closer relationship in the 1990s. However, cooperation between individual unions in collective bargaining and joint action in industrial disputes are still the exception, particularly at industry level. This has led to the duplication of bargaining in many sectors, adding to the fragmentation caused by the growth of separate negotiations with independent unions.

Since there are no recognition procedures and the law does not stipulate any criteria of representativeness (the few legal requirements are not enforced, on the grounds that they may be unconstitutional), all unions are considered to be representative and have the same rights. Thus collective bargaining depends largely on the employers' willingness to negotiate with a particular union. This situation has permitted the employers, including public enterprises and the government, to help new UGT or independent unions get off the ground by rapidly reaching agreements with them; as a result, Intersindical's virtual 'bargaining monopoly' in manufacturing, construction, electricity, road and urban transport, post and telecommunications and large sections of the civil service, has been broken. UGT is dominant only in banking, insurance, white-collar occupations in industry and services, and some sectors of the public administration; while the independent unions organize professional and managerial staff and several categories of higher-paid workers with special bargaining power, mainly in the public sector.

Membership, Organization and Finances

According to probably somewhat inflated estimates, nearly 30 per cent of all wage and salary earners are unionized, corresponding to roughly one million people, but with a very unequal distribution across industries, between public and private sectors and between large and small enterprises. This places Portugal in the group of western European countries with the lowest union densities, but ahead of Spain, France and Greece.

Intersindical may represent 60 per cent of unionized workers, the UGT 30 to 35 per cent and the independent unions less than 10 per cent. All the largest organizations belong to Intersindical or UGT, which together account for 210 of the 370 unions.

Overall membership has fallen continuously since the late 1970s, although the effects of the old system of compulsory dues, abolished in 1975, continued to keep density artificially high until about 1977. In 1977, the compulsory check-off system was abolished by a socialist government, explicitly as a way of weakening Intersindical. While many public enterprises have agreed to deduct dues since then, private sector employers' associations have opposed cooperation in this field and contributions are now mostly collected by the unions.

Several other factors are more important in explaining declining membership. One is the very significant rise since 1976 of temporary work and of informal employment in the black economy. The phenomenon, as in Spain, reflects the pressure of high unemployment, but has been aggravated in Portugal by the persistence of rigid regulations on dismissals. The estimated proportion of informal employment in construction is 50 per cent, consisting overwhelmingly of (often illegal) immigrants from the former African colonies, but it is also significant in the clothing and footwear industries and certain services. Probably as a consequence, construction (the largest industry in employment terms, with over 300,000 wage earners) has a union density of barely 10 per cent, the lowest in the country. The loss of many thousands of jobs in union strongholds, poor member services, inter-union competition, union politicization and factionalism, the reluctance of younger workers to join unions, and employer pressures, are also commonly cited by union officials as explanations for falling membership.

The unions have experienced increasing financial difficulties. Added to the 'natural' causes of low union density, declining membership, the low level of dues, low wages, and the lack of resources inherited by most corporatist unions, the situation is considerably worsened by the duplication of resources and hence costs as a result of union pluralism. One consequence is that strike funds are relatively rare. Only small, cohesive, mostly independent unions with comparatively well-paid memberships (pilots, air traffic controllers, train drivers and so on) have such funds, and they use them to great effect.

The scarcity of resources obviously affects the confederations too. A considerable number of unions are unable to pay their affiliation fees and both UGT and Intersindical, as well as several primary unions, have always had to rely on 'international solidarity' in the form of substantial assistance from foreign union movements. UGT is notable in that over 50 per cent of its income from union contributions in 1990 came from just one of its 60 affiliates, the Union of Banking Employees of Southern Portugal, the richest and largest primary organization in the country, with 46,000 members.

The Lisbon-based banking union, prominent in the creation of Intersindical in 1970, and subsequently of UGT in 1978, has been governed successively by all the main factions and since 1988 has been led by an unusual alliance of socialists and communists. The singular success of banking unionism in Portugal (unionization approaches 90 per cent) is partly due to relatively privileged treatment under the corporatist regime, but membership has more than doubled since the revolution, in sharp contrast to the general trend. The Union of Metal Workers of Lisbon, for example, has lost nearly half of its former 70,000 members since 1975, when it was the leading union in Intersindical. In the banking unions, services to members are well developed, and the conduct of collective bargaining and industrial disputes has been very effective. Strikes are subject to ballots, internal factions cover the whole political spectrum, and the governing bodies are directly elected in well-contested elections with high turnouts. Very few unions combine the same features, none with a comparable membership.

Nevertheless, the multiplication of new domestic and foreign banks since the 1980s and the current privatization programme may pose a serious threat to the banking unions too. Private banks, where union density appears to be much lower, are offering considerably higher wages and adopting different approaches to personnel management and work organization; as a result, collective bargaining is losing some of its significance. New policies include greater job mobility, more flexible working hours, and, in the case of the largest new private bank, the Banco Comercial Português, the rejection of female employment; this flouts equal opportunity laws which have often not been enforced in practice, and has provoked a condemnatory report by the Commission for Equality in Work and Employment (*Comissão para a Igualdade no Trabalho e no Emprego*), a tripartite body created in the early 1980s.

The changes taking place in the banking sector may be duplicated in other industries as state monopolies are dismantled, and further developments are likely in response to the single European market. In the medium term, however, a drastic fall in unionization in privatized enterprises seems unlikely.

The number of full-time officials in Portuguese unions is very low – only 300 out of Intersindical's 5,000 officers are union employees, though some 'lay' representatives in large, mainly public, enterprises also work full-time for the union – and in general they are poorly qualified. The recruitment of younger officers is becoming increasingly difficult. A lack of resources and discrimination against activists (in the form of loss of pay and promotion) makes union jobs extremely unattractive, at least to skilled workers, and most activists are motivated primarily by strong political commitment. Party militancy may be viewed as a major force sustaining union organization within Intersindical and even in UGT. Religious motivation is also still important: although the church failed in its long-term attempts to promote Catholic trade unions, a considerable number of current union leaders and activists, including confederal officers, began their careers in the 'schools' of the *Juventude Operária Católica* and the *Liga Operária Católica*, particularly prior to the 1970s.

Union leaders and activists are given party responsibilities and political jobs (and even appointed to party executive bodies, although this is formally prohibited under the union law). Formally, only personal ties exist between unions and parties; the unions do not provide financial support to the parties, nor have they any right of representation in party bodies. During the 1980s, 5–9 per cent of members of parliament were UGT and Intersindical union officers or confederal leaders. In theory, the three political parties receiving the most votes are all pro-labour (Socialists, Communists and Social Democrats), though none of them emerged historically out of the union movement, which practically disappeared for a half century until the 1970s. With the advent of democracy, all the main parties sought to establish roots in the working class, and party activists played a large part in building and running the emerging union movement. As a result, the unions have functioned largely as vehicles of political influence. Over the last decade union action has become less ideologically determined, but the links between unions and party politics still prevail, except in the case of independent unions.

In the confederal bodies of UGT and in most of its affiliated unions there are formally organized political factions (*tendências*). They have constitutional rights such as the nomination of candidates to the leadership, and they are generally represented on union bodies on a proportional basis; in practice, the union's top executive body (the *secretariado executivo*) is composed of an equal number of socialists and social democrats. The factions are nevertheless considered to be independent from the corresponding party leaderships. Intersindical rejects organized factions, but permits a limited pluralism in confederal bodies, with a clear majority of communists and a minority of left-wing socialists, Catholics and other small groups.

The dominant communist influence in Intersindical makes it more centralized, cohesive and disciplined than UGT, where the main tendencies are more balanced and the ideological cement is far less important, even within the factions (several sub-factions exist). The UGT leadership finds it much harder than Intersindical to lay down common positions for its member unions on issues such as political action, tripartite concertation, collective bargaining and union structure (demarcations, mergers, etc.).

The predominance of political action in Portuguese trade unionism results from several structural features: the historically minor role of societal self-regulation (including collective bargaining) compared to statutory regulation, partisan control of the unions, the prevailing weakness of unions and a chronic bias of employers' associations towards lobbying and reliance upon government. Following the 1974 revolution, these factors were reinforced by economic crisis and a much larger state role in the economy. Unable to prevent the rise in unemployment or the fall in real wages between 1976 and 1985, the unions directed their energies to preventing the watering down of the labour legislation passed after the revolution, a legal framework which Intersindical praised as the most advanced in western Europe. The unions have been only partially successful in their aim, but they used political action, including a successful general strike in 1988, to secure what may well be their major achievement in the 1980s: the maintenance of union rights and the protection of the main legal provisions on job security and the right to strike. For UGT, the creation of the Permanent Council for Social Concertation by the coalition government in 1984 was another outstanding achievement.

Union pluralism, which does not have solid traditions in Portugal, was largely a reflection of the deep political divisions of the revolutionary period. Subsequent domestic political developments and major international events have helped soften those divisions: socialists and communists have remained together in opposition to the PSD government since 1985, while the crisis of the communist world has had a great impact on the PCP and particularly on Intersindical. Despite the ousting of reformists in the PCP, the party has not been able to purge the union organization in the same way, and Intersindical has, for the first time, been displaying considerable autonomy from the party. The ascendancy of the reformists over the orthodox communists in the leadership permitted Intersindical to join the Permanent Council for Social Concertation in 1987 and to establish formal relations with UGT in 1988. The earlier sharp antagonism between the union confederations is generally giving way to more muted differences of approach, except perhaps on the question of the law on dismissals and the issue of flexibility. These developments mean that the costs of pluralism may soon appear unacceptable to the unions. In 1990, the leader of UGT appealed personally to Intersindical for the two organizations to merge by the end of the century, but both unions are aware of the complex political issues that have to be settled before this can be achieved. More pragmatically, in 1991 the union confederations agreed to develop a joint strategy for confronting the problems of European integration and in particular its 'social dimension'.

Collective Bargaining

In the late 1970s, collective bargaining was almost paralysed, partly as a result of Intersindical's unwillingness to make concessions to the employers and its preference for direct government intervention in wage regulation. The emergence of the 'parallel' unions and the pragmatism of UGT led to the resumption of collective bargaining in the 1980s and by the end of the decade it was widespread. In 1989 nearly two million wage and salary earners – 98.5 per cent of those in legal employment in private and public enterprises[1] – were covered by industry agreements, government extensions of industry agreements, company agreements and statutory regulations in individual industries or occupations. Taking all wage and salary earners (over three million in 1989), 61 per cent were covered by collective agreements or government extensions, 3 per cent by direct statutory regulations in private industries, 17.5 per cent by civil service statutory regulations and 18.5 per cent were not covered by any collective regulation or were workers in the black economy. Only 5 per cent of all wage earners were covered by company agreements, mostly in public enterprises.

The reform of the legal framework of collective bargaining has long been on the political agenda, and consensus was apparently reached in 1990 on the changes to be made. However, in 1991 the law still regulated collective bargaining in a very detailed way, laying down a host of regulations covering procedures, time periods, and the scope and content of bargaining. Public enterprises have been subject to further controls: managements must follow strict bargaining guidelines laid down by the government for each set of negotiations and, when an agreement is reached, the sponsoring minister's final approval is required.

The negotiation process is voluntary, since practically no sanctions can be imposed on parties unwilling to negotiate or to participate in mediation or arbitration. During the 1980s, the government gradually ceased to issue direct statutory regulations in cases of bargaining impasses, a legal expedient dating from the corporatist system when strikes were prohibited. However, once both sides agree to bargain formally, they must comply with all legal requirements. When an agreement is reached, it has to be registered and published by the Ministry of Employment, thus becoming legally enforceable and extendible to other employers and workers or related industries. Its validity only expires when it is replaced by a new agreement, which according to the legislation cannot be less favourable overall to the workers than the existing one. The first negotiation of a formal company agreement is viewed by individual employers as a step with far-reaching implications; since once an agreement is concluded, it is likely to form the basis of further union claims.

The legal position on the applicability of collective agreements is somewhat confused. In theory, agreements apply only to the workers represented by the signatory unions. In practice, however, since only one agreement is enforceable for the same group of employees within a company (conditions cannot be differentiated according to union membership), workers may find themselves covered by an agreement reached by a union of which they are not members. Moreover, in the absence of recognition procedures or criteria of representativeness – reflecting government attempts since 1976 to foster the role of 'parallel' unions in collective bargaining – this union may be in a minority position in the sector. This tends to arise because high inflation systematically encourages employees to opt for the agreement in which wage scales have been more recently adjusted, which then applies to the whole of the affected workforce. The current legal ambiguity has allowed UGT and some independent unions – even where they are in a minority position – to oust Intersindical in the bargaining process of several large enterprises and sectors (most notably in textiles and clothing), by negotiating a rapid adjustment of wages in exchange for giving up provisions and improvements dating from the revolutionary period. Intersindical has resorted to strike action in an attempt to keep both the earlier provisions and the adjusted pay, but it has often failed to win rank-and-file support. Recently the Textile Federation, affiliated to Intersindical, has been challenging the implementation of an agreement between the minority Sindetex (UGT) and the employers' associations introducing flexible working hours. Such inter-union rivalry, with each union trying to obtain more favourable settlements than its competitor, may have tempered the employers' initial enthusiasm for UGT's growing role in collective bargaining.

A deadlock in collective bargaining is usually followed by voluntary, though legally regulated, 'conciliation' procedures before a strike is called. Conciliation and mediation services, established by the corporatist regime in 1969, are provided free of charge by officials of the Ministry of Employment. The procedure gives unions and employers the opportunity to involve the government in their disputes, a traditional practice largely unchanged by the revolution. The arbitration mechanism is private (no permanent arbitration service exists) and expensive, and it became increasingly unpopular during the 1970s, especially among the employers. In the 1980s very few disputes were submitted to arbitration, even in public enterprises, where the government had the power to order it. In 1990, the unions, the government and the employers' confederations agreed to set up a compulsory arbitration system.

The tension between an over-regulated and highly legalistic framework and voluntary collective bargaining may help explain why formal company bargaining is so rare in the private sector, and why industry bargaining has so little impact on working conditions and terms of employment in leading or even average enterprises. The role of government extensions, the absolute dominance of industry collective bargaining over company bargaining and the lack of articulation between the two levels are also legacies of the corporatist system.

The multiplication of bargaining processes and agreements resulting from union pluralism and independent unions, and the development of company bargaining in the nationalized sector, are the main innovations in bargaining structure since the 1970s. There has also been a move from regional to national industry agreements in a few cases. Despite the attempts made by large industry-based unions to unify the bargaining process within each sector, office employees and such occupations as sales representatives, drivers, managers, technicians, engineers and other professionals are very often covered by separate industrial agreements. The same occurs in several public and private enterprises: in the national railway company, for example, the various occupations are now covered by five different company agreements, instead of one until the 1970s.

While many public enterprises have yearly-amended company agreements, similar agreements in the private sector are very rare, covering less than 1 per cent of the total labour force. Industry agreements stipulate minimum conditions well below those prevailing in each sector. Wage levels in the main urban areas have been estimated to be around 25 per cent higher than those laid down in industry agreements; the figure is lower for blue-collar workers and much higher for managerial and professional staff.

Employers' associations have consistently opposed regular and formal company-level bargaining, so as to discourage union activity within the enterprise and maximize employer control over employment conditions. The scope for employer flexibility at company level also provides a means of mitigating the rigidity of employment legislation. Nevertheless, employers have supported those aspects of labour legislation that favour them, preferring such issues to be regulated by law rather than by collective bargaining, even at industry level.

Given that the main subject of industry agreements is minimum rates of pay, collective bargaining at this level is almost redundant in Portugal, at least when unemployment is not too high. The national minimum wage, revised annually by the government since 1974, forces employers to adjust their lowest rates of pay and, consequently, the entire pay scale. Thus in practice only the gap between national and industry minimum rates is the subject of bargaining. Between 1977 and the early 1980s the government introduced a statutory incomes policy, in an attempt to curb inflation, leaving even less room for real bargaining. Annual 'wage ceilings' or *tectos salariais* set a maximum rate of nominal wage growth for all industries, on the basis of inflation forecasts that proved to be unrealistically low. The ceilings soon became counter-productive, since the unions regarded them as lower limits above which bargaining should take place. The policy also paralysed collective bargaining and the government was compelled to intervene more directly.

Economic recovery since the mid-1980s has sustained a high level of investment and employment, assuring real wage growth particularly in the major urban areas irrespective of union action and collective bargaining. Actual earnings have increased faster than negotiated wage scales for several consecutive years. In a tighter labour market favouring skilled or semi-skilled workers in particular, collective bargaining may be significant only in as far as government extensions accelerate the effects of market mechanisms on the lowest wages. Under such conditions, especially if earnings are increasing more rapidly than productivity growth, the government and employers may regard industry agreements as a moderating force on pay levels. For the unions, the value of industry-level collective bargaining is felt in periods of recession, when it inhibits decreases in real wages (the annual adjustment of the national minimum wage has been outstripped by inflation on several occasions: according to Intersindical estimates, it has lost over 30 per cent of its real value since 1974).

Apart from the very impressive but short-lived gains of 1974–5 the unions have generally been unable to influence the level of wages and the share of national income – which fell continuously between 1981 and 1990 – either in the very unstable economic conditions that prevailed after the establishment of democracy or under the prosperity of the last five or six years. The effects of the egalitarian wage policies of the 1970s failed to last: activities of the independent unions and a tighter labour market have led to a restoration, or even a widening, of differentials (except possibly in the civil service).

For more than a decade after the revolution, Intersindical unions did not press for the expansion of formal company-level bargaining. On the contrary, the clear preference was for industry agreements, since union strength was concentrated in a few large enterprises and the majority of workers, with lower wages, were employed in the smaller ones. Ideological reasons (egalitarianism, uniformity) also had a part in this strategy, although Intersindical continued to support informal or unofficial bargaining at the workplace. In the mid-1980s, UGT (partially followed by Intersindical) began to support the introduction of a multi-level or articulated system of collective bargaining. The employers were predictably hostile to bargaining at workplace level, but in 1990 the employers' confederations agreed with the unions on the general desirability of collective bargaining at all levels, including the company. None the less, there are indications that future employers in companies to be privatized will welcome an end to company agreements and a return to industry bargaining.

The rigidities of official collective bargaining can be evaded at company level by a variety of 'informal' or unofficial practices: avoiding written agreements or not complying with other legal requirements. The 'social contracts' concluded in several private and public enterprises in difficulties during the 1980s, despite being written agreements, should also be put in this category, as they temporarily suspended certain provisions and rights (the law prohibits such abrogations by collective agreements). These negotiations were conducted by the workers' commissions, not the unions, although the former are not legally entitled to bargain. Generally, however, informal bargaining involves the negotiation of a 'list of demands' or *caderno reivindicativo* submitted by the labour representatives. Frequently, management will only deal with the workers' commissions which, unlike the unions, are exclusively internal to the enterprise; moreover, only one workers' commission may be elected in each enterprise or establishment, while there may be several unions. The concessions made by the employer in informal bargaining are embodied in management minutes, avoiding the appearance of bilateral agreements. Demands are frequently backed up by different forms of union action, including stoppages.

Informal bargaining practices are not as widespread and regular as formal bargaining, but they are much more flexible and fill a visible gap in industrial relations by providing a complement to industry bargaining. A sharp distinction between the two practices is that informal bargaining is totally dependent on union strength and bargaining power in each company, while in formal industry bargaining the unions can rely on government extensions. As a rule, however, the unions lack sufficient strength to establish informal bargaining as a customary practice. In several industries informal company bargaining has not developed at all.

Detailed data on the frequency and scope of informal bargaining are unavailable even in sectors such as chemicals, engineering and clothing where it is said to be more common. One reason may be that such data would disclose the strengths and the weaknesses of union organization in a crucial area of activity.

Against a background of corporate restructuring, company agreements on redundancies, temporary wage freezes and increased job mobility, sometimes with virtual no-strike clauses, have been signed in some private companies (e.g. in Lisnave, the largest national shipyards). But given the severity of the effects of rationalization on the work force in the private sector, a consensus is less likely to be reached than in the public enterprises where company bargaining has traditionally been the norm.

The predominance of company bargaining in nationalized enterprises reflects the fact that they are among the largest employers, often dominating entire sectors. In other cases, state enterprises have abstained from industry-level bargaining as a result of government decisions reflecting economic policy objectives. In sectors such as banking and insurance, industry bargaining determines actual (rather than minimum) employment conditions, in an attempt to ensure uniform labour costs and provisions across state enterprises in those sectors; and it covers a far larger range of negotiating issues than does industry bargaining in the private sector, which is largely confined to wages.

The vitality of collective bargaining in public enterprises also reflects greater union strength: unionization averages 80 per cent, according to official data, the check-off system is widespread, and discrimination against activists is rare. The attitude of public enterprise management towards the unions and the workers' commissions (which are active mainly in the public sector) is more legalistic and cooperative than in private firms. Well-staffed personnel, industrial relations and human resource departments have been created in most state enterprises, reflecting the importance of company-level bargaining, but also management concern to avoid disputes and to provide rapid solutions to grievances and problems arising at the workplace. Personnel departments have also been developing new hiring, training, promotion and remuneration policies, mostly in dialogue with the unions, the workers' commissions or both. The receptiveness of workforce representatives to changes and new working methods has increased drastically since the privatization process began; for example, in the state-owned Petrogal (oil refining and distribution), which is soon to be privatized and exposed to fierce international competition, the great majority of the 6,000 staff agreed in a work-force ballot to give up the company's collective agreement in return for a large compensation payment.

A further feature of collective bargaining in public administration and public utilities is that it is 'informal bargaining', leading to non-enforceable agreements; the final document (if there is one) takes the form of a recommendation, signed by both parties, which is in theory not binding on the government. The bargaining process, regulated by legislation in

1984, takes place every year before the state budget is approved by parliament. The legal justification for this hybrid system is the 'sovereignty' of the state, although civil servants have the same right to strike as other groups of workers (and perhaps use it more often).

Strikes

After 1974 the number of strikes increased to several hundred a year. The frequency of disputes, numbers of workers involved and days lost rose to a peak between 1980 and 1983. This period coincided with the first centre-right government since the revolution and with a deteriorating economic and social situation after the second oil shock. The main target of industrial action was the wage ceilings. Another cause of disputes was the alarming spread of a new phenomenon: the failure of employers to pay wages. Unable to adjust the size of their work force by cutting jobs, a growing number of firms delayed payment for several months; by 1984 over 100,000 workers were affected. Intersindical organized a massive and effective campaign over the issue. The deflationary economic policies of the following government, the PS–PSD grand coalition, exacerbated the effects of recession, worsened unemployment, and led to a fall in real wages below the 1974 level. In 1984, at the peak of the crisis, the indicators of industrial disputes began to show a decline and in 1987, when the economy was already rapidly recovering, they reached their lowest overall level for the 1974–90 period (see table 14.5).

Despite the fall in the number of industrial disputes, the first successful general strike ever organized in Portugal was held in 1988. According to the unions, nearly 80 per cent of the work force took part. The action was called simultaneously, though not jointly, by Intersindical, UGT and a large number of independent unions, unifying all the main factions, including a sector of the social democrats themselves, against the PSD government. It was motivated by the proposed reform of the law on dismissals. The strike changed the PSD's optimistic assessment, following its landslide victory in the 1987 general elections, of its capacity to push through changes in the law against union opposition: following the threat of a new general strike, the law eventually underwent only minor amendment in 1989.

The main sectors in terms of total working days lost between 1986 and 1990 were transport, engineering, banking, textiles and clothing, in that order. Over the last five years, transport and banking, both highly unionized sectors dominated by public enterprises, have together accounted for well over half of total working days lost (42 per cent and 14 per cent respectively), while basic metals, metal products, machinery, transport equipment, textiles, clothing, footwear, leather and construction together accounted for less than 25 per cent.

These statistics relate only to public and private enterprises, excluding public administration, health, public education, etc. for which reliable

Table 14.5   Industrial disputes, workers involved and working days lost (1974–1990)

Year	Number of strikes	Workers involved/ strike	Working days lost (total)	Average duration (days)	Working days lost/1,000 wage earners
1974[a]	313	–	–	–	–
1975	340	–	–	–	–
1976	367	–	–	–	–
1977	357	–	–	–	–
1978	333	478	580,419	3.6	236
1979	381	885	621,792	1.8	252
1980	374	1,066	734,536	1.8	283
1981	756	671	941,220	1.8	349
1982	563	609	595,654	1.7	217
1983	532	608	767,676	2.3	271
1984	550	514	331,100	1.2	120
1985	504	478	335,664	1.4	122
1986[b]	363	638	381,917	1.6	136
1987	213	382	113,228	1.4	39
1988	181	859	197,902	1.3	66
1989	307	965	357,377	1.2	115
1990	271	476	146,532	1.1	46

[a]Last 8 months only.
[b]From 1986 on, public administration and public services not included.
Sources: MESS, INE.

strike data are unavailable; in 1986 the government even ceased to issue statistics on strikes in the civil service. It is possible nevertheless to say that the public sector as a whole is much more affected by strikes than the private sector, with a high strike frequency in the civil service and recurring industrial disputes in chronically loss-making public enterprises, particularly in the transport sector. In the last decade, however, many public enterprises have established a more equable relationship with the unions.

The number of sector (or industry-wide) strikes has decreased sharply from an annual average of 87 in 1980–2 to only 22 in 1988–90, a faster decrease than that of single-firm strikes (from 468 to 230 over the same period), suggesting that formal collective bargaining in the private sector has led to very few strikes in recent years. The emergence of independent unions was reflected in a noticeable increase in strikes by occupational groups in the 1980s, mostly in the public sector. The average duration of strikes in public and private enterprises fell, in line with the trend in other indicators of conflict, from 3.6 days in 1978 to 1.1 in 1990, probably the lowest figure since 1974. Again, the main exceptions seem to be the stoppages called by small, occupational or grade-based unions in the public sector, though accurate comparisons are not possible due to deficiencies in the statistics.

The Legislation on Dismissals and Redundancies:
The Crucial Issue of Flexibility

Perhaps the most insistent demand of the employers' organizations since the 1970s has been the complete overhaul of the legislation on dismissals, which CIP viewed as a major obstacle to domestic and foreign investment and to resolving the problems of unemployment, unpaid wages, absenteeism, low productivity and poor employee motivation. The virtual prohibition of redundancies, the narrow definition of fair dismissal, the legal procedures relating to conflicts on this matter and the rules on severance pay make the Portuguese legislation, despite some changes since the 1970s, very favourable to workers with a permanent contract of employment.

Even during the rapid economic growth and full employment of the corporatist regime, employers considered the law restrictive, but in 1975, at the height of the recession, individual and collective dismissals became virtually impossible (except on disciplinary grounds) without the consent of the work force or the approval of the government. The constitution of 1976 also enshrined the 'right to job security', which has prevented centre-right governments from introducing more flexible legislation. High inflation meant that adjustment to the crisis from 1977 took the form of a reduction in real wages rather than in employment, largely the opposite of what occurred in Spain after the oil shocks.

Nevertheless, the problems of declining private investment and growing unemployment evident in the early 1980s have disappeared without major changes in the legislation. Since 1976, when the legal rules on temporary work became more permissive, employers have been able to rely on a massive influx of workers on fixed-term contracts. Since the early 1980s over two-thirds of all hirings have been on fixed-term contracts; about 19 per cent of all wage earners have now a contract of this kind, not counting other forms of precarious and temporary work (subcontracting, for example) and the mass of workers in the black economy without any contract at all. This has eased the problem of labour market rigidity, although it has also led to sharp labour market segmentation favouring those on permanent contracts. The unions, particularly Intersindical, have shown little sensitivity to this question, blaming problems on the legislation on fixed-term work rather than on the inflexibilities caused by the law on dismissals.

Another consequence of the legislation on dismissals is that private enterprises have become increasingly selective in the hiring of new employees. This has been one factor behind the expansion of personnel management and the creation of human resource departments in Portuguese companies. Since EC entry, vocational and apprentice training in companies has also developed rapidly, largely financed by European Social Fund grants which currently amount to 1 per cent of GDP.

CIP's attitude to job security is that workers must compete to retain their jobs in the same way that entrepreneurs must be competitive to preserve their businesses. Nowhere else in the European Community, CIP argues, does the law guarantee the workers' 'ownership of jobs' to the same extent (although the Greek legislation was, until recently, similar). The unions for their part claim that employers are seeking to restore the old authoritarian relations within firms. The comparison with European standards, they argue, should be extended to wages, working conditions, unemployment benefits and welfare services which all lag behind those of Portugal's EC partners. For example, the coverage of the system of unemployment benefits, introduced in Portugal only in 1975, is by far the worst in western Europe. In 1988, unemployment compensation represented 0.32 per cent of GDP, with only 22 per cent of registered unemployed in receipt of benefit. Total government expenditure in support of the labour market (training, direct job creation and unemployment benefits) was less than 1 per cent of GDP, lower than in any other western European country.

A further revision of the law on dismissals has recently been completed. The change broadens the criteria of fair dismissal to include the worker's inability to adapt to changes in the nature of the job. The UGT is not opposing the reform; in 1990 it signed a wide-ranging tripartite agreement (Economic and Social Agreement – see below) which included proposals to amend the law on dismissals. Intersindical refused to sign the agreement, allegedly because of the dismissal provisions, although it participated in discussions until the last moment.

Social Concertation: The New Paradigm of Industrial Relations?

The foundation of UGT in 1978, the creation of the CPCS in 1984 and the conclusion of tripartite agreements between the government, UGT and the employer confederations in 1986, 1987 and 1990 are frequently cited as milestones along the road from the impasse of class conflict to the present era of social concertation characterized by dialogue, compromise and participation (Pinto 1991; Nascimento Rodrigues 1991). One hypothesis is that the emerging 'new paradigm of the industrial relations sub-system', when considered alongside other developments such as the profusion of national and regional consultative bodies, signals the imminent arrival of a new wave of corporatism, this time under the auspices of liberal democracy.

Undoubtedly, some important changes have taken place since the troubled 1970s and early 1980s. However, the neo-corporatist scenario fails to take account of other recent developments. The general strike of March 1988, supported by the overwhelming majority of unions, is also a milestone and one that does not fit easily with the notion of social concertation. Furthermore, while UGT has played the leading role in the concertation process, Intersindical remains the more representative union body. Finally, the climate of relative detente in industrial relations since the mid 1980s must be seen less as a product of the new concertation policies than as the combined effect of steady economic growth, rapidly declining unemployment and rising real wages.

In addition, the tripartite agreements reached so far seem less significant than enthusiastic assessments have claimed. The first two important agreements produced by the CPCS, in 1986 and 1987, under the guise of 'recommendations on incomes policy', dealt almost exclusively with the rate of growth of nominal wages in collective bargaining for 1987 and 1988 respectively. Only the minority UGT signed the agreements on behalf of labour, while CIP refused to sign the second recommendation. The recommendations were based on forecasts of inflation which proved correct for 1987; as a result, the first agreement was widely considered a success and a decisive contribution to curbing inflation. But in 1988, contrary to expectations, inflation stopped falling despite only moderate pay settlements, and UGT withdrew its support when the government refused to adjust the recommended wage increase. No agreements were reached for 1989 and 1990, but moderation continued to prevail in collective bargaining. Inflation, in turn, rose once more, fuelled by huge budget deficits, external constraints and, to a lesser extent, the rise in actual earnings relative to negotiated wage rates. The experience of 1987–90 illustrates the limitations of unions' participation in a concerted incomes policy or in centralized bargaining, when they are unable to influence significantly the level of actual earnings through industry or company bargaining. Under current economic conditions, the most likely consequence of voluntary wage restraint through centralized bargaining is an increase in wage drift.

The employers' confederations have shown relatively little interest in concerted incomes policies, arguing that the causes of inflation lie in excessive public expenditure. In any case, given the decentralized nature of employer organization, the confederal bodies lack the necessary authority to enforce a strict incomes policy on their affiliates (Pinto 1990). At the CPCS the employers' principal objective has been the reform of labour market regulation rather than centralized pay determination.

With the Economic and Social Agreement (AES) of 1990, the CPCS became a forum for government and the social partners to negotiate changes in labour legislation. The AES covered a wide range of issues to be regulated by future legislation: dismissals, weekly working hours (cut from 48 to 44 hours, with a further gradual reduction to 40 hours by 1995), working-time flexibility, vocational training, unemployment benefits, child labour (minimum age raised from 14 to 15), health and safety at the workplace, supplementary social security in cases of industrial restructuring, and collective bargaining (removing restrictions on the scope of bargaining and the establishment of a compulsory arbitration system). A recommendation on pay policy for 1991 was also approved (leading to conflict between the UGT leadership and some of its affiliated unions in the public sector). For the first time, the annual revision of the national minimum wage was also subject to tripartite negotiation and included in the AES (for details, see EIRR 208, May 1991: 10–12).

At first sight, therefore, the AES appears a major step forward in the development of social concertation. Behind most of the legislative proposals in the AES lies the desire of the parties to reduce the glaring discrepancies between Portuguese provisions on social and labour affairs and those prevailing in other EC countries. It may be argued that such measures would have had to be introduced, sooner rather than later. But significantly, social concertation has been the procedure chosen to implement them. Thus while the content of current Portuguese industrial relations reflects the external pressures of greater European integration, its form may indicate the consolidation of the social concertation paradigm. None the less, tensions are already apparent between the logic of concertation and that of interest representation through the party system; for example, social concertation has made it hard for the largest opposition party, the PS, with its close links to UGT, to criticize the government's social policies. Indeed, the PCP itself had a hard job in persuading Intersindical not to sign the AES in 1990. From a political standpoint therefore it is easy to understand the PSD government's attachment to social concertation, which it has been able to exploit for electoral purposes.

It is still premature to suggest that a new, more stable and coherent system of industrial relations has developed since the establishment of democracy. Different layers and patterns continue to interact within a heterogeneous and as yet ill-defined system, against a background of successive phases of historical development and a fast-changing environment (Caire 1987). In particular, it is still not clear whether current trends such as social concertation will persist in the future, nor, if they do, whether they will consolidate the traditionally dominant role of the state in Portuguese industrial relations, or, on the contrary, permit the social actors to assert their autonomy.

Notes

[1]   The figures do not include employment in central and local government, public education and health, where the rules and working conditions are established by the government after consultations with the unions; nor most rural workers or, of course, employment in the black economy.

Abbreviations

AES	*Acordo Económico e Social* – Economic and Social Agreement, signed in1990
AIP	*Associação Industrial Portuguesa* – Portuguese Association of Industry
CAP	*Confederação da Agricultura Portuguesa* – Confederation of Portuguese Agriculture

CCP	*Confederação do Comércio Português* – Confederation of Portuguese Commerce
CDS	*Partido do Centro Democrático e Social* – Democratic and Social Centre Party, also known as Christian Democrats
CIP	*Confederação da Indústria Portuguesa* – Confederation of Portuguese Industry
CGT	*Confederação Geral do Trabalho* – General Confederation of Labour (outlawed in 1927)
CGTP	or CGTP-IN *Confederação Geral dos Trabalhadores Portugueses* – General Confederation of Portuguese Workers, usually known as *Intersindical*
CNEP	*Conselho Nacional das Empresas Portuguesas* – National Council of Portuguese Enterprises
CPCS	*Conselho Permanente de Concertação Social* – Permanent Council for Social Concertation
INE	*Instituto Nacional de Estatística* – National Statistical Institute
MESS	*Ministério do Emprego e Segurança Social* – Ministry of Employment and Social Security
PCP	*Partido Comunista Português* – Portuguese Communist Party
PSD	*Partido Social Democrático* – Social Democratic Party
PS	*Partido Socialista* – Socialist Party
UGT	*União Geral de Trabalhadores* – General Workers' Union

References

Barreto, J. 1991: *A Formação das Centrais Sindicais e do Sindicalismo Contemporâneo em Portugal (1968–1990)*. Unpublished.

Caire, G. 1987: Naissance d'un système de relations professionnelles: le Portugal après avril 1974. *Travail et Société*, 12, 2, 367–86.

Cardoso, J. L., Brito, J., Mendes, F. and Rodrigues, M. 1990: *Empresários e Gestores da Indústria em Portugal*. Lisbon: Dom Quixote.

Gaspar, C. 1988: *As Aventuras das Associações Empresariais e a Democracia Portuguesa*. Unpublished.

Lucena, M. 1988: La herencia de dos revoluciones. *Revista de Estudios Políticos*, 60–1, 467–516.

Makler, H. 1976: The Portuguese industrial elite and its corporative relations: a study of compartmentalization in an authoritarian regime. *Economic Development and Cultural Change*, 24, 3, 493–526.

Nascimento Rodrigues, H. 1991: Da luta de classes à concertação social. *Diário de Notícias – Empresas*, Outubro 1991, 36–8.

Pinto, M. 1988: *Caracterização do Modelo Jurídico-Institucional da Contratação Colectiva em Portugal*. Lisbon: UGT.

Pinto, M. 1990: Trade union action and industrial relations in Portugal. In G. Baglioni and C. Crouch (eds), *European Industrial Relations. The Challenge of Flexibility*. London: Sage, 243–64.

Pinto, M. 1991: Ensaio sobre a concertação social e a mudança do paradigma sindical e social. In *Portugal em mudança. Ensaios sobre a actividade do XI Governo Constitucional*. Lisbon: INCM, 337–63.

Rodrigues, M. J. 1988: *O Sistema de Emprego em Portugal. Crises e Mutações*. Lisbon: Dom Quixote.

Stoleroff, A. 1988: Sindicalismo e relações industriais em Portugal. *Sociologia*, 4, 2, 147–64.

15

Spain: Constructing Institutions and Actors in a Context of Change

Miguel Martínez Lucio[1]

Introduction

In the aftermath of four decades of authoritarian rule, Spain has been attempting to establish liberal-democratic institutions and a new model of industrial relations along typical 'European' lines. The dilemma it faces, like Greece and Portugal, is that it is doing so just as the European industrial relations models themselves are undergoing major transformations.

The development of a successful industrial relations system is not a straightforward process: the existence of an appropriate legal framework, formal structures and collective actors does not in itself guarantee that the system is functioning according to the tenets of the liberal-democratic model, that is, based on clearly articulated economic interests and a mutual acceptance of the joint regulation of work. From the death of Franco in 1975 to the present, Spanish industrial relations have been in a state of flux, and the fluid attempts to construct actors and processes constitute the central theme of contemporary Spanish industrial relations, and of this chapter.

The construction of the model has coincided with major political change and social and industrial restructuring, in a period when there has been little consensus between industrial relations actors on questions such as the economic and social role of the state, the prerogatives of management, or the position of trade unions as representatives of worker interests. Thus there has been a close interaction between political, social and economic changes on the one hand, and industrial relations developments on the other. Particularly important is the historical dimension of past strategies and choices (cf. Lange et al. 1982) that have contributed to the forging of organizational identities and to the expectations and interests that underpin the relationship between organizations and their constituencies; this legacy continues to constrain or facilitate present courses of action.

This chapter begins with the historical evolution of contemporary industrial relations, looking in turn at the Francoist dictatorship and the political transition from the mid- to late-1970s. As in Portugal, the evolution of industrial relations under the dictatorship has had a continuing impact on subsequent developments; but in contrast to the Portuguese case, the transition to democracy was premised on the attempt to forge liberal-democratic industrial relations practice, and this too has had lasting consequences.

Then follows an overview of the main actors and institutions of industrial relations, and of the industrial and labour market context. This section outlines the key characteristics of the Spanish system and highlights the tensions between evolving industrial relations institutions and the transformations in industrial structure and the economy.

Third, the chapter examines aspects of the development of industrial relations institutions with reference to the diverse political and ideological projects of the principal actors. One element is the way in which industrial relations actors – employers and unions – relate to the state, which is itself undergoing critical changes. This is explored through an examination of a key feature of democratic Spanish industrial relations: 'social concertation' involving the state, unions and employers in various forms of 'political exchange' at national level. A second element is the way in which institutional structures of industrial relations have evolved to handle issues of joint regulation, particularly through collective bargaining. A final element is the impact of structural changes in the labour market and in society. Unemployment has been a salient political issue of the last decade in Spain, and has formed a key reference point for relations between management, unions and the state; whilst other labour market developments such as the changing occupational structure, and the 'casualization' of employment have had profound consequences for the organization and strategies of industrial relations actors.

Our analysis stresses the complexities facing the key actors as they struggle to construct their own distinct visions of the emerging industrial relations model and to establish appropriate practices within it. All this is taking place at the same time as the metaphors and practices of the 'postwar' model are unravelling: economic and political transformation, the crisis of a social-democratic model of the welfare state, and the growth of labour market deregulation, are eroding the political foundation of the liberal-democratic model just as it is becoming established in Spain. One consequence has been that, despite the institutionalization of industrial relations structures, political influences still shape industrial relations strategies.

Industrial Relations under Franco

Many of the characteristics of the current industrial relations system have their origins in Francoist structures and in the events of the dictatorship years. The Nationalist victory in the civil war of 1936–9 brought a complete break with the traditions of the Second Republic. Hundreds of thousands of Spaniards fled into exile, and up to a quarter of a million supporters of the republic are believed to have been executed in the years immediately after the civil war. The old autonomous unions – notably the socialist-linked UGT and the anarcho-syndicalist CNT –were crushed. Remnants of pre-civil war organization were still to be found: Maravall (1978: 77–109) has pointed to the clandestine activities of UGT members in the 1940s and 1950s, contributing to heroic if ineffectual industrial struggles in their once traditional strongholds. But on the whole, neither the union nor the Socialist Party (PSOE) put a high priority on industrial struggle within Spain: foreign intervention was still unrealistically expected until 1956 (Gillespie 1989), and the unions operated mainly in exile, supported by an ineffectual and divided opposition. Like the socialists and anarchists, the communists did not initially support those who wished to reconstruct their organization within Spain, being more concerned with building a centralized apparatus in exile and isolating elements ambivalent towards Moscow (Preston 1976).

The regime developed an authoritarian, hierarchical system of labour relations institutions whose point of departure was the 1938 Labour Charter, based on a mish-mash of Italian fascist and native Spanish corporatist and 'social Catholic' ideas (Fina and Hawkesworth 1984). The Francoist system was centred on 24 (subsequently 28) 'vertical' unions (*sindicatos verticales*) in different sectors of production. The vertical unions compulsorily organized employers and workers alike around the principles of 'unity, totality and hierarchy', and the submergence of class antagonisms. This *Organización Sindical Española* (OSE) remained the preserve of the 'Falangist' wing of the Francoist political alliance (Carr and Fusi 1981: 24–8).

In the new system, the traditional features of liberal-democratic industrial relations were rejected: strikes were considered an attack on the 'normality of production' and were banned as seditious acts under the penal code, autonomous workers' organizations and collective bargaining were illegal; the Ministry of Labour set wages through compulsory official norms or *reglamentaciones*, and it imposed a detailed and rigid regulation of all aspects of employment by means of labour ordinances (*ordenanzas laborales*).

At the micro-level, the 'national-syndicalist' system organized labour within structures that denied any autonomy of representation: a command structure of appointed officials ran the national, provincial, and local offices of the OSE (Amsden 1972; Foweraker 1989). Even when indirect elections were introduced, they were tightly controlled by the Falangists. In short, the state penetrated deeply into civil society, preventing its autonomous organization in the sphere of production. Behind the obsession with order, hierarchy and discipline lay a concern for the development of production: Francoist state elites were conscious that the Republic had not just threatened the 'traditional' Spain of conservative,

Catholic values, but that it had failed as a project to modernize Spain and control the working class. The Francoist state thus sought to coerce the economic classes and organize them and the economy through a strict model of bureaucratic regulation (Estape and Amade 1986) that facilitated the accumulation of capital.

The burden of Francoist labour legislation was not solely repressive but sought also to establish a certain legitimacy in the eyes of workers. Rigid state control of workers was to be balanced by a paternalist supervision of employees' welfare. In 1953, compulsory *jurados* or works councils were introduced in individual firms and establishments; their official function was, however, limited to advisory and administrative matters, and they acted as extensions of the official unions (Fina and Hawkesworth 1984: 6). In the area of substantive rights, a law passed in 1944 made it formally difficult for employers to dismiss workers, while detailed labour ordinances restricted labour mobility in the workplace or enterprise. However, the reality was rather different: the use of contractual clauses and of provisions in the employment legislation concerning political activity, probationary periods, etc., provided employers with the necessary flexibility to overcome employment rigidities.

The bureaucratization of micro-level employment structures and the enshrinement of individual 'rights' were designed to contain autonomous initiatives within the workplace. But the system regulated employment in a way that would not always serve the interests of employers, especially when economic development subsequently necessitated a more flexible model of labour control. Moreover, despite the authoritarian context, the vertical unions provided scope for autonomous worker activity; and during the transition to democracy, labour regulations provided rights that could be exploited by the emerging independent unions.

Franco managed to impose industrial order – although, despite the draconian nature of labour legislation, strikes were not eliminated even in the 1950s (Fina 1978) – but was less successful in the 1940s and 1950s in promoting industrial development. There were various reasons for this: Spain's international isolation, its technological backwardness, and the continuing legacy of the destruction caused by the civil war. The attempt to trigger 'autarchic' economic development, led by a state productive sector on Italian lines, was a failure: bureaucratic regulation resulted in uneven and constricted economic growth.

This stagnation prompted the reforms of the late 1950s that sought to integrate Spain into the booming world market. While the state retained an active role in industrial development, the country was opened up to foreign capital and there was a move away from the corporatist regulation of prices and incomes. These reforms laid the basis for the so-called 'economic miracle' of the 1960s, based particularly on the growth of tourism and other services, but also on rapid industrialization.

Industrialization, and the large-scale internal migration (particularly from the under-developed south to the developing centres of Catalonia and Madrid) that accompanied Spain's transformation from a rural to an urban economy, brought a new work force into the expanding sphere of waged labour. In some areas, like Asturias, Madrid and Barcelona, new, sporadic, *ad hoc* forms of workers' organization were developing outside the OSE. The mass meeting or *asamblea* was the main vehicle for collective action, an institution of almost mythological status in modern Spanish labour history. Autonomous action gradually crystallized into the so-called *comisiones obreras* (workers' commissions) in certain larger factories and public enterprises, and into *comisiones de barrio* (neighbourhood commissions) in local areas (Villasante 1984; Castells 1983). The *comisiones oberas* began to engage in informal negotiations with employers – indeed, some were set up to conduct such negotiations. For many employers, particularly in larger, more modern enterprises, informal bargaining with semi-clandestine but more representative groups was seen as a way of reducing workplace conflict at a time of rapid company growth. In other firms (such as the state railway, RENFE, in which formal collective bargaining was still banned), the pressure of clandestine workplace organizations transmitted growing wage pressures from the wider economy (Ferner and Fina 1988).

Alongside these developments, the first cracks appeared in the monolithic mould of the national-syndicalist labour system. The 1958 Law on Collective Agreements permitted the controlled development of collective bargaining as an alternative to state regulation of pay and working conditions. The law created in effect a dual structure (Fina and Hawkesworth 1984: 6) of multi-firm bargaining (at local, provincial or regional levels) and of company or plant bargaining. The former was conducted by the vertical unions, and the latter by management and labour representatives of the *jurado*. But in all cases, the official unions retained close control over the procedures and processes of bargaining, while the Ministry of Labour had to ratify agreements. As a consequence, collective labour disputes through the courts were subsequently recognized, and strikes were decriminalized (in 1965), although not legalized.

This easing of the system was both a reflection of the changes in Spanish economy and society induced by the 1950s liberalization policies, and an encouragement to further developments. Bargaining became quite extensive; in 1969 for example, 3.8 million workers were covered by nearly 1,600 agreements (Martín Valverde 1991: 8). And the prospect of real bargaining for the first time made the *jurados* and other vertical institutions much more significant bodies from the point of view of the incipient autonomous workplace organizations. The *comisiones obreras* – like their counterparts in the clandestine workers' movement in Portugal – also adopted a strategy of electing workers to the *jurado* and other workplace posts, and to regional bodies of the official union system (Giner and Sevilla 1979; Martino de Jugo 1980). Independent representatives and union activists negotiated formally and informally with management through the company-level *jurados de empresa* or even in certain provincial tiers of the OSE. Although the extent of these activities was uneven, and they rarely attained any permanence, the presence of workers' commission members and other independent activists was vexatious enough for the government to crack down hard in the 1960s on what had become semi-tolerated activity; in 1968 the authorities expelled 1,800 elected representatives from the OSE.

Yet such experiences were never generalized. Much of the clandestine labour movement was concentrated in the larger factories where it was easier to organize. In addition, the Spanish Communist Party (PCE), which dominated the workers' commissions by the late 1960s, saw these factories as the basis for the anti-Franco struggle. The unions concentrated their efforts on key firms in specific sectors: shipbuilding, steel, cars, public transport and chemicals. The consequences were to become apparent when the economic crisis of the 1970s and 1980s challenged the centrality of these sectors and types of firms.

Another key sector was construction, which was the first stopping-off point for a great part of the influx of agricultural labour into industrial employment. These workers inhabited areas with the worst living conditions produced by rapid urbanization and industrialization; thus they acted as a bridge between the labour and urban struggles. This social/urban dimension was a pivotal aspect of the labour movement from the 1960s, given the limitations imposed on union action by the authoritarian nature of lower management, the lack of implementation of collective agreements, and the dismissals on political grounds of great numbers of activists. The rise of the urban movement pulled in workers whose conditions at work did not permit them to organize, and there was an emphasis on regional, non-workplace organization and leadership. The strategy of the PCE, which became central in both movements, was to link these distinct arenas of action together in the struggle against Franco. Thus an extensive dialogue took place during the dictatorship between labour and community movements on issues such as housing, and points of convergence were constructed that were to be central to the later and more open mobilizations (Martínez Lucio 1989).

In the period before 1975 characteristics and traditions therefore developed in the Spanish industrial relations system, some of which were to be reinforced by subsequent developments. First, the structure of worker representation was strongly oriented to the workplace and company. This reflected the nature of state intervention and the limited formal space for autonomous worker representation, coupled with the strategies of key actors such as the PCE. As a result, certain industries such as metalworking and chemicals had a level of workplace activity which would later obstruct the construction of centralized national labour organizations. In addition, as Balfour (1984) argues, though these lower tiers were to be highly active in industrial conflicts and in trade union politics in the later 1970s, the clandestine and authoritarian context may have actually facilitated political control of bodies like the workers' commissions by the PCE.

Despite these limitations, workplace organization in key sectors was a central feature of the anti-Francoist movement. Collective action to de-

mand changes in work organization, working-time arrangements, or production bonuses, coupled with the role of the *asamblea*, became integral to
the workers' commissions' strategy. Indeed, it became central to their
very organizational identity, reinforced in the years immediately preceding Franco's death; in the eyes of members and lower tiers of leadership,
the commissions, and the more coordinated, centralized movement to
which they eventually gave rise, were differentiated from other union
organizations in that they simultaneously negotiated and applied industrial pressure. In the later phases of Francoism, the commissions united in
an organization that considered itself a union with a 'socio-political'
identity (Zufiaur 1985; Martínez Lucio 1989).

Second, following the liberalization of the late 1950s and 1960s, an
uncoordinated and inefficient system of ritualistic collective bargaining
developed, producing a vast range of collective agreements. This emerging system accentuated later problems of developing representative
organizations (Casas 1984). Semi-autonomous informal bargaining tended
to deal with wages. Such was the centrality of the wage issue that when
wages were not increased following a collective agreement, usually at a
higher level, some workers would strike and have the Ministry of Labour
intervene and set an improved compulsory award (Foweraker 1989). This
decentralized structure of bargaining was reinforced by employer strategies to offset rigidities in employment with flexibility in the area of wage
relations, through the use of bonus payments, health and safety compensation payments, and an array of other payment forms (Serrano and Malo
de Molina 1991; Toharia 1988: 121; Ferner and Fina 1988). As a result of
such developments, the basic wage had only a limited role in determining
actual pay, and central, institutional control over this element of employment was particularly weak. None the less, aspects of state regulation,
particularly covering individual rights in areas such as employment termination and job classification, caused increasing problems for employers
in the later years of the dictatorship and in the post-Francoist period as
employers sought greater flexibility at work and in the labour market.

Third, this shifting, amorphous industrial relations environment was
used by autonomous collectives of workers and opposition forces for
political purposes. As a consequence, economic, social and political demands were never clearly differentiated. The years of the political transition
never totally eradicated these characteristics of the industrial relations
system.

Political Transition and the Establishment of
Democratic Industrial Relations

The critical years of transition from 1975 to 1978 saw the development of
new, more direct forms of representation in unions and broader social
movements. Franco's death in November 1975 was followed by an escalation of industrial and social militancy in which protests against government

economic policies were combined with demands for political democracy. The outcome was the legalization of the opposition parties and the holding of free elections in 1977.

In this transitional period of struggle against Franco's immediate successors, Spanish trade unionism acquired its contemporary shape. In 1976 the workers commissions were transformed into a centralized trade union, the *Comisiones Obreras* (CCOO). Its hopes of sustaining a monopoly of representation were dashed, however, when the UGT was re-established, and the rivalry between the two movements paralleled that between their associated parties, the PCE and PSOE. Electorally, the socialists soon overshadowed the communists, winning a majority in the 1982 elections. Support for their respective unions was more evenly divided, but the UGT – benefitting from preferential treatment by employers and the government – was able to consolidate the larger membership.

In the formative phase of trade union reconstruction, union strategy was formulated in the context of general mobilization against the regime and the demand for democracy. Political mobilization was accompanied by demands for pay rises – as exemplified by the wave of strikes in early 1976 against the government's economic policies and limited wage increases. Economic demands were intensified by the emerging union leaderships' lack of real control over their local activists, and by inter-union competition at the lower levels in factories and local areas, where the developing local elites of each union competed with each other in putting forward claims and calling for strike action. Until 1978, these lower-level union representatives had no legal basis. Local action was still interwoven with the vestiges of Francoist labour organization: in some cases, local leaders were individuals who had been members of the old *jurados*; in others, they had emerged as a result of more informal elections, or through mass meetings, strike movements, and other forms of action.

Thus national trade union action rested upon a compromise with local organizations and struggles; during the period of widespread mobilization of 1976–7, this situation could be tolerated and indeed exploited, since 'mobilization' constituted the basis for union strategy and action. But the change of national union strategy in 1977, towards national political compromise and concertation, led to a widely-noted phenomenon of *desencanto* – 'disenchantment' – among workers who saw the transition and its nascent organizations in terms of material and economic improvement rather than merely democratic consolidation. One outcome was the dramatic fall in union membership, from over 50 per cent of employees in the early phase of the transition to under 15 per cent by the 1980s.

Union strategies and actions must be seen in the context of attempts to create national organizational structures. There was intensive internal debate over the form of worker representation within unions and the relationship between different organizational levels. UGT was constructed 'from above' on the basis of groups of non-communist workers and activists, and it adopted more moderate strategies than its communist-dominated rival, CCOO. UGT had close links with the Socialist Party PSOE (*Partido Socialista Obrero Español*), and the party cells promoted workplace union branches (*secciones sindicales*). This institutionalized workplace action, insulating the union from the 'volatility' of local mobilization; a volatility encouraged by caucuses of radical activists. UGT's approach to organization was in stark contrast to that of CCOO and other left groups. CCOO favoured unitary representation at the workplace through works councils (*comités de empresa*) – the successors of the old *jurados* – and through the *asamblea*. At the national level, there was also a debate as to whether the labour movement should have a unitary structure or distinct national confederations; differences of ideology and strategy between the socialist and communist-dominated wings of the movement meant, inevitably, the formation of two distinct structures.

Even CCOO, in its search for more permanent, institutionalized structures, was beginning steadily to redefine the nature of the workplace *asamblea*: it came to be used more as a channel of communication, and for taking decisions on specific issues. This was partly a consequence of the tensions arising out of the earlier, more spontaneous and less controlled arrangements in which frequent mass meetings were used by *ad hoc* worker councils (*consejos obreros*). In 1977–8, such spontaneous forms of organization were brought under control or dismantled by political cells within the unions. Increasingly, the alliance between union organization and local community action was broken and labour issues were disentangled from wider concerns. Struggles over pay ceased to have their earlier political resonance and became more economistic in nature, allowing them to be incorporated into national union strategies whether of conflict or of tripartite concertation.

Parallel changes took place in the perspectives and identities of workers themselves: attitudes became more consensual, less cynical with regard to the socio-economic system, more accepting of managerial legitimacy, less sympathetic to the position of the communists (Pérez Díaz 1979). However, there was no straightforward relationship between such attitudinal changes and the unions' organizational strategies. Moreover there were ambiguities, tensions and conflicting expectations which fuelled conflicts over unemployment and redundancy, wages, workplace grievances and local community issues channelled by CCOO and the PCE.

However, such traditions caused organizational problems for CCOO in the late 1970s when national concertation obliged it to dampen down worker mobilization. This 'demobilization' went against its 'trade union culture' (Aguilar and Roca 1989; Roca 1991), and clashed with the expectations of the rank and file and with emerging forms of worker representation both inside and outside the workplace (Martínez Lucio 1987); it also failed to eliminate the organizational and ideological resources that were to fuel a resurgence of rank-and-file activity in the mid- to late 1980s.

UGT developed a different set of organizational practices that emphasized 'negotiation' rather than 'mobilization', encouraging a more moderate set of worker attitudes. Thus UGT's relation to its membership during the late 1970s and early 1980s was distinct from CCOO's: its rank and file was less active and more dependent on the regional and industrial tiers of the organization. Politically, the union emphasized the role of macro-level social wage negotiations as part of tripartite political exchange. UGT's higher industrial relations profile in these years also reflected its increasing closeness to the employers, both at the level of the firm and in bipartite relations with the employers' association. This was symbolized by the 1980 multi-industry framework agreement, signed by the employers and UGT without the participation of CCOO. Such exclusionary tactics became a hallmark of the UGT in the competitive struggle for supremacy between the two unions. It was used at lower levels as well, for example in company agreements on redundancy and restructuring.

The depoliticization of industrial relations, the reduction in levels of conflict, and the construction of 'traditional' institutional arrangements for collective bargaining, were key UGT priorities (Maravall 1981), against a background of strong social and economic demands (and the destabilizing effects of military insurrection, terrorism and radical Basque nationalism). The result, for some observers, was to neuter industrial relations and to subordinate them to broader political objectives (Martínez Alier 1983). Moreover, UGT's conception of the structure and content of industrial relations was somewhat restricted; collective bargaining was narrowly defined as primarily concerned with wage issues and, to a lesser extent, with working hours (Casas 1984).

The Institutions and Actors of Modern Spanish Industrial Relations: An Overview

The legacy of Francoism and of the period of transition to democracy has contributed to an industrial relations system with a peculiar set of characteristics. This section provides an overview of industrial relations institutions and actors, and of the economic context in the 1980s; subsequent sections will look at the more specific issues that shaped the development of this model.

The Economic Context

Spain, like Portugal, made the transition to democracy at a time of growing economic crisis, with rising inflation and unemployment, a worsening balance of payments and stagnating or even falling GDP. The recession knocked Spanish output per head back to 72 per cent of the European average, the lowest relative level since 1968. Unemployment – which had been insignificant in the early 1970s – rose sharply from 4.7 per cent in 1976 to 14.4 per cent in 1981, reaching a peak of almost 22 per cent in 1985.

These problems were seriously aggravated by the Francoist legacy of an economy that was 'peripheral' to the rest of Europe. It was based on an inefficient, backward productive structure and that had initiated a strong process of industrialization only from the 1950s. Industry was biased towards consumer goods and traditional sectors, was labour-intensive, used outdated technology and had low levels of productivity and international competitiveness. Between 1981 and 1986, the shake-out in the 'traditional' declining sectors led to the net loss of over 150,000 jobs in mining, steel and textiles, clothing and footwear alone (Vázquez Barquero 1991: 11). Radical state-sponsored restructuring was carried out in steel, shipbuilding, and mining and also in consumer durables such as the household electrical goods sector. Traditional industrial regions such as the Basque country were badly hit. The total shake-out in manufacturing employment over the same period was around 450,000 jobs. From the mid-1980s, Spain began a phase of economic recovery and growth, with annual growth rates of over 4 per cent. Unemployment began to decline, albeit slowly, and was still among the highest in Europe in 1989 at more than 17 per cent, while employment rose by 1.5 million between 1985 and 1989 (Fernández et al. 1991).

The structure of production and employment has been gradually approaching that of the 'advanced' European economies. Agriculture still accounted for more than a fifth of the working population at the time of Franco's death; by 1989, it was around 13 per cent (Martín Valverde 1991: 198), still about twice the EC average. Services reached half of total employment in the mid-1980s and have continued their progression since, although their 1990 level of 55 per cent was still below the Community average of 62 per cent. Public administration has been a major area of expansion (up by more than 50 per cent as a proportion of total employment between 1976 and 1989, in large part a reflection of the long-delayed development of a welfare state, and the creation of new state structures in the autonomous regions or *autonomías* set up under the 1978 Constitution). Meanwhile, industry has continued its slow decline as a source of employment (see table 15.1). Further structural adjustments are likely as Spain faces the challenges of growing deregulation – for example of financial services – and competition accompanying European integration.

A striking characteristic of the Spanish labour market is the relatively low participation rate of 14.8 million or 49 per cent of those of working age in 1989 (in a total population approaching 40 million); and of the

Table 15.1   Employment by sector of production 1970–89

	Agriculture	Industry	Construction	Services
1970	29.2	28.6	8.3	33.9
1975	21.9	28.0	10.0	40.1
1980	19.1	26.8	8.9	45.1
1985	18.2	24.2	7.3	50.2
1989	13.0	23.5	9.2	54.3

Sources: Instituto Nacional de Estadística, *Anuario Estadístico*.

economically active population, wage earners make up only 72 per cent, some nine percentage points below the EC average. For men, the participation rate was 66.6 per cent. Only 32.7 per cent of women were economically active in 1989, although the figure had been steadily increasing from less than a quarter at the beginning of the 1970s. Women also suffered a much higher unemployment rate than men – peaking at 27.6 per cent in 1988. A further feature, especially significant given the salience of the issue of mass unemployment in political debate since the early 1980s, is the poor coverage of state unemployment benefit; indeed, coverage fell between 1976 and 1988. The unemployed receive direct benefits only for two years. This has to be seen against the extremely high rate of long-term unemployment: in 1988, 43 per cent of jobless had been out of work for two years or more, with young people particularly hard hit. The extent of youth unemployment has seriously restricted young people's experience of liberal-democratic industrial relations and of jointly regulated workplaces; they are exposed to relatively inferior work conditions especially if they lack higher education (Montero 1985).

A second major development in the labour market has been the upsurge in 'atypical' employment contracts (Pérez Amorós and Rojo 1991; Recio 1991). The Workers' Statute of 1980, and subsequent reform in 1984, opened the way for a range of more flexible contracts and eased the regulation that was seen by employers as an impediment to restructuring and a contribution to the rise in the black economy in sectors such as textiles and footwear. By 1990, 30 per cent of the labour force – more than 2.75 million – were on fixed-term contracts, up from 16 per cent in 1987; in the public sector, the proportion of non-permanent employees was much lower, but rising fast (from 8 per cent in 1987 to 14 per cent in 1989). The increase affected all industrial sectors, with particularly notable rises in services and construction. However, unlike other EC countries, part-time employment is little used (it affects 6 per cent of the wage-earning population compared with 13 per cent in the Community as a whole).

Employers were prohibited from keeping workers on a temporary contract for more than three years, in an attempt to limit employer reliance on – and abuse of – this form of contract. But in practice employers were able to switch between more than a dozen different kinds of short-term contract (including work experience, job-training and work-sharing contracts) to evade the restrictions of the law; for example, a young person coming into the labour market might be placed on a training contract before going on to another short-term form of employment. More exposed, less well organized groups such as new entrants and women were the main components of the temporary labour force. Trade unions unsurprisingly saw these developments as an intense casualization of employment; but it has also been argued that the high rate of fixed-term employment will leave Spanish enterprises unprepared to cope with challenges of the single European market (Pérez Amorós and Rojo 1991).

Other observers have taken a more sanguine view of developments, however. Segura et al. (1991: 110) suggest that in 1988–90 there was a reversal of the previous trend, with a higher proportion of workers gaining permanent contracts. These authors also stress that temporary contracts can act as a transition to more stable employment, and a form of regulation of the conditions of non-core workers. Public policy is intended to induce greater flexibility in the employment relation as a way of avoiding the expansion of the uncontrolled black economy, although some members of the political elite (including the former PSOE Minister for the Economy, Miguel Boyer) have praised the role of the submerged economy in allowing new entrepreneurs a breathing space to establish their activities.

There has been some attempt to mobilize and unionize pockets of 'peripheral' workers. But in general, the apparent lack of relevance of trade unions to the lives of a growing proportion of the work force, and the disenchantment with both unions and government over their failure to provide more stable employment, provide a key theme in the evolution of the new industrial relations in Spain; a theme that is taken up further below.

The Employers

Characteristics of Spanish Employers

The debate on the role of small-scale enterprise, as a major initiator of new trends in industrial development and in the politics of work, has had echoes in Spain, where small enterprise is particularly significant (e.g. Castillo 1991). The predominance of smaller firms has been increasing: in 1961, 38 per cent of employees worked in firms of fewer than 50 workers; in 1989, the figure was 53 per cent, while only 19 per cent worked in firms of over 500 employees. Using a different basis of calculation (percentages of total work force rather than of wage earners), Sisson et al. (1991: 97) show that Spain had the highest proportion of any EC country of workers (41 per cent) in firms with under ten workers, and the lowest proportion by far (8 per cent) in companies with over 500 workers. However, this does not necessarily imply that Spain – despite the hopes of policy-makers – is taking the Italian road to economic growth based on flexible specialization and the dynamism of a modern small-firm sector. Despite the emergence of incipient 'industrial districts' in Catalonia and Madrid, it would appear that conservatism and paternalistic employment relations remain the dominant characteristics of small-scale capital in Spain. The rise in the proportion of small firms probably reflects the elimination of large production units in the course of the restructuring of traditional industries. Union membership and organization tend to be much weaker in small firms. Work forces are generally dependent on union bodies external to the workplace, even where elected union representatives exist, and the extensive network of local union offices of the 1970s has been substantially reduced, in great part as a result of financial difficulties and low membership. None the less, the predominance of small-scale enterprise means that their industrial relations and personnel management practices are the prevalent pattern, if not in the forefront of innovation within the industrial relations system (cf. Prieto 1991: 193–4). Unfortunately, empirical data on the industrial relations of small firms are relatively scarce.

A second notable feature of Spanish employers is the relative weakness of domestic capital *vis-à-vis* foreign ownership, again a legacy of the country's late and dependent pattern of industrialization. In the late 1970s, foreign-controlled companies – largely from North America and, within Europe, from France, Germany, the UK – accounted for about 47 per cent of turnover and 43 per cent of employment in major Spanish industries (Buckley and Artisien 1988: 116–18). They were particularly dominant in chemicals, vehicles, machinery, oil and mining. Since the 1970s, their role has increased still further: for example, with the sale of the state-owned SEAT, foreign companies now totally dominate the car industry. Direct foreign investment in Spain as a proportion of GDP doubled between 1980 and 1987 to 1.2 per cent (Durán 1989: 342). Conversely, with the exception of the (partly state-owned) Telefónica, no Spanish companies figured in a list of the 100 largest private-sector European Community multinationals (by size of work force) in 1990 (Sisson et al. 1991: 104–7). The dominance of foreign multinationals raises the question of how far they act as importers of new industrial relations, personnel and human resource management policies into Spanish industry. Under Franco, multinationals were in the forefront of developing *de facto* bargaining with their workforces, and there is some evidence that today they are among those adopting modern HRM practices such as the use of quality circles and performance-related pay. However, the diffusion of such practices in Spain still appears limited, and hard data are difficult to come by.

State enterprise, largely created in the 1940s under the Francoist strategy of economic autarchy, has traditionally played a key role in the industrialization process, notably through the state industrial holding company INI (*Instituto Nacional de Industria*) modelled on the Italian IRI, and subsequently the petrochemical holding INH (*Instituto Nacional de Hidrocarburos*). In the early years of the transition, INI in particular was used as an instrument of state employment policy, softening the effects of the mounting recession by absorbing failing companies; between 1978 and 1980 its total work force rose by some 25,000 to a peak of almost a quarter of a million at a time when unemployment was rising sharply. Subsequently (and particularly after the consolidation of democracy with the defeat of the coup attempt in February 1981), political and social objectives took second place to economic policies of rationalization and restructuring. In INI, numbers fell from their peak to 170,000 in 1986. Other public enterprises, notably the railway company, RENFE, also played a significant role in the politics of the transition. At a time when the actors were feeling their way towards new post-Francoist institutions, the resumption of peaceful collective bargaining in RENFE after a forty-year hiatus was seen as a symbol or model of successful democratic industrial relations (Ferner 1988).

Employers' Organizations

The organization of business interests in Spain is highly unitary (see especially Pardo and Fernández 1991). The *Confederación de Organizaciones Empresariales de España* (CEOE) has established a near monopoly of representation since its foundation in 1977. Even at the time of its creation it could claim a 60 per cent coverage and by 1987 some 1.4 million firms (95 per cent of the total) were members of affiliated bodies. It represents large and small, foreign and national, public and private firms alike, although there has been a tendency to rely on small and medium capital since the large-firm sector is dominated by multinationals that tend to be less active in the organization. CEOE fought off a challenge by a rival confederation of small and medium firms by founding its own confederation (CEPYME) for such firms, incorporated into CEOE as a semi-autonomous organization in 1980.

CEOE was the product of an amalgam of various territorial and sectoral organizations, some of them with their roots in the old OSE system. This element of continuity allowed it to establish an organizational structure very quickly. But there was also a clear break with the past: the confederation was promoted by a group of forward-looking entrepreneurs aware of European models of industrial relations and forms of interest group representation. Its structure continues to be based on a combination of around 100 territorial and 50 sectoral bodies that combine the economic functions of trade associations with the industrial relations role of employers' associations. An engineering company in Valencia will be a member of the Valencian Metalworking Employers' Federation which in turn will have a double affiliation to CEOE through the provincial intersectoral Valencian Employers' Confederation and the national-sectoral Metalworking Confederation, CONFEMETAL. Exceptionally, the powerful subsector of car manufacturing, represented by ANFAC, is directly affiliated to the CEOE, rather than through the sectoral organization CONFEMETAL, a reflection of intra-sectoral differences of interest. The decentralization of the Spanish state has encouraged a corresponding decentralization of member organizations, and the 'mesogovernmental' level of the regional autonomous communities is an important arena of employer action; one of CEOE's most powerful members is the Catalonian FNT (*Fomento del Trabajo Nacional*).

CEOE's inclusive nature and the wide variety of employer interests that it represents have prompted a particular organizational style that leaves considerable autonomy to member associations, and avoids conflict and controversy on issues sensitive to its diverse constituents. Differences between member associations over restructuring, notably in the steel industry and in shipbuilding, led to breakaways in the early 1980s. Though CEOE has tended to follow a more directive line in industrial relations than in other matters, its loose organizational structure has sometimes created problems in getting its member organizations to follow central policy, for example on wage increases: as in the 1990 dispute with the influential National Construction Confederation over the latter's agreement to increases 2.5 percentage points above CEOE's recommendations.

CEOE was very much a response to the political conditions of the transition. In the context of an explosion of industrial conflict, the employers felt the need for an effective political voice to confront powerful and politicized unions and to deal with the state. It has actively attempted to forge an employer identity around deregulatory labour market policies (Martínez Lucio 1991). As a result, it has at times made direct forays into politics, but political intervention decreased after the consolidation in power of a PSOE government increasingly favouring market principles, labour market deregulation, and pay restraint.

CEOE has played an important role in constructing the new framework of industrial relations, pursuing a strategy of collective bargaining and social concertation, and accepting the trade unions as valid interlocutors. Through bipartite and tripartite social pacts in the late 1970s and early 1980s, the employers helped institutionalize industrial relations. Thus the bipartite agreement of 1979 formalized mutual recognition of unions and employers' organizations, while that of 1980 established for the first time criteria of representative status in the application of collective agreements (see below). Indeed, for Pardo and Fernández (1991: 170), 'the policy of social concertation initiated in 1979 in collaboration with the UGT has without doubt been the most significant contribution of [CEOE] to the consolidation of the democratic order, by increasing the country's governability in this crucial and uncertain period'.

The Institutional Framework of Industrial Relations

The period since 1976 has witnessed the creation of liberal-democratic institutions of industrial relations, and an appropriate legal framework (e.g. Baylos 1991; Falguera i Baró 1991). The process has not been a mere technical exercise in model-building but has been intricately bound up with the political struggles of the transition and with each actor's attempt to pursue its own interests and vision of its place in the system. Labour legislation was based on formal and informal processes of negotiation in which the unions as well as political parties were intimately involved. In particular, PSOE was generally able to ensure that the organizational interests of UGT prevailed and were embodied in legislation: a notable example is the support that the law gives to the union workplace branch. Nor was it a system created entirely from scratch: the influence of history is strong, for example in the key role of the labour courts in the regulation of conflict, in the forms of employee representation at the workplace, and in the regulation of collective agreements.

The first major step towards the new industrial relations occurred in 1977 with the legalization of unions and recognition of the right to strike, subsequently embodied in the 1978 Constitution. The Constitution also provided for a basic framework in the shape of the Workers' Statute (*Estatuto de los Trabajadores*) which was finally passed in March 1980. Amended on several occasions, it still constitutes the 'centrepiece of Spanish labour law' (Martín Valverde 1991: 89). It is concerned, first, with the key issues of the individual employment relationship, introducing some flexibility into the rigid Francoist system of regulation. Second, it lays down the procedures and scope of collective bargaining, consolidating the role of the *erga omnes* principle whereby agreements apply to all workers and employers in a given bargaining domain, whether or not they are members of their respective associations. This type of agreement has been the most common throughout Spanish labour history. Third, the Statute formalizes workers' participation within the enterprise through workers' committees and delegates, bodies which yet again have their historical antecedents in the Francoist institutions of *jurados* and *delegados sindicales*.

A second major statute is the Law of Trade Union Freedom (LOLS – *Ley Orgánica de Libertad Sindical*) of 1985 which develops the right of freedom of association and regulates the activities of unions. It provides statutory support for workplace union branches (*secciones sindicales*) and union delegates, and stipulates the facilities they are entitled to. Most importantly, it extends the notion of union representativeness by granting the status of 'most representative union' to those unions that win at least 10 per cent of representative posts nationally in workplace elections (or 15 per cent in individual Autonomous Communities). The status confers several important rights. First, 'most representative' unions have the right to negotiate generally applicable collective agreements. Second, they are entitled to certain facilities within the enterprise, such as time off for union duties. Third, they are represented on tripartite public bodies such as the National Employment Institute (INEM) which runs unemployment offices and administers the benefit system, and the National Institute of Social Security (INSERSO) which administers social security benefits. 'Most representative' status has also been a major criterion for redistributing the accumulated assets of the old Francoist *Organización Sindical* to the democratic unions.

A further notable feature of the institutional framework is the continuing role of labour law in the conduct of industrial relations. Recourse to the labour courts rather than (or in addition to) internal company disputes procedures has been a common form of individual grievance-handling on matters ranging from overtime pay to compensation for dismissals; more recently, however, extra-judicial mechanisms have been used more (see below). The courts also play a large part in the settlement of collective disputes of rights, for example over the application or interpretation of collective agreements.

The Unions

At the end of the 1970s, trade unionism was 'extraordinarily complex' (Miguélez 1991: 214). According to Martín Valverde (1991: 10), 'On the trade union side, the most remarkable event over the past few years has been the clarification of the landscape of representation', with the increasing duopoly of the two large national confederations, UGT and CCOO. As was described earlier, CCOO emerged out of the spontaneous growth of semi-clandestine workplace organization from the 1960s, slowly institutionalizing its structures in the early years of the transition (Almendros et al. 1978). UGT has a much longer history. Founded in 1888, it has always been closely linked to the Socialist Party, PSOE, founded a few years earlier. Since the transition, UGT has been able to recover a leading role, despite its near total eclipse during the dictatorship years, relying heavily on the support of the state in establishing a favourable institutional framework.

The old, powerful anarcho-syndicalist tradition has withered. It was best represented by the CNT (*Confederación Nacional del Trabajo*) founded in 1910, which claimed 1.2 million members at the time of the Second Republic. It re-emerged with the return of democracy, but has failed to regain past glories, although it has influence in particular regions and individual plants, together with breakaways such as the CGT (*Confederación General del Trabajo*); and the CGT, with its more 'realistic' brand of anarcho-syndicalism, has had some notable successes in works council elections.

Other smaller unions emerged from the transition, but their significance has tended to decrease. One example is USO (*Unión Sindical Obrera*), founded in 1960 and strongly influenced by the progressive Catholic currents then active in the clandestine labour movement. It claimed 100,000 members in 1983, but has suffered from splits, and a section has since merged with UGT. More significant are the regionally based unions, especially ELA-STV (*Solidaridad de Trabajadores Vascos*) in the Basque country, and INTG (*Intersindical Gallega*) in Galicia. These unions have tended to play a central role in action against state-led restructuring projects in their *autonomías*. The future of the regional unions depends on how the regional structure of the state evolves, and on the political 'spaces' that are left to them by the growing unity of action between UGT and CCOO which are both present in substantial numbers within their territories. Other regionally based organizations are important, particularly in agriculture, where the radical SOC (*Sindicato de Obreros del Campo*) was a serious rival of the main unions among Andalusian land labourers in the early 1980s.

An important recent development has been the growth of independent unions, especially among more skilled, highly paid occupational groups in air and rail transport, health, education and communications. There is also a separate body for professional and managerial staff, the CGC (*Confederación General de Cuadros*), although it lags behind the two main confederations in representing this group of employees.

Membership and Electoral Strength

Union membership is, in the absence of widespread use of check-off arrangements, difficult to assess (see Miguélez 1991; also Sagardoy and León 1982; Lawlor and Rigby 1986); unpaid dues are a serious problem. The high point of union membership was around 1977–8, when the two main unions amassed 2.6 million between them. Figures for 1985 suggest that CCOO had about 500,000 members, down from over 700,000 in 1982, and UGT was stable at around 660,000 (Lawlor and Rigby 1986: 254). In 1982 the regional unions are estimated to have had about 103,000 members, independents 50,000, USO 99,000 and others (including CNT) 140,000.

The unions' own figures and survey findings suggest that in the industrial sector, density reached 40–45 per cent of the working population in the period of mass mobilization of the late 1970s. Thereafter, unionization fell sharply; by 1982, it was around 20 per cent, and it is currently believed to be below 15 per cent, comparable with France. Density appears to vary considerably between sectors and different groups of employees, being lower among white-collar and technical staff, especially in private industry; workers in small firms; workers in insecure employment, particularly women and new entrants to the labour market; and, of course, workers in the burgeoning black economy (Miguélez 1991: 219). Total membership at the end of the 1980s was probably less than two million.

The reasons for the fall in unionization are complex (see Miguélez 1991: 218). First, mass unemployment, the decline in heavily unionized sectors (engineering, textiles and construction) and the rise in 'precarious' forms of employment have eroded the traditional bases of union organization. A study in the early 1980s suggested that union strength was concentrated in the traditional sectors. Metalworking accounted for 27 and 23 per cent in CCOO and UGT respectively, while construction, transport, textiles and mining were another 33 per cent in CCOO and 29 in UGT (Rijnen 1984). Second, the benefits of bargaining extend to unionized and non-unionized workers alike (see the section on collective bargaining below), and although the law allows the parties to agree that non-members pay a 'negotiation fee' (*canon de negociación colectiva*), the requirement that individual workers must accept the levy in writing has limited its use (Martín Valverde 1991: 43). More generally, falling unionization may be one symptom of the 'disenchantment' with collective action which followed the demobilization of the late 1970s.

Plummeting membership and mounting financial difficulties have led observers to talk of a 'crisis of representation' in Spanish unions. None the less, membership figures give an incomplete impression of the unions' position and influence. As in France, formal union 'representativeness', for the purposes of reaching collective agreements and for participation in tripartite bodies, is judged according to the results in workplace elections in which all the employees, whether union members or not, take part. Elections for works councils (*comités de empresa*) and workers' delegates (*delegados de personal*) take place every four years (formerly every two years). The Spanish labour movement has consequently been labelled a ' "voters' trade unionism" rather than a "members' trade unionism"...since this underlines the significance of electoral results in the union context and at the same time suggests the blurring or disappearance of the importance of union membership' (Martín Valverde 1991: 24–5).

As in Germany, the system of workplace representation, while formally separate from the structure of union representation, has come to be so closely linked with it in practice that 'they might rightly be considered facets of a single system of representation' (Martín Valverde 1991: 13). First, the unions are very strongly represented on the *comités* and among workers' delegates (see table 15.2), and have a key role in the electoral process; this is important since it is the works council that is empowered to reach collective agreements with the company. It should be noted, however, that candidates backed by a particular union are not necessarily members of that union – two-fifths of delegates standing for election on the UGT platform in 1986 were not in affiliated unions. Second, the unions' organization at the workplace through the *sección sindical* is generally linked closely with the works council, and provision has been made under labour legislation for union workplace delegates to attend meetings of the council.

What is notable, especially in contrast with France, is that the two major unions have consolidated their position in works council elections and the non-union representatives have fallen away. The combined share of UGT and CCOO rose from 56.2 per cent in 1978 to 75.2 in 1986, with UGT the main gainer; while the non-affiliated representatives were not much more than a third of their 1978 strength by 1986 and were no longer a significant force. Moreover, participation of the work force in these elections is high. Four million employees voted in the 1986 elections, together with one million public sector workers in their separate elections the following year – about half the total number of employees. In the companies where elections take place (in many smaller companies, elections are not held because of a lack of union resources), participation is

Table 15.2 Results in workers' committee elections 1977–90 (% of votes)

	1978	1980	1982	1986	1990
CCOO	34.5	30.9	33.4	34.5	
UGT	21.7	29.3	36.7	40.9	
USO	3.9	8.7	4.6	3.8	
Non-members	18.2	14.6	12.1	6.7	
ELA-STV	0.9	2.4	3.3	3.3	
INTG	–	1.0	1.2	0.7	
Miscellaneous	20.8	13.1	8.7	10.1	

Note: Separate elections are held in the public sector where, in 1987, the public servants' confederation CSIF was the single largest union with 25 per cent; CCOO won 24.2 per cent, UGT 23.1 per cent.
Source: Martín Valverde (1991: 203).

around 80 per cent of the work force. These data together suggest that unions as an institution are more favourably regarded by workers than their membership figures might indicate.

In most companies, the works council is under the majority control of the two main unions. In smaller companies, one electoral slate commonly monopolizes workplace representative bodies, although in larger companies the effect is much less marked (Alós-Moner and Lope 1991: 246) and it is common for neither union to have a majority. As a result, the effectiveness of the committees has varied with the quality of the relationship between the two unions. This is particularly important when it comes to negotiating formal company collective agreements, since under the Workers Statute, agreements must be signed by more than 50 per cent of works council members in order to be legally binding on all employees in the company, rather than just on the members of signatory unions. When unity or cooperation between the two major unions is not possible, as in the mid-1980s, the role of the councils is therefore weakened. In such circumstances the UGT in particular has sometimes used the trade union workplace branch as the vehicle for negotiations with management (Martínez Lucio 1989). This has allowed it to keep open its channels of communications with the employer, especially during critical periods of restructuring.

Union Organization

A notable feature of Spanish union organization is the close link with political parties, although the two main unions have somewhat different patterns of political activity. Despite its highly centralized disciplinary mechanisms, CCOO has been relatively more tolerant of internal opposition – its constitution emphasizes the concept of pluralism – and the play of politics is more diverse and complex than initial appearances might suggest. The union has also had to accommodate the fall-out of the crisis of the non-PSOE left in Spain which has resulted in the fragmentation of the traditional communist party. Political factions exist within UGT, usually organized on the basis of their degree of support for the PSOE government; but factionalism has not been so sustained and formalized as in CCOO.

Despite subsidies from the state and foreign union movements and the distribution of the *patrimonio sindical* (i.e., the assets of the Francoist OSE, and those of the traditional unions seized by the Nationalists after the civil war), the financial and organizational resources of Spanish unionism are poor. This reflects declining membership, low dues (the annual subscription is around 0.4 per cent of wages for both UGT and CCOO) and widespread non-payment (in 1983 only 58 per cent of UGT members and 66 per cent of CCOO's were paid up) (Lawlor and Rigby 1986: 259). Head office facilities for research and organizational support are undeveloped compared with those of German or even British unions. At workplace level, there is a scarcity of able activists – the same few people often run both works councils and union branches, even in large, highly unionized companies – and representatives are generally poorly trained and lacking in qualifications (Alós-Moner and Lope 1991). One reason is the relatively weak link between the sectoral union organization and the branches.

The union confederations are organized on a dual structure: industrial or sectoral, and territorial. Thus a particular union is a member of both a sectoral federation and geographical multi-sectoral body; though at provincial level there is a considerable overlap of union activists. Generally, the sectoral structure has tended to assume the main responsibility for industry negotiations in a particular province, with the territory playing a larger role in the unions' area organization and in relations with regional and local government (Lawlor and Rigby 1986: 258–9). More recently, core industrial federations at territorial level have begun to dominate the regional and provincial structures. For example, the UGT structure in the province of Guadalajara is virtually dominated by its public sector federation which constitutes about half its membership there. Both sets of structures feed into the policy-making process of the national confederal organization.

Despite different nuances, the Spanish trade union picture resembles the French case. State institutional support – through representation in tripartite bodies, legally extendable collective agreements, state-defined representativeness, financial support, a legal framework of facilities – may have provided a minimum basis for union action and allowed the movement to consolidate in the aftermath of dictatorship. But at the same time, institutionalization may be seen to have weakened the unions' autonomous capacity to organize and mobilize workers (cf. Estivill and de la Hoz 1990: 284–9); their recognition, legitimacy and influence derive more from the state than from their own members. State-assisted consolidation may have been more advantageous to UGT; indeed it was probably the only way to re-establish it as a major force, given its extreme organizational weakness at the end of the Francoist period. Conversely, institutionalization has forced CCOO to play down the alternative model of organization that its successful grassroots activism had made viable at the start of the transition.

Macro-Level Relations between State, Labour and Capital

This section looks at one of the key elements of the institutionalization process in Spain, political concertation between state, capital and labour. With the democratic transition, the 'incomplete' character of Spanish capitalism and state organization became increasingly apparent. The state had to be reconstructed along northern European lines – just when the northern European model was itself entering into crisis. A double transition was therefore required. Emerging political elites had to manage diverse regional, social and economic demands arising from new and often spontaneous forms of social organization. At the same time, the unions were conscious of the need to strengthen the legitimacy of the new social and economic system, in the face of uncertainties and dangers. The response was to impart a peculiar set of characteristics to Spanish industrial relations at the macro-level. Between 1977 and 1986, there was a process of national concertation (see table 15.3) which involved, at various times, the government, political parties, CEOE, and one or both of the major union confederations. These agreements can be seen as an attempt at tripartite or bipartite exchange in which wage control was accepted by the unions in return for government or employer concessions or reforms in areas like trade union law and job creation. Successive pacts laid down bands for wage increases usually in line with or a little below projected increases in inflation.

The Moncloa Pacts of October 1977 were, in the first place, a political response to the wage explosion of 1975–7 and the high level of industrial conflict (see below). They were signed by the political parties alone, although they had the backing of the main union confederations which were anxious to see the stabilization of the democratic regime. The Pacts were an attempt by the main political parties to tie the modernization of the state to wage restraint. They established a framework for policies on pay, employment and social security during the transition years. However, as with many later agreements, while the wage controls were generally implemented effectively, the broader reforms were not.

Concertation was also an arena of inter-union rivalry, and a complex three-way politics was played out as the actors fought to consolidate their position. One significant aspect was the marginalization of CCOO, which allowed UGT to establish itself institutionally and politically. This partly reflected CEOE's policy of favouring UGT and encouraging rivalry between the two confederations. Thus in the Basic Interconfederal Agreement (ABI) of 1979 and the Interconfederal Framework Agreement (AMI) of 1980, for example, CCOO was isolated and excluded. CCOO had its own reservations about concertation, not least because it undermined the union's preference for developing strong unity of action built upward

Table 15.3   Political concertation in Spain, 1977–86

Agreement	Date	Signatories
Moncloa Pacts	1977	parties
ABI	1979	CEOE/UGT
AMI	1980	CEOE/UGT/USO
	1981	CEOE/UGT/USO
ANE	1982	Govt/CEOE/CCOO/UGT
AI	1983	CEOE/UGT/
AES	1985	CCOO
	1986	Govt/CEOE/UGT CEOE/UGT

from the workplace. But this tendency was interrupted when the stability of the system as a whole was threatened. The 1981 National Agreement on Employment (ANE) was truly tripartite, involving government, employers and both major unions. It was signed during the political crisis following the attempted military coup d'état of February 1981, and offered employment creation and a range of other social measures in return for wage moderation. Similarly, CCOO participated in the Interconfederal Agreement (AI) of 1983, following the socialists' election victory in 1982. But when PSOE invited all the economic actors to discuss a new tripartite agreement, the AES (Economic and Social Agreement), CCOO once again felt unable to sign: it preferred to negotiate on the basis of the commitments made in the Socialist Party's electoral programme!

The unions supported concertation, first, as a means of consolidating democracy. Second, however, they saw it as a way of legitimizing themselves as actors within the new regime, of achieving their own consolidation as organizations, and of institutionalizing the rules of industrial relations. Thus some of the unions' recompense for wage moderation took the form of 'organizational benefits' (Roca 1991): for example, UGT and CCOO took part in the deliberations leading to the 1980 Workers' Statute and had a considerable influence on its content. Third, the unions hoped for more substantive benefits. The main substantive commitment of the national agreements was contained in the 1981 ANE, which promised to create 350,000 more jobs. Subsequently, however, unemployment continued to rise, and few new jobs were created.

More often than not, union hopes were disappointed, and this was one of the principal causes of the decline in union interest in concertation from the mid-1980s, and the growing rapprochement between the two major confederations. The break between UGT and the PSOE government was triggered by the government's refusal to accede to union demands at the time of the Economic and Social Agreement of 1984–6. The unions wanted a surplus from taxation and social security contributions to be used for welfare expenditure (Gillespie 1990), at a time when at least 60 per cent of the unemployed received no benefit whatsoever. On the pay front, too, the unions felt disillusioned by concertation. Generally, the large majority of lower-level collective agreements stayed within the bands established by successive national pacts. For example, only 21 per cent of workers in 1985 and 8 per cent in 1986 were covered by agreements that exceeded the levels laid down in the AES, despite CCOO's opposition to the pact (Roca 1991: 367). Moreover, from the AMI of 1981, national pacts permitted pay increases above inflation on the basis of improvements in productivity at enterprise level. Companies were to introduce systems to measure changes in productivity, but in practice employers were reluctant to negotiate on the distribution of productivity gains. This led UGT to press for higher pay bands to be set in national bargaining, and the ensuing disagreement was a principal cause of the breakdown of concerted incomes policy (Espina 1991). Since 1987, pay bargaining has taken place – for the first time since 1977 – on a decentralized basis, without any national framework of wage bands for the private sector.

The advantages of concertation for employers were, of course, the moderation of wage demands, the increased predictability of wage costs and inflation, and the negotiation of an institutional framework of industrial relations. As Roca (1991) argues, concertation was a rational employer response at a time of union strength when no actor wished to see an all-out confrontation in view of the political fragility of democracy. By the mid-1980s, however, the disadvantages were outweighing the benefits. Recession and the unions' own organizational difficulties had weakened the labour movement considerably since the late 1970s, so the employers had less incentive to contain the demands of labour through concertation. Nor were employers happy to pay the price of wage moderation in terms of improved social provision and possibly expansionist economic policies, and they resisted implementing national agreements that committed the state to action (the Moncloa Pacts, ANE in 1981 and AES in 1984–6); thus they gave priority to bipartite agreements that did not involve broader social policy commitments by the government. In any case, the employers believed that they themselves had gained little from government involvement. CEOE argued that the government was failing to implement its agreed commitments to reform corporate taxation, employers' social security contributions and labour market regulation: all aspects which CEOE considered vital for maintaining the competitiveness of Spanish business following EC membership in 1986 (Pardo Avellaneda and Fernández 1991: 175). In addition, the employers' agenda had changed. Corporate restructuring and international competitiveness were replacing inflation and pay restraint as their principal concerns. National concertation was thought to help maintain labour market rigidities inherited from Francoism, and thus to impede the process of rationalization, particularly in the sectors worse hit by the crisis. Concertation was also seen as encouraging excessively centralized, standardized collective bargaining outcomes when the situation demanded arrangements tailor-made to the needs of different firms (López Novo 1991).

The employers' lack of commitment to concertation reflects a political as well as an economic rationale. From the outset, CEOE resisted strong forms of corporatist representation at state level, sacrificing its own role in order to prevent the development of a strong state-labour relation (Martínez Lucio 1991). CEOE's strategy reflected its position as an organization trying to represent a highly fragmented employer class in which a proliferation of small and medium-sized concerns coexisted with large enterprises dominated by state and foreign capital. In addressing the problem this posed for forging a political identity and 'voice' for itself, CEOE chose to depict employers as a force for social progress prevented from fulfilling their mission by the restrictions imposed by state and labour. The representation of employers' interests thus assumed a highly antagonistic quality – as in the vehement support for labour market deregulation. Nor could the employer class look for salvation to political parties of the right, since these tailored their economic policies to the prized centre ground of Spanish politics, and were in any case too ineffectual to appear as a government-in-waiting.

For government, too, the value of concertation diminished from the mid-1980s. With the PSOE government under Felipe González (continuously in power since 1982) providing political and economic stability, democratic institutions were more soundly entrenched; the need for tripartite peak bargaining as a political stabilizer was therefore diminished. The socialists felt secure enough following their second election victory in 1986 to risk their close alliance with UGT. Moreover, as in Mitterrand's France, the early expansionary thrust of government economic policy was soon replaced by a variant of Thatcherite economic and monetary discipline in which – especially as the recession deepened and unemployment rose – concertation had no place. This was symbolized by a notorious leaked letter in which the government's economics minister put the case for not having a social contract in 1984, on the grounds that 'no concertation was cheaper than concertation'.

The decline of concertation puts into perspective the academic debate on the subject. On the one hand, writers such as Pérez Díaz (1984) see concertation as evidence of the creation of a Spanish neo-corporatism, albeit of a weaker kind than that of northern or central Europe; a neo-corporatism based on the *de facto* if not explicit commitment of the social actors to jointly negotiated social and economic policies, and their ability in turn to commit their members. Roca (1991) has pointed to the danger of assuming that corporatism was the only rational response to the requirements of the transition, and more generally that it is an inevitable tendency in parliamentary-democratic systems. Rather, corporatism has to be seen more as a 'strategy' than a 'system': a strategy for coping with social conflict and generating consensus, initiated by government in response to a particular conjuncture (Roca 1983).

The absence of corporatist arrangements after 1986 tends to support Roca's interpretation. Indeed, it may be argued that the success of neo-corporatism as a governmental strategy in Spain has resided precisely in its contingent, non-institutionalized character. The role of more formal institutions has been fairly limited. The formation of the tripartite Economic and Social Council, specified in the Constitution to advise government on economic planning and social affairs, was repeatedly delayed (*IDS European Report* 361, January 1992: 11), while participation in existing state bodies such as the National Employment Institute (INEM) has tended to be limited and ritualistic, dealing with the implementation of policy rather than policy-making (Martínez Lucio 1991). The informality of corporatist arrangements has given the government considerable flexibility, allowing it to convene negotiations at some junctures and to keep its distance from them at others. Thus when national concertation did not accord legitimacy to government policy, within the constraints of monetarist orthodoxy and the primacy of the market, the government sought legitimacy elsewhere: for example by exploiting its parliamentary majority, as it did in the crises over cutbacks in state pensions in 1985 and over the state-sponsored industrial restructuring programme of 1983.

One implication of this fluidity is that when conditions are appropriate, the government is likely to turn once again to concertation as a political tool. Indeed, this seems to have been the case since the beginning of the 1990s (see below), in response to the external economic challenge of European integration, and to changes in the internal balance of political power following the December 1988 general strike.

Collective Bargaining and the 'Formal' Dimension of Industrial Relations

The politics of incomes was one of the principal obsessions of Spanish industrial relations in the 1980s. It was played out in terms of a ritualistic debate about percentage increases in which the parties put forward arguments either about the need to maintain Spain's comparative advantage as a low-wage producer in Europe or, alternatively, to improve the workers' standard of living. Measures of inflation, past and forecast were a key reference point (e.g. Espina 1991), becoming part of the internal organizational politics of unions and employers' associations (Martínez Lucio 1989). Union branches showed their loyalty by accomplishing the percentages laid down by their national leadership, either by restraining increases as part of the 'social wage' logic of the UGT for most of the 1980s, or by breaking the national objectives set in tripartite or bipartite national bargaining between government, UGT and CEOE, as was the case of CCOO for most of the period. The unions' politics of 'class solidarity' through incomes policy, together with the importance of sectoral collective bargaining, gave rise to claims in the mid-1980s that union organization (and industrial relations generally) was becoming more centralized at the expense of works councils and company-level bargaining (Miguélez 1985).

The official statistics of the Ministry of Labour and Social Security present an apparently healthy picture of collective bargaining in Spain. Thus in 1990, 4,273 collective agreements were concluded, applying to 949,531 companies and 6,919,805 workers, out of an active work force of around 12.3 million. According to these statistics and the analysis of official bodies such as the National Commission for Collective Agreements, the number of agreements showed a steady increase on the previous two years, having risen by 5.7 per cent in 1989 and 9.5 per cent in 1990. Likewise the number of workers covered by agreements rose by 2.7 per cent in 1989 and by 13.4 per cent in 1990, maintaining the trend of the 1980s (see table 15.4).

The statistics also suggest a relatively centralized pattern of collective bargaining. Although 3,015 of the agreements signed in 1990 (around 75 per cent of the total) were concluded at company level, these affected only just over a million workers, the remaining 5.9 million being covered by

Table 15.4 Collective bargaining in Spain 1977–89

	No. of agreements	000s of employees	000s of companies
1977	1,349	2,876	557
1980	2,564	6,070	878
1981	2,694	4,435	673
1982	3,385	6,263	889
1983	3,655	6,226	870
1984	3,796	6,182	837
1985	3,834	6,131	847
1986	3,790	6,275	892
1987	4,112	6,868	997
1988	4,039	6,805	958
1989			
1990	4,273	6,920	950

Source: Ruesga (1991: 389); Ministry of Labour and Social Security.

agreements signed at a level above the company. The coverage of company agreements declined from 21 per cent of workers in 1981 to 16.6 per cent in 1987 and 14.8 per cent in 1990. In many instances company bargaining was conducted within the framework of a higher-level agreement. Above the company there were two main types of agreement: provincial-sectoral, numbering 1,108 and covering just under 4 million workers; and national-sectoral (notably in the chemicals industry) numbering 61 and covering 1.6 million workers.

The impression of a relatively centralized collective bargaining system was underlined by the behaviour of the bargaining parties. The annual collective bargaining round appeared to be directed from the head offices of the employers' organizations and the main trade unions, either by imposing centrally agreed wage increases or through recomm-endations delimiting negotiations at lower levels. However, this picture of a system dominated by higher levels of organization ignores some key contradictions and problems of collective bargaining in Spain.

National sectoral agreements were relatively underdeveloped in terms of content and the effectiveness of implementation. Such agreements increased in number during the 1980s and were seen as a vehicle for the orderly restructuring of many aspects of sectoral employment conditions (gradings, disciplinary measures, etc.) which had rested on outmoded and inflexible regulations and often predated the advent of democracy. Sectoral agreements seemed an effective means of adjusting incomes and tying them to changes within an industry. Thus, negotiated wage increases barely kept pace with inflation, even in the late 1980s in the absence of concerted incomes policy, although there was considerable variation from sector to sector: for example in 1989, average negotiated increases (in large companies) were 9.6 per cent in financial institutions compared with 5.4 per cent in commerce, hotels and catering (EIRR 204, January 1991: 23). Wage drift, facilitated by the lack of articulation between different levels of bargaining, was modest, amounting to 2–3 percentage points on pay per employee for the early 1980s, and considerably less in the latter part of the decade (Espina 1991: 345; EIRR 204, January 1991: 22). Agreements also dealt with other conditions such as working hours (just under 40 hours a week since the mid-1980s). For the unions the attraction of such agreements was that they 'regulated' intransigent and paternalistic small and medium-sized employers while also strengthening the sectoral dimensions of their organizations, the effectiveness of which had been limited by the territorial dimension.

For many trade unionists and employers, the national industry agreement for the chemicals sector served as a model. Running for much of the 1980s, the agreement allowed the 'social partners' to deal consistently with wages, such conditions as working hours, and the replacement of the labour ordinances, and in so doing to develop a strong consensual relationship. This was not, however, typical of sectoral agreements. For example, the negotiation of an agreement in the engineering industry between the employers' organization CONFEMETAL and the metalworking federation of UGT was marked by conflict between the leadership of CONFEMETAL and its regional organizational tiers who viewed it as a threat to their own bargaining role and to their objective of restricting the areas jointly regulated with the union. In the construction industry, likewise, resistance on the part of provincial employers who were initially sceptical of developments outside their immediate control proved a stumbling block. As a result, these agreements did not provide an effective, centralized model of bargaining regulating a broad range of employment issues (Martinez Lucio 1989).

Although provincial-sectoral bargaining has been the most important level in terms of the numbers of workers covered, it is also, paradoxically, the least studied by Spanish industrial relations analysts. In theory it is the vital level for the millions of workers in small and medium-sized concerns who have no company agreement or effective representation structures at the workplace.

The bargaining effectiveness of union organization varies widely between provinces and regions. While Barcelona, Madrid, Valencia, and a few other regions are well organized by the unions, they are considerably weaker elsewhere. At establishment level, moreover, works council members and workers' delegates often have an ambiguous representative role in smaller companies. According to some observers many elections are ritualistic in nature. Given the unions' concern with 'representative' status, and their lack of financial resources nationally, the principal objective of the major confederations has often been to maximize their representatives in the four-yearly elections, rather than to ensure that existing committees operate effectively. In many small firms, the representative arrangements appear to be inoperative, while even in larger ones, most works council delegates fail to use their allocation of time for workplace activity. Thus the structures necessary for implementing sectoral agreements at company level are often underdeveloped, and show considerable regional variation. Even in a relatively well-organized region such as Madrid, employers in the metal trades have tended to implement the wage element of the agreement while ignoring other provisions.

In short, the national and provincial sectoral agreements cannot be considered a fully effective system of centralized bargaining; even in the early 1980s, observers had begun to note a certain 'impoverishment' of the content of collective bargaining.

Company bargaining is largely the preserve of larger concerns, which have a much richer experience of both procedural and substantive bargaining. The extent of company bargaining has remained fairly steady during the 1980s: since 1982, each year has seen between two and three thousand company agreements, covering about one million employees. The annual studies of collective bargaining in companies with over 200 workers, conducted by the Ministry for the Economy, provide the most consistent data on bargaining at this level. These point to a limited negotiating agenda, and to difficulties in bringing subjects other than pay and working hours to the bargaining table. As a result important issues have been neglected.

In some firms, for instance in the domestic electrical goods and motor-manufacturing sectors, bargaining appears to have been broadened to cover restructuring and voluntary redundancies through company 'viability' plans. However, this does not signify an extension of the unions' negotiating role to areas of managerial decision-making such as the introduction of new technology: the little research that has been conducted in this area suggests that such involvement was minimal (Martínez Lucio 1989). Agreements covering other issues, such as training, types of labour contract, pensions, and so on, were few and far between in the 1980s, and were concentrated in a few key firms. Negotiated pay increases in company-level agreements appear, if anything, to be slightly below those in higher-level agreements (Ruesga 1991: 395).

Overall, despite the centralization of the rituals of pay determination, collective bargaining has been less centralized and more uneven and fragmented than would at first appear. The strategy of both CCOO and UGT has been to promote the rationalization of bargaining structures, particularly through sector agreements, while at the same time broadening their training programmes for local negotiators and attempting to introduce a wider category of issues into the bargaining arena. However, CCOO has always been less hostile to decentralized bargaining, which it sees as enhancing the participation of workers, allowing local mobilization to be tied into the broader dynamics and issues of collective bargaining, and as forming the basis for union activity during workplace elections.

The employers and CEOE began to show a growing interest in decentralized bargaining in the late 1980s – for rather different reasons. In their view higher-level agreements enforced excessively homogeneous conditions across a wide range of companies. One particular area of 'rigidity' has been the application of pay increases equally across different occupations and grades, restricting the flexibility of employers to award differential increases to different segments of the labour force (the chemicals industry agreement is one of the few that permits the negotiated pay increase to be applied to the total wage bill of a company, rather than to each occupational grouping). Especially in the early days of the transition, union pressure had been responsible for the erosion of pay differentials; employers responded with intra-company bargaining on the margins of formal negotiations, involving particular workplaces and occupational groups, in order to restore differentials for key groups of skilled employees (Ruesga 1991: 392). The Ministry of Economy survey for 1989 shows continuing widening of differentials in bargaining in large companies. Another aspect of higher-level bargaining that has encouraged decentralization is the loading of increases on to the basic, fixed elements of pay, inhibiting employers' efforts to strengthen performance incentives (López Novo 1991: 143). Thus, as in many other European countries, company bargaining is increasingly seen as a way of addressing issues of corporate rationalization and implementing strategies of greater flexibility.

A final aspect of collective bargaining is its role in the institutionalization of conflict. In the late 1970s, the mass mobilizations that linked political and economic demands resulted in a major upsurge in conflict: at the 1979 peak, for example, 5.7 million workers participated in 2,680 strikes (see table 15.5). Spain has continued to have one of the highest rates of strike action in Europe, although as elsewhere there has been a decline in numbers of strikes, strikers and hours lost since the mid-1980s (with the exception of 1988, year of the general strike). But the picture has been one of progressive 'Europeanization' of the strike pattern in which

Table 15.5   Industrial conflict in Spain 1976–89

	Strikes	*Participants (000s)*	*Working days lost (000s)*
1976	1,568	3,639	13,752
1977	1,194	2,956	16,642
1978	1,128	3,864	11,551
1979	2,680	5,713	18,917
1980	1,365	1,710	6,178
1981	1,307	1,126	6,154
1982	1,225	875	2,788
1983	1,451	1,484	4,417
1984	1,498	2,242	6,358
1985	1,092	1,511	3,224
1986	914	858	2,279
1987	1,497	1,881	5,025
1988	1,193	6,692	11,641
1989	863	1,223	3,165

Note: Figures exclude Catalonia 1983–5 and the Basque country 1986–9; figures for 1989 are provisional.
Source: Alonso (1991: 424).

conflict is an accompaniment of the collective bargaining process. A notable example is the recurring pattern of public sector negotiations accompanied by programmes of strikes and other forms of industrial action (Ferner 1988); the ritual element is strong, since conflict reflects union pressure on the employer as part of the bargaining process, rather than the breakdown of negotiations, and in any case many public services are subject to limitations on industrial action through 'minimum service' provisions. The conflictuality of collective bargaining also reflects continuing rivalry between the two main confederations, and the rise of independent, grade-based unions. This has created a dynamic of competitive bidding in negotiations that has often led to conflict. CCOO tends to call more strikes than UGT (22 per cent and 14 per cent respectively in 1988), but around 50 per cent of strikes are called by workers' committees rather than by the unions. Lockouts are rare in Spain, largely because of legal restrictions.

Despite the 'institutionalization' of conflict, figures for 1986–8 suggest that a minority of strikes arise out of the negotiation process (though in 1987 they involved about two-thirds of striking workers) (Alonso 1991: 426). One major cause of conflict in Spain has been industrial restructuring affecting workers in mining, shipbuilding, steel, and other sectors, most recently in the state-owned mining company Hunosa, in Asturias (EIRR 215, December 1991: 11–13). These disputes have often been part of a wider mobilization by regional interests against the impact of rationalization.

Crisis in the Labour Market: A Destabilizing Influence

The profound qualitative and quantitative transformation of the labour market in Spain has been outlined above. But the way in which the changes have been managed through industrial relations actors and institutions requires closer scrutiny, especially because of their potential to destabilize the evolving institutional framework of Spanish industrial relations.

A number of explanations have been put forward for the peculiar intensity of Spanish unemployment (Fina 1987; Comisión de Expertos 1988; Bentolila and Blanchard 1990; Sagardoy 1987): for example, the breakdown of the Francoist model of economic growth based on protected markets, labour-intensive industries and the strict regulation of labour markets; the persistence of elements of the archaic industrial relations legacy of the dictatorship, including labour market rigidities; the absence of a coherent economic policy in the early years of the transition, particularly in response to the wage explosion at a critical economic and political juncture; and the rapid increase in Spain's population (from 34 million in 1970 to nearly 40 million two decades later) requiring the extensive creation of new jobs merely to maintain existing ratios of employment. Thus, while explanations vary widely, the legacy of the dictatorship and of the transition play a prominent role.

One major effect of labour market changes and increasingly segmented employment has been to reinforce the diversity of workers' experiences. In a peculiar manner this limits the impact of unemployment. First, in larger concerns the economic crisis, coupled with the state restructuring programmes of the 1980s, posed problems for company industrial relations. In key sectors such as motor manufacturing, a feature of the 1980s was the drawing up of 'viability' plans that tied collective bargaining into broader agreements on restructuring (Martínez Lucio 1989). Wages, hours and even working practices were negotiated within a 3–5 year business planning framework in companies such as Peugeot, Pegasa (the truck manufacturer) and the aeronautics firm CASA. Higher than average redundancy payments, largely financed – directly or indirectly – through the state were a central element in these agreements.

In the critical period of the early to mid-1980s, this approach to restructuring was underpinned by UGT's strategy of cooperation that, in contrast to CCOO, rejected workers' mobilization and emphasized negotiation with the employer to establish long-term corporate viability. On occasion, UGT acceptance forced CCOO to go along with viability agreements. The PSOE's industrial policy depended on UGT's cooperative role which in many cases exposed the union to the wrath of workers affected by redundancy. Though there were parallels with national concertation, 'micro-corporatism' at company level was not a precise analogue of the pacts of the early 1980s: it was more crisis-led, and less the outcome of a 'social wage' strategy of political exchange. The effect was to exclude large groups of organized workers, in core sectors and segments of the work force, from active involvement in the struggle against unemployment.

The state's role in this area is also illuminating. Spanish legislation put obstacles in the way of redundancies: the mandatory special redundancy procedure (*expediente de crisis* or *expediente de regulación de empleo*, which like so many aspects of Spanish industrial relations has a long tradition in labour law) required redundancies to be officially authorized in the absence of agreement by workers' representatives. In addition to the restrictions on employers' freedom of action, the high cost of shedding labour on permanent contracts was a further deterrent to 'adjustment' of employment in firms. However, alternative forms of state regulation facilitating contract termination were developed. The creation of IMAC (*Instituto de Mediación, Arbitraje y Conciliación*) in January 1979 was a response to union reactions to the use of redundancy procedures. Individualized contract terminations through IMAC became far more significant than the more collective *expediente de crisis* (the latter accounting for little more than a quarter of total redundancies and dismissals). The termination of a contract via IMAC created a space whereby workers could reach an individual agreement with their employer: the employer recognized that the termination was unjustified and hence that the employee had a legal right to compensation; in return workers were compensated and permitted to receive their legally entitled social security benefits without having to go through the usual route of the labour courts.

Although redundancy payments were often relatively high, employers' costs were more predictable and the process more speedy than the legal route, permitting easier planning for the introduction of new technology and other changes. Employers also avoided the 'opening up of the books' and the more extensive union involvement traditionally associated with the *expediente de crisis*. Thus, as Bilbao (1991) argues, conflict between labour and capital was individualized. Such developments, allowing a cumulative total of 3.1 million workers to be dismissed from their jobs between 1978 and 1988, have led Falguera i Baró (1991: 285) to speak of a 'vertiginous' process of liberalization of the legal framework of dismissal and redundancy.

Other innovations were available to employers and unions seeking to limit potential conflict in key areas of industry undergoing change. An example is the Employment Promotion Funds, agreed by UGT and the PSOE in 1983, which guaranteed redundant workers in certain cases three years' unemployment benefit (instead of the usual maximum of two) so long as redundancy payments were placed in a fund that could be used by a potential employer to provide subsequent employment on the same terms and conditions as before; in practice they were little used (and were criticized for limiting the access of new entrants to the labour market – García-Perrote and Desdentado 1983).

Thus the strategies of UGT, employers and the state managed to isolate and defuse this potentially disruptive sphere of industrial relations. It was mainly CCOO and minority unions close to it that utilized the issue for worker mobilization and political engagement during the 1980s.

Qualitative changes in the labour market have also been important. Spain, like other southern European countries, represents a classic example of increasing labour market duality and fragmentation. Many employers have called for further flexibility and company-oriented approaches to industrial relations. A growing disillusionment with macro-level and corporatist relations, and with 'politicized' trade unionism, was paralleled by a growing interest in individual relations and human resource management (González 1991). According to a recent international survey of firms with over 200 workers, Spanish firms tend explicitly to use the 'human resources' label for personnel departments, in comparison with other European countries. They are also much readier than their French counterparts to use individual payment methods for managerial staff and for technical and professional employees (Price Waterhouse/Cranfield 1991; Filella 1991; Hegewisch 1991). Multinational firms seem to have been in the vanguard of implementing individualistic approaches to industrial relations, often influenced by experience of developments elsewhere. For example, they led in the development of quality circles (e.g. Delgado 1990), and of individualized payment systems, team-working and multiskilling, as in the proposed regime for SEAT's new plant at Martorell (EIRR, 210, July 1991: 9). Smaller employers were also looking to the techniques and practices of human resource management as a way of pre-empting strong and independent labour representation.

The development of individualistic strategies of labour management is likely to create new problems for the organization of labour at enterprise level, as is the changing occupational structure of employment. Both UGT and CCOO have developed structures for women and youth (and in the case of CCOO, for immigrants as well). But these have yet to be fully integrated into organizational power structures: for example, through voting rights at conference. In general, the unions' strength is, as described earlier, still located in a few key sectors such as metalworking, transport or chemicals, and in a few key regions. The organizational weight of other sectors, such as the traditionally important construction industry, has been diminished by the labour market developments described but it is still considerable.

Thus in general, far-reaching industrial transformation has not immediately challenged the internal order of the major unions. Criticism of the influence of core groups of workers in key industries and large companies, with their protectionist interest in permanent and protected employment (Recio 1991) may be valid; but it has to be understood in the context of complex organizational dynamics and the wider political strategies of the two major unions. Indeed, more recent developments, particularly the increasing importance of public sector members, often facing casualization of employment, may influence the internal politics of the unions on substantive issues such as welfare rights and encourage decentralization and other organizational restructuring to give greater weight to new interests and groups within the union.

Trade Unions, Employers and the Broader Responses to the Dilemmas of Spanish Industrial Relations

Key actors have been trying to develop strategies to surmount the perceived limitations of bargaining relations at macro- and micro-levels and to avert a crisis of socio-economic representation. The election in 1982 of the PSOE majority government on a programme based on the 'social market' and economic and political modernization signalled a shift in the nature of Spanish politics. But restructuring of core sectors of industry provoked widespread popular mobilizations. These were not as extensive as those of the latter part of the 1970s, nor did they have the unifying element of demands for democratization; but the cause of protecting employment did serve to bring together a variety of disparate interests, with CCOO acting as a focal point. CCOO was also involved in other mobilizations in the 1980s, notably the 24-hour general strike (together with CNT and USO) in June 1985 over proposed government reforms of the pensions system, for which the unions claimed the support of 50 per cent of the work force.

Thus the two main unions pursued conflicting strategies, cementing their contrasting identities. UGT consistently pursued neo-corporatist relations with employers and the state, and became closely linked with economic modernization through its willingness to sign redundancy and restructuring agreements in companies. CCOO on the other hand was able to hark back to its older identity of the 1960s and 1970s, and to end its brief flirtation with moderation (a reflection of the Eurocommunist line imposed by the PCE).

However, relations between UGT and PSOE began to sour from the mid-1980s as a result of the government's increasing economic conservatism and the abandonment of socially progressive policies, and relations between the two major confederations improved. This prepared the way for joint action over social and economic demands in the 'Trade Union Priority Programme'. Subsequently, the relationship between the unions was not as smooth, and arguments over the timing of the 1990 round of workplace elections prevented them from drawing up a joint collective bargaining strategy in 1991. But with the government stressing economic austerity and liberalization in preparation for European integration, the basis for union cooperation persists, and more recently they have moved closer together again, and are even talking of a gradual integration of the two organizations (EIRR 213, October 1991: 9).

The high point of cooperation was the joint 24-hour strike of 14 December 1988, which paved the way for negotiations over a variety of social issues including pensions, social security, education reform, youth training, and the control of temporary employment contracts. The unions' role in such matters reflects the nature of political representation in Spain, in which economic interest groups pick up issues neglected by the political parties in their struggle for the liberal centre ground of Spanish politics. CCOO, followed by UGT, has been central to the construction of these political 'counterpoints', subtly altering the unions' identities as social actors. Indeed, given the continuing legitimacy of the unions, as shown by the massive support for the 1988 general strike and by their share of the vote in workplace elections, it is not too far-fetched to argue that the unions have acted as the main opposition force to the Socialist government (Martínez Lucio 1990; Gillespie 1990).

Trade unions in the 1980s contributed to a peculiar set of relations between organized labour and the state, with a limited reappearance of concertation, both in the regional governments of the *autonomías*, and at national levels.

After the 1988 general strike, a range of discussions and negotiations took place around the unions' main demands, and around the government's concerns in the face of European integration. Thus in 1991 the government initiated tripartite discussions for a 'competitiveness' agreement in response to the completion of the single European market and problems posed by membership of the European Monetary System; the so-called 'Social Pact for Progress' foundered on the unions' opposition to its emphasis on wage restraint (EIRR 211, August 1991: 8). (The government also proposed to use the Economic and Social Council (CES) as a forum for tripartite discussion on pay restraint, a move rebuffed by both unions and employers on the grounds that the CES's role was consultation rather than negotiation (EIRR 213, October 1991: 9).) The previous year, attempts at social dialogue had borne fruit: government and unions reached agreement on the introduction of contentious legislation to institutionalize the unions' role at firm level by permitting union monitoring of labour contracts (EIRR 198, July 1990: 9; 206, March 1991: 9). A key aim of the measure was to reduce fraud and abuses·by employers that occurred – even with the plethora of legal forms of temporary contract – in sectors such as construction. Companies are obliged to pass a copy of a new employment contract to worker representatives within ten days so that they can verify its legality, prior to official notification to the local offices of INEM. CEOE, which had been marginalized in discussions, reacted with bitter hostility to what it saw as an assault on the basic rights of employers and a step towards the 'sovietization' of industrial relations, mounting a challenge at the Constitutional Court and through the ILO.

A second new area of institutionalized union involvement beyond the realm of the state involves pensions. Under 1989 legislation, if employers decide to set up corporate pension funds, the unions have statutory rights of participation in the funds' management committee. While the legislation offers considerable advances in protecting pensioners' rights – by comparison, for example, with notoriously lax British standards – it may also be seen as an indication of the state's anxiety to share the increasing burden of administering the pension system through the use of private and company-based arrangements.

Thus recent developments suggest that labour and social welfare legislation is being implemented through the participation of social actors in new institutions at firm level, rather than solely through the state; the trend to enterprise-based micro-corporatism appears to be confirmed. A further feature of current industrial relations is the continuing lack of consensus among the actors. For example, with CEOE demanding a transfer of funds from social welfare to infrastructural investment, the unions have complained of a CEOE-government common front against the workers' social demands (*El País* 28 June 1991), though on other issues (such as contract monitoring), the alliance is between government and unions. Such antagonisms are likely to colour the impact on Spanish industrial relations of the EC Social Charter (Montero Cortes 1991). If the union movement sees the EC as the basis for establishing a stronger commitment to social rights in Spain – they have advocated, for example, an enhanced role for ETUC – the employers regard it rather as the basis for a freer set of labour market arrangements and are hostile to the 'social dimension'. Their overwhelming concern with deregulation suggests that human resource management strategies based on undermining collective forms of worker representation may have increasing appeal for Spanish companies.

Conclusions

The Spanish case illustrates the diversity, rather than the convergence, of emerging industrial relations in Europe. In many ways it may be subsumed under a 'Latin European' model of industrial relations, with weak institutional structures, and the pervasive legacy of authoritarian rule. But it differs in several substantial respects from such cases as Portugal and Greece, largely reflecting the different experiences of the transition to democracy. The nature of the transition has continued to exert a profound influence on the industrial relations system and on the way in which the actors have constructed their own identities.

The central problem of Spanish industrial relations has been the need to build the system at a time of intense and uneven economic development, in the context of growing international competition and the pressures of European integration. The increasing fragmentation of the working class, as a result both of short-term economic policy and of secular changes in economic structure, and the fragmentation and weakness of indigenous employers, have added to the difficulties of the process.

While micro-relations between employers and unions have become more institutionalized, notably through the consolidation of collective bargaining, this broader political context has given rise to a complex national pattern of Spanish industrial relations: temporary alliances necessary for the stabilization of the new socio-economic order were interspersed with periods of controlled mobilization and conflict. These reflected profound ambiguities in the strategies of all the main actors. On the one hand, employers and unions pursued confrontation as part of the process of forging an organizational and ideological coherence and identity. On the other hand, they saw the need for political action to appeal to the state on behalf of often poorly organized internal constituencies. Political action at the state level was also a reflection of their own organizational weakness: as in France, the industrial relations actors relied heavily on the state to create a legal framework of support. For the unions this meant a legitimation of their status and 'representativeness'; for the employers it meant state intervention in creating the conditions for economic growth under the aegis of free enterprise.

At the same time, the state had an interest in political alliances, first to shore up the shaky democracy, subsequently to prepare the ground for meeting the challenge of Europe. In addition, the state was forced to respond to the political head of steam created by mass mobilization in the periods of political exclusion: hence the concessions to social concertation in the wake of the 1988 general strike. Thus periods in which the state excluded the social actors from influence alternated with phases of greater involvement. This dynamic was also complicated by the nature of the governing party. In pursuing a conservative policy of rationalization, deregulation and monetarism, the PSOE government did not have quite the same freedom of action as a conventional conservative administration but was to an extent bound by its credentials as a social-democratic party, and its close historical links with UGT; as a consequence, to take one example, labour market deregulation was softened by the concession of a key union role in monitoring employment contracts. In short, the government was caught between the welfare politics of the unions and their expectations concerning the 'social dimension' of European integration, and the constant demands of the employers for freer labour market relations and a less statist approach to economic issues.

The government's approach was also conditioned by the legacy of the Francoist state, apparent in industrial relations, the labour market and employment matters generally. Yet it could be argued that over the past fifteen years, these very archaic, inflexible state structures have provided an important means of containing conflict by limiting the speed and extent of deregulation, and providing a culture of central control – for example through the factory inspectorate, and in general through the persistence in some areas of a highly legalistic framework of industrial relations.

Notes

[1]   I would like to dedicate this chapter to the memory of my father, Miguel Martínez Fernández. I am also grateful for the support Anthony Ferner has given me in writing the chapter. As mentioned in the Preface, the original Spanish team of Víctor Pérez Díaz, Modesto Escobar and Joaquín López Novo, continued to contribute to the chapter by providing a number of working papers, and I would like to thank them for their help.

Abbreviations

ABI	*Acuerdo Básico Interconfederal* – National Multi-Industry Basic Agreement, 1979
AES	*Acuerdo Económico y Social* – Economic and Social Agreement, 1984
AI	*Acuerdo Interconfederal* – National Multi-Industry Agreement, 1983
AMI	*Acuerdo Marco Interconfederal* – National Multi-Industry Framework Agreement, 1980
ANE	*Acuerdo Nacional de Empleo* – National Employment Agreement,1981
CCOO	*Comisiones Obreras* – Workers' Commissions
CEOE	*Confederación Española de Organizaciones Empresariales* – Spanish Confederation of Employers' Organizations
CES	*Consejo Económico y Social* – Economic and Social Council
CEYPME	*Confederación Española de la Pequeña y Mediana Empresa* – Spanish Confederation of Small and Medium-Sized Enterprises
CGC	*Confederación General de Cuadros* – General Confederation of Professional and Managerial Staff
CNT	*Confederación Nacional del Trabajo* – National Confederation of Labour
FTN	*Fomento del Trabajo Nacional* – Promotion of National Labour
IMAC	*Instituto de Mediación, Arbitraje y Conciliación* – Institute of Mediation, Arbitration and Conciliation
INEM	*Instituto Nacional del Empleo* – National Employment Institute
OSE	*Organización Sindical Española* – Spanish Syndical Organization
PCE	*Partido Comunista Español* – Spanish Communist Party

PSOE   *Partido Socialista Obrero Español* – Spanish Socialist Workers' Party
UGT   *Unión General de Trabajadores* – General Workers' Confederation
USO   *Unión Sindical Obrera* – Workers' Trade Union Confederation

References

Aguilar, S. and Roca, J. 1989: 14-D. Economía política de una huelga. *Bulletí Informatiu 1989*. Barcelona: Fundación Jaume Bofill.

Almendros, F., Jiménez-Asenjo, E., Pérez Amorós, F. and Rojo, E. 1978: *El Sindicalismo de Clase en España (1939–1977)*. Barcelona: Península.

Alonso, L. 1991: Conflicto laboral y cambio social. Una aproximación al caso español. In Miguélez, F. and Prieto, C. (eds), 403–23.

Alós-Moner, R. and Lope, A. 1991: Los sindicatos en los centros de trabajo. In Miguélez, F. and Prieto, C. (eds), 233–50.

Amsden, J. 1972. *Collective Bargaining and Class Conflict in Spain*. London: Weidenfeld & Nicolson.

Balfour, S. 1984: The Origins of *Comisiones Obreras*. *Spanish Studies*

Baylos, A. 1991: La intervención normativa del estado en materia de relaciones colectivas. In Miguélez, F. and Prieto, C. (eds), 289–306.

Bentolila, J. and Blanchard, O. 1990: Spanish Unemployment. *Economic Policy*, April, 233–81.

Bilbao 1991: Trabajadores, gestión económica y crisis sindical. In Miguélez, F. and Prieto, C. (eds), 251–71.

Buckley, P. and Artisien, P. 1988: Policy Issues of Intra-EC Direct Investment: British, French and German Multinationals in Greece, Portugal and Spain, with Special Reference to Employment Effects. In Dunning, J. and Robson, P. (eds) *Multinationals and the European Community*, 105–28. Oxford: Blackwell.

Carr, R. and Fusi, J.P. 1981. *Spain. Dictatorship to Democracy* (2nd. edn.) London: Allen & Unwin.

Casas, J.I. 1984: La contratación colectiva en la crisis económica española. Paper presented to Conference at Instituto de Estudios Laborales.

Castells, M. 1983: *The City and the Grassroots*. London: Edward Arnold.

Castillo, J.J. 1991: Restructuración productiva y organización del trabajo. In Miguélez, F. and Prieto, C. (eds), 23–42.

Comisión de Expertos sobre el Desempleo 1988: *El Paro: Magnitud, Causas, Remedios*. Madrid.

Delgado, F. 1990: Industrial Relations and Human Resource Management in the Spanish Car Industry: The Case of Quality Circles. Unpublished MA Dissertation. Coventry: University of Warwick.

Durán Herrera, J.J. 1989: Inversion directa y resultados de las empresas multinacionales españolas, *Papeles de Economía Española*, 39, 339–53.

Espina, A. 1991: Política de rentas en España. In Miguélez, F. and Prieto, C. (eds), 331–60.

Estape, F. and Amade, M. 1986: Realidad y propaganda de la planificación indicativa en España. In Fortina, J. (ed.) *España bajo el Franquismo*. Barcelona: Crítica.

Estivill, J. and de la Hoz, J. 1990: Transition and Crisis: The Complexity of Spanish Industrial Relations. In Baglioni, G. and Crouch, C. (eds) *European Industrial Relations*, 265–99. London: Sage.

Falguera i Baró, M. 1991: La legislación individual de trabajo. In Miguélez, F. and Prieto, C. (eds), 271–87.

Fernández, F., Garrido, L. and Toharia, L. 1991: Empleo y paro en España. In Miguélez, F. and Prieto, C. (eds), 43–96.

Ferner, A. 1988: *Governments, Managers and Industrial Relations. Public Enterprises in their Political Environment*. Oxford: Blackwell.

Ferner, A. and Fina, L. 1988. La Dinámica Salarial durante el franquismo. El caso de RENFE. *Revista de Historia Económica*, 6, 1, 133–61.

Filella, J. 1991: Is there a Latin Model in the Management of Human Resources? *Personnel*

Review, 20, 6, 15–24.

Fina, L. 1978. Política salarial i lluita de classes sota el franquisme, *Materiales,* 7.

Fina, L. 1987. Unemployment in Spain: Its Causes and the Policy Response. *Labour,* 1, 2, 26–39.

Fina, L. and Hawkesworth, R. 1984. Trade Unions and Collective Bargaining in Post-Franco Spain. *Labour and Society,* 9, 1, 3–27.

Foweraker, J. 1989. *Making Democracy in Spain.* Cambridge: Cambridge University Press.

García-Perrote, I. and Desdentado, A. 1983: Los medidas laborales en la reconversión industrial. *Economía Industrial,* no. 232, 31–57.

Gillespie, R. 1989: *The Spanish Socialist Party. A History of Factionalism.* Oxford: Clarendon.

Gillespie, R. 1990: The Breakup of the 'Socialist Family': Party-Union Relations in Spain. *West European Politics,* 13, 1, 47–62.

Giner, S. and Sevilla, E. 1979: From Despotism to Parliamentarism: Class Domination and Political Order in the Spanish State. *Iberian Studies,* Autumn, 69–82.

González, B. 1991: Administración y patronales denuncian el giro sindical hacia partidos paralelos. *La Gaceta,* 3 June 1991.

Hegewisch, A. 1991: The Decentralisation of Pay Bargaining: European Comparisons. *Personnel Review,* 20, 6, 29–36.

Lange, P. et al. 1982: *Unions, Change and Crisis.* London: Allen & Unwin.

Lawlor, T. and Rigby, M. 1986: Contemporary Spanish Trade Unions. *Industrial Relations Journal,* 17, 3, 249–65.

López Novo, J. 1991: Empresarios y relaciones laborales: una perspectiva histórica. In Miguélez, F. and Prieto, C. (eds), 131–47.

Maravall, J. 1978: *Dictadura y Disentimiento Político.* Madrid: Alfaguara.

Maravall, J. 1981: *La Política de la Transición.* Madrid: Taurus.

Martín Valverde, A. 1991. *European Employment and Industrial Relations Glossary: Spain.* London/Luxembourg: Sweet & Maxwell/Office for Official Publications of the European Communities.

Martínez Alier, J. 1983: The Old Corporatist Ideology and the New Corporatist Reality in Spain. Paper presented to Conference, European University Institute.

Martínez Lucio, M. 1987: El sindicalismo madrileño en un contexto de cambio. *Alfoz,* January/February, 44–51.

Martínez Lucio, M. 1989: *The Politics and Discursive Struggles of Trade Union Development and the Construction of the Industrial Relations Arena. A Reassessment of Concepts and Problems.* Unpublished Ph.D. Dissertation. Coventry: University of Warwick.

Martínez Lucio, M. 1990: Trade Unions and Communism in Spain: The Role of the CCOO in the Political Projects of the Left. *Journal of Communist Studies,* December, 80–99.

Martínez Lucio, M. 1991: Employer Identity and the Politics of the Labour Market in Spain. *West European Politics,* 14, 1, 41–55.

Martino de Jugo, J. 1980: *Los Ferroviarios en Comisiones Obreras. Datos para la historia del movimiento obrero 1964–80.* Madrid: CCOO.

Miguélez, F. 1985: Sindicalismo y conflicto social en la España de la transición. *Mientras Tanto,* 24.

Miguélez, F. 1991: Las organizaciones sindicales. In Miguélez, F. and Prieto, C. (eds), 213–32.

Miguélez, F. and Prieto, C. (eds) 1991: *Las Relaciones Laborales en España.* Madrid: Siglo Veintiuno.

Montero, R. 1985: *La Inserción el la Actividad Económica: Emplo y paro juvenil.* Madrid: Ministerio de Cultura, Instituto de Juventud.

Montero Cortes, M.-T. 1991: *Social Policies in the Context of the Single Market and Spanish Industrial Relations.* Unpublished MBA Thesis. Cardiff: University of Cardiff Business School.

Pardo, R. and Fernández, J. 1991: *Las organizaciones empresariales y la configuración del sistema de relaciones industriales en la España democrática, 1977–1990.* In Miguélez, F. and Prieto, C. (eds), 147–84.

Pérez Amorós, F. and Rojo, E. 1991: Implications of the Single European Market for Labour and Social Policy in Spain. *International Labour Review*, 130, 3, 359–72.

Pérez Díaz, V. 1979: *Clase Obrera, Partidos y Sindicatos*. Madrid: Instituto Nacional de Industrias.

Pérez Díaz, V. 1984: Políticas económicas y pautas sociales en la España de la transición: la doble cara del neocorporatismo. In Linz, J. (ed.) *España: un presente para el futuro*, 21–55. Madrid: Instituto de Estudios Económicos.

Preston, P. 1976: La oposición anti-franquista: la larga marcha hacia la unidad. In Preston, P. (ed.) *España en Crisis*. Madrid: Fondo de Cultura Económica.

Price Waterhouse/Cranfield 1991: *The Price Waterhouse Cranfield Project on International Strategic Human Resource Management. Report 1991*. Price Waterhouse/Cranfield.

Prieto, C. 1991: Las prácticas empresariales de gestión de la fuerza de trabajo. In Miguélez, F. and Prieto, C. (eds), 185–210.

Recio, A. 1991: La segmentación del mercado de trabajo en España. In Miguélez, F. and Prieto, C. (eds), 97–115.

Rijnen, H. 1984: Industrial Relations and Trade Unions in Spain. Unpublished paper. Madrid.

Roca, J. 1983: Economic Analysis and Neo-Corporatism. Paper presented at European University Institute.

Roca, J. 1991: La concertación social. In Miguélez, F. and Prieto, C. (eds), 361–77.

Ruesga, S. 1991: La negociación colectiva. In Miguélez, F. and Prieto, C. (eds), 379–402.

Sagardoy, J. 1987: Labour Market Flexibility in Spain. *Labour and Society*, 12, 1, 55–67.

Sagardoy, J. and León, D. 1982: *El Poder Sindical en España*. Madrid: Planeta.

Segura, R. and Malo de Molina 1991: *Analisis de la Contratación Temporal en España*. Madrid: Ministerio de Trabajo y Seguridad Social.

Sisson, K., Waddington, J. and Whitston, C. 1991: Company Size in the European Community. *Human Resource Management Journal*, 2, 1, 94–109.

Toharia, L. 1988: Partial Fordism: Spain between Political Transition and Economic Crisis. In Boyer, R. (ed.) *The Search for Labour Market Flexibility. The European Economies in Transition*. Oxford: Clarendon.

Vázquez Barquero, A. 1991: Dinámica económica y reestructuración productiva en España. In Miguélez, F. and Prieto, C. (eds), 3–22.

Villasante, T. 1984: *Comunidades Locales*. Madrid: Instituto de Estudios de Administración Local.

Zufiaur, J. 1985. El sindicalismo español en la transición y la crisis. *Papeles de Economía Española*, 22.

16

Italy: Between Political Exchange and Micro-Corporatism

Anthony Ferner and Richard Hyman[1]

Introduction

The dynamics of Italian society constitute an enigma, straining the comprehension of participants and foreign observers alike. Themes which are central to the understanding of many other European countries – federalism, pillarization, corporatism – are likewise of importance in the history of modern Italy, but in forms which are at best loosely structured and semi-institutionalized. The contrast between constitutional principle and actual practice is exceptionally marked.

Though Italy's national boundaries have altered relatively little since unification in the 1860s, national identity is qualified by sharp internal differentiation. Economic and occupational structures, standards of living, political loyalties, cultural traditions and even language vary substantially between parts of the country. Only since the 1970s has there existed a comprehensive system of regional government with financial and legislative authority. However, the division of powers between central and regional governments is imprecise, and in practice the latter depend on substantial resources from the former. In the absence of clear and effective rules governing the devolution of powers, 'relations among the regions and between the regions and the central government are not determined by institutional rules but by a process of political bargaining' (Sassoon 1986: 214). In this process, political alliances and personal linkages play a vital role. In this respect, the Italian system may be defined as tacit federalism.

Major cleavages of politics and ideology have long pervaded Italian society: Catholic and anti-clerical, communist and anti-communist, collectivist and individualist. Distinctive ideologies are linked not only to specific political parties but also to newspapers, trade unions, social and cultural organizations. In this respect, the 'pillar' structure characteristic of such countries as The Netherlands is replicated, but without the stable and accepted system of mutual accommodation which the Dutch have evolved. Here too, the coexistence of competing interests and identities rests upon a process of informal and often covert deals and bargains; hence one may speak of tacit pillarization.

The relationship between state and civil society – discussed in more detail below – is similarly ambivalent. In many areas of social and economic life, legislative prescription connects only loosely with the actual rules of the game. The accommodation of organized interests is a central priority of the process of governance. As in many other countries, the practice of 'macro-concertation' or 'neo-corporatism' has been an obvious feature of union-employer-government relations in Italy in recent decades. Perhaps in part because of the distinctive historical resonances of Mussolini's corporate state, however, tripartism in Italy has not been formalized in bodies with the influence and status of the Austrian Parity Commission, the Dutch Social and Economic Council, or the Swedish Labour Market Board. Rather, concertation has been informal and *ad hoc*: a process of tacit corporatism.

These characteristics of the social and political structure contribute to the paradoxical nature of Italian industrial relations. Some observers (e.g. Cella 1989) speak of the 'weak institutionalization' of collective bargaining in Italy; yet others emphasize that there exists a dense network of shared understandings and a common adherence to rules of the game. The major national organizations on each side – despite their forceful representation of opposing economic interests, and their traditional association with radically contrary political projects – have long adhered to mutually accepted norms of action. In many respects, trade unions – including the largest, traditionally communist-led confederation – and employers' organizations have functioned as a source of national stability and order. As we argue below, this helps explain why major changes in the structure of the economy and the organization of production have been achieved in the past dozen years with a high degree of consent.

This quasi-institutionalization has permitted a degree of flexibility in the accommodation of cross-cutting divisions of local, ideological and economic interests. The Italian system nevertheless has obvious disadvantages: the tendency for informal bargaining to shade into clientelism, criminality and corruption; and the unpredictability which can at times result in explosive instability. The deficiencies of quasi-federalism have assisted the dramatic rise of the right-wing separatist movement in the northern provinces; those of quasi-pillarization were revealed in the rancorous divorce referendum of 1974, when long dormant hostilities between Catholic and secular identities erupted. In industrial relations, the inadequacies of quasi-corporatism are repeatedly stressed within the Italian literature, and in recent years have been symbolized by such dramatic episodes as the bitter conflict at Fiat in 1980, the national confrontation over the revision of wage indexation in 1984–5, and latterly by the upsurge of public-sector conflict outside the control of the main trade unions. All these aspects of weak 'institutionalization' are discussed in more detail below.

Any account of Italian industrial relations faces a choice of emphasis: is the central issue the intermittent crises, or their successful avoidance during the normal operation of the system? As in all other countries, analysts must also address the issue of change as against continuity, when both are evident features of recent historical experience. 'As we look back over the last twenty years, we are ever more struck by an apparent paradox: the extent of change, even transformation, over these years seems great, yet within each phase the prevalent impression was one of the viscousness of Italian society, of the difficulty of change, even of inertia' (Regini and Lange 1990: 4). The interpretative focus necessarily influences the relative stress laid on innovation as against stasis, the identification of turning points, and hence the periodization underlying any history of post-war Italian industrial relations.

There is, indeed, a broad consensus that a major paradigm shift occurred around the time of the successful strike wave of 1969, the 'hot autumn'. Before then, it was not too misleading to bracket Italy with France as an instance of a 'southern European model' of industrial relations marked by management authoritarianism, weak and politically divided unions, and underdeveloped collective bargaining. Thereafter, the two national paths diverged radically. But precisely how the pattern of Italian industrial relations has subsequently evolved – and in particular, how far the combination of economic restructuring, high unemployment and new management initiatives has transformed the system in the 1980s – is strenuously debated.

In this chapter we explore some of these controversies. After sketching the economic and political background to Italian industrial relations, we discuss in successive sections the role of government, legislation and 'political exchange'; trade unions and the processes of workplace representation; and employers and their organizations. In Italy, more than most other countries, the interlinkages between industrial relations 'actors' and their strategies are so complex that much cross-referencing between sections will be unavoidable. We then outline the different levels of collective bargaining and their changing interrelationship, and the country's notable strike record. We end by identifying some key themes in the recent development of industrial relations and major issues for the 1990s. Our tentative conclusion is that the 1980s have indeed seen a radical change, far less clear-cut than that which followed the 'hot autumn' but of comparable long-term significance. This second transformation has involved a simultaneous reconstruction of organized relations at macro and micro levels, with the evolution of centralized patterns of 'tacit political exchange', and decentralized forms of company-level 'micro-corporatism'. The interrelationship between the two levels has also altered; but whether a coherent and resilient pattern of articulation has emerged remains as yet uncertain.

Socio-Economic Background

Italy is, in terms of population, the second largest country in western Europe. Its post-war history has seen an incomplete socio-economic transformation from the most industrially backward member of the original EEC to a successful modern economy. However, internal disparities are among the most extreme in any European country. Large-scale manufacturing is geographically concentrated; early post-war industrialization was firmly rooted in the 'industrial triangle' between Milan, Turin and Genoa, and while the dominance of the north-west is now less decisive, regional contrasts in industrial structure remain marked. Agriculture has declined in significance since the 1940s, when it occupied some 40 per cent of the labour force, to 14 per cent in 1980 and 9 per cent in 1990. However, in the *Mezzogiorno* – the six southern mainland provinces, together with Sicily and Sardinia – some 17 per cent still work on the land.

As elsewhere in southern Europe, a substantial service sector developed while industrial employment was still relatively small (table 16.1). In 1990, 59 per cent of the labour force worked in services, as against 32 per cent in manufacturing and construction. Labour force participation rates, particularly for women, are relatively low, though as in other countries the female rate has been rising in recent decades. There is little part-time employment, though the removal of obstacles to such employment has been an important recent policy issue. Self-employment is high: accounting for 29 per cent of the total occupied labour force, but 63 per cent in agriculture and 46 per cent in market services.

As we indicate in more detail below, the structure of the Italian economy is markedly bi-polar. On the one hand there is a significant group of large, often multi-plant and multinational enterprises, many of them within the ambit of state holding companies; on the other, a very extensive number of small establishments. In part, the contrast between large and small overlaps that between north and south, and manufacturing as against agriculture and much of the service sector. However, artisan and small-firm production – what has been termed 'high-technology cottage industry' (Sabel 1982: 220) – has played an important role in the development of some of the most advanced sectors of Italian manufacturing. In particular, the 'Third Italy' (the provinces to the immediate north of the geographical centre) has often been viewed as the exemplar of a modern type of 'industrial district' in which a network of interdependent small producers permits flexible, adaptable and innovative economic performance. Nevertheless, as a rough generalization it is fair to characterize large employers in terms of relatively formal industrial relations policies (whether innovative or bureaucratic), while small employers are more likely to display informal, personalized, and often irregular employment practices. In this sense there exist two major systems of industrial relations in Italy: the first, largely typical of the north and of large firms, is shaped by the characteristic Italian mix of legal regulation and collective bargaining; the second, associated with

Table 16.1 Labour market indicators 1970–90

	1970	1980	1985	1988	1989	1990
Total employment (000s)	18,956	20,487	20,894	21,253	21,154	21,454
Participation rate[a] (%)	59.5	60.8	59.8	61.2		
male	86.8	82.8	79.3	78.8		
female	33.5	39.6	41.0	43.9		
Unemployment rate (%)	3.1	7.8	10.6	12.0	12.0	10.9
male	–	4.7	7.0	8.0	8.5	
female	–	13.0	17.3	18.6	19.1	
youth (16–24 years)	–	25.2	26.1	34.5		
North-centre	–	7.6	8.7	7.7		
South	4.9	11.5	14.7	20.6		
Sectoral share of employment (%)						
agriculture, forestry & fishing	19.4	14.2	11.1	9.8	9.3	8.9
industry (incl. construction)	43.3	37.6	33.2	32.2	32.2	32.1
services	37.3	48.3	55.7	58.1	58.6	59.0

[a]Labour force as percentage of population of 16–64 years.
Sources: EUI (1991); OECD *Economic Surveys*; ILO *Yearbook of Labour Statistics*.

the south and small employers, is largely non-union and often escapes the regulatory net. 'The decisive locus of industry-level bargaining is in the North, in the major factories and the major services firms, and in any case is determined essentially by the state of the Northern labour market' (*Ministero del Lavoro* 1990: 26). Research concentrates overwhelmingly on the former system. We must perforce follow suit, and in this chapter our main concern is with trends and variations in industrial relations in large-scale industry and the public sector.

Accurate discussion of the labour force and its distribution is obstructed by the prevalence of an extensive 'black economy'. Particularly in the south, there exists 'a massive underground and irregular economy, with its concomitant tax and social security evasion and widespread illegal and undocumented employment, the violation of labour rights legislation and the limitation of economic freedom' (*Ministero del Lavoro* 1990: 27). Calculation is of necessity imprecise; but the national labour force survey provides data which are unlikely to overstate the dimensions of the problem. It is estimated that the numbers of irregularly employed, dual job-holders and illegal immigrant workers amounted to almost 5 million in 1980, over 20 per cent of national employment; and that there was an increase of 650,000 by 1987. 'More than half of the increase in the economy's labour requirement between 1980 and 1987 was met by an increase in moonlighting, and about a third of it by non-resident foreigners' (*Ministero del Lavoro* 1990: 204). According to the same source, irregular employment is concentrated in 'tiny enterprises' in manufacturing, and more generally in other sectors such as agriculture, construction and private services, notably in the south, and for the most part involving unskilled labour.

Unemployment has been a serious problem throughout the 1980s, with a level of over 10 per cent for most of the decade (see table 16.1). Levels are particularly high among first-job seekers – the proportion of youth among the unemployed is the highest in the EC. Female unemployment is more than double the male rate, in part reflecting the growth in female labour force participation. Similarly, unemployment in the south is more than double the rate in the rest of Italy. These figures have combined to produce an unemployment rate of over 50 per cent for women aged under 24 in southern Italy (*Ministero del Lavoro* 1990). Inflation in the last two decades has been very high, reaching a peak annual rate of over 20 per cent in 1980; and though the figure was soon reduced, at over 6 per cent in the early 1990s it remains above the European average.

The State, Law and Political Exchange

The Political System

The political system in Italy is extremely complex. The Chamber of Deputies and the Senate – both elected by proportional representation, though by different systems – have co-equal status; the legislative process therefore requires delicate coordination between the two chambers. The electoral system generates a multiplicity of parties with parliamentary representation; governments are invariably coalitions, and the inter-party alliances on which they rest lack stability. Thus there have been more than fifty governments since the war – though in practice, changes of government rarely involve major alterations either in political composition or in personnel.

The pivotal role in Italian government is played by the Christian Democrats (DC), who have achieved the largest vote in every national election. Despite a decline in support since 1948, when they won almost half the votes, in recent decades they consistently received a third or more of votes. The DC have provided the head of every post-war government, except for the two periods 1981–2 and 1983–7 (when they were nevertheless the largest government party). The DC benefit from their traditional links with the powerful Catholic church, and from the system of patronage and clientelism associated with control of public agencies at national (and often regional and local) level. However, the *Democristiani* are less an integrated ideological bloc with a common policy orientation than a coalition of factions covering a broad spectrum of right–left politics. As the 'communist threat' which once held together the DC as a counter-force has waned, so the internal conflicts have become more severe and more manifest.

After the war the communists, whose standing was boosted by their prominent role in the wartime anti-fascist resistance, became the second main political force, and the largest and most influential communist party in western Europe. From the onset of the cold war the Italian Communist Party (PCI) was excluded from government, but nevertheless attracted roughly a quarter of the popular vote throughout the 1950s and 1960s, and won control of local government in a number of important cities. The Italian party was the first to question established communist orthodoxies, calling in the 1970s for a 'historic compromise' whereby communists would join with progressive tendencies in other parties and the Catholic church in order to defend democracy and achieve social and economic reform. Despite some sympathy within the governing parties for the proposal to admit the PCI to the coalition this was never approved; but between 1976 and 1979 a half-way house was agreed, whereby the party was allowed control of some important parliamentary committees in return for its support for the government. The new strategy initially brought the PCI over 30 per cent of the vote in parliamentary elections. In the 1980s the party lost popular support while continuing to distance itself from the communist tradition, and after bitter internal debates in 1990 and 1991 changed its name to the Democratic Left Party (PDS). However, the change resulted in a split, with a new party – *Rifondazione Comunista* (RC) – emerging to the left of the PDS and drawing the support of some of the most committed PCI activists.

The exclusion of the communists from government despite the level of their popular support created a situation commonly described as 'blocked democracy'. Effective government depends on the ability of the DC to sustain alliances with minority parties. The Social Democrats (PSDI), whose popular vote for the last 20 years has been below 5 per cent, the Republicans (PRI), who until recently attracted even less support, and the tiny Liberals (PLI) have been able to exercise disproportionate influence as components of multi-party coalitions. More notably, the Socialist Party (PSI), which in the 1970s never achieved 10 per cent of electoral support in general elections, and reached a peak of just over 14 per cent in 1987, was able to hold the premiership between 1983 and 1987 and may well do so again. At local and regional level, the PSI is often able to act as a power-broker between the two main parties, choosing which to partner in a coalition administration; in consequence, it has been able to hold key positions in local government. Like the DC, the PSI has recently been involved in major scandals concerning links with the mafia and other criminal elements, and diverting public funds to party coffers.

As indicated earlier, the strength of party identities has generated a quasi-pillarization of Italian society. While the main employers' confederation, Confindustria, has traditionally had close links with the Christian democrats, on the trade union side the pattern has been one of complex political affiliations. As in many other southern European countries, the Italian labour movement has been divided on ideological lines for most of its existence. The main unions which developed at the end of the nineteenth century were linked to the growing socialist movement, and a class-political orientation was expressed both in the local chambers of labour and the national confederation which was established in 1906. Catholic unions, formed to counter socialist influence among workers, followed suit by creating a rival confederation. The communist-socialist split did not lead to a further fracturing of trade unionism; but after the fascist seizure of power in 1922, all independent workers' organizations were soon suppressed. In 1944 the main political forces in the struggle for national liberation – socialists, communists and Christian democrats – agreed to create a unified trade union, CGIL (*Confederazione Generale Italiana del Lavoro*). But unity did not survive the cold war: in 1948 CGIL split three ways. The Christian democrats formed CISL (*Confederazione Italiana dei Sindacati Lavoratori*), and social democrats and republicans created UIL (*Unione Italiana del Lavoro*), leaving CGIL under the control of the communists, though retaining a significant left-socialist tendency. The evolution, and implications, of political identities and divisions are explored further below.

At the beginning of the 1990s, Italian politics appeared to have entered a new phase of instability; and this has been reinforced by the results of the 1992 general election. All the main parties lost support. The PDS registered only just over 16 per cent; even adding on the 5.6 per cent gained by RC, this was the worst 'communist' performance since

1946. The DC lost a similar level of support, falling below 30 per cent for the first time ever. The PSI, which had been expected to improve its national position, lost votes overall, despite a considerable advance in the south. The main beneficiary was the Lega Nord (LN), an alliance of the various 'leagues' in the northern provinces, which argued for autonomy within a formal federal structure, curbs on immigration, and lower taxes. The LN emerged with 9 per cent of the national vote, 18 per cent in the northern provinces (where all its candidates were standing), and became the largest party in its main stronghold of Lombardia. Politically, Italy has become almost bifurcated, with the DC and PSI dominating the south, and PDS and LN ascendant in the north. In a country where party loyalties have traditionally been extremely stable, so that a shift of two or three per cent in a party's support is regarded as a landslide, this result was seismic in its implications. A variety of scenarios for the 1990s have emerged: radical constitutional reform; entry of the PDS into government; the break-up of the DC. Whatever the outcome, the implications for industrial relations are imponderable, but could be highly disruptive.

The State in the Italian Economy

The distinctive politics of Italian industrial relations are shaped by the contradictory combination of a tradition of state interventionism and a post-war history of weak and indecisive government. The boundaries between state and civil society are fluid and imprecise: and indeed, economic efficacy depends in large degree on a network of relations between the two spheres which bedevil analysis or even description.

In Italy, in marked contrast to Germany, there was no sharp post-war break with the institutional framework of the fascist era. The 1943 palace revolt which ousted Mussolini (leaving him to head a rump government in the north) permitted a constitutional continuity between pre-war fascism and post-war democracy. While the trappings of the corporate state were discarded, much of its infrastructure survived. Despite the economic liberalism of the DC government, it retained the state holding company IRI: a vehicle, as shown below, for strategic intervention in industrial development as well as innovation in industrial relations. Post-war governments also inherited a 'state apparatus which had not changed much since fascist times and was less at home with general economic management and macro-economic policy than with direct deals between government and single firms' (Ranci 1987: 117). Particularistic relationships between government and economic actors extended seamlessly – particularly at regional and local level – into systems of clientelism and corruption.

The strategic role of the state in the Italian economy coexists with governmental weakness and legislative sclerosis. 'Blocked democracy' leads to permanent difficulties in achieving policy consensus within unstable and disparate coalitions; and the loss of legitimacy for the governmental process, combined with the institutional checks and balances in the Italian parliamentary system, poses serious obstacles to radical policy initiatives. Change typically occurs incrementally, requiring *ad hoc* compromises to ensure the consent of the interests affected. This has meant, in particular, that industrial relations policy must normally be acceptable both to unions and to employers' organizations.

The implementation of policy and law reflects the same tensions. As Lange and Regini have emphasized (1989: 250), the linkages between state and economy in Italy involve 'mixes of regulatory modes and principles'. Control and exchange relationships interconnect with the mobilization of consent. The search for legitimacy typically qualifies the application of power.

Law and Industrial Relations

These general characteristics are of specific relevance for industrial relations. The Italian labour market is subject to a complex web of legal regulation, which has evolved in particularistic fashion rather than being shaped – with the dramatic exception of the 1970 Workers' Statute – by comprehensive legislative initiative. Giugni (1982: 383), in a well-known analysis, refers to Italian labour law as an alluvial deposit (*formazione alluvionale*); in similar vein, Reyneri (1989a: 135) refers to a 'geological stratification' of legal instruments, with a succession of new regulations being 'casually added onto the old norms'. He cites the existence of 'ten different modes of hiring and five or six different forms of unemployment insurance, not to mention the eight or nine different tripartite commissions (unions, business and state bureaucrats) that are meant to oversee aspects of the labour market'. In the last two years, further legislation has compounded the complexity.

The individual employment relationship is thus governed by extensive legal norms and administrative mechanisms. The post-war regulative system (in some respects inherited from pre-war corporatist controls) prescribed, for example, that firms were required to recruit labour via the official employment exchange; hence private employment agencies are illegal. Part-time and short-term contracts were permitted only in narrowly specified circumstances. A variety of 'protective' restrictions – for example, the prohibition of night-work – applied to women workers. No specific minimum wage legislation was ever enacted, but article 36 of the Constitution which refers to 'proportionate' and 'decent' wages has been interpreted by the courts as requiring adherence to the minima contained in collective agreements. Also relevant is the notion of *erga omnes*, which denotes the universal applicability of the terms of collective agreements. This is one of those provisions of article 39 of the Constitution which has never been embodied in legislation. However, some lawyers argue that a 'more courageous use' of article 36 could form a vehicle for the extension of collective agreements, thus bringing firms which are not members of employers' associations within the scope of industry-wide agreements (Napoli 1989: 68). Considerable protection of individual employment was provided by law 604 of 1966, which permits dismissal only when justified by 'subjective' reasons (the employee's conduct) or 'objective' (situations of redundancy) (Sciarra 1986: 56–62).

In two main respects, the legal framework has altered in recent decades. Attempts have been made, from the late 1970s, to introduce greater flexibility, and hence some of the previous controls have been relaxed. However, as is argued below, this process has been more limited in Italy than in many other countries, and deregulation has occurred in a regulated fashion. More noteworthy in many respects was the radical extension of employee rights contained in the *Statuto dei Lavoratori* (Workers' Statute, law 330/1970). This reflected the dramatic shift in the relation of forces in industry following the 'hot autumn' of 1969, and was intended to re-stabilize Italian industrial relations within a new institutional framework. Employment security was reinforced, with remedies of both substantial compensation and reinstatement prescribed in cases of unjustified dismissal; unilateral changes in job definitions were also tightly restricted. Various forms of surveillance were prohibited: the use of security guards to observe workers (except for the purpose of protecting property); monitoring employee performance by audio-visual devices; enquiries into workers' political, religious or trade union opinions. Disciplinary procedures and sanctions are tightly regulated under the Statute, which also provides for educational and other forms of leave. In sum, the 1970 Statute provides the most radical body of individual employment rights in Europe.

Yet the reality of the Italian labour market involves an extensive 'informal' economy with widespread dual job-holding and illegal and irregular employment practices. 'The labour market appears subject to rigid legal guarantees and pervasive administrative control but in fact a diffuse social spontaneity prevails, rooted in familial or community micro-systems; without competent and efficient mechanisms of public intervention, legal norms remain a dead letter' (Reyneri 1989b: 377). As noted earlier, large factories and public agencies, particularly in the north, and where effective workplace unionism exists, may comply with the legal provisions; elsewhere, systematic non-observance may be the norm. The law is a resource, at times indeed important, in the dynamics of the labour market; but other, often conflicting forces also exert a major influence.

Collective Labour Law

Despite the elaborate system of individual labour law in Italy, collective aspects of industrial relations are subject to very little direct legal regulation. The 1948 Constitution defined Italy as 'a democratic republic founded on labour', and declared (articles 39 and 40) that employees have the right to organize collectively and to strike; but the subsequent DC governments failed to enact specific legislation giving detailed force to these principles (though Italy did adopt the relevant ILO conventions). Clearly there was a fear among employers and the political right that such legislation would strengthen the labour movement in general and CGIL in particular; but among trade unionists there was also some concern that legally enshrined rights would be accompanied by unpalatable regulations and restrictions. Technically, too, legislation on trade union rights would involve considerable difficulties in a national context of union pluralism and inter-confederal competition.

In general terms, therefore, trade union organization and action in Italy are today less regulated than elsewhere in Europe. If unions enjoy few specific rights they are subject to even fewer obligations. Their internal organizational arrangements and their objectives (such as political involvements) are not externally regulated. Until the 1990 law on disputes in essential services (discussed below), strike action was virtually unconstrained by law. While jurists have debated whether collective agreements impose some form of peace obligation, this possibility has never been of practical significance. As in Britain, such agreements are 'binding in honour only' (Wedderburn and Sciarra 1988).

Trade unions derive ambiguous rights from the legal concept of 'most representative union' (*sindacato maggiormente rappresentativo*). This imposing status lacks precise statutory definition, and has therefore to be interpreted by specific judicial or administrative decision. In practice, the 'most representative' unions are the three main confederations and their affiliated sectoral organizations, though on occasion the neo-fascist CISNAL is also so designated. The status entitles the favoured unions to various legally prescribed rights, and is also the basis for appointment to various tripartite administrative agencies.

The most notable source of collective employment rights is the *Statuto dei Lavoratori*. However, as a legal support for unions the Statute has been variously described as 'promotion without regulation' (Treu 1987a: 170) and 'a victory for imprecision' (Wedderburn 1991: 248). In general, a variety of collective rights are specified in the form of protections and resources for employees at workplace level, rather than specifically for their organizations. Workers are legally authorized to establish and join unions and carry out trade union activities, and may participate in meetings at the workplace. Employers are prohibited from discriminating against union members, and from attempting to form company unions. Any action by an employer likely to obstruct the right to freedom of association and collective action can result in a complaint to the local judge (*pretore*), who may issue an immediate judgment on the matter.

The law also established a new institution, the *rappresentanza sindacale aziendale* (RSA); while scarcely translatable, this concept may be roughly rendered as 'workplace union representative structure'. Workers are entitled to establish these bodies 'within the ambit' of the 'most representative' unions, or those which are parties to collective bargaining arrangements which cover the enterprise. The law is silent on the actual constitution of RSAs or the manner of their election, but states that representatives are entitled to both paid and unpaid leave of absence for different union functions, to protection against victimization and facilities for communication with the workforce, and (in larger firms) to be provided with an office.

These rights constitute a powerful and extensive set of supports for trade union organization, and have contributed to the relative resilience of Italian unions despite radical industrial restructuring and adverse labour market conditions (see below). The fact that most rights adhere to individuals (as is true, in Italy, of the right to strike itself) rather than unions as organizations does not appear to weaken their effect, and may be seen as a reflection of the problems of trade union pluralism and inter-union rivalry. The difficulty of identifying a specific 'bargaining agent' also helps explain why the Statute 'did not impose any general duty to bargain, but ensured that the *rappresentanza* clung like a limpet to the walls of every enterprise' (Wedderburn 1991: 252).

Hence in a unique fashion, 'voluntarism' and 'juridification' are both strong features of Italian industrial relations, complementary as much as contradictory. 'Bargaining coexists with law, leading a parallel life' (Sciarra 1987: 128). This coexistence has become increasingly important since the late 1970s: 'law and collective bargaining are moving more and more in the direction of mutual interpenetration' (Napoli 1989: 72).

Social Protection and Special Employment Measures

The Italian system contains a complex variety of instruments and institutions designed to facilitate economic restructuring, support those made redundant, and improve the labour market position of the unemployed (and in recent years, particularly school-leavers). As in other aspects of industrial relations, statutory provisions and collective agreements interconnect, and unions and employers are involved in the operation of the official machinery.

The most notable instance of social protection in the labour market is the *Cassa Integrazione Guadagni* (CIG – earnings maintenance fund). This fund, administered by a tripartite agency, the *Istituto Nazionale per la Previdenza Sociale* (INPS – National Institute for Social Insurance), dates from 1941. Its purpose was to provide income support for employees affected by short-time working or lay-offs as a result of temporary market difficulties. After the war the scope of the scheme was extended on a number of occasions. Under the 'ordinary' CIG system, the employer can apply for support from the fund following consultations with the relevant trade unions, and workers can receive up to 80 per cent of their wages for twelve months.

An 'extraordinary' version of the scheme was established in 1968, and extended in 1977, to support workers affected by company reorganization. New tripartite bodies were established to oversee the application of the fund, at national and regional levels (Tronti 1991: 127). In effect, the 'extraordinary' CIG could operate without time limits (despite a notional two-year maximum); and by the 1980s it was functioning less as a support fund for those affected by temporary reductions in production than as a form of redundancy compensation for those whose jobs were permanently eliminated by corporate restructuring. Despite some limited restrictions on payments from the fund, expenditure increased rapidly: in the peak year of 1984 a total of over 800 million working hours were paid for under the scheme in the manufacturing and construction industries, though the figure fell by more than half by the end of the decade (Tronti 1991: 128). At the peak, roughly 10 per cent of all workers in large companies were permanently laid off and supported by the CIG; in major manufacturing industries the proportion was far higher (Negrelli and Santi 1990: 161).

Such concealed redundancy made it relatively easy for firms to agree restructuring initiatives, as well as reducing the official unemployment figures (since workers affected are still legally employees of their firms). The system gave unions a far more favourable bargaining position in responding to radical restructuring of employment than existed in most other countries, since the state income guarantees cushioned those members who were made redundant and provided a floor of benefits; additional payments above the 80 per cent level might sometimes be negotiated. But as already indicated, this was achieved at considerable financial cost: in the mid-1980s, public expenditure on CIG was some 4,000 billion lire a year. In addition, some critics (e.g. Padoa Scioppa 1987) argued that the system reinforced labour market divisions between protected 'insiders' and jobless 'outsiders', particularly the young.

After lengthy debates on possible reforms to the system, changes were finally enacted in 1991. These placed a two-year limit to payments from the fund, required companies to rotate those laid off and receiving benefits across the whole work force, and provided incentives for early retirement in firms pursuing technological restructuring. In particular, the unions have long supported the principle of rotation on grounds of equity, but major employers such as Fiat had found this unacceptable (Padoa Schioppa 1987: 105).

Of the numerous forms of special employment measures introduced in the 1980s (a reflection of the process of 'incrementalism' discussed previously) the most important in terms of coverage have been the 'trainee contracts' introduced by law 863 of 1984. The scheme permits employers to offer temporary contracts to young persons (aged below 30), and provides substantial exemptions from social security contributions; further incentives are offered to employers who convert the temporary contract into permanent employment. The specific training requirements are modest; in practice, the scheme is simply designed to facilitate the recruitment of young unemployed persons. In this respect it has achieved some success; in its first five years of operation, over one and a half million such contracts were issued. Minor legislative changes have also been made to encourage apprenticeships, the numbers of which declined in the first half of the 1980s but subsequently recovered.

Less numerically significant, but in some ways a greater breach with past practice, was the provision in the same legislation for part-time contracts. The aim is to spread job opportunities by relaxing legal restrictions on such employment: firms may either fill vacancies on a part-time basis, or allow existing staff to transfer to part-time working. The annual number of contracts under this scheme reached almost 200,000 by the late 1980s, the great majority involving women workers.

A particularly ambitious project, also initiated in the 1984 legislation, involved 'solidarity contracts' whereby individual working hours could be reduced either to create new employment or else to minimize or avert redundancies. Half of the loss of income resulting from the reduced hours is compensated from public funds. However, the use made of these contracts has been negligible. Other special employment measures have been directed towards young persons and to the unemployed in the south of Italy; to encouraging self-employment; and to assisting early retirement. Subsidies have also been provided for employment in 'socially useful' activities (for a detailed review of special employment measures see *Ministero del Lavoro* 1990: ch. V).

Any overall assessment of the initiatives of the past decade must conclude that the impact has been modest indeed. Officially recorded part-time and fixed-term contracts cover only some 6 per cent of Italian employment in each case (EIRR 1990). Yet as was seen in the introduction to this chapter, irregular forms of employment have increased far more rapidly, particularly in the south where unemployment is highest. Outside the control of either legal regulation or collective bargaining, the labour market has adapted to changed circumstances in ways which are informal and usually illegal.

Flexibility and Deregulation

Many of the special employment initiatives have involved a relaxation of traditional legal restrictions on 'atypical' labour contracts. In this respect, they can be seen as part of a more general process of labour market deregulation, in response to pressures for enhanced flexibility from employers in particular. A major landmark of this process was law 903 of 1977 which modified the previous prohibition on night-work for women. Reyneri (1989b: 383) has referred to the 1980s as a decade of 'creeping deregulation' (*deregolamentazione strisciante*, rendered perplexingly as 'rampant deregulation' in Reyneri 1989a: 140).

Given the elaborate and extensive system of labour market regulation which has traditionally existed in Italy, the trend to deregulation has indeed been more limited and gradual than in many other European countries, and has sustained the dual features of reform by agreement and the mutual interaction of legislation and collective bargaining. The central prerequisite for permitting enhanced employer flexibility – in extending night-work, overriding normal seniority rules, introducing temporary and short-term contracts – is that the initiatives should be approved by collective agreement. Hence 'the implementation of flexibility is subject to collective control, usually coupled with public control' (Treu 1987a: 178).

Wedderburn (1991: 254) has referred to the process as 'articulated deregulation', and this concept may be interpreted in at least two different ways. First, the relaxation of legal restrictions is merely provisional, depending on the re-regulation of the relevant issue by collective agreement; but second, the major deregulatory initiatives have represented statutory enactments of changes already agreed by unions and employers in bilateral or trilateral national discussions. This complex interaction of legislation and negotiation fits within the far broader pattern of 'political exchange' which was characteristic of Italian industrial relations in the late 1970s and early 1980s, and which arguably has persisted in more tacit and covert form.

Political Exchange and Tripartism

It is no accident that the notion of political exchange (*scambio politico*) originated in Italy. To overcome the problems inherent in Italy's 'blocked democracy', the formal political process has always required elaborate channels of informal negotiation with socio-economic interest groups. As emphasized at the outset, informality is a persistent theme in the Italian context: the formal institutions of tripartite concertation and regulation established in many European countries in the 1960s and 1970s have no parallel in Italy. The closest analogue, the *Consiglio Nazionale dell'Economia e del Lavoro* (CNEL – National Council for the Economy and Labour) has an imposing title but few significant functions, operating principally as a research and information institute. Real decisions are taken elsewhere.

In an influential discussion, Pizzorno (1978) explored the phenomenon of political exchange through a distinction between three types of bargaining. The individual bargain between worker and employer involves an exchange of wages for work performance; in the collective bargain between unions and a company (or employers' association), the trade-off is between the gains achieved for the workers represented, and the order and predictability achieved by the employer. In both types of exchange, market power – individual and collective – plays an important role. In political bargaining, by contrast – for example, a campaign to prevent a factory closure – unions may achieve gains even when market power does not exist. Here, what unions offer is 'consensus and support...the threat is withdrawal of the wider social consensus or social order' (1978: 279).

In this sense, political exchange is relevant to industrial relations only in contexts where governments require support in mobilizing consensus, and where trade unions have the capacity to facilitate or obstruct this process – both conditions which have generally applied in post-war

Italy. At the very least, even governments which feel no need for active trade union support normally wish to avoid their opposition: 'obtaining union neutrality has been important for almost every Italian government in the last two decades' (Perulli 1990: 28). One corollary is what Treu (1987b: 361) has termed 'the unwritten rule that any major legislation on labour matters must have the largely unanimous consent of the trade union movement (including its communist fraction)'. This principle, he suggests, was 'applied since the 1950s to make up for the exclusion of the Communist Party from national government....This arrangement was an imperfect functional equivalent of a pro-labour government.'

These considerations are essential for an understanding of the complex processes of peak-level bargaining between unions and employers, and the overt and covert involvements of the government, since the mid 1970s. Much of the detail – and in particular the complex struggles and negotiations over wage indexation – forms the subject of later discussion. At this point, however, it is appropriate to offer some broad assessment of the way that politics and industrial relations have interconnected in the evolution of political exchange.

Arguably, the 'internal' and the 'external' accounts of the weakness of macro-concertation identifiable in the Italian literature – the one emphasizing the unions' difficulties in securing rank-and-file compliance with restraint, the other their difficulties in securing worthwhile compensation for restraint – should be seen as complementary rather than contradictory. As Pizzorno indicated in his early discussion of political exchange (1978: 284–5), the trade-off between immediate, calculable self-restraint in wage bargaining and more diffuse and longer-term gains in organizational status and political influence may be differentially regarded at leadership and rank-and-file levels. For this reason, analysts of neo-corporatism have often viewed unified, centralized and encompassing trade unions as a prerequisite for stable political exchange. Yet as Regini (1984: 133–4) has argued, Italian unions have possessed 'functional equivalents' which have facilitated tripartite concertation: most notably, the degree to which rank-and-file activists share the political perspectives of union leaders and are thus receptive to a defence of political exchange in terms of solidaristic class interests.

In assessing the experience of the last two decades, three main phases require consideration: first, the agreements reached during the period of 'national solidarity' government, and the more difficult efforts to reach an economy-wide deal which led eventually to the 'Scotti' agreement of 1983; second, the February 1984 agreement/decree, and the resulting rupture between the communists and the other participants; third, the gradual, more tacit return to the search for accommodation in a process which may perhaps be termed 'passive political exchange'.

In the first phase, the goal of consensus in the face of economic and political crisis was initially of overwhelming significance. This is the major explanation for the tripartite 1977 agreement, in procedural terms path-breaking though imposing few firm obligations on any of the parties. Later the costs and benefits of concertation – the exchange dimension – became increasingly significant, and contributed to the growing tensions within peak-level relationships. Class solidarity has a material dimension; hence Regini's emphasis (1984: 139) on the importance, in this first phase of political exchange, of 'the unions' growing awareness of their miscalculation of the benefits which could in fact be obtained from concertation'. Certainly the decision of the PCI in 1979 to withdraw support from the government reflected both political considerations (the electoral costs of consensus) and dissatisfaction with the limited material concessions to working-class interests by the government. It is significant that this break did not put an end to the pursuit of macro-agreement. Though the changed political environment, and the employers' offensive which was symbolized by the Fiat dispute, made settlement extremely difficult, the attempts continued. In terms of content – the limitations on the distinctive Italian wage indexation system, the *scala mobile* (which dated from 1956 but had been put on a more generous basis under the multi-industry collective agreement of 1975), the freezing of company-level wage bargaining, and the acceptance of deregulation – the agreement brokered by the government at the outset of 1983 was no less significant than that of 1977. In the view of Rehfeldt (1991: 329), 'the agreement constitutes in effect the first *explicit* application of the strategy of political exchange inaugurated by the EUR line' – the joint union programme of 1978, discussed below, which marked the shift from the militancy of the first half of the 1970s to far greater restraint.

The following year, under the new socialist-led government, another agreement was proposed, further restricting indexation in exchange for tax concessions by the government. CISL and UIL, together with the socialist minority in CGIL, were prepared to acquiesce; but the latter's communist majority, under strong pressure from the PCI leadership which demanded a more militant stance, rejected the deal. In the absence of agreement, the government imposed the proposed terms by decree; the PCI demanded a national referendum; but after a protracted and bitter campaign it was defeated, though achieving a 45.6 per cent vote against the changes.

The rupture of 1984 reflected, in part, the absence of compensating benefits for unions in the 1983 deal (Giugni 1987: 381). 'All three unions seemed substantially convinced of the need for a centralized agreement to combat inflation, but were uncertain and divided over its contents' (Regalia and Regini 1989: 395). But the breakdown also stemmed from an 'over-politicization' of political exchange: the desire of the new government under Craxi (and no doubt also of CISL, UIL and the socialist minority in CGIL) to outmanoeuvre the PCI to the advantage of the socialists. The immediate decision to impose by decree-law the deal from which CGIL had withdrawn, but on which a compromise solution might presumably have still been possible, was a dramatic provocation, breaching the 'unwritten rule' of consensual legislation (Treu 1987b: 361). Nevertheless, it is significant that the PCI rather than CGIL made the running in the parliamentary filibustering and the referendum campaign. The CGIL leaders distanced themselves from the party's actions and remained interested in macro-concertation, as their acceptance of the IRI agreement of December 1984 clearly indicates. Thus while the consensus of interpretations was that the end of formal tripartism (and the collapse of the unitary CGIL–CISL–UIL federation) reflected the renewed primacy of party-political considerations, there is disagreement whether it was the PCI which imposed on CGIL an objection in principle to a pact, or on the contrary the pro-government political leanings of CISL and UIL which made them willing to accept an agreement regardless of content (cf. Regalia and Regini 1989: 394–5).

While explicit trilateral concertation was not subsequently resumed, political exchange in more covert guise has continued. As one employers' representative has commented (Olivieri 1987: 376), 'no one mentioned the words concertation or social pact but it would appear that, in the space of three years, taking the Scotti Protocol as the point of departure, Italy has progressed from the "authoritarian" concertation typical of the times of emergency to a free and conscious concertation for purposes of development'. Hence it is possible to speak of 'the actuation of an "implicit" incomes policy through the central government budget, while employer and worker organizations reached agreement through ordinary collective bargaining' (*Ministero del Lavoro* 1988: 8). From the outset, taxation decisions and incomes policies have been closely linked, with governments rewarding trade union restraint by adjustments to tax scales to compensate for 'fiscal drag' (Somaini 1989: 344). Even if at arms' length, such reciprocity would seem to have remained an important feature.

Additional elements in an 'implicit incomes policy' are the unions' acquiescence in the gradual dismantling of the *scala mobile*, and the reluctant acceptance by Confindustria of its legislative extension in 1986, 1989 and 1990. Other recent initiatives are evidence of passive political exchange: the 'Giugni law' of 1990 designed to curb *cobas*-led strikes (discussed below); the extension of employment protection rights in 1991 to workers in firms with fewer than 15 employees, an agreed change which avoided a referendum called by the left-wing *Democrazia Proletaria* party; the curbs on the CIG in the same year; and the law 125 of 1991 on equal opportunities for women, following a variety of other initiatives regarding female employment rights (*Ministero del Lavoro* 1990: 437–47). The consensus underlying these legislative changes – with very different balances of costs and benefits for unions and employers – is a strong indication of a continuing process of tripartite trade-offs.

Political exchange, then, 'has not totally disappeared in recent years; it has simply developed more pragmatic and flexible forms' (Negrelli and Santi 1990: 186). Rather than direct tripartite concertation, what is often involved is a more or less articulated set of bilateral trade-offs (employers–government, government–unions, unions–employers). The dangers of breakdown or prolonged deadlock over any issue encourage compromise on all sides, as the history of the *scala mobile* clearly demonstrates. More positively: in procedural terms, unions benefit from government confirmation of their (increasingly problematic) representative status, the government from the legitimacy bestowed on its economic programme; in substantive terms, the trade-off between wage restraint, employment creation, labour market flexibility and a favourable tax and welfare regime offers all parties the possibility of a positive-sum game (De Marinis 1991: 12). Yet the very complex dynamics of intra- and inter-organizational interest divisions and accommodation, together with the tensions between political and industrial relations identities, pose major obstacles to agreement. In a context of weak institutionalization (Cella 1990), political exchange is unstable. 'The policy of concertation cannot be consolidated without institutional reform' is the persuasive conclusion of one of the key actors in the shaping of modern Italian labour law (Giugni 1987: 382).

Trade Unions

A Divided Movement

Trade unions have been central actors in the double transformation of industrial relations in the past quarter-century, both as subjects and as objects of change. The evolution of Italian unionism since the late 1960s has involved a complex interplay of industrial and political interests and activities, through which the labour movement – and more specifically the largest organization, CGIL – has moved from marginalization to a pivotal role in contemporary socio-economic relationships (Lange et al. 1982). But enhanced power and status have been associated with new debates and uncertainties: questions of collective identity, internal democracy and representativeness acquired new prominence in the 1980s, and as yet remain unresolved.

As was noted previously, for almost all its existence the Italian trade union movement has been ideologically divided. The present system with the main confederations CGIL, CISL and UIL, a small neo-fascist rival, and various 'autonomous' unions, dates from the period of the cold war. The intervening years have, however, seen considerable variations in the meaning and significance of union pluralism, with relations between the major unions varying between bitter antagonism and amicable cooperation. Inter-union relations at different levels (confederal, sectoral union and workplace) have also displayed distinctive characteristics. For example, the struggles of the 'hot autumn' of 1969 encouraged the formation of unitary factory committees (see below), reinforced existing moves towards a common front of the three unions in engineering, and subsequently gave rise to united action at confederal level. More recently, workplace trade union unity has often proved resilient even in the case of national disagreements, most notably during the period of political confrontation in 1984–5.

In the 1950s and 1960s, inter-confederal conflicts were intense. Those opposed to CGIL accused it of subordinating industrial policy to the political objectives of the PCI. CGIL in turn denounced CISL for its compliance with (Christian democrat) government policies of wage restraint, and its readiness to sign agreements with (Christian democrat) employers, many of whom systematically victimized CGIL militants while favouring their rivals. A complex set of issues which transcend the question of party-political links and extend to the very meanings and philosophies of trade unionism may be seen, in retrospect, as taking shape in this period. Should unions be concerned primarily with their current membership, or is their constituency the working class as a whole? Is their goal to represent the general interests of their members as wage-earners, citizens and consumers, or should the emphasis focus primarily on workers' status as employees of a particular firm or public-sector organization? Does collective bargaining always carry the risk of stifling workers' collective vigour, so that it should always be subordinated to mass mobilization and struggle; or can unions serve their members' interests more effectively as pragmatic, reliable bargaining partners of the employers? The new cadres of CISL sector-union officials in the 1950s and 1960s, as they attempted to weaken the ties to DC politics, evolved a practice influenced by American-style business unionism. The relative priority of collective bargaining was to become a line of division *within* CGIL. In the latter case, differences were to some extent reconciled by cloaking the reality of an increasing bargaining orientation under the continued rhetoric of class struggle. Such conflicts of trade union philosophy were to re-surface in the 1980s.

In any event, CGIL lost badly in membership terms during these earlier decades, both absolutely and relative to its rivals. In particular, by the mid 1950s CISL was clearly succeeding in negotiating real improvements in some of its company agreements, attracting membership, while initial CGIL resistance to such 'sectional' bargaining weakened its appeal to the less ideologically committed (Romagnoli and Della Rocca 1989: 96). Since there are no independent data to verify the unions' own statements, membership figures have to be treated with scepticism; but CGIL claimed 4.6 million members in 1950, only 2.4 million in 1967; while CISL numbers increased from 1.2 to 1.5 million members. UIL did not issue membership figures until 1970, when it was less than half the size of CISL (see table 16.2). (The neo-fascist confederation CISNAL, based mainly in the public sector, possessed negligible membership.) At first sight (and without correcting for the probable exaggeration in the confederations' competing claims) this would imply a density of roughly 35 per cent in the latter 1960s. However, Italian unions – particularly CGIL – have long had a disproportionate strength of membership in agriculture, extending to tenant farmers and share-croppers – a reflection of traditions of rural radicalism in parts of the country, and of the

Table 16.2 Membership of the three main confederations 1950–86 (000s)

Year	Aggregate membership CGIL	CISL	UIL	Total	Employed membership CGIL	CISL	UIL	Total	Density %
1950	4,641	1,190	-	5,830					50.8
1951	4,491	1,338	-	5,829					50.9
1952	4,342	1,322	-	5,664					48.8
1953	4,075	1,305	-	5,380					45.6
1954	4,134	1,327	-	5,461					44.6
1955	4,194	1,342	-	5,536					43.9
1956	3,666	1,707	-	5,374					42.0
1957	3,138	1,262	-	4,400					34.2
1958	2,596	1,654	-	4,250					32.7
1959	2,601	1,284	-	3,885					29.7
1960	2,583	1,324	-	3,908					28.5
1961	2,531	1,399	-	3,930					28.2
1962	2,611	1,436	-	4,046					28.2
1963	2,626	1,504	-	4,129					28.6
1964	2,712	1,515	-	4,227					29.7
1965	2,543	1,468	-	4,011					28.5
1966	2,458	1,491	-	3,949					28.0
1967	2,424	1,523	-	3,946					27.7
1968	2,461	1,627	-	4,088					28.7
1969	2,626	1,641	-	4,268					29.4
1970	2,943	1,808	780	5,530					38.5
1971	3,138	1,973	825	5,937					41.1
1972	3,215	2,184	843	6,242					43.2
1973	3,436	2,214	902	6,553					44.6
1974	3,827	2,473	965	7,264					47.2
1975	4,081	2,594	1,033	7,708					48.5
1976	4,313	2,824	1,105	8,242					48.7
1977	4,475	2,810	1,160	8,445					49.0
1978	4,528	2,869	1,285	8,682					48.9
1979	4,584	2,906	1,327	8,817					48.4
1980	4,599	3,060	1,347	9,006	3,484	2,508	1,146	7,138	49.0
1981	4,595	2,989	1,357	8,941	3,387	2,371	1,143	6,901	47.6
1982	4,576	2,977	1,358	8,910	3,267	2,287	1,134	6,688	46.2
1983	4,556	2,953	1,352	8,860	3,134	2,224	1,121	6,479	45.2
1984	4,546	3,097	1,345	8,988	3,030	2,262	1,114	6,406	44.9
1985	4,592	2,953	1,306	8,851	2,939	2,056	1,064	6,059	42.0
1986	4,647	2,975	1,306	8,928	2,825	1,967	1,046	5,838	40.3
1987	4,743	3,080	1,344	9,167	2,768	1,952	1,069	5,789	39.9
1988	4,867	3,288	1,398	9,554	2,733	2,018	1,100	5,851	40.0
1989	5,027	3,379	1,439	9,845	2,718	1,994	1,104	5,815	39.4
1990	5,150	3,508	1,486	10,145	2,725	2,024	1,124	5,872	39.3

Note: UIL membership not available before 1970. Density refers to the membership of the confederations listed, excluding retired, unemployed and self-employed members.
Source: Romagnoli and Della Rocca 1989; Squarzon 1992.

trade union role as a political focus and agency of social insurance. Excluding agriculture from the picture, density was probably at most 25 per cent.

The 'Hot Autumn' and Trade Union Consolidation

The wave of conflict and mobilization at the end of the decade culminating in the 'hot autumn' of 1969 brought a revival of trade union organization which was both quantitative and qualitative. Ten years of continuous membership growth allowed CGIL to recoup its losses of the previous two decades; aggregate density, on the unions' own claims, rose to 49 per cent by the end of the 1970s. In terms of ambitions and self-confidence, the 'hot autumn' 'represented a rupture in Italian work relations and in their relationship to politics, a historical break-point which set off a series of changes which we still do not fully understand' (Regini and Lange 1990: 4).

Three aspects of the qualitative transformation of Italian trade unionism deserve emphasis. The first is the dramatic rise in union effectiveness at workplace level within key sectors of industry, linked to the pursuit of an agenda of 'new demands' encompassing control of the organization of production, employment security, and the reduction in inequalities of pay and status (Regalia et al. 1978). These gains became consolidated through the new institutions of workplace representation and the provisions of the 1970 Workers' Statute, both of which are discussed in more detail below.

Second, relations *within* the rival confederations were affected. Traditionally, the Italian labour movement was characterized by 'highly centralized trade unions, organized vertically and giving great predominance to the top echelons' (Farnetti 1978: 422). Each of the three organizations possesses a dual structure: 'horizontal' confederal bodies at local, regional and national levels, and 'vertical' industrial unions within their own internal hierarchies of decision-making. CGIL, with its emphasis on class unity, traditionally attached greater priority to the confederal as against the industrial units of organization. CISL – defined in its title as a confederation of unions – placed greater emphasis on the bargaining autonomy of its industrial components; nevertheless, both CISL and UIL were also relatively centralized by comparison with confederations in many other European countries. However, the increased importance of collective bargaining at industry and company level had the effect, in all three confederations, of shifting the balance of power towards the 'vertical' organizations; while the upsurge of rank-and-file activism and the resulting structures of workplace representation had a decentralizing effect within industrial unions.

Third, the growing attention to 'industrial relations' as against 'political' functions tended to weaken party-political dominance over the unions. In the case of CGIL this change can be traced back to the early 1960s when the PSI, previously committed to many of the communists' anti-capitalist and anti-government positions, participated in the 'opening to the left' and joined a centre-left coalition (though itself suffering a left-wing breakaway over the issue). The broad political consensus among socialists and communists within CGIL was inevitably ruptured; to prevent a split within the confederation itself it was necessary to dilute its political identity. Although CISL did not undergo the 'deconfessionalization' of the French CFDT, the increasing emphasis of a new generation of leaders on organizational independence and professional collective bargaining eroded the close links with Christian democracy. There also developed a significant socialist tendency, increasingly influential in policy formulation; and some far-left groups which rejected the PCI's new line (or were expelled from the party) also became active in CISL. In the engineering industry, which as in most countries played a leading role in industrial relations, the respective unions of all three confederations were cooperating closely in collective bargaining by the late 1960s.

In all confederations, the aftermath of the 'hot autumn' brought support for the principle of 'incompatibility': that those occupying leading positions in the unions should not simultaneously hold party or parliamentary office. This principle was in turn a necessary basis for a re-unification of the three confederations: a goal seen as rapidly attainable in the enthusiasm of the early 1970s. The new cooperative relationship was symbolized in 1972 by the creation of a 'unitary federation' of CGIL, CISL and UIL, though the aim of complete unification advanced no further. Fears within both CISL and UIL that their distinctive identities would be overwhelmed within a single confederation, and political tensions resulting from the collapse of the centre-left government in 1974, set firm limits to unity.

While growing inter-union agreement on the importance of collective bargaining encouraged a loosening of party ties, this cannot be equated with a depoliticization of trade unionism. Not only were negotiating objectives, in the first half of the 1970s, extremely ambitious; the aim was also to underwrite, extend and generalize the outcome of negotiations with employers through engagement in the political arena. The 'struggle for reforms' embraced by the unitary federation went far beyond immediate employment issues, and involved concerted pressure on the government. In a sense, collective bargaining – backed by strikes and demonstrations if necessary – was raised to the level of the state.

The Corporatist Experiment

A stronger, more integrated trade union movement was soon confronted by the challenges of economic and political instability. The combination of the international economic crises of the early 1970s and the unions' own successes in raising wages and curbing managerial control was reflected in one of the highest inflation rates in Europe together with rising unemployment; the competitiveness of the Italian economy seemed in question.

Concurrently, the highly visible activities of the neo-fascist right and the 'autonomist' left – with terrorist groups at both extremes – created fears of escalating political violence which could undermine constitutional order and end in an authoritarian coup (the Chilean example was particularly salient for the PCI, encouraging its pursuit of the 'historic compromise').

The fear of social collapse, which led to the 'national solidarity' government of 1976–9, encouraged the unions to collaborate in a process of macro-economic concertation. This did not – as in Britain, say – involve radical institutional innovation: as described below, a pattern had developed of extensive centralized negotiation over a wide agenda (for example, reforms to the CIG system or the reformulation of the *scala mobile* system of wage indexation) with the government actively involved behind the scenes. The effect of the crisis was to reverse the direction of pressure within peak-level bargaining, as governments and employers rather than the unions took the initiative.

In 1977 the unions agreed with the employers a programme for improving productivity, and a moratorium on company-level pay bargaining which was seen as a major source of inflation. In the following year the three confederations reached an agreement – known as the 'EUR-line' – of which the central principle was a commitment to wage restraint in order to facilitate government policies which would aid economic recovery and protect jobs.

As has been seen, this strategy of 'political exchange' proved disappointing in its effects. On the one hand, all unions faced problems in delivering restraint when faced with the need to manage a 'trade-off between responsiveness and responsibility' (Romagnoli 1990: 17). In many of the organizational strongholds which had been consolidated during the previous decade, union activists were understandably reluctant to reverse the militant orientation which had hitherto brought dramatic gains; and union leaderships therefore equivocated in their commitment to restraint (Golden 1988; Mershon 1990). Conversely, government and employers proved unwilling or unable to deliver the macro-economic policies which would satisfy union aspirations (Regini 1984; Kreile 1988). The withdrawal of PCI support for the government ended the brief Italian experiment in German-style concertation.

The 1980s: A Decade of Crisis?

The event which cast a shadow across Italian industrial relations during the following decade was the bitter Fiat dispute of 1980, in opposition to the company's proposals for restructuring accompanied by heavy job losses. Ironically, the CGIL leaders (like those of the other confederations) were anxious to achieve a negotiated solution to an issue on which they felt the union could not win; but the local leadership in this the unions' principal stronghold insisted on a more militant response (Golden 1990; Locke 1990, 1992). The outcome was a 35-day stoppage which ended in defeat after the company had mobilized an anti-strike demonstration, largely involving middle managers, acclaimed with some exaggeration as the 'march of the 40,000'. This was seen as a devastating division within the unions' ranks, given their previous insistence that 'managers are workers too', and paved the way for more far-reaching debates concerning union representativeness.

The 1980s proved a decade of relative union weakness and defensiveness in the face of high unemployment and managerial initiatives to restructure and reorganize production; and a continuing uneasy but informal collaboration between the rival unions despite tensions which at times brought temporary breakdown.

Superficially, union membership proved stable despite hard times. From just over 9 million in 1980, total membership fell to a low of 8.85 million in 1985 (a decline of less than 2 per cent) before rising to a record level of over 10.1 million in 1990. However, membership of employed workers fell substantially in the early and mid 1980s: by 1986, over a third of all union members were retired, self-employed or unemployed, while members in employment fell by 1.3 million or 17 per cent (Santi 1988: 157–9). The position has since stabilized; the total of *employed* members of the confederations has fluctuated at just under the six million mark. The fortunes of the three organizations during the 1980s differed considerably. CGIL lost over a fifth of its employed membership, CISL suffered almost as badly, whereas UIL has remained almost stable. The recent expansion of union membership has come wholly from retired workers: by 1990 the proportion in all the unions was 38 per cent, and no less than 46 per cent in CGIL. Overall density (in terms of the ratio of employed unionists to employment) fell between 1980 and 1990 from 49 to 39 per cent. By comparison with several other European countries, this may be regarded as a fairly modest decline; the unions have doubtless been assisted by the widespread operation of the check-off system, under the provisions of the 1970 legislation (Romagnoli and Della Rocca 1989: 111).

Membership in manufacturing was affected by closures and redundancies, and more aggressive managerial policies in many factories which in the 1970s had become strongly unionized; but density slipped little (from 44 to 42 per cent). In agriculture, numbers fell with the continued decline in the sector; however, the phenomenal level of unionization fell only from 98 to 85 per cent. In private services there was a sharp drop in union membership, despite the expansion of employment in the sector; density fell from 39 to 24 per cent. Only in public services did both absolute numbers, and density rates, increase (Romagnoli and Della Rocca 1989: 98); this may well owe much to the strengthening and reorganization of bargaining relations in the public sector under law 93 of 1983 (see below). Density in the three confederations rose from 45 per cent in 1980 to 50 per cent in 1985, though by 1990 it had slipped to 48 per cent. Given the growing membership of the *autonomi*, however, aggregate unionization was almost certainly still increasing.

The adverse climate of the 1980s had contradictory implications for intra- and inter-union relations. On the one hand, a common front was necessary in order to respond effectively to new challenges; on the other, the continuing pressure from government and employers for moderation strained the tolerance of union militants (particularly in CGIL) and of rank-and-file workers – particularly those in relatively favourable labour market situations – who chafed at imposed restraint. Cooperation and conflict, both among unions and between unions, employers and the state, have marked the past decade.

Divisions became sharpest in 1984, with CGIL's rejection of the draft tripartite agreement, the resistance to the government's decree-law leading to the referendum of 1985. The CGIL–CISL–UIL unitary federation collapsed in recriminations, but after this traumatic experience the confederations edged back towards more cooperative relations, for the most part agreeing to further initiatives to contain inflation and encourage productive flexibility, but on occasion mobilizing common resistance (see above).

'Representativity'

In the 1980s it became common for Italian commentators to speak of a 'crisis of representativity' in trade unionism. Unions have always claimed to represent a broader constituency of interests than those formally recorded as members; and as indicated above, the law adopts the notion of 'most representative' unions without any necessary quantitative criterion. However, the decline in active membership in the first half of the 1980s, following the previous decade of growth, weakened their claims to speak for labour in the national arena.

The problem was compounded by both internal and external challenges, to some extent interconnected. Internally, leadership acquiescence in the rolling back of many of the gains of the 1970s has provoked rank-and-file opposition to the official negotiating positions of the unions (Accornero 1992: 15–16). To help legitimize their position, from 1986 unions began to organize membership ballots on their negotiating programmes and draft settlements, but were often embarrassed by the level of recorded opposition. Externally, the three confederations have been faced with new rivals for workers' loyalties. 'Autonomous' unions – based mainly in public administration, the health and education services, and public transport – have become increasingly assertive in the past decade. They possess significant membership among key employee groups; Romagnoli (1989: 270) suggests that they covered 15–20 per cent of public service employees in the mid-1980s. More important than sheer numbers, however, is their ability to exert a leadership role in strikes, when many members of the main confederations have followed their call and rejected their own unions. Also of growing significance are separate confederations of managerial and professional staff. Separatist tendencies among craft, professional and managerial employees – commonplace in some other countries – raise distinctive problems in Italy. The claim of the three confederations to act as national representatives of a broad working-class constituency – and to be taken seriously by the state – rests upon the credibility with which they can present themselves as representatives of every category of worker. At a different level, this has also been the prerequisite of an effective bargaining commitment – expressed in radical form in the 1970s, and underlying many of the conflicts over the *scala mobile* – to a substantial narrowing of differences of pay and status. Fragmentation of occupational interests threatens the ideal of proletarian unity which – albeit with different accents – has been part of the common language of post-war Italian unionism (Garofalo 1988: 278).

Perhaps even more serious was the rise in the late 1980s of rank-and-file committees (*cobas*) which have mobilized effective strike action particularly in the public services, in support of more ambitious demands than the main confederations have been willing to sanction. For some observers these movements reflect a new form of craft trade unionism, challenging the role of the confederations as representatives of the skilled or professional sections of employees with a strong labour market position (*Lavoro 80* 1989). The role of such 'unofficial' militancy – which however has become increasingly institutionalized, for example with the emergence of 'guilds' (*gilde*) in the education sector – is discussed further below. It may also be noted that the new political assertions of regionalism have had an impact on industrial relations. The *Lega Lombarda* has established its own 'autonomous' trade union, SAL, which has gained support in some of the major industrial centres of the northwest.

These challenges coincide with major dilemmas for a trade union movement torn between traditions of class militancy and social partnership. The role conflict is undoubtedly most acute for CGIL in an era of post-communism. Its October 1991 congress approved by a large majority a programme which in effect abandoned the traditional principle of class struggle, embraced a philosophy of collective bargaining in which strike mobilization retains only a subsidiary tactical role, and adopted German-style industrial democracy as a key union objective. The disciplined factional organization through which the communists controlled CGIL for almost half a century has been dissolved. The transformation of CGIL has obvious implications for the other confederations, which now need a new justification for their independent existence. The differences in union self-definition in the 1990s are far more subtle than in the past: CGIL emphasizes the defence of workers' rights, CISL the pursuit of social solidarity, UIL the representation of workers as citizens (Accornero 1992: 37). The key question for Italian trade unionism in the 1990s is whether the differences – and the force of institutional vested interests – are sufficient to sustain a divided movement.

Workplace Representation

The representation of employee interests at workplace level has a long tradition, within an institutional framework which has altered significantly at key moments in the history of Italian industrial relations. As in many other countries, the balance between relative autonomy on the one hand and subordination to the priorities of management or outside unions on the other has often been complex and uncertain.

The first institution of workplace representation was the *commissione interna* (CI), established by collective agreement in the engineering industry in 1906, and extended widely in Italian industry in the years surrounding the First World War. Suppressed under the fascist regime (which created its own corporatist institutions), the CIs were reconstituted under an agreement between Confindustria and the newly emerging union organizations at the end of 1943. This agreement was revised on several subsequent occasions.

Members of the CI were nominated by the trade unions (with separate manual and white-collar constituencies) but elected by the whole of the work force. After the split in the Italian trade union movement, the annual CI elections served – as with the ballots for works committees in France – as a popularity contest between the rival organizations. (The loss by CGIL of its majority of representatives at Fiat in 1955 had a traumatic impact, forcing the union to reassess its policy on company-level collective bargaining.) The *commissioni* possessed few powers; militant representatives (typically CGIL members) were exposed to victimization by employers, who conversely could encourage the election of more compliant nominees who might be fostered as an alternative focus of employee loyalty to the external unions. On several occasions in the 1950s and early 1960s, CGIL pressed for legal recognition of the CIs in order to strengthen their powers and allow greater protection for members; but CISL (which no doubt feared that any statutory machinery could be dominated by CGIL) was opposed. Its preferred strategy was to build up union sections (*sezioni aziendali sindacali*) at workplace level, as the basis for company bargaining under its own control (Sciarra 1977: 38; Romagnoli and Della Rocca 1989: 116).

Legal support for workplace representation was provided for the first time under the 1970 Workers' Statute, and followed radical changes which had occurred during the 'hot autumn'. The largely spontaneous upsurge within the factories gave rise to two new representative mechanisms: the *delegati*, chosen by work groups to express their grievances and demands to management; and the rank-and-file committees in which shop-floor delegates, members of any union or of none, acted collectively to negotiate with the company and if necessary to organize strikes and other protests. These soon became consolidated into the *consiglio di fabbrica* (CdF, factory council), a body with resonant antecedents in the militant struggles around the end of the First World War. The 1970 legislation both generalized some of the gains achieved unilaterally in the leading centres of militancy, and served to institutionalize previously autonomous insurgency within the formal mechanisms of trade unionism and collective bargaining.

As outlined previously, the 1970 law formally established a new institution, the *rappresentanza sindacale aziendale* (RSA). The constitution of the RSAs is imprecise, and the right to create them is assigned to employees rather than unions. In practice, the RSA has provided legal backing for the mechanism of the *consiglio di fabbrica*. In some cases the new councils sustained the grassroots impetus of the phase of mobilization; but elsewhere, 'once the confederations had joined to officially embrace the new structure, councils were typically "imported" into workplaces, at the initiative of extra-factory unionists and in the absence of plant-level collective ferment' (Mershon 1990: 48). Nevertheless, the legal underpinnings of the RSA are an obstacle to external union control: delegates are elected by workers (whether union members or not) and must take account of work force views. Divided loyalties can readily ensue.

The 'normalization' of workplace representation was consolidated in 1972, at the time of the pact establishing the CGIL–CISL–UIL unitary federation, when the unions also agreed that the CdF should constitute their common mechanism of shop-floor organization. The council was to be the model for union workplace activity, not only in manufacturing but across the economy more generally. Formal recognition was seen by some commentators as a source of centralization and bureaucratization in the councils. Delegates tended to represent larger constituencies than at the height of initial activism, and councils elected their own executive committees which took over many of the functions originally performed by the CdF as a whole. Close links were often established with the full-time officials of the unions, who were appointed in large numbers during the 1970s (giving Italian unions a ratio of one official for every 700 members, 'one of the highest rates of bureaucratization in the western world') (Romagnoli and Della Rocca 1989: 103). Where union membership was strong, the CdF soon developed an important role as the agent of workplace collective bargaining. In the process, though, a set of distinct and indeed contradictory roles developed. One, inherited from the 'hot autumn', was the mobilization and representation of a collective identity shaped by the production relations of each workplace; a second, the more passive channelling of information from the workplace to the outside unions, and decisions from the unions down to the membership; a third, participation in a system of joint regulation of management-worker relations (Regalia 1988: 356–7; Romagnoli and Della Rocca: 118–19).

The pressures on trade unions to exercise bargaining restraint, the collapse of the unitary federation, and more general inter-union tensions, have made the status of the CdF ever more problematic since the late 1970s. Many councils – particularly those which maintained close collective links with a militant work force – opposed national union policies to moderate pay bargaining and cooperate with company re-structuring (Mershon 1989).

After the traumatic confrontations of the early 1980s, new forms of workplace representation were established or discussed. The IRI Protocol of 1984 (see below) provided for the creation of joint committees as a channel of employee participation in technical and organizational change within public companies, and this pioneering initiative was followed by a wide range of other agreements for workplace union participation in company reorganization. A key trend of workplace industrial relations in the 1980s, according to Negrelli (1991a), has been the 'formalized proceduralization', through rights of information and consultation, of issues which in the previous decade were often the focus of resistance and conflict. The evolution of mechanisms of joint problem-solving, as Saba (1992) has argued, generates a process half-way between negotiation and participation, but within which managerial rationality sets the parameters for decision-making. Here again, the external union is increasingly involved in overseeing or even displacing shop-floor delegates in the process of workplace regulation (Windolf 1989).

The double-edged nature of such participation – a vehicle for the articulation of employee interests, but at the same time a means of blunting oppositional action – may be seen as contributing to the general problem of representativity in the 1980s. Inter-union divisions compound the difficulties of sustaining stable micro-corporatist solutions. The common perspective of the confederations has been that the structures of union representation themselves must be reformed if mutually damaging competition in the workplace is to be avoided; but as in the past, there is no obvious mechanism which can provide a strong relationship between representatives and rank-and-file while avoiding CGIL dominance over the smaller confederations. In 1989 the three confederations agreed to create a new type of organization, the *consiglio aziendale di rappresentanza sindacale* (CARS – works council of union representatives), partly directly elected and partly appointed by the unions; but this initiative was bedevilled by recriminations over electoral procedures. In 1991 a more elaborate inter-union agreement was reached, providing for a rather more democratic system, the *rappresentanza sindacale unitaria* (RSU – unitary trade union representative structure). Unions may nominate delegates either jointly or separately, for election by the whole work force; but each of the three confederations will be guaranteed a proportion of seats. Elaborate procedures are specified to ensure that RSUs maintain a mandate from the work force while undertaking their negotiating functions, yet at the same time preserve agreement between the three confederations. Whether the new mechanism will really help attain these objectives – which in the past have so often proved contradictory – and at the same time allow the main confederations to ward off the challenge of autonomous unions and rank-and-filist oppositional movements within the workplace remains as yet untested.

The Employers

The fragmented structure of production in Italy has given rise to diverse interest groups among employers, and they have pursued divergent business strategies and a variety of approaches to labour and industrial relations. In this section, the principal characteristics of Italian employers in terms of size and ownership are sketched. Their main representational organizations are then outlined. The remainder of the section describes the main lines of fragmentation between different employer interests, and the way they have been represented in – and sometimes against – the central employers' body Confindustria. Subsequent sections will deal in detail with bargaining processes and outcomes, and with the evolution of employers' strategies since the 1980s.

The Characteristics of Italian Employers

As noted in the introduction, the Italian economic structure differs sharply from that of the other major European economies. To a far greater extent it is characterized by the coexistence of a small number of large enterprises with large numbers of small and medium companies, including an extensive artisan sector (OECD 1991: 61–4). In 1990, the proportion of the work force employed in very small firms (under 10 employees) was, at over 40 per cent, about twice that in France, Germany or Britain; the figure of 17 per cent employed in large firms (500 employees or more) was about half that in the other major European economies. Italy has a third fewer very large companies (employing over 1000 workers) than The Netherlands, while only six Italian companies figure in the list of the top 100 employers in Europe, and only nine in the world's top 500 in 1989 (compared with 55 for UK, 38 for Germany and 23 for France) (Sisson et al. 1991: 97, 99).[2] One result is that a few large companies – Montedison, Olivetti, Pirelli and above all Fiat – have played a very important role in the development of employer strategy in Italy. In the 1980s, while there has been a notable increase in industrial concentration (Poscetti 1988), large firms have been rationalizing their activities and sharply reducing their work forces. As a result, the role of small firms in employment has been growing (e.g. Contini and Revelli 1990).

Italian firms, much more than British, concentrate their activities within particular industrial sectors. Despite forays into 'non-core' activities in the 1970s and early 1980s, companies now appear to be retreating back to their core business (Poscetti 1991: 84). At the same time, Italian companies have responded to growing competition and to European integration by increasingly 'internationalizing' their activities through foreign acquisitions, joint ventures, marketing agreements and so on (Poscetti 1988). During the 1980s, large companies such as Fiat, Olivetti and Montedison generally consolidated a 'multi-divisional' structure in which separate business sectors or sub-sectors were given operational autonomy within overall corporate strategic and financial control. (Regini and Sabel 1989a; Grant and Martinelli 1991: 75–6). They also resorted to more flexible market and production strategies. Such changes were of course taking place in many other European countries. What was notable about the Italian case was the speed of the process, 'in companies which at the beginning of the 1980s appeared completely paralysed, and in a country in which only a few years ago it had become almost a cliché to talk of a "structural" economic and industrial crisis' (Regini 1991b: 181).

A notable feature of the Italian economy has been the much-vaunted dynamism of a significant subgroup of small and medium enterprises. In the so-called 'Third Italy', in regions such as Veneto, Tuscany and Emilia Romagna, specialized networks of companies have grown up since the 1960s in industrial sectors ranging from clothing and textiles through furniture and ceramics to agricultural machinery and machine tools (Trigilia 1986). One factor in the growth of this sector was the desire of leading manufacturing companies to escape the constraints imposed by employees' growing workplace power in the late 1960s and early 1970s. Many industrial jobs were subcontracted to small firms supplying marketing, engineering, information technology and other services (Cipolletta 1990: 420-3). Thus the growth of an important segment of the small-firm sector was organically linked to the development of large companies.

A final important characteristic of economic structure in Italy is the role of public enterprise. State-controlled firms were responsible for 25 per cent of total employment in non-agricultural and non-financial enterprises (of 20 employees or more) in 1987 (OECD 1991: 117). A number of state holding companies, of which IRI (*Istituto per la Ricostruzione Industriale*) and ENI (*Ente Nazionale Idrocarburi*) are the most important, control hundreds of subsidiaries which operate like private firms. These subsidiaries are themselves organized into industrial groups, for example in steel, telecommunications or the financial sector. Together, they employ about half-a-million people, two-thirds of them in IRI enterprises. In the 1960s and 1970s, IRI in particular was used as a 'social buffer', taking over troubled private sector firms and their employees. This process was reversed in the 1980s: a major rationalization saw IRI employment fall some 40 per cent between 1980 and 1989, and a measure of privatization was introduced as the holding companies rationalized their portfolios. The importance of the public enterprise sector has meant that its representatives have been major actors on the Italian political scene, and in the development of industrial relations.

Employer Representation

The main private sector peak organization is Confindustria (*Confederazione Generale dell'Industria Italiana*), which represents leading firms in manufacturing and construction.[3] Formed after the First World War out of a looser confederation of associations, it supported fascism after 1922, becoming the

Confederazione Fascista dell'Industria in 1925, but was reconstituted at the end of the war on a more 'apolitical' basis. Confindustria is made up of around 100 industry (so-called 'category') associations, and more than 100 geographically based multi-industry organizations. Since reforms in the early 1970s, the provincial bodies have been grouped into about 20 units, roughly corresponding to administrative regions, and the industry associations into the same number of broad product market units (Sisson 1987: 56–64). In 1987, Confindustria's member associations in manufacturing industry had 112,000 affiliated firms with 3.7 million employees, compared with 81,000 firms and 2.7 million employees in 1980.

Leading affiliates are Federmeccanica in engineering, Federchimica in chemicals and Federtessile in textiles; and Assolombarda (the employers' organization for the province of Milan). Members may either be 'economic' bodies (see Chiesi and Martinelli 1989), or perform an employers' association or industrial relations (*sindacale*) role; Confindustria and other peak associations, and territorial bodies, perform both functions, while national category associations may be either. Federmeccanica is an example of an association concerned solely with industrial relations. Confindustria's new statute of 1983 defined the industrial relations role as activity concerned with employment legislation, collective bargaining, training, relationships with international bodies, and social welfare functions. In collective bargaining, the peak organization has responsibility for interconfederal negotiations, the sectoral associations for national industry bargaining, and the territorial bodies for local and company bargaining. The economic role concerns sectoral policy and general economic policy, including supranational issues and foreign trade (Becchi Collidà 1989: 143–4).

The polarization of industrial structure between large and small firms has laid the basis for a more fragmented pattern of employer representation in Italy than in other European countries. In Italy – unlike in Spain, with a similarly fragmented economic structure –Confindustria has been unable to build itself into an encompassing interest organization, even though structural reforms in the 1980s were followed by a rise in membership. Although half of small firms are affiliated to Confindustria associations, there is also an independent organization for small and medium-sized enterprise, CONFAPI (*Confederazione della Piccola e Media Industria*), which was set up in 1947. It is strong in regions such as Emilia Romagna and Tuscany, and its 30,000 affiliated firms covered around 850,000 workers in 1987. In addition, there are employers' confederations for the artisan sector, for agriculture, and for the service sector; these bodies often have strong links to political parties (Confcommercio is affiliated to the DC, for example, and Confesercenti, to parties of the left). A new employers' confederation, the Federation of Advanced Service Industries (*Federazione del Terziario Avanzato*), emerged in the 1980s, although it has failed to attract important companies from Confcommercio, and it has not so far signed any major collective agreements. Even within large manufacturing industry, Confindustria's influence is weakened by the low profile of foreign subsidiaries, which tend to keep their distance from employers' associations in order to reduce their exposure to sectoral conflicts, and to follow the personnel and industrial relations policies of their parent companies (Becchi Collidà 1989: 139).

The public enterprise sector also has a separate structure of representation, further weakening the representativity of Confindustria. This goes back to the *distacco* (parting, separation) of the 1950s, when the public enterprises withdrew from Confindustria following the law of December 1956 that set up the Ministry of State Participation. The withdrawal of IRI enterprises reflected the role in IRI of senior figures close to the reformist sectors of DC which were preparing for the move towards the centre-left. The unions, especially CISL, also played a role and actively campaigned in parliament and elsewhere for separate representation for state firms whose industrial relations policies were more progressive (Becchi Collidà 1989: 148–9). Nearly 300 firms under IRI and the small holding company EFIM are currently members of Intersind, created in 1958. Firms under the energy sector holding company, ENI, are in ASAP, which was set up in 1960.

Sectoral employers associations such as Federchimica and Federmeccanica are the important players in national industry bargaining. However, the territorial level is also significant, particularly in sectors such as construction with strong regional labour markets, and in the 'micro-corporatist' relationships between firms, unions and local authorities in the industrial districts (e.g. Trigilia 1989). Moreover, with the growing importance of workplace and enterprise bargaining in the 1980s, lower organizational levels of employers' associations began to acquire new functions.

Employers' Interests and Strategies

The fragmentation of economic structure and of interest representation has given rise to several lines of cleavage: between large and small firms, between capital-intensive and labour-intensive sectors, between exporters and importers, between public and private capital (Becchi Collidà 1989). One major strand of tension within the private sector has been the battle for control of employers' representation between the capital-intensive and labour-intensive sectors. In the 1960s and 1970s, the major protagonists of this were Montedison (and its predecessors) on the one hand, and Fiat on the other (Contini 1991; Martinelli 1980).

In the early post-war period, employer representation was fairly unified and homogeneous under the aegis of Confindustria. Confindustria was dominated by a 'traditional' alliance in which the major element was the group of large firms, especially in the electricity supply industry and in basic chemicals. It proved resistant to social change and to broader political strategies for incorporating new social groups within the system. Operating in capital and intermediate goods sectors, it was less affected by union struggles and less concerned to seek employee consensus. It was supported in its resistance to change by the small-firm sector (Martinelli 1980).

As economic development progressed, however, different interests became more influential within Italian capital, in particular large companies in labour-intensive sectors, producing consumer goods and hence interested in the expansion of the domestic market. The existing forms of interest representation were increasingly unable to reconcile the conflicting strategies of the different groups, leading to pressures for reform of Confindustria. Firms like Fiat employed large work forces concentrated in relatively few establishments and were faced with stronger unions. They thus had an interest in institutionalizing industrial relations as a way of reducing labour conflict, and developed strong links, independently of Confindustria, with the reformist wing of DC that was advocating the integration of new social groups in the economy and polity. These groups were slow in adopting a more progressive approach to industrial relations: Fiat, for example, even while swimming against the tide of Confindustria and pursuing a policy of high wages, maintained a fiercely repressive regime in its plants until the 1960s – a strategy summarized as 'the iron fist at Mirafiori and the velvet glove in Rome' (Contini 1990). None the less, these new groups increasingly adopted a more modern industrial relations philosophy and practices. Within Confindustria, the power of the old guard was decisively weakened when the electricity trusts were nationalized in 1963 to allow government control over development strategy, especially in the south.

From the late 1960s, as union strength began to increase with full employment, eroding still further the influence of Confindustria, the modern group of large companies pursued a strategy of institutional reform, culminating in Giovanni Agnelli's presidency of Confindustria between 1972 and 1975. Under the inspiration of the modernizers, the 1970 Pirelli report on the future of Confindustria proposed a more constructive relationship with the unions, arguing that Italy was a pluralist society in which conflicts of interest were inevitable, that trade unions had to be recognized and that they had to be engaged through new institutions of dialogue (Becchi Collidà 1989: 141–2). Fiat itself proposed an 'alliance of the productive classes' in the modernization of Italy. One outcome of the reform process was the creation of Federmeccanica in 1971. Until then, Confindustria had itself conducted negotiations on behalf of the metalworking employers, but the modernizers were anxious for the organization to withdraw from the immediate industrial relations fray and to concentrate on relations with government.

A second great fault line running through Italian employers' organizations has been that between state and private capital. The DC centre-left saw public enterprise as a tool of economic and social development: the expansion of public enterprise under IRI and (from 1953) ENI was a victory for the Catholic political class's strategy of occupation of the state and colonization of the economy and its accompanying spoils system (Maraffi 1980). State capital developed into a strong interest group, with close personal and political links with factions within DC, on the basis of a systematic exchange of political support for financial aid (Martinelli 1981).

In the strategy of the DC, public enterprise was entrusted with a 'political' role, independent of the private sector, in carrying out politically defined activities in the general interest. One aspect of this was the adoption of more modern industrial relations practices. In a 1968 document, Intersind stressed that conflicts of interest were inherent in modern industrial society, and saw its role as furthering the rationalization of industrial relations through a voluntary collective bargaining system that could channel conflicts (cited in Sisson 1987: 22–3 fn.). Objectively, therefore, the interests of the state-controlled enterprises converged with those of the modernizing private sector group in promoting the reform of Italian institutions and of industrial relations specifically. State enterprises were in the forefront of major industrial relations developments, and their innovations were a prime factor in undermining the traditional power group in Confindustria. They pursued a policy of coexistence with the unions, especially with the Catholic CISL, and in the early 1960s Intersind led the way in signing 'articulated' company-level agreements, particularly in engineering.

During the 1970s, the public enterprise sector increasingly suffered economic difficulties and political scandals as 'managerial' goals were subordinated to a variety of political objectives of the ruling DC and indeed of public enterprise managers themselves (Martinelli 1980). As a result, the sector lost its previous role as trend-setter in industrial relations. But in the 1980s, the sector again played a prominent role from the time of the signing of the IRI Protocol in 1984 (see below).

Collective Bargaining

Three basic levels of collective bargaining – national (interconfederal), industry, and company or plant – have each played a central role in post-war developments. The salience of each, the relationship between them, and the balance between centralization and decentralization, have shifted constantly, a manifestation of the relatively low institutionalization of Italian industrial relations. A persistent feature has been the 'bipolarity' of bargaining: at any one time, two of the three levels have tended to be more prominent (Cella and Treu 1989b; Baglioni 1991a; Negrelli 1991d). In addition, the regional or 'territorial' level has been important at certain times and in certain sectors, notably construction, commerce and agriculture.

Phases in the Development of Collective Bargaining in Post-war Italy

Cella and Treu (1989b: 162–74) identify several broad phases in the development of collective bargaining. In the immediate postwar period, bargaining was 'centralized, weak and static' (p. 162), dominated by union and employer confederations. Pay levels and differentials were determined rigidly at central level until 1954, when the so-called 'category' – that is, industrial sector – federations were given limited powers to negotiate on pay issues; but the main determinant of pay continued to be the *scala mobile* pay indexation system established in the interconfederal agreement of 1945 (see below). At company level, bargaining was not formally recognized; and if it took place at all, was hidden from view. This pattern of bargaining was underpinned by the strategies of unions and employers, and by the condition of the labour market. In a context of high and persistent unemployment, fuelled by a large pool of surplus agricultural labour, employers had an interest in avoiding sectoral pay differences so as to keep increases to the level of the least dynamic sectors; the political and economic weakness of the unions also prompted them to concentrate their limited resources on national bargaining.

These structural factors were changing in the late 1950s with economic growth and the rise of mass production, the emergence of a new class of industrial manual workers, and more favourable labour market conditions. A new phase was initiated that was to last for most of the 1960s. The bargaining structure began to exhibit the bipolarity that was to become typical, with a decentralization to the industry level, which henceforth became the 'fulcrum' of the system (Treu 1991: 13), and the decline in importance of interconfederal negotiations. At the same time, plant bargaining had been spreading under the coordination of provincial union officials. Following the metalworking conflict of 1962–3, the right of provincial sector unions to negotiate at the workplace was formally recognized. Under the system of 'articulated bargaining', issues such as piece rates, bonuses and job evaluation could be devolved to company level, although within a framework laid down at national sector level. This produced an 'uprecedented institutionalization' of the Italian industrial relations system (Cella and Treu 1989b: 166). Institutional arrangements included so-called 'delegation' clauses (*clausole di rinvio*) devolving to lower level the competence to negotiate over specific issues, and peace obligations (*clausole di tregua*) preventing conflict between contract renewals.

The Italian model of economic development in the 1960s, based on low wages and the intensification of work in the factories, generated considerable tensions, compounded by the failure of social welfare, housing and other public services to keep pace with economic growth. At the political level, the experience of the centre-left governments of the 1960s had enabled the unions to consolidate their position. These tensions ushered in the third phase in the development of the collective bargaining system, the 'cycle of struggle' lasting from 1968–73, dominated by the events of the 'hot autumn' of 1969.

The rigid legal framework of coordinated bargaining levels fell apart throughout manufacturing industry. Bargaining became both highly decentralized and highly informal (Cella and Treu 1989b: 167–8). While the national industry level of bargaining remained important, the company level assumed the 'leadership' role (Negrelli 1991d: 4). The defining feature of the period was the explosion in the number of company or plant agreements after 1967: in 1971, for example, some 1.6 million workers were covered by 7,600 agreements. With the 1970 Workers' Statute giving unions the right to establish plant-level structures and protecting workplace union representatives against dismissal, the early 1970s were the 'golden age' of plant bargaining. Enterprise bargaining dealt not only with pay – with an emphasis on egalitarian flat rate increases and the reduction of differentials – but also with such issues as work organization and union rights at the workplace. Such bargaining increasingly escaped the control of higher levels of the union. In a novel version of bipolarity, sectoral agreements often became the means for generalizing the outcome of company bargaining. Even non-union or weakly unionized small and medium-sized firms came within the ambit of industry agreements as a result of the high level of worker mobilization, and bargaining also spread in sectors other than manufacturing, particularly services.

From the mid-1970s, the mounting economic crisis, rising unemployment and corporate restructuring were weakening the unions, and their bargaining strategies became increasingly defensive. This fourth phase was marked by a *de facto* recentralization of control over bargaining by both unions and employers' organizations, leading to a new bipolarity comprising interconfederal and industry levels of bargaining: according to Chiesi and Martinelli (1990: 204–5), employers pursued a double strategy, with Confindustria acting as a 'protective umbrella' helping reduce levels of conflict, while the larger, more highly unionized companies pursued strategies of restructuring and decentralization (these are analysed in detail below). The scope for company bargaining on pay matters was significantly reduced by the renewed importance of the *scala mobile*. Centralization occurred also at the company level itself, with the negotiating role moving from union delegates to works councils, and external union officials at provincial or even national level. The centralizing tendencies reached their peak in the interconfederal negotiations of the late 1970s and early 1980s (see below). For the first time in many years, there were attempts to reduce the autonomy of lower bargaining levels – for example, through the provision agreed in 1983 forbidding lower levels to reopen issues already defined at higher levels.

If the first half of the 1980s was marked by the 'decisive shift of the centre of gravity of industrial relations into the political and institutional arena', the second half of the decade 'saw collective bargaining restored to its former importance with the resumption of economic growth, the successful completion of restructuring and the moderation of inflation' (Baglioni 1991a: 89–90). From the mid- until the late 1980s, the interconfederal level once more receded in importance; while the sectoral level reaffirmed its key position within the bargaining structure. After 1988, concern over inflation and comparative labour costs in the context of European integration, as well as the need to reform industrial relations structures, were creating pressures for renewed national bargaining, and indeed for a return to tripartite concertation, as well as for a greater institutionalization of bargaining (Bellardi 1991). At the same time, however, corporate strategies of innovation were continuing to push the system towards lower levels of bargaining (Negrelli 1991d), while matters were complicated by the increasing role of union actors outside the main confederations, particularly the *cobas*.

In the following sections, the characteristics of bargaining at each of the three major levels since the 1980s are examined in more detail. The section concludes by looking at the special case of bargaining in the public sector.

The National Interconfederal Level

Interconfederal agreements have been seen as the response to 'times of crisis or serious economic difficulties, when pay regulation and/or restructuring of employment and the labour market are the predominant issues' (Cella and Treu 1989b: 175). In the period of crisis and restructuring from the mid-1970s until the mid-1980s, the national interconfederal level achieved a centrality that it had not had since the immediate post-war phase of Italian industrial relations (pp. 174–84). In the second half of the 1980s, central bargaining faded in importance, only to re-emerge at the end of the decade as inflation rose and wage costs became increasingly sensitive in the context of European integration and membership of the narrow band of the EMS.

In central bargaining, the state has played an important role. In some cases this has involved participating formally in tripartite accords (as with the January 1983 'Scotti' agreement on pay costs and the *scala mobile*), in others exerting considerable informal influence over bipartite bargaining between the peak organizations, whose agreements are often subsequently endorsed in legislation.

The key interconfederal agreement of the 1970s was that of January 1975 which harmonized the cost-of-living allowances (*contingenza*) of blue- and white-collar workers; thus all employees received automatic flat-rate payments or 'points', regardless of individual pay levels (Flanagan et al. 1982: 542–6). The agreement was, on the union side, the culmination of the egalitarian impulses of the 'hot autumn', and on the employers' side, of the pressures of large labour-intensive employers such as Fiat, influential at this time in the leadership of Confindustria, who had been subjected to pay bargaining at company level since the late 1960s and who wished to see a more centralized control of pay costs.

One of the primary concerns of subsequent interconfederal negotiations has been to address the legacy of the 1975 deal, which in combination with high inflation severely compressed differentials, thus hindering companies' labour market policies. In the February 1977 agreement on labour costs, the unions made important concessions in order to retain the *scala mobile* mechanism; the agreement also contained provisions on more flexible working-time arrangements, such as extended shift-working.

The reform of the *scala mobile* and the containment of inflation were the main concerns of a series of tripartite and bipartite agreements between 1983 and 1986, and again at the turn of the decade. The triangular agreement of January 1983 and the February 1984 agreement tightened the working of the *scala mobile*. However, the opposition of CGIL to the 1984 deal led to the changes being embodied in legislation – provoking the Communist Party's unsuccessful referendum campaign (see above). In 1985 Confindustria agreed to stay in the *scala mobile* on condition that a more restrictive public sector agreement on indexation was extended to the private sector (Faustini 1987).

Towards the end of the decade, with inflation rising again – and faster than forecast – the parties returned to interconfederal negotiations on the *scala mobile* and pay costs. Against a background of wider attempts to reform the structures of industrial relations and pay bargaining, the results have been patchy and inconclusive. On a number of occasions, Confindustria attempted to withdraw from the mechanism, but the *scala* was reprieved by legislation or by new tripartite accommodations such as that of July 1990. Finally, however, under the agreement of December 1991, the unions accepted the expiry of the *scala mobile* at the end of 1991, in exchange for the negotiation of an as yet unspecified replacement mechanism in the future (EIRR 216, January 1992: 15–16).

Interconfederal bargaining has been important in other areas, particularly labour market issues and the framework of industrial relations. The former have traditionally been regulated through legislation on the basis of prior interconfederal negotiations. In the 1980s, agreements on atypical employment forms, such as training contracts, 'solidarity' contracts (reducing pay and hours in return for maintenance of employment levels) and part-time working, have likewise been embodied in legislation (Cella and Treu 1989b: 180–1; see also above). The latter role of interconfederal agreements, in drawing up procedural frameworks of industrial relations, has traditionally been less well developed, partly because a framework of rights was contained in the Workers' Statute. Provisions on procedures for regulating collective bargaining at lower levels have always been rudimentary, especially with the low level of institutionalization of bargaining in the 1969–73 period. In the 1980s, interconfederal bargaining was used to establish more formal procedural arrangements. The January 1983 agreement defined the relationships between lower bargaining levels through so-called 'functional coordination' clauses (subsequently embodied in sectoral agreements), prohibited renegotiation at company level of issues already bargained over in industry negotiations, and imposed a moratorium on company pay bargaining; the effectiveness of these provisions was mixed, however. At the end of the decade, the parties were again discussing the structure of the industrial relations system. Reform was perceived as necessary to maintain international competitiveness, but as with the *scala mobile*, it has been repeatedly postponed by differences between the parties.

Industry Bargaining

The national industry agreement (*contratto di categoria*) has been called the 'loadbearing axle', the most stable element of the collective bargaining system (Cella and Treu 1989b: 184–200). The agreement for 1.5 million workers in engineering (which covers a wide range of sectors including cars, heavy engineering, steel, shipbuilding, and electronics) has been the 'pilot' agreement, the 'contract par excellence' of Italian industry. Together with the major agreements in textiles, chemicals and construction, the contract of the *metalmeccanici* dominates bargaining in manufacturing. However, its influence has been tempered by the difficulties of applying a single set of provisions across such a wide range of industries, and there have been several proposals to fragment the engineering sector into several separate bargaining groups (Giugni 1987: 233).

Contracts tend to last for three years, although a four-year textile agreement in 1987 exemplified a more recent trend to longer agreements. Contract renewals generally take place in a more or less synchronized bargaining round. Though there is no formal coordination, informal contacts encourage a convergence of provisions of different agreements around particular themes – for example, union information rights in the late 1970s. The provisions of interconfederal agreements also ensure a certain homogeneity of outcomes in sectoral bargaining, as on the issue of working time in the early 1980s. Since the mid-1980s, however, there have been signs of a growing fragmentation in industry bargaining which 'for the first time lost its traditional unifying role' (Negrelli 1991d: 5).

A legacy of the struggles of 1969 has been the decay of the commitment to avoiding industrial action while negotiations are in progress; this is reflected in patterns of conflict synchronized with contract renewal (see below). Government mediation has become increasingly common, as for example in the long-running 1990 dispute in the banking and finance sector.

Industry agreements generally establish minimum pay scales that lower-level bargaining may improve upon. But their content on pay issues has been constrained, especially since the late 1970s, by the operation of the *scala mobile*, and they deal more with the structure than the level of increases. The inflexibility caused by the high proportion of automatic pay elements such as seniority has led to attempts since 1982 to reduce their weight by cutting the number of increments and ending inflation-linking. National agreements also determine minima for various bonuses, allowances and length-of-service increments.

Other issues dealt with include working time, skill levels and job classifications. On the first of these, the renewals of 1969–70 marked the general achievement of the 40-hour week in Italian industry. More recently the treatment of working time has reflected employers' concern with greater flexibility and cost reduction. Reductions in hours have been accompanied by union concessions allowing greater utilization of plant and management freedom to meet production peaks by exceeding weekly working hours (Cella and Treu 1989b: 193–4). Following the 1987 bargaining round, average working time was around 1750 hours a year.

Bargaining on job classifications has seen a tendency towards a simplification of schemes through a reduction in the number of levels, as in the engineering and chemical industries, and towards a harmonization of treatment of blue- and white-collar workers. The spirit of 1969 was reflected in the narrowing during the 1970s of differentials between manual and white-collar jobs, although from the 1980s, industry bargaining has tended to widen the so-called pay 'fan' (*ventaglio*) once more, and to make special provisions for middle managers (Giugni 1987: 234).

A further important area treated in national industry agreements has been the question of trade union rights, information and participation (Cella and Treu 1989b: 194–7). Industry agreements specified the detailed application of rights contained in the Workers' Statute of 1970 on the work of union delegates and meetings, union facilities in the workplace and so on. From the mid-1970s union rights to information about the economic situation of companies above a certain size, which first developed in a number of large firms such as Fiat and Zanussi, were generalized through sectoral bargaining. Agreements set out the sort of company information to which provincial unions and union workplace representatives are entitled: generally it includes data on the restructuring or decentralization of production, technological and organizational change, production plans and state financial assistance; and agreements also specify the rights of regional and national unions to information from employers' associations on the general prospects of the industry (for examples from the food and textiles industries, see Zoccatelli and Marin 1992a: 237–40 and 1992b: 264–7). In some agreements, employers are required to submit information to joint examination with the unions, especially concerning the impact of company decisions on employment levels and working conditions. In practice, the results of these rights, stipulated in the so-called 'first part' of collective agreements, have been uneven, especially in smaller companies (Giugni 1987: 234–5), and they have not lived up to union hopes that they would provide an 'Italian path to industrial democracy' (Cella and Treu 1989b: 196).

The latest round of sectoral bargaining, in 1990, was marked by the confused context of national interconfederal negotiations over the reform of industrial relations discussed above. In the so-called 'war of the contracts', Federmeccanica took a hard line, reflecting its desire to contain rising wage costs at a time when the industry was having to adapt to the single European market. At one point it broke off negotiations on renewal of the engineering contract, provoking the industry's first national strike since 1982 (EIRR 199, August 1990: 11).

Recent sectoral agreements have also confirmed the tendency towards the (re)institutionalization of bargaining through a more formal definition of bargaining issues and procedures. This, according to Bellardi (1991), has been closely linked with the parties' concern to achieve a higher degree of consensus and participation of the unions and work force in economic restructuring. One aspect has been the definition in industry agreement of the respective roles of different levels (Bellardi 1991: 4–6). Thus the moratorium imposed on the handling of 'economic' issues at company level has been extended in several recent agreements, and rules stipulating that matters dealt with at one level which may not be reopened at lower levels have become more explicit and formalized. Some agreements, as in chemicals and metalworking, lay down time periods within which company negotiations on working time must be completed, and during which the status quo is applied in the enterprise and the union remains under an obligation not to resort to collective action. Thus there appears to have been a partial return to the 'articulated' bargaining structures of the 1960s, within more highly developed structures.

Recent developments in the private sector have paralleled and in some cases borrowed from the model provided by the state-owned sector. As mentioned earlier, Intersind and the state holding companies IRI and ENI have played a significant role in the modernization of industrial relations at various times. The *Protocollo IRI* of 1984 (renewed in 1986) was a pathbreaking procedural agreement. Similar agreements were signed for other state groups, including ENI. The IRI Protocol was a response to upheavals caused by the rationalization and restructuring of operations in industries such as steel, shipbuilding and engineering, and by rapid technological change, for example in telecommunications. The aim of the Protocol was to increase the stability, predictability and 'governability' of industrial relations through the creation of a formal structure of 'joint consultative committees' (*comitati consultativi paritetici*) at group, sector, enterprise and plant levels. Cross-sectoral regional committees were also set up. Management was required to inform union representatives about strategic decisions on new investment, the introduction of new technology, acquisitions and divestments, and employment. The committees had the right to discuss and evaluate corporate strategies. Committees also had the power to make proposals on work organization, industrial relations and labour market policies. Finally, they were responsible for implementing a disputes procedure intended to reduce the levels of small local conflicts, *micro-conflittualità*.

Although the IRI Protocol has been called 'a major innovation for Italy's traditionally highly informal and rather unstable system of industrial relations' (Treu and Negrelli 1987: 84), its operation has been uncertain in practice. While the Protocol makes consultation obligatory, it does not make its outcome binding on the employer. Research has pointed to the ritualism of meetings, the limited possibilities of affecting decisions, the uncertain relationship of the joint committees to existing union structures in the enterprise, and the inappropriateness of a uniform system of consultation for such a heterogeneous group of companies (Negrelli 1989a: 239); in ASAP, a different approach was taken, with varying arrangements for groups of ENI companies. None the less, the IRI Protocol has had widespread influence on Italian industrial relations by providing a model of institutionalized 'neo-contractual' relationships, particularly at company level.

Recent agreements within the state-owned sector have contained innovative provisions pointing to a further 'proceduralization' of industrial relations (Bellardi 1991; Morese 1991). The 1990 agreement for the state-owned engineering industry (between Intersind and ASAP and the three union confederations) lays down a fuller, more 'articulated' framework for the conduct of negotiations. This includes the definition of appropriate bargaining issues at industry and enterprise levels; the establishment of timetables for the renewal of contracts in order to increase predictability; mechanisms for ensuring that agreements are respected; and procedures for reducing conflict.

Bargaining at Company and Workplace Level

According to a Federmeccanica survey of the engineering industry in 1972, when decentralized plant bargaining was at its peak, there were negotiations in a third of small firms (10–50 employees), almost three-quarters of small-medium firms (50–100), and virtually all firms over 100 employees (Cella and Treu 1989b: 204–5). By the end of the decade, company bargaining was playing a less significant role, although it remained important in larger companies where issues of working hours and the development of union information and consultation rights were dealt with. However, company bargaining has played an increasingly important part since the early 1980s as enterprises have adopted what Regini (1991a) calls 'eclectic pragmatism' in their relations with the unions in order to address the problems of corporate restructuring and the need for greater flexibility (see below).

Inevitably, as in Britain, 'a good part of decentralized bargaining takes place in a totally informal manner', without any written record, at plant section level between union representatives and middle managers or supervisors (Cella and Treu 1989b: 207), although such 'submerged' bargaining has been in decline since the 1970s. The main source of information on the extent and nature of formal company bargaining is the CESOS Observatory whose annual survey records developments since 1984 (Milani 1990; Baglioni 1991b). The surveys reveal a significant degree of company bargaining, even in smaller firms. In 1989, 51 per cent of companies with 500 or more employees negotiated at least one company agreement; 40 per cent of medium-sized firms (100–499 employees) and 26 per cent of small-medium (20–99) firms did so. In the late 1980s, companies in the food, engineering, chemicals and financial services were more likely to bargain than those in textiles, printing and publishing, transport or distribution. The changing structure of corporate work forces, with a decline in the proportion of manual workers, appears to have promoted rather than hindered company bargaining. Thus for most of the period covered by the CESOS surveys, firms in which there was a higher proportion of white-collar employees were significantly more likely to conclude agreements.

External unions (usually at provincial level) played an increasing formal role in company bargaining. The change was particularly marked in large companies where external union officers were sole signatories in 28 per cent of agreements in 1989, compared with 0.4 per cent in 1984–5. This tendency may reflect union efforts to respond in a coordinated way to widespread management-initiated change at company level, especially where technically complex issues – such as linking pay to company performance – are involved (cf. Baglioni 1991b: 7). By contrast, external employers' associations were only very rarely involved, being sole signatories in less than one per cent of agreements in 1989. Nevertheless, there was a tendency for agreements to be reached at more centralized levels *within* companies, certainly compared with the *repartismo* of the early 1970s (e.g. Negrelli 1991a: 190–1). In international comparison, such findings appear to be confirmed by survey data from ten European countries showing that bargaining over pay in large companies in Italy is more likely to take place at corporate headquarters (as opposed to subsidiary, site or establishment) than is the case in any other country (Hegewisch 1991: 31).

The most common subjects of company bargaining have been pay, working time, and union rights, followed by labour market issues, the working environment, work organization (including new technology and internal mobility), job classification, company welfare services, and vocational training. Labour market issues were proportionately more important for companies in economic difficulties, as were questions of work organization. The most common labour market subjects were employment guarantees, new forms of employment contract (such as job training, fixed-term, and part-time contracts), job reductions, and the use of the CIG.

Bargaining over pay has been constrained, as noted, by decisions at higher levels. An employers' association in the Milan region reported that company bargaining in 1988 accounted for about 14 per cent of total pay of workers covered, a proportion well below the 20 per cent recorded in the mid-1970s, though higher than the 10 per cent trough of 1984 following the January 1983 national agreement on the suspension of company pay bargaining (Negrelli 1991e: 235). The proportion of pay determined at company level was much higher for white-collar staff than for manual workers. Fixed-sum payments, such as the company or plant payments known as *superminimi*, are by far the most common subject of company agreements on pay issues. However, there has been a notable rise in the significance of variable pay elements. CESOS data suggest that variable pay was dealt with in 42 per cent of agreements in 1989, compared with 17 per cent in 1984–5. An Intersind survey of 60 'gainsharing' agreements in large companies between 1984 and 1988 indicates that they provide a wide variety of bonuses linked to various physical and financial performance indicators such as productivity, quality, sales revenue and operating profit (Cugini 1989; Prosperetti and Cossentino 1989). Such agreements were more likely in public than in private sector companies and were particularly common in the engineering industry. One example is Fiat's 1989 agreement under which a variable bonus amounting to about 2 per cent of annual pay is determined by a weighted index of measures of company performance, including net revenue per employee (Bianchi 1990).

With legislation allowing statutory working hours provisions to be exceeded only by collective agreement, working-time flexibility was a major feature of company bargaining in the late 1980s. Works councils have in many cases accepted longer working hours and flexible arrangements – such as '6x6' six-day, three-shift working, in return for additional payments or job security guarantees (EIRR 190, November 1989: 14).

Collective Bargaining in the Public Sector

In 1989 public employees in Italy made up 17.4 per cent of total employment, compared with 12.3 per cent in 1970. Although it continued to grow throughout the 1970s and 1980s (a reflection of the relatively late development of welfare services in Italy), the public sector[4] still represented a somewhat smaller proportion of total employment than in France, or even in Britain after a decade of Thatcherism (Oxley and Martin 1991: 168). Nevertheless, its industrial relations have been disproportionately influential, partly because of its general image of inefficiency and slowness to reform. In recent years, institutional reforms of industrial relations have had a major impact on collective bargaining, leading to what Treu and de Felice (1990) have referred to as a process of convergence with private sector industrial relations, although observers have reservations about the success of these changes.

As in many other European countries, the doctrine of the sovereignty of the state curtailed the development of collective bargaining for 'public employees'. It was only from the late 1960s that formal rights and structures of collective bargaining developed: in the public health sector from 1969, in the state and 'parastate' sectors from 1975 and in local government from 1978. The major legislative measure institutionalizing industrial relations machinery across the public sector was the framework law for public employment (Law 93) of 1983. Even before this, however, the public sector had traditionally high levels of unionization compared to the private sector. Alongside the main confederations (among which the DC-linked CSIL'played the dominant role), there were many independent unions, organizing specific occupational groups and in individual ministries: fragmented patterns of representation reflected the fragmentation of the employers into numerous separate bureaucratic units, each with different administrative traditions. In the absence of formal bargaining rights, the unions were 'indispensable interlocutors' (Romagnoli 1989: 267) in an informal system of participation. They had a degree of 'co-responsibility for the effectiveness of administrative action' (p. 270) through multifarious consultative bodies, some going back to the turn of the century, especially on personnel questions such as discipline, job classifications, careers and working-time. At the 'micro-level' of the workplace, there was informal *de facto* bargaining on such questions as work allocation; unions also put pressure on employers to grant the most favourable terms within the public sector's 'remuneration jungle' in which highly fragmented job structures sprouted hundreds of pay levels, with 'enormous, incongruous disparities in treatment and earnings both between sectors, and between grades' (*Ministero del Lavoro* 1988: 173). Earnings tended to be higher than in the private sector until the end of the 1960s; combined with higher job security, this meant that public employees were relatively 'privileged' (Treu 1987: 115). At the macro-level, unions lobbied government and parliament and engaged in informal bargaining over pay and employment legislation.

In the context of growing concern about the control of public expenditure, the impetus for the 1983 law appears to have come from pressure to reform the chaotic remuneration systems of the public sector, and to rationalize the structure of employer organization, in which structural and cultural distinctions between different parts of the state were 'exacerbated by political competition' (Treu 1987: 119) – for example, between central bodies linked to the governing DC and local bodies often controlled by other parties. In addition, there were increasing union demands for collective bargaining to be put on a regular footing; in the 1970s, the gains of private sector workers were threatening the privileged position of public employees and, while real wages continued to increase, they slipped back significantly relative to the private sector, especially in the second half of the decade (Oxley and Martin 1991: 166).

The 1983 law established the structures, procedures and actors of collective bargaining for the whole of public employment. The more than three million public employees are divided up into eight sub-sectors or *comparti*: schools (1,145,000 employees), universities (44,000), state research institutions (16,000), the postal service and other *aziende autonome* (300,000), parastatals (80,000), local government (*autonomie locali*) (620,000), health (620,000) and central government (270,000) (figures from EIRR 181, February 1989: 22). Each *comparto* has its own collective agreement which has to be authorized by the cabinet. In addition, a number of agreements cover the whole public sector, on issues such as inter-sector mobility, training, and equal opportunities (Russo 1990).

Law 93/1983 reserved to the state powers over organizational structures, hiring and firing, job classification, training, maximum working hours, the size of the work force, the organization of work, and discipline (although in most of these areas there is employee involvement, as before, through bipartite consultation machinery). The authorities retain the power to modify agreements which infringe the state's prerogative in such areas. The structure of bargaining within each subsector remains centralized, although the law allows some devolution of issues such as work organization and training to local levels. Pay is explicitly excluded from local bargaining, a reflection of the imperative of public expenditure control. This concern is also seen in the requirement that the employers' side in bargaining must include top-level government representatives, and in the power of the cabinet to refuse approval of agreements that exceed budgetary constraints.

The impact of the new framework has been mixed. A 1987 report by a Ministry of Labour committee (the Carniti Report) found that the long-familiar 'dysfunctions' remained: 'lack of transparency on wages and salaries, an excessive incidence of automatic mechanisms, and a stress on security and employee guarantees at the expense of efficiency' (*Ministero del Lavoro* 1988: 173). According to Romagnoli (1989: 271), old-style informal bargaining through the joint committee system continues. The parties have been reluctant to make use of the provisions for local bargaining, although a 1983 agreement set up a fund amounting to 0.8 per cent of the pay bill to finance productivity projects at local level. The classic public sector division between the 'employer' and the 'paymaster' has dogged union efforts to identify specific bargaining partners with the power of the purse. Dispersion of authority among several employers encourages 'phantom' and 'multilateral' bargaining' among the employers, for example between national and local governments over national pay guidelines, leading to a very protracted bargaining process; while the unions themselves are worried about a loss of influence to the *autonomi* should they try to coordinate and rationalize bargaining in too centralized a manner (Treu 1987: 120; Romagnoli 1989: 271–2).

A study of bargaining rounds in the public sector *comparti* (Cecora 1990) suggests that the parties have had problems in keeping to the time periods laid down in the law, not only for reaching agreement, but for authorization. The Court of Accounts had the task of monitoring the legitimacy of agreements, and its failure to ratify significant elements of agreements (for example, the provisions of the state police contract on seniority in the 1985–7 round) put a question mark against the autonomy and status of public sector bargaining. After a worsening of delays in the late 1980s that led Cecora (1990: 6) to speak of the 'progressive degeneration of the entire system of regulation of bargaining relationships in public employment', revisions to the law in 1990 were thought likely to improve the situation.

Pay and pay structures have been a major concern of collective bargaining since the introduction of the 1983 law. One objective of bargaining has been to reduce the weight of the biennial seniority payments (*scatti*):

according to the Carniti report, some 50 per cent of career earnings in the public sector were determined by seniority, compared with 20–5 per cent in private industry. However, in individual *comparto* agreements, there has been a tendency to re-establish the weight of seniority in determining pay (Cecora 1989: 6). A second concern of policy-makers and bargainers has been to relate pay more closely to productivity. Commonly, those bonuses that exist 'turn out to be more in the nature of automatic perquisites than a true reward for skill or merit', and even overtime payment tended to function as a 'sort of lump-sum additional compensation', not conditional on additional hours actually worked (*Ministero del Lavoro* 1988: 175). In various parts of the public administration there have been a number of experiments in recent years with productivity measurement, appraisal and reward (Pennella 1989). But, as Cecora (1990: 5) remarks, while formally incentives are linked with the achievement of specific projects or tasks, in reality 'the final outcome has not been dissimilar to the disappointing attempts made in the past': the problem residing largely in the difficulties of measurement and supervision.

A final aspect of pay is the overall level of settlements. In a number of agreements, particularly in the schools and health subsectors, there has been a tendency to breach pre-established limits for pay increases. Indeed, the IMF (1990: 9) was moved to warn that 'progress towards the convergence of [Italian] rates of inflation with those of major partners within the EMS by 1994 will not be possible unless the public sector sets the example by reining back the rate of increase of earnings in line with the established guidelines'; and it unsuccessfully requested the Italian government to freeze collective contract renewals for public employees in 1991. In 1990, the pay of public employees increased by an average of 16 per cent, compared with about 7 per cent in private industry and services (De Luca, P. 1992: 5–7), and the trend continued in 1991 (Negrelli 1992).

In short, therefore, although there have been important industrial relations reforms in the public sector, the context of European monetary integration and a public sector agenda of retrenchment have inhibited the development of collective bargaining for public employees since the early 1980s. Currently, further reform is being discussed in tripartite talks. Among the proposals are the extension of the areas of collective bargaining and the restriction of legal regulation to staffing policy and general organizational guidelines (EIRR 210, July 1991: 7), and a greater decentralization of bargaining to bring the public sector more into line with private industry.

Strikes

Measured across the whole of the post-war period, Italy clearly heads the European strike table. It has ranked high in terms of all three conventional indicators of conflict: number of stoppages, workers involved, and working days lost. This reflects a combination of forms of strikes of varying size and duration: company and workplace disputes, industry-level stoppages, demonstrative general strikes. The sectoral distribution of disputes is rather more even than in most other countries, and the secular trends – despite obvious peaks and troughs – less dramatic. Certainly there has been a significant decline in strike activity in the past decade; but less drastic than in many other European countries.

Official statistics are available from 1949 – a year of particularly intense and politicized conflict as the cold war ruptured the fragile unity of the immediate post-war years. In principle the data cover every strike and lockout, regardless of size or duration; though as in most countries, small and short stoppages may fail to be reported.

In the late 1940s and early 1950s, just over 1,000 disputes a year were recorded. The numbers climbed persistently in the next two decades, reaching almost 2,000 a year in the mid-1950s, rising rapidly to over 4,000 in 1963, and after falling back before the 'hot autumn' reached the record figure of 5,598 in 1971. There was then a sharp decline, to 2,000 in 1979, followed by further reductions in the 1980s. The figure for 1990 – just over 1,000 – was the lowest since the war; while the number of disputes is likely to have fallen below this level in 1991.

The trend in workers involved has been rather different. Initially around 3 million a year, with a peak of 4.7 million in 1953, involvement fell during the 1950s to under 2 million. For most of the 1960s the figure was between 2 and 3 million a year, but jumped to 7.5 million in 1969. This record was in turn exceeded in most years in the 1970s, with a peak of over 16 million in 1979. The figure subsided somewhat in the 1980s, but still averaged 4 million in the latter half of the decade.

The number of working days lost was 16.5 million in 1949, but around 5 million a year in the following decade. Levels were considerably higher in the 1960s, with a record of almost 38 million in 1968. The figure did not fall below 10 million in any subsequent year until 1984, and in the latter 1980s settled at around 4 million (table 16.3).

Franzosi (1989) has argued, in an analysis of the years 1955–78, that the 'shape' of post-war strikes in Italian manufacturing has undergone three major transformations. Until the 1960s their average duration was fairly short, but then increased sharply. The second change, from the end of the 1960s, was in the average size: the number of workers involved increased significantly. From the mid- 1970s a third shift occurred, towards shorter but larger strikes: a pattern which continued through the 1980s.

It is a familiar observation, which nevertheless bears repetition, that there is no such thing as an 'average' strike: the notion is merely a statistical artefact. In fact, at least four different types of dispute have been common in Italy. First, as in other southern European countries, there is a tradition of short (at most, one-day) political protests, which aim to involve large numbers of workers and hence register a large total of days lost. Since 1975 the official statistics have identified disputes 'not concerned with industrial relations'; though few in number, these often account for a sizable proportion of days lost (in 1985, the majority). Second, there are token strikes associated with industry-level bargaining: these may be large, but relatively limited in their impact on figures of days lost. Third are more extended industry-level stoppages; these are exceptional in Italy, not least because of the lack of union strike funds; but were important in contributing to the average length of strikes in the 1960s. Given the tradition of two- or three-year national agreements, industry-wide strikes – whether short or long – tend to 'bunch' in particular years of contract renewal. Fourth are company-level strikes: large or small, short or protracted. These have always accounted for the great majority of stoppages in post-war Italy, though for a far smaller proportion of workers involved and days lost (Bordogna and Provasi 1989: 287).

Franzosi has argued that a variety of explanations are needed to interpret the trends in Italian strikes: the economic situation, changes in bargaining institutions, the dynamics of political exchange. Given the complex interconnections between politics and industrial relations, it is impossible to interpret trends and patterns of disputes simply in terms of the contingencies of collective bargaining: changes in the political climate, in party-union linkages, and in inter-party relations all have an important impact. In particular, the shifts in PCI priorities between oppositional mobilization and the pursuit of consensus, as well as the changing forms of party influence within CGIL, have been of major significance in the post-war decades. However, developments at the point of production also exert an autonomous impact. Accounts of the explosion of militancy in 1969 have always emphasized the immediate grievances of 'the young, mostly immigrant, semi-skilled workers, who had been almost excluded from the industrial relations system until 1968' and who were subject to intense pressures at work as well as intolerable living conditions (Regalia et al. 1978: 109). The radicalism of many of the forms of action –lightning strikes, selective and rolling stoppages, various types of work-to-rule – reflected spontaneous collective decisions within the workplace rather than deliberate union strategy. The growth in organization and confidence at company level associated with the 'hot autumn', and consolidated under the Workers' Statute, in turn contributed to the upsurge in all dimensions of disputes in the 1970s. The relative independence of factory trade unionism from external union control, as was noted above, created problems for CGIL in particular when its strategy shifted towards political compromise and bargaining restraint.

The three factors emphasized by Franzosi are all relevant for understanding strike trends since the late 1970s. High levels of unemployment, the new insecurity of much industrial employment, and a more aggressive managerial approach have transformed the context of company-level industrial relations. The experience of symbolic defeats, such as Fiat in

Table 16.3 Industrial disputes 1955–89: Number, workers involved (000s) and hours lost (000s) by type of dispute

Year	Workplace			Single-industry			Multi-industry			Total		
	N	W	H	N	W	H	N	W	H	N	W	H
1955[a]	1,357	346	5,441	584	667	37,272	40	370	2,265	1,981	1,383	44,978
1956	1,214	271	4,502	649	998	26,565	41	409	2,026	1,904	1,678	33,093
1957	1,134	269	5,498	579	774	29,953	18	184	1,499	1,731	1,227	36,950
1958	1,267	258	4,817	644	854	27,541	26	171	1,017	1,937	1,283	33,375
1959	1,243	220	4,686	649	1,487	67,705	33	193	1,132	1,925	1,900	73,523
1960	1,707	368	8,583	709	949	31,422	55	1,021	6,284	2,471	2,338	46,289
1961	2,478	505	15,554	966	1,863	61,650	58	330	1,923	3,502	2,698	79,127
1962	2,536	496	16,310	1,088	1,990	155,494	28	424	9,928	3,652	2,910	181,732
1963	3,413	691	18,313	710	2,131	68,516	22	872	4,329	4,145	3,694	91,158
1964	3,128	750	15,487	673	2,050	80,109	40	445	9,113	3,841	3,245	104,709
1965	2,675	696	15,873	494	1,539	39,721	22	75	349	3,191	2,310	55,943
1966	1,953	460	9,423	418	1,207	104,893	16	220	1,472	2,387	1,887	115,788
1967	2,251	483	10,381	391	1,623	56,117	16	137	2,050	2,658	2,243	68,548
1968	2,860	847	21,704	489	1,256	25,477	28	2,759	26,737	3,377	4,862	73,918
1969	3,219	754	21,408	548	2,910	230,620	21	3,843	50,569	3,788	7,507	302,597
1970	3,537	1,153	30,214	614	2,543	115,842	11	26	156	4,162	3,722	146,212
1971	4,831	1,465	35,284	725	2,243	67,476	42	183	830	5,598	3,891	103,590
1972	4,099	1,073	23,164	639	2,480	108,434	27	852	4,882	4,765	4,405	136,480
1973	3,225	938	15,483	523	2,698	138,429	21	2,497	10,023	3,769	6,133	163,935
1974	4,465	1,704	34,001	691	2,067	41,638	18	4,053	60,628	5,174	7,824	136,267

Year	Industrial issues			Other issues			Total		
	N	W	H	N	W	H	N	W	H
1975	3,568	10,717	181,381	33	3,392	8,943	3,601	14,109	190,324
1976	2,667	6,974	131,711	39	4,924	45,932	2,706	11,898	177,643
1977	3,259	6,434	78,767	49	7,369	37,196	3,308	13,803	115,963
1978	2,465	4,347	49,032	14	4,427	22,207	2,479	8,774	71,239
1979	1,979	10,521	164,914	21	5,717	27,799	2,000	16,238	192,713
1980	2,224	7,428	75,214	14	6,397	39,987	2,238	13,825	115,201

Year	Industrial issues			Non-industrial issues			Total		
	N	W	H	N	W	H	N	W	H
1981	2,176	3,567	42,802	28	4,660	30,889	2,204	8,227	73,691
1982	1,741	7,490	114,889	6	2,993	15,051	1,747	10,483	129,940
1983	1,550	4,625	82,626	15	2,219	15,395	1,565	6,844	98,021
1984	1,759	3,540	31,786	57	3,816	29,137	1,816	7,356	60,923
1985	1,336	1,224	11,036	5	3,619	15,779	1,341	4,843	26,815
1986	1,462	2,940	36,742	7	667	2,764	1,469	3,607	39,506
1987	1,146	1,473	20,147	3	2,800	12,093	1,149	4,273	32,240
1988	1,767	1,609	17,086	2	1,103	6,120	1,769	2,712	23,206
1989	1,295	2,108	21,001	2	2,344	10,052	1,297	4,452	31,053
1990	1,094	1,634	36,272	0	0	0	1,094	1,634	36,272

a 1955–74 statistics include only 'industrial' disputes.
Source: Annuario Statistico.

1980, has reinforced the erosion of worker combativity, and may help explain in particular why the number of workplace strikes has fallen, and why those which do occur seem increasingly to take the form of token demonstrations rather than sustained engagements.

The evolution of bargaining institutions is also important. Most commentators stress the weak institutionalization of Italian industrial relations, and certainly the volatility apparent in the last three decades reflects the absence, or inadequacy, of mechanisms to contain new challenges and aspirations. Nevertheless, the past decade has seen a significant trend towards the 'proceduralization of conflict' (Sciarra 1988: 670), together with a formalization of company-level bargaining, and its re-articulation with higher levels of industrial relations. The IRI protocol of 1984, subsequently revised and elaborated, has served as a model for the public enterprise sector and beyond in generating 'new "techniques" and instruments of mediation' (Negrelli and Santi 1990: 172). The 'new forms of regulation' (Negrelli 1988), discussed in more detail below, include formalized workplace grievance procedures, and machinery of conciliation and arbitration. In principle, unions and employers accept the obligation to exhaust the possibilities of peaceful resolution of disputes before resorting to strikes or lockouts; and though each side accuses the other of failure to respect these commitments, it would seem that the increased institutionalization has indeed contributed to a reduction in conflict.

The demonstrative general strike has been a traditional vehicle of political protest in Italy, and since the 1970s also a resource in political exchange. As is apparent from table 16.3, there was a sharp fall in the number of political strikes during the period of national solidarity government (though the few which did occur had a substantial impact on the statistics). In 1980, after the PCI returned to opposition, political stoppages accounted for over a third of total days lost. The breakdown of tripartism and inter-union cooperation in 1984 brought an upsurge in political stoppages, accounting for almost half of all days lost. In 1985 – the year of the *scala mobile* referendum – the number of political strikes was smaller, but they contributed (in a year when the impact of collective bargaining disputes was by far the lowest of the decade) the majority of days lost. Thereafter there have been far fewer political stoppages, but on occasion they still serve as both a vehicle of mass mobilization and a symbol of inter-union cooperation in pursuit of demands related to social and fiscal policy. As in 1989, such stoppages can have a considerable impact on the statistics. However, the confederations have currently abandoned the general strike as a political weapon.

The theme of the 'tertiarization of conflict', proposed in an influential analysis by Accornero (1985), has been taken up by many subsequent writers (e.g. Bordogna and Provasi 1989: 286; Negrelli and Santi 1990: 191). The argument is that disputes are increasingly located in the service sector, and particularly in transport, public administration and social services; but also that with new actors, the issues and targets have altered. As against the solidaristic and egalitarian emphasis underlying the collective bargaining (and strike) agenda of the 1970s, the new conflicts often involve higher-status craft and professional groups pressing for restoration of differentials squeezed by past collective agreements and by flat-rate wage indexation. At the same time, the tactics of public service strikes – often imitating those pioneered by factory workers in 1969 – are designed to cause maximum public disruption in order to put pressure on management and the government. Such stoppages, led by 'autonomous' unions and *cobas*, are widely interpreted as signs of a change in the character of the strike from a vehicle of popular mobilization to an instrument of competitive inter-group conflict (Sciarra 1988). They can be seen as a major cause of the main union confederations' crisis of representativity, undermining the credibility of their appeals to a common working-class interest, and gravely weakening their public standing.

The recent pattern of public-service conflicts has also provoked the first post-war legal restrictions on strike action, law 146 of 1990. Introduced by Gino Giugni – law professor, CISL advisor and PSI senator, who helped draft the 1970 Workers' Statute – the new law is intended to regulate disputes in a specified number of essential services. There is a requirement to maintain a minimum level of service (which should be determined by collective agreement) during any strike, and to ensure this minimum, specific individuals may be required to remain at work. Strike organizers must give ten days' notice to the employer, who must in turn warn the public. Individual workers who break the law may be fined or suspended from work, but not dismissed; organizations can be temporarily deprived of their benefits under the Workers' Statute. The legislation, while a major symbolic break with the voluntarist tradition, is scarcely draconian in content; its main objective is to encourage self-regulation by unions and public employers. It is still early to judge its efficacy. On the negative side, it appears that agreements on minimum standards of service have been difficult to achieve; and *cobas*-led strikes recurred in the summer of 1991 without the law being invoked. However, far fewer days were lost in such disputes than in previous years, and most observers see this as an index of the law's success – perhaps complementing a weakening of employee support for militant oppositional organization (Negrelli 1992).

Despite the recent emphasis on *conflitto terziarizzato* as a novel phenomenon of the 1980s, it is important to recognize significant continuities in the sectoral distribution of Italian strikes. As table 16.4 shows, public and private services (including transport) accounted for over 40 per cent of strikes in most years of the 1980s, and reached half the total in 1988. The proportion of workers involved was lower in most years (usually between a quarter and a third), indicating that stoppages were usually smaller than in manufacturing. Conversely, disputes in services were longer on average, accounting for 60 per cent of days lost in 1986 and 1989 (both years of major public-sector conflicts).

Table 16.4 Disputes by sector 1960–89 (5-year averages): Number, workers involved (000s) and days lost (000s)

	Total	Agriculture, forestry, fishing	Mining, quarrying	Manufac-turing	Electricity, gas, water	Construction	Transport, storage, communication	Hotels, catering, commerce	Community, social & personal services	Services as %
1960–64 N	3,522	123	172	1,876	59	366	329	92	587	29
W	2,977	327	86	1,321	25	305	251	68	593	31
D	12,576	2,059	360	6,583	128	1,035	678	160	1,572	19
1965–69 N	3,080	103	61	1,736	50	170	352	85	567	33
W	3,762	378	39	1,856	63	307	342	140	637	30
D	15,420	1,323	167	9,172	174	1,128	919	511	2,024	22
1970–74 N	4,694	92	73	2,589	73	218	538	236	926	36
W	5,195	354	47	2,976	84	347	346	221	820	27
D	19,614	1,340	155	11,163	287	910	1,284	993	3,480	29
1975–79 N	2,819	62	51	1,506	59	157	366	199	570	40
W	12,964	835	75	7,659	125	1,074	533	710	1,934	25
D	21,368	1,811	104	10,750	93	1,745	1,107	1,318	4,440	32
1980–84 N	1,914	58	33	1,011	42	102	285	125	370	41
W	9,347	563	41	5,428	68	641	437	664	1,505	28
D	13,651	720	45	8,178	65	835	1,597	1,041	1,988	34
1985–89 N	1,405	41	27	626	35	65	235	98	329	47
W	3,977	248	35	1,993	46	245	297	320	792	35
D	4,366	232	30	1,686	48	267	638	427	1,033	48
1980 N	2,238	82	34	1,199	44	158	253	196	385	37
W	13,825	751	52	8,775	109	995	472	681	1,990	23
D	16,457	1,082	63	10,544	96	1,010	4,544	721	2,486	47
1981 N	2,204	55	54	1,212	39	111	314	141	407	39
W	8,227	549	36	4,933	58	411	487	323	1,429	27
D	10,527	756	48	5,437	60	370	1,325	581	1,951	37

Table 16.4 (cont.)

1982 N	1,747	56	41	885	55	91	267	94	336	40
W	10,483	722	45	5,944	84	863	468	665	1,693	27
D	18,563	863	58	12,012	82	1,336	672	1,713	1,827	23
1983 N	1,565	39	24	861	31	82	301	84	283	43
W	6,844	402	26	3,693	31	482	397	400	1,413	32
D	14,003	461	23	8,851	26	1,007	764	437	2,434	26
1984 N	1,816	56	11	896	41	68	289	109	437	46
W	7,356	393	46	3,793	60	454	1,360	1,250	1,001	35
D	8,703	439	32	4,048	60	451	1,678	1,751	1,244	42
1985 N	1,341	43	29	694	31	73	176	82	274	40
W	4,843	296	90	2,711	82	389	213	356	706	26
D	3,831	200	60	2,137	59	303	323	199	551	28
1986 N	1,469	42	22	614	32	88	242	108	359	48
W	3,607	168	10	1,622	52	313	250	194	998	40
D	5,644	229	18	1,634	75	327	649	637	2,081	60
1987 N	1,149	32	27	526	44	33	229	73	245	48
W	4,273	285	40	2,295	34	278	351	332	657	31
D	4,606	207	31	1,943	33	449	773	341	819	42
1988 N	1,769	43	37	764	38	59	330	127	433	50
W	2,712	222	13	1,399	42	88	235	199	514	35
D	3,315	344	22	1,336	37	75	586	183	703	44
1989 N	1,297	45	22	632	28	74	198	101	334	44
W	4,452	269	20	1,940	21	155	434	525	1,087	46
D	4,436	179	17	1,380	34	183	859	773	1,013	60

Source: ILO, *Yearbook of Labour Statistics.*

The share of services in the strike figures is certainly noteworthy. However in Italy, unlike most other European countries, manufacturing has never overwhelmed the strike record; both agriculture and services have traditionally been more strike-prone than in other national contexts. In the 1960s – when employment in the service sector was proportionately much smaller than today – it was responsible for 30 per cent of all strikes. Moreover, the proportion actually increased during the upsurge of factory militancy of the late 1960s and early 1970s. As Regalia et al. comment (1978: 109–10), 'after 1969 conflictual action spread to sectors of the labour force which were not traditionally "strike prone".... New protagonists emerged: white-collar workers, public service employees and civil servants.' As in the 1980s, 'a common attempt was made to achieve salary increases which would re-establish differentials over industrial workers'; and 'where the unions were strongest and attempted to control mobilization, some ex-union leaders associated with left-wing groups formed autonomous rank-and-file committees which could call strikes for wage demands'.

Thus the novelty of recent experience can be exaggerated. Lightning stoppages of train drivers or air-traffic controllers are highly visible and disruptive; but whatever their symbolic importance they contribute relatively little to the aggregate strike statistics. The increased prominence of services within the overall figures stems not so much from increased militancy on the part of service workers as a relatively stable pattern of strike activity in a period when manufacturing disputes fell sharply. In particular, the increased share of services in the total of working days lost does not mean that stoppages have become larger and longer in the tertiary sector, but rather that manufacturing strikes have become shorter since the mid 1980s. Hence in 1990, with a major conflict over the new engineering agreement, the proportion of days lost in 'tertiary' strikes fell to 16 per cent.

The issue is thus not that service-sector militancy has increased in the 1980s, but that it has failed to decline to the same extent as in manufacturing. To explain this, one may refer in part to processes familiar in public employment throughout Europe: increased budgetary stringency leading to managerial efforts to rationalize and economize, and to a tougher climate for wage bargaining. Of specific relevance in the Italian context is the background of weak and unstable government. Public-sector unions in some European countries have discovered painfully that their governments are willing and able to stand firm in the face of strike action; for their Italian counterparts, militancy can still bring success. In the Italian case, moreover, it is possible to identify a problem of over-rapid and hence unsuccessful institutionalization. The reformed system of collective bargaining, codified by law 93 of 1983 (see above), rests on the principle of self-regulation by the negotiating parties, and ties admission to the bargaining process to adherence to the norms of self-restraint. Yet in a sector where the main confederations have traditionally faced autonomous rivals, the exclusion of the latter from the

machinery of negotiation merely confirms their status as poles of opposition and resistance. Hence the agonized debates among the main
confederations in such sectors as the railways and airlines on whether to
admit their rivals to a seat at the bargaining table. Whether such a
strategy of incorporation of the militants will be widely pursued, and
whether it will work, remains uncertain.

Changing Management Strategies:
Is Micro-concertation the New Italian Model?

The restructuring of the corporate economy since the late 1970s has had a
profound effect on management strategies and industrial relations in the
enterprise. Like their counterparts in other European countries, Italian
employers have responded to market competition and internationalization
by rationalizing corporate organization, introducing new technology, and
pursuing more flexible market and production strategies. What is surprising, however, given the historical legacy of poorly institutionalized,
conflictual, low-trust industrial relations, is that there appears to have been
a growth of more consensual, formalized relationships operating not only
through the increased bargaining activity described above, but also through
mechanisms of consultation and participation (Negrelli 1991a, Ambrosini
et al. 1992). How, as Regini (1987: 7) asks, may one explain that 'following
the rigidities of the 1970s and the union defeats of the early 1980s, the
majority of employers have not pursued to its conclusion the strategy of
breaking with existing forms of regulation and bypasssing the unions?'
Before attempting to answer the question, we sketch some of the major
changes in corporate personnel and industrial relations since the beginning
of the 1980s.

Employers' Flexibility Strategies

Italian employers, both large and small, have been implementing increased
flexibility in many areas of industrial relations and work organization. As
suggested above, company bargaining on pay has increasingly covered
new performance-related forms of remuneration. It appears to be a particularly important phenomenon among higher white-collar employees.
According to a survey of large companies in ten European countries, a
considerably higher proportion (86 per cent) of technical and professional
employees in Italy receive merit pay than in any other country (Price
Waterhouse/Cranfield 1991: 34); in addition, there was a marked increase
in the weight of the performance-related element for white-collar employees, from 13 per cent in 1983 to 20 per cent in 1988, much higher than in
France or Britain. This has been attributed more to the flattening of differentials than to 'a fundamental shift towards a performance culture' (Hegewisch
1991: 33). None the less, the 1989 collective agreement for Italy's 90,000
industrial managers represented 'a change in the pay philosophy of the

major industrial concerns', with an increasing weight given to '*superminimi individuali*', the individually-negotiated element of remuneration based (for senior managers) on performance and company ability to pay. A survey by the managers' organization FNDAI showed that *superminimi* already accounted for about 21 per cent of the total pay packet on average (*IDS European Report* 338, February 1990: 9–10). In general, the proportion of pay determined individually has risen relative to the part determined through company bargaining: while the latter remained fairly constant at 14–15 per cent, the former doubled from 5.8 to 11.4 per cent between 1983 and 1988, according to a survey by the Milan region engineering employers' organization Assolombarda (Negrelli 1991d: 7); by 1991 it had risen to 14 per cent (Negrelli 1992).

The true extent and significance of merit and performance-related pay is more uncertain (cf. Della Rocca 1991; 1992). For example, there is little evidence that it forms a major element in the pay packet of most staff in the companies where it has been introduced. The Intersind survey of 'gainsharing' agreements suggests the variable element in practice amounts to about 3 per cent of earnings for manual workers and slightly less for middle-level white-collar employees (apparently contradicting the IDS findings) (Prosperetti and Cossentino 1991: 8). None the less, there is little doubt that 'flexible pay' has become more widespread and important (cf. Negrelli 1989a: 251–2; Saba 1992: 94–102), and remuneration policy directed to corporate objectives is of growing importance in Italian companies.

A second area of flexibility is in levels and forms of employment. Companies have pursued 'numerical' flexibility with considerable cuts in work forces. For example, Fiat reduced numbers by 46 per cent between 1979 and 1985 (Locke and Negrelli 1989: 66). The blow of redundancy and lay-offs was softened, however, by the institution of the CIG (see above) which in practice covered situations where there was no prospect of a return to work; in Fiat, nearly 21,000 workers were paid by the CIG in 1980 (ibid.). In addition, large Italian companies were among the most likely in Europe to use voluntary redudancy and early retirement, and the least likely to use compulsory redundancy, as means of reducing the work force (Price Waterhouse/Cranfield 1991: 12).

A recent CENSIS survey of 600 companies shows that the use of fixed-term and part-time contracts, flexitime, and other forms of flexible employment is significant in Italian firms (Camusi 1991), if not as widespread as in other European countries: Italy had a rate of part-time employment of 5.6 per cent in 1987, the second lowest rate in Europe after Spain (EIRR 1990: 13); a similar proportion were on fixed-term contracts in 1988, a figure more in line with most other European countries (p. 28). Much of this flexibility is, as suggested above, the result of collective agreements both at national industry and company level. The CENSIS survey reveals greater flexibility in the service sector than in manufacturing, in large companies than in small, and in the north than in the south. A notable finding is the recourse of many companies to external consultancy contracts for skilled professional functions such as planning, research and development.

Camusi (1991: 4) cautions against automatically interpreting atypical forms of employment as indications of flexibility. For example, part-time work, which was rising rapidly in the second half of the 1980s especially in the service sector (*Sysdem Bulletin*, 4, 1991: 28–9), is commonly employed in Italy as the first step to full-time permanent employment and as such may point to rigidity rather than flexibility. Moreover, survey data suggest that companies lack the necessary skills and experience to handle flexible arrangements, which often, partly for that reason, lead to more micro-level conflict and increased overall costs (Camusi 1991: 6–8).

There were major changes in work organization in Italian companies in the 1980s, partly as a result of new technologies including robots (Regini and Sabel 1989a). However, case studies suggest that advanced electronics did not always lead to 'post-Taylorist' forms of flexible work organization but often created increased rigidity; in some cases there was a return to assembly-line operation following experiments with teamworking (Regini and Sabel 1989b: 33–44; Locke and Negrelli 1989: 67–73; Berta and Michelsons 1989: 144–51).

The Pursuit of Flexibility and Industrial Relations

A basic question is whether this flexibility is achieved through the strengthening of unilateral management prerogative and the application of human resource policies oriented to the individual worker; or through more consultative, cooperative means involving unions and the work force collectively. These two ends of the spectrum were encapsulated in two contrasting strategies in the first half of the 1980s, which Giugni has labelled the *modello Prodi* (after the head of IRI at the time of the 1984 Protocol – see above) and the *modello Romiti* (after the managing director of Fiat at the beginning of the 1980s).

The crushing defeat of the unions in the 1980 Fiat strike appeared to set the seal on a phase of unilateralism. This strategy was given programmatic expression by Federmeccanica in its 1984 'manifesto'. The association depicted a future for Italian industrial relations in which waning collective relations would be replaced by individual employer-employee bargaining; union intervention was regarded as often imposing bureaucratic constraints on 'the free circulation of [entrepreneurial] energies' (cited in Negrelli 1991a: 34). For the first half of the 1980s, unilateralism, and the marginalization of the unions, appeared to be prevailing strategy at Fiat (Locke and Negrelli 1989). But Fiat was in many ways a special case: managerial strategy was a response to a specific combination of international product market pressures and intense union militancy in the 1970s. Even when managerial assertiveness was at its height, from the defeat of the 1980 strike until the middle of the decade, there was no sweeping rejection of the unions: the company did not renege on formal agreements, and made only fairly desultory efforts to develop 'human resource management' oriented to the individual employee (Locke and Negrelli: 79–84). Fiat, in short, was not typical, and its phase of unilateralism was neither total nor long-lasting.

In general, commentators point to a widespread increase in the 'average rate of cooperation' in Italian companies (Regini 1991a: 15). Regini (1987: 6) identifies a model of '"*de facto* cooperation"', often tacit and informal, but highly effective', leading to the development of a 'micro-concertation' that paralleled (and in some ways depended on) concertation at the macro-level. Even in Fiat from 1985, management and unions cooperated in the introduction of some aspects of flexibility. Generally, micro-concertation was seen in the rapid extension of company bargaining, described above, and more specifically in the 'institutionalization' of industrial relations within the firm. One factor behind the formalization of participative structures was the increasing introduction of performance-related pay systems, which necessitated discussion of indicators, the fixing of objectives and the monitoring of outcomes (Galeone 1992: 222–4). Alongside more formalized bargaining procedures, mechanisms for information and consultation were increasingly developed (Negrelli 1991a; Ambrosini et al. 1992), sometimes through elaborate formal structures, as in the IRI Protocol.

The new element was the favourable attitude of unions to more direct forms of communication and consultation, which were seen as coexisting pacifically with traditional industrial relations structures rather than being in opposition to them (Regini and Sabel 1989b: 46–7). Recent case studies of a range of industries suggest that direct employee involvement, bypassing the unions, is rare in Italian firms, although it does occur in the subsidiaries of some foreign multinationals (Ambrosini 1992: 140–3). There were some signs of elements of 'human resource management': changes in work organization were sometimes accompanied by the introduction of quality circles – originally imported by multinationals such as Philips and Thomson. A number of large companies in the food industry adopted them in the 1980s, some – such as the state-owned Italgel – going on to introduce 'total quality management' (Zoccatelli and Marin 1992a). But the level of such activity in Italy remained extremely low at the end of the 1980s (Negrelli 1989a: 253–4; Ambrosini et al. 1992). More important, as a study of engineering firms concludes, 'while one may observe a growing [employer] attention to human resource management, this does not involve a strategy of deunionization, does not appear to narrow the scope for union action, and does not come into direct conflict with union interests' (Galeone 1992: 220). In the food company, Italgel, for example, the unions were formally involved in the system of quality circles, and the introduction of total quality management was seen as a source of growing consensus (Zoccatelli and Marin 1992a: 253). In general, there has been what Regini (1991b: 188) calls a 'peaceful superimposition' of direct relations with employees on management–union relations. This in turn reflects the notable willingness of Italian unions – including, in recent years, CGIL – to engage in the collaborative management of change.

Case-study evidence points to a very wide variety of practices within this general model. Even similar companies within the same sector could choose different solutions to the problems of change and restructuring; even in the state industry sector, the *'modello Prodi'* was by no means a homogeneous phenomenon. Negrelli (1991a: ch. 9) proposes a classification of employer industrial relations strategies into the 'instrumental', the 'bureaucratic' and the 'processual'. The first is exemplified by Fiat (Locke and Negrelli 1989), or by the French-owned brewery Wührer, studied by Treu and Negrelli (1987). Companies use bilateral means of resolving issues of flexibility in an opportunistic fashion, when other means prove inadequate. In Fiat, for example, the company negotiated with the unions over Saturday working when individual forms of persuasion failed to produce sufficient volunteers. Thus 'instrumental' managements will involve unions on particular issues (and for particular groups of workers), and generally at operational rather than strategic levels.

Negrelli (1991a: 133–86, 241–2) argues that the second, 'bureaucratic', approach is typical of certain state sector companies (such as ENEL, the state electricity company, and to an extent the telephone company, SIP) that were attempting to restructure their operations in a centralized manner, reflecting the nature of their operations. At corporate level, both management and unions were fearful of centrifugal tendencies, and left little scope for either management or unions in the operating units to influence decision processes. The bureaucratization of industrial relations is also a reflection of the imposition of the unitary, centralized IRI model under the 1984 Protocol. As mentioned, subsequent framework agreements, such as that in ENI, adopted a more decentralized approach, allowing different formats to emerge in different sectors.

In the third model, of 'processual participation', relationships are based on trust, and mechanisms of consultation are developed at different levels of the company, with a high degree of articulation between them. Participation may extend from issues of immediate work organization to broad corporate strategies of restructuring. Examples are found not only in state companies such as the telecommunications equipment manufacturer Italtel (Negrelli 1989b; 1991a: ch. 7), but also in large private companies like Pirelli – which pioneered a consultative approach in the second half of the 1970s as a response to corporate crisis (Negrelli 1991a: ch. 4) – or the steel company Falck (Regalia 1989) and even the small-firm sector in industrial districts such as Modena and Prato (Perulli 1989; Trigilia 1989). Zanussi has recently introduced an innovative agreement which concedes several areas of managerial prerogative to joint committees (*organismi paritetici*) dealing with issues such as the impact of new technology and job classifications (EIRR 217, February 1992: 16–17). In Italtel, where the participative strategy predated the IRI Protocol, joint committees at corporate level discuss areas of corporate strategy such as diversification or regional specialization, while 'technical commissions' examine issues such as work organization, health and safety, training, and equal opportunities. In such companies, formal agreements in the negotiating machinery tend to depend on a prior consensus being reached within the joint consultative machinery. Indeed, Negrelli (1991a: 275) talks of an 'uninterrupted process of engagement, with the formal company agreement constituting merely one phase in an endless sequence of overlapping and iterative phases'; Bordogna, for example, observed intense and continuous bargaining during the restructuring process in a petrochemicals company in the Montedison group (Bordogna 1989: 115–18). Elsewhere, consultative practices have had a less profound influence on negotiating systems: either the two machineries coexist uneasily in parallel, or the unions exploit consultation opportunistically in local bargaining (Negrelli 1991a: 276–8).

Thus the dichotomy between the public enterprise Prodi model, and the (implicitly) private sector Fiat model is far too simple a description of reality. Differences between corporate strategies are not to be explained simply by the public-private division: although many of the public enterprises have 'participative' industrial relations, there are significant variations, and indeed, some state-owned companies – in the food and clothing sectors, for example – have tried to reaffirm managerial prerogative in the restructuring process (Treu and Negrelli 1987: 93). Nor, as Regini and Sabel (1989b) argue, can companies neatly be divided between small and large firms (corresponding to unilateral management action versus bargained change). Researchers (Trigilia 1989; Perulli 1989) have argued that small firms, operating through their local employers' organizations, have often built on the solidaristic relationships embedded in the social fabric of the 'Third Italy' where the growth of small enterprises has been greatest. There was an upsurge in enterprise agreements in areas like Modena and Prato in the first half of the 1980s, covering issues of flexibility (subcontracting, internal mobility, work reorganization). In general, researchers have observed a pragmatic attitude by both small enterprise management and local union leaderships to cooperation, and both have often engaged in tripartite 'micro-bargaining' with the local state.

How then may the variants be explained? One possibility is that managerial styles are influenced by market situation: that companies faced with critical competitive pressures were more likely to adopt unilateral or at best 'instrumental' approaches to industrial relations. This cannot, however, explain why companies such as Italtel, or Petrolchimico Montedison, in the throes of major restructuring and work-force reductions and operating in rapidly changing market sectors, should adopt a highly participative approach. A further explanatory factor may be industrial sector. The case studies reported by Ambrosini et al. (1992) suggest that there are considerable sectoral variations: in chemicals, for example, there is greater participation in business decisions, while in engineering or textiles, it is more limited to questions of work organization. This may reflect such factors as the chemical industry's high capital intensity, and the predominance of white-collar employees (Famiglietti 1992). Despite the sectoral factor, however, there are clearly wide variations between individual firms within sectors.

Regini (1991a) suggests that differences may reflect the extent to which unions are able to help companies in the task of constant work reorganization. There may thus be greater 'procedural participation' in companies with 'diversified quality production', while 'neo-fordist' firms might 'choose to return to an older model of bargained management' (p. 20). Differences in industrial relations and union history appear to be important in explaining different approaches to restructuring. High unionization, particularly among core groups of staff has been seen as likely to encourage more cooperative industrial relations (Negrelli 1989a: 230–1; Treu and Negrelli 1987: 92); while Bordogna (1989) emphasizes the importance of having unions which mangement felt it could do business with.

However, the lesson of many case studies appears to be the *instability* of managerial approaches: Italtel's consultative strategy followed a change in management in 1981, and a period of conflictual industrial relations. Similarly, Zanussi's engagement with participation dates from the company's takeover by Electrolux in 1985 (Galeone 1992). Olivetti's tradition of union-management dialogue, and of a more 'technical', less 'political' approach to personnel management, was curtailed with the change of ownership in the late 1970s (Berta and Michelsons 1989). Falck was seen as a model of the consultative approach in the mid-1980s, but its relationships with the unions seemed more formalistic and strained at the beginning of the 1990s as it pursued new market strategies and continued to restructure its capacity (De Luca, M. 1992: 171–3). Fiat has veered, as described, from unilateralism to opportunist collaboration. Latterly, faced with the removal of trade barriers and far eastern penetration of the domestic market, it appears to be heading in the direction of 'Japanization' and the philosophy of 'total quality'. When it seemed likely that the European Social Charter provisions would be based on the German model, the company pragmatically declared itself ready to adopt a participation model. At the end of the 1980s the company relaunched the former system of joint 'commissions', bodies charged with analysing specific issues such as working time and health and safety, and arriving at agreed solutions (Galeone 1992); and at the beginning of 1992, Fiat reached an agreement with the unions on quality and worker participation in suggestions schemes, an initiative that would have been unthinkable in the Fiat of the early 1980s. New pressures for restructuring, from the completion of the single European market, from the continuing internationalization of production, and from competitiveness implications of the movement to the narrow band of the

European Monetary System, may all put added stress on existing cooperative relationships.

This possible instability raises a question about the broader interpretation of the changes in enterprise industrial relations since the 1980s. On the one hand are 'optimists' such as Negrelli (1990) or Ghera (1990) who identify a process of increasingly institutionalized and consolidated positive-sum 'participative bargaining'. Negrelli, for example, talks of flexibility as almost 'a value in itself', helping 'enrich social dialogue' (1990: 381). On the other hand are more sceptical observers like Regini (1991a: 15), who argues that 'most Italian employers in this period were not so much concerned with greater or lower degrees of consensus to the company's general objectives as they were in need of some *de facto* collaboration in restructuring specific aspects of the work relationship.... Irrespective of their general style of labour relations, most employers were driven pragmatically to seek (limited) collaboration in the specific aspects of the work relationship which were to be re-regulated.' Thus managements were interested in finding satisfactory solutions to specific work organization problems as they arose, rather than in the affirmation of a general style of industrial relations. Moreover, micro-concertation was in practice based more on the exchange of flexibility for increased material rewards than on a real increase in union participation in management decision-making (Zoccatelli and Marin 1992b: 256). None the less, even the sceptics identify an increase in *de facto* cooperation since the early 1980s.

A further consideration is how effective the new structures of company-level participation are in practice. Recent case studies suggest that a note of caution is warranted. Company agreements may not be fully implemented in practice, while *de facto*, informal relationships may continue to be more important means of collaboration especially where management is mistrustful of divided unions (Ambrosini 1992: 136–7; Galeone 1992: 218). Observers suggest that the unions – and indeed middle management – are often culturally unprepared for operating developed structures of participation (e.g. Galeone 1992: 225–9).

A final question is why there should have been an upsurge –whether permanent or transitory – in cooperative enterprise relations in Italy from the late 1970s, compared with, say, the generally more exclusionary or marginalizing strategies of British employers towards the unions. A number of explanations have been put forward. Regini (1991a: 17–19) argues that managements were caught in two minds. The weakening of the unions after 'a decade of union power' tempted management to exclude the unions from a role in restructuring; and international market pressures made employers less tolerant of rigidities. On the other hand, the very weakness of unions – and possibly the baleful lesson of the 1980 defeat at Fiat (cf. Regini 1987: 13) – induced them to moderate their opposition to change and even to internalize the company's need for flexibility. The Fiat strike also carried warnings for management of the costs of confrontational policies. Meanwhile, the company level was no longer in the spotlight as it had been a decade or so earlier: events at that level had lost their symbolic resonance (cf. Regini and Sabel 1989b: 55); restructuring and constant technological innovation made companies vulnerable and more in need of alliances. The importance of company-level accommodations was increased following the splits between the main unions in 1984, which disrupted not only interconfederal relations but also national sectoral bargaining. At the company level, however, unitary factory councils largely persisted, providing management with a coherent bargaining partner. The unions' position in the enterprise was in any case protected – to a greater extent than in, say, Britain – by the higher-level framework of legislation and central and industry agreements that defined a structure of workplace representation (see above) (cf. Regini 1987). Finally, there was a learning process, in which management saw restructuring being carried out at least as successfully in companies with strong unions and participative industrial relations.

At a more general level, what appears to have tipped the employers towards cooperation rather than unilateralism is the weakness of the Italian state. The tradition since the 1960s of inter-class political coalitions and the perceived need for social consensus ruled out a Thatcherite legislative and political programme for curbing union power and bolstering management prerogative. The pragmatism of Italian employers was thus an appreciation of wider political realities as much as of the micro-politics of the firm.

Conclusion: Italian Industrial Relations in the 1990s

In the introduction to this chapter we emphasized the complexities in the development of industrial relations since the revolution in practices and institutions precipitated by the 'hot autumn'. From the late 1970s a second transformation has occurred. Yet in contrast to the earlier paradigm break, the second transition cannot be identified with a single historical turning point. Rather, the last fifteen years have seen a series of incremental shifts, at times indeed temporarily halted or even reversed, from a phase of centralized, largely labour-initiated regulation of employment relations to one of employer-initiated, decentralized but still centrally regulated responses to external challenges.

The 1990s, in Italy as in so much of Europe, are a decade of increasing unpredictability; but the uncertainties are if anything greater than in most other countries. In the party-political sphere, the pattern which persisted for almost half a century seems to be disintegrating, and it is as yet unclear what may replace it. The DC has lost its status as a hegemonic national party, with a mutually reinforcing process of declining electoral support and escalating internal conflict. Anti-communism was a major element of the party's political appeal and the rationale for its internal cohesion; without the PCI as a point of reference, its future must be questioned. With a growing geographical polarization of party loyalties, the task of assembling a parliamentary majority which can claim legitimacy in both north and south has become increasingly problematic. Post-communism appears to create the possibility, and perhaps also the necessity, of admitting the PDS into the governing coalition. With the end of 'blocked democracy' and a restructuring of the political establishment, will the rise of new, less 'reliable' vehicles of political opposition receive a dangerous impetus?

As suggested, new political alignments remove the rationale for the triple division of the main union confederations. Faced with serious challenges to their representative status, there is an obvious logic to moves to greater unification. At the very least, it seems reasonable to predict a reconstitution of the unitary federation; the obstacles to more fundamental unity may, however, prove as great as twenty years ago.

As in most of Europe, the main confederations face two different challenges in their claims to representativeness. On the one hand there is the growth of irregular and often illegal forms of employment, for the most part outside the scope of union organization. It is as yet unclear how far the increasing significance of this underground labour force threatens to undermine the 'defensive rigidity' (Reyneri 1989a) which the unions, and in particular CGIL, attempted to sustain during the 1980s. Nor is it evident how far such workers could in principle be brought within the scope of collective organization, or how far they regard unions as protectors of the interests of 'insiders' whose efforts to control the labour market threaten their own position.

The second challenge is more dramatic: collective organization and action, independently of and often in opposition to the main federations, by highly qualified groups of employees, particularly in the public sector. It was precisely the threat to their own representative status posed by 'autonomous' unions and *cobas* which led all three confederations to support the 'Giugni' law regulating strikes in public services. It remains in doubt whether the confederations can regain the allegiance of these advantaged groups, and hence restore their claim to speak for all categories of employee: the dilemma is that any endorsement of the anti-egalitarian demands of strategic groups is likely to alienate the unions' core constituency. One possibility, then, is the continued growth of separate organizational representation of craft, professional and managerial interests. The institutional consolidation of such representation within a single rival federation would be a serious blow to the 'most representative' status of CGIL, CISL and UIL. A Scandinavian scenario, in which such occupational interests are articulated by separate organizations with their own distinctive 'political' programmes, cannot be ruled out.

Is fragmentation inevitable? It has been seen that a feature of Italian industrial relations in the past decade has been the extent of controlled deregulation and articulated decentralization. Faced with centrifugal pressures, the state, Confindustria and the union confederations have recognized a common interest, and hence mutual interdependence, in striving to maintain some form of centralized regulation and control. It remains uncertain whether the relatively effective articulation of centralized and decentralized regulation can be maintained in the 1990s. Much will depend on developments in company strategy. As indicated above, Italian managements have not in the main sought total autonomy from external regulation, either by law, employers' associations or trade unionism. For the most part they have found it possible to achieve sufficient flexibility within the framework of national regulation, and to establish systems of 'micro-corporatism' in which the unionized work force and its representatives cooperate in the pursuit of corporate objectives.

A delicate, and perhaps precarious balance has prevailed for the past dozen years: sustaining on the one hand an articulation between micro-corporatism and national political exchange; on the other, a negotiated accommodation between managements and unions. For those involved at both levels and on both sides, there has been a constant need to adjust to the shifting strategies of their counterparts, and to manage a tension between programmatic rhetoric and the often rather different policy realities. That the contradictions have been kept largely under control for so long suggests the possibility, but not indeed the certainty, that industrial relations will remain relatively orderly in the 1990s.

This relative order reflects, first, the institutional context of industrial relations. For example, the Workers' Statute lays down a fundamental floor of rights for employees in the workplace, making it difficult for employers, at least in larger companies, to ride roughshod over collective employee representation. Second, the employers have not had the backing of a strong, partisan state capable of altering the institutional framework in their favour: the Italian state has neither the mandate, nor the effective apparatus, to achieve such a radical shift of power relations. Instead, it has been cautious and controlled in its deregulatory thrust, strengthening labour market mechanisms such as the CIG that are capable of encouraging collaborative economic adjustment and corporate restructuring. Thus unions – weakened by economic crisis and the crisis of representation – and management have both had an incentive to cooperate in change. As Baglioni has argued (1987: 85), 'though Italy is not in the group of countries with an established tradition of political exchange, it appears to be one of the very few in which such exchange is unavoidable, since no alternative solutions involving the rupture of relations appears possible'.

This points to an apparent paradox in depictions of the 'Italian model'. On the one hand, observers commonly stress the *weakness* of institutions. On the other hand, institutions appear strong enough to influence the direction of change and set limits to the alternatives available. Thus despite the protean quality of industrial relations, allowing them to change from one form into quite another in the course of a couple of decades, there appears to be a deeper stability in relationships. What is more problematic is whether the institutional arrangements will have the strength and flexibility to accommodate new challenges.

A key imponderable is the impact of the single European market, which will inevitably restructure the terrain of Italian industrial relations. Preoccupation with short-term and domestic issues has meant that the industrial relations actors have given less central attention to '1992' in Italy than in many other countries. As was seen previously, some major employers such as Fiat sought external barriers as a complement to inner-EC free trade: 'Fortress Europe' was necessary to keep American, and especially Japanese, competition at bay. This was a minority view, and the Italian government has been a major contributor to the mainstream of EC policy development. Yet almost certainly the debate reflects very different interests between traditional price-competitive manufacturers in mass markets, and more advanced and specialized producers. Hence 1992 may accentuate the traditional divisions among Italian employers.

Italian trade unions have played a relatively minor part in the debate over the new Europe. All three confederations have declared a general commitment to European integration, but with an emphasis on the need for enhanced employee and union rights to counteract pressures towards cost-cutting, deregulation and social dumping. CGIL in particular has expressed optimistic aspirations for enhanced union participation in EC policy-making, a strong social dimension and an increased co-ordination of collective bargaining at European level. The mechanics of achieving such ambitious goals have received far less attention.

In the 1990s, then, industrial relations in Italy continue to evolve. The main actors seem increasingly uncertain of their future strategies, and their authority is under challenge. Analogous difficulties have of course occurred in the past, and the system has survived. In Italy, more than any other major European country, predicting the future of industrial relations must be extremely hazardous.

Notes

1   We are most grateful to Paul Edwards for reading and commenting on the whole chapter, and to Keith Sisson for his observations on the section dealing with employers. Above all, we are extremely grateful to Mike Terry for his encouragement, constructive criticism and practical help.

2   These figures exclude the great state holding companies IRI and ENI since they are not quoted companies, although a number of their quoted subsidiaries are included.

3   This description of employers' organization draws heavily on Becchi Collidà 1989.

4   The 'public sector' in Italy includes those working in central and local government, the non-trading state agencies such as the institutions administering social security (the 'parastatals'), education, and the public health service. Following the Italian usage, the term excludes workers in the enterprises of 'state participation' under IRI, ENI and EFIM, though it includes municipal-owned enterprises and the postal services. The 'public sector' also used to include the railways (Ferrovie Statali) which were part of the central state administration until 1986 when they were given corporate status. The broad description of

public sector employment in this section draws heavily on Romagnoli 1989 and Treu 1987. See also Minstero del Lavoro 1988: 171–5.

Abbreviations

ASAP	*Associazione Sindacale per le Aziende Petrolchemiche e Collegate a Partecipazione Statale* – Employers' Association for Public Sector Oil and Petrochemical Enterprises
CdF	*consiglio di fabbrica* – factory council
CGIL	*Confederazione Generale Italiana del Lavoro* – Italian General Confederation of Labour
CI	*commissione interna* – workplace commission
CIG	*Cassa Integrazione Guadagni* – earnings maintenance fund
CISL	*Confederazione Italiana dei Sindacati Lavoratori* – Italian Confederation of Workers' Unions
CISNAL	*Confederazione Italiana dei Sindacati Nazionali Lavoratori* – Italian Confederation of National Workers' Unions
CNEL	*Consiglio Nazionale dell'Economia e del Lavoro* – National Council of the Economy and Labour
cobas	*comitati di base* – rank-and-file committees
CONFAPI	*Confederazione della Piccola e Media Industria* – Confederation of Small and Medium-Sized Industry
Confindustria	*Confederazione Generale dell'Industria Italiana* – General Confederation of Italian Industry
DC	*Democrazia Cristiana/Democristiani* – Christian Democracy / Christian Democrats
ENI	*Ente Nazionale Idrocarburi* – National Petrochemical Agency
Intersind	*Associazione Sindacale Intersind* – employers' association for public sector enterprises
IRI	*Istituto per la Ricostruzione Industriale* – Institute for Industrial Reconstruction (state industrial holding company)
PCI	*Partito Comunista Italiano* – Italian Communist Party
PDS	*Partito Democratico della Sinistra* – Democratic Party of the Left
PLI	*Partito Liberale Italiano* – Italian Liberal Party
PRI	*Partito Republicano Italiano* – Italian Republican Party
PSDI	*Partito Socialista–Democratico Italiano* – Italian Social-Democratic Party
PSI	*Partito Socialista Italiano* – Italian Socialist Party
RC	*Rifondazione Comunista* – Communist Reconstruction Party
RSA	*rappresentanza sindacale aziendale* – union workplace representative structure
UIL	*Unione Italiana del Lavoro* – Italian Union of Labour

References

Accornero, A. 1985: La 'terziarizzazione' del conflitto e i suoi effeti. In G.P. Cella and M. Regini (eds), *Il Conflitto Industriale in Italia*, Bologna: Il Mulino.

Accornero, A. 1992: *La Parabola del Sindacato*. Bologna: Il Mulino.

Ambrosini, M. 1992: Partecipazione e coinvolgimento dei lavoratori: le politiche manageriali. In M. Ambrosini et al. (eds), 116–152.

Ambrosini, M., Colasanto, M. and Saba, L. 1992: *Partecipazione e Coinvolgimento nell'impresa degli anni '90*. Milan: FrancoAngeli.

Baglioni, G. 1987: Constants and Variants in Political Exchange. *Labour*, 1, 57–94.

Baglioni, G. 1991a: An Italian Mosaic: Collective Bargaining Patterns in the 1980s. *International Labour Review*, 130, 1, 81–93.

Baglioni, G. 1991b: Cinque anni di contrattazione aziendale nell-industria italiana. L'osservatorio CESOS. *Industria e Sindacato* 19/20, 1–19.

Becchi Collidà, A. 1989: Le associazioni imprenditoriali. In G.-P. Cella and T. Treu (eds), 135–56.

Bellardi, L. 1991: Rinnovi contrattuali e 'nuove regole' delle relazioni industriali. *Industria e Sindacato*, 17, 3–8.

Berta, G. and Michelsons, A. 1989: Il caso Olivetti. In M. Regini and C. Sabel (eds), 133–70.

Bianchi, G. 1990: Nuove forme di incentivazione salariale: gli accordi in alcune grandi aziende Fiat, Zanussi, Olivetti. In G. Baglioni, P. Feltrin and G. Pisu (eds), *Relazioni Sindacali in Italia 1988/89*, Rome: Lavoro, 271–82.

Bordogna, L. 1989: Il caso del Petrolchimico Montedison di Ferrara. In M. Regini and C. Sabel (eds), 95–132.

Bordogna, L. and Provasi, G.C. 1989: La Conflittualità. In G.-P. Cella and T. Treu (eds), 275–306.

Camusi, M.-P. 1991: La flessibilità nel sistema aziendale italiano. *Industria e Sindacato*, 28, 3–8.

Cecora, G. 1990: Pubblico impiego: motivazioni e opportunità per la riforma. *Industria e Sindacato*, 43, December, 3–8.

Cella, G.-P. and Treu, T. 1989a: *Relazioni industriali. Manuale per l'analisi dell'esperienza italiana*. Bologna: Il Mulino.

Cella, G.-P. and Treu, T. 1989b: La contrattazione colletiva. In G.-P. Cella and T. Treu (eds), 157–217.

Cella, G.P. 1989: Regulation in Italian Industrial Relations. In P. Lange and M. Regini (eds), 167–86.

Cella, G.P. 1990: The Institutions in the Italian System of Industrial Relations. *Labour*, 4, 9–15.

Chiesi, A. and Martinelli, A. 1989: The Representation of Business Interests as a Mechanism of Social Regulation. In P. Lange and M. Regini (eds), 187–213.

Cipolletta, I. 1990: Italian Industry in the Eighties: Reflecting on the Changes. *Review of Economic Conditions in Italy*, 3, 411–39.

Contini, B. and Revelli, R. 1990: Turbolence [sic] in Italy's Industrial Structure and Labour Market in the Eighties: Reflections on Labour Policies. *Review of Economic Conditions in Italy*, 1, 85–105.

Contini, G. 1991: Enterprise Management and Employer Organization in Italy: Fiat, Public Enterprise and *Confindustria* 1922–1990. In S. Tolliday and J. Zeitlin (eds), *The Power to Manage? Industrial Relations in Comparative Perspective*, London: Routledge, 204–27.

Crouch, C. and Pizzorno, A. (eds) 1978: *The Resurgence of Class Conflict in Western Europe Since 1968*. London: Macmillan.

Cugini, A. 1989: Retribuzione e produttività aziendale. *Industria e Sindacato*, 30, 7–12.

De Luca, M. 1992: La partecipazione nel settore siderurgico. In M. Ambrosini et al. (eds), 153–84.

De Luca, P. 1992: Rapporto sui salari. Dinamiche retributive e competitività. *Notiziario del Lavoro*, 52, February, 3–8.

De Marinis, N. 1991: Prassi e teoria della rappresentanza sindacale nell'evoluzione del sistema di relazioni industriali. *Industria e Sindacato*, 28, 9–13.

Della Rocca, G. 1991: Incentivi: quale salario e quale partecipazione? *Industria e Sindacato*, 17, 9–19.

Della Rocca, G. 1992: Le ricerche sulle retribuzioni ad incentivo: risultati e problemi. *Notiziario del Lavoro*, 52, February, 51–62.

EIRR 1990: *Non-Standard Forms of Employment in Europe*. EIRR Report 3. London: IRS.

Famiglietti, A. 1992: La partecipazione nei settori chimico ed energia. In M. Ambrosini et al. (eds), 185–208.

Farnetti, P. 1978: The Troubled Partnership: Trade Unions and Working-Class Parties in Italy, 1948–1978. *Government and Opposition*, 13, 416–36.

Faustini, G. 1987: A New Method of Indexing Wages in Italy. *Labour*, 1, 2, 71–91.

Flanagan, J., Soskice, D. and Ulman, D. 1983: *Unionism, Economic Stabilization, and Incomes*

Policies: European Experience. Washington D C: The Brookings Institution.

Franzosi, R. 1989: Strike Data in Search of a Theory: The Italian Case in the Postwar Period. *Politics and Society*, 42, 453–87.

Galeone, P. 1992: La participazione nel settore metalmeccanico. In M. Ambrosini et al. (eds), 209–29.

Garofalo, M.G. 1988: Osservazioni sulla democrazia sindacale *Lavoro e Diritto*, April, 269–88.

Ghera, E. 1990: Le nuove relazioni industriali: dalla contrattazione rivendicativa alla contrattazione partecipativa. In G. Baglioni, P. Feltrin and G. Pisu (eds), *Relazioni Sindacali in Italia 1988/89*, Rome: Lavoro, 283–91.

Giugni, G. 1982: Il diritto del lavoro negli anni '80. *Giornale di Diritto del Lavoro e di Relazioni Industriali*, 15, 373–409.

Giugni, G. 1987: Social Concertation and the Political System in Italy, *Labour and Society*, 12, 379–83.

Golden, M. 1988: *Labor Divided: Austerity and Working-Class Politics in Contemporary Italy.* Ithaca: Cornell UP.

Golden, M. 1990: Political Attitudes of Italian Workers: Twenty Years of Survey Evidence. *European Journal of Political Research*, 18, 305–23.

Grant, W. and Martinelli, A. 1991: Political Turbulence, Enterprise Crisis and Industrial Recovery: ICI and Montedison. In A. Martinelli (ed.), *International Markets and Global Firms.* London: Sage, 61–90.

Hegewisch, A. 1991: The Decentralisation of Pay Bargaining: European Comparisons. *Personnel Review*, 20, 6, 28–35.

IMF (International Montary Fund) 1989: Italia: consultazioni 1990. (Preliminary conclusions of the IMF mission in Italy). *Industria e Sindacato*, 43, December, 9–11.

Kreile, M. 1988: The Crisis of Italian Trade Unionism in the 1980s. *West European Politics*, 11, 54–67.

Lange, P. and Regini, M. (eds) 1989: *State, Market, and Social Regulation. New Perspectives on Italy.* Cambridge: Cambridge University Press.

Lange, P., Ross, G. and Vanicelli, M. 1982: *Unions, Change and Crisis: French and Italian Union Strategy and the Political Economy, 1945–1980.* London: Allen & Unwin

Lavoro 80 1989: Dopo i Cobas: Questioni sulla rappresentatività sindacale. *Quaderno 8.*

Locke, R. and Negrelli, S. 1989: Il caso Fiat Auto. In M. Regini and C. Sabel (eds), 61–94.

Locke, R.M. 1990: The Resurgence of the Local Union: Industrial Restructuring and Industrial Relations in Italy. *Politics & Society*, 18, 347–79.

Locke, R.M. 1992: The Demise of the National Union in Italy: Lessons for Comparative Industrial Relations Theory. *Industrial and Labor Relations Review*, 45, 229–49.

Maraffi, M. 1980: State / Economy Relationships: The Case of Italian Public Enterprise. *British Journal of Sociology*, 31, 4, 507–24.

Martinelli, A. 1980: Organised Business and Italian Politics: Confindustria and the Christian Democrats in the Postwar Period. In P. Lange and S. Tarrow (eds) *Italy in Transition. Conflict and Consensus*, London: Frank Cass, 67–87.

Martinelli A. 1981: The Italian Experience: A Historical Perspective. In Vernon, R. and Aharoni, Y. (eds) *The State-Owned Enterprise in the Western Economies*, London: St Martin's Press, 85–98.

Mershon, C.A. 1989: Between Workers and Unions: Factory Councils in Italy. *Comparative Politics*, January, 215-35.

Mershon, C.A. 1990: Relationships among Union Actors after the Hot Autumn. *Labour*, 4, 35–58.

Milani, R. 1990: Contrattazione aziendale. In G. Baglioni, P. Feltrin and G. Pisu (eds), *Relazioni Sindacali in Italia 1988/89*, Rome: Lavoro, 127–36.

Ministero del Lavoro 1988: *Report '88: Labour and Employment Policies in Italy.* Rome: IPZS.

Ministero del Lavoro 1990: *Report '89: Labour and Employment Policies in Italy. Rome:* IPZS.

Morese, R. 1991: Il valore innovativo del Ccnl metalmeccanici a partecipazione statale. *Industria e Sindacato*, 16, 1–5.

Napoli, M. 1989: Il quadro giuridico-istituzionale. In G.-P. Cella and T. Treu (eds), 47–83.

Negrelli, S. 1988: Management Strategy: Towards New Forms of Regulation? In R. Hyman and W. Streeck (eds), *New Technology and Industrial Relations*, Oxford: Blackwell, 89–100.

Negrelli, S. 1989a: Le relazioni industriali nell'impresa. In G.-P. Cella and T. Treu (eds), 219–55.

Negrelli, S. 1989b: Il caso Italtel. In M. Regini and C. Sabel (eds), 171–206.

Negrelli, S. 1990: Flessibilità economica e solidarietà sociale. *Stato e Mercato*, 30, December, 373–406.

Negrelli, S. 1991a: *La Società dentro l'impresa*. Milan: FrancoAngeli.

Negrelli, S. 1991b: Introduzione. Il dificile cammino verso l'equilibrio tra centralizzazione e decentramento. In G. Baglioni, A. De Sanctis and S. Negrelli (eds), *Le Relazioni Sindacali in Italia 1989/90*, Rome: Lavoro, xi–xxv.

Negrelli, S. 1991c: Dai diritti di informazione ai diritti di consultazione. *Industria e Sindacato*, 37, 1–18.

Negrelli, S. 1991d: La contrattazione colletiva in Italia. Unpublished paper. Brescia.

Negrelli, S. 1991e: La contrattazione decentrata delle retribuzioni nel settore privato in Europa: tre metodi e quattro modelli. In R. Brunetta (ed.), *Retribuzione, Costo del Lavoro, Livelli della Contrattazione*, vol. 2, 227–48.

Negrelli, S. 1992 (forthcoming): Temporeggiare in attesa di quale accordo? In CESOS, *Le relazioni sindacali in Italia. Rapporto 1991*, Roma: Lavoro.

Negrelli, S. and Santi, E. 1990: Industrial Relations in Italy. In G. Baglioni and C. Crouch (eds), *European Industrial Relations*. London: Sage, 154–98.

OECD 1991: *OECD Economic Surveys. Italy 1990/1991*. Paris: OECD.

Olivieri, R. 1987: Social Concertation and Tripartism in Italy. *Labour and Society*, 12, 367–77.

Oxley, H. and Martin, J. 1991: Controlling Public Spending and Deficits: Trends in the 1980s and Prospects for the 1990s. *OECD Economic Studies*, 17, Autumn, 145–89.

Padoa Schioppa, F. 1988: Underemployment Benefit Effects on Employment and Income Distribution. *Labour*, 2, 101–24.

Pennella, G. 1989: Productivity in the Italian Administration. Methods, Comparisons and Results. *Labour*, 3, 3, 169–87.

Perulli, P. 1989: Il distretto industriale di Modena. In In M. Regini and C. Sabel (eds), 249–82.

Perulli, P. 1990: Italian Unions as a Stabilising Force of the Political System. *Labour*, 4, 25–34.

Pizzorno, A. 1978: *Political Exchange and Collective Identity in Industrial Conflict*. In C. Crouch and A. Pizzorno (eds) 1978, Vol. 2, 277–98.

Poscetti, M. 1988: Highlights of the 21th CENSIS Report on Italy's Social Situation. *Review of Economic Conditions in Italy*, 1, 93–101.

Poscetti, M. 1991: Highlights of the 24th CENSIS Report: Phenomena and Trends in Italy in 1990. *Review of Economic Conditions in Italy*, 1, 81–90.

Price Waterhouse/Cranfield 1991: *The Price Waterhouse Cranfield Project on Indternational Strategic Human Resource Management. Report 1991*. Price Waterhouse/Cranfield.

Prosperetti, L. 1991: I 'premi di produttività': perchè la diffusione? Paper presented to III European Regional Congress of the International Industrial Relations Association, Bari, September 1991.

Prosperetti, L. and Cossentino, F.: 1989: La diffusione di accordi di *gainsharing* in Italia. Tendenze, problemi e prospettive. *Industria e Sindacato*, 34, 3–12.

Ranci, P. 1987: Italy: The Weak State. In F. Duchêne and G. Shepherd (eds), *Managing Change in Western Europe*, London: Frances Pinter, 111–44.

Regalia, I. 1988: Democracy and Unions: Towards a Critical Appraisal. *Economic and Industrial Democracy*, 9, 345-71.

Regalia, I. 1989: L'area di Sesto S. Giovanni. In M. Regini and C. Sabel (eds), 207–48.

Regalia, I. and Regini, M. 1989: Sindacati, istituzioni, sistema politico. In G.-P. Cella and T. Treu (eds), 389–414.

Regalia, I., Regini, M. and Reyneri, E. 1978: Labour Conflicts and Industrial Relations in Italy. In Crouch and Pizzorno (eds), Vol. 1.

Regini, M. 1984: The Conditions for Political Exchange: How Concertation Emerged and Collapsed in Italy and Great Britain. In J.H. Goldthorpe (ed.), *Order and Conflict in Contemporary Capitalism*, Oxford: Clarendon, 124–42.

Regini, M. 1987: Tendenze recenti delle relazioni industrali di impresa. Alcuni spunti interpretativi. Collana 'Discussioni' 9. Milan: IRES.

Regini, M 1991a: Employers' Reactions to the Productivity Drive: The Search for Labour Consensus. Paper presented to III European Regional Congress of the International Industrial Relations Association, Bari, September 1991.

Regini, M. 1991b: *Confini mobili. La costruzione dell'economia fra politica e società*. Milan: Il Mulino.

Regini, M. and Lange, P. 1990: Twenty Years after the Hot Autumn. *Labour*, 4, 3–8.

Regini, M. and Sabel, C. (eds) 1989a: *Strategie di riaggiustamento industriale*. Bologna: Il Mulino.

Regini, M. and Sabel, C. 1989b: Le strategie di riaggiustamento industriale in Italia: uno sguardo d'insieme in chiave comparata. In M. Regini and C. Sabel (eds), 11–59.

Rehfeldt, U. 1991: L'échange politique difficile. Les stratégies syndicales en Italie 1975–1990. *Sociologie du Travail*, 3/91, 323–49.

Reyneri, E. 1989a: The Italian Labour Market: Between State Control and Social Regulation. In Lange and Regini (eds), 129–46.

Reyneri, E. 1989b: Mercato e politiche del Lavoro. In Cella and Treu (eds), 345–88.

Romagnoli, G. 1989: Le relazioni sindacali nel settore pubblico. In Cella, G. and Treu, T., 257–73.

Romagnoli, G. 1990: A Few Notes on the Representativeness of Italian Trade Unions over the Last Twenty Years. *Labour*, 4, 17–23.

Romagnoli, G. and Della Rocca, G. 1989: Il sindacato. In Cella and Treu (eds), 85–134.

Russo, C. 1990: Contrattazione di categoria nel pubblico impiego. In G. Baglioni, P. Feltrin and G. Pisu (eds), *Relazioni Sindacali in Italia 1988/89*, Rome: Lavoro, 111–15.

Saba, L. 1992: Il sindacato e la partecipazione: forme, istituti e organismi partecipativi nel rapporto con l'impresa. In M. Ambrosini et al. (eds), 51–115.

Santi, E. 1988: Ten Years of Unionization in Italy (1977–1986). *Labour*, 2, 153–82.

Sassoon, D. 1986: *Contemporary Italy. Politics, Economy and Society since 1945*. London: Longman.

Sciarra, S. 1977: The Rise of the Italian Shop Steward. *Industrial Law Journal*, 6, 35–44.

Sciarra, S. 1986: Restructuring Labour in the Enterprise: Italy. *Bulletin of Comparative Labour Relations*, 15, 53–84.

Sciarra, S. 1987: Plant Bargaining: The Impact of Juridification on Current Deregulative Trends in Italy. *Comparative Labour Law Journal*, 8, 123–38.

Sciarra, S. 1988: Il 'conflitto fra gruppi' nei servizi pubblici essenziali. *Lavoro e Diritto*, II, 667–98.

Sisson, K. 1987: *The Management of Collective Bargaining. An International Comparison*. Oxford: Blackwell.

Sisson, K., Waddington, J. and Whitston, C. 1991: Company Size in the European Community. *Human Resource Management Journal*, 2, 1, 94–109.

Squarzon, C. 1992 (forthcoming): La sindacalizzazione e la rappresentanza nel 1990. In CESOS, *Le relazioni sindacali in Italia. Rapporto 1991*, Rome: Lavoro.

Treu, T. 1987a: Italian Industrial Relations in the Past Ten Years. *Bulletin of Comparative Labour Relations*, 16, 167–81.

Treu, T. 1987b: Ten Years of Social Concertation in Italy. *Labour and Society*, 12, 355–66.

Treu, T. 1987c: Labour Relations in the Public Service in Italy. In T. Treu (ed.) *Public Service Labour Relations. Recent Trends and Future Prospects. A Comparative Survey of Seven Industrialised Market Economy Countries*, Geneva: ILO, 111–43.

Treu, T. 1991: *European Employment and Industrial Relations Glossary: Italy*. London/Luxembourg: Sweet & Maxwell/Office for Official Publications of the European Communities.

Treu, T. and de Felice, A. 1990: The Future of Labour Relations in the Public Service in Italy. In W. Dercksen (ed.) *The Future of Industrial Relations in Europe*, Netherlands Scientific Council for Government Policy, 65–75.

Treu, T. and Negrelli, S. 1987: Workers' Participation and Personnel Management Policies in Italy. *International Labour Review*, 126, 1, 81–95.

Trigilia, C. 1986: *Grandi partiti e piccole imprese*. Bologna: Il Mulino.

Trigilia, C. 1989: Il distretto industriale di Prato. In M. Regini and C. Sabel (eds), 283–333.

Tronti, L. 1991: Employment Protection and Labour Market Segmentation. *Labour*, 5, 121–45.

Wedderburn, K.W. (Lord) 1991: *Employment Rights in Britain and Europe*. London: Lawrence & Wishart.

Wedderburn, K.W. (Lord) and Sciarra, S. 1988: Collective Bargaining as Agreement and as Law. In A. Pizzorusso (ed.), *Law in the Making*, Berlin: Springer.

Windolf, P. 1989: Productivity Coalitions and the Future of European Corporatism. *Industrial Relations*, 28, 1, 1–20.

Zoccatelli, M. and Marin, U. 1992a: La partecipazione nel settore alimentare. In M. Ambrosini et al. (eds), 230–57.

Zoccatelli, M. and Marin, U. 1992b: La partecipazione nel settore tessile. In M. Ambrosini et al. (eds), 258–80.

17

Greece: From State Authoritarianism to Modernization

Nicos D. Kritsantonis

Greece today is in the throes of a crucial social and economic transition. After a post-war history marked by political authoritarianism and dictatorship, and by profound economic backwardness, the country must now adapt to membership of the EC and integration within a competitive international economy. Survival after 1992 requires a comprehensive modernization of Greek institutions; and as part of the process, a transformation in industrial relations.

Historical background

The history of Greece since the formation of an independent state in 1830 may be divided into four stages. Until 1890 the economy was pre-capitalist, and agriculture remained the dominant sector. Between 1890 and 1922 there was a considerable inflow of capital, mainly from Greek emigrés, as part of the widespread process of capitalist investment in peripheral countries. This facilitated the development of transportation and related infrastructure, as well as initial stages of industrialization. The domestic economy expanded rapidly during the third phase (1922–40). An important factor was the influx of over a million ethnic Greek refugees from Asia Minor, dramatically expanding the industrial labour force. However, the economy still remained primarily agrarian. Only since 1945 – and the crushing of the left in the civil war of 1944–9 – has Greece become a decisively capitalist economy.

The post-war years may in turn be perceived as four distinct phases. In the first, external capital investment under the Truman Doctrine and the Marshall Plan helped consolidate the Greek economy and integrate it within international trade: a strategy symbolized by the 50 per cent devaluation of the drachma in 1953. The state was closely involved in the process, undertaking infrastructural development, investing in strategic industries, and offering incentives for foreign investment.

The second phase, after 1960, saw impressive economic growth. The inflow of foreign capital continued, entailing control of key positions in the economy by overseas multinationals. At the same time, domestic capital formation was encouraged by state loan finance and other incentives and subsidies. GNP increased by 7 per cent a year between 1950 and 1973, or 6.3 per cent per capita; the comparable figures for Spain were 6.7 and 6.3 per cent, for Brazil 6.7 and 3.7 per cent (Weisskopf 1978: 144). Thus Greece was clearly a successful entrant to the international economy. Economic expansion, however, was achieved by dint of political repression, particularly following the military coup of 1967, when trade unions and opposition parties were driven underground.

The downfall of the military dictatorship in 1974 coincided with the global oil crisis. The policies of the conservative New Democracy government compounded the problems of the Greek economy. Unemployment and inflation both rose rapidly. Towards the end of the period a series of bankruptcies engulfed whole sectors of the economy (e.g. 80 per cent of the paper industry, 45 per cent of the cement industry).

The economic crisis helped encourage a mass movement which culminated in the election in 1981 of the PASOK (Panhellenic Socialist Movement) government. In this fourth phase, the new government attempted to raise workers' living standards, develop a welfare state, and modernize Greek institutions. But the inheritance of economic crisis and institutional backwardness frustrated the attempt (Vergopoulos 1986: 99). This in turn contributed to PASOK's defeat by the right in 1990. The new government's neo-liberal policies (privatizations etc.) have caused economic instability, with increased unemployment and a fall in real wages.

Uneven Development

The Greek economy performed increasingly well for most of the post-war period, and in particular between 1955 and 1975, as measured by the growth of GNP, exports and invisible earnings. After 1975, however, the position deteriorated. And throughout the post-war decades, economic development has displayed considerable internal imbalance. This is evident if one compares the relative performance of the agricultural, manufacturing and service sectors.

Agriculture has always been important for the Greek economy. It accounted for 30.3 per cent of GNP in 1951, and though the figure had fallen to 13.2 per cent in 1988, this is still high by comparison with other countries. Traditionally farming has been based on small family units with low productivity. More modern methods have brought some improvement: for example, through the growing use of tractors (the numbers increased tenfold between 1962 and 1988). However, there remains a serious imbalance between arable and livestock farming; Greece is self-sufficient in cereals, fruit and vegetables, but depends heavily on imports of meat and dairy products.

There are also imbalances within the manufacturing sector. Total production almost tripled between 1962 and 1978, rising as a proportion of GNP from 25 to 32.5 per cent. But manufacturing remains dominated by traditional industries, in particular consumer goods (textiles, clothing, and foodstuffs still accounted for 43 per cent of manufacturing output in 1983). Conversely, the engineering industry is very underdeveloped, and Greece depends almost totally on imports of machinery. The high levels of investment in recent decades have done little to alleviate this imbalance, since only a small proportion (only one-seventh in the period 1958–80) is channelled into manufacturing. By contrast, 30 per cent of total investment was in the construction industry.

Since 1961 the service sector has accounted for more than half the Greek GNP. The rapid expansion of banking, commerce, import-export services, as well as tourism, has not encouraged the development of the rest of the economy. On the contrary, the service sector has diverted capital and other resources from industrial production.

Despite impressive aggregate growth, the lack of structural integration is a fundamental weakness in the Greek economy. For example, the importance of agriculture is not matched by the development of an agricultural machinery industry; such equipment must still be imported. Similarly, the rapid expansion of electricity generation has depended on expensive imports of fuel and technology. No attempt has been made to develop a local electrical engineering industry, or to utilize natural energy sources. Or again, there has been a successful development of metal mining, but not of associated processing and manufacturing activities; most of the output is exported in, at best, a semi-processed state.

Hence Greek industry remains polarized between production of domestic consumer goods, and the export of primary commodities. This structural imbalance has combined with the openness of the Greek economy and the dominance of overseas capital to cause a deteriorating balance of payments. The value of visible exports as a proportion of imports fell from 71 per cent in 1938 to 48 per cent in 1958 and 37 per cent in 1969, and has since stabilized at just over 40 per cent. The visible trade deficit in 1988 was 7,600 million drachmas, equivalent to 20 per cent of the national income. External equilibrium has thus depended on invisible earnings – tourism, shipping, and remittances from Greek migrant workers overseas. This has made Greece particularly vulnerable to vicissitudes in the world economy, as is currently all too apparent.

The Structure of Employment

The labour force has been expanding rapidly: by more than 4 per cent a year in the recent past. The structure of employment reflects the characteristics of the national economy which have already been discussed. The annual labour force survey for 1987 provides data on the percentage distribution of the working population by occupation and sector. Only one worker in five is engaged in manufacturing; the combined work force of mining, manufacturing, construction and public utilities is only 28 per cent of the economically active total (see table 17.1). The proportion working in agriculture – still almost 30 per cent – is four times the EC average. (The low productivity of Greek agriculture is shown in the fact that the contribution of farming to GNP is only half the proportion represented by agriculture in the labour force.) The work force in the service sector has been rising continuously, and now stands at 45 per cent.

Table 17.1   The sectoral distribution of the Greek labour force 1987

	Male		Female		Total	
	Number *(000s)*	*%*	*Number* *(000s)*	*%*	*Number* *(000s)*	*%*
Agriculture, Forestry, Fishing	533	22.6	438	35.4	971	27.0
Mining	22	0.9	2	0.2	24	0.7
Manufacturing and Handicraft	512	21.7	203	16.4	715	19.9
Electricity, Gas and Water	30	1.3	5	0.4	35	1.0
Construction and Public Works	230	9.8	2	0.2	232	6.4
Commerce, Restaurants and Hotels	371	15.7	221	17.9	592	16.5
Transport and Communications	220	9.3	24	2.0	244	6.8
Financial and Related Services	91	3.8	55	4.5	146	4.0
Other Services	351	14.9	286	23.2	637	17.7
Total	2,361	100.0	1,236	100.0	3,597	100.0

Source: NSSG, Labour Force Survey for 1987.

Female participation has increased rapidly: from 24 per cent in 1974 to 27 per cent in 1980 and 36 per cent in 1987; but the level is still low by comparison with other European countries. Nearly half (47.5 per cent) work in services, almost all of these in shops, catering and public services. No less than 35 per cent work in agriculture, as against only 18 per cent in manufacturing.

This relates to the most distinctive feature of the Greek labour force: only half (49.3 per cent) are employees (compared with an EC average of 82 per cent), while 31 per cent are self-employed, 15 per cent are unpaid family workers and 5 per cent are employers. Just over half the self-employed are in agriculture, and a fifth work in shops and tourism. These figures contribute to the unusually small size of work units: 93 per cent of establishments have fewer than 10 employees, only 0.3 per cent have over 200.

Finally, the labour market is highly urbanized: in 1987, 31.5 per cent of the labour force worked in the Athens area, and 27.2 per cent in other urban centres (i.e. locations with 10,000 or more inhabitants). But in this respect also, imbalance and polarization are evident. At one extreme, 4 million workers – 41 per cent of the labour force – live in the four largest urban areas of Greece. But conversely 30.3 per cent live in rural settlements (under 2,000 inhabitants) and a further 11.6 per cent in semi-rural (under 10,000). Modern Greece is thus a contradictory mixture of milieux.

Multinational Companies and Large Employers

Despite the great preponderance of small enterprises, the dominant role in the economy is increasingly played by a small number of large, often foreign-owned enterprises, and in some sectors by state enterprises. Increasingly the dominant firms are conglomerates, straddling several sectors of the economy. The influx of foreign capital has increased rapidly over recent years: it constituted 11.4 per cent of investment in 1950–9, 16.5 per cent in 1960–9, 24.8 per cent in 1970–9, and reached 40.6 per cent in 1980–5 (Perakis 1987: 40).

In 1972 foreign multinationals were already dominant in several sectors of industry, controlling 96 per cent of production in petroleum products, 60 per cent in transport, 57 per cent in steel, 45 per cent in chemicals, 42 per cent in electrical equipment; the proportion for manufacturing as a whole was 30 per cent (Karantzas 1985: 38). A more recent assessment by Tolios (1987) shows a restructuring of multinational activity in the context of Greek membership of the EC: foreign companies controlled 30 per cent of the assets of the 550 largest manufacturing firms in 1981, but received 61 per cent of total profits. In the service sector, foreign ownership is also substantial. In 1983, foreign banks controlled 25 per cent of loan capital, while foreign insurance companies controlled 35 per cent of the market. In the retail and tourist sectors, multinationals also have a significant and increasing stake.

Table 17.2   The dominance of the 100 largest firms in Greek manufacturing

	Total number of firms with 10 or more employees	Stake of top 100 in total (%):			
		Assets	Sales	Profits	Employment
1973	1,759	56	54	56	40
1978	2,944	46	51	64	32
1981	3,210	52	58	75	34

Source: Karantzas (1985: 39).

The dominance of large companies, both Greek and foreign-owned, has become increasingly marked in the last two decades (see table 17.2). In manufacturing, while the number of small firms has also increased rapidly, the 100 largest enterprises account for over half the total assets and sales, and three-quarters of net profits; their declining share of total employment reflects their success in rationalizing production.

In mining, four companies in 1983 owned 65 per cent of assets and employed 51 per cent of the labour force. Similarly, highly concentrated ownership exists in construction and civil engineering, in road haulage – where giant multinationals have increasingly taken over local small owners as subcontractors – and in shipping. In the service sector, the two main banking groups owned 84 per cent of total assets in 1984. Five companies controlled half the insurance market in 1983. The ten biggest exporting firms controlled over a third of foreign trade in the same year. Even in agriculture, with its proliferation of small farmers, there has been a rapid rise in the proportion of large units, most notably in livestock; in poultry farming, four companies control half the total production.

In the past decade, state economic activity has become very important. The PASOK government assigned publicly owned companies a key role in its 'strategic plan of national independence'. A new State Business Reconstruction Organization was also established to take over domestic firms in economic difficulties. The state has a monopoly in telecommunications and in electricity supply (DEH). In oil refining and distribution ELDA-EKO, together with a handful of multinationals, dominates the domestic market. The state railways (OSE) and airline (Olympic) each has a monopoly. The state also has majority control in banking and insurance. Of the 200 largest manufacturing firms, 67 are state-controlled.

Class Relations and the Greek State

The character of Greek economic development can be viewed in the context of the distinctiveness of Greek politics. For half a century – from the inter-war military dictatorships, through wartime Nazi occupation, the right-wing administration which held control after the civil war of 1946–9, to the regime of the colonels between 1967 and 1974, authoritarian, anti-labour and pro-capitalist rule was the norm. The implications for the evolution of trade unionism and industrial relations will be discussed later in this chapter. Here the consequences for Greek capital will be indicated.

Between the wars, government policy had encouraged the development of the Greek manufacturing base, leading to the emergence of a significant class of industrial capitalists. But under German occupation a different type of capitalist emerged: described in 1947 by Paul Pater, head of the US Economic Mission in Greece, as a 'new generation of speculators, opportunists and black marketeers that emerged after the war with large fortunes and luxury' (Tsoukalas 1986: 19). This new generation dominated the period of post-war reconstruction by their key role in managing the inflow of Marshall Plan funds, directing investment to commercial, financial and speculative activity.

This new class of commercial capitalists was closely linked to the Greek state throughout the 1949–67 period of 'restricted democracy' (or as Mouzelis (1976: 60) called it, 'repressive parliamentarianism'). The crushing of the left in the civil war (partly through foreign intervention) gave political control to the extreme anti-communist right, many of whom had collaborated with the Nazis. Though interventionist in economic orientation, the regime had no rational strategy for the development of the Greek economy. The priorities were, first, to implement policies attractive to foreign capital; second, to sustain a mutually advantageous relationship with local capitalists. This relationship operated, not in an institutionalized form, but rather through networks of personal bribery and patronage (Petmetzidou-Tsoulouvis 1984: 28).

In a context where Greek post-war economic expansion was driven by subsidies, incentives and state-sponsored monopoly prerogatives, the business culture encouraged the pursuit of easy profits. Capitalists turned primarily to non-productive activities because profits were higher.

After the restoration of democracy in 1974, Greek capitalists pursued a strategy which became known as 'autocratic modernization'. This involved a new basis for integration of the Greek economy within the new international division of labour, symbolized by Greece's accession to the EC in 1981. Throughout the period of PASOK government (1981–9) Greek capital resisted the policies for economic reconstruction by engaging in an effective investment strike – even though the government rapidly turned from its initial radicalism to more orthodox economic policies (Spourdalakis 1986).

Employers' Organizations

The 1955 legislation which defined the main framework of post-war industrial relations specified the organizations entitled to represent employers in national collective bargaining. These are the Federation of Greek Industries (SEB), the Commercial Employers' Associations of Athens, Piraeus and Thessaloniki (now combined in the Federation of Greek Commercial Associations, EESE); and the General Confederation of Greek Artisans and Handicrafts (GSEBEE).

In addition to the functional division between industrial, commercial and artisan employers there are other lines of division. The ship-owners, traditionally a key section of Greek capital, have two separate organizations: the London-based Greek Shipping Co-operation Committee; and the smaller Federation of Greek Shipowners, in Piraeus. In commerce, the local employers' associations, linked in a national Federation of Commercial Associations (EESE) face rivalry from strong breakaway groups. The Artisans' Confederation also opened its membership to shopkeepers in 1987, causing representational conflicts. EESE attacked the move, but GSEBEE insisted that the former merely represented the interests of large concerns, and neglected smaller trades, 80 per cent of whom were unorganized.

The SEB was established in 1917 as the Federation of Greek Industrialists and Handicrafts. The title was shortened in 1946, when handicraft producers formed their separate confederation; the present name was adopted in 1979, reflecting a change of rule permitting only corporate, and not individual membership. This seemingly minor change reflected a modernization strategy within SEB. Traditionally the organization had been largely a vehicle for the personal interests of the wealthy and powerful families who both owned and controlled the companies which dominated pre-war industrialization. Their leadership was subject to three challenges: the collapse or decline of many of the traditional family-owned firms; the growth of modern, professional management with a different conception of corporate interests; and the growing popular denunciations in the 1970s (which culminated in the PASOK election victory) of the relationships of personal patronage between the state and leading industrialists.

The current structure of the SEB is complex. It comprises some 500 directly affiliated companies, a number of sectoral organizations, and five geographical associations from peripheral regions of Greece. Some 2,000 firms are indirectly represented through these sectoral and regional affiliates. Every two years, a General Assembly of SEB elects the 20-member Administrative Board, which in turn appoints a smaller Executive Committee. There is also a variety of sub-committees and consultative councils, including a General Council which meets monthly.

SEB represents its member companies in centralized collective bargaining and negotiations with government; it also provides information services, seminars and conferences for member firms. As well as coordinating the investment strike against the policies of the PASOK government, SEB organized a National Council of Private Enterprise (ESIP) during 1984–7 to lead protest demonstrations. More conventional initiatives in recent years include the adoption of an 'Enterprise Charter', and the submission of detailed proposals relating to the EC single market.

In 1978 there were some 380,000 small businesses and artisan producers, the majority with fewer than five employees. Since 1919 GSEBEE has existed as a national confederation for this sector. Under the corporatist arrangements established in 1946, it acquired a legal monopoly of representation together with payment from the state insurance fund (TEBE) to which contributions were obligatory (Mavrogordatos 1988: 164). With quasi-compulsory membership and no effective internal democratic structures, GSEBEE – like the trade unions at this time – was run by a caste of state-sponsored leaders.

The situation changed in 1981 when the new government abolished compulsory affiliation payments, subsequently enforcing a more democratic structure through the law 1712/1987. The confederal leadership is now accountable to the lower levels of organizations.

GSEBEE is composed of three types of organization: local single-sectoral, local multi-sectoral, and national single-sectoral. Like the trade unions, in the past it operated on the bases of compulsory membership, with contributions collected through the state insurance fund for traders. Total membership in 1990 was 131,548, almost half of these affiliated via local artisan unions.

GSEBEE policy is determined by a general assembly of 242 representatives, who in turn elect an administrative board with 51 members. A distinctive feature is that factions associated with different political parties nominate slates, and the election is decided by proportional representation. In this way, a unitary organization is maintained despite the existence of ideological differences.

The EESE is a recent creation. Only in 1961 did the local commercial associations form a loose umbrella body, the Coordinating Council of Greek Commercial Associations, comprising the 15 largest associations then in existence. Collective bargaining in the commercial sector was undertaken by the three largest local associations (Athens, Piraeus and Thessaloniki). National organizations have also operated in specialized sections of commerce: SELPE, founded in 1977, for supermarkets; POEKO, in 1981, for 14 organizations of importers and wholesalers. The national federation, EESE, was established only in 1987.

However, it has proved impossible to reconcile the different interests of separate commercial organizations. EESE has 52 affiliates, and is certainly the most representative organization in the commercial sector; but SELPE, SESME and POEKO all remain outside, and Mavrogordatos (1988: 60) estimates that it includes only 10 per cent of eligible firms. Attempts to establish an umbrella confederation of the four organizations have proved unsuccessful. EESE is governed by a general assembly and administrative board, on both of which the three main local associations are directly represented. As in GSEBEE, these governing bodies are elected from rival political slates, and political factionalism is often a divisive influence.

Greek Employers' Organizations and the EC

The single European market poses serious challenges for Greek employers, whose traditional policies are unsuited to the increasingly competitive environment. Large firms are best prepared for 1992, and SEB has possessed a Brussels office ever since Greek membership of the EC was first discussed in 1962. It has also lobbied the Commission over the allocation of regional development funds. SEB policy on 1992 calls for improved support for research and development, telecommunications and vocational training, as well as a taxation regime favourable to investment, and a switch of resources from the public to the private sector. Outside the large manufacturing firms, 1992 is generally regarded as a serious threat, which will involve widespread take-over activity of smaller firms by both Greek and foreign capital in a process of vertical and horizontal integration. The relevant employers' organizations – in particular, GSEBEE – see the only options as a joint protective strategy with state support. Within the EC, representatives of GSEBEE press for protective measures for countries and sectors which would suffer from unrestricted competition. Collaboration with small-business representatives from other EC countries – for example, in the European Federation of Handicraft and Manufacturing Enterprises – is one vehicle for such demands. GSEBEE has been forced to modernize its organization, building up its information and educational services.

In the commercial sector the employers' organizations have reacted similarly. Because of the trend of Greek economic activity towards the tertiary sector, their influence may be increasing as the constituency of SEB has shrunk. However, the different interests of the various fractions of capital in the face of 1992 make any unification of employers' organizations unlikely at present.

Personnel Management and Industrial Relations in Greek Companies

The factors already discussed are reflected in the very limited development of personnel management in Greece. As in other countries of the Mediterranean periphery, the post-war alliance between the new capitalist class and the state allowed the marginalization of organized labour and the adoption of an autocratic and authoritarian management style. In addition, the dominant tradition – most obviously, but by no means exclusively, among the numerous small employers – was one of owner-management; control was exercised by the owner, and perhaps other members of his immediate family.

In this context there was no space for personnel management as the function is understood in Britain; in Greece, those given this title had no more than a policing role. Customarily the position was filled by a junior member of the owner's family, or by a retired military or police officer. Formalized personnel policies were very much the exception. Not until the 1970s did different management policies emerge. The restoration of political democracy in 1974 and the rapid growth of trade union organization helped stimulate more sophisticated labour relations practices, with the establishment of specialist personnel departments in larger firms. Nevertheless, a management consultancy survey found that as recently as 1986 only 9 per cent of Greek companies with 100 or more employees had a separate personnel department; only 11 per cent had an explicit personnel planning policy. By contrast, 52 per cent of foreign-owned companies undertook personnel planning. A further weakness is that personnel departments tend to be staffed by managers without formal training in personnel and industrial relations; for there is a complete lack of such courses in Greece, at least at graduate level. A study by Kanellopoulos (1990) found that 61 per cent of Greek personnel managers were graduates and 15 per cent possessed a (foreign) postgraduate degree. Half the latter were MBAs; only 10 per cent had specific personnel qualifications. Companies have increasingly recognized this gap in management development in the approach to 1992.

There has been a dramatic change in policies towards company industrial relations. The 1955 legislation (Act 3239/1955) which set the main framework for post-war labour law prescribed collective bargaining only at multi-employer level, and companies resolutely refused to recognize unions at workplace level. This was consistent with the priority of employers in most countries to 'neutralize the workplace' from collective bargaining (Sisson 1987). But after 1975 employers were forced to come to terms with the shopfloor strength of the resurgent trade union movement, legally underpinned in 1982 by Act 1264/1982 which established union rights in the workplace. Other recent legislation has also encouraged a shift in the focus of industrial relations to company or plant level. In the public sector, Act 1365/1983 provided for employee representation on company boards. In private companies, Act 1876/ 1990 has encouraged company negotiations by bringing these within the statutory framework of conciliation and arbitration.

It is unclear how far multinational companies are an exception to the trend, and perhaps an obstacle to its generalization. Certainly most foreign multinationals are non-union, and some have applied sophisticated human resource management programmes as a way of integrating employees within the company. However, the more modern generation of Greek managers does not object in principle to the formal rights of unions at company level, which do not seriously inhibit managerial prerogative in practice. Significantly, the February 1990 law was supported by all the main political parties. On the other hand, since the fall of the PASOK employers have pressed for legislative changes to permit more employment flexibility and curb the right to strike. The latter was achieved with Acts 1892 and 1915/1990.

Labour

As has already been noted, the Greek class structure is distinctive in the low proportion of employees and the high proportion of self-employed and family workers in artisan production, trade and agriculture. Not only are employees a minority of the active labour force, but the larger part of the wage-labour force are themselves employed in the public sector with its wide array of state-controlled companies. This has important implications for working-class mentality and identity. In a context of employment insecurity throughout the post-war decades, the permanency attached to state employment was a source of patronage used by the government party to sustain clientelist relations. At the same time, wage levels were lower than in the private sector, encouraging dual job-holding (also common in agriculture), even though the law until 1990 in theory restricted part-time employment. Workers in such a position develop a 'split personality' (Tsoucalas 1986: 175) which can inhibit effective social and political mobilization.

Conversely, small-business owners and other self-employed form a relatively cohesive and effective socio-political group. They are almost as numerous as waged and salaried employees; moreover in most cases the self-employed are not simply individual economic actors but represent a family production unit. Hence, as Simitis (1989: 13) argues, it is very difficult to apply conventional notions of class structure and class politics to Greece. Rather, there exists a diversity of bases of interest and lines of division, which may cut across simple criteria of class in terms of locations in the production system. Correspondingly, groups relate to the state not as a protagonist in a struggle between capital and labour, but as the potential defender of their special rights and interests. Politics itself becomes primarily an arena for the mobilization of sectoral economic interests.

The Development of Greek Trade Unions

Contemporary Greek trade unionism has inevitably been shaped, both by the late and limited development of an industrial working class, and by the central role of the state in the formation of the modern economy. Occupational and industrial union organization first emerged in the 1880s, with multi-union local federations being created in the early years of the present century. The Greek General Confederation of Labour (GSEE) was established in 1918. Though nominally the confederation has continued to function uninterruptedly since then, in fact its character and status have fluctuated repeatedly in the face of state regulation and repression, and the vagaries of internal union politics.

As in many other European countries, unions suffered internal political splits after 1920, notably between socialists and communists. The latter acquired considerable strength in Greece, but were outlawed by the Metaxas dictatorship in 1936 and legalized only after the restoration of democracy in 1974. After 1968 Greek communists themselves were split between 'Eurocommunists' and the orthodox communist KKE (Spourdalakis 1986: 263–5). Subsequent divisions (caused in particular by conflicts after the period of PASOK government) have resulted in four separate communist and ex-communist parties. The recent complex patterns of internal political tendencies and tensions in GSEE itself are discussed below.

The initial formation of a national structure of trade unionism was the outcome of a period best described as one of state paternalism, when different political parties sought organized popular support. In particular, liberals and socialists cooperated in formulating a system of labour legislation in the period 1909–22, including a law of 1914 which regulated union organization.

Regulation was later reinforced by a system of financial control. In 1931 the state established a Workers' Housing Trust (*Ergatiki Estia*: literally, Workers' Hearth) with a reserve fund drawn from compulsory contributions of 0.25 per cent of every employee's pay (with equivalent contributions from employers). The Minister of Labour received the power to distribute 8 per cent of this fund to trade unions. Under the Metaxas regime in 1936, this procedure was used to subordinate unions to the government. GSEE became, in effect, a state institution with exclusive jurisdiction. The Minister of Labour became responsible for appointing union officials, who were then no longer democratically accountable but on the contrary required to support government policies. Unions were thus transformed in this corporatist system into mere 'rubber-stamp' organizations.

An attempt after the war to reconstitute GSEE as an independent and pluralistic confederation broke down in 1946 when the new royalist government overturned the executive elected by conference and imposed its own nominees. Repressive state control was slightly relaxed two decades later under the Centre Union Party government, but reasserted with a vengeance after the colonels' coup. Thus over several decades up to 1974, supporters of independent trade unionism were subject to police surveillance, arrest, imprisonment and sometimes worse (see, for example, Catephores and Tzannatos 1986).

While genuine activists were persecuted, a caste of leaders developed who were ironically known as *ergatopateres* (workers' fathers). Sustained by patronage relations with the government, they also confected a spurious legitimacy by convening rigged conferences, de-registering troublesome branches, and similar stratagems. Since their income was received from the government rather than from members' subscriptions, they were under no real pressure to act effectively as workers' representatives.

Trade Unions under Democracy

The fall of the military dictatorship in 1974 brought important changes in the trade union situation, but some distinctive features persisted.

An important novelty was the rise of factory organization, independently of the official GSEE structures. This provided for the first time a significant basis for rank-and-file initiative within Greek trade unionism, and a pressure point for greater union democracy. Factory unionism was a spontaneous movement, reflecting both the material effects of a growing concentration of urban industrial workers and the political-ideological context of the protest movement which resulted in the fall of the military dictatorship. The movement sought effective collective protection against dismissals (not provided by the existing unions), improvements in wages and working conditions, and a shorter working week. Disparate strike movements in 1975, organized by workplace strike committees, led to the formation of autonomous factory unions. These coordinated their activities, forming OBES (Federation of Factory Unions) in 1979. This was too late, however, to stem the collapse of the movement: the repercussions of the political defeat symbolized by Law 330/1976, the hostility of the Communist Party to the movement's 'syndicalist' character, and the opposition of the SEB, with victimization and black-listing of union activists.

At a different level, totalitarian control of the unions was fractured by the introduction of explicit political factionalism in which all main left parties – newly legalized after thirty years – were represented. Maintaining a unitary organization despite these complex organized divisions has been a continuous, and not always resoluble, problem for GSEE since 1974. Detailed instances will be examined below.

While the corporatist character of union dependence on the state was modified after 1974, however, a close inter-relationship persisted. Unions continued to receive their finance from the state social welfare system. It was open to them to supplement their income through membership subscriptions, but most made no attempt to do so (major exceptions being unions for seafarers, bank employees and public utility workers – all of whom benefit from a dues check-off system). Hence in 1984, GSEE received a total income of 200 million drachma (£620,000), a mere 45,000 drachma (£140) coming from membership subscriptions (Koukoules 1988: 26). Local and sectoral unions obtained a higher proportion of income from subscriptions; but the contribution levels in Greek unions are remarkably low by international standards.

With no financial basis to membership, union claims to numbers represented cannot readily be validated. Since payments from the state reserve funds were intended to be proportional to membership, unions had every incentive to exaggerate. Only with the trade union legislation of 1990 was this system of state subsidy finally abolished – together with the similarly funded union official' pension scheme, traditionally an important resource for the *ergatopateres*. The result is that Greek unions are now in desperate financial straits. From the restoration of democracy in 1974, GSEE notionally supported the abolition of state subsidy; but most unions were reluctant to require realistic levels of contribution (even after law 1264/1982 facilitated check-off agreements) for fear of losing members. Governments irrespective of party were willing to maintain the former system, even if as a notionally 'temporary' arrangement. The abolition of state funding in 1990 was a punitive response to the GSEE campaign against government policy. Deprived of the source of all but a fraction of their income, unions are now in a parlous state: with difficulties in paying officials' salaries, affiliation fees to international organizations, and expenses of union delegations.

The structure of Greek trade unionism has changed little since 1918. The basic level of organization consists of 'primar' unions, representing workers of a particular industry, occupation, craft or company in each locality. A decade ago almost 5,000 were registered, but at its 1989 Congress GSEE reported 3,020. The decline reflects the elimination of many of the 'ghost' unions which existed on paper in the era of the *ergatopateres*. As suggested above, actual membership is difficult to determine; Katsanevas (1984: 13) estimated a density of between 27 and 33 per cent, and this still seems a reasonable assessment. However, some sectors are far more strongly unionized than others; in banking, public utilities, local government and education density is probably 80 per cent or higher.

Traditionally, most primary unions were based on craft or occupation, reflecting the very limited development of mass-production industry in Greece. This form of organization was favoured by the authorities during the period of state paternalism, as less likely than industrial unionism to present a class-political challenge to the regime. However, craft organization has been weakened by technological change, which has displaced or de-skilled traditional craft occupations. Conversely, membership has expanded in industrial or sectoral unions; by 57 per cent between 1975 and 1989 in the two largest industry federations, those of metal- and textile workers. A new type of primary union also came to prominence from 1975, the factory union. To an important extent this represented a spontaneous rank-and-file reaction to the corrupt nature of the old unions, and the factory organizations were resisted by the state, the employers and some sections of the official union leadership. The rapid growth of factory unionism in the 1970s was halted in the 1980s, largely because many were rooted in the so-called 'problematic' sectors of traditional manufacturing where heavy job losses have occurred in the past decade. (Thus membership of OBES, the national federation of factory unions, fell from 11,600 in 1983 to 6,300 in 1989.) Finally, there exist some primary unions which are general in coverage, though at present their significance is slight.

Primary unions are able to affiliate to either of two types of secondary organization. One is the national federation, organized on the basis of sector, industry or occupation. GSEE contains 60 such federations, which represent 1,439 local unions – just under half the total number of primary organizations within its ranks. In membership terms, however, the national federations are the key component of GSEE. In 1989, the 15 largest federations accounted for 47 per cent of the total GSEE membership of 564,000. The largest federations cover such sectors as construction, metalworking, banks, telecommunications, electricity, railways, health care and public services.

The alternative line of affiliation for primary unions is to the labour centres, a type of local or regional body to some extent modelled on the French *bourses du travail*. Though such centres antedate the GSEE itself, their role has been marginalized by the developmemnt of collective bargaining. The 69 labour centres in 1989 encompassed the majority of primary unions, but only a third of total GSEE membership. Those in the three major cities – Athens, Piraeus and Thessaloniki – contain 11 per cent of the members of GSEE; the others are for smaller bodies, often in peripheral regions.

At national confederal level, GSEE is the one organization of note. Apart from certain rival bodies with no more than a paper existence, there is a separate confederation – ADEDY – which covers public employees whose status is formally defined in the Greek Constitution. It should also be noted that amongst a number of professional groups (in engineering, law, medicine etc.) there exist independent associations some of whose functions resemble those of trade unions.

Internal Organization

The internal organization of Greek unions has, from the outset, been subject to detailed legal regulation. Any association of workers with more than 20 members can register as a union. The governing body is an executive board, while an audit committee also exists to oversee the financial administration. The law 1264/1982 redefined electoral procedures. The main official positions (President, Vice-President, and Secretary/Treasurer) must be open to election at least every three years, and no individual may hold more than one of these offices.

A worker is permitted to belong to two different primary unions (e.g. one occupationally and the other industrially based), but may vote or stand for office in only one of these. Members of primary unions have the right to vote, and stand for election, at secondary level (regional labour centre or national federation), according to how the union decides to affiliate.

Political Factionalism

As in earlier periods when state control was relaxed, 1974 saw the formation of a variety of organized political tendencies within GSEE, attached to different political parties. Originally aiming to challenge the corrupt leadership of the *ergatopateres*, these political factions now act primarily as 'transmission belts' for their respective parties. From one perspective, political factionalism may be seen as the source of an active, campaigning democracy within Greek unions. But from a different perspective, it can be regarded as leading to an over-politicization of unionism, with policy debates reflecting party-political loyalties rather than specifically trade union interests and priorities. Recruitment can also be inhibited, if political activists are reluctant to 'dilute' the membership with non-partisans.

Realistically, political factionalism may be considered the necessary price to pay if GSEE is to survive as a unitary federation. Since union governing bodies are elected by systems of proportional representation, all significant tendencies are able to achieve some positions of leadership. While disputes over the representation of specific tendencies are not uncommon, these have never gone so far as to threaten the break-up of GSEE itself.

The main political groupings are PASKE, linked to PASOK; DAKE (formerly ADISK), linked to the conservative New Democracy party; ESAK, orthodox communist; and AEM, linked to the Eurocommunist left, now known as the Renewal Left. Following the split in PASKE in 1985 (see below), a new grouping – SSEK – was formed, but it is no longer significant.

From the restoration of democracy until 1983, GSEE congresses were dominated by the right, partly because a number of left-oriented federations were excluded, and the left groupings complained of under-representation. In effect, the New Democracy government, within the framework of the 330/1976 law, was able to facilitate control of the unions by its own supporters.

With the change of government in 1981, 'the Socialists inherited a markedly corporatist labour relations system in which compulsory government mediation, and other direct involvement in trade union procedures were the rule, and free collective bargaining and open-democratic trade union structures the exception' (Spourdalakis 1988: 229–30). The new law 1264/1982 on trade union democracy provided the basis for a successful legal challenge to the GSEE leadership elected in 1981 (when key left unions were excluded). The court judgment gave a majority of seats on the GSEE executive to PASKE, but some also to ESAK and AEM (which provided the new President). In protest at this decision, the right boycotted the 1983 congress at which PASKE was the dominant force.

In 1985 a major crisis occurred when the PASOK government introduced its austerity measures (see below). A minority of the PASKE leadership, representing public sector unions, opposed the measures, and were promptly expelled from PASOK. Together with ESAK and AEM representatives, the oppositionists held a majority on the GSEE administrative board but were out-voted on the governing council, which installed a new leadership, boycotted by the anti-government factions. With two rival ruling committees each claiming legitimacy, a court ruling backed the government supporters. Only in 1989 was the split finally overcome, when all main factions – left and right – participated in the GSEE congress. The outcome was an administrative board in which no one faction was dominant: PASKE gained 18 seats, against 27 for the other factions combined.

Workplace Representation

While statutory or voluntary machinery of workplace employee representation is an established part of most European industrial relations systems, there is no sustained tradition of such institutions in Greece.

Attempts to establish workplace structures with functions complementary to those of the unions can be identified at historical phases of trade union advance (Koutroukis 1987: 54). There were some instances in the 1920s, followed by more extensive initiatives at the height of the national liberation struggle against the Nazis and the collaborationist government. The factory union movement after 1974 gave a major impetus to demands for worker participation, with both PASOK and the Eurocommunists supporting proposals for socialization and workers' self-management.

After the Socialist election victory, the 1264/1982 legislation was designed to encourage union-based workplace representation. Employers were obliged to provide facilities for union meetings at the workplace (outside working hours), and notice-boards for union announcements. Workers elected to representative positions in their local union were protected against dismissal and entitled to time off work (without pay) to carry out their duties. Employers were also obliged to hold discussions with employee representatives, if so requested, at least once a month. Union representatives were also entitled to attend any workplace inspection by Ministry of Labour officials.

A subsequent law, 1586/1985, provides for statutory health and safety committees with employee representation. This was followed by a more general law, 1767/1988, prescribing workers' councils in all enterprises – both private and public – with more than 50 employees. The councils are only consultative, and all employees – whether or not union members – can vote and stand for election. In any difference between councils and unions, the latter are guaranteed precedence.

The introduction of workplace representatives in the 1980s occurred only slowly in the private sector, but much faster in public enterprises. A special law, 1365/1983, provided a number of new mechanisms of employee representation including a general assembly (ASKE, representative assembly of social control), a central workers' council, and representation on the administration board and management council. However, the implementation of the new institutions merely stimulated intense competition for representation among the different political factions and high hopes for employee democracy degenerated into petty antagonisms. Union leaders, of whatever political persuasion, came to view the new machinery as a threat, and the government itself diluted a number of the provisions. The sorry episode seems to support the conclusion of Metropoulos (1987: 101) that employee participation can function in a positive manner only in industrial relations systems where an institutionalized relationship between capital and labour already exists.

Trade Unions and Politics

Greek unions are exceptional, in Europe, for the continued role of class politics as their dominant point of reference. In part this reflects the unusual degree of political polarization in Greece and – to some extent as a corollary – the intensity of industrial conflicts. The long heritage of political repression, linked to an unusually autocratic set of employers, never made 'free collective bargaining' an option for Greek trade unions. Rather, 'industrial' and 'political' aspirations and demands were interconnected and mutually conditioning. For example, the operation of compulsory arbitration prescribed in the 3239/1955 law, and the restrictive impact of government incomes policies meant that simple wage bargaining could readily lead to confrontation with the state. Unions could not avoid politics, and experience of the alliance between state and capital in post-war Greece encouraged most political tendencies in the unions to adopt a radical anti-capitalist stance.

This orientation was perhaps most clear-cut in the years 1976–81, between the fall of the dictatorship and the election of the PASOK government. Labour movement activists had played an important part in resistance to the colonels' regime, but saw themselves eclipsed by the New Democracy government which failed to make a complete break with the old regime and consolidated the existing economic order. After 1981, the unions were split between those committed in principle to support for the PASOK government, and others – PASOK dissidents and other leftists – willing to oppose government policies if these appeared to contradict workers' interests.

The election of a conservative government has helped to re-unite the political tendencies in the unions and sharpen their radicalism. The immediate focus has been the 'Balkan Thatcherite' policies of the new government – economic austerity and privatization; all political tendencies, except – predictably – DAKE, oppose the neo-liberal policies adopted by the new government. But there has also been a general radicalization of union policies, encompassing such issues as peace and disarmament, ecology, and solidarity with struggles in the Third World. For the first time, unions are also giving serious attention to the interests of women workers. In the past decade there have been important advances on such questions as maternity leave, parental allowances, insurance rights and legal protection. However, women are still mainly confined to low-paid, low-skilled occupations, and have remained largely unrepresented in the governing bodies of the unions: women constituted 4.5 per cent of the leadership of local labour centres and 4.3 per cent in national union federations; in the GSEE, 5 of the 45-person administrative board were women. There are signs of change, however: two women have recently been elected to the GSEE's 15-member executive committee, while in OTOE (the banking union) it was recently agreed to ensure proportional representation for women on governing bodies.

Since 1976, GSEE has been a member of the ETUC. It joined ICFTU in 1950, though membership was suspended during the military dictatorship, but also retained an association with the WFTU. The main sectoral federations are also affiliated to the relevant international bodies. The approach of 1992 has brought to the fore many issues concerning the role of Greece and Greek labour in broader European developments, and it is generally recognized that Greek unions have been slow to develop a response to the new issues. Hurried efforts are now being made to formulate policy positions appropriate to European economic integration, and to strengthen links with other European unions.

In recent decades, Greek trade unions have been the most party-dependent in the whole of western Europe. Recently this has been increasingly identified as a problem. The debate continues as to whether, and how, unions might attain greater independence – in terms of membership, finance and policy formulation – from political institutions.

State and Law

Industrial relations in Greece is subject to a comprehensive and complex framework of legal regulation. Ever since 1909 the law has defined in detail the relationships between employers, unions and the state, in ways which – according to the political context – have been sometimes progressive but more usually repressive.

For most of the post-war period, the rules of the game were defined by Law 3239/1955 which prescribed a centralized system of collective bargaining with provision for state intervention via compulsory arbitration. After 1974 New Democracy enacted some revisions, and PASOK initiated some more radical and pro-union changes, but without replacing the previous legal framework.

The new act 1876/1990, passed under the three-party conservative/socialist/communist coalition government, was a radical step towards industrial relations modernization. The 1955 law was abolished and a more voluntaristic set of procedures established. The right and duty of the parties directly involved to engage in collective bargaining are now legally enshrined. Compulsory arbitration is replaced by a new voluntary system of conciliation, mediation and – on the initiative of either party – arbitration, by an agency independent of the government. The overall effect of this law is to detach collective bargaining from the state, and to devolve the key level of negotiation to the individual employer.

The changes in Greek labour law since the restoration of democracy have been rapid and confusing. Numerous acts have affected individual employment rights. The main issues involved have been working hours and holidays; the position of women and young workers; and health and safety.

Regulation of the labour market has been another important area of intervention. The OAED (Labour Force Employment Organization) was authorized by law 1403/1983 to organize employment training. Under the Act 1545/1985, OAED acquired far more extensive powers of labour market regulation including administration of unemployment benefits. The provisions for vocational training were considerably expanded by law 1839/1989. To control job losses, the law 1387/1983 imposed rigid limits on collective dismissals. However, the new conservative government has pursued a policy of deregulation, and law 1892/1990 introduces new forms of flexibility in the labour market, including the authorization – for the first time in Greece – of part-time employment.

In terms of collective labour law, the Act 330/1976 soon after the fall of the dictatorship provided a very restrictive framework. Trade union rights were severely circumscribed, job security was reduced and strikes were subject to serious limitations. Law 1264/1982, passed in the early months of the PASOK government, radically enhanced trade union rights. As has been seen, the union position in the workplace was strongly reinforced. Extensive rights to strike were provided, and where a strike was called according to specified procedures the employer was prohibited from dismissing strikers, hiring strike-breakers, or imposing a lockout. However, the law imposed additional restrictions in the public sector and in certain essential services; and this was compounded between 1983 and 1988, under a legal provision specifying that strikes in newly nationalized services required a majority of all employees to vote in favour of action. Much more comprehensively restrictive is the new law 1915/1990 passed by a narrow majority by the conservative government. In effect, the act abolishes most of the rights acquired by the unions in 1982, restricting the scope of lawful strikes, permitting the dismissal of unlawful strikers, and imposing new limitations on strikes in public services.

Public Sector Activity

Under the current government, the economic role of the state is a question of intense controversy, privatization being justified by reference to the 'unproductive' nature of state activity.

The economic role of the state may be assessed by a variety of criteria (Magliveras 1987: 4). As an agency of income distribution, the state in Greece is of considerable importance compared with other European countries: state expenditure was 40.6 per cent of GNP in 1980 and rose to 55.5 per cent in 1985. But in terms of business activity, the state is much more marginal in Greece. Public enterprises accounted for 6.6 per cent of total added value in 1975, 11.2 per cent in 1982; and for 15.4 per cent of total investment in 1975, 27.3 in 1982.

State-owned firms employed 7.8 per cent of the wage-labour force in 1975, 8.8 per cent in 1981, and 9 per cent in 1985. But for the public sector as a whole the figures were far higher: 17 per cent in 1971, 30.5 per cent in 1981 and 32.1 per cent in 1985. By 1990 the proportions may have reached 40 per cent. Almost three-quarters of public employees are on fixed-term contracts: in part a reflection of the insecurity of Greek workers generally, but also an indication of the way that Greek governments have always used employment as a means of patronage.

Employment status varies in different parts of the public sector. Direct employees of the state have a status as civil servants specified in the Constitution. This imposes a number of obligations and restrictions, but also guarantees security of employment. Until 1981, public employees required a formal certificate of 'civic reliability' issued by the local police authority; and though this has been abolished, political acceptability still remains a significant influence on employment. In other parts of the public sector – nationalized companies, banks, etc. – employment status is the same as in the private sector. In practice, however, employees have achieved considerable employment security irrespective of the formal contractual position.

Special legal regulations affect collective organization in the public sector. Trade unionism is prohibited in the police and fire service and the military. Permanent civil servants are not allowed to join the same trade unions as other workers. However, the 1982 legislation enabled the formation of civil service unions on the same structural basis as other unions. The primary unit of organization is the individual section with national federations for particular government departments. These 59 federations are in turn members of the Confederation of Civil Servants, ADEDY. Founded in 1945, ADEDY has a history of internal politics which parallels GSEE. Until 1983 it was controlled by a right-wing leadership unaccountable to the membership, but their position was eventually challenged successfully in the courts. As in GSEE, political factions linked to the various parties now compete for leadership positions.

Union density in the civil service is very high. In 1989, ADEDY claimed 200,000 members, representing 65 per cent of those with permanent contracts as civil servants. Density is particularly high among primary and secondary schoolteachers, whose federations together make up some 40 per cent of ADEDY membership.

Under the terms of a recent reform, public servants in Greece are covered by a unitary grading system, consisting of five job grades and 28 pay scales. Basic pay is supplemented by a variety of allowances, which serve to widen differentials. Until 1990, pay was adjusted automatically every four months on the basis of the official cost-of-living index; now the adjustment is decided unilaterally by the government.

Collective bargaining does not formally occur in the public service, and the right to strike is more restricted than for other types of employee. Unions can submit schedules of demands relating to terms and conditions of employment, but all governments have regarded it as an issue of state sovereignty that they retain absolute jurisdiction on these matters. Greece has not therefore ratified the relevant ILO conventions, despite repeated demands from the unions. There are some signs, however, that government policy may change.

The issue of privatization and deregulation, important in many European countries during the 1980s, did not arise in Greece while PASOK was in government. On the contrary, its strategy for economic development involved a central role for state intervention. The aim was to 'socialize' the existing public sector; rescue the bankrupt sector of the economy through state reconstruction, subsidies and protected markets; and build up a modern welfare state. But the grand strategy failed: rather than modernization, state intervention seemed to result in bureaucracy and low productivity. Later than in the rest of Europe, neo-liberal views eventually gained ground; and the current conservative government is committed to an extensive programme of deregulation and privatization. There are already signs that this is provoking confrontation with public sector unions.

Trends in Collective Bargaining

The law of 1955 which formed the main basis for post-war Greek industrial relations supported a fundamentally unrepresentative and undemocratic trade union structure; restricted the agenda of collective bargaining and the right to strike; and enabled governments to intervene repeatedly to impose incomes policies.

In practice these limitations were partially transcended after 1975 with the rise of the factory union movement. A decree issued during the period of dictatorship (186/1969) had provided for the appointment of a tripartite mediation committee to resolve workplace disagreements, and this procedure was utilized by the factory unions to press a far wider range of demands than specified under the law. The decisions of the tripartite committee then served as the *de facto* equivalent of company collective agreements.

There has now developed a variegated structure of collective bargaining in Greece. Four levels of negotiation occur: single-company; local craft or occupational; national industry-level; and national multi-industry. Until 1990 there was no legal right to negotiate at company level, apart from provisions for 'special collective agreements' for 'such clearly specified organizations as banks, public utilities, local government, and so forth, which belong to the public or semi-public sector' (Ioannou 1989: 209). The abolition in 1990 of the previous restrictive legislation appears to have stimulated a considerable expansion in the scope of bargaining. Issues covered in recent agreements include trade union rights and facilities at the workplace, supplementary social welfare benefits, company investment and the introduction of new technology.

Table 17.3   Collective agreements and arbitration decisions 1961–91

Year	Total C.A.	Total A.D.	National General	National Craft	Local Craft	'Special'	Company	Sector
1961	63	69	1	12	36	14		
1962	70	66	2	14	19	35		
1963	61	75	–	10	31	20		
1964	97	93	–	27	41	29		
1965	121	93	1	21	59	40		
1966	105	96	–	28	40	37		
1967	63	78	1	10	26	26		
1968	63	91	2	14	24	23		
1969	50	81	–	13	16	21		
1970	53	57	–	20	3	30		
1971	46	60	–	17	7	22		
1972	88	45	–	44	11	33		
1973	158	60	–	47	18	93		
1974	70	85	–	21	15	34		
1975	131	143	3	30	13	85		
1976	144	120	1	30	24	90		
1977	146	179	1	29	15	101		
1978	166	214	–	37	14	115		
1979	173	247	(2)**	42	15	116		
1980	221	299	(1)**	56	25	140		
1981	233	330	–	54	26	153		
1982	300	232	(1)**	70	42	188		
1983	57	80	–	7	8	40		
1984	252	264	1	47	22	182		
1985	175	167	1	51	29	194		
1986	44	82	1	18	7	18		
1987	76	84	(1)**	21	11	44		
1988	*	*	1	53	20	49		
1989	276	111	1	90	24	161		
1990	236	106	1	65	20	51	53	46
1991	283	87	1	37	33	–	123	89

* 1988 figures are for agreements up to 27 July.
** National General agreements reached after Arbitration.
Source: Ministry of Labour.

Table 17.3 shows the figures for agreements and arbitration awards in the last three decades. It indicates clearly the weakness of 'free collective bargaining' in the Greek context. In most years, more claims have been resolved through arbitration than by negotiation; as Ioannou (1989: 211) insists, 'compulsory arbitration has played a dominant role in the process of wage determination and job regulation'. Excluding from consideration the 'special' agreements in the public and semi-public sector, the weakness of 'voluntary' collective bargaining is even more obvious: during the 1970s and 1980s, an average of only some 50 agreements a year. In the last few years, however, there have been signs of a considerable increase in the effectiveness of collective bargaining.

The articulation of the different levels of bargaining is a potential source of problems. In the past, agreements were negotiated mainly at two levels: centrally, between SEB and GSEE and locally, for individual occupational groups. The recent growth of company and single-industry agreements is a prospective source of inter-union tension and rivalry – even though there are few signs that Greek employers are pursuing the decentralization strategy evident in other European countries.

Conflict

The exceptional political background to industrial relations in Greece, and the very limited institutionalization of 'free collective bargaining', are reflected in distinctive patterns of industrial conflict. Strikes are not, in the main, used as a means of applying sustained pressure on employers in the course of collective bargaining. Unions do not have the resources for a trial of strength in this manner and their use of the strike is conditioned as much by political as by industrial relations considerations.

In applying pressure on employers, Greek unions resort to a variety of 'cut-price' sanctions: short workplace stoppages, withdrawal of goodwill, go-slows, working-to-rule, refusal to perform specific duties, sit-ins.

The period up to 1981 was marked by an increase in the frequency and size, though not duration, of strikes (Ioannou 1989: 96) (see table 17.4). At the peak, almost one worker in two was involved in strike action. This reflected not bargaining strength but the escalating political radicalism of the years following the fall of the dictatorship and resistance to government attempts to impose pay constraint in a period of high inflation. Almost all these strikes were unsuccessful.

Recently there has been a major upsurge in strike activity. The early years of the PASOK government saw low strike figures, as the government met many of the unions' demands. But after the imposition of austerity measures in 1985 strikes escalated, making Greece one of the most strike-prone of all OECD countries (EIRR 191, December 1989: 6). A significant feature of this period was the key role of public employees in industrial conflict. As table 17.5 shows, the public sector share in the

Table 17.4   Strikes in Greece 1976–90

Year	Strikes	Strikers	Hours Lost
1976	829	241,142	5,187,783
1977	401	393,572	8,217,864
1978	405	349,969	6,477,117
1979	372	638,635	9,950,074
1980	472	1,317,917	20,494,944
1981	313	361,106	5,341,961
1982	447	246,543	7,892,094
1983	361	148,174	2,986,957
1984	268	107,957	2,690,879
1985	453	785,725	7,660,879
1986	218	1,106,330	8,839,363
1987	235	1,576,520	16,353,463
1988	320	363,864	5,596,123
1989	202	765,115	8,903,863
1990	200	1,405,497	20,435,313

Source: Ministry of Labour

number of disputes has increased, and the impact in terms of number of strikers and days lost is particularly high. This characteristic has continued under the conservative government, in reaction to its restrictive economic programme and privatization initiatives.

Table 17.5   State-owned companies' share of strike activity 1982–90 (%)

	Strikes	Strikers	Hours Lost
1982	6	47	43
1985	10	36	28
1986	18	37	37
1987	23	23	34
1988	19	23	39
1989	24	26	38
1990	33	43	49

Source: Ministry of Labour

Conclusion

Greece remains marked by an 'immature' system of industrial relations. Organized labour has not yet achieved a position of influence in socio-economic development. Workers and unions have therefore had to react, often destructively, against the policies of employers and governments, rather than being able to play a more positive role. Factional rivalry within the union movement and the considerable decentralization of power which has arisen are additional obstacles to the unions adopting a more 'responsible' role in Greek industrial relations.

Abbreviations

GSSE	General Confederation of Greek Workers
NSSG	National Statistics Service of Greece
OBES	Federation of Industrial Unions
SEB	Federation of Greek Industries
GSEBE	General Confederation of Greek Artisans and Independent Handicraft Producers
EESE	Federation of Greek Commercial Associations
ADEDY	Confederation of Greek Civil Servants

References

Catephores G. and Z. Tzannatos 1986: Trade Unions in Greece: 1949–81 and 1981–83. In Z. Tzannatos (ed.) *Socialism in Greece*, Aldershot: Gower.

ETUI 1984: *The Trade Union Movement in Greece*. Brussels: ETUI.

EUROSTAT 1986: Employment/Unemployment Survey 1986. Luxembourg: EUROSTAT.

Fakiolas, R. 1987: Interest Groups: An Overview. In K. Featherstone and D.K. Katsoudas (eds) *Political Change in Greece*, London: Croom Helm.

GSEE 1986: Act 1264/82: Trade Union Rights and Freedoms. Athens (in Greek).

GSEE 1989: Women Secretariat: Demands for a Contemporary Role of the Working Woman in Production, the Family, Life and Society. Athens (in Greek).

GSEE 1989: 25th Congress of GSEE. Athens (in Greek)

Ioannou C. 1989: *Salaried Employment and Trade Unionism in Greece*. Athens: Foundation for Mediterranean Studies (in Greek).

Kanellopoulos, C. 1990: Personnel Management and Personnel Managers in Greece. Athens: ELKEPA (in Greek).

Karantzas, G. 1985: Data on the Greek Economy in 'Leaflet' No. 4. Athens (in Greek).

Katsanevas, T. 1984: *Trade Unions in Greece*. Athens National Centre of Social Research (in Greek).

Koukoules, F. 1988: Seventy Years of Recent Trade Union History. *Trade Union Review*, 45, September (in Greek).

Koutroukis, T. 1987: Worker Participation in Greece 1910–1981. *Trade Union Review*, 34, October (in Greek).

Magliveras, S. 1987: Public Sector of the Economy: Development Tendencies and Problems. *Scientific Thought*, 32.

Mavrogordatos, G. 1988: *Between Pityokamptis and Prokroustis: The Occupational Organizations in Contemporary Greece*. Odysseus: Athens (in Greek).

Metropoulos, A. 1987: The Future of the Trade Unions. *Positions*, 19 (in Greek).

Mouzelis, N. 1976: Capitalism and Dictatorship in Greece. *New Left Review*, 96, March-April.

Mouzelis, N. 1978: *Modern Greece: Facets of Under-Development*. London: Macmillan.

NSSG 1985, 1987: Labour Force Surveys of Greece. Athens.

OBES 1984: *The Factory Movement*. Athens: OBES (in Greek).

Petmetzidou-Tsoulouvis, M. 1984: Approaches to the Issue of Under-Development of the Greek Social Pattern. *Contemporary Issues*, 22 (in Greek).

Perakis, C. 1987: The Foreign Capital in Greece. Types and Evolution Tendencies. *Scientific Thought*, 32.

Simitis, C. 1989: Introduction. In N. Mouzelis et al. (eds), *Populism and Politics*, Athens: Gnosis (in Greek).

Spourdalakis, M. 1986: The Greek Experience. *Socialist Register, 1985–6*, London: Merlin.

Spourdalakis, M. 1988: *The Rise of the Greek Socialist Party*. London: Routledge.

Tolios, C. 1987: The New Phenomenon of Monopoly Sovereignty in the Greek Economy. *Scientific Thought*, 32 (in Greek).

Tsoukalas, C. 1986: *State, Society and Labour in Post-War Greece*. Athens: Themelio (in Greek).

Vergopoulos, C. 1986: Economic Crisis and Modernization in Greece and the European South. In *Les Temps Modernes, Greece in Evolution*, Athens: Exantas (in Greek).

Weisskopf, T. 1978: Imperialism and the Third World. In C. Wilber (ed.), *The Political Economy of Development and Under-Development*, New York: Random House.

Index